UML™ 2 Toolkit

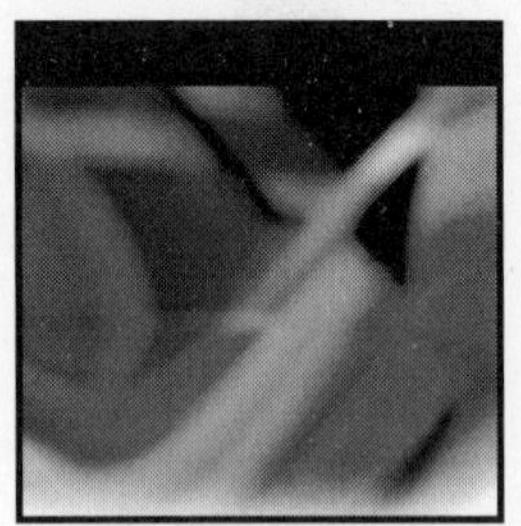

UML™ 2 Toolkit

Hans-Erik Eriksson
Magnus Penker
Brian Lyons
David Fado

Wiley Publishing, Inc.

Publisher: Joe Wikert
Executive Editor: Bob Elliott
Development Editor: Kevin Kent
Editorial Manager: Kathryn Malm
Production Editor: Pamela Hanley
Permissions Editors: Carmen Krikorian, Laura Moss
Media Development Specialist: Travis Silvers
Text Design & Composition: Wiley Composition Services

Published by Wiley Publishing, Inc., Indianapolis, Indiana
Published simultaneously in Canada

For general information on our other products and services please contact our Customer Care Department within the United States at (800) 762-2974, outside the United States at (317) 572-3993 or fax (317) 572-4002.

Library of Congress Cataloging-in-Publication Data:

Library of Congress Control Number: 2003015155

ISBN: 0-471-46361-2

Printed in the United States of America

10 9 8 7 6 5 4 3 2 1

Contents

OMG Press Books in Print

For complete information about current and upcoming titles, go to www.wiley.com/compbooks/omg/.

- *Building Business Objects* by Peter Eeles and Oliver Sims, ISBN: 0-471-19176-0.
- *Business Component Factory: A Comprehensive Overview of Component-Based Development for the Enterprise* by Peter Herzum and Oliver Sims, ISBN: 0-471-32760-3.
- *Business Modeling with UML: Business Patterns at Work* by Hans-Erik Eriksson and Magnus Penker, ISBN: 0-471-29551-5.
- *Common Warehouse Metamodel Developer's Guide* by John Poole, Dan Chang, Douglas Tolbert, and David Mellor, ISBN: 0-471-20243-6.
- *CORBA 3 Fundamentals and Programming, 2nd Edition* by Jon Siegel, ISBN: 0-471-29518-3.
- *CORBA Design Patterns* by Thomas J. Mowbray and Raphael C. Malveau, ISBN: 0-471-15882-8.
- *Enterprise Application Integration with CORBA: Component and Web-Based Solutions* by Ron Zahavi, ISBN: 0-471-32720-4.
- *Enterprise Integration: An Architecture for Enterprise Application and Systems Integration* by Fred A. Cummins, ISBN: 0-471-40010-6.
- *Enterprise Java with UML, Second Edition* by C.T. Arrington and Syed H. Rayhan, ISBN: 0-471-26778-3.
- *Enterprise Security with EJB and CORBA* by Bret Hartman, Donald J. Flinn, and Konstantin Beznosov, ISBN: 0-471-15076-2.

- *The Essential CORBA: Systems Integration Using Distributed Objects* by Thomas J. Mowbray and Ron Zahavi, ISBN: 0-471-10611-9.
- *Instant CORBA* by Robert Orfali, Dan Harkey, and Jeri Edwards, ISBN: 0-471-18333-4.
- *Integrating CORBA and COM Applications* by Michael Rosen and David Curtis, ISBN: 0-471-19827-7.
- *Java Programming with CORBA, Third Edition* by Gerald Brose, Andreas Vogel, and Keith Duddy, ISBN: 0-471-24765-0.
- *Mastering XMI: Java Programming with XMI, XML, and UML* by Timothy J. Grose, Gary C. Doney, and Stephen A. Brodskey, ISBN: 0-471-38429-1.
- *Model Driven Architecture: Applying MDA to Enterprise Computing* by David S. Frankel, ISBN: 0-471-31920-1.
- *The Object Technology Casebook: Lessons from Award-Winning Business Applications* by Paul Harmon and William Morrisey, ISBN: 0-471-14717-6.
- *The Object Technology Revolution* by Michael Guttman and Jason Matthews, ISBN: 0-471-60679-0.
- *Programming with Enterprise JavaBeans, JTS and OTS: Building Distributed Transactions with Java and C++* by Andreas Vogel and Madhavan Rangarao, ISBN: 0-471-31972-4.
- *Programming with Java IDL* by Geoffrey Lewis, Steven Barber, and Ellen Siegel, ISBN: 0-471-24797-9.
- *Quick CORBA 3* by Jon Siegel, ISBN: 0-471-38935-8.

About the OMG

The Object Management Group (OMG) is an open membership, not-for-profit consortium that produces and maintains computer-industry specifications for interoperable applications. To achieve this goal, the OMG specifies open standards for every aspect of distributed computing, from analysis and design through infrastructure to application objects and components defined on virtually every enterprise middleware platform. OMG's membership roster includes virtually every large company in the computer industry, and hundreds of smaller ones. Most of the companies that shape enterprise and Internet computing today are represented on OMG's Board of Directors.

OMG's flagship specification, and the basis for future OMG specifications, is the multiplatform Model Driven Architecture (MDA). Unifying the modeling and middleware spaces, the MDA supports applications over their entire life cycle from Analysis and Design, through implementation and deployment to maintenance and evolution. Based on normative, platform-independent Unified Modeling Language (UML) models, MDA-based applications and standards may be expressed and implemented, equivalently, on multiple middleware platforms; implementations are produced automatically, for the most part, by MDA-enabled tools, which also generate cross-platform invocations, making for a truly interoperable environment. Because the UML models remain stable as the technological landscape changes around them over time, MDA-based development maximizes software ROI as it integrates applications across the enterprise, and one enterprise with another. Adopted by members as the basis for OMG specifications in September 2001, the MDA is truly a unique advance in distributed computing. To learn more about the MDA, visit www.omg.org/mda.

The OMG's modeling specifications form the foundation for the MDA. These include the UML, the Meta-Object Facility (MOF), XML Metadata Interchange

(XMI), and the Common Warehouse Metamodel (CWM). The industry's standard for representation of analysis and design, the UML defines use case and activity diagrams for requirements gathering, class and object diagrams for design, package and subsystem diagrams for deployment, and six other types of diagrams. The MOF defines a standard metamodel for applications, allowing UML models to be interchanged among tools and repositories, and XMI standardizes the format for these interchanges. Finally, CWM establishes metamodels in the field of data warehousing, completing OMG's standardization in the modeling space.

The Common Object Request Broker Architecture (CORBA) is OMG's vendor-neutral, system-independent middleware standard. Based on the OMG/ISO Interface Definition Language (OMG IDL) and the Internet Inter-ORB Protocol (IIOP), CORBA is a mature technology represented on the market by more than 70 ORBs (Object Request Brokers) plus hundreds of other products. Scalable to Internet and Enterprise levels, CORBA more than meets business computing requirements through its robust services providing directory, distributed event handling, transactionality, fault tolerance, and security. Specialized versions of CORBA form the basis for distributed real-time computing, and distributed embedded systems.

Building on this foundation, OMG Domain Facilities standardize common objects throughout the supply and service chains in industries such as telecommunications, health care, manufacturing, transportation, finance/insurance, biotechnology, utilities, space, and military and civil defense logistics. OMG members are now extending these Domain Facilities, originally written in OMG IDL and restricted to CORBA, into the MDA by constructing UML models corresponding to their underlying architecture; standard MDA procedures will then produce standards and implementations on such platforms as Web Services, XML/SOAP, Enterprise JavaBeans, and others. OMG's first MDA-based specification, the Gene Expression Facility, was adopted less than 6 months after the organization embraced the MDA; based on a detailed UML model, this specification is implemented entirely in the popular language XML.

In summary, the OMG provides the computing industry with an open, vendor-neutral, proven process for establishing and promoting standards. OMG makes all of its specifications available without charge from its Web site, www.omg.org. Delegates from the hundreds of OMG member companies convene at week-long meetings held five times each year at varying sites around the world, to advance OMG technologies. The OMG welcomes guests to their meetings; for an invitation, send your email request to info@omg.org or visit www.omg.org/news/meetings/tc/guest.htm.

Membership in OMG is open to any company, educational institution, or government agency. For more information on the OMG, contact OMG headquarters by telephone at +1-781-444-0404, by fax at +1-781-444-0320, by email to info@omg.org, or on the Web at www.omg.org.

2003 OMG Press Advisory Board

Preface for the Second Edition

The first edition of the *UML Toolkit* in 1998 provided readers with a view of the Unified Modeling Language (UML) as it first emerged. UML answered the industry's need for a common language to discuss information technology. This proved a remarkable success. UML is now the standard for object-oriented development, and with UML 2 the language seeks out new frontiers.

The first edition of the *UML Toolkit* provided helpful explanations of how to use UML from two practicing software professionals, Hans-Erik Eriksson and Magnus Penker. The book went beyond the factual description of the language and explained the meaning and context of its features. However, the evolution of the modeling discipline and the adoption of UML 2 leaves the first edition in need of an update to reflect these advancements.

When we were asked to take a look at revising the first edition, we eagerly jumped at the chance to bring the work up to date to reflect UML 2. With Number Six Software, we make our living through the practical application of object-oriented design to deliver high-quality software solutions. This project gave us the chance to update a useful book while also assessing how UML 2 can help our clients and the software-development industry.

The revision fulfills our three core goals:

- Updating the text to reflect UML 2
- Adding new materials to explain the reasons behind UML 2 and the significant new features, which resulted in a new content throughout the book and a new chapter on Model Drive Architecture (MDA)
- Injecting our own practical experience into new examples and a case study, which resulted in a thoroughly revised case study and supporting artifacts on the CD

The notion of a UML toolkit is one with which we are comfortable, even if we have extended the meaning of the term a bit from the first edition. The notion of a toolkit fits very well for this book. Number Six Software's technical staff often stresses that the goal of training in any skill is to get it into your "toolkit." Then you can comfortably review all the items in your "toolkit" to find the best fit for each situation. Clients, as a rule, do not appreciate perfectly formed UML that does not further their goals. As with any other language, just because your grammar is correct does not make your statement intelligent or helpful.

Note on UML 2 Tools

The authoring of this book coincides with the final review of the UML 2 proposal; therefore, we did not have the benefit of UML 2–compliant tools. This book focuses on good modeling with UML, relying on the UML 2 features that make sense logically. While we looked at a few early versions of tools, we did not find the support for features we are accustomed to in the current UML support tools. However, we have included a set of links to vendor sites on the CD for this book. With the speed of development of these tools, we are confident that the reader will find demonstration versions that support UML 2 at practical levels.

UML 2 allows greater variation in the way diagram elements look. The validation and interchange of UML files now uses a mark-up language, so the actual look of a feature might change between tools. However, with better support for model management and with clearer rules for connecting all the different diagrams, UML 2 should be far easier to use in tools than UML 1.

Overview of the Second Edition

This revision follows the general outline of the first edition, starting with a broad overview of UML followed by more-detailed chapters on advanced topics and completed by a case study. Where possible, we sought to retain the structure of the first edition and the broad focus on using UML elements on successful projects.

Chapter 1 answers the question "What is UML?" The chapter explains the roots of UML and describes the method wars that made standard notation so attractive. The chapter also explains some of the main goals for UML 2.

Chapter 2 provides a broad-brush portrait of all the main UML features. This introduction explains UML as a system, providing the needed context for the more detailed coverage of individual diagrams and specific themes in the rest of the book. The chapter also reviews the features to look for in a modeling support tool.

Chapter 3 explores use-case diagrams. These stick figures and bubbles focus on the functionality delivered to users. Good use cases focus a project on what the system needs to deliver. Use cases can provide an organizing unit for the more detailed analysis of a system in static and dynamic models. Here we cover how to organize, describe, assess, test, and realize use cases.

Chapter 4 covers classes and their relationships. Classes define the things in a system. Classes represent only the type of things in a system; to represent a specific thing, UML uses objects as the specific instance of a class. The relationships between classes provide substantial information about a system. Some classes are organized hierarchically, while others depend on other elements to work properly. This chapter reviews the variety of mechanisms in UML to describe these relationships. The chapter also covers ports and interfaces, static structures that define a working relationship with the environment or other classes.

Chapter 5 reviews the basic features of the dynamic diagrams. These diagrams reveal the dynamic flow in a system, showing how specific objects interact to produce a result. Activity diagrams often focus on high-level system flow. State machines show the life-cycle "states" of a class. Interaction diagrams show the messages between the objects collaborating in a system.

Chapter 6 covers advanced dynamic modeling related to real-time systems. The real-time theme provides a practical focus on mechanisms related to communication, synchronization, fault tolerance, and concurrency. Activity diagrams, state machines, and interaction diagrams provide features to handle these common issues.

Chapter 7 reviews architecture and the modeling techniques appropriate to represent architecture. Both logical and physical architecture are covered. The section on logical architecture covers patterns and revisits a number of diagrams already described to explain how they can be used to render the logical architecture. The physical architecture section covers component diagrams and deployment diagrams that show how the system is manifested into actual artifacts that ultimately reside on physical processors.

Chapter 8 shows how to extend UML features for specific environments or domains. UML includes stereotypes, tagged values, and constraints as extension mechanisms. These extensions can be grouped into a coherent set, called a profile, targeted to a specific environment or theme, such as Java or real-time systems. Users can also define their own mechanisms. The chapter also reviews the model for UML and the language used to define a modeling language, the Meta Object Facility (MOF).

Chapter 9 reviews the Model Driven Architecture initiative (MDA). This chapter explains how UML helps support MDA and how MDA in turn helps to guide new features in UML. The MDA initiative provides guidance on how to manage effectively the proliferation of models and diagrams for complex systems. With effective management of models and targeted profiles, UML provides an essential tool for the modern organization.

The first nine chapters review the usage and application of UML in terms of a modeler producing effective diagrams. However, diagrams alone don't work well without a process to support their effective use. Chapters 10 and 11 look at the use of UML as part of an effort to deliver a software product.

Chapter 10 presents a process for using UML. No one "correct" process for using UML exists, so the chapter starts with characteristics of a process and some criteria of a process that the authors of UML had in mind when designing the language. The disciplines that must be covered in such a process are covered, and then their application within the Unified Process is described. The chapter ends with issues of applying the process: the usage of tools and the assessment of model quality.

Chapter 11 provides a practical example of UML at work with the case study of a library system. The companion CD to this book includes the artifacts for this deployment, as well as all the source code needed to make the system run.

Finally, the visual glossary and glossary appendixes provide a handy reference for the elements used in this book.

About the Authors

Hans-Erik Eriksson (Sweden) has over 15 years' experience in system development and software architecture. He is the author of six books in the field, including *Business Modeling with UML: Business Practices at Work,* and is also a highly skilled trainer and practitioner of UML.

Magnus Penker (Sweden) is senior advisor and consultant to both public authorities and international top management. He is also a former senior management consultant and methodologist with over 10 years' experience in business processes and object-oriented analysis and design. In addition to working on the *UML Toolkit* and *UML 2 Toolkit,* Penker has also collaborated with Hans-Erik Eriksson on *Business Modeling with UML: Business Practices at Work.*

Brian Lyons is Chairman, CTO, and cofounder of Number Six Software, Inc., a Washington, D.C.–based software development outsourcing company. Mr. Lyons has been a leading expert in object-oriented technology and iterative development techniques since the mid-1980s. Much of his career has been spent as a trainer, product-centered consultant, methodologist, and mentor, but he has always stayed close to the pragmatic issues of the software developer.

David Fado works as a software architect for Number Six Software, Inc., of Washington D.C., focusing on information and financial management systems. Starting in software development after an academic career in economic and diplomatic history, Dr. Fado worked as a project manager and architect on a variety of complicated global projects dealing with financial information. Since that time, Dr. Fado has focused on using UML and development support tools for successful projects, joining Number Six Software because of their focus on the practical application of UML and object-oriented processes.

About the Contributors

Mike Bonamassa is a practice manager at Number Six Software. Mr. Bonamassa has been working in the software engineering field for more than 20 years. He was an early employee of Rational Software Corporation and has been involved in helping corporations understand the UML and Rational Unified Process (RUP) for the past 14 years. Mr. Bonamassa has been a leader on large projects at key accounts that needed to navigate through change into a more productive and culturally considerate software-development process.

Robert J. Daly has been applying UML since it was little more than stick figures on cave walls. For his entire career in software, Rob has been standing on the shoulders of smarty-pants and pragmatically using that collective power to make his clients' software endeavors succeed. Reasonably successful at it, he cofounded Number Six Software with Lyons in 1994 and served as its president until spring 2003, when he left to help launch a Number Six derivative, 5AM Solutions, Inc., whose mission is to build custom software solutions to serve the biosciences and translational research communities.

Paul M. Duvall is a software architect with Number Six Software, a leading software development company in the Washington, D.C. area. He has over nine years of applied software-engineering experience. As a developer, inventor, and architect, he has contributed design and development expertise to several complex system development efforts in various domains. Prior to Number Six, Paul was a software engineer with Robbins-Gioia and EDS Corporation. In addition to the *UML 2 Toolkit*, he has written several technology white papers. He holds a bachelor of science degree in Management Information Systems and has earned multiple professional certifications in Java technology, Web technology, and software-development methodology.

Greg Gurley works as a project manager at Number Six Software of Washington, D.C., managing the development of custom Web applications for Number Six and their clients. Gurley has applied object-oriented technologies, use-case modeling, and object modeling for over 15 years. As trainer, mentor, analyst, developer, architect, and project manager, he has extensive experience in iterative software development applied to many domains

Stephen M. Matyas III is a software consultant for Number Six Software, a leading software development company based in the Washington, D.C. area. He has spent most of his time designing and developing software applications using UML, software-engineering processes, objected-oriented technologies, and open-source technologies. He graduated in 2001 from the Virginia Polytechnic Institute and State University with a bachelor of science degree in Computer Science and now lives in Fairfax, Virginia.

Acknowledgments

Delivering this book felt much like delivering a software project: We relied on a large cast playing a variety of roles to get the product out (almost) on time.

Above all, we wish to acknowledge the contributing authors, who were instrumental in getting this book done in a timely manner. Paul M. Duvall organized the case study, a project all its own, and did a great job translating a typical application into a practical illustration of UML. Stephen M. Matyas III spent many tireless hours performing all aspects of developing the Library application implemented as a part of the case study. Robert J. Daly, Greg Gurley, and Michael G. Bonamassa each contributed significant sections to the revision. The authors from the first edition, Magnus Penker and Hans-Erik Eriksson, reviewed all the chapters and provided many helpful suggestions.

We also wish to thank reviewers from Number Six Software: Joe Hunt, Paul Moskowitz, Leslie Power, Kevin Puscas, and David Sisk. In addition, we would like to thank Lisa A. Porter for providing her technical writing expertise and Melissa C. Wood for her userinterface design, development, and advice.

We also want to provide a special thanks to Jim Odell for walking us through some of the trickier parts of UML 2.

We wish like to thank Robert Elliot, Kevin Kent, and the staff at Wiley for all their help producing this book.

A number of others who helped along the way also deserve mention; these include Conrad Bock, Grady Booch, Robert Boylan, Carolyn Fado, Kelly Fado, Mark D. Flood, William Graeter, Øystein Haugen, Amy Henry, Cris Kobryn, Brian Lawler, Terry Quatrani, Mike Rosen, Bran Selic, and Richard Soley.

CHAPTER

1

What Is UML?

What is the UML? In short, the Unified Modeling Language (UML) provides industry standard mechanisms for visualizing, specifying, constructing, and documenting software systems. However, such a static definition does not convey the tremendous growth of UML and the exciting opportunities of recent advances in the language. UML organizes thought with a dynamic set of features that support continuous evolution. This evolution has seen UML through a number of minor new releases (versions 1.0, 1.1, 1.2, 1.3, and 1.4, referenced as UML 1.*x*) into a major release (2) designed to extend UML's growth into new areas. The latest UML specification now spans hundreds of pages, with links to other specifications bringing the total into the thousands. The long answer to the question "What is the UML?" is found in the specifications that define the current edition of UML. However, those specifications, freely available for download, do not provide a practical overview of the key features of UML. This book seeks to address this need. This chapter provides some general background on software modeling, the historical roots of UML, and the basic goals of UML 2.

UML provides a language for describing system interactions, supported by a cohesive set of definitions managed by an official group, the Object Management Group (OMG). In this, UML at first resembles a software product more than a language; software versions improve "bugs" in the specification and add new "features" just like UML. However, like a language, UML has evolved dialects beyond the reach of official standards for such needs as data modeling, business modeling, and real-time development. The designers of UML intentionally gave UML the power for such evolution; UML has extension mechanisms that allow for creative new approaches. The implementation of UML, and especially UML 2, allows flexible language evolution that can keep up with the pace of change in software development. UML seeks to define concepts, to establish notation for communicating those concepts, and to enforce the related grammatical rules for constructing software models, allowing for automated tool support. The goal is to have the flexibility to apply to all software development while providing coherent enough definitions for automation. UML 1.*x* made a giant step toward this goal, and UML 2 furthers this effort. Put another way, UML provides a set of tools for all those involved in using information technology. This set of tools involves a rich set of graphical elements, including notation for classes, components, nodes, activities, ports, workflow, use cases, objects, states, and the relationships between all these elements.

Just as a dictionary does not explain how to write a book, UML itself offers no process for developing software. Just as a toolbox does not tell you how to use a hammer, UML does not recommend how to use the notation it provides in a model. Using UML to enhance project success requires skill, talent, and creativity. This book explains how to use the UML toolkit to improve software systems. So, this book not only discusses the specific elements of the UML specification, but also shows how to use these to model within a process to develop good software.

The Purpose of Modeling

A model represents highly creative work. There is no final solution and no correct answer that is checked at the end of the work. The model's designers, through iterative work, ensure that their models achieve the goals and the requirements of the project under construction. But a model is not final; it is typically changed and updated throughout a project to reflect new insights and the experiences of the designers. During the modeling, the best solutions are often achieved by allowing a high degree of brainstorming, during which different solutions and views are modeled and tested. By discussing different possibilities, the designers reach a deeper understanding of the system, and can finally create models of the systems that achieve the goals and requirements of the system and its users.

Communicating a model in a clear way to the many people involved in a software project represents a core feature of UML. The term *modeling* can lead to confusion, because it also applies to a number of different levels. Modeling shows not only the detailed specifications of software elements, but also high level analysis, providing mechanisms to link the different layers of abstraction. A model can reduce complexity by decomposing a system into easy-to-understand elements. In software engineering, modeling starts with a description of a problem, an analysis, and then moves to the proposition of a solution to solve the problem, a design, along with an implementation and a deployment.

Models have driven engineering disciplines for centuries. One assumes the ancient Egyptians worked up a model before starting on a pyramid. Any building project includes plans and drawings that describe the building. This model also provides essential instructions to the workers implementing the design. For a model, the object under development may be a house, a machine, a new department within a company, a software program, or a series of programs. Diagrams specify how you want the finished product to look and to act. Plans for implementation, including estimation of cost and resource allocation, are made based on the information contained in the model. A poor model makes accurate estimation and planning impossible.

During the work of preparing a model, the model's designers must investigate the needs, preferences, structure, and design for the finished product. These needs and preferences, called *requirements*, include areas such as functionality, appearance, performance, and reliability. The designers create a model to communicate the different aspects of the product. Good designers will take advantage of the tools offered by UML to improve their design and get feedback from their clients. In order to allow this feedback loop between those who need the software, those who design the software, those who build the software, and those who deploy the software, a model is often broken down into a number of views, each of which describes a specific aspect of the product under construction.

A model not only represents a system or organization, promotes understanding, and enables simulation, but it is also a basic unit of development. It specifies a part of the function, structure, and the behavior of a system. A model is not directly observable by its designer or its user, but can be expressed in terms of diagrammatic notation, text, or a combination of both.

Many models for software engineering are displayed using a graphical language expressed by shapes, symbols, icons, and arrows, and supported by labels. In fact, models are usually described in a visual language, which means that most of the information in the models is expressed by graphical symbols and connections. The old saying that "a picture speaks a thousand words" is also relevant in modeling. Using visual descriptions helps communicate complex relationships; it also makes the practical modeling work easier.

NOTE **Not everything is suitable for a visual description, some information in models is best expressed in ordinary text.**

In short, usable models are:

- **Accurate.** They must precisely and correctly describe the system they are representing.
- **Understandable.** They must be as simple as possible, but too simple to accurately fulfill their purpose, and must be easy to communicate.
- **Consistent.** Different views must not express things that are in conflict with each other.
- **Modifiable.** They must be easy to change and update.

Software Development, Methods, and Models

Many software projects fail. They can fail in many ways.

- Excessive cost
- Late delivery
- Absolute failure to meet the requirements and needs of customers

Some projects fail in terms of budget, schedule, and functionality, the three major factors to track in managing a software project. Such total failures appear far too often in software development. Effective modeling and sound management practices can help avoid such failures.

Technical advances, such as object-oriented programming, visual programming, and advanced development environments, have helped to increase productivity of coding, but have not solved these problems. Such technical advances have improved efficiency at the lowest level of system development, the programming level, not at the level of the analysis, design, or implementation.

One of the main problems with today's software development is that many projects start programming too soon and concentrate too much effort on writing code. Many managers lack an understanding of the software development process and become anxious when their programming team is not producing code. Programmers also tend to feel more secure when they're programming rather than when they are building abstract models of the system they are to create. In many cases, fundamental industry practices created many of these problems by measuring the performance of a programmer by lines of code rather than by solutions.

The use of modeling in software development is the difference between mature software engineering and hacking up code for a temporary solution. Systems are becoming much larger, integrating many different hardware and software components and machines, and distributed over complex architectures and platforms. The need to integrate extremely complex systems in distributed environments requires that systems be designed carefully, not coded haphazardly.

Before UML, many approaches, called *methods*, were developed that attempted to inject engineering principles into the craft of software engineering. The most worthwhile engineering techniques are those that can be described both quantitatively and qualitatively, and used consistently and predictably. The method must achieve better results than using no method, must be able to be applied to many different problems, and must be able to be taught to others relatively easily.

The multitude of different methods, each with its own unique notation and tools, left many developers confused and unable to collaborate. The lack of a well-established notation upon which creators of many methods and tools could agree made it more difficult to learn how to use a good method. Furthermore, most of the early object-oriented methods were immature and best suited for small systems with limited functionality. They did not have the capability to scale up to the large systems that are now common. Indirectly, modeling can encourage a designer or software architect to adopt a more disciplined development process. Directly, models serve as a repository of knowledge.

The trends of the software industry still point to the need for creating models of the systems we intend to build. Visual programming is a technique by which programs are constructed by visually manipulating and connecting symbols; so it is that modeling and programming are highly integrated. Systems are becoming larger and are distributed over many computers through client/server architectures (with the Internet as the ultimate client/server architecture). The need to integrate complex systems in distributed environments requires that systems have some common models. Business engineering, where the business processes of a company are modeled and improved, requires computer systems that support these processes to implement the business models. Building models of systems before implementing them is becoming as normal and accepted in the software engineering community as it is in other engineering disciplines.

UML has helped improve modeling, making software engineering more mature as a discipline. Now, those who want to work as a software architect *must* know UML. The Java architecture exam, for example, assumes a knowledge of UML. Such progress, in a little over 60 months since initial adoption, represents a remarkable achievement. It is worth knowing how UML evolved, to understand the core elements of the language. Basically, three prominent methodologists in the information systems and technology industry—Grady Booch, James Rumbaugh, and Ivar Jacobson—cooperated in developing UML. UML combined the most effective diagramming practices applied by software developers over the past four decades. This combination put an end to competing styles that had clashed in the so-called "method wars."

The Method Wars

Antecedents of object-oriented (OO) modeling languages first appeared in the mid-1970s, and continued during the 1980s as programmers and project managers tried different approaches to analysis and design. Object orientation was initially spawned by the programming language Simula, but it didn't become popular until the late 1980s with the advent of programming languages such as C++ and Smalltalk. When object-oriented programming became a success, the need for methods to support software development followed. More than 50 methods and modeling languages appeared by 1994, and a growing problem became finding a single language to fulfill the needs of many different people and projects.

In the mid-1990s, the modeling languages started to incorporate the best features of previous languages, and few languages gained prominence over the field. These included OOSE (Object-Oriented Software Engineering), OMT-2 (Object Modeling Technique), and Booch'93. OOSE established the use of use cases, making it suited to business engineering and analysis. OMT-2 was strongly oriented toward analysis, and proved to be better at modeling data-intensive information systems. Booch'93 focused on the design and construction phases of projects, and proved especially applicable to engineering applications. Some prominent methods from this era and their contributions are listed as follows:

- **Coad/Yourdon.** This method, also known as OOA/OOD, was one of the first methods used for object-oriented analysis and design. It was simple and easy to learn, and worked well for introducing novices to the concepts and terminology of object-oriented technology. However, the notation and method could not scale to handle anything but very limited systems. It was not heavily used.
- **Booch.** Booch defined the notion that a system is analyzed as a number of views, where each view is described by a number of model diagrams. The method also contained a process by which the system was analyzed from both a macro- and microdevelopment view, and was based on a highly incremental and iterative process. Although it was very strong in architecture, there were those that argued that it didn't nail requirements issues.
- **OMT.** The Object Modeling Technique (OMT) was developed at General Electric by James Rumbaugh and is a straightforward process for performing tests based on a requirements specification. The system is described by a number of models, including the object model, the dynamic model, and the functional model, which complement each other to give the complete description of the system. The OMT method

also contained practical instructions for system design, taking into account concurrency and mapping to relational databases.

- **OOSE/Objectory.** The OOSE and Objectory methods both build on the same basic viewpoint formed by Ivar Jacobson. The OOSE method (I. Jacobson et al., 1992) was Jacobson's own vision of an object-oriented method. The Objectory method was used for building a number of systems from telecommunication systems for Ericsson to financial systems for Wall Street companies. Both methods were based on use cases, which are then implemented in all phases of the development. Objectory was also adapted for business engineering, where the ideas are used to model and improve business processes.
- **Fusion.** This method came from Hewlett-Packard (D. Coleman, 1994) and was called a second-generation method, as it was based on the experiences of many of the initial methods. Fusion enhanced a number of important previous ideas, including techniques for the specification of operations and interactions between objects.

Each of these methods had its own notation (the symbols used to represent object-oriented models), process (which stipulates the activities to perform in different parts of the development), and tools. This made the choice of method a very important decision, and often led to heated debates about which method was "the best," the "most advanced," and "the right" method to use in a specific project. As with any such discussion, there seldom was a good answer, because all the methods had their own strengths and weaknesses. Experienced developers often took one method as a base, and then borrowed good ideas and solutions from others. In practice, the differences between the methods were not significant, and as time passed and the methods developed, they began to integrate the best ideas. Still, the method confusion took up time, prohibited the development of a common notation, and prevented common tool support for visual modeling.

This was recognized by several of the method gurus, who began to seek ways to cooperate. A primary goal of UML was to put an end to the "method wars" within the object-oriented community. In October 1994, Grady Booch and Jim Rumbaugh of the Rational Software Corporation began work on unifying the Booch and OMT methods, resulting in a draft version of the Unified Method in October 1995. OOSE was incorporated into the Unified Method when Rational bought the Swedish company Objectory.

Earlier in 1995, Ivar Jacobson, the Chief Technology Officer of Objectory, and Richard Soley, Chief Technology Officer of the Object Management Group (OMG), decided to work together to achieve an independent, open standard in the methods marketplace. OMG hosted a meeting attended by most of the major methodologists at the time, with the one goal of achieving an industry standard modeling language. Jacobson joined Booch and Rumbaugh's unification work and the three became known as the "Three Amigos." The three then recognized that their work was more suited to creating a standard modeling language than a method and began work on the Unified Modeling Language. They submitted a number of preliminary versions of UML to the object-oriented community and received more ideas and suggestions to improve the language. Version 1.0 of the Unified Modeling Language was released in January 1997.

Even though the main parts of UML are based on the Booch, OMT, and OOSE methods, these designers also included concepts from other methods, for example, the work of David Harel on state charts adopted in the UML state machines, the parts of the Fusion notation for numbering operations included in collaboration diagrams, the responsibilities and collaborations from Wirfs-Brock, and the work of Gamma-Helm-Johnson-Vlissides on patterns and how to document them that inspired details of class diagrams. UML 2 has been additionally improved by the work of a number of designers with practical experience. The ability of UML to incorporate so many different thinkers into a framework of cooperation and improvement helps to explain the language's success.

The goals of UML, as stated by the designers, are:

- To model systems (and not just software) using object-oriented concepts
- To establish an explicit coupling to conceptual as well as executable artifacts
- To address the issues of scale inherent in complex, mission-critical systems
- To create a modeling language usable by both human beings and machines

Acceptance of UML

To establish UML, the designers realized that the language had to be made available to everyone. Therefore, the language is nonproprietary and open to all. Companies are free to use it with their own methods. Tool vendors are free to create tools for it, and authors are encouraged to write books about it. During 1996, a number of organizations joined to form the UML Partners consortium. These companies included the Digital Equipment Corporation, Hewlett-Packard, I-Logix, Intellicorp, IBM, ICON Computing, MCI Systemhouse, Microsoft, Oracle, Texas Instruments, Unisys, and Rational. These organizations saw UML as strategic to their businesses and contributed to the definition of UML. The companies also supported the proposal to adopt UML as an Object Management Group (OMG) standard. This made UML independent of any one company's business plan, making it more likely to act as a standard throughout the industry. This approach brought peace and ended the wasteful method wars. For UML 2, this list of companies has expanded significantly. At this point, UML has far outgrown its initial founders, and it will outlast Rational as an independent company, now that IBM has purchased Rational.

The Object Management Group

The Object Management Group was founded in 1989 by 11 member companies, including 3Com Corporation; American Airlines; Canon, Inc.; Data General; Hewlett-Packard; Philips Telecommunications N.V.; Sun Microsystems; and Unisys Corporation, and now has over 800 members. The OMG is a not-for-profit corporation that is dedicated to establishing a component-based software industry through vendor independent specifications. Its goal is to produce industry guidelines and specifications in order to provide a common framework for application development.

The OMG does not produce software; it produces and then distributes specifications that are developed by an open community of contributors. Members can submit technology or concepts for review, contribute to open discussions, provide commentary, and review submissions from other members. Members of the organization then vote on contributions, adoptions, and versions of specifications in Task Forces and Technology Committees.

Unified Modeling Language Elements

With OMG support, the UML is now very well documented with a formal specification of the semantics of the language. Chapter 2 provides a high-level overview and is followed by chapters that look at these features more closely. At a high level, the details of UML are as follows:

- All UML diagrams describe object-oriented information.
- Class and object diagrams illustrate a system's static structure and the relationship between different objects.
- Interaction diagrams, state machines, and activity diagrams, show the dynamic behavior of objects, as well as messages between objects.
- Use-case and activity diagrams show system requirements and process workflows.
- The composite structure diagram shows the collaborating features as they combine at run time to implement a specific UML element.
- Deployment diagrams help with the deployment of the software in a specific environment.

These features of UML enable business analysts and software architects to collaborate on a design, and specify, construct, and document applications in a standard way. Modelers can make sure that requirements are effectively captured, business problems are addressed, and the solutions are workable and practical.

Because no notation can cover every possible type of information, UML also supports the use of comments and defines their notation. One can also extend UML for specialized environments. UML 2 encourages a modeler to develop a Platform Specific Model tuned to the deployment environment. However, these language elements are not enough; they must be used within a sound process to take advantage of their main features to enhance communication.

Methods and Modeling Languages

There are important differences between a method and a modeling language. A *method*, also called a methodology, is an explicit way of structuring one's thinking and actions. It consists of a process, a standard vocabulary, and a set of rules and guidelines. It tells the user what to do, how to do it, when to do it, and why it is done. The method defines a set of activities that will accomplish the goals of the project, including the purpose of each specific activity, and what resulted from that activity. Examples include the Unified Process, Shlaer-Mellor, CRC (Class, Responsibilities, and Collaborators), and Extreme Programming. A mature and effective methodology for object-oriented development will encompass many different elements:

- A full life-cycle process
- A language defining concepts and models that are consistent, including notation for how ideas are presented
- Defined roles with prescribed responsibilities
- Rules and guidelines that define activities and how they are performed, including the work products and deliverables they produce
- Defined analysis, design, development, and test strategies

Methods contain models, and these models are used to describe something and to communicate the results of the use of a method. The main difference between a method and a modeling language is that the modeling language lacks a process or the instructions for what to do, how to do it, when to do it, and why it is done. Though UML standardizes models and has incorporated elements gathered from many different methods, the development approaches that use UML are as diverse as the environments in which it is used. It can provide the underlying notation and language of the process. Still, different projects will emphasize different diagrams and extensions to UML. A project that demands accurate real-time execution will have different modeling needs than a project that provides reports at predefined intervals, for example. The real-time project will likely use extension mechanisms found in profiles for the advanced and specialized concepts needed in the project.

A model is expressed in a *modeling language*. A modeling language consists of notation—the symbols used in the models—and a set of rules directing how to use it. The rules are syntactic, semantic, and pragmatic.

- Syntax tells us how the symbols should look and how the symbols in the modeling language should be combined. The syntax can be compared to words in natural language; it is important to know how to spell them correctly and how to put different words together to form a sentence.
- Semantic rules explain what each symbol means and how it should be interpreted, either by itself or in the context of other symbols.
- The pragmatic rules define the intentions of the symbols through which the purpose of a model is achieved and becomes understandable for others. This corresponds in natural language to the rules for constructing sentences that are clear and understandable. To use a modeling language well, it is necessary to learn all of these rules. Fortunately, UML is a lot easier to comprehend than a natural language. Though naturally, even when the language is mastered there is no guarantee that the models produced will be effective.

Object-Oriented Software Development

UML comes from an object-oriented background. One answer to the question "What is the UML?" could be the following: "It is an object-oriented modeling language for modern software systems." As an object-oriented modeling language, all the elements and diagrams in UML are based on the object-oriented paradigm. Software development that is object-oriented depicts the real world and solves problems through the interpretation of "objects", digitally mimicking and representing the tangible elements of a system. The object-oriented approach considers a system as a dynamic entity comprising components, which can really only be defined with respect to one another. What a system is and does can be described only in terms of its components and how they interact.

Concepts of Object Orientation

The principal concepts of object orientation are as follows.

- Object orientation is a technology for producing models that reflect a domain, such as a business domain or a machine domain, in a natural way, using the terminology of the domain.
- Object-oriented software development has five underlying concepts: objects, messages, classes, inheritance, and polymorphism. Software objects have a state, a behavior, and an identity. The behavior can depend upon the state, and the state may be modified by the behavior. Messages that provide the communication between the objects of a system, and between systems themselves, have five main categories: constructors, destructors, selectors, modifiers, and iterators.
- Every object is a real-world "instance" of a class, which is a type of template used to define the characteristics of an object. Each object has a name, attributes, and operations. Classes are said to have an association if the objects they instantiate are linked or related.
- Object-oriented models, when constructed correctly, are easy to communicate, change, expand, validate, and verify.
- When done correctly, systems built using object-oriented technology are flexible in response to change, have well-defined architectures, and provide the opportunity to create and implement reusable components. The requirements of the system are traceable to the code of the system.
- Object-oriented models are conveniently implemented in software using object-oriented programming languages. Using programming languages that are not object-oriented to implement object-oriented systems is not recommended. However, it's important to realize that object-oriented software engineering is much more than just a couple of mechanisms in a programming language.
- Object orientation is not just a theory, but a well-proven technology used in a large number of projects and for building many different types of systems. The field still lacks standardization to show the way to an industrialization of object technology. The work provided by OMG strives to achieve such standardization.
- Object orientation requires a method that integrates a development process and a modeling language with suitable construction techniques and tools.

In UML, objects and classes are modeled by object and class diagrams. The interaction between objects is represented by communication or sequence diagrams. Communication diagrams more effectively display the physical layout of objects within a system, while sequence diagrams show the interactions between objects across time. Classes may be placed into hierarchies by means of generalization and specialization relationships, which are usually implemented using inheritance. UML perfectly complements the object-oriented development philosophy, as it was designed with object orientation as its foundation.

Business Engineering

The use of object-oriented modeling for the purpose of business engineering has generated a lot of interest. Object-oriented models have proven to be an excellent method for modeling the business processes in a company. A business process provides some value to the customer of the business (or perhaps the customer's customer). When a company uses techniques such as Business Process Reengineering (BPR) or Total Quality Management (TQM), the processes are analyzed, improved, and implemented in the company. Using an object-oriented modeling language to model and document the processes also makes it easier to use these models when building the information systems in the company.

CROSS-REFERENCE **For more on business engineering, see the book *Business Modeling with UML: Business Patterns at Work* by Magnus Penker and Hans-Erik Eriksson (Wiley 2000).**

UML 2 offers a number of new features designed to make it easier to move from business process modeling to software development. Activity diagrams and state machines include more features for accurate system description and flow control. In addition, a first-class extension mechanism with profiles makes it easier to tailor UML in a standard way to support specific domains.

Disciplines of System Development

There are numerous methods and processes applied to develop systems. Disregarding particular phases, milestones, or artifacts created, you can consider that a set of disciplines will always be applied. These disciplines are:

- Requirements
- Analysis
- Design
- Implementation
- Test

No matter when the disciplines are applied in an end-to-end process, no matter how much or little emphasis each discipline might receive in a process, one must work on the system from each of these perspectives.

CROSS-REFERENCE **Chapter 10 describes a process for using UML. In the next sections, we will just introduce how UML supports each of these disciplines.**

Requirements

UML has use cases to capture the requirements of the customer. Through use-case modeling, the external actors that have interest in the system are modeled along with the functionality they require from the system (the use cases). The actors and use cases are modeled with relationships and have communication associations with each other or are broken down into hierarchies. The actors and use cases are described in a UML use-case diagram. Each use case is described in text, and that specifies the requirements of the customer, what he or she expects of the system, without considering how the functionality will be implemented. Extra detail of the system can be described using behavioral diagrams, such as state machines and activity diagrams, plus structural diagrams, such as high-level class diagrams showing relationships among business entities. The requirements discipline can also be exercised with business processes, not only for software systems.

Analysis

Analysis is concerned with the primary abstractions (classes and objects) and mechanisms that are present in the problem domain. The classes that model these are identified, along with their relationships to each other, and described in a UML class diagram. Collaborations between classes necessary to perform the use cases are also described, via any of the dynamic models in UML. In the analysis, only classes that are in the problem domain (real-world concepts) are modeled—not technical classes that define details and solutions in the software system, such as classes for user interface, databases, communication, concurrency, and so on.

Design

In design, the result of the analysis is expanded into a technical solution. New classes are added to provide the technical infrastructure: the user interface, database handling to store objects in a database, communication with other systems, interfacing to devices in the system, and others. The domain problem classes from the analysis are "embedded" into this technical infrastructure, making it possible to change both the problem domain and the infrastructure. The design results in detailed specifications for the implementation activities.

Implementation

In implementation, the classes from the design phase are converted to actual code in an object-oriented programming language (using a procedural language is *not* recommended). Depending on the capability of the language used, this can be either a difficult or an easy task.

When creating analysis and design models in UML, it is best to avoid trying to mentally translate the models into code. The models are a means to understand and structure a system; thus, jumping to early conclusions about the code can be counterproductive to creating simple and correct models. The programming is a separate activity, during which the models are converted into code.

Test

A system is normally exercised via unit tests, integration tests, system tests, and acceptance tests.

- The *unit tests* are of individual classes or a group of classes and are typically performed by the programmer.
- The *integration test* integrates components and classes in order to verify that they cooperate as specified.
- The *system test* views the system as a "black box" and validates the end functionality of the system expected by an end user.
- The *acceptance test* is conducted by the customer to verify that the system satisfies the requirements. It is similar to the system test.

The different test teams use different UML diagrams as the basis for their work: unit tests use class diagrams and class specifications, integration tests typically use component diagrams and collaboration diagrams, and the system tests implement use-case and activity diagrams to verify that the system behaves as initially defined in these diagrams.

Relevant Changes in UML 2

The initial versions of UML blended a number of different modeling methods into a standard, freeing software engineers to focus on software and allowing tool vendors to provide automated support for software development. More importantly, UML improved software engineering by supporting effective management of information and communication about system elements. The model took center stage. Such success created an appetite for more. Software engineers now want additional features for describing behavior, portraying alternate paths, supporting component development, and showing the complex distributed deployments that mark enterprise applications. Tool vendors want an unambiguous specification so that all tools claiming to implement UML actually do. Further, the worlds of automated support tools and software modeling continue to grow closer. Some look for an architecture driven by models with enough technical sophistication to generate more code automatically and with enough flexibility to evolve with continuous change. UML 2 seeks to deliver these additional features, and more.

The OMG set out well-defined goals for UML 2 in a set of requirements that reflected issues found by users of UML 1.*x*. UML 2 supports the initiative for a model-driven architecture by providing the stable technical infrastructure that allows for additional automation of the software development process. From the requirements specification, four goals have emerged as prominent drivers in the evolution of UML:

- Make the language for modeling software entities more executable.
- Provide more robust mechanisms for modeling workflow and actions.
- Create a standard for communication between different tools.
- Reconcile UML within a standard modeling framework.

UML 2 has four separate specifications to address these main goals. Of these, the superstructure provides the main specification for UML elements and diagrams. Most of the information relevant to this book comes from the superstructure specification. That said, the other specifications help make UML easier to implement with support tools. They are of more interest to tool vendors and those with a passion for modeling, but merit brief mention here to explain the increasing complexity of UML behind the notation definition. Indeed, the OMG wanted to clearly separate the definition of the UML notation from the metamodel semantics.

The infrastructure specification provides a clearer mapping between UML and a general framework for all modeling from the OMG, the Meta Object Facility (MOF). This will allow the production of additional types of modeling languages that will all use the same basic elements. Additionally, this makes it easier for UML to rely on Extensible Markup Language (XML) Metadata Interchange (XMI) to define the rules for validating models and moving them between tools. While UML 1.*x* enhanced communication between people with visual diagram, UML 2 will enhance automated communication with the ability to express UML models in XML. If UML 1.0 attempted to end the method wars among those in object-oriented design, UML 2 seeks to be part of a system that allows modeling of all information technology systems and communication within a complex enterprise, a very lofty goal

The Object Constraint Language (OCL) defines instructions for specifying constraints and actions in a model. UML diagrams, however, do not require the use of OCL. The Diagram Interchange Model is a brief statement that specifies what you would anticipate: rules for diagram interchange.

UML 2 seeks to build on UML 1.*x*, not replace elements for no reason. OMG specified that changes should have as little impact as possible to users of current languages. Any change requires a clear statement of how this helps UML attain the specified goals. We can summarize the requirement's specification goals for the superstructure as follows.

- Support component-based development, including full definition for plug substitutability.
- Allow fuller modeling of the component execution context, especially needed with the proliferation of middleware and Web applications.
- Provide standard profiles or extensions for important languages.
- Support automated implementation of common interaction patterns.
- Enhance UML for runtime architecture, including support for the modeling of internal structure, especially communication paths, as well as the description of the dynamic behavior of that internal structure.
- Improve state machines, with clearer specifications for links to behavior and rules for specialization.
- Improve activity graphs with better control and data flow features.
- Support the composition of interaction mechanisms; define sequences of interactions, alternate interactions, and parallel execution.

Summary

UML 2 has a number of changes to diagrams that reflect behavior and deployment. New features, such as the port, explicitly support component-based development. Indeed, each of the changes in UML 2 in some way furthers these stated high-level goals discussed in the preceding section. Readers will find a more detailed summary of these changes at the end of each modeling chapter. The next chapter, Chapter 2, provides a high-level overview of the main elements in UML as background for the more detailed chapters on the specific types of modeling. The emphasis remains on understanding how to use the basic tools of UML, giving the reader an effective toolkit for software success.

CHAPTER 2

An Overview of UML

The Unified Modeling Language (UML) can capture a stunning array of processes and structures related to business and software. UML has such power that a modeler can use it for the general architecture of any construction that has both a static structure and dynamic behavior. A project can rely on UML as the standard language to express requirements, system design, deployment instructions, and code structure. The UML practitioner can capture ideas using visual tools, efficiently share these ideas with others, and effectively respond to change. UML provides a powerful set of tools to capture the lightning of information technology in a bottle. To achieve these wide-ranging capabilities, the language has features that do not apply in all circumstances. On a project using UML, the modeler will emphasize a subset of the potential diagrams. However, to know which features to emphasize on a project, a modeler needs to be familiar with all the general elements in UML. This will allow the modeler to know which "tool" to select from the UML "toolkit." This chapter provides an overview of UML to demonstrate its scope and structure. The elements of the language are described only briefly here, with more in-depth explanations and details included in later chapters. Because of this organization, not all the pieces may fall into place for you at once, but they will come together gradually as you continue with the book. You are not expected to fully understand the diagrams shown in this chapter, but rather to just get a glimpse of UML and its possibilities. When you are reviewing what might at first appear as rather boring and impractical structures, recall that the general goal of UML is to be a mechanism to capture and to manage ideas about information technology systems. UML diagrams represent the collective wisdom of some of the best minds of the last 20 years. They provide powerful tools that have succeeded in making the information technology revolution more manageable.

Software development and information technology change rapidly, so a successful language must work with this change. For example, since UML first emerged in the late 1990s, software has gone through another transformation with the proliferation of distributed systems and Web application architectures using complex deployments. UML has adapted to this with more formal mechanisms for showing the deployment information of specific platforms. When a system model requires specialized information like this, UML has formal extensions called profiles to apply UML to specific sectors, software problems, or language platforms.

The following overview describes UML by looking at these organizational features:

- **Views.** Views show different aspects of the system. A view is not a graphical element or diagram but an abstraction consisting of a number of diagrams. Only by defining a number of views, each showing a particular aspect of the system, can you construct a complete picture. The views also link the modeling language to the method or process chosen for development.
- **Diagrams.** Diagrams include the graphical elements that describe the contents in a view. UML has about a dozen different diagram types that are used in combination to provide all views of the system.
- **Model elements.** The concepts used in the diagrams are model elements that represent common object-oriented concepts such as classes, objects, and messages, and their relationships, including associations, dependencies, and generalization. These are the basic elements for modeling an object-oriented software system. A model element is used in several different diagrams, but it always has the same meaning and symbol.
- **General mechanisms.** General mechanisms provide extra comments, information, or semantics for a model element; they also provide extension mechanisms to adapt or to extend the UML to a specific domain, language, method or process, organization, or user.
- **Model Driven Architecture (MDA) features.** The group that manages UML, the Object Management Group (OMG), wraps UML within a broader initiative called MDA. MDA seeks to make UML models more executable and better integrated with development support tools. As part of the MDA initiative, UML complies with general efforts to manage multiple models.

Views

It takes a lot of effort to model a complex system. In an ideal world, you might represent the entire system clearly in a single picture that all understand without confusion. This ideal is impossible; only a trivial system could achieve such a goal. No modeler can generate a single diagram that defines the entire system unambiguously and is understandable by all human beings looking at it. A single graph cannot capture all the information needed to describe a system. A system has many different aspects: functional (its static structure and dynamic interactions), nonfunctional (timing requirements, reliability, deployment, and so on), along with organizational aspects (work organization, mapping to code modules, and so on). A system description requires a number of views, where each view represents a projection of the complete system that shows a particular aspect.

Each view requires a number of diagrams that contain information emphasizing a particular aspect of the system. A slight overlap does exist, so a diagram can actually be a part of more than one view. By looking at the system from different views, it is possible to concentrate on one aspect of the system at a time. A diagram in a particular view needs to be simple enough to communicate information clearly, yet coherent with the other diagrams and views so that the complete picture of the system is described by all the views put together. Each diagram contains graphical symbols that represent the model elements of the system. Figure 2.1 shows the views often used with UML. They are:

- **Use-case view.** A view showing the functionality of the system as perceived by external actors.
- **Logical view.** A view showing how the functionality is designed inside the system, in terms of the system's static structure and dynamic behavior.
- **Implementation view.** A view showing the organization of the code and the actual execution code.
- **Process view.** A view showing main elements in the system related to process performance. This view includes scalability, throughput, and basic time performance and can touch on some very complex calculations for advanced systems.
- **Deployment view.** A view showing the deployment of the system into the physical architecture with computers and devices called *nodes*.

When you choose a tool to draw and to manage the diagrams, make sure it's one that makes it easy to navigate from one view to another. In addition, to see how a function is designed to work within a diagram, the tool must make it easy to switch to either the use-case view to see how the function is described by an external user or to the deployment view to see how the function is distributed in the physical structure. The tool makes it easier to follow from one view to the other.

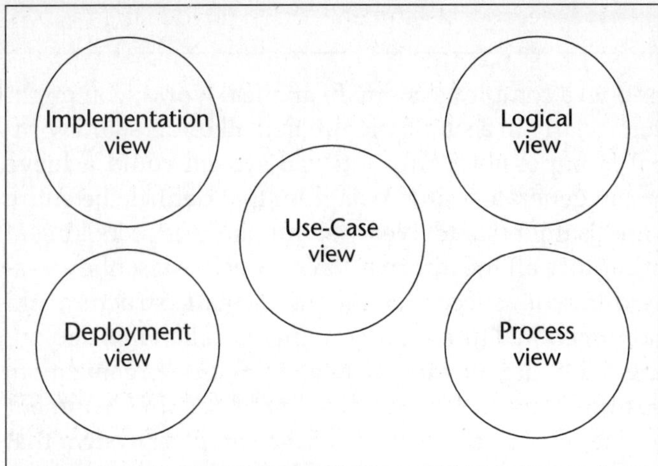

Figure 2.1 The views in UML.

Note that other views can be used, including static-dynamic, logical-physical, workflow, and others. UML doesn't require the views described in this chapter, but they are those that the initial designers of UML had in mind, so most tools provide some variant of these views. Modern UML tools also include features to define your own views and relate different models within a common system or project. A later section in this chapter has more on development support tools.

With the evolution of UML and its growing use across all sorts of processes, the focus has moved away from trying to capture the complete system all within the views of one model. MDA promotes the notion of different model levels that can use appropriate extension packages, or profiles, fit to the purpose of the model. At a high level, a system might have a general model that reflects the domain and business concerns for a client. This independent model then links to one or more specialized models better able to implement UML instructions in the proper target environment. However, to keep these models from spiraling out of control, it is important to keep them linked. In addition, it is important that the models be managed so that they can implement the main functionality of the system. It is the use-case view that is used to capture the functions needed by the client.

Use-Case View

The use-case view describes the functionality the system should deliver, as perceived by external actors. An actor interacts with the system; the actor can be a user or another system. The use-case view is used by customers, designers, developers, and testers; it is described in use-case diagrams, sometimes with support from activity diagrams. The desired usage of the system is described as a number of use cases in the use-case view, where a use case is a generic description of a function requested.

The use-case view is central, because its contents drive the development of the other views. The final goal of the system is to provide the functionality described in this view—along with some nonfunctional properties. Hence, this view affects all the others. This view is also used to validate the system and finally to verify the functioning of the system by testing the use-case view with the customers (asking, "Is this what you want?") and against the finished system (asking, "Does the system work as specified?").

Logical View

The logical view describes how the system's functionality is provided. It is mainly for designers and developers. In contrast to the use-case view, the logical view looks inside the system. It describes both the static structure (classes, objects, and relationships) and the dynamic collaborations that occur when the objects send messages to each other to provide a given function. Properties such as persistence and concurrency are also defined, as well as the interfaces and the internal structure of classes.

The static structure is described in class and object diagrams. The dynamic modeling is described in state machines, and interaction and activity diagrams.

Implementation View

The implementation view describes the main modules and their dependencies. It is mainly for developers and consists of the main software artifacts. The artifacts include different types of code modules shown with their structure and dependencies. Additional information about the components, such as resource allocation (responsibility for a component) or other administrative information, such as a progress report for the development work, can also be added. The implementation view will likely require the use of extensions for a specific execution environment.

Process View

The process view deals with the division of the system into processes and processors. This aspect, which is a nonfunctional property of the system, allows for efficient resource usage, parallel execution, and the handling of asynchronous events from the environment. Besides dividing the system into concurrently executing threads of control, this view must also deal with the communication and synchronization of these threads.

The emphasis on a view that shows concurrency provides critical information for developers and integrators of the system. The view consists of dynamic diagrams (state machines, and interaction and activity diagrams) and implementation diagrams (interaction and deployment diagrams). A timing diagram, as is described in Chapter 6, also provides a specialized tool for the process view. A timing diagram provides a way to show the current status of an object in terms of time. For example, this diagram can show how synchronized objects can queue to use a thread or process as a result of different strategies for implementing priority usage of resources.

Deployment View

Finally, the deployment view shows the physical deployment of the system, such as the computers and devices (nodes) and how they connect to each other. The various execution environments within the processors can be specified as well. The deployment view is used by developers, integrators, and testers and is represented by the deployment diagram. This view also includes a mapping that shows how the artifacts are deployed in the physical architecture, for example, which programs or objects execute on each respective computer.

Diagrams

The diagrams contain the graphical elements arranged to illustrate a particular part or aspect of the system. A system model typically has several diagrams of varying types, depending on the goal for the model. A diagram is part of a specific view, and when it is drawn, it is usually allocated to a view. Some diagram types can be part of several views, depending on the contents of the diagram.

This section describes the basic concepts behind each diagram. Additional details about the diagrams, their syntax, their meaning, and how they interact are described in the later chapters.

NOTE The diagrams throughout this book are taken from different types of systems to show the diversity of UML.

Use-Case Diagram

A use-case diagram shows a number of external actors and their connection to the use cases that the system provides (see Figure 2.2). A use case is a description of a functionality (a specific usage of the system) that the system provides. The description of the actual use case is normally done in plain text or as a document linked to the use case. The functionality and flow can also be described using an activity diagram. The use case description only views the system behavior as the user perceives it and does not describe how the functionality is provided inside the system. Use cases define the functional requirements of the system.

CROSS-REFERENCE **Use-case diagrams are described in greater detail in Chapter 3.**

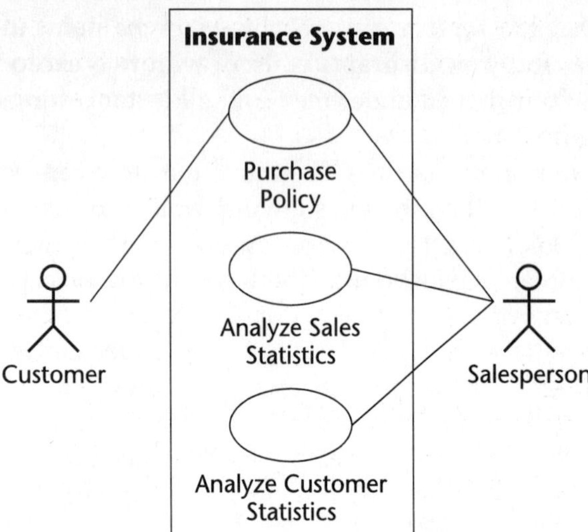

Figure 2.2 Use-case diagram for an insurance business.

Class Diagram

A class diagram shows the static structure of classes in the system (see Figure 2.3). The classes represent the "things" that are handled in the system. Classes can be related to each other in a number of ways: They can be associated (connected to each other), dependent (one class depends on or uses another class), specialized (one class is a specialization of another class), or packaged (grouped together as a unit). All these relationships are shown in a class diagram along with the internal structure of the classes in terms of attributes and operations. The diagram is considered static in that the structure described is always valid at any point in the system's life cycle.

A system typically has a number of class diagrams—not all classes are inserted into a single class diagram—and a class can participate in several class diagrams.

CROSS-REFERENCE **Class diagrams are described in Chapter 4.**

Object Diagram

An object diagram is a variant of a class diagram and uses almost identical notation. The difference between the two is that an object diagram shows a number of object instances of classes, instead of the actual classes. An object diagram is thus an example of a class diagram that shows a possible snapshot of the system's execution—what the system can look like at some point in time. The same notation as that for class diagrams is used, with two exceptions: Objects are written with their names underlined and all instances in a relationship are shown (see Figure 2.4).

Object diagrams are not as important as class diagrams, but they can be used to exemplify a complex class diagram by showing what the actual instances and the relationships look like. Objects are also used as part of interaction diagrams that show the dynamic collaboration between a set of objects.

State Machines

A state machine is typically a complement to the description of a class. It shows all the possible states that objects of the class can have during a life-cycle instance, and which events cause the state to change (see Figure 2.5). An event can be triggered by another object that sends a message to it—for example, that a specified time has elapsed—or that some condition has been fulfilled. A change of state is called a *transition*. A transition can also have some sort of behavior connected to it that specifies what is done in connection with the state transition.

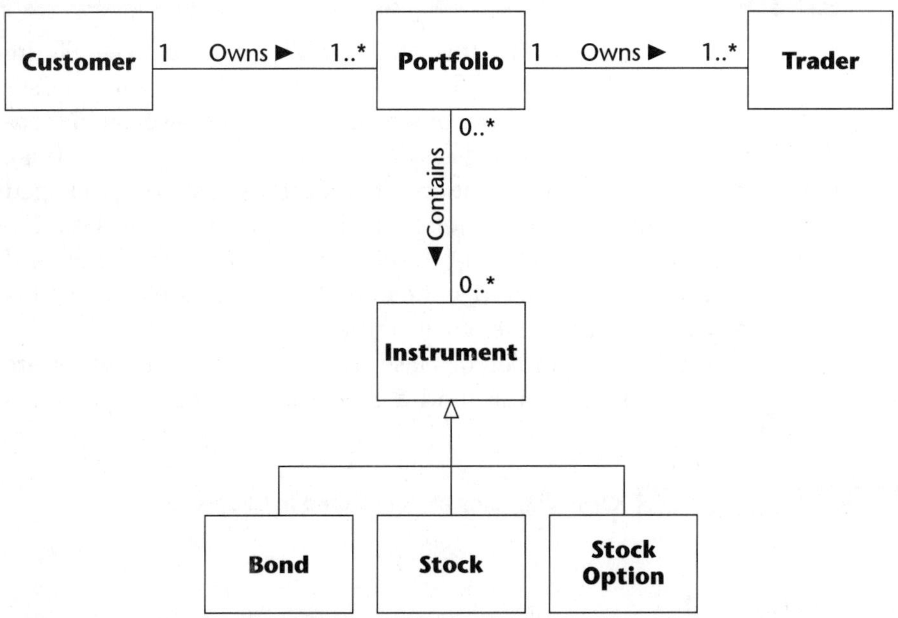

Figure 2.3 A class diagram for financial trading.

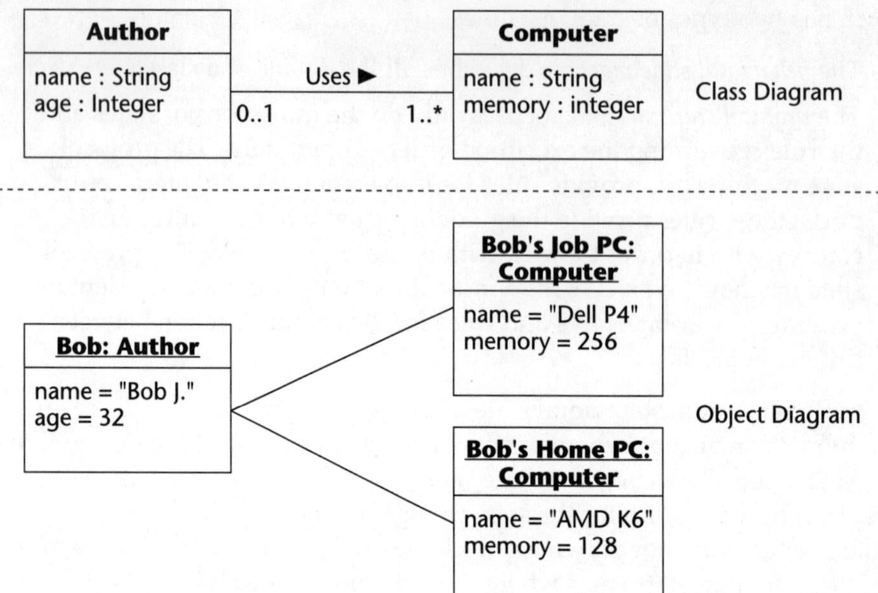

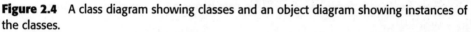

Figure 2.4 A class diagram showing classes and an object diagram showing instances of the classes.

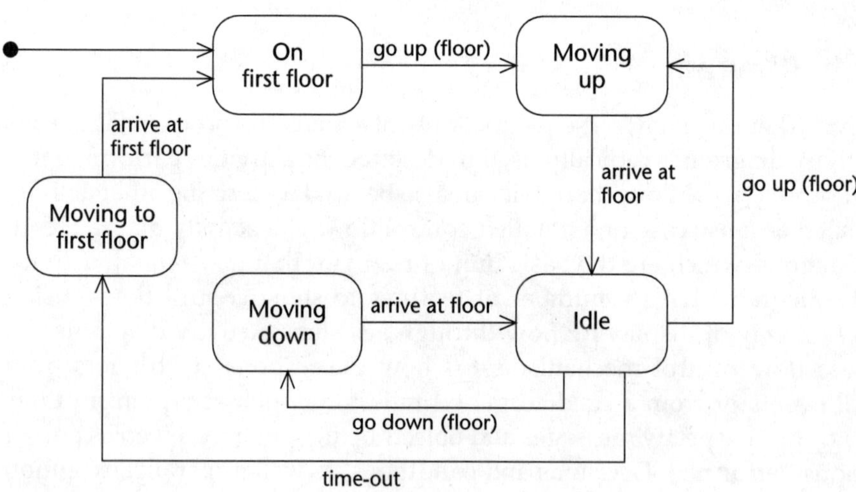

Figure 2.5 A behavioral state machine for an elevator.

UML has two types of state machines.

- The *behavioral state machine* describes all the details of a class's life cycle.
- The *protocol state machine* focuses only on the transitions of states and the rules governing the execution order of operations. The protocol state machine can provide rules for implementation by interfaces or ports; these rules provide the guidelines that other systems must comply with in order to work with the associated class. The protocol state machine helps UML support component-based development by providing clear interfaces and rules for the communication between different objects.

In implementation, behavioral state machines can get quite complex as they try to model concurrent behavior, show nested states, and allow for redefinition. At the core, however, the state machine represents a relatively simple concept to show the rules for the state change of an instance.

State machines are not drawn for all classes, only for those that have a number of well-defined states and where the behavior of the class is affected and changed by the different states. State machines can also represent the system as a whole.

CROSS-REFERENCE **State machines are described in more detail in Chapters 5 and 6.**

Activity Diagram

An activity diagram shows a sequential flow of actions, as shown in Figure 2.6. The activity diagram is typically used to describe the activities performed in a general process workflow, though it can also be used to describe other activity flows, such as a use case or a detailed control flow. The activity diagram consists of actions, which are the basic unit of behavior that make up an activity. Activity diagrams have a number of features to show control flows, using tokens as a way of displaying flow through a system. Activity diagrams can use these flow control mechanisms to show the response to triggers from external events or from a predetermined milestone, such as a point in time. The diagram can specify messages and objects being sent or received as part of the actions performed. Decisions and conditions, as well as parallel execution of actions, can also be shown in the diagram.

CROSS-REFERENCE **Activity diagrams are described in Chapters 5 and 6.**

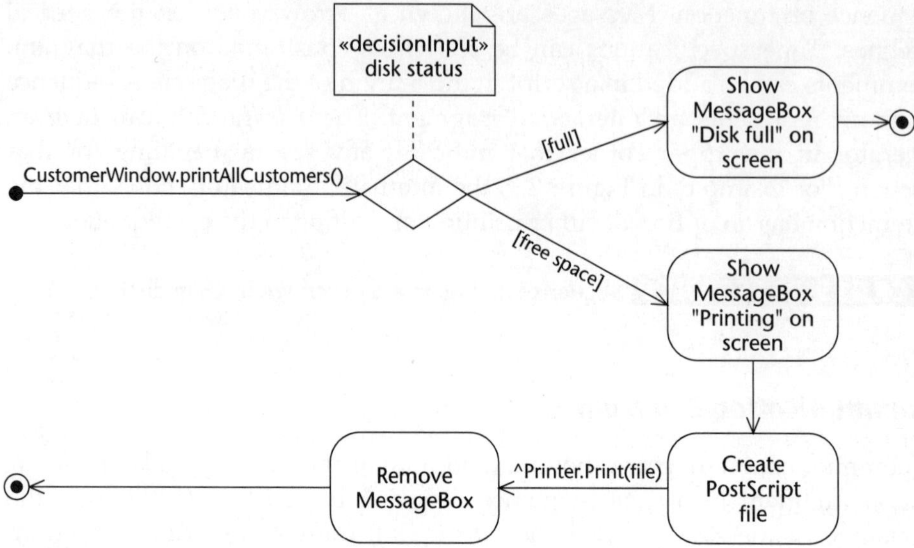

Figure 2.6 An activity diagram for a printer server.

Interaction Diagrams

UML provides a number of diagrams that show the interaction between objects during the execution of the software. These diagrams include sequence diagrams, which emphasize modeling the potential ordering options of an interaction; communication diagrams, which look at the structures of the interacting objects; and interaction overview diagrams, which place interaction fragments, or fragments of sequence diagrams, in a high-level workflow. UML also provides a timing diagram specialized for real-time systems.

CROSS-REFERENCE **Interaction diagrams are reviewed in Chapters 5 and 6.**

Sequence Diagram

A sequence diagram shows a dynamic collaboration between a number of objects, as shown in Figure 2.7. The important aspect of this diagram is that it shows a sequence of messages sent between the objects. It also shows an interaction between objects, something that happens at one specific point in the execution of the system. The diagram consists of a number of objects shown with vertical lifelines. Time passes downward in the diagram, and the diagram shows the exchange of messages between the objects as time passes in the sequence or function. Messages are shown as arrows between the vertical lifelines. Time specifications can be shown as constraints on the diagram. Comments can be added in a script in the margin of the diagram. A sequence diagram represents an interaction fragment. These fragments can take an operator in the upper corner that indicates any special handling for that section. For example, in Figure 2.7, the alternative indicator shows that the interaction has an option of either printing or waiting in the print queue.

CROSS-REFERENCE **Sequence diagrams are described in Chapters 5 and 6.**

Communication Diagram

A communication diagram shows a dynamic collaboration, just like the interaction fragment in a basic sequence diagram. In addition to showing the exchange of messages (called the *interaction*), the communication diagram shows the objects and their relationships (sometimes referred to as the *context*). Whether you should use a sequence diagram or a communication diagram can often be decided by the main goal for the exercise. If time or sequence is the most important aspect to emphasize and you need to show multiple interaction fragments, choose sequence diagrams; if the context is important to emphasize, choose a communication diagram. The interaction among the objects is shown on both diagrams.

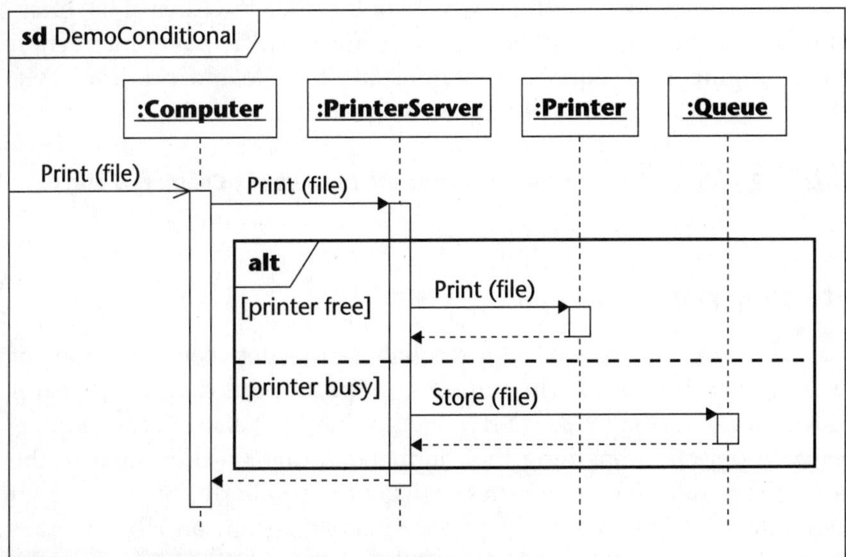

Figure 2.7 A sequence diagram for a print server.

The communication diagram shows a number of objects along with their relationships. Message arrows are drawn between the objects to show the flow of messages. Labels are placed on the messages, which show among other things the order in which the messages are sent, but not necessarily the order in which the messages are received. It can also show conditions, iterations, return values, and so on. When he or she is familiar with the message label syntax, a developer can read the communications and follow the standard execution flow and the exchange of messages. Note, however, that the communication diagram cannot handle the case when the reception order of a message is unknown. Figure 2.8 shows a communication diagram for a print server with some conditional messages.

CROSS-REFERENCE **Communication diagrams are described in Chapters 5 and 6.**

Interaction Overview Diagram

The interaction overview diagram provides the modeler with an opportunity to review the main flow of interactions at a high level. This feature can prove helpful when you are trying to make sure that the design has captured all the main flow elements defined in a use case. An interaction overview diagram is basically an activity diagram with main nodes replaced by the interaction fragments, or parts of sequence diagrams, placed in a specific order. The diagram also provides another method to show flow control during an interaction. The point of the interaction overview diagram is to show in one place the options that exist for the interaction.

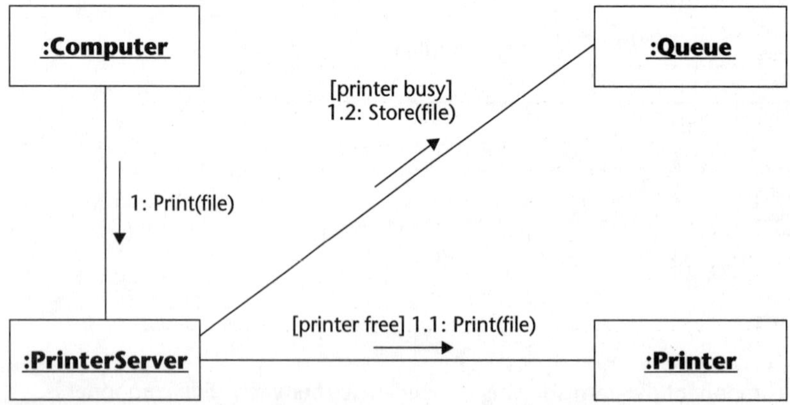

Figure 2.8 A communication diagram for a printer server.

Component Diagram

A component diagram shows the physical structure of the code in terms of code components. A component can be a source code component, a binary component, or an executable component. A component contains information about the logical class or classes it implements, thus creating a mapping from the logical view to the component view. Dependencies between the components are shown, making it easy to analyze how other components are affected by a change in one component. Components can also be shown with any of the interfaces that they expose, such as OLE/COM (object linking and embedding/Component Object Model) interfaces, and they can be grouped together in packages. The component diagram is used in practical programming work (see Figure 2.9).

CROSS-REFERENCE **Component diagrams are described in more detail in Chapter 7.**

Deployment Diagram

The deployment diagram shows the physical architecture of the hardware and software in the system. You can show the actual computers and devices (nodes), along with the connections they have to each other; you can also show the type of connections. Inside the nodes, executable components and objects are allocated to show which software units are executed on which nodes. You can also show dependencies between the components.

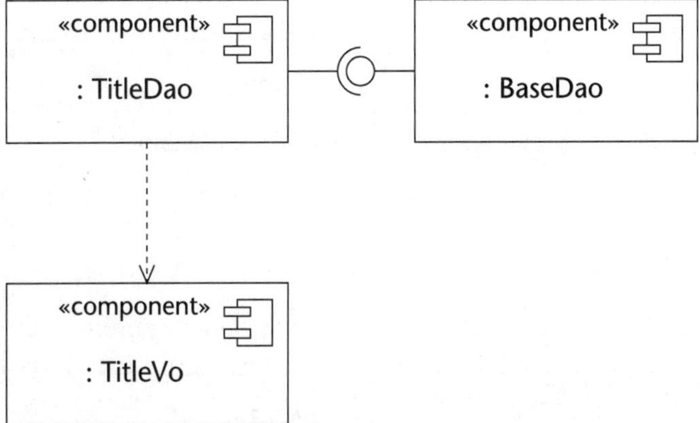

Figure 2.9 A component diagram showing dependencies between code components.

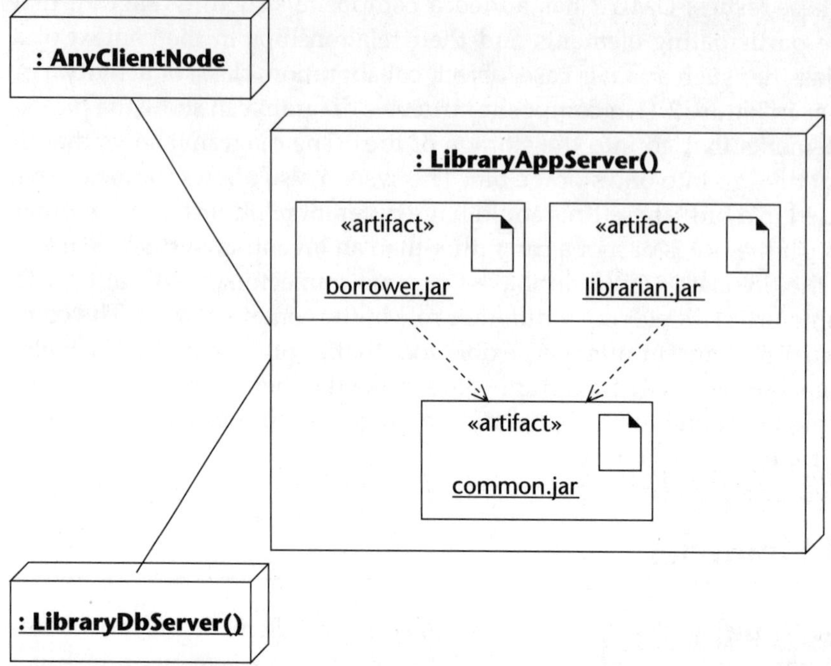

Figure 2.10 A deployment diagram shows the physical architecture of a system.

As stated previously, the deployment diagram, showing the deployment view, describes the actual physical architecture of the system. This view is far from the functional description in the use-case view. However, with a well-defined model, it's possible to navigate all the way from a node in the physical architecture to its components to the class it implements to the interactions that objects of the class participate in and finally to a use case. Different views of the system are used to give a coherent description of the system as a whole (see Figure 2.10).

CROSS-REFERENCE **Deployment diagrams are described in Chapter 7.**

Composite Structure Diagram

A well-defined model clearly communicates the roles and responsibilities of the elements. What about runtime architectures, where the system has parts and connectors not necessarily known at design time? For example, some systems produce a runtime architecture that isn't clear from a typical object or class diagram. The specific collaboration of elements might involve different relationships and rules from the information in the other static diagrams. To address these issues, UML 2 has added a composite structure diagram that shows the participating elements and their relationships in the context of a specific classifier such as a use case, object, collaboration, class, or activity. For example, as in Figure 2.11, a composite structure diagram can show the participating elements that go into the storage of tires. The diagram shows that in storage, 10 tires go into one storage bin. The system also allows for loose tires not included in a bin. These tires could have different relationships in another context. So, if the tire is part of a car, rather than an inventory system as in this diagram, the tire class would not have the same connectors. See Chapter 7 to see the same tire class playing a different role in the context of a car. The composite structure diagram offers a flexible tool that applies to many UML elements. For example, such a diagram could make it easier to apply the classes in your domain model to a collaboration occurrence without having to redefine them for each new context.

Model Elements

The concepts used in the diagrams are called model elements. A model element is defined with semantics, a formal definition of the element or the exact meaning of what it represents in unambiguous statements. A model element also can have a corresponding graphical element, which is the visual representation of the element or the graphical symbol used to represent the element in diagrams. An element can exist in several different types of diagrams, but there are rules for which elements can be shown in each type of diagram. Some example model elements are class, object, state, node, package, and component, as shown in Figure 2.12. Extensions to these model elements are also important, such as with artifacts on deployment diagrams. Chapter 8 includes more information on extensions.

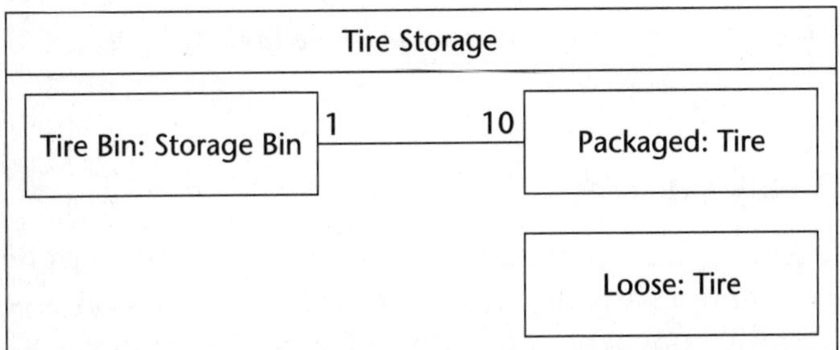

Figure 2.11 A sample of a composite structure diagram for a tire-storage system.

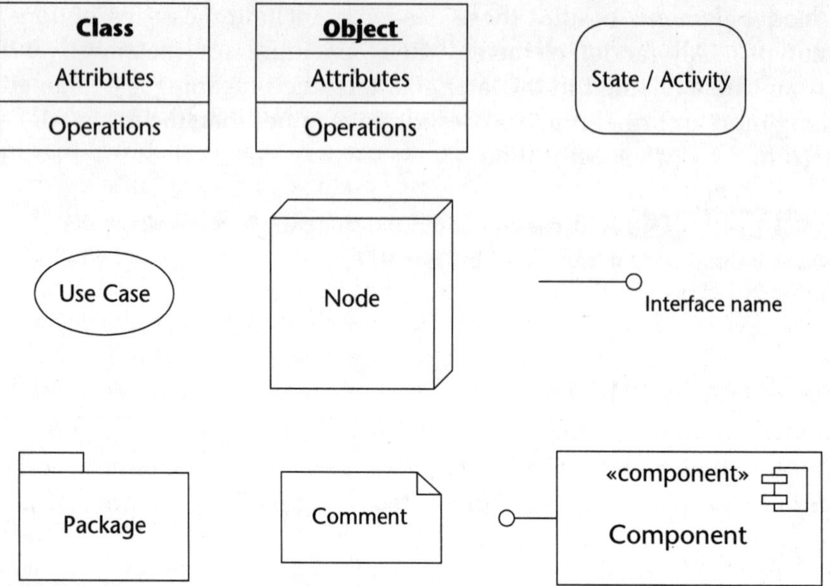

Figure 2.12 Some common model elements.

Figure 2.13 shows examples of relationships, which are also model elements and are used to connect other model elements with each other. Some different relationships are as follows:

- **Association.** Connects elements and links instances.
- **Generalization.** Also called inheritance, it means that an element can be a specialization of another element.
- **Dependency.** Shows that one element relies in some way on another element.
- **Aggregation.** A form of association in which an element contains other elements.

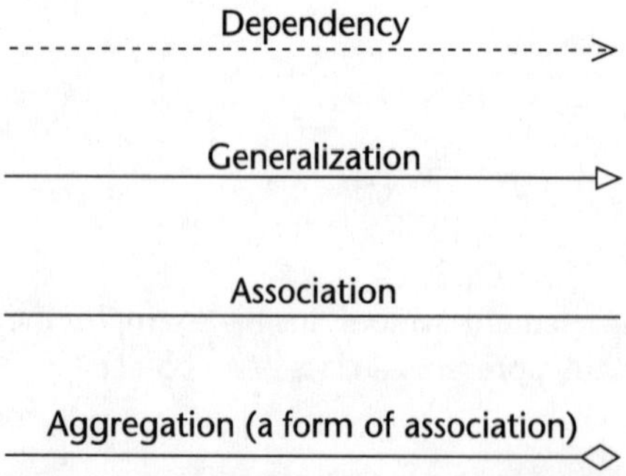

Figure 2.13 Examples of some relationships.

Other model elements besides those described include messages, actions, and stereotypes. All model elements, their semantics (or meaning), and allowed usage are explained in the later chapters; their meaning is explained emphasizing more informal practical descriptions rather than the formal definitions used in the UML specification.

CROSS-REFERENCE A discussion about the semantic framework, or the metamodel, behind UML is contained in Chapter 8.

General Mechanisms

UML utilizes some general mechanisms in all diagrams. These supply additional information that cannot be represented using the basic abilities of the model elements.

Adornments

Graphical adornments can be attached to the model elements in diagrams. The adornments add visual impact to the element. An example of an adornment is the technique used to separate a type from an instance. When an element represents a type, its name is displayed in boldface type. When the same element represents an instance of the type, its name is underlined and may specify both the name of the instance as well as the name of the type. A class rectangle, with the name in bold representing a class and the name underlined representing an object, is an example of this. The same goes for nodes, where the node symbol can be either a type in boldface, such as **Printer,** or an instance of a node type, such as `John's HP 5MP-printer`. Other adornments specify the multiplicity of relationships, where the multiplicity is a number or a range that indicates how many instances of connected types can be involved in the relation. Adornments are written close to the element to which they add information. All the adornments are described in conjunction with the description of the element that they affect (see Figure 2.14).

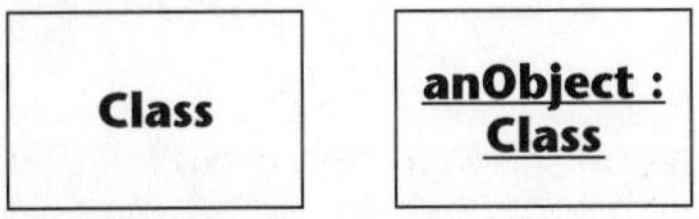

Figure 2.14 Adornments add information to an element symbol. In this example, the boldface and underlining specify whether the symbol represents a class or an object.

Comments

Not everything can be defined in a modeling language, no matter how extensive the language. To enable adding information to a model that otherwise cannot be represented or just to explain the design direction chosen on a diagram, UML provides a comments capability. A comment can be placed anywhere in any diagram, and it can contain any type of information. Its information type is an uninterpreted string that has no particular meaning in UML. The comment is typically attached to some element in the diagram with a dashed line that specifies which element is explained or detailed, along with the information in the comment (see Figure 2.15). The dashed line is not necessary if it is clear on the diagram what the comment means.

A comment often contains explanations or questions from the modeler as a reminder to resolve a dilemma at a later time. Comments also help to explain the goals and general features of a diagram.

Specifications

Model elements have properties that hold data values about the element. A property is defined with a name and a value called a *tagged value*, which is of a specified type such as an integer or a string. A number of predefined properties exist, such as CallConcurrencyKind, which indicates whether an operation can execute concurrently, sequentially, or guardedly.

Properties are used to add additional specifications about element instances that are not normally shown in the diagram. Typically, a class is described with some text that more informally itemizes the responsibilities and capabilities of the class. This type of specification is not normally shown in the diagram itself, but is available in a tool usually accessed by double-clicking an element that brings up a specification window with all of the element's properties (see Figure 2.16).

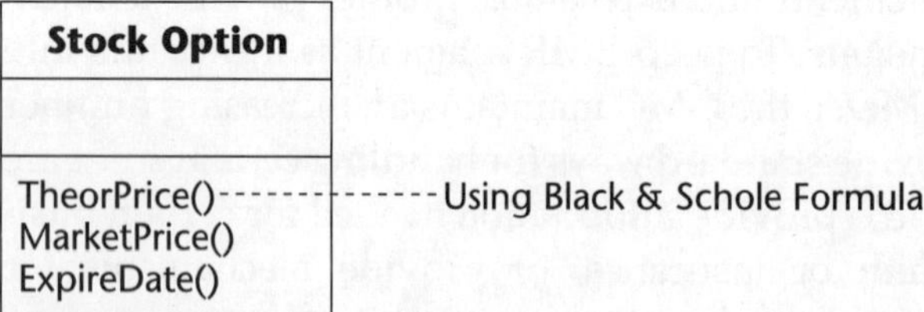

Figure 2.15 A comment contains any additional information such as a simple explanation of the element.

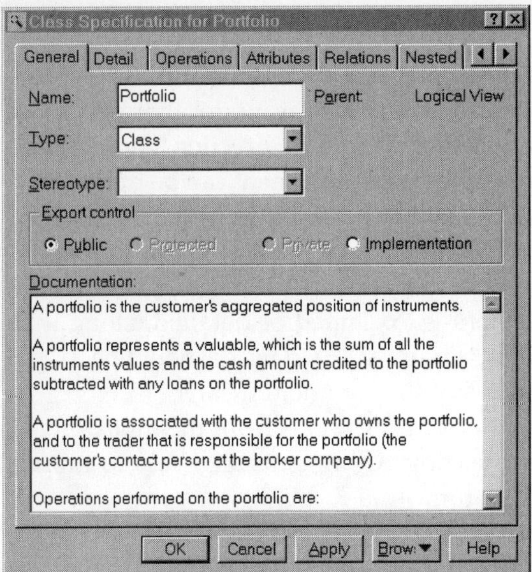

Figure 2.16 A specification window in a tool that shows the properties of the class.

Extending UML

UML can be extended or adapted to a specific method, organization, or user. We touch on three extension mechanisms here: stereotypes, tagged values, and constraints.

CROSS-REFERENCE **These mechanisms are described in more detail in Chapter 8.**

The extension mechanisms of UML have been very successful, leading to a proliferation of new model elements and extensions. Profiles provide a mechanism to manage these extensions. To keep UML coherent as it expands into new areas with the focus on MDA, the OMG maintains an increasing number of profiles. These profiles provide standard ways for handling certain software languages, such as Java or .NET; provide information needed for certain business domains, such as health or insurance; or provide mechanisms for advanced concepts, such as frameworks, enterprise architecture, or complex real-time systems.

Stereotypes

A stereotype extension mechanism defines a new kind of model element based on an existing model element. Thus, a stereotype is "just like" an existing element, with some extra semantics that are not present in the former. A stereotype of an element can be used in the same situations in which the original element is used. Stereotypes are based on all types of elements—classes, nodes, components, and packages, as well as relationships such as associations, generalizations, and dependencies. A number of stereotypes are predefined in the UML, and they are used to adjust an existing model element instead of defining a new one. This strategy keeps the basic UML language simple.

A stereotype or set of stereotypes on an element is described by placing its name as a string—for example, <<StereotypeName>>—around the name of the element, as shown in Figure 2.17. (For multiple stereotypes this would read <<StereotypeName1, StereotypeName2>>.) The angle brackets are called *guillemets*. A stereotype can also have its own graphical representation, such as an icon, connected to it. An element of a specific stereotype can be shown in its normal representation with the stereotype name in front of the name, as a graphical icon representing the stereotype, or as a combination of both. Figure 2.17 shows an artifact stereotype, one of the standard stereotypes in UML. A few stereotypes have common notation, but many don't because they are defined by the user. Tools supporting UML provide users with options for implementing their own icons. Whenever an element has a stereotype name or icon connected to it, it's read as an element type of the specified stereotype. For example, a class with the stereotype <<Window>> is read as "a class of the Window stereotype," meaning that it is a window type of class. The particular characteristics a Window class must have are defined when the stereotype is defined.

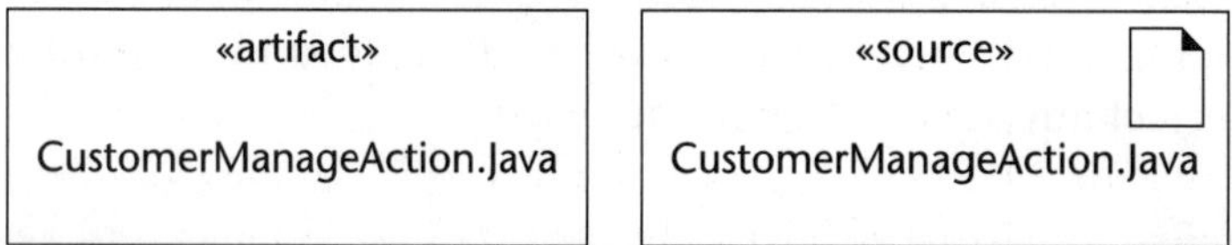

Figure 2.17 The source code file for the class CustomerManageAction.java can be represented as a class with the stereotype <<Artifact>>. Alternately, the element can also be shown with the artifact icon of a sheet of paper and with the stereotype <<source>>, as that is the type of artifact in play, or with both stereotypes listed. The stereotype adds extra semantics to the base UML element.

As we stated previously, a stereotype is an excellent extension mechanism, and one that prevents the UML from becoming overly complex, yet enables the necessary extensions and adaptations. UML evolution has sparked an explosion of stereotypes, many now organized into the profiles mentioned earlier. Most requested new model elements have a basic prototype in the UML. A stereotype can then be used to add the necessary semantics required in order to define the missing model element.

Tagged Values

As described earlier in the chapter, elements can have properties that contain name-value pairs of information about them (see Figure 2.18). These properties are also called *tagged values*. A number of properties are predefined in UML, but users can define additional properties to hold information about elements. Any type of information can be attached to elements: method-specific information; administrative information about the progress of modeling; information used by other tools, such as code generation tools; or any other kind of information that the user wants to attach to elements.

Constraints

A constraint is a restriction on an element that limits the usage of the element or the semantics (meaning) of the element. A constraint is either declared in the tool and repeatedly used in several diagrams or identified and applied as needed in a diagram.

Figure 2.19 shows an association between the Senior Citizen Group class and the Person class, indicating that the group might have persons associated to it. However, to express that only people older than 60 years of age can be attached to it, a constraint is defined that limits participation to only persons whose age attribute is greater than 60. This definition constrains which people are used in the association. Without it, someone interpreting the diagram might misunderstand it. In a worst-case scenario, such misunderstanding could lead to an incorrect implementation of the system.

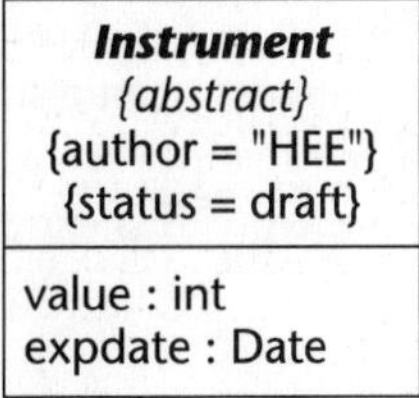

Figure 2.18 Properties on an Instrument class. Abstract is a predefined property; author and status are user-defined tagged values.

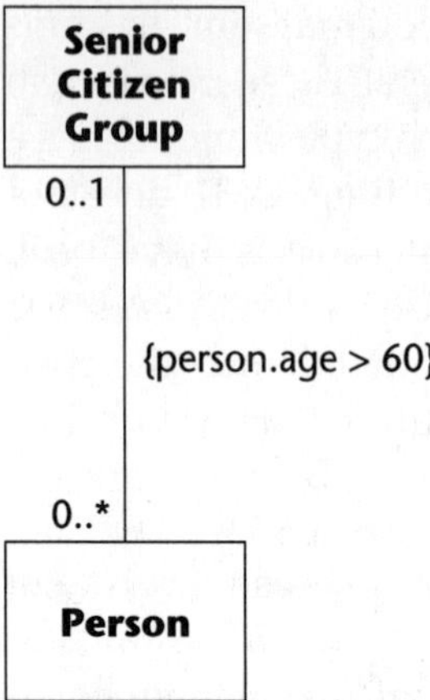

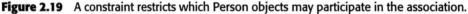

Figure 2.19 A constraint restricts which Person objects may participate in the association.

In this case, the constraint is defined and applied directly to the diagram in which it is used, but it can also be defined as a constraint with a name and a specification, such as "Senior Citizen" and "Person.Age > 60," and used in several diagrams. Some predefined constraints exist and can be used. In addition, UML relies on another language for expressing constraints, called the Object Constraint Language (OCL). UML does not enforce the use of OCL because constraints can be expressed in any form, using any language.

CROSS-REFERENCE **Constraints and OCL are described in Chapter 8.**

Model Driven Architecture with UML

When building systems with UML, sometimes you need more than a single model. You might need distinct models for different platforms or various projects in the life cycle of the system. The purpose of the models will differ. In a project focused on business-process analysis, the purpose of the model is to capture the rules and main functions of the system and to model the basic "real-world" actions and collaborations without reference to the specific implementation details. In later projects, the purpose might be to expand the model into a working technical solution with consideration for the implementation environment. In implementation projects, a model includes the source code compiled into programs. Deployment of artifacts on a system also requires sophisticated modeling. The tracking between the views, phases, and models is maintained through properties or refinement relationships. Although some projects might well cover an entire system and all the different phases in one model, you will find it easier on many projects to break these up into separate models.

Model Driven Architecture, or MDA, includes the notion that some systems need multiple models arranged in a standard set of layers. These models can contain the multiple views described previously, but each type of model has a different focus, requiring its own set of profiles and handling. UML does not require a modeler to use MDA, and many successful projects have been founded on sound analysis using UML without MDA. Generally, MDA starts with a broad Computation Independent Model, or CIM, that defines the business domain for the system. The CIM is often a given for a software project. The Platform Independent Model, or PIM, shows the main business process with computational detail but without implementation information. The next layer is the Platform Specific Model, or PSM, that gives implementation detail tuned to a specific deployment environment. In MDA there can be a number of PSMs, usually one for each platform in the system. At the layer below the platform is the implementation language, so a model can also be implementation language independent or specific. For example, a project deployed on a J2EE platform might employ more than one scripting language.

The goal is to encapsulate the model elements that relate directly to the deployment code so they can take advantage of precise notation in a relevant profile or a specialized UML tool. The goal of MDA is to make UML more precise and executable, like a software language, not to add more complex model layers for no practical reason. MDA breaks down a larger system into component models that retain a link to the other models. These separate models are more than separate views of the same system; each model also has its own collection of views and may rely on different UML profiles for definition. Each model can have a number of different diagrams and ways of providing instructions for system implementation.

Although the models are different, they are normally built by expanding the contents of earlier models. With the variety of model levels, MDA proposes an information-management system taking advantage of automated modeling tools to achieve interoperability (see Figure 2.20). With all these levels, MDA seeks to apply UML to large systems. MDA is unlikely to be of much use for a modeler maintaining a legacy application for, say, updating a data application with a few new fields. However, when that legacy system is replaced, modelers will require the additional information provided with the MDA approach.

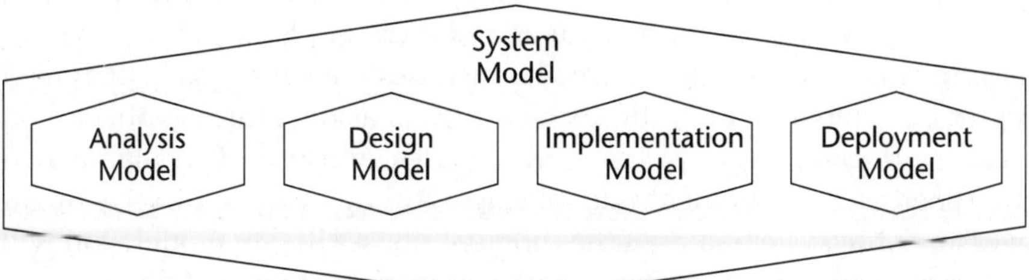

Figure 2.20 An MDA system is described in several models.

With MDA influencing the latest set of OMG specifications, UML is now part of a larger modeling universe, defined by the Meta-Object Facility (MOF), an abstract language for defining modeling languages. Reliance on MOF will make it easier for very specialized languages to still work with the same general concepts, allowing for communication about models and a standard way of querying model information, even across multiple models. Scrubbing away the ambiguity comes with a cost: The UML specification, or set of specifications, is now much bulkier and the language less ambiguous. The UML 2 suite of specifications is over twice as large as the specification for UML 1.4. If you include the specifications for profiles, UML has nearly 10 times more material than it did in version 1.0. The explosion of pages makes it harder to review the specification and understand UML as a whole, but the precision and clear definitions make possible the management of incredibly complex enterprise applications.

All of this extra detail is in support of the MDA initiative, which organizes the disparate efforts in the OMG related to UML. Getting the work on the different profiles and the different UML packages to focus on a common goal is not easy. The focus of MDA on using a number of different models with the goal of these models providing a clear and current picture of the enterprise helps channel these efforts in a way that encourages maximum participation and communication.

Software Development Process and UML

UML is independent of any software-development process, although the diagrams do encourage and support certain approaches to development. UML is also independent of any phase in any software life cycle, which means the same generic language and the same diagrams are used to model different things in different phases. It's up to the modeler to decide the purpose and scope that a model covers. The modeling language provides only the ability to create models in an expressive and consistent manner.

When one is modeling with the UML, the work is governed by a method or process that outlines the different steps to take and how these steps are implemented. Such a process typically divides the work into successive iterations comprising the traditional disciplines of software development (requirements, analysis, design, implementation, deployment, test). (Chapter 10 offers object-oriented software development processes and examples.) However, a smaller process exists that concerns the actual modeling work. Normally, when you are producing a model or a single diagram, you start the work by collecting a suitable group of people who present the problem and the goals; they engage in an informal brainstorming and sketching session during which ideas about a possible model are exchanged. The tools used could even be very informal, such as notes and a whiteboard. This session continues until the participants feel they have a practical suggestion for the basis of a model (an early hypothesis). The result is then put into a tool; the hypothesis model is organized, and an actual diagram is constructed according to the rules of the modeling language. Next, the model is detailed through iterative work, through which more details about the solution are discovered and documented. As more information is acquired about the problem and its solution, the hypothesis gradually becomes a diagnosis for a usable model. When the model is almost finished, an integration and verification step is taken, which leads to the model or diagram being integrated with other diagrams or models in the same project to ensure that no inconsistencies exist. The model is also validated to verify that it solves the right problem (see Figure 2.21).

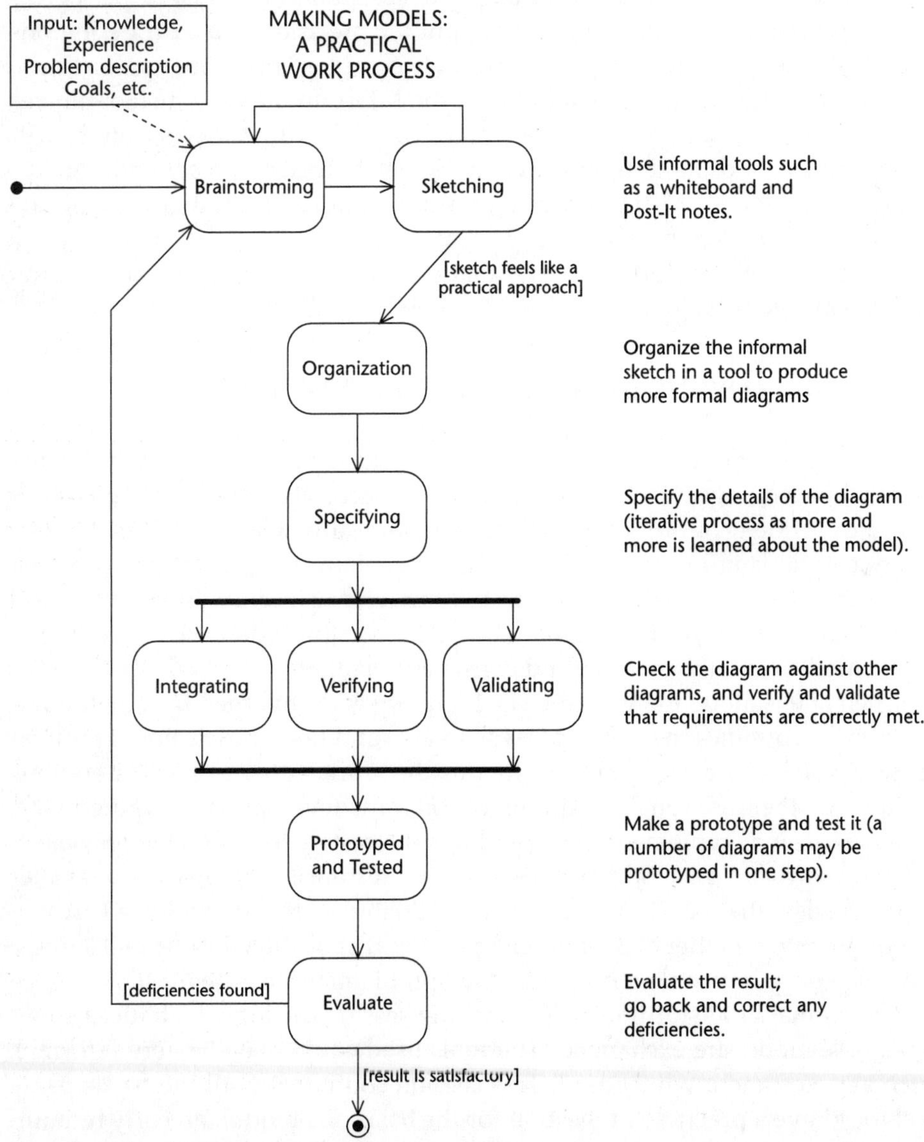

Figure 2.21 A practical modeling work process.

Finally, the model is implemented as some kind of prototype that is evaluated for any deficiencies in the actual solution. Deficiencies include such things as missing functionality, bad performance, or high development costs. The deficiencies lead the developers back to the respective step(s) in order to remove them. If the problems are major, the developers might have to go all the way back to the brainstorming/sketching phase. If the problems are minor, the developers probably just have to change parts of the organization or specification of the model. Note that the prototype step cannot be performed immediately after the diagram is finished; it should be taken when a number of diagrams can be prototyped together. The prototype can be a throwaway, constructed just for evaluation, or if the prototype step is successful, it can become an iteration in the real development process.

We are not aware of all the possibilities of UML. Traditionally, designers of programming or macro languages are surprised at how people use the new language. For example, James Gosling told us that his macro language is used in the Emacs editor to write satellite navigation systems and basic compilers! Early versions of UML quickly outgrew the language, requiring additional features to support complex distributed architectures and large systems. Given the versatility of UML, it will continue to evolve in unexpected ways to support the creation of dynamic and complex systems.

Tools

Using a modeling language as complex and extensive as UML requires the support of tools. Even if the first sketches of a model are done using a whiteboard (drawing the models manually), the work of maintaining, synchronizing, and providing consistency in a number of diagrams is almost impossible without a tool.

The modeling tool or software-development support-tool market has exploded since the release of UML and the new generations of programs used to produce programs. The first edition of this book included a wish list of features for a development-support tool, most of which are now commonly available, with even a few additional features. This list still provides a good practical guideline for what a software team needs in a UML tool. Some basic tools using UML notation are little more than drawing tools, with few consistency checks or knowledge of the method or modeling language present. Not all tools will fully support UML. You will find different levels of support, ranging from basic to advanced. At the time of publication, vendors have not yet produced a tool that implements UML 2 features. As UML 2 becomes standard, tools will implement an increasing number of features. Tools will also continue to help define UML, as automation reveals ambiguity in the UML specification that requires clarification.

A modern software-development support tool should provide these functions:

- **Draw diagrams.** The tool must support easy rendering of the diagrams in the modeling language. The tool should be intelligent enough to understand the purpose of the diagrams and know simple semantics and rules so that it can warn the user or prohibit the inappropriate or incorrect use of the model elements.
- **Act as a repository.** The tool must support a common repository so that the collected information about the model is stored in one place. If the name of a class is changed in one diagram, the change must be reflected in all other diagrams in which the class is used. The integration with a configuration management system keeps the repository information consistent and synchronized.
- **Support navigation.** The tool should make it easy to navigate the model, to trace an element from one diagram to another, or to expand the description of an element.
- **Provide multiuser support.** The tool should support multiple users and enable them to work on a model without interfering with or disturbing each other.
- **Generate code.** An advanced tool should be able to generate code, where all the information in the model is translated into code skeletons that are used as a base for the implementation phase.
- **Reverse engineer.** An advanced tool should be able to read existing code and produce models from it. Thus, a model could be made from existing code, or a developer could iterate between working in the modeling tool and programming.
- **Integrate with other tools.** A tool should integrate with other tools, both with development environments such as an editor, compiler, and debugger, and with other enterprise tools such as configuration-management and version-control systems.
- **Cover the model at all abstraction levels.** The tool should be easy to navigate from the top-level description of the system (as a number of packages) down to the code level. Then, to access the code for a specific operation in a class, you should be able to click the operation name in a diagram.
- **Interchange models.** A model or individual diagrams from a model should be able to be exported from one tool and then imported into another tool, as Java code is produced in one tool and then used in another tool. The same interchange should apply to models in a well-defined language.

Drawing Support

A tool must make the drawing of diagrams easy and fun. The time is long gone when an advanced drawing tool could call itself a full development-support tool, for not only must the tool provide excellent mechanisms for selecting, placing, connecting, and defining the elements in a diagram, but it must also have support to assist the modeler in rendering a *correct* diagram. The tool should "have an understanding" of the semantics of the elements so that it can issue a warning if an element is incorrectly used or if a specific operation is inconsistent with some other operation; for example, if a proposed change in one diagram conflicts with another diagram in the same model.

The tool should also have support for laying out the design for the diagrams. This support should include allowing the modeler to rearrange the elements and automatically rearranging message lines so that they don't cross each other. Many CAD systems have very elegant algorithms for doing this, and many modeling-tool vendors could learn a lot by looking at those systems.

Model Repository

A support tool must maintain a model repository that provides a database with all information about the elements used in a model, regardless of which diagram the information comes from. This repository should contain the base information about the entire model, which is then viewed through a number of diagrams, as shown in Figure 2.22.

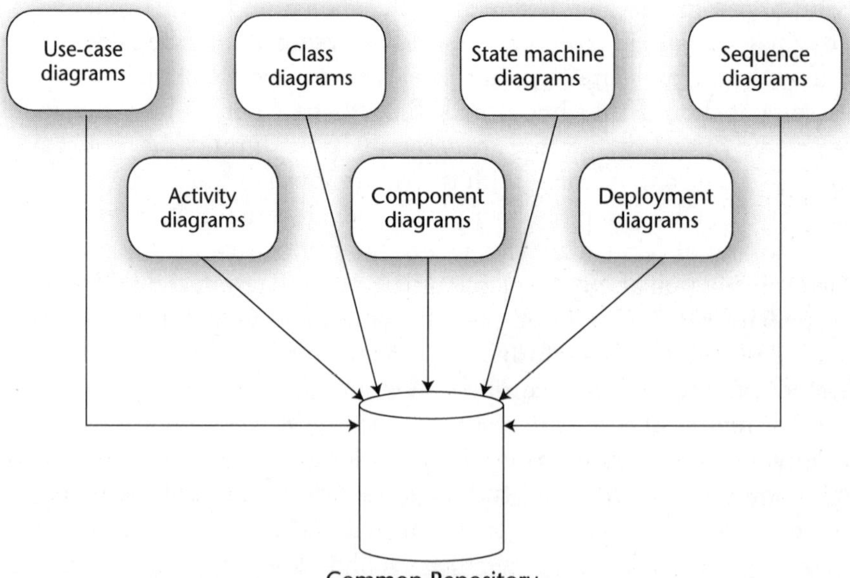

Figure 2.22 A repository contains all the information from all the diagrams necessary to make sure the model is consistent and enables the use of generic tools for documentation and reuse.

Some tasks that the tool can perform with the help of a repository are:

- **Checking for inconsistency.** If an element is used inconsistently in different diagrams, the tool must warn the user of or prohibit this. If the modeler tries to delete an element in one diagram and it is used in other diagrams, the developer must be warned about this. If the developer insists in deleting the element, it must be deleted from all diagrams where it is referenced, and the developer must go back and update these diagrams to make them valid.
- **Critiquing.** Using the information in a repository, a tool can critique the model, pointing out parts that haven't been specified or applying model heuristics that show possible mistakes or inappropriate solutions.
- **Reporting.** The tool can automatically generate complete and extensive documentation about all elements, such as classes or diagrams in a model, similar to term catalogs of all data.
- **Reusing elements or diagrams.** A repository can support reuse so that modeling solutions or parts of a solution in one project can be easily reused in another project. Components in a UML model are directly connected to the source code so that both the model and the actual code can be reused in different projects.

Navigation

When several views and diagrams are used together to describe a system, it's very important to navigate between them. Therefore, the tool must support easy navigation, both in terms of scale and browsing. It must be easy to browse the different diagrams and to perform searches for model elements.

An element should have hyperlinks, links that are not visible when looking at the printed diagrams, but that are accessible only through the tool. It should be possible to click an element with the right mouse button and get a pop-up menu that displays common operations and gives navigation possibilities, such as looking at other diagrams where the element is present or accessing detailed information about the element. Parts of a diagram should be expandable or collapsible. It should be easy to expand and view the contents of the package, and collapse this information to view the surrounding package.

Another way to handle a complex diagram is to define filters, which can separate or highlight some interesting aspect of the diagram, for example, to show only one type of relationship or class. Modelers should have control over what is shown so that they can study only the part that is important at a given moment.

Multiuser Support

A tool should enable several users to work cooperatively on the same model, that is, without disturbing or interfering with each other. Typically, a user working on a diagram should lock it so that no one else can change it at the same time. Furthermore, any changes made to shared elements in the repository should be identified by the tool. But decisions about which change is valid must be resolved by the users. Multiple users will find the best support to be a strong configuration-management system. For projects that share models among teams dispersed geographically, even half the world away, such management aids in the success of the project.

Code Generation

Modern tools have support for code generation, so that those parts of the work worth saving from the modeling phase don't have to be recreated when the implementation phase begins. These tools typically generate *code skeletons* in a target language and transfer the information from the models into code in that language. The type of code generated usually is static information, such as class declarations, including attributes and method declarations. The bodies of the methods containing the actual code are normally left blank, to be filled in by the programmer—though it is theoretically possible that parts of dynamic models can be translated into body code. As UML evolves under the guidance of MDA, such generation of code will become more common, though it will only enhance the importance of accurate modeling. The MDA effort stresses the use of a model compiler that will produce code from UML diagrams.

Different types of target languages are used. Naturally, object-oriented programming languages such as C++ or Java are used, but languages such as SQL (Structured Query Language, for the schema definition of a relational database) or IDL (Interface Definition Language for interfaces in a CORBA-compliant system) can also be generated. Therefore, a tool should have the capability to plug in different code generators, or model compilers, for different languages.

What happens if you generate code from a model, start coding the bodies of the methods, and then make a change in the model? Is the code work lost when you generate the code skeleton from the updated model? Luckily, that is not always the case. The generated code contains marks that show which sections of the code are generated from the model and which are manually coded. When the code is generated anew, the sections that contain manual code should not be touched by the code generator. However, some model compilers require 100 percent usage of generated code. Such an approach can lack flexibility and make it hard to optimize a system. In such an approach, most of the software coding work is then done at the level of improving the model compiler. Such compilers currently are in the early phases of development but are likely to come into more widespread use provided they can successfully deliver high-quality code all the time, which remains a matter of some debate. For the near future, a team should have a code generator that supports human as well as machine coding.

Reverse Engineering

A reverse-engineering functionality shows the other side of the code-generation functionality. Code is read and analyzed by the tool, and diagrams are created that show the structure of the code. Typically, only static structure diagrams such as class diagrams are constructed from the code: No dynamic information is extracted from the code. The reverse-engineering function is used for both unknown code that is bought or coded manually and for code generated with the code-generation function. When applied to unknown code, the result is either uplifting or depressing, depending on the structure of the code. Code that is unstructured is inevitably unveiled when reverse-engineered into a diagram. When buying class libraries, reverse engineering is often used to get a diagram that represents the structure of the library, so that the classes in the library can be used in diagrams.

When code generation and reverse engineering are combined, it's commonly referred to as *round-trip engineering*. Using round-trip engineering, a developer can iterate between modeling and implementation, so that a model is defined; code is generated, explored, and changed in the development environment; and then the code reverse-engineered back to a model. The development process then truly becomes iterative.

Integration

Traditional modeling tools are quickly becoming more integrated with other tools used in system development. Since the modeling tool actually stores a model of the entire system, it's really the natural hub for all the other tools, such as these:

- **Development environment.** With these tools, it's possible to go directly from a model element in a diagram to a development environment, where the code is edited, compiled, and debugged. The opposite is also true. The tool should go directly from editing a code module to determine its location in the logical and physical models of the system. Also, some development environments use UML notation to show basic software elements, such as Java classes. Here, UML represents a feature added to a development environment, not a complete UML set of features for modeling a system.

- **Configuration and version control.** These are tools for handling several different configurations of the system and different versions of both the system and individual elements. The tool should provide version control for both the models and the code.
- **Documentation tools.** These tools can automatically generate documentation from the model repository. The tool should also be able to generate statistics based on the information found there.
- **Testing tools.** Testing tools are mainly for the administration of the test process—collecting and maintaining test reports. Testing is really the validation (Did we build the right system?) and verification (Did we build the system the right way?) of the development process. Thus, the models contain a lot of information for the testing process that should transfer to the testing tools.
- **GUI builders.** A good idea is to have associations from classes in the model to their GUI representations in a GUI builder, where the organization of the user interface is stored. It should also be possible to automatically generate GUI forms for classes in the model. For example, if the attributes in a class are read, the fields of appropriate types in a form are generated for those attributes.
- **Requirement specification tools.** UML has use cases to capture the functional requirements of a system. However, nonfunctional aspects of the system also exist, and these could be described using requirement specification tools. Some methods prefer techniques other than use cases for requirement engineering and, therefore, need other tools.
- **Project management and process support tools.** A project management tool is devised to help the project manager define time schedules and resource allocation plans and perform follow-ups on the progress. Since the production of models is a large part of a project, it is beneficial when the project manager can easily check the progress of the modeling work.

Note that not all of these tools need to be used in every project. The options available for development support will continue to expand. Still, development projects should continue to look for these basic support features.

Interchange of Models

It used to be impossible to create a model in one tool and then export it to another tool. To do this, modelers require a standardized format for storing and sharing a model. Standard XML Metadata Interchange (XMI) schema provides this for UML. XMI gives the modeler a tool for sharing complex information about objects. An XMI schema defines the standard format for model objects. XMI relies on XML as the mechanism for sharing the data. XML, or

Extensible Markup Language, provides a way to communicate not only information but also the structure, or the metadata, about that information. The OMG has defined an XMI specification to allow for the expression of models in XML, which enforces a common way to store and to exchange UML files. For more on XMI, see the XMI specification from OMG.

As the OMG worked on a standard for communicating UML models, it became clear that not all tool vendors implement UML in the same fashion. Rigid standards remaining impractical, UML specifications now include a number of "semantic variation points" where different methods of handling the information remain UML compliant. Thus, tool vendors can apply their own notions to the handling of certain events. However, there still remains the concept of complying with UML, enforced by rules expressed in XMI. For example, UML does not dictate to tool vendors how to handle unexpected behaviors in a state machine, but each UML tool still needs to explain a transition in the same manner.

UML also has different levels of compliance with the UML specification. The designers of UML recognized that there would be a basic level of compliance required of all vendors claiming to implement UML. Beyond that, there are intermediate and complete compliance levels that show increasing conformity to the complete UML specification. Review the details of any UML 2 tool to see what parts of the language they support. With UML 2 the rules for such support are now clear, so a product can prove they comply at a certain level with the specification.

XMI schemas not only allow the interchange of models, but they also verify that a tool has properly formed UML information. If a user has adopted a number of profiles, a properly constituted tool should be able to interpret these profiles without negative consequence to the model. The idea is for UML models not to become burdened with proprietary or company information that forces a modeler to use a specific tool exclusively. Rather, supported by defined XMI schema, UML can be a language used in multiple tools, a true standard for the software industry.

Tool Options

Any list of available tools and their respective features ages poorly in print media. This is especially true at the time this text is being written because UML 2 is bound to shake up the visual modeling marketplace.

Rather than outlining the capabilities of various tools, we have chosen to simply give a list of tools recognized in the marketplace today, along with Web addresses to additional information. Simple drawing tools that might have a template of UML icons have been excluded. This list is not exhaustive. For more vendor resources, see the list on the accompanying CD.

- **ArgoUML.** http://argouml.tigris.org
- **Borland Together.** www.borland.com/
- **Codagen Architect.** www.codagen.com/
- **Embarcadero Describe.** www.embarcadero.com/
- **Kennedy-Carter iUML.** www.kc.com/
- **Rational Rose.** www.rational.com/
- **Rational XDE.** www.rational.com/
- **Tau UML Suite.** www.telelogic.com/

Relevant Changes in UML 2

In each chapter where it is appropriate, we include a brief overview of the new features in UML 2 relevant to the chapter. In this chapter, a few comments on the main features in UML 2 as they reflect on the current user of UML 1.*x* are in order.

On one level, UML has not changed tremendously, which is in part by design because the OMG specified they wanted UML 2 to comply with earlier versions and demanded only minor departures from common practice for current users. That said, UML 2 represents a substantial milestone in the evolution of UML in support for enterprise systems, as explained with the review of the goals for UML 2 reviewed in Chapter 1. Many will continue to use UML 1.*x* features, while increasingly using the enhancements. Basic items in UML, such as the class diagram, remain easy to learn, while the more advanced features require increasing amounts of training and expertise.

For the UML 1.*x* user, the biggest changes to the existing feature set occur in the dynamic area for the interaction diagrams and activity diagrams.

- The UML 1 collaboration diagram is now gone, having turned into a communication diagram.
- The sequence diagram now has fragments, allowing it to show more complex options on one diagram. Fragments also support reuse of sequence diagram elements.
- Two new interaction diagrams, the time diagram and the interaction overview diagram, provide new tools to look at dynamic behavior.
- The activity diagram now represents a first-class construct and is no longer lumped together with the state machine. The new activity diagram includes support for a number of additional flow features and no longer focuses on transitions but rather on token flow along activity edges.

The behavioral specification components of UML have changed more than the static portions. The static portions, the class and object diagrams, have already effectively helped produce code from software development tools. The behavioral specifications have been less successful, in part because the syntax for these elements remains incomplete or too ambiguous to work with actual software code. In the quest to make UML more precise, the UML specification includes much more information in the dynamic diagrams.

UML is no longer defined in terms of UML but rather in terms of a more abstract language for specifying model languages called MOF. This will make it easier to manage information across multiple platforms and diverse systems. The clearer definition will also make it easier to use XMI to manage models and use multiple UML tools.

In terms of extensions, UML 2 emphasizes the use of profiles as well as multiple model levels to keep models focused on their main purpose and to take advantage of common approaches to problems. These extensions make it easier for some model levels to produce code.

UML 2 has a number of other important enhancements, including the following.

- The introduction of the composite structure diagram enables you to show the connection between a high-level classifier, such as a use case, and the runtime elements needed for that classifier.
- The protocol state machine and the port provide a number of features to support component development by providing clear rules for the environmental requirements of the component.
- Rules for defining the internal structure of a classifier are now clearer, making it easier to decompose a classifier.

As tool vendors apply the new UML 2 standards, features will find uses not predicted by the designers, just as in UML 1. In addition, as the software industry changes, UML will change to address new issues. The core idea of UML as a common language to manage a model of a system remains. UML provided standards that made it easier for humans to communicate model elements. UML 2 includes a number of features that will make it easier for machines to communicate about model elements, responding to the queries and the needs of people.

In order to produce great software, modelers should still look to use the elements in the UML toolkit that best achieve the goal at hand. With UML 2, that toolkit is now substantially larger with a number of specialized tools. The modeler will not need to master the intricacies of each of these tools, but rather understand the general approach of UML. Much as a carpenter still uses a saw for most of his cutting, software designers will still rely on the core features of UML 1.*x* for their modeling work. UML 2 might make it easier to use that saw safely or automate it for more efficient production, but it does not represent a substantial redefinition of the modeling elements.

Summary

UML organizes a model in a number of views that present different aspects of a system. Only by combining all the views can a complete picture of a system be achieved. A view is not a graph; its contents are described in diagrams that are graphs with model elements. A diagram typically shows only a part of the contents in a view, and a view is defined with many diagrams. A diagram contains model elements such as classes, objects, nodes, components, and relationships such as associations, generalizations, and dependencies. The elements have semantics—a meaning—and graphical symbols to represent them.

The UML diagrams include class, object, use case, state machine, sequence, communication, timing, interaction overview, activity, component, and deployment. The purpose of the diagrams and the rules for drawing them are described in the chapters to come.

UML has some general mechanisms with which to add information not visible in the diagram drawings. These include adornments placed next to elements, notes that can hold any type of information, and specification properties. Extension mechanisms, including tagged values, constraints on elements, and stereotypes, that define a new kind of model element based on an existing model element also exist.

A system is described in several different model types, each with a different purpose. UML also allows communication between a number of different models targeted at different levels of the enterprise. The analysis model describes the functional requirements and the modeling of real-world classes. The design transforms the analysis result into a technical solution in terms of a complete working software design. The implementation model implements the system by coding it in an object-oriented programming language. And, finally, the deployment model places the programs constructed in a physical architecture with computers and devices (called nodes). The work is done iteratively and not in sequence.

NOTE **The development process is explained in Chapter 10.**

You need a tool to use UML seriously in real-life projects. A modern tool has the capability to draw the diagrams, store the overall information in a common repository, allow easy navigation in the model between different views and diagrams, create reports and documentation, generate code skeletons from the model, read unknown code and produce models, and be easily integrated with other development tools.

CHAPTER

3

Use-Case Modeling

Use-case modeling describes what a system does to benefit users. The use-case diagrams help to focus mounds of technical information on a tangible value. Properly done, use cases provide the glue that holds a model together and show concisely and efficiently, even with stick figures and circles, what a system can provide. A use-case model is built through an iterative process, during which discussions between the system's developers and the stakeholders (customers and/or end users) lead to a requirement specification on which all agree. Use-case modeling was created by Ivar Jacobson based on his experiences developing the AXE system at Ericsson, specifically the OOSE and Objectory methods. Since this time, use cases have received a lot of interest from the object-oriented community and have influenced many object-oriented methods. Currently, a number of books are devoted to modeling with use cases.

This chapter provides an overview of use cases, relying on a number of examples from the case study (see Chapter 11). The case study provides a practical example of a working software project that starts with a set of use cases and illustrates a development process that relies on UML. The case study and the supporting material on the CD show the practical benefits of use-case modeling.

Although use cases offer a number of technical features, focus on these should not detract from the main goal of clarifying and documenting the key system needs. More than any other UML diagram, use-case diagrams stress flexibility and a focus on quickly gathering system information. Use-case diagrams will never have the richness of meaning to allow for automatic code generation as is done with class diagrams, so you need not get bogged down debating details. Use the additional use-case features to improve models by encouraging reuse, enhancing clarity, and implementing better organization of model elements.

Basics of Use Cases

The primary components of a use-case model are use cases, actors, and the system modeled, also called the subject. Each use case specifies a complete functional unit. This means that the use case handles the entire process, from its initiation by an external actor until it has performed the requested functionality. A use case must always deliver some value to an actor, something the actor wants. The actor is any external entity that has an interest in interacting with the subject. Often, it is a human user of the system, but it can also be another system or some kind of hardware device that needs to interact with the system.

In use-case modeling, the system, or subject, is looked upon as a "black box" that provides use cases. How the system does this, how the use cases are implemented, and how they work internally is not important. In fact, when the use-case modeling is done early in the project, the team might have no idea how the use cases will be implemented. The primary purposes for use cases are:

- To decide and describe the functional requirements of the system, resulting in an agreement between the stakeholders and the software developers who are building the system.
- To give a clear and consistent description of what the system should do, so that the model can be used throughout the development process to communicate to all developers those requirements, and to provide the basis for further design modeling that delivers the requested functionality.
- To provide a basis for performing system tests that verify that the system works appropriately and validate it. For example, by asking, does the final system actually perform the functionality initially requested?
- To provide the ability to trace functional requirements into actual classes and operations in the system. To simplify changes and extensions to the system by altering the use-case model and then tracing the use cases affected into the system design and implementation.

The actual work required to create a use-case model involves defining the system, finding the actors and the use cases, describing the use cases, defining the relationships between use cases and actors, and finally validating the model. It is a highly interactive format that should include discussions with the customer and the people representing the actors. The use-case model consists of use-case diagrams showing the actors, the use cases, and their relationships. These diagrams give an overview of the model, but the actual descriptions of the use cases are typically textual. Visual models can't provide all the information necessary in a use-case model, so rely on both use-case diagrams and text specifications. Use-case modeling is often a part of a wider requirements-gathering effort. Arriving at a reasonably complete use-case model diagram set typically involves at least an order of magnitude less effort than detailing the individual use-case specifications, detailed requirements, and supplementary specifications.

A number of different people have an interest in the use-case models.

- The stakeholders are interested because the use-case models specify the functionality of the system and describe how the system can and will be used. It is helpful when the stakeholders play an active role in the use-case modeling because then models can be adapted in detail to the stakeholders' wishes. The use cases are described in the language and terminology of the customer or user.
- The developers need the use-case models to understand what the system should do, and to provide them with the foundation for more detailed modeling work and coding.
- Project managers who apply an iterative and incremental life cycle build their iteration plans around the successful implementation of use cases; since the customers understand the essence of the use-case model, they can visualize what functionality should be present at the close of any planned iteration.
- The integration and system test teams need the use cases to test the system to ensure that it performs the functionality specified in the use cases.
- And, finally, anyone involved in activities connected to the functionality of the system may have an interest in the use-case models; this may include marketing, sales, support, and documentation teams.

The use-case model represents the use-case view of the system. This view is very important, as it affects all other views of the system. Both the logical and physical architecture are influenced by the use cases, because the functions specified in the use-case model are implemented in those architectures. A successful design can then produce a product that satisfies the users.

Use-case modeling is used not only to capture requirements of new systems; it is also used when new generations of systems are developed. When a new generation (version) of a system is developed, the new functionality is added to the extant use-case model by inserting new actors and use cases, or by modifying the specifications of current use cases.

WARNING **When augmenting an extant use-case model, be careful not to remove any functionality that is still needed.**

Use-Case Diagram

A use-case model is described in UML with a number of *use-case diagrams*. A use-case diagram contains model elements for the system, the actors, and the use cases, and shows the different relationships such as generalizations, associations, and dependencies among these elements, as shown in Figure 3.1. Each of the elements is described in more detail in the sections of the chapter that follow.

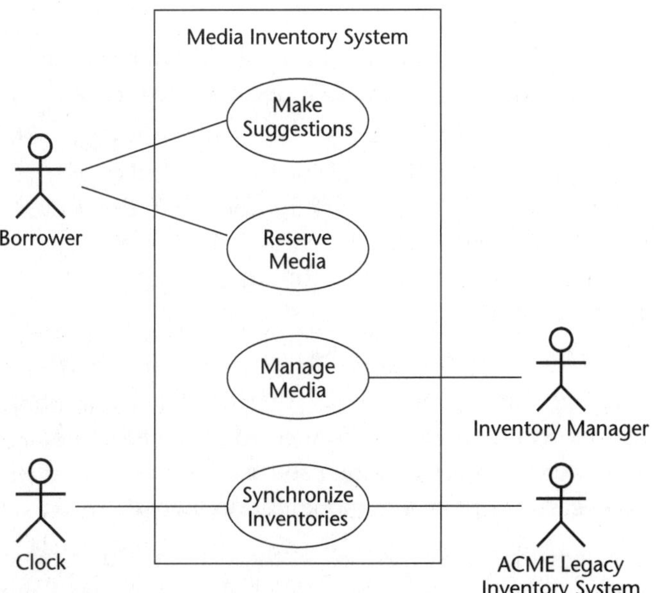

Figure 3.1 A use-case diagram shows actors, use cases, and their relationships. The system is defined through the system boundaries.

The actual description of the use-case contents is usually given in plaintext. This description contains vital information for defining the actual requirements and functionality. Some development support tools provide effective management of this text or link the use case to a requirements repository in a database. This text and the use case can provide the requirements for the system. In addition to describing the use case in text, you can draw an activity diagram.

CROSS-REFERENCE **Activity diagrams are described in more detail in Chapter 5 and Chapter 6.**

However, it's important to remember that a use case should be easy to communicate to an end user, and a more formal structure, such as an activity diagram, can be intimidating to people not used to interpreting them. In addition, the enhanced activity diagrams in UML 2 can carry much more information than activity diagrams in previous iterations of UML, taking them beyond the focus on functionality into flow analysis. It is best to use activity diagrams to clarify the text rather than replace it.

System

As part of use-case modeling, the boundaries of the system, or subject, developed are defined. The system can itself be a classifier, or subject, that owns the set of use cases.

NOTE **A subject in a use-case model does not necessarily have to be a software system; it can be a business or a machine. Indeed, the subject or system is also a classifier.**

Defining the boundaries and the overall responsibility of the system is not easy, because it's not always obvious which tasks are best automated and which are best handled manually or by other systems. Another consideration is how large the system should be in its first generation. It's tempting to be ambitious for the first release, but such lofty goals can make the system too large and the time to delivery much longer. A better idea is to identify the basic functionality and concentrate on defining a stable and well-defined system architecture to which more functionality can be added in future generations. You can always capture some general use cases and address these in more detail at a later date.

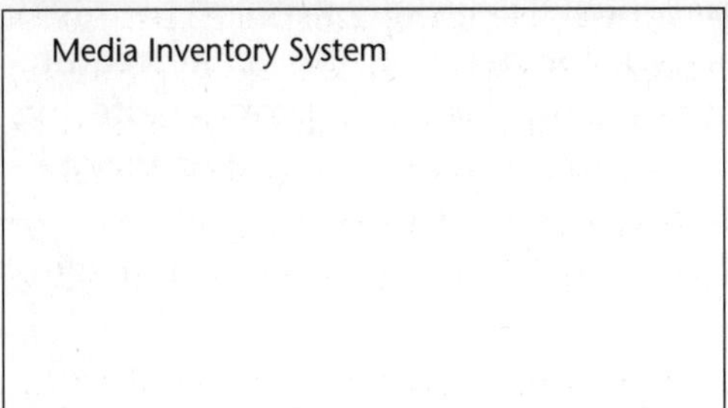

Figure 3.2 A system, or subject, in a use-case model.

It is essential to compile a catalog of central concepts (entities) with suitable terms and definitions at an early stage. This is not a domain object model, but rather an attempt to describe the terminology of the system or the business modeled. The terminology then describes the use cases. The catalog can also be used to begin the domain analysis that follows later. The extent of this catalog can vary; it can be a conceptual model showing simple relationships or just a glossary containing terms and a short description of what each is in the real world.

A subject in a use-case diagram is described as a box; the name of the subject appears above or inside the box, as shown in Figure 3.2. The box also contains symbols for the use cases.

Actors

An *actor* is someone or something that interacts with the system; it's who or what uses the system. By "interacts with the system," we mean that the actor sends or receives messages to and from the subject, or exchanges information with the system. In short, actors carry out use cases. Again, an actor can be a human being or another system (such as another computer to which the system is connected or some kind of hardware device that communicates with the system).

An actor is a type (a classifier), not an instance. The actor represents a role, not an individual user of the system. If John Doe wants to get auto insurance from an insurance company, it is his *role* as the insurance buyer or policyholder that we want to model, not John Doe. In fact, one person may be different actors in the system, depending on his or her role in the system. And the roles a person may have in the system can be restricted. For example, the same person can be prohibited from both entering an invoice and approving the invoice. An actor has a name, and the name should reflect the actor's role. The name should not reflect a specific instance of an actor, nor reflect the functionality of the actor.

The actor communicates with the system by sending and receiving messages, which are similar to those found in object-oriented programming, though they are not formally specified in a use case. A use case is always initiated by an actor that sends a message to it. This is sometimes called a *stimulus*. When a use case is performed, the use case might send messages to one or more actors. These messages may also go to other actors in addition to the one that initiated the use case.

Actors can also be defined as active or passive. An *active actor* is one that initiates a use case, while a *passive actor* never initiates a use case, but only participates in one or more use cases.

Finding Actors

By identifying the actors, we establish those entities interested in using and interacting with the system. It is then possible to take the position of the actor to try to identify the actor's requirements for the system and which use cases the actor needs. The actors can be identified by answering a number of questions:

- Who will use the main functionality of the system?
- Who will need support from the system to do their daily tasks?
- Who will need to maintain and administer the system, and keep it working?
- Which hardware devices does the system need to handle?
- With which other systems does the system need to interact? This could be divided into systems that initiate contact with the system and the systems that this system will contact. Systems include other computer systems as well as other applications in the computer in which this system will operate.
- Who or what has an interest in the results (the value) that the system produces?

When looking for the users of the system, don't consider only individuals sitting in front of a computer screen. Remember, the user can be anyone or anything that directly or indirectly interacts with the subject and uses the services of the system to achieve something. Keep in mind that use-case modeling emphasizes tangible value; actors can be the customers of the business. Actors are not just users in the computer sense of the term.

As a means of identifying different actors, conduct a study of users of the current system, asking what different roles they play when they perform their daily work. The same user may perform several roles at different times.

To repeat, an actor is a role (a classifier), not an individual instance. However, by providing examples of a couple of instances of an actor, you can verify that the actor really exists. An actor must have some association with one or more use cases. Although that actor might not initiate a use case, that actor will at some point communicate with one. The actor is given a name that reflects the role in the system.

Actors in UML

Actors are classifiers with the stereotype <<actor>>. The actor's name reflects the role of the actor. An actor can have both attributes and behavior, as well as a note describing the actor. An actor class has a standard stereotype icon, the "stickman" figure, with the name of the actor beneath the figure, as shown in Figure 3.3.

There are alternative presentation options to the stickman, though without any associated stereotype/classification adjustments. In other words, though one can use alternative depictions of actors, there exists no analogous semantic element to support the differences. If the model is exported electronically, no meaning will be given to the different icons. Figure 3.4 illustrates some alternatives to the mundane stickman. As a modeler, you can use whatever icon best communicates the information about the system. We suggest that you do not use the blockhead icon to show the client, but you might be encouraged to provide other visible clues as to who is using the system.

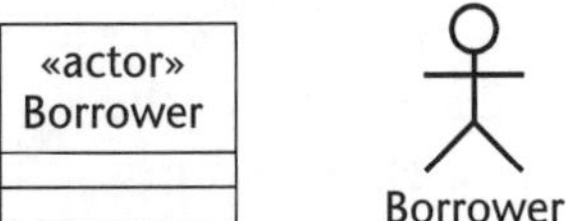

Figure 3.3 An actor is a classifier, and is shown as a class rectangle with the stereotype <<actor>>. The standard stereotype icon of a stickman is normally shown in use-case diagrams. The stickman icon has the actor's name below the figure.

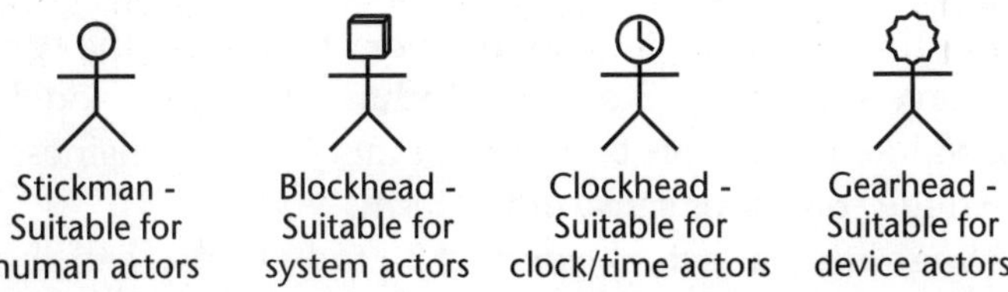

Figure 3.4 Some alternate presentation options to the stickman.

Relationships between Actors

An actor typically has associations to use cases that must be binary. Actors can also have generalization relationships among themselves, with the typical semantic expectation that the child can do what the parent does and then some.

When several actors, as part of their roles, also play a more generalized role, it is described as a *generalization*. This occurs when the behavior of the general role is described in an actor superclass. The specialized actors inherit the behavior of the superclass and then extend that behavior in some way. Generalization between actors is shown as a line with a hollow triangle at the end of the more general superclass, as shown in Figure 3.5. This is the same notation used for generalization between any classifiers in UML. Note that this use case shows the functionality for the case study in Chapter 11.

Actor generalization can improve the understandability of a use-case model. On the other hand, it should not be used when the system is best understood as having independent roles. For example, in our business a Manager might be able to do everything a Clerk can do and then more. But it might be simpler to accept that when a particular person is doing those Clerk tasks, then he or she is playing the role of Clerk, even if that person could also play the role of Manager.

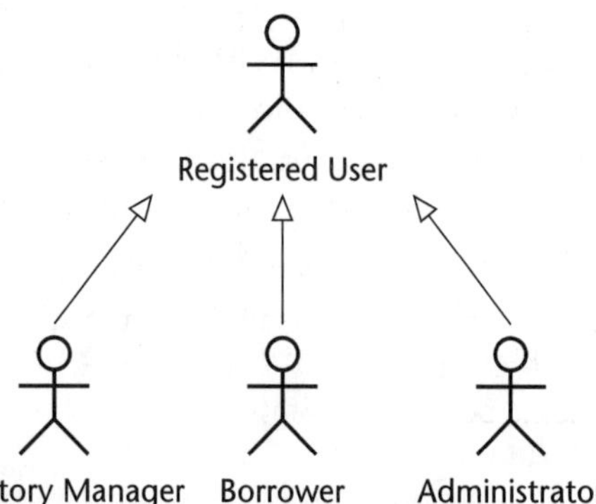

Figure 3.5 The actor base Registered User describes the general role played by Inventory Manager, who manages the inventory, and by Borrower, who reserves media. Use cases such as Login (of a Registered User) can be described in terms of the base Registered User.

Use Cases

A use case represents functionality for an actor. A use case in UML is defined as "a set of actions performed by a system, which yields an observable result that is, typically, of value for one or more actors or other stakeholders of the system." The actions can involve communicating with a number of actors (users and other systems), as well as performing calculations and work inside the system. The characteristics of a use case are:

- **A use case is always initiated by an actor.** A use case is always performed on behalf of an actor. The actor must directly or indirectly order the system to perform the use case. Occasionally, the actor may not be aware of initiating a use case.
- **A use case provides value to an actor.** A use case must deliver some kind of tangible value to an actor or actors. The value doesn't always have to be salient, but it must be discernible.
- **A use case is complete.** A use case must be a complete description. A common mistake is to divide a use case into smaller use cases that implement each other much as functions call each other in a programming language. A use case is not complete until the end value is produced, even if several communications (such as user dialogs) occur along the way.

Use cases are connected to actors through *associations*, which are sometimes referred to as *communication associations*. Associations show which actors the use case communicates with, including the actor that initiates the execution of the use case. The association should always be binary, implying a dialog between actor and system. Additionally, UML permits using multiplicity on the ends of associations (such as one actor communicates with one or more instances of a use case). A use case is named for which instance the use case performs, such as Signing Insurance Policy, Updating Register, and so on, and is often a phrase rather than a one-word label.

A use case is a classifier (specifically, a *BehavioredClassifier*), not an instance. It describes the functionality as a whole, including possible alternatives, errors, and exceptions that can occur during the execution of the use case. An instantiation of a use case is often called a *scenario*, and it represents an actual usage of the system (a specific execution path through the system). A use case represents a set of actions, which can be further modeled in an activity diagram. For example, a scenario instance of the use case Signing Insurance could be "John Doe contacts the system by telephone and signs for car insurance for the Toyota Corolla he just bought."

Finding Use Cases

The process for finding use cases starts with the actors previously defined. For each of the actors identified, ask the following questions:

- Which functions does the actor require from the system? What does the actor need to do?
- Does the actor need to read, create, destroy, modify, or store some kind of information in the system?
- Does the actor have to be notified about events in the system, or does the actor need to notify the system about something? What do those events represent in terms of functionality?
- Could the actor's daily work be simplified or made more efficient by adding new functions to the system (typically functions currently not automated in the system)?

Other questions to ask that don't involve one of the current actors are:

- What input/output does the system need? Where does this input/output come from or go to?
- What are the major problems with the current implementation of this system (perhaps it is a manual system instead of an automated system)?

The last questions are not meant to infer that the use cases identified don't have an actor, just that the actors are recognized first by identifying the use case and then the actor(s) involved. A use case must always be connected to at least one actor. If unconnected to an actor, you can never tell the beneficiary of the functionality in the use case, and you can't test the system.

Use Cases in UML

A use case is represented in UML as an ellipsis containing the name of the use case, or with the name of the use case below it. A use case is normally placed inside the boundaries of a system, and can be connected to an actor with an association or a communication association that shows how the use case and the actor interact.

Because each use case represents a complete unit, UML provides for no associations between use cases, but only between an actor and a use case. Use cases do have three types of relationships that allow for more complex modeling, as explained in the next section.

Relationships between Use Cases

There are three types of relationships between use cases: extend, include, and generalization. The relationship definitions are as follows:

- **Generalization.** Following the same semantics as other UML elements that permit generalization, a use-case generalization is a relationship from a child use case to a parent use case, specifying how a child can specialize all behavior and characteristics described for the parent. See Chapter 4 for a discussion of generalization.
- **Extend.** This relationship specifies that the behavior of a use case may be augmented by an additional use case. The extension takes place at one or more specific extension points defined in the extended use case. Note, however, that the extended use case is defined independently of the extending use case. Use-case extension is intended to be used when there is some additional behavior that should be added, conditionally, to the behavior defined in another use case.
- **Include.** This relationship indicates that a use case contains the behavior defined in another use case. Further, Include is a directed relationship between two use cases, implying that the behavior of the included use case is inserted into the behavior of the base use case. The base use case depends on the externally observable behavior of the included use case. The use case that is included is always required in order for the base use case to execute.

When using these relationships, you must always keep clarity as a primary concern. Modeling with these techniques can result in a simpler use-case model with reduced redundancy and increased extensibility. Modeling with these techniques can also result in a use-case model that is so intricate that it cannot be understood by the nontechnical stakeholders. Use cases are a means for human beings to communicate. A correct model that is too difficult to understand is a poor-quality model. For more on model quality, see Chapter 10.

Generalization Relationship

As mentioned earlier, generalization can help you manage a model. Since both actors and use cases are types of classifiers, UML allows for a generalization relationship between these elements. In the context of a use case, where each use case represents a complete set of actions, what does a parent-child relationship mean? It shows that a set of children has the same relationship as the parent to an actor. In addition, it shows that the children do not simply reuse the same procedures as those in the parent (in which case you would have an include relationship), but modify the behavior in some manner. In the example in Figure 3.6, the inventory manager needs to generate formatted output, which can at times mean generating an export set or generating a report. When using generalization, remember that use cases represent a function delivering a benefit, so you will not get the detailed meaning of parent-child relationships that you will from other UML elements. In most cases, the include and extend relationships will provide much more help in a use-case model.

Extend Relationship

Don't overdo it, but the extend relationship can come in handy in two distinct situations:

- When a system to be developed will potentially be deployed with varying sets of optional behavior
- When the deployment schedule of a system's use cases requires deployment of functional, though not complete, use cases

In either case, the base use case should describe essential behavior and note specific *extension points* with defined conditions where extending use cases are expected to fill in the details. The base use case must be able to operate in lieu of any extending use cases, and for that matter, has no knowledge of any extending use cases, only of the potential to be extended.

An extend relationship between use cases is shown as a dependency (a dashed line with an arrowhead pointing at the use case being extended) with the stereotype <<extend>>, as shown in Figure 3.7. Note also that the base use case can identify any number of extension points and that those extension points can be illustrated in the compartment of the use-case symbol (whether oval/ellipsis or rectangle). In an alternate form of notation, the extension points can be listed as part of the classifier rectangle, and the use case can be shown with an ellipse icon in the right-hand corner. You should use this notation, as shown in Figure 3.8, if you have a number of extension points on one use case.

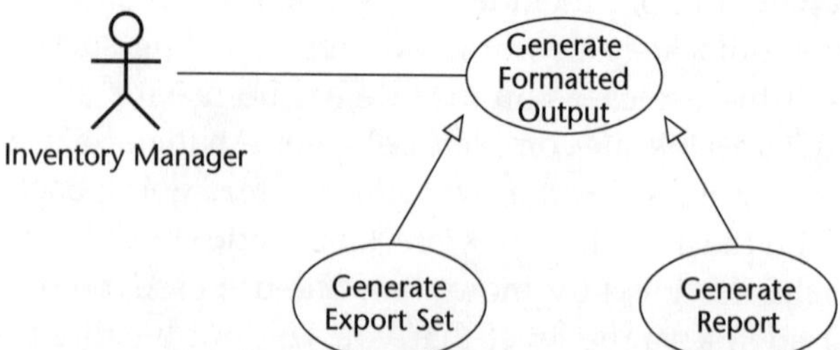

Figure 3.6 Example of a generalization relationship between use cases, where Generate Formatted Output is the base use case.

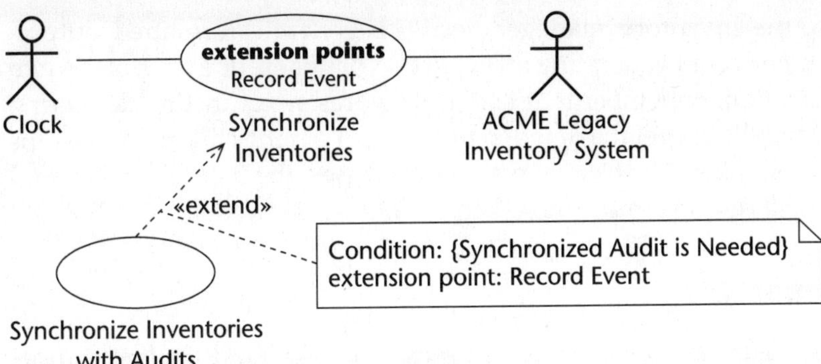

Figure 3.7 An extend relationship shows how one use case can extend the behavior of the base use case through specific extension points specified in the base use case.

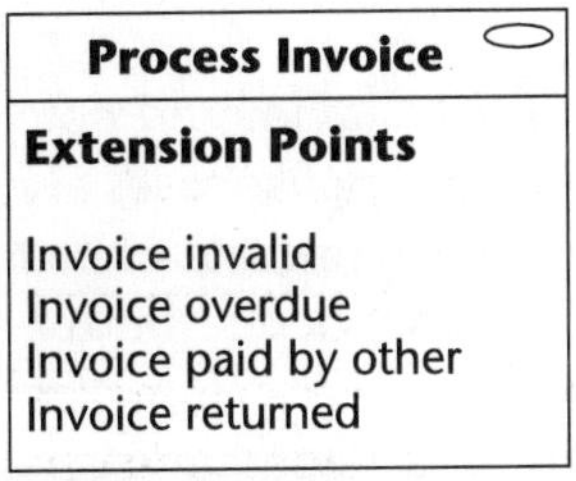

Process Invoice

Extension Points

Invoice invalid
Invoice overdue
Invoice paid by other
Invoice returned

Figure 3.8 A use case shown with alternate classifier notation showing the extension points of the use case.

Include Relationship

When a number of use cases have common behavior, this behavior can be modeled in a single use case that is *included* by the other use cases. When a use case includes another, the entire use case must be included. The idea of the include relationship is to model common behavior, such as logging information, that many use cases depend on, or "include." This relationship encourages reuse, and the modeler should keep this in mind when creating such a relationship. In other words, if the use case you include has no use for other use cases, don't separate it out as a separate complete behavior. An include use case represents a complete unit of behavior that will finish before going back to the base use case that relies on the include. Therefore, an include should represent a discrete subset of behavior used by more than one use case. Sometimes, use cases will start at such a vague level that you will not be able to break down the behavior. In such a situation, do not use include, but work on further definition of the use cases.

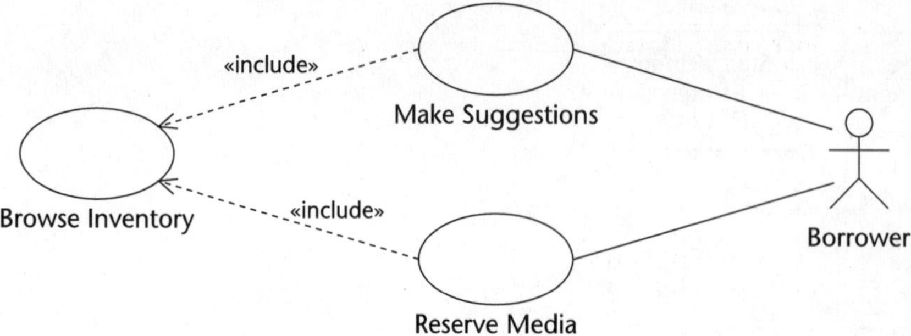

Figure 3.9 An include relationship shows how common behavior in a number of use cases can be described in a shared use case that is included in other use cases.

An include relationship is shown through the dependency relationship (a dashed line with an arrowhead pointing at the use case being included) with the stereotype <<include>>, as shown in Figure 3.9, which models part of the system in the case study.

Organizing Use Cases

How can you package a use case? How do you organize a use case so it makes sense to your clients and the rest of the team? UML offers two options: You can have a package own a use case or, with UML 2, you can also have a classifier own use cases. Use cases and actors can and often are placed into a substantial package structure. It is often useful to organize them along either functional lines or by use cases performed by specific actors. Keeping in mind that this represents a requirements model and that the use cases will influence subsequent development activities, significant care should be taken to ensure that the packaging makes sense to the consumers of the use cases. Figure 3.10 shows a high-level package structure for a review of the information technology of a general university-wide portal. In this case, the actors have been stored separately in their own package because they are reused in many situations and they require review by the client. Drilling down on the student-related use cases, you can see a number of additional packages in Figure 3.11. Note that any number of package organizations could have been used. Rely on what makes the most sense to the client and move on quickly; excessive debate about package organization wastes time. Another view of this same system is shown in Chapter 9 on Model Driven Architecture (MDA), which shows the relationships between all the packages on one diagram. Even if an element is in a package structure, you can still use it on many diagrams.

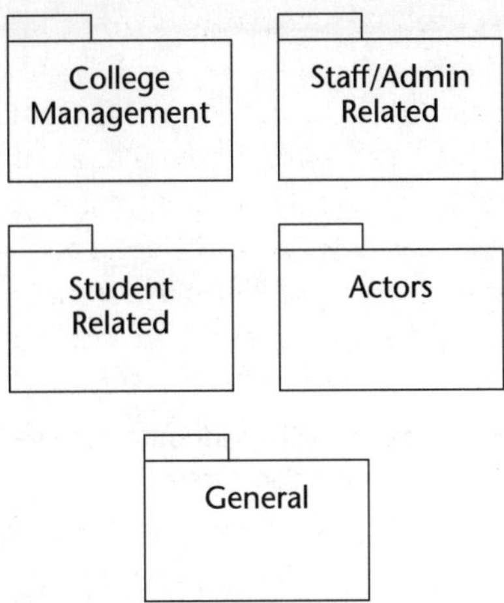

Figure 3.10 High-level package structure for a general portal at a University.

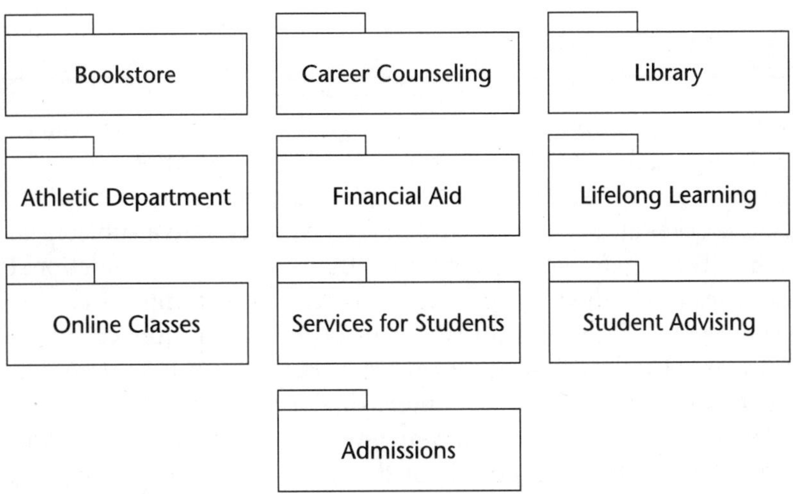

Figure 3.11 The package structure for the student-related packages for the general portal.

Figure 3.12 shows the use-case diagram for one package. In this library package, you can see how the library could use the new portal. In brief, the library will provide access to library information, while also getting relevant

information on whether a student is eligible to check out materials. Note that the diagram can include use cases that are from other packages, as it does here, showing that the use case for updating student status includes registration providing the latest information. This project had well over 20 packages of related use cases, so it required understandable organization. Such a large effort could also employ other UML diagrams or rely on an MDA approach with layered models. However, if the client understands use cases and wants a focus on observable benefits in a large system, the use-case view provides a great way to get this information quickly. It is not a substitute for detailed workflow analysis, but it can indicate where such analysis will likely bring the most benefit.

While a package can own a use case, a classifier can also own a use case. So, a general classifier called Financial Aid Office could own a set of use cases. In other words, the package layers in Figure 3.11 could also be modeled as classifiers. Figure 3.13 shows the Financial Aid Office, a classifier, owns four use cases. A use-case diagram could show how the actors interact with these use cases.

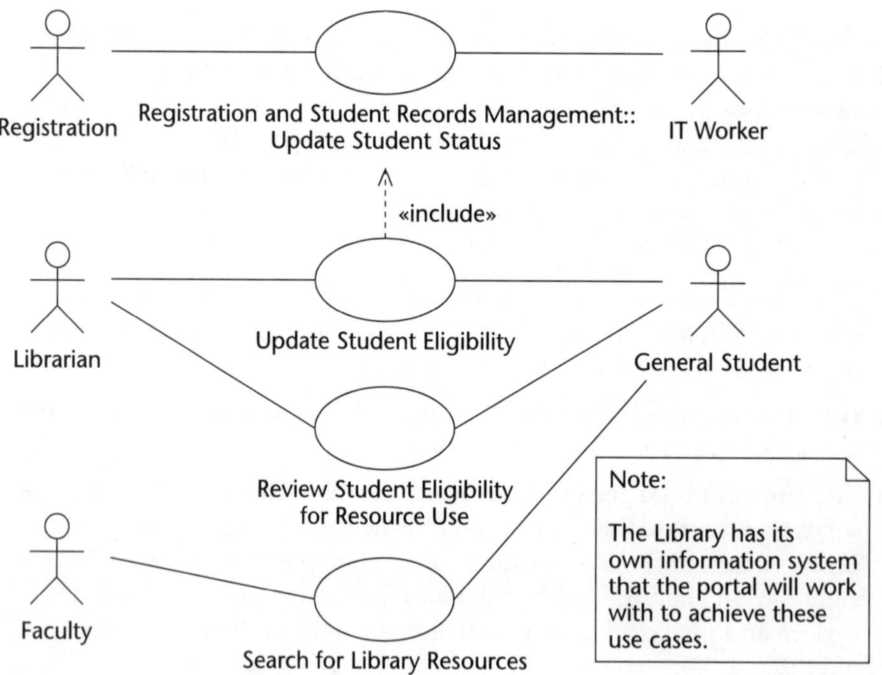

Figure 3.12 Use-case diagram for the library package of the portal.

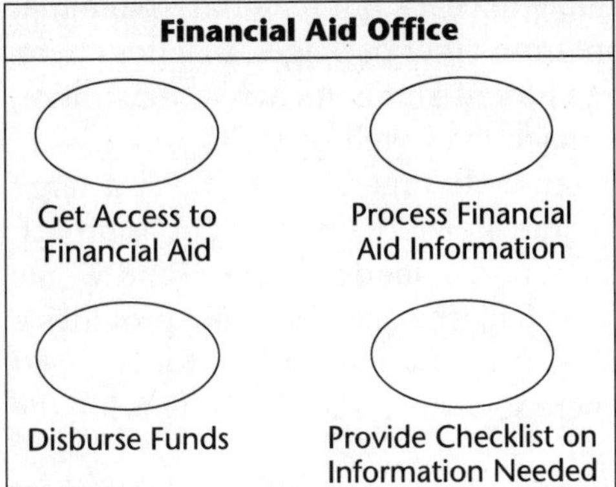

Figure 3.13 A classifier can own use cases, providing another way to organize use cases in a model.

Describing Use Cases

As we've noted, the description of the use case is normally done through text. This description is a simple and consistent specification about how the actors and the use cases (the system) interact. It concentrates on the external behavior of the system and ignores how things are actually performed inside the system. The language and terminology used in the description are the same as those used by the customer or user of the system.

The text description should include:

- **Objective for the use case.** What are the ultimate objectives of this use case? What is it trying to achieve? Use cases are goal oriented, and the goal of each use case should be apparent.
- **How the use case is initiated.** Which actor initiates the execution of the use case, and in which situations?
- **The flow of messages between actors and the use case.** Which messages or events do the use case and the actor exchange to notify each other, update or retrieve information, and help each other with decisions? What should describe the main flow of messages between the system and the actors, and which entities in the system are used or modified?
- **Alternate flow in the use case.** A use case can have alternate executions depending on conditions or exceptions. Care should be taken to

delineate normal flow from alternate and exceptional flow so that readers are not overwhelmed with the potentially distracting wealth of information supporting the detail of the alternate or exceptional flows. Typically, separate sections of the description are used to detail these variants.

- **Special/supplementary requirements applicable to the use case.** These are the requirements that provide detail, though not necessarily behavior, that is specific to the use case. Examples include data definitions, performance requirements of specific steps, security requirements, and so on. For more complex systems with real-time requirements, these will have more definition in later diagrams (see Chapter 6 on real-time and performance issues in behavior models). At the use-case level, the idea is to capture the requirements, not to lay out the design.
- **How the use case finishes and its value to the actor.** Describe when the use case is considered finished and the kind of value delivered to the actor.

Remember that the description identifies what is done relevant to the external actor, not how things are done inside the system. The text should be clear and consistent so that a customer can understand and validate it (agree that it represents what he or she wants from the system). Avoid complicated sentences that are hard to interpret and easy to misunderstand.

A use case can have internal structure that can be described with a composite structure diagram (see Chapter 7). You can also describe a use case with an *activity diagram*, as shown in Figure 3.14. The activity diagram (described in more detail in Chapters 5 and 6) shows a sequence of activities, their ordering, and optional decisions that are made to indicate which activity is performed next.

NOTE Keep in mind that a use-case model must be easy to communicate to a user and should not be described too formally.

As a complement to a use-case description that contains the complete and general description, a number of actual scenarios are used to illustrate what happens when the use case is instantiated. The scenario description illustrates a specific case, with both the actors and the use cases involved as actual instances. Customers can better understand a complex use case when a more practical scenario describes the behavior of the system. But note, a scenario description is a complement to, not a substitution for, the use-case description.

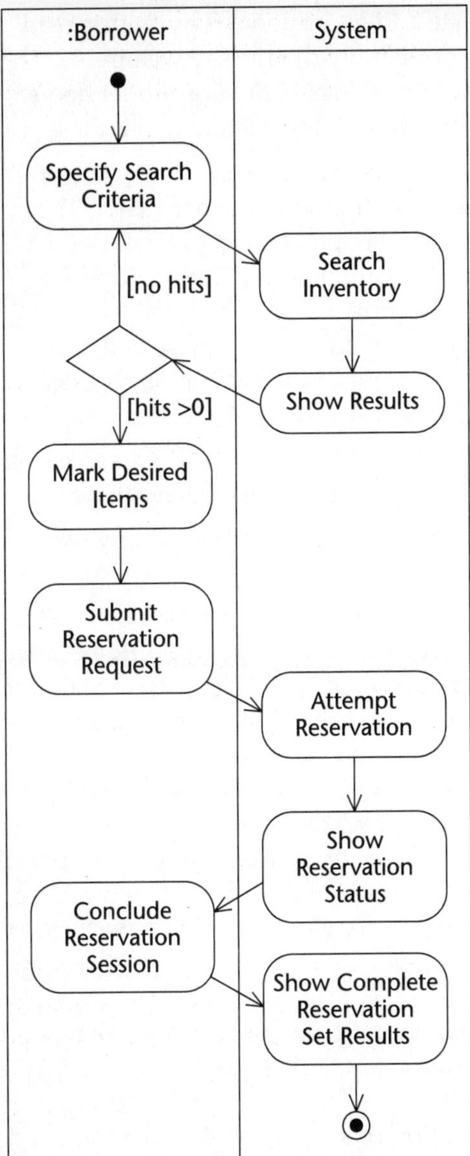

Figure 3.14 An activity diagram used to describe the interaction between the actor and the use case.

Assessing Use Cases

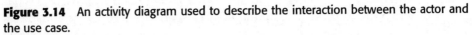

After the use cases are described, a specific activity reveals whether the relationships previously described are identified. Not until the use cases are at least partially described do the developers have the knowledge to identify suitable relationships. Even if you are not able to get all the detail of the use cases, at least be able to articulate the general needs the user has from the system. During this activity, answer the following questions:

- How do the actors involved in a use case communicate with the system?
- Are there similarities between a number of actors that represent a common role and thus could be described as a *base class actor*?
- Do a number of use cases rely on a common flow of activities that could be described as an include relation to a use case?
- Do special cases of a use case exist that could be described as an extend relation?
- Are there any actors or use cases without an association? If so, something is wrong. Why are the actors there? Why is the use case there?
- Are any functional requirements known, but not handled by any use case? If so, create a use case for that requirement.

NOTE More detailed requirements might not fit in a use case, while some general performance issues will find their way into the supplementary specifications. At this level, look for any substantial portions of functionality missed in the review.

Testing Use Cases

The use cases also have a purpose in testing. Testing involves two different but related goals: *verification* and *validation*. Verification confirms that the system is implemented correctly according to the requirements specifications and the design. Validation ensures that the system under development actually addresses the customer's needs. Use cases help validation by providing a method to test the system for observable benefits to actors.

Use cases provide the functional view of a software project from the start, making it the main source for validation. However, if the use cases don't reflect the needs of the users, then validation is impossible. The project may technically deliver what the specification outlined, but not achieve what the client wanted. As soon as use cases have been prepared, the model should be presented to and discussed with customers and end users. They must validate the model, indicating that this model correctly meets their expectations of the system; specifically, the way the system provides the functionality for them. For some clients, this may require a number of iterations and frequent reviews during the software development life cycle. To do this, the modeler must ensure that the customers really understand the model and its meaning, to avoid obtaining approval for something that is not acceptable. During this process, questions and ideas will no doubt arise that will need to be added to the use-case model before final approval. Having a valid set of use cases as early as possible helps projects succeed. If you wait until later to make sure that the use cases are valid, it could turn out that the system doesn't meet the correct user requirements, so the whole project may have to be reworked from scratch. Use cases can work against this risk by keeping the focus on the high-level functionality in a way that is easy to review. Of course, full validation will happen with the actual adoption of the system by the users to fulfill their needs.

Verification of the system tests that it works according to the specifications. Thus, verification can't be carried out until there are working parts of the system. Then, it is possible to test that the system behaves as specified by the users, that the use cases described in the use-case model perform, and that they behave as described in the use-case description.

Use cases play an integral part in helping testers organize their tests; projects that employ use cases to communicate requirements typically have test cases that reflect the use-case model. For testers who are devising test cases from use cases, much of what exists in a use case can be exploited. For example, for every use-case scenario, there will be at least that many test scenarios. Bear in mind that varying input values will be required to provide boundary/edge condition test coverage, so there will likely be more than one test scenario for each use-case scenario. Use-case elaboration conditions or any other flow rules will also prove helpful for test cases.

Use Cases and Requirements Management

Use cases provide an excellent way to capture and to organize requirements. However, systems will almost always get requirements from additional sources, not just documented use cases. Indeed, UML does not require use cases, and some projects find success without use-case modeling. The point we make here is that use cases keep the focus on delivering value to clients, so the model helps drive project success. However, use cases do not represent a magic bullet that will automatically meet all the requirements of the users.

Other sources of requirements include change requests for an existing system, mandated rules for a system, or a database of desired features. Additional requirements-gathering efforts are likely needed for many projects, especially those that rely heavily on a graphical user interface (GUI). Many Web projects or data-entry screens require sophisticated work on the GUI to satisfy the client. One effective method for gathering requirements is to produce storyboards, scrawls, or a graphic click-through that shows the users how they will interact with the system. This uncovers many implicit notions of how to use the system.

With a click-through presented to a client, all that remains is for the development team to provide the detailed connections at a later time. Use caution, then, when working with the client to avoid leaving unrealistic expectations of system performance. Avoid making the demonstration too realistic because it could cross the line into the unsavory practice of producing vaporware before the system even has a proven architecture.

CROSS-REFERENCE **The case study in Chapter 11 provides a good example of how a project evolves from a set of use cases through analysis and design. The case study includes some typical project artifacts and working code based on experience.**

Realizing Use Cases

Use cases link to the design and analysis of the system under construction. This section describes a basic approach to elaborating use cases and connecting them to objects in the system. This means that the use cases are *realized* in the system, that the responsibilities to perform the actions described in the use-case descriptions are allocated to collaborating objects that implement the functionality.

NOTE **This section relies on some concepts and features described in later chapters. We present this explanation here to offer one approach to working with use cases and to set the stage for later chapters.**

As with many things in UML, the language makes no demands on using all the diagrams but offers services to use according to the needs of the modeler. The widespread adoption of UML has expanded the ways to use the language, making UML a flexible set of tools. However, to understand how to use the set of tools in the UML toolkit you need to see them in action. This section, coupled with the case study in Chapter 11 and on the CD, provides an overview of a standard approach to implementing use cases.

The principles for realizing use cases are:

- **A collaboration realizes a use case.** A collaboration shows an internal implementation-dependent solution of a use case in terms of the relationships between classes and objects (called the *context* of the collaboration) and their interaction to achieve the desired functionality (called the *interaction* of the collaboration). The symbol for a collaboration is a dashed ellipse containing the name of the collaboration.

- **To explain a collaboration requires a number of diagrams showing both the context and the interaction between the collaboration elements.** Participating in a collaboration are a number of elements that can be used in many ways. Typical diagrams used include communication, sequence, interaction overview, activity, and state machines, as covered in later chapters. The type of diagram to use to give a complete picture of the collaboration depends on the actual case. In some cases, one diagram may be sufficient; in other cases, a combination of different diagrams may be necessary.
- **A scenario is an instance of a use case.** The scenario is a specific execution path (a specific flow of events) that represents a specific instantiation of the use case (one usage of the system). When a scenario is viewed as a use case, only the external behavior toward the actors is described. When viewed as a collaboration occurrence, the scenario includes the interaction between the parts inside the system, or the runtime architecture, as shown in a composite structure diagram. For more on collaborations, composite structures, and runtime architecture, see Chapter 7.
- **A use case can own diagrams that detail its internal structure.** A use case can own diagrams to describe the actions that take place to deliver the benefits of the use case. These can emphasize the runtime architecture or other elements that emerge with the implementation of the use case. For example, Figure 3.15 shows a use case that owns a state machine. Such devices make use cases more flexible and link them to other diagrams that can more precisely map actions.

Realizing a use case requires the designer to transform the different steps and actions in the use-case description (as described in text or other diagrams) to classes, operations in these classes, and relationships between them. This is described as allocating the responsibility of each step in the use case to the classes participating in the collaboration that realizes the use case. At this stage, a solution is found that gives the external behavior the use case has specified; it is described in terms of a collaboration inside the system.

Each step in the use-case description can be transformed into operations on the classes that participate in the collaboration realizing the use case. A step in the use case is transformed to a number of operations on the classes; it is unlikely that there is a one-to-one relationship between an action in the use case and an operation in the interaction between objects of the participating classes. In fact, there are almost always more messages represented in a collaboration than there are steps in a scenario of a use case, simply because the collaboration adds several classes that are needed to support the realization of the use case. Also note that a class can participate in many use cases. The total responsibility of the class is the integration of all roles it plays in the use cases.

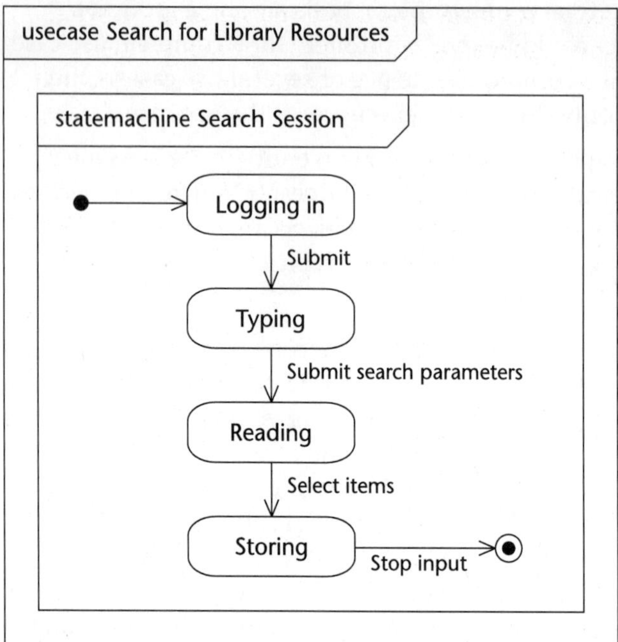

Figure 3.15 A use case can own diagrams that detail the internal structure of the use case. In this example, the use case has a state machine to elaborate the detailed meaning of the use case.

The relationship between a use case and its implementation in terms of a collaboration can be shown through a *realize relationship* (a dashed line with a hollow triangle arrow pointing at the use case being realized). The relationship can also be shown by a use case owning a composite structure diagram.

Allocating responsibilities to classes successfully requires common sense, experience, and hard work. The rest of this book outlines additional tools to help design a system. As always, when object orientation is involved, it is highly iterative work. The modeler tries different possibilities, gradually improving on his or her solution until he or she has a model that performs the functionality desired and that is flexible enough to allow for future changes (model quality is discussed in Chapter 10).

Many successful projects, including the case study in Chapter 11, employ a method pioneered by Jacobson that defines three analysis class stereotypes: boundary, control, and entity. For each use case, these objects are used to describe a collaboration that implements the use case. The responsibility for each of these stereotypes is as follows:

- **Boundary.** This object type lies close to the boundary of the system (though still within it). It interacts with the actors outside the system and passes messages to and from them to the other object types inside the system.

- **Control.** This object type controls interactions among a group of objects. Such an object could be the "controller" for a complete use case, or it could implement a common sequence of several use cases. Often such an object exists only during the execution of the use case.
- **Entity.** This object type represents a domain entity in the area the system handles. It is typically passive in that it doesn't initiate interactions on its own. In information systems, entity objects are normally persistent and stored in a database. Entity objects typically participate in many use cases.

The stereotypes for these classes have their own icons (see Figure 3.16) and can be used when drawing the diagrams that describe a collaboration or in a class diagram. After defining the different types of objects and specifying the collaboration, a specific activity can be made to look for similarities between them so that some classes can be used in a number of use cases. Applying the use cases in this way can also be the basis for analysis and design of the system; this development process is what Jacobson calls use-case driven.

Methods vary on when to allocate responsibilities to classes from the use cases. Some methods suggest that a domain analysis be made, showing all the domain classes with their relationships. Then, the software architect takes each use case and allocates responsibility to classes in the analysis model, sometimes modifying it or adding new classes. Other methods suggest that the use cases become the basis for finding the classes, so that during the allocation of responsibilities, the domain analysis model is gradually established.

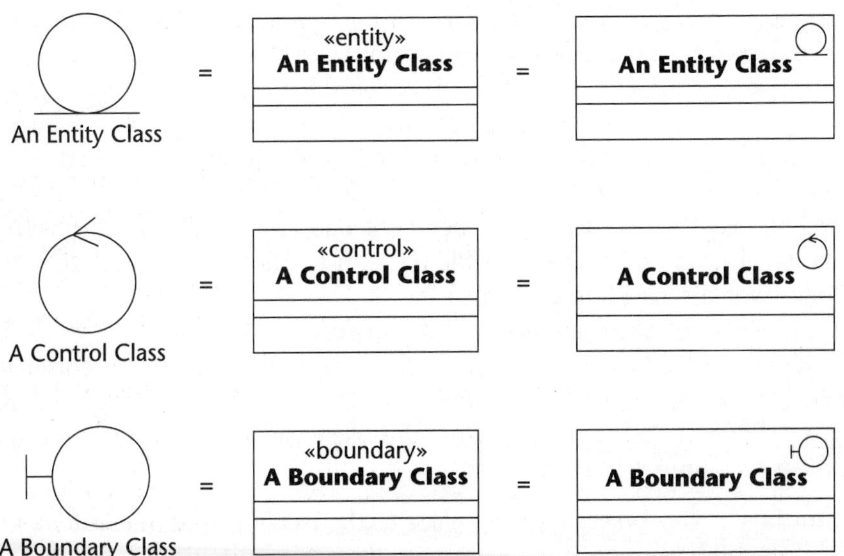

Figure 3.16 Analysis class stereotypes used for initial use-case realizations.

It is important to emphasize that the work will be done a number of times as part of an iterative process that will uncover additional requirements and issues not recognized at the start of the a project. For example, when responsibility is allocated to classes, errors and omissions in the class diagrams may be discovered and lead to modification of the class diagrams. New classes will surely be identified in order to support the use cases. In some cases, it might even be necessary to modify the use-case diagrams because a deeper understanding of the system has made the team recognize that a use case is incorrectly described. Therefore, reviews of modeling work provide a great way to make certain that all the issues emerge as soon as possible.

Use cases help you to focus on the functionality of the system, so that it is correctly described and correctly implemented. One problem with several object-oriented methods that don't have use cases is that they concentrate on the static structures of classes and objects (sometimes called conceptual modeling), while ignoring the functional and dynamic aspects of the system being developed. Use cases keep the team focused on the functionality delivered to the user. Software engineers have devised a variety of methods to link use cases to design. How to leverage the use cases to best focus on a project depends on individual style and the goals of the project. Remember that even if the stick figures and circles can seem silly, especially during long debates on whether to use <<include>> or <<extend>>, they do focus the project. Keep in mind that more projects and software products fail from the inability to appreciate what the client really needs from a system than from a failure to code a Java class correctly. Use cases provide a tool to address this issue.

Relevant Changes in UML 2

UML 2 adds a few additional features to use cases that allow a modeler to more easily integrate a use case with other elements in a model.

UML 2 allows for classifiers to own use cases. This provides an alternative to organizing use cases by packages. In addition, it allows a use case to be part of something other than the abstract system. UML 2 introduces the notion of the subject, which is a classifier that has a relationship to the use case. A use case does not have to be connected to a subject, but it can be. Because use cases are linked more strongly to classifiers in UML 2, it enables easier integration of use cases with other model elements because classifiers have a wider array or relationships than packages.

Therefore, a use case can more easily work with other modeling elements, furthering the initial requirement, or use case for the UML 2 product, of making the modeling elements broadly compatible for standard extensions and machine communication. This lets use cases focus on what they are best at, describing the benefit to the users. Other UML diagrams break down the details of how that is implemented. As an example of increased communication with other elements, a use case can now own internal structure diagrams to show the relevant architectural elements related to the use case. They can also own a diagram showing the runtime architecture of a collaboration with the composite structure diagram, explained in Chapter 7.

The way that the details of an extension are represented has been changed slightly to include a note attached to the extend relationship. In addition, the condition for the extension should be indicated on the diagram. For use cases with a number of extensions, the use of an alternate notation that details the extensions and the conditions for the extensions is encouraged.

For modelers who have familiarity with earlier versions of UML or the first edition of this book, there were some evolutionary changes of note between UML 1.3 and UML 1.4 that have carried over into UML 2.

- The uses relationship was replaced by the include relationship.
- The extends relationship was simply renamed "extend."
- The generalization relationship was added.

Summary

Use-case modeling is a technique used to describe the functional requirements of a system. Use cases are described in terms of external actors, use cases, and the subject modeled. Actors represent a role that an external entity such as a user, hardware, or another system plays in interacting with the system. Actors initiate and communicate with use cases, where a use case is a set of sequences of actions performed in the system. A use case must deliver a tangible value to an actor and is normally described through text documentation. Actors and use cases are classifiers. An actor is typically connected to one or more use cases through associations, and both actors and use cases can have generalization relationships that describe common behavior in superclasses inherited by one or more specialized subclasses. A use-case model is described in one or more UML use-case diagrams.

Figure 3.17 provides a summary diagram that sets the stage for the rest of the book. Use cases are realized in collaborations, where a collaboration is a description of a context showing classes/objects and their relationships (see Chapter 4) and an interaction showing how the classes/objects work together to perform a specific functionality. A collaboration is described with activity diagrams, communication diagrams, composite structure diagrams, and sequence diagrams (as described in Chapters 5, 6, and 7). When a use case is implemented, the responsibility of each of the action steps in the use case must be allocated to classes participating in the collaboration, typically by specifying operations on these classes, along with how they interact. A scenario is an instance of a use case, or a collaboration, showing a specific execution path. As such, a scenario is an illustration or an example of a use case. When viewed as an instance of a use case, only the interaction between the use case and the external actor is described, but when viewed as a collaboration occurrence, the interaction between the parts inside the system, the runtime architecture, is described. The composite structure diagram reviewed in Chapter 7 provides a tool to model the collaboration occurrence.

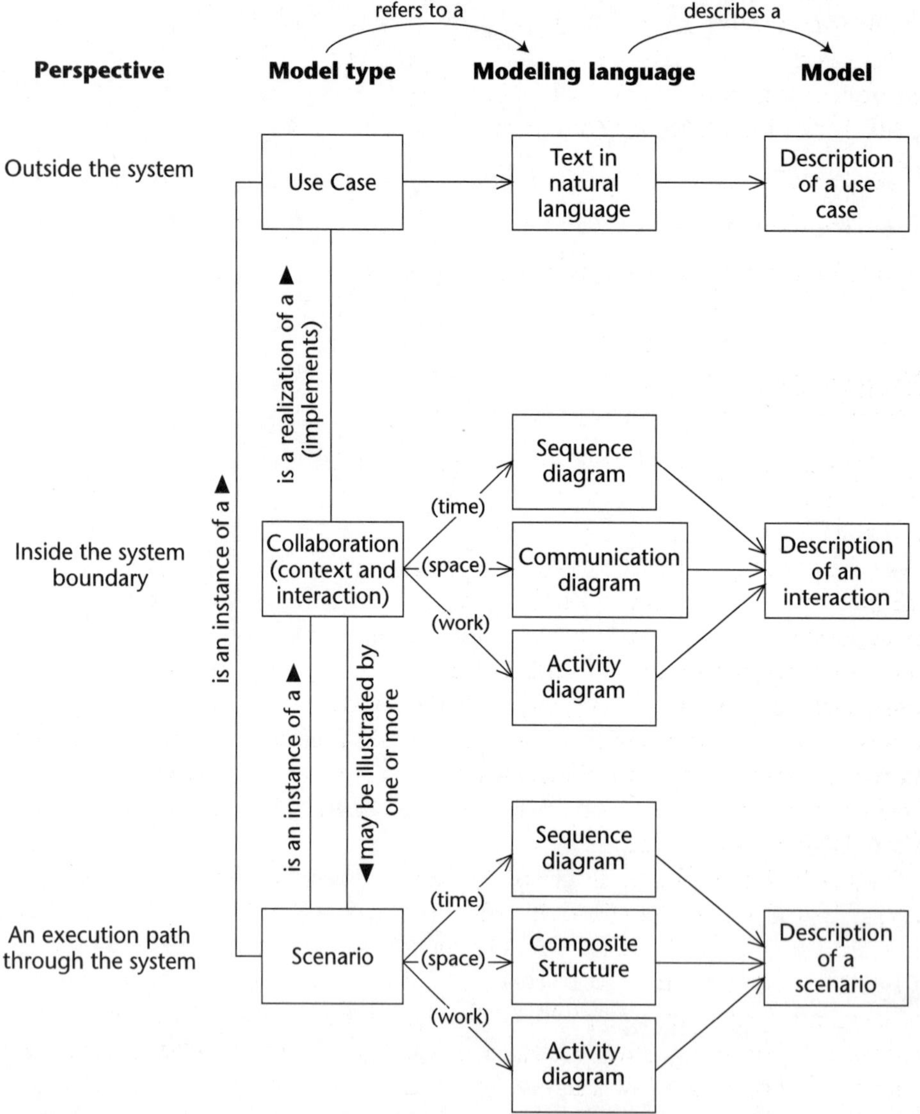

Figure 3.17 The relationships between use case, collaboration, and scenario.

CHAPTER

4

Classes, Objects, and Their Relationships

Object-oriented modelers use classes, objects, and their relationships to describe things and how they work. Classes and objects describe the elements in the system, while the relationships reveal communication and interaction. People have used classes and objects in classification for thousands of years to describe complex systems. Although modeling is not new, using a specialized modeling language to capture thought and transfer these models into working systems responding to change is new. When using object-oriented programming to build software systems, classes and relationships provide the core information of the software product.

Classes and Objects

You can talk about an object and manipulate it. An *object* exists in the real world (or more precisely, in your understanding of the real world). It can be a part of any type of system, for example, a machine, an organization, or a business. Some objects tend toward the theoretical (such as implementation objects in a software system): You can derive them by analyzing the structure and behavior of objects in the real world. Objects, in one way or another, represent your understanding of the real world.

A *class* describes the properties and behavior of a type of object. All objects can reflect some class. From a class, a system will create individual instances, or objects. Put another way, objects are instantiated from a class. An object relates to a class similarly to a variable relating to a type in an ordinary programming language or a cookie relating to a cookie cutter in a kitchen. You use classes to discuss systems and to classify the objects you identify in the real world.

So far, this is nothing new. Consider Darwin, who used classes to describe biological groups. He combined his classes via inheritance to describe his theory of evolution. Object-oriented design classifies information in a similar manner, with inheritance between classes. Going further back, one could claim Plato used classes when describing reality as reflection of ideal types: Human beings lived in a cave viewing "reflections" of the pure realm. In object-oriented terms, the ideal type is the class, and the images on the cave wall are the objects. Plato lacked a precise semantic mapping between these realms, and, of course, he had no need to model software entities. Fortunately, for the software designer, UML provides something new: a clearer relationship between class and object than a vague and shadowy resemblance. When it comes to software, designers must move quickly and precisely from the abstract to the real and back again.

In UML, objects reflect real software entities. With UML, a designer has the power to take objects and show how to build or to refine systems. UML provides a powerful set of tools, but a modeler must still mold these elements into a clear model. An object-oriented model of any system—business, information machines, or anything—relies on real concepts from the problem domain, making the models understandable and easy to communicate. If you build a system for an insurance company, it should reflect the concepts in the insurance business. If you build a system for the military, the concepts from that world should be used to model the system. With a clearly modeled understanding of the primary concepts of a business, the designer can also adjust to change. At this level, modeling reflects an art of capturing a system; no perfect model for a system exists.

You can redesign a model to fit new laws, strategies, rules, and so on by adjusting the differences between the core classes of the old business and the new business. In any model, it is useful to mimic as closely as possible real-world elements, to make them easier to understand. To get the most from the customer, the model elements should be easy to discuss, easy to verify against functional requirements, and easy to maintain. Use cases, as seen in Chapter 3, provide a great way to keep the model focused on items important to the user. When models reflect the look of their real-world counterparts and embody the core needs of the users as well as the concepts in the problem domain, you have a great chance to produce a healthy object-oriented system. Figure 4.1 shows classes, objects, and the relationships among them in a high-level class diagram.

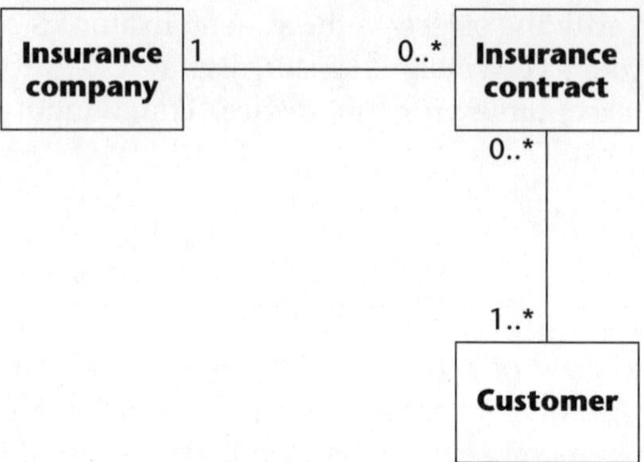

Figure 4.1 A simple model of an insurance business. One insurance company has many (zero-to-many) insurance contracts. An insurance customer has many (zero-to-many) insurance contracts. An insurance contract is related to one insurance company. The insurance contract is related to many (one-to-many) insurance customers. The entities shown in the model are classes.

In UML, a class is the most common classifier. UML includes a large number of other classifiers, such as use cases, signals, activities, or components.

NOTE **Many features in this chapter, such as templates and generalization, apply to other classifiers even though this chapter focuses on their application to classes.**

A class is the most general of classifiers as it can describe an object in any type of system—information, technical, embedded real-time, distributed, software, and business. Artifacts in a business, information that should be stored or analyzed, and roles that the actors in the business play often turn into classes in information and business systems. Examples of classes in business and information systems include:

Customer

Agreement

Invoice

Debt

Asset

Quotation

Even if another specialized UML diagram or element can handle an entity, such as a component, many modelers still initially set these up as classes to get a complete picture of the system during analysis. At the least, this lets the designer know that he or she has to handle an interface or wrapper for these system objects. Also, they help to verify the objects in the system. Examples of classes in technical and software systems can include sensor, display, I/O card, engine, button, control class, file, executable program, device, icon, window, and scrollbar.

Class Diagram

A *class diagram* describes the static view of a system in terms of classes and relationships among the classes. Although it might look like a data model filled with entities and attributes, remember that classes not only show the structure of your information but also describe behavior. The class diagram can define a foundation for diagrams showing other aspects of the system, such as the states of the objects and the collaboration between objects shown in the dynamic diagrams. In addition, an object-oriented programming language can directly implement a class, making the class diagram one of the core diagrams for generating code and making UML executable (see Chapter 9 on Model Driven Architecture [MDA]). A class diagram shows only classes, not objects. The object diagram shows that actual object instances of the classes.

To create a class diagram, you need to identify and describe the main items in the system. After the definition of a number of classes, the modeler can define the relationships between classes. A class is drawn with a rectangle, often divided into three compartments (as shown in Figure 4.2):

- The name compartment
- The attributes compartment
- The operations compartment

Finding Classes

The modeler must use the knowledge of experts in the problem domain along with an understanding of the user and system in a creative endeavor to capture the system. Good classes reflect the problem domain and have real names, not confusing or fake names from literature or sports. Believe it or not, we have seen a few projects that don't follow this simple rule, making the model hard to read. When you are looking for classes, a good use-case model helps tremendously. Rely on the use-case model and requirements specification in the search for classes. Pose the following types of questions:

- Do I have information that should be stored or analyzed? If there is any information that has to be stored, transformed, analyzed, or handled in some other way, then it is a possible candidate for a class. The information might include concepts that must always be registered in the system or events or transactions that occur at a specific moment.
- Do I have external systems? If so, they are normally of interest when you model. The external system might be seen as classes that your system contains or should interact with.
- Do I have any reusable patterns, class libraries, or components? If you have patterns, class libraries, or components from earlier projects, colleagues, or manufacturers, they normally contain class candidates.
- Are there devices that the system must handle? Any technical devices connected to the system turn into class candidates that handle these devices.
- Do I have organizational parts? Representing an organization can be done with classes, especially in business models.
- Which roles do the actors in the business play? These roles can be seen as classes, such as user, system operator, customer, and so on.

Looking for classes may well prompt questions that will improve the use-case model or requirements specification.

Name Compartment

The top compartment of the class rectangle contains the name of the class; it is capitalized and centered in boldface. Again, the name should be derived from the problem domain and should be as unambiguous as possible. Therefore, it should be a noun, for example, Invoice or Debt. The class name should not have a prefix or a suffix.

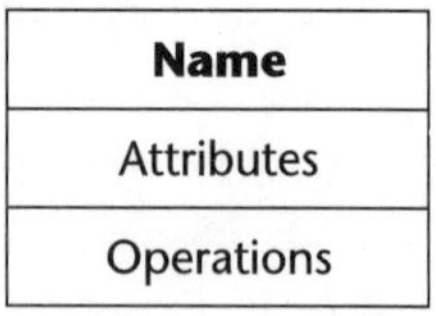

Name
Attributes
Operations

Figure 4.2 A class in UML.

Attributes Compartment

Classes have *attributes* that describe the characteristics of the objects. Figure 4.3 shows the class Car with attributes of registration number, data, speed, and direction. The correct class attributes capture the information that describes and identifies a specific instance of the class. However, only the attributes that are interesting within the system being modeled should be included. Furthermore, the purpose of the system also influences which attributes should be used. Attributes have values in object instances of the class.

An attribute has a type, which tells you what kind of attribute it is, as shown in Figure 4.4. Typical attribute types are integer, Boolean, string, date, real, point, and enumeration, which are called *data types*. Their instances are values (not objects). They can be specific for a certain programming language; however, any type can be used, including other classes.

The attributes can have different *visibility*. Visibility describes whether the attribute can be referenced from classes other than the one in which they are defined.

- If an attribute has the visibility of public, it can be used and viewed outside that class.
- If an attribute has the visibility of private, you cannot access it from other classes.
- If an attribute is protected it is private to the class, but visible to any subclasses through generalization and specialization.

Car
registration number data speed direction

Figure 4.3 A class, Car, with the attributes registration number, data, speed, and direction. Attribute names typically begin with a lowercase letter.

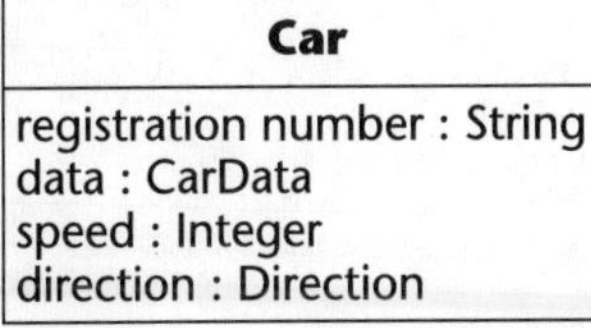

Figure 4.4 A class with typed attributes.

Additional kinds of visibility might be defined using a profile, or extension, for a particular programming language, but public and private are normally all that are necessary to express your class diagrams. Public is usually expressed with a plus sign (+), private with a minus sign (–), as shown in Figure 4.5. Protected is generally shown with the pound (#) sign. If no sign is displayed, this means that the visibility is undefined (there is no default visibility). Individual tool vendors implementing UML often use their own notation for the different types of visibility.

Figure 4.6 shows an attribute with a default value. It's assigned at the same time an object of the class is created.

An attribute can also be defined as a class-scope attribute, as shown in Figure 4.7. This means that the attribute is shared between all objects of a certain class (sometimes called a *class variable*). By convention, display the class-scope attribute with an underline. UML tools might display class-scoped attributes in different ways, and the meaning of these will differ in models fitting a profile for a specific programming language. For example, in Java a class variable will mean a static variable.

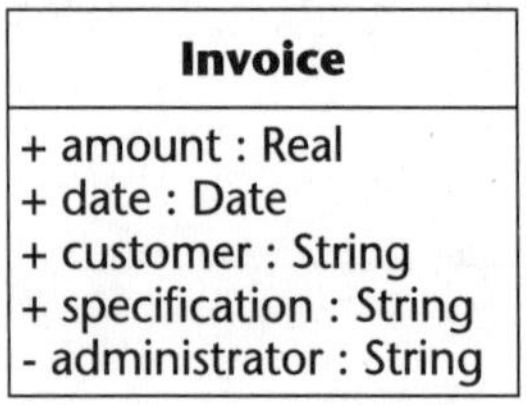

Invoice
+ amount : Real
+ date : Date
+ customer : String
+ specification : String
- administrator : String

Figure 4.5 A class with public and private attributes.

Invoice
+ amount : Real
+ date : Date = Current date
+ customer : String
+ specification : String
- administrator : String = "Unspecified"

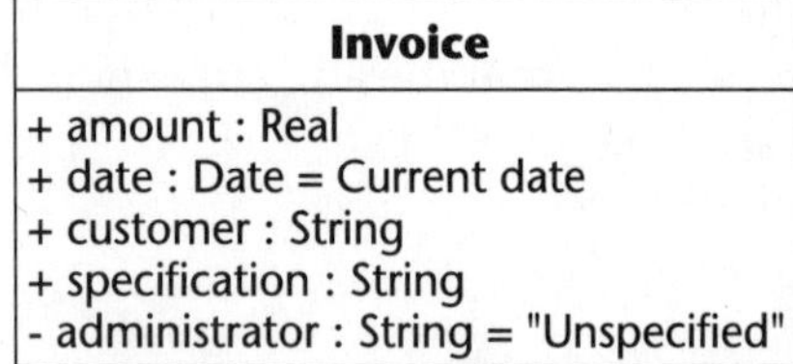

Figure 4.6 A class with attributes and their default values.

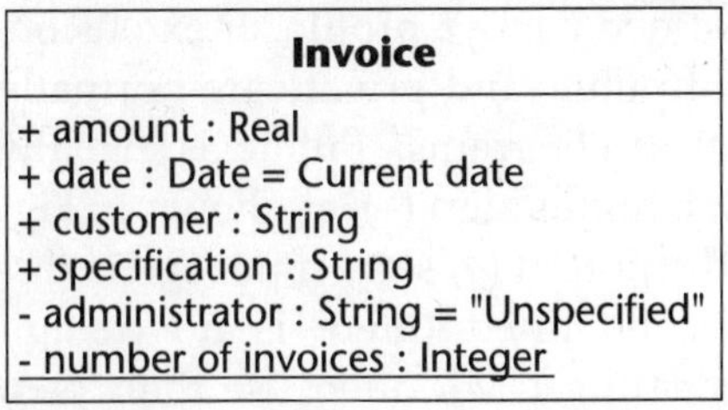

Invoice
+ amount : Real + date : Date = Current date + customer : String + specification : String - administrator : String = "Unspecified" - number of invoices : Integer

Figure 4.7 A class with a class-scope attribute. The attribute number_of_invoices is used to count the invoices; the value of this attribute is the same in all objects because the attribute is shared between them.

A property-string can be used to further describe an attribute. A property-string is written within curly braces; it is a comma-separated list of property values that apply to the attribute. For example, as shown in Figure 4.8, an attribute can have a property of {readOnly}. Other properties include {ordered}, {sequence} and others. The property-string on an attribute shows how, in this case, the UML designers use an extension mechanism in a standard way to enhance the language. Users can further extend the types of properties using the same extension mechanisms. See Chapter 8 for more details on UML extension mechanisms.

UML has formal syntax for the description of an attribute:

```
visibility / name : type [multiplicity] = default-value { property-
string }
```

You must have a name, but all other parts are optional. A "/" indicates that the attribute is derived. For example, the age of a person might be derived as the current date minus the date of birth. Multiplicity shows the number of instances of the attribute in square brackets (for example, [0..1]) and can be omitted for multiplicities of exactly one. The property-string can be used to specify other information about the attribute, such as that the attribute should be persistent. For more on these properties, see Chapter 8.

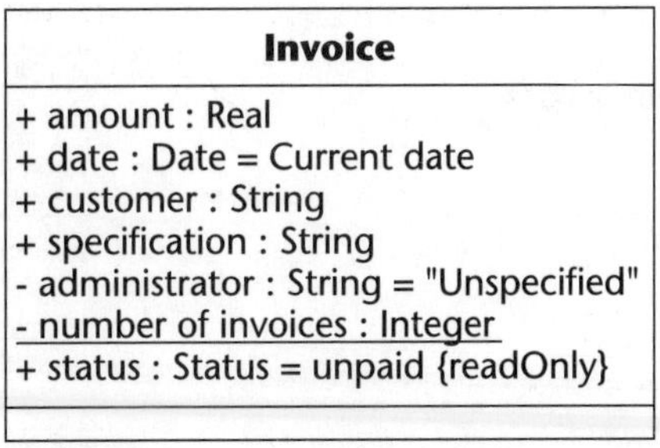

Invoice
+ amount : Real + date : Date = Current date + customer : String + specification : String - administrator : String = "Unspecified" - number of invoices : Integer + status : Status = unpaid {readOnly}

Figure 4.8 An attribute with a property-list of {readOnly}.

Java Implementation

Java, or another object-oriented language, can implement a class. All object-oriented programming languages have support for classes and objects. Translating the model class into code requires specific details, as shown in Figure 4.9 and represented in code below.

```
public class Invoice
{
    public double amount;
    public Date date = new Date();
    public String customer;
    static private int number_of_invoices = 0;

    // Constructor, called every time an objects is created
    public Invoice ()
    {
        // Other initialization

        number_of_invoices++; // Increment the class attribute
    }
    // Other methods go here
} ;
```

Operations Compartment

Figure 4.10 demonstrates that a class has both attributes and operations. As we've discussed, attributes characterize objects of the class and can describe the state of the object. *Operations* manipulate the attributes or perform other actions. Operations are normally called functions, but they are inside a class and can be applied only to objects of that class. An operation is described with a return-type, a name, and zero or more parameters. Together, the return-type, name, and parameters are the *signature of the operation*. The signature describes everything needed for the operation. To perform an operation, an operation is applied to an object of that class (is called on an object). The operations in a class describe what the class can do (not how), that is, what services it offers; thus they could be seen as the interface to the class. Just like an attribute, an operation can have visibility and scope.

Invoice
+ amount : Real + date : Date = Current date + customer : String - number of invoices : Integer = 0

Figure 4.9 An Invoice class.

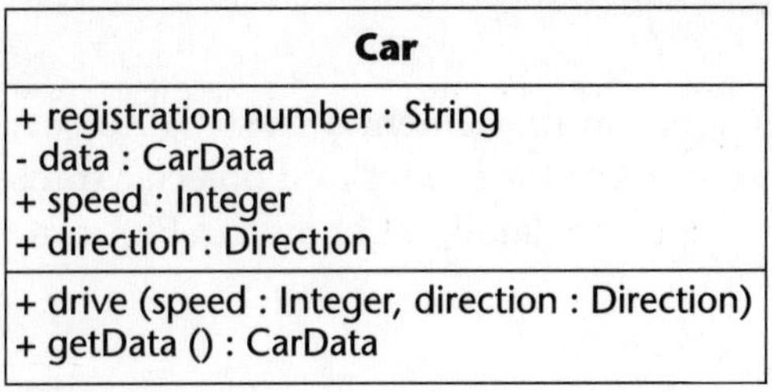

Car
+ registration number : String - data : CarData + speed : Integer + direction : Direction
+ drive (speed : Integer, direction : Direction) + getData () : CarData

Figure 4.10 The class Car has attributes and operations. The operation drive has two parameters, *speed* and *direction*. The operation getData has a return type, CarData.

A class can also have class-scope operations, as shown in Figure 4.11. A class-scope operation can be called without having an object of the class, but it is restricted to accessing only class-scope attributes. Class-scope operations are defined to carry out generic operations such as creating objects and finding objects when a specific object is not involved (except as possibly the result of the operation).

The formal syntax for an operation is:

```
visibility name ( parameter-list ) : return-type-expression { property-
string }
```

where parameter-list is a comma-separated list of formal parameters, each specified using the syntax:

```
direction name : type-expression [multiplicity] = default-value
{ property-string }
```

Visibility is the same as for attributes (+ for public, – for private, # for protected). Not all operations need to have a return-type, parameters, or a property-string, but operations of the same name must always have a unique signature (return-type, name, parameters). Figure 4.12 shows public operations with varying signatures.

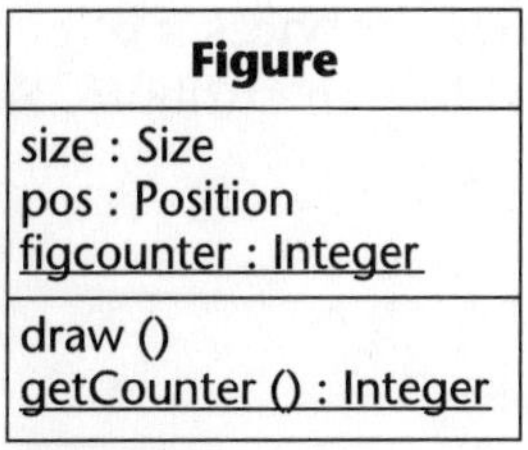

Figure
size : Size pos : Position figcounter : Integer
draw () getCounter () : Integer

Figure 4.11 Class-scope operation getCounter.

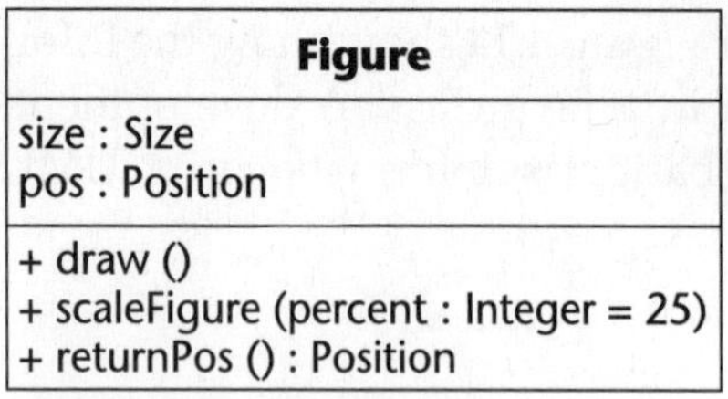

Figure
size : Size pos : Position
+ draw () + scaleFigure (percent : Integer = 25) + returnPos () : Position

Figure 4.12 Operation signatures.

A parameter's direction indicates whether it is being sent into or out of the operation (in, inout, out). It is also possible to have default values on parameters, which means that if the caller of the operation doesn't provide a parameter, the parameter will use the specified default value, as shown in Figure 4.13.

NOTE The operation is a part of the interface for a class; the implementation of an operation is called a *method*.

A *persistent* class is one whose objects exist after the program that created it ends. Persistent class objects store themselves in a database, a file, or some other permanent storage, and typically have a class-scope operation to handle the storing of the objects, for example, store (), load (), create (). A class can be described as persistent by using one of the UML extensions. Many modelers put the persistent property in the name compartment (when shown in a class diagram, a property is put within curly braces, as in {persistent}). If you are modeling for a specific platform, that platform likely has mechanisms for indicating persistence. For example, for Enterprise JavaBeans (EJB), you would use a stereotype for an entity bean to show persistence.

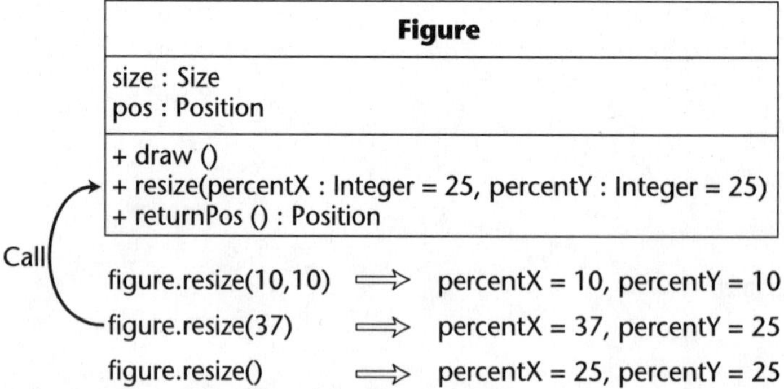

Figure 4.13 Default values for parameters.

A simple translation from UML to Java for Figure 4.14 shows how the information in the diagram reflects information in a Java class. A development-support tool can enable the generation of such basic class information from UML. The Java code for the class in Figure 4.14 is:

```
public class Figure
{
    private int x = 0;
    private int y = 0;

    public void draw ()
    {
        // Java code for drawing the figure
    }
} ;
```

The Java code for creating figure objects and calling the draw operation is:

```
Figure fig1 = new Figure();
Figure fig2 = new Figure();
fig1.draw();
fig2.draw();
```

When objects are created, normally they should initialize attributes and links to other objects. It is possible to have an operation called create that is a class-scope operation used to create and initiate the object. It is also possible to have an operation with the same name as the class, which would correspond to a constructor in a programming language (such as in C++ or Java). A constructor is called to create and initiate an object of the class. The class in Figure 4.14 would typically have a constructor to initialize the attributes x and y to some suitable start values.

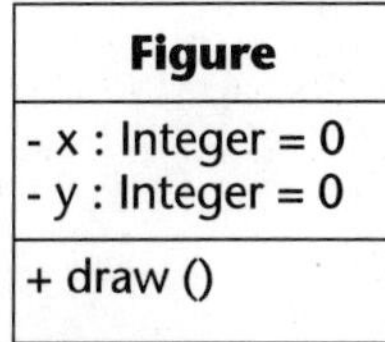

Figure 4.14 A Figure class.

Using Primitive Types

A primitive type is not a class and has no substructure but defines a data type. UML uses a handful of primitive types, including "string" for a set of characters, "integer" for numbers, and "Boolean" for true/false values. Users and tool vendors can define additional primitive types. Normally, the tool used for drawing the UML diagrams can be configured for a specific programming language by using a profile, in which case, the primitive types for that language become available. In a model without deployment detail, a simple subset of normal types could be used (for example, integer, string, float). The primitive types are used for return-types, parameters, and attributes. Classes defined in any class diagram in the model can also be used to type attributes, return-types, or parameters. A modeler or a profile could further define general types such as date, real, long, and so on for a specific language.

Relationships

Class diagrams consist of classes and the relationships among them. The relationships that can be used are *associations*, *generalizations*, *dependencies*, and *abstractions/realizations*.

- An *association* is a connection between classes, which means that it is also a connection between objects of those classes. In UML, an association is defined as a relationship that describes a set of links, where link is defined as a semantic connection among a tuple of objects.
- A *generalization* is a relationship between a more general and a more specific element. The more specific element can contain only additional information. An instance (an object is an instance of a class) of the more specific element may be used wherever the more general element is allowed.
- A *dependency* is a relationship between elements, one independent and one dependent. A change in the independent element will affect the dependent element.
- An *abstraction* is a relationship between two descriptions of the same thing, but at different levels. A *realization* is a type of abstraction that shows a model element that realizes a more general element.

In the next sections, association, aggregation (which is a special case of association), generalization, dependency, and abstraction relationships are presented and discussed.

Associations

An association is a connection between classes, a semantic connection (link) between objects of the classes involved in the association. An association is normally bidirectional, which means that if an object is associated with another object, both objects are aware of each other. An association represents that objects of two classes have a connection between them, meaning, for example, that they "know about each other," "are connected to," "for each X there is a Y," and so on. Classes and associations are very powerful when you model complex systems, such as product structures, document structures, and all kinds of information structures. UML refers to a specific instance of an association as a *link*.

Normal Association

The most common association is just a connection between classes. It is drawn as a solid line between two classes, as shown in Figure 4.15. The association has a name (near the line representing the association), often a verb, although nouns are also allowed. When a class diagram is modeled, it should reflect the system that is going to be built, meaning that the association names should come from the problem domain as do class names.

It is possible to use navigable associations by adding an arrow at the end of the association. The arrow indicates that the association can be used only in the direction of the arrow. However, associations may have two names, one in each direction. The direction of the name is shown by a small solid triangle either preceding or following the name, depending on the direction. It's possible to read an association from one class to the other, as in Figure 4.15: "An author uses a computer."

Figure 4.16 shows an example where a car can have one or more owners, and a person can own zero or more cars. This can be expressed as part of the association in a class diagram. To express how many, you use *multiplicity*, a range that tells you how many objects are linked. The range can be zero-to-one (0..1), zero-to-many (0..* or just *), one-to-many (1..*), two (2), five to eleven (5..11), and so on. It is also possible to express a series of numbers such as (1, 4, 6, 8..12). If no multiplicity is specified, then it is one (1) by default. The multiplicity is shown near the ends of the association, at the class where it is applicable (see Figure 4.17).

Figure 4.15 An author uses a computer. The Author class has an association to the Computer class.

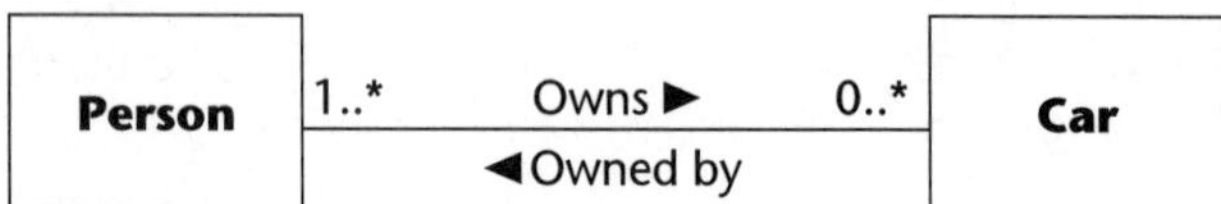

Figure 4.16 A person owns many (zero-to-many) cars. A car can be owned by many (one-to-many) persons.

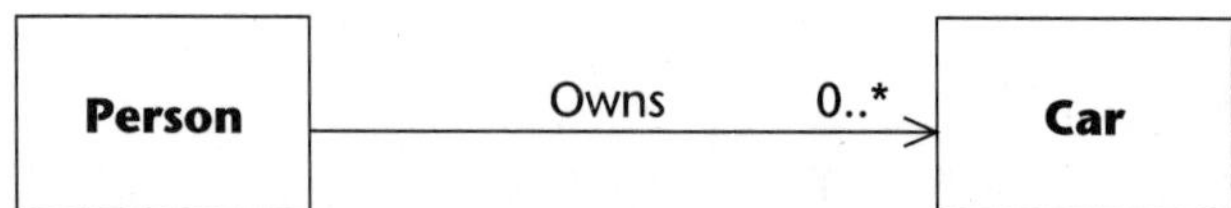

Figure 4.17 A navigable association says that a person can own many cars, but it does not say anything about how many people can own a car.

When you model very complex systems, communicate results effectively and keep the entire model up to date. If you keep your use cases and other model elements current, you can continue to verify and validate the model. When creating a diagram, many decisions must be made that otherwise would not be in text. Even a small model contains a lot of information, and it is always possible to translate the model into natural language. For example, the model in Figure 4.18 leads to the following statements:

- An insurance company has insurance contracts, which refer to one or more customers.
- A customer has insurance contracts (zero or more), which refer to one insurance company.
- An insurance contract is between an insurance company and one or more customers. The insurance contract refers to both a customer (or customers) and an insurance company.
- The insurance contract is expressed in an (zero or one) insurance policy (a written contract of insurance).
- The insurance policy expresses an insurance contract.

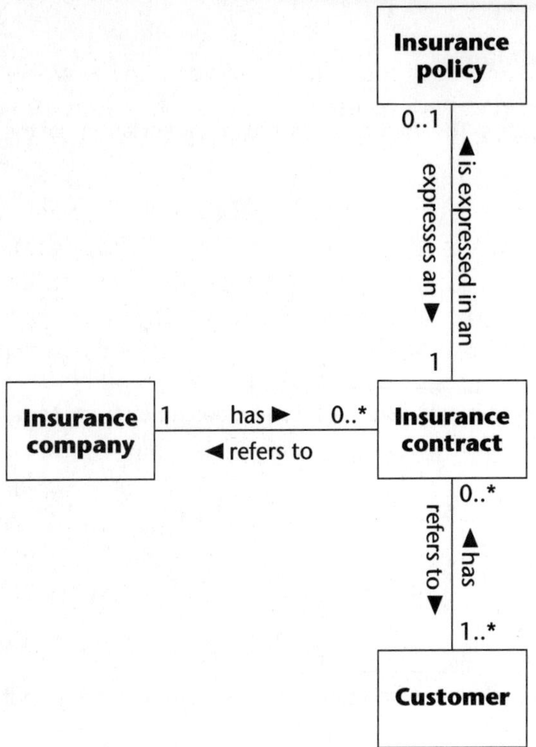

Figure 4.18 A class diagram describing an insurance business.

The multiplicity specifies that the insurance contract is expressed in an (zero or one) insurance policy (written contract of insurance). If you call the insurance company and insure your car, there is an insurance contract, but no insurance policy. The insurance policy will be sent to you later. The point is, it is very important to model the real business, not just what it seems to be. If you model the insurance business based on the insurance policy, you might have problems. For instance, what would happen if a customer insured his car then crashed it a minute later (there is no insurance policy yet, but there is an oral agreement with the insurance agent)? Alternately, what would happen if the insurance business instituted other types of insurance policies (insurance on the Web)? If you model the "soul" of the business (the real business), you can easily handle business changes because of new laws, competition, or economic shifts. In the case of insurance on the Web, you could add a new class called Web insurance policy. The new class could have a different behavior than normal insurance policies (for example, that customers can change them by themselves, and the changes will automatically affect the insurance contract; and the insurance policy can be sent directly to the customer by email).

Object Diagram

So far, only classes have been shown in your models. Objects can be shown in an object diagram. An object diagram in UML uses the same notation and relationships as a class diagram, since the objects are just instances of the very same classes. Where a class diagram shows the class types and their relationships, the object diagram shows specific instances of those classes and specific links between those instances at some moment in time. An object diagram can thus be viewed as an example of a class diagram, and as such it is often drawn to illustrate how a complex class diagram can be instantiated into objects (see Figure 4.19). The object diagram also shows how objects from a class diagram can be combined with each other at a certain point in time.

An object is shown as a class, and the name is underscored, although an object's name can be shown optionally preceding the class name as: `objectname : classname`. The object does not have to be named, in which case only the class name is shown underscored, preceded by a colon to indicate that it is an unnamed object of the specified class. The third alternative is that only the object name is specified (underscored); the class name is not shown in the diagram.

Recursive Association

It's possible to connect a class to itself via an association. The association still represents a semantic connection between objects, but the connected objects are of the same class. An association from a class to itself is called a *recursive association* and is the basis for many complex models used to model things such as product structures, as shown in Figure 4.20. Figure 4.21 shows a possible object diagram for the class diagram described in Figure 4.20.

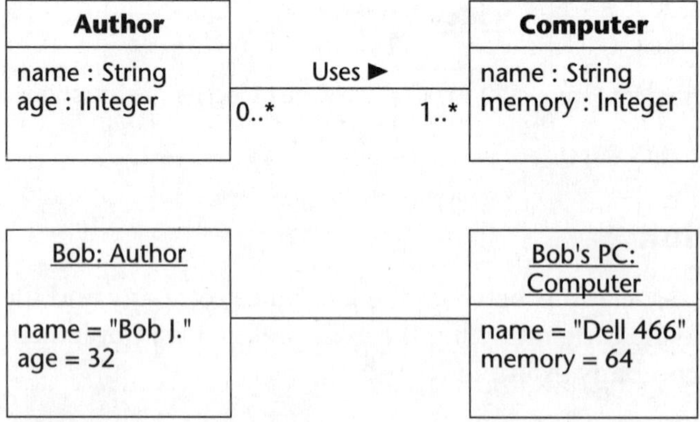

Figure 4.19 A class diagram and an object diagram, and an example of the class diagram being instantiated.

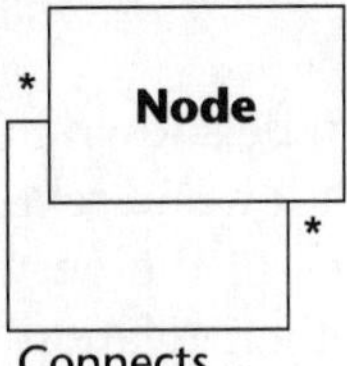

Figure 4.20 A network consists of many nodes connected to each other.

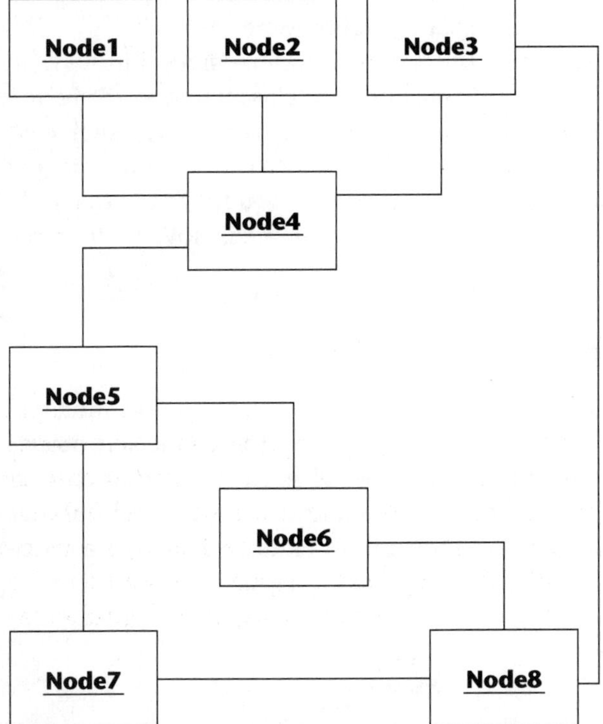

Figure 4.21 An object diagram for Figure 4.20, in which only the object names are shown.

Java Implementation

Figure 4.22 displays the associations between the Insurance company and the Insurance contract, while the code following the example is a Java implementation of that insurance company example.

Figure 4.22 Insurance company has associations to Insurance contract.

```
// Insurance_company.java file
public class Insurance_company
{
    /* Methods */

    // Insurance_contractVector is a specialization of the
    // Vector class ensuring hard typing. Vector is a standard
    // Java class for dynamic arrays.
    private Insurance_contractVector contracts;
}

// Insurance_contract.java file
public class Insurance_contract
{
    /* Methods */

    private Insurance_company refers_to;
}
```

It is easy to implement an association that is navigable or a bidirectional one-to-many association. However, in some languages, it is not that easy to implement a bidirectional many-to-many association. On the other hand, a bidirectional many-to-many association can be transformed to two one-to-many associations, as shown in Figure 4.23. For clarity, you should use the approach in Figure 4.23, although you may see both methods of implementation when you review a model.

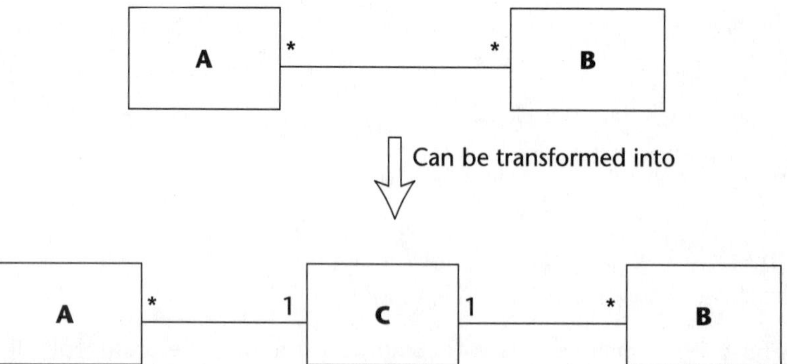

Figure 4.23 A bidirectional many-to-many association can be transformed into two one-to-many associations.

Roles in an Association

An association can have roles connected to each class involved in the association, as shown in Figures 4.24 through 4.26. The role name is a string placed near the end of the association next to the class to which it applies. The role name indicates the role played by the class in terms of the association. Roles are a useful technique for specifying the context of a class and its objects. Role names are part of the association and not part of the classes. Using role names is optional.

Qualified Association

Qualified associations are used with one-to-many or many-to-many associations. The qualifier distinguishes among the set of objects at the many end of an association. The qualifier specifies how a specific object at the many end of the association is identified, and may be seen as a kind of key to separating all the objects in the association. The qualifier is drawn as a small box at the end of the association near the class from which the navigation should be made. Remember that the qualifier represents an addition to the association line, not to the class. Qualified associations reduce the effective multiplicity in the model from one-to-many to one-to-one by indicating with the qualifier an identity for each association. As shown in Figure 4.27, although the Canvas class will have a number of figures, each figure will have a qualifier.

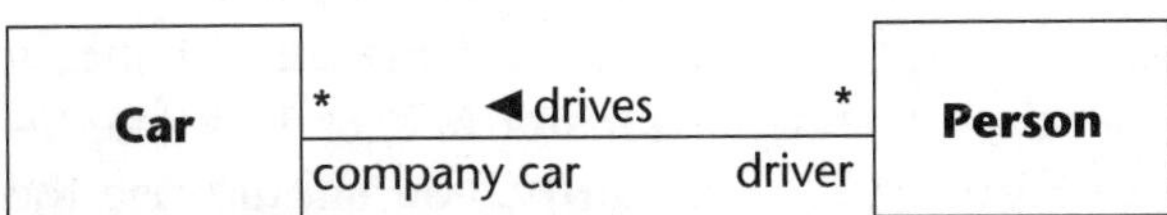

Figure 4.24 A person plays the role of a driver and a car plays the role of a company car in terms of the drives association between Car and Person. Roles are the context in which objects act. A car can play other roles in another context, such as ambulance, police car, and so on.

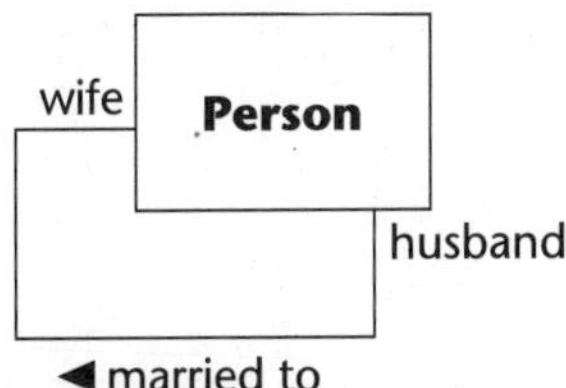

Figure 4.25 A husband is married to a wife. Both husband and wife are people. If a person is not married, then he or she cannot play the role of husband or wife, which means that the married to association is not applicable.

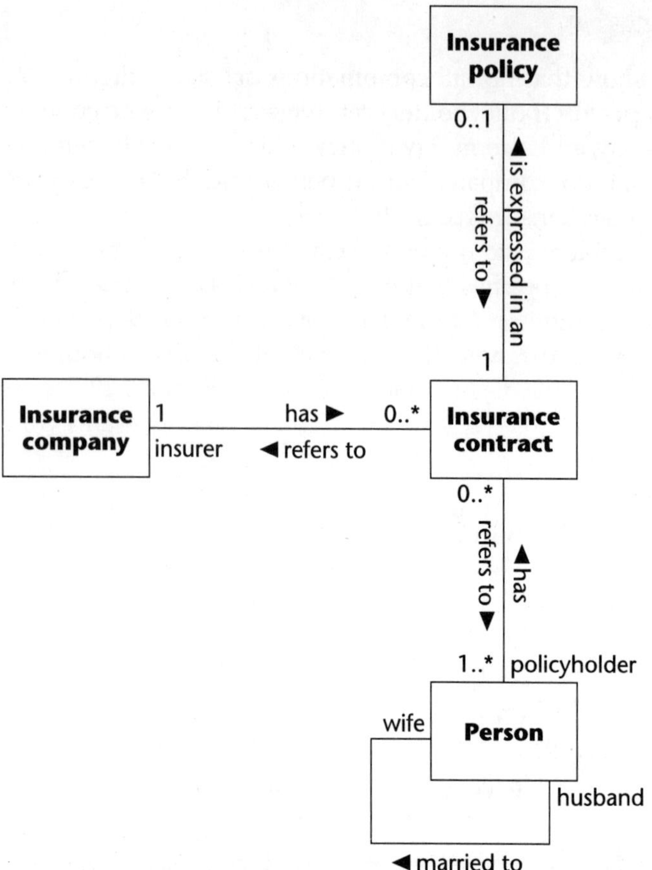

Figure 4.26 A class can play different roles in different associations. The model from Figures 4.18 and 4.25 are combined. In this model, a person can play the role of husband, wife, or policyholder. The insurance company plays the insurer role.

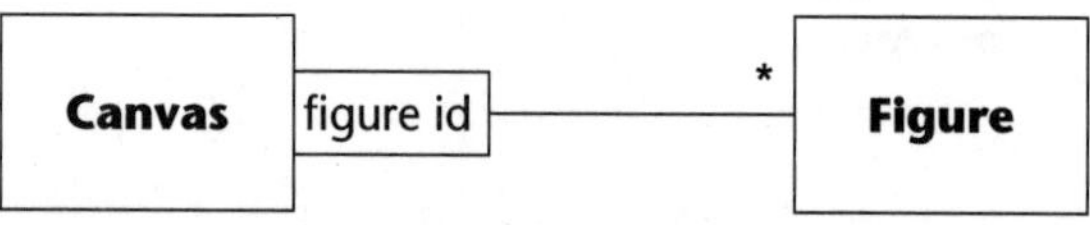

Figure 4.27 In the Canvas class, the association is represented with a unique identification for each figure (figure id).

Xor Constraint

The class diagram can show that not all combinations are valid. Figure 4.28 shows such a model. A person (policyholder) can have an insurance contract with an insurance company, and a company (policyholder) can have an insurance contract with an insurance company, but the person and the company are not permitted to have the *same* insurance contract.

A way of solving the problem is to use or-associations or an either/or (xor) constraint. The xor constraint specifies that objects of a class may participate in, at most, one of the associations at a time. The xor constraint is depicted by a dashed line between the associations that are part of the association, and with the specification {xor} on the dashed line, as shown in Figure 4.29.

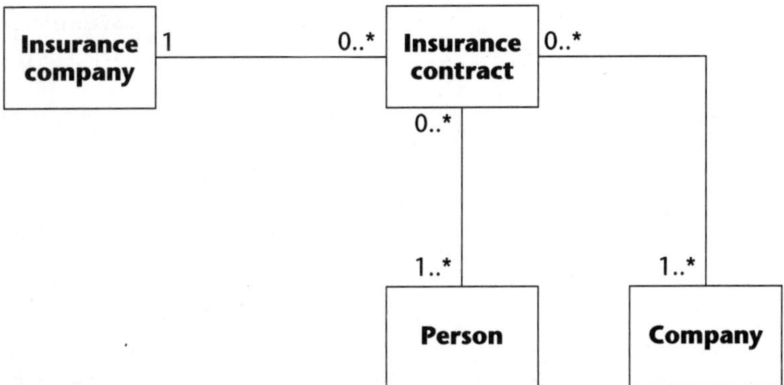

Figure 4.28 An insurance contract cannot have associations to both company and person at the same time.

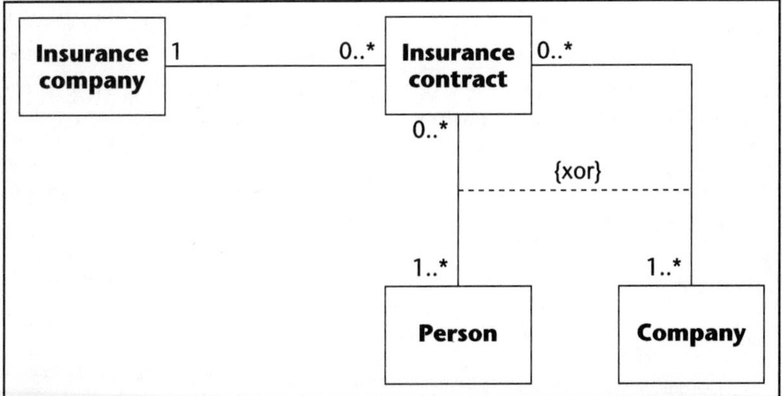

Figure 4.29 A xor constraint shows that only one of the associations is valid at a time.

Ordered Association

As indicated earlier in the chapter, in UML a specific instance of an association is called a link. UML offers a variety of ways to indicate the properties of the links in an association. One of the more common is an ordered association. The links between objects may have an implicit order; for example, windows can be ordered on a screen (one is on the top, one is at the bottom, and so on). The default value for an association is unordered. It can be shown explicitly that an association is unordered, but this is not normally the case. If there is an explicit order between the links, it is shown by putting {ordered} next to the association line near the class of the objects that are ordered, as shown in Figure 4.30. How the ordering is done (sorted) is specified either with a property of the association or inside the braces (for example, {ordered by increasing time}). Other property strings to attach to an association include {bag} to show that the same element can show up more than once and {sequence} to indicate an ordered bag. See Chapter 8 for additional material on these standard extensions to associations.

Association Class

A class can be attached to an association, in which case it is called an *association class*. The association class is not connected at any of the ends of the association, but is connected to the actual association. The association class is just like a normal class; it can have attributes, operations, and other associations. The association class is used to add extra information on a link, for example, the time the link was created. Each link of the association is related to an object of the association class. The model in Figure 4.31 shows an elevator system. The elevator control manipulates the four elevators. On each link between the elevators and the elevator control, there is a queue. Each queue stores the requests from both the elevator control and the elevator itself (the buttons inside the elevator). When the elevator control chooses an elevator to perform a request from a passenger outside the elevator (a passenger on a floor), the elevator control reads each queue and chooses the elevator that has the shortest queue. The choice could also be made by using some clever algorithm.

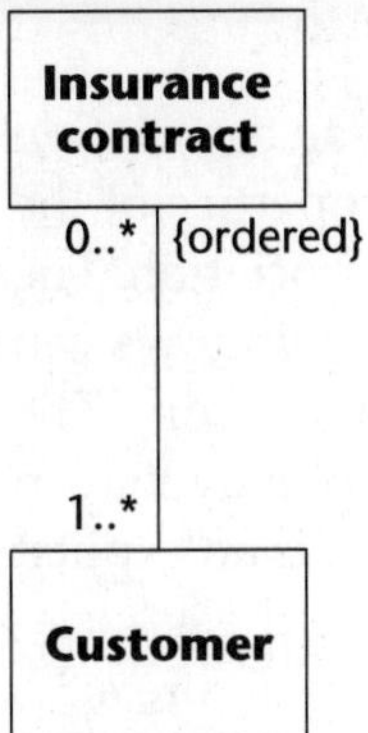

Figure 4.30 An ordered association.

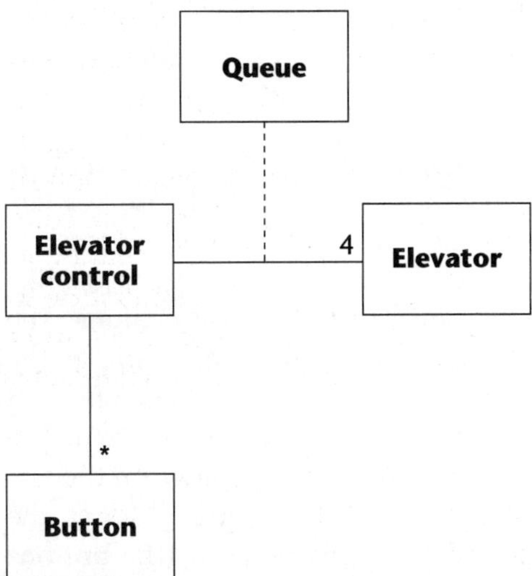

Figure 4.31 The association class Queue could be extended with operations to add requests to the queue, to read and remove requests from the queue, and to read the length. If operations or attributes are added to the association class, they should be shown as in a class.

Ternary Association

More than two classes can be associated with each other; the *ternary association* associates three classes. The model in Figure 4.32 shows that a customer who plays the role of policyholder has many (zero-to-many) insurance contracts, and each insurance contract is associated with an insurance company that plays the role of insurer. On the association between customer and insurance contract, there is an (zero or one) insurance policy. The ternary association is shown as a large diamond. Roles and multiplicity may be shown, but qualifiers and aggregation (see next section) are not allowed. An association class may be connected to the ternary association by drawing a dashed line to one of the four points on the diamond.

Aggregation

Aggregation is a special case of association. The aggregate indicates that the relationship between the classes is some sort of "whole-part." One example of an aggregate is a car that consists of four wheels, an engine, a chassis, a gear box, and so on. Another example is a binary tree that consists of zero, one, or two new trees. When aggregation is used, it often describes different levels of abstraction (car consists of wheels, engine, and so on). The keywords used to identify aggregates are "consists of," "contains," "is part of," that is, words that indicate a whole-part relationship between the classes involved (and naturally also on their object counterparts). Special kinds of aggregation—the shared aggregate and composition aggregate—will be described next. Aggregation reflects a composition relationship distinct from the constellation of cooperating elements found in a composite structure diagram. The composite structure diagram, discussed in Chapter 7, does not show the structure of an aggregation but rather the way the different system elements communicate to achieve a task in the context of a classifier. An aggregation represents a strict relationship indicating the composition of a class, not the runtime architecture.

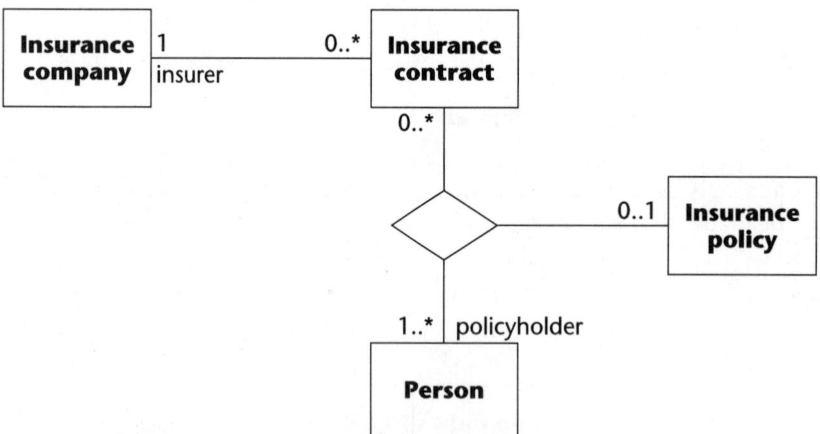

Figure 4.32 A ternary association connects three classes.

Aggregate

Figure 4.33 shows an aggregate as a line with a hollow diamond attached to one end of the line (at the wholeside, the class that contains the other class, the partside). Note, the diamond may not be attached to more than one end. Since aggregation is a special case of association multiplicity, roles (on the partside) and qualifiers may be attached to the aggregate, as in an association. An aggregate can be implemented in the same way as an association, that is, with some kind of object reference from the wholeside to the partside (and vice versa). The aggregate can also have a name (with direction) and be navigable.

Shared Aggregation

A *shared aggregation* is one in which the parts may be parts in any wholes, as shown in Figures 4.34 and 4.35. That an aggregation is shared is shown by its multiplicity. The aggregation is shared if the multiplicity on the wholeside is other than one (1). Shared aggregation is a special case of a normal aggregation.

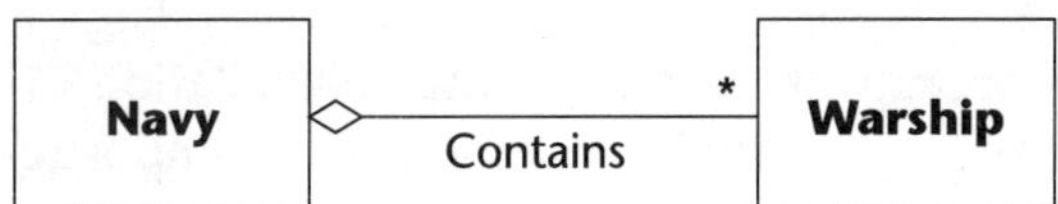

Figure 4.33 The Navy contains many warships. Some warships can be removed, and it is still a navy; and some warships can be added, and it is still a navy. This is significant for a normal aggregation (but not for a composition aggregation, as described later). The parts (the warships) compose the whole (the Navy). The hollow diamond shows the aggregation.

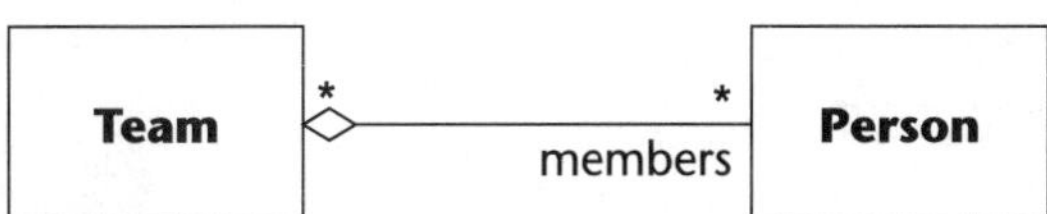

Figure 4.34 A team is composed of team members. One person could be a member of many teams. The model shows an example of a shared aggregation, where the people are the shared parts.

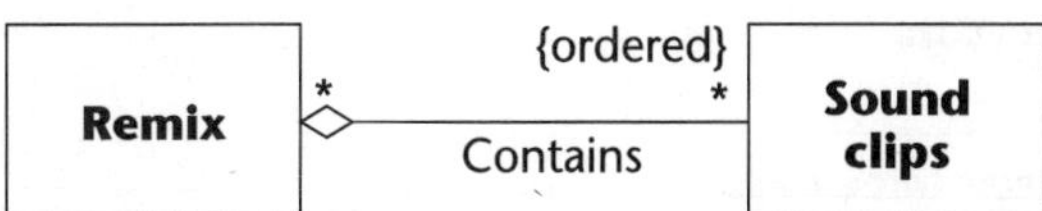

Figure 4.35 A remix is composed of many sound clips; the same soundtrack could be a part of many remixes.

Composition Aggregation

A *composition aggregation* owns its parts. The composition aggregation is one with strong ownership. The parts "live" inside the whole; they will be destroyed together with its whole. The multiplicity on the wholeside must be zero or one (0..1), but the multiplicity on the partside may be any interval. A composition aggregation forms a tree of parts, whereas a shared aggregate forms a net.

There are two ways of showing a composition aggregate. First, it can be shown with a line and a solid diamond attached to the wholeside. Second, if there is more than one part in the same aggregate (whole), they may be drawn as a tree by merging the aggregation ends into a single end. This notation is allowed for all types of aggregates. These notations are illustrated in Figures 4.36 and 4.37.

Figure 4.38 shows an example of when an aggregate can have only one role name. The role name is at the partside. Part "a" in the figure is a compound aggregation with role names. Part "b" in the figure shows the attribute syntax used to show compound aggregation. The roles turn into attribute names, and the classes turn into attribute types.

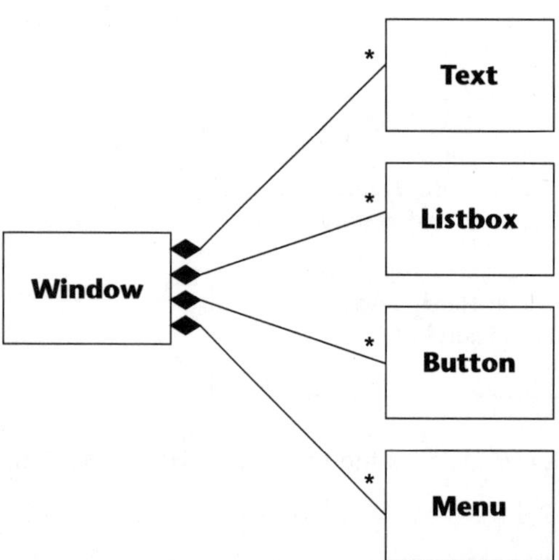

Figure 4.36 The diamond shows the composition aggregate; the window contains (is aggregated of) many menus, buttons, listboxes, and texts. All types of aggregation can have a name.

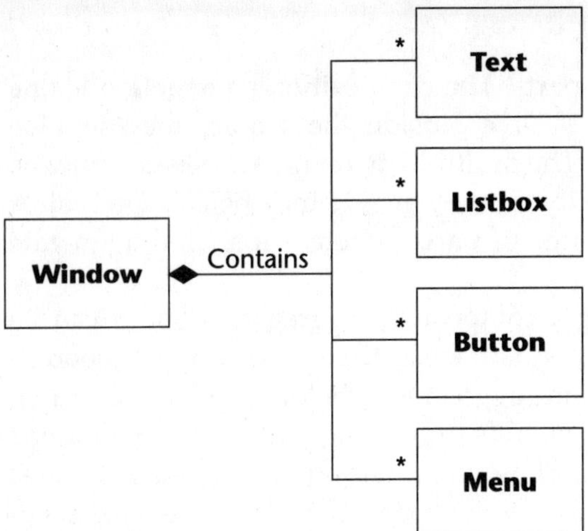

Figure 4.37 If there is more than one part in the same aggregate (whole), they may be drawn as a tree by merging the wholeside into a single end. This is allowed for all types of aggregates. An aggregate has only one role name, and that is at the partside.

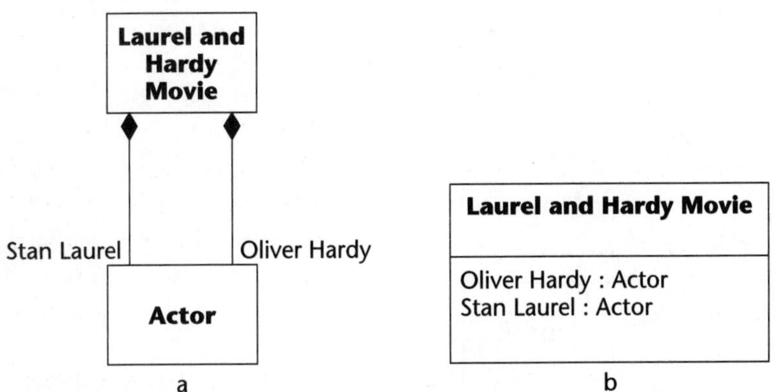

Figure 4.38 A Laurel and Hardy movie always includes the roles Oliver Hardy and Stan Laurel.

A compound aggregate could be implemented in the same way as an association, but the whole class must control the life cycle of its parts; thus, the class must destroy its parts at the same time it is destroyed. An alternate way of implementing a compound aggregate is to implement the parts as member objects of the class, that is, physically encapsulating the parts inside the whole class (see Figure 4.39).

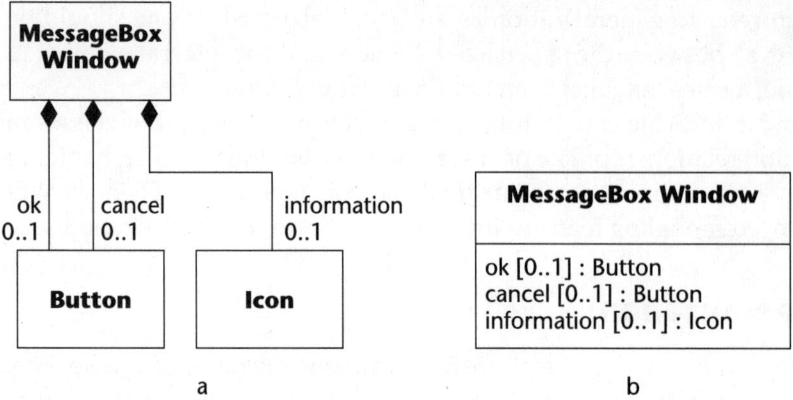

Figure 4.39 A MessageBox Window consists of zero or one ok Button, zero or one cancel Button, and zero or one information Icon. A compound aggregate is shown as attributes in a class. The multiplicity is shown in Part "b" of the figure.

Generalization

Generalization allows for hierarchical classification, an essential element of UML that makes it possible for the modeler to describe a system. UML defines generalization as follows: "A taxonomic relationship between a more general classifier and a more specific classifier. Each instance of the specific classifier is also an instance of the general classifier. Thus, the specific classifier indirectly has features of the more general classifier." Put another way, generalization describes a relationship between groups of things with something in common. Software languages implement generalization by allowing inheritance from a parent class to a child class. Those modeling complex systems will need to portray complex and overlapping sets of inheritance relationships.

Generalization allows classes to be specialized into new classes. A modeler can then handle special cases or extensions as separate classes, while maintaining the key elements of the parent class. Generalization applies to many classifiers in addition to class. Generalization, as implemented in classes, makes effective reuse and efficient software evolution possible.

NOTE In this section, we will primarily consider generalization in terms of classes, but the relationship applies to other elements, such as state machines and use cases.

Generalization applies only to classifiers or types, not to specific instances. In other words, a class can inherit another class, but an object cannot inherit another object, even though the instances are indirectly affected through their type. You can refer to generalization as an "is a" relationship; one should be able to say "is a" between the specialized element and the general element (a car *is a* vehicle, a sales manager *is an* employee, and so on).

A modeler can indicate constraints on a generalization or a set of classes in a generalization relationship. The next section describes the basic mechanics of generalization with a discussion of abstract and concrete classes. Then, we will review advanced modeling features for generalization and generalization sets.

Basic Generalization

Generalization shows a close relationship between a general and a specific class. The specific class, called the *subclass,* inherits everything from the general class, called the *superclass.* The attributes, operations, and all associations of the superclass become a part of the subclass. So, attributes and operations with public visibility in the superclass will be public in the subclass as well. Members (attributes and operations) that have private visibility will also be inherited, but are not accessible within the subclass. To protect attributes or operations from access from outside the superclass and the subclass, you can assign these with protected visibility. A protected member cannot be accessed from other classes, but is available from the class and any of its subclasses. A private member is typically preceded by a minus sign (–); a public member is preceded by a plus sign (+); a protected member is preceded by the pound sign (#). A modeler can suppress the visibility marker so that it is not shown on the class diagram.

A class can be both a superclass and a subclass as part of a class hierarchy. A class hierarchy graphs the generalization relationships between a set of classes. A class can inherit from one class (in which case, it is a subclass to that class) and at the same time be inherited from another class (in which case, it is a superclass to that class). However, a modeler cannot implement a generalization cycle: a classifier may not relate to itself as part of a generalization tree. UML represents generalization as a solid line from the more specific class (the subclass) to the more general class (the superclass), with a large hollow triangle at the superclass end of the line (see Figure 4.40). As in the case with aggregation, inheritance could be shown as a tree, where the triangle is shared between all the subclasses (see Figure 4.41).

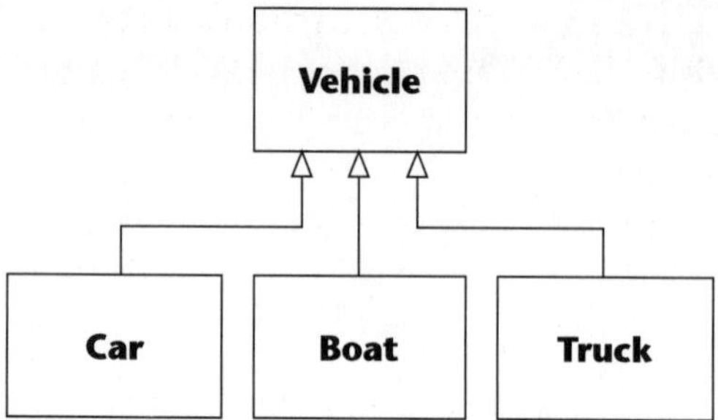

Figure 4.40 Vehicle is a general class (superclass) derived to specific classes (subclasses) via inheritance (generalization-specialization).

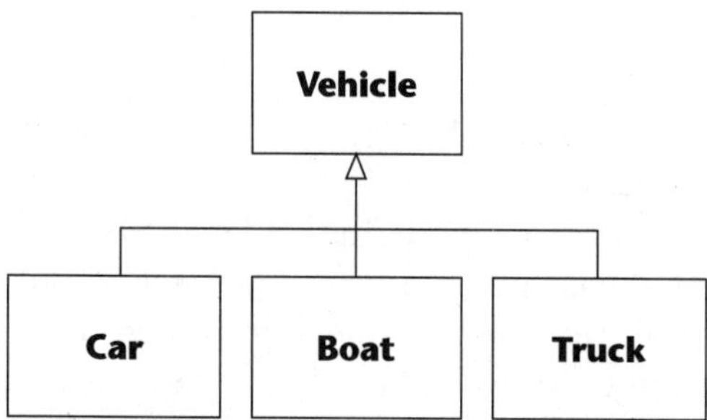

Figure 4.41 The same model as in Figure 4.40, but the inheritance takes the form of a tree (with only one hollow triangle).

An *abstract class* is one that does not have any objects; or, more precisely, it is not allowed to have any object instances. An abstract class describes common attributes and behavior for other classes. In the class hierarchy in Figure 4.42, it is hard to imagine objects that are vehicles that you cannot further distinguish as being a car or a boat. However, the Vehicle class captures commonalities between the car and boat. Vehicle represents an abstract class, which doesn't have any objects, but shows common features of a set of classes. A class can be specified explicitly as abstract by italicizing the class name or by putting the keyword {abstract} within the name compartment of the class, under the class name.

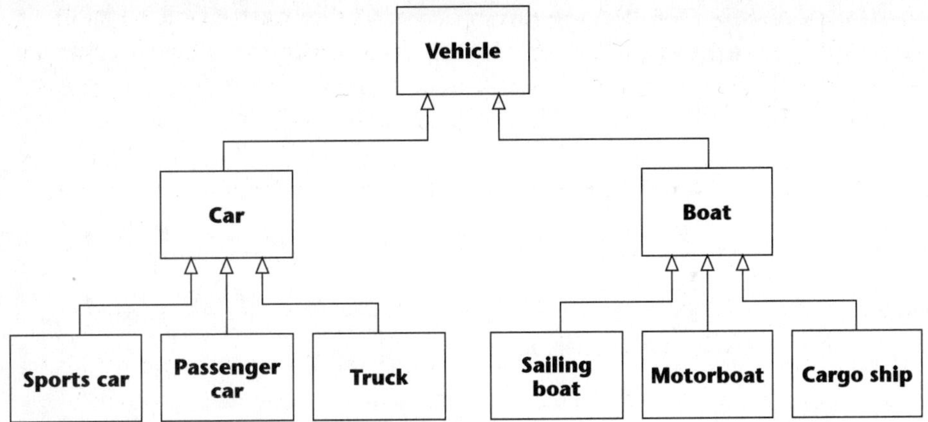

Figure 4.42 A class hierarchy for vehicles. The Car class is a subclass to Vehicle, but the superclass to Sports car, Passenger car, and Truck.

An abstract class usually has abstract operations. An *abstract operation* has no implementation method where it is specified; only the signature is shown. A class that has at least one abstract operation must by definition be an abstract class. A class that inherits from a class that has one or more abstract operations must implement those operations (provide methods for them) or itself become an abstract class. Abstract operations can be shown with the property string {abstract} following the operation signature. They can also be shown with the operation signature in italics. Abstract operations are defined in abstract classes to specify behavior that all the subclasses must have. A Vehicle class could have abstract operations to specify that all vehicles must have the ability to drive, to start, and to stop. Thus, all classes inheriting from Vehicle must provide methods for those operations (or themselves become abstract).

Some modelers strive always to provide a layer of abstract classes as parents, looking for common elements in any inheritance relationship that could then be extended to other children. For complex items, this provides additional flexibility to provide for the evolution or expansion of the system. In this case, both "car" and "boat" would represent abstract classes requiring a child class to implement the abstract operations of drive and stop. Boat may have an additional abstract operation to show that all boats must also float. One can continue to model such abstractions indefinitely, but will quickly face diminishing returns. To avoid excessive abstractions, look for the useful abstractions that link to the real objects in the system and look to satisfy the use cases gathered that show the purpose of the system.

With generalization, you link abstractions to implementation. The opposite of an abstract class is a *concrete class*. In a concrete class, it is possible to create objects from the class that have implementations for all operations. If the Vehicle class has specified an abstract operation drive, then both cars and boats must implement that method (or the operations themselves must be specified as abstract). The implementations are different, though. When a person tells the car to drive, the wheels move. When someone tells the boat to drive, the propeller moves (see Figure 4.43). It is easy to express that subclasses inherit an operation from a common superclass, but that they implement it in different ways.

A subclass can redefine the operations of the superclass, or the class can just implement the superclass as defined. A redefined operation must have the same signature (return type, name, and parameters) as the superclass. The operation being redefined can be either abstract (not have an implementation in the superclass) or concrete (have a implementation in the superclass). In both cases, the redefinition in the subclass will be used for all instances of that class. New operations, attributes, and associations can be added to the subclasses. An object of a subclass may be used in any situation where it is possible to use the superclass objects. In this case, the subclass will have a different implementation depending on the object involved.

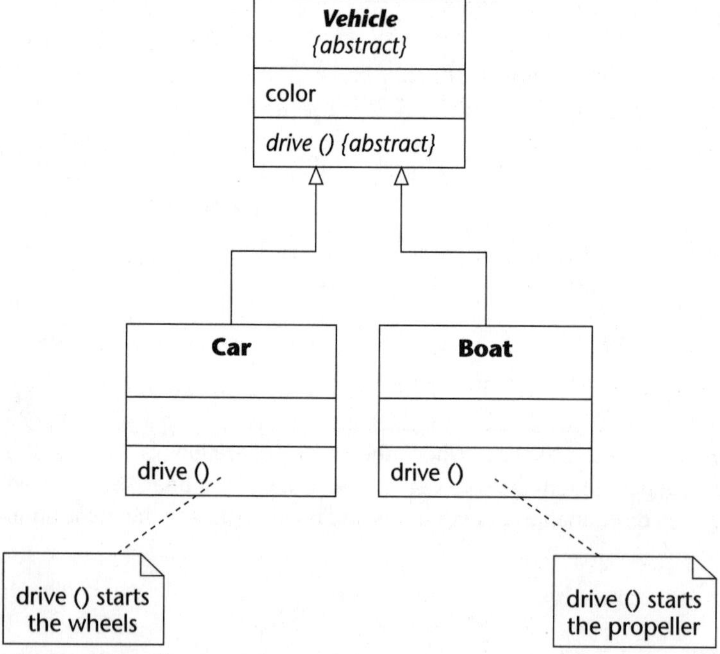

Figure 4.43 The Car inherits the attribute color and the operation drive. The operation drive is redefined in the classes Car and Boat. The class Vehicle is abstract, which also is marked. The notes below the classes are used to comment on a class diagram.

Figure 4.44 shows a Person class that has a drives association to the Vehicle class.

The Vehicle class is abstract; that means that the actual objects that the Person drives are from the concrete subclasses Car and Boat. When the person calls (performs) the drive operation, the result depends on whether the object used in that situation is a car or a boat. If it is an object of the class Car, it will start the wheels (using the implementation as specified in the Car class). If it is an object of the class Boat, it will start the propeller (using the implementation as specified in the Boat class). This provides an example of the standard object-oriented technique called *polymorphism*. With polymorphism, the object from a subclass acts as an object from a superclass, and one or more of the operations in the superclass are redefined (or morphed). Polymorphism (which is Greek for many forms) means that the actual implementation used depends on the type of object that owns the operation. Figures 4.45, 4.46, and 4.47 illustrate the combination of these elements in a model.

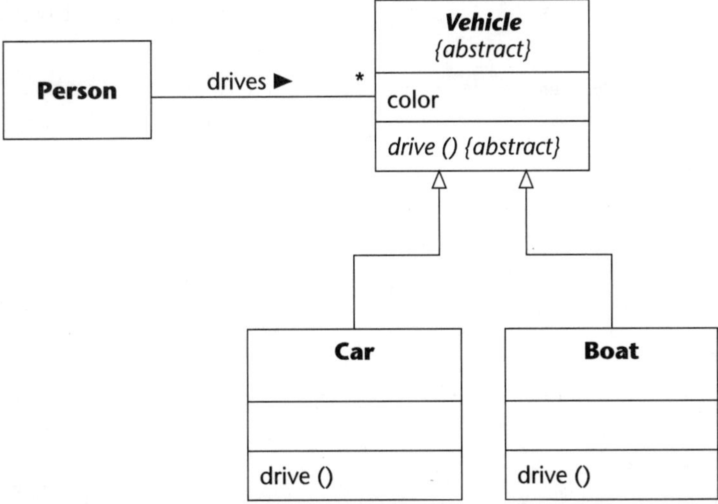

Figure 4.44 A person drives vehicles. When the drive operation is called, the implementation used depends on whether the object used is a car or a boat. Vehicle is an abstract class showing the commonalties between cars and boats, including the association relationship to the Person class.

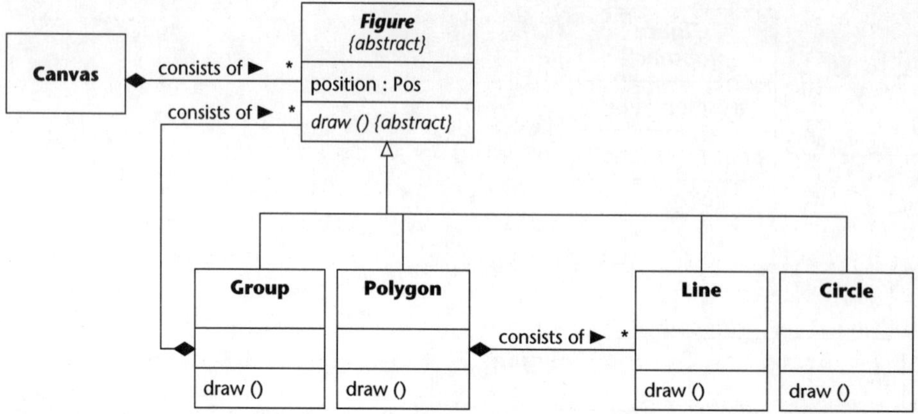

Figure 4.45 A canvas consists of many figures. Figures could be circles, lines, polygons, or groups. A group consists of many figures. When a client asks the canvas to draw itself, the canvas asks its associated figures to draw themselves. Each figure (circles, line, polygons, or groups) is responsible for drawing itself in an appropriate way. The group draws itself through calling the draw operations in the figures that make up the group. Note that the canvas does not have to ask each figure which kind of figure it is; it just has to call the draw operation and everything else works automatically.

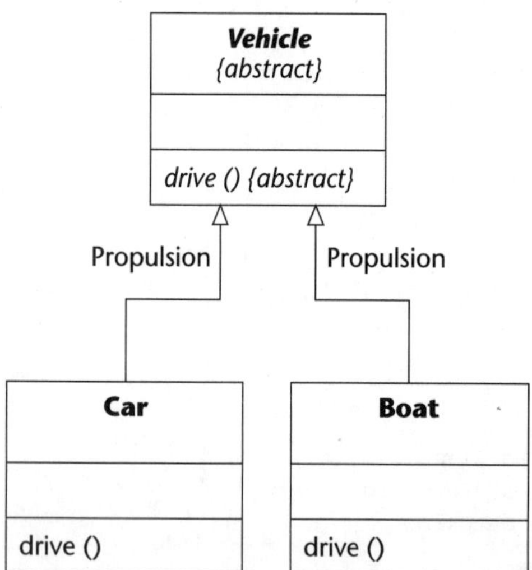

Figure 4.46 Generalization-specialization with a discriminator that specifies that it is with respect to the propulsion that the subclasses differ.

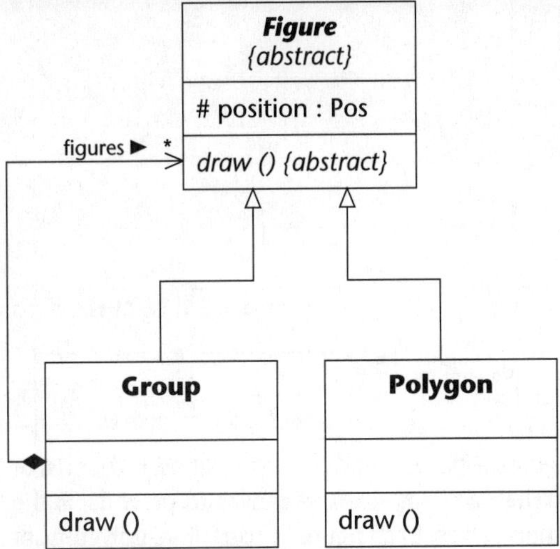

Figure 4.47 A class hierarchy with a superclass Figure and two subclasses Group and Polygon.

The Java code for implementing the model in Figure 4.47 might look like:

```
abstract public class Figure
{
    abstract public void draw();
    protected Pos position;
}

public class Group extends Figure
{
     public void draw ()
     {
            for (int i = 0; i < consist_of.size(), i++)
            {
                 consist_of[i].draw();
            }
     }
     // FigureVector is a specialized class of the standard
     // Vector class which implements a dynamic array.
     // FigureVector adds hard type checking
     private FigureVector figures;
}

public class Polygon extends Figure
{
     public void draw ()
     {
       /* Draw polygon code */
     }
}
```

Advanced Generalization

UML provides some enhanced features to manage generalization relationships. The generalization set and powertype provide mechanisms that allow the modeler to define different types of generalization relationships.

Generalization Set

UML offers a feature to organize different relationships between a parent and a child class. The *generalization set* defines the rules for partition of the superclass. This allows the modeler to organize different sets of subclasses that inherit from a common superclass. A superclass can have one or more generalization sets to reflect the fact that child classes could resemble the parent in a number of different ways. When working at a high level of abstraction, a modeler could derive a number of generalization sets depending on system requirements. So, for example, the superclass "vehicle" could have one generalization set partitioned based on the method of propulsion. This would not preclude another generalization set partition based on the type of license needed to operate the vehicle.

To display these generalization sets in the model, either apply the generalization set name to the line connecting the two classes or draw a dashed line across all the lines in the set connecting the superclass to the subclass. If you are using a generalization tree where a number of lines end in the same generalization triangle, signify the generalization set with one name. Figure 4.48 shows these relationships in both notation styles to illustrate your options. For clarity, a real model should adopt one of the styles consistently.

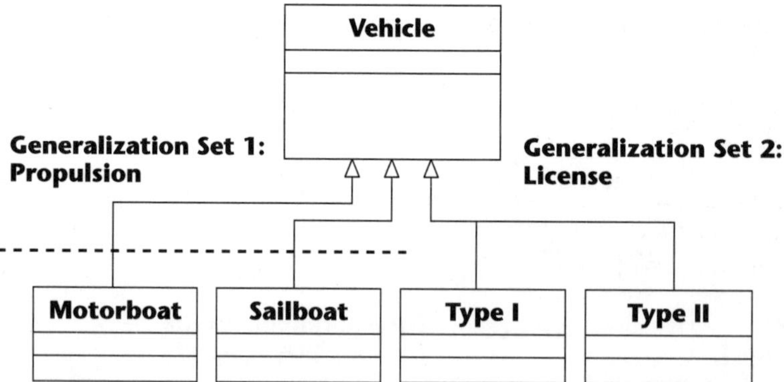

Figure 4.48 Generalization set visually showing the partition as part of a tree or set off by a dashed line. Both forms are correct. Use the approach that best communicates the partition to your audience.

All generalization sets have an attribute to indicate whether they can overlap with other classes. Overlapping means that any further subclasses in the inheritance relationship can inherit from more than one source (that is, can use multiple inheritance with a common superclass in the inheritance tree). For example, the Amphibian in Figure 4.49 can have more than one parent. Disjoint generalization is the opposite of overlapping, which means that the subclasses are not allowed to be specialized into a common subclass. They cannot have multiple inheritance.

A generalization set also has an attribute indicating if the set is complete. If it is complete, this means that all subclasses have been specified, and that no further subclassing can be done, as shown in Figure 4.50.

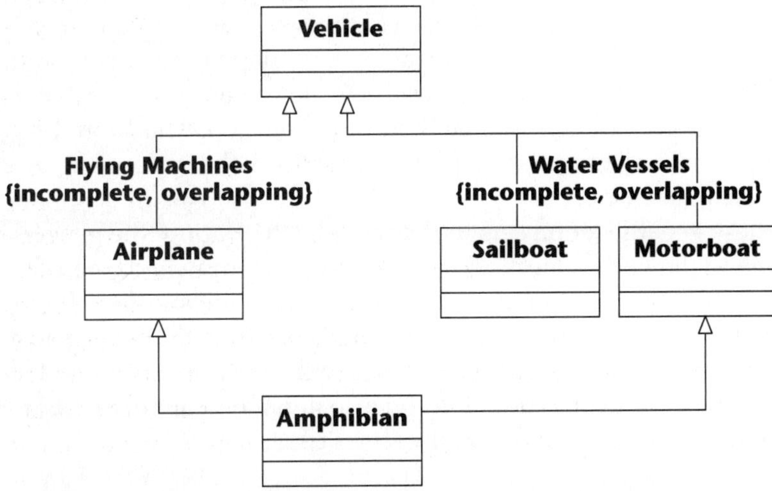

Figure 4.49 Because the inheritance is specified as overlapping, the Amphibian class can inherit from both the airplane and the sailboat/motorboat classes.

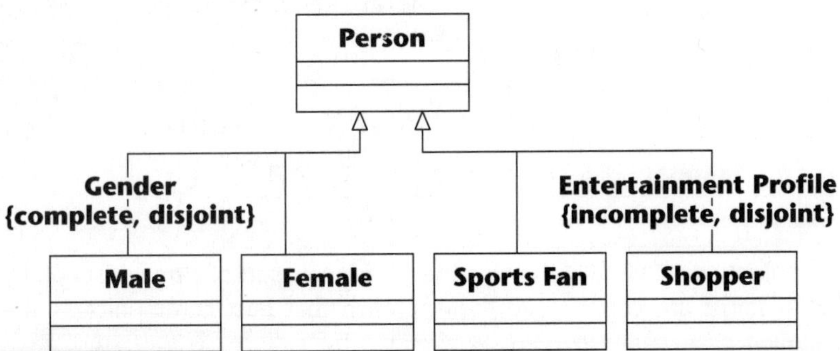

Figure 4.50 The gender generalization set is constrained to be complete, which means that no new subclasses may be added. The entertainment profile generalization set, in contrast, is incomplete.

An incomplete generalization, the default, means that subclasses may be added later on. Because one of the main goals of generalization is to allow for future extensions and flexible expansion, incomplete generalizations are the norm.

With the definition of generalization set, it is easier to model two separate sets of inheritance relationships with different constraints specified on each of the generalization sets. The two attributes allow for four types of generalization sets. A model displays these options by showing the attributes between braces. A {complete, disjoint} set will cover all permissible permutations (it is complete) while having no common instances. An {incomplete, disjoint} generalization set will have no common instances, while allowing additions to the set. The {complete, overlapping} generalization set allows subclasses to share common instances, while allowing no additions to the set. The {incomplete, overlapping} set differs by allowing additional elements. By default, a generalization set is {incomplete, disjoint}.

Powertype

UML allows for generalization with the powertype, a mechanism to model classes made of subclasses. So, as shown in Figure 4.51, breaking down vehicles according to methods of propulsion likely results in a powertype called propulsion. All instances of this powertype are also subclasses of vehicle. Those classes partitioned based on license requirements specify a version of the powertype for licensed vehicle. You specify a powertype by indicating the name of the superclass preceded by a colon on the generalization relationship. Depending on the powertype, the class can inherit different attributes and operations.

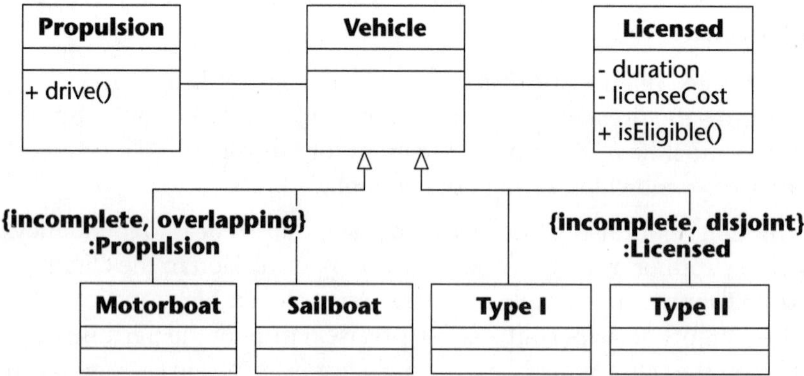

Figure 4.51 Display of powertype.

The powertype provides the greatest benefit during analysis at a high level, when the same item may be considered in a number of different ways. Complex generalization relationships producing a number of powertypes provide a flag for the modeler to review closely. Such a situation indicates a potential data integrity situation to address during system design. Powertypes also provide a powerful analytic tool for handling business entities based on the mathematical notion of the power set. For more on powertypes in business modeling, see *Business Modeling With UML: Business Patterns at Work* (2000) by Magnus Penker and Hans-Erik Eriksson, authors from this book.

Dependencies and Abstractions

UML provides dependency relationships to show that a model element requires another model element for some purpose. The precise nature of the relationship varies, depending on the elements involved and the type of dependency requirement described. In a dependency relationship, one element represents the client that requires a supplier element. This supplier/client relationship can take on a number of different forms, but in general a dependency indicates that a client is not complete without the supplier. For example, when a class takes an object of another class as a parameter or one class accesses a global object of another class, you have a dependency from one class to the other, even without an explicit association between them. A change in the supplier class may affect the client class.

UML represents a dependency relationship as a dashed line with an arrow (and possibly a label) between model elements. The tail end of the line shows the client, and the arrowhead end shows the supplier. UML has a number of standard stereotypes to identify the kind of dependency, and modelers can define their own stereotypes for dependencies. Some of the more common types of dependencies follow:

- A basic "usage" relationship between two elements indicates that a class requires the presence of another class. In Java, for example, this client class must have an import statement for the supplier. The stereotype <<uses>> indicates a usage dependency.
- A permission relationship shows another standard type of dependency, where the supplier must grant some level of permission to the client. Figure 4.52 shows an example of a permission dependency, indicated with the stereotype <<permit>>. The precise nature of the permission depends on the deployment language. So, for example, in C++, you can code special access for a "friend."

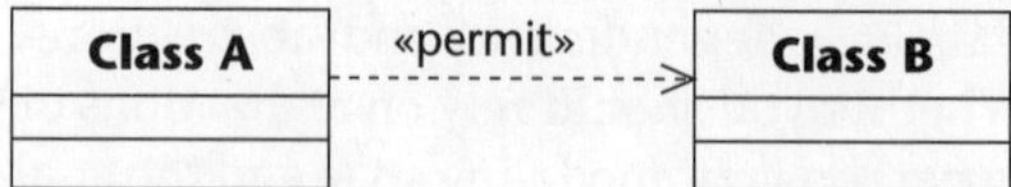

Figure 4.52 A dependency relationship between classes. The type of dependency is shown as stereotype; in this case, it is a <<permit>> dependency.

- Dependencies can also indicate relationships between model elements at different levels of abstraction. A model element may refine or realize a more general description of the system at a different layer of the analysis. For example, a collaboration of classes may provide the details for a general class. So, a car class actually results in a number of classes to make up the car. The <<refine>> stereotype shows a mapping between two sets of model elements at different semantic levels. So, a design class will <<refine>> a class described during analysis.
- The <<trace>> relationship typically shows that two elements represent the same concept in different models. A <<trace>> relationship shows an information mapping between elements, useful for tracking requirements.
- The <<derive>> relationship shows that one can compute the client from the supplier.

In addition to these stereotypes, UML also offers the more precisely defined realization relationship, a type of dependency that has special notation. In a realization, the supplier provides the specification that the client implements. UML shows a realization relationship as a dashed line with a hollow triangle between two model elements (a dashed generalization symbol; see Figure 4.53). Realization can model optimizations, templates, framework composition, and even refinement. Realization often provides a mechanism to coordinate different model elements. The relationship between a collaboration of classes and a Use Case specification provides a typical example. In such a case, a collaboration realizes a Use Case. A component can also realize elements defined during design.

Figure 4.53 Realization relationship.

With all these different tools to analyze dependencies and abstractions, which should the modeler choose? Whether you should rely on realizations or other forms of abstraction depends in part on your modeling style and the goal of the model. These tools work best when pointed toward the goal of coordinating model elements to enhance communication about what the client needs. Model coordination should seek to do the following, regardless of the precise notation implemented:

- Show how models on different abstraction levels are related
- Show how models from different phases (requirement specification, analysis, design, implementation, and so on) are related
- Support configuration management
- Support traceability in the model

CROSS-REFERENCE **The OMG's Model Driven Architecture (MDA) initiative provides a common approach for model management. For more on MDA, see Chapter 9.**

Constraints, Expressions, and Derivations

It is possible to capture rules in the form of expressions and constraints in UML. A constraint is stated to return a true/false value, so a model element either complies or does not comply. An expression returns a set of values depending on the context. Capturing these rules in a model provides information crucial for software development.

UML defines a few constraints, such as the xor constraint, ordered association, and the restrictions on generalization sets already discussed. Users can also define their own constraints using their own guidelines. Expressions can show how to derive attributes, such as the age of a person (current date minus the date of birth). Such rules are especially useful for attributes, associations, inheritance, roles, and time constraints in the dynamic models that we will describe later in this book (state machines, sequence diagrams, communication diagrams, and activity diagrams). Rules appear inside curly braces ({ }) near the model element or in braces in a comment connected to the model element.

Constraints can also apply to associations. For example, if a company has contracts with many customers, a derived association could show the rules that indicate who qualifies as VIP customers. The derived association goes directly from the class company to the class customer. A derived association has a label placed near the association, beginning with a slash followed by the name of the derivation, as shown in Figure 4.54. A constraint association can be established when one association is a subset of another association, as shown in Figure 4.55.

Attributes can also have constraints or be derived, as shown in Figure 4.56. A typical constraint for an attribute is a value range, as shown in Figure 4.57. A value range is like a property list for an attribute that specifies the possible values. The property list is a string in any format. For example, a property string for the color attribute is {red, green, yellow}. As a constraint, a property string for the color attribute could be {0<= color <= 255}. A derived attribute is calculated in some way from other attributes. The formula for the calculation is given inside the braces under the class. A derived attribute begins with a slash, and is not stored with that class because it is always calculated.

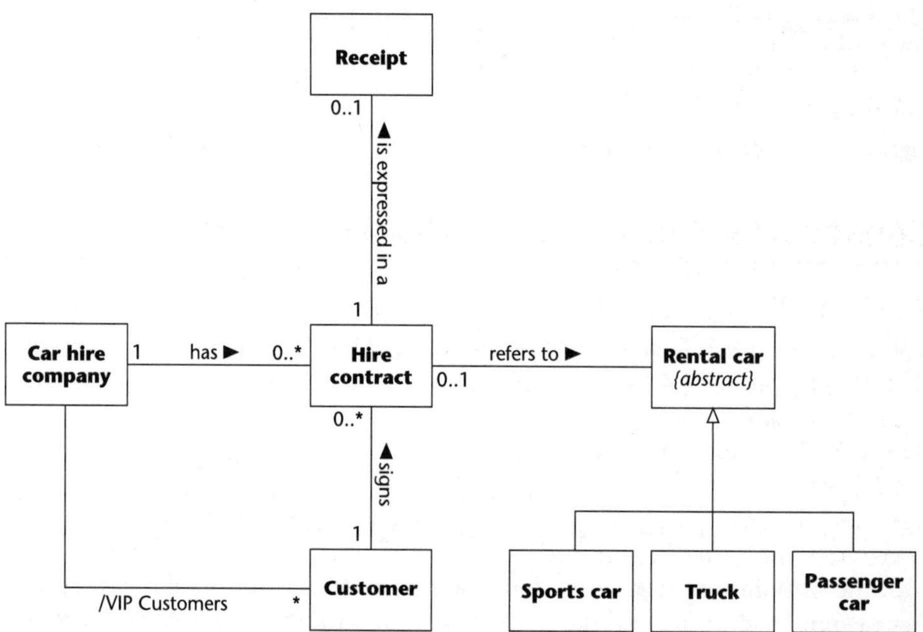

Figure 4.54 The VIP customers are a derived association.

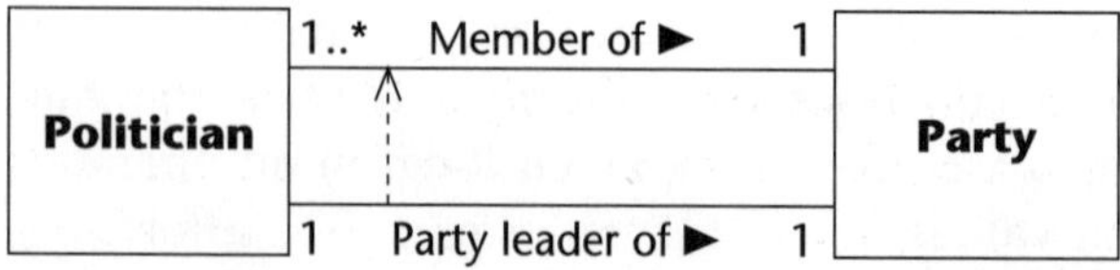

Figure 4.55 A constraint association. The party leader of association is a subset of the member of association.

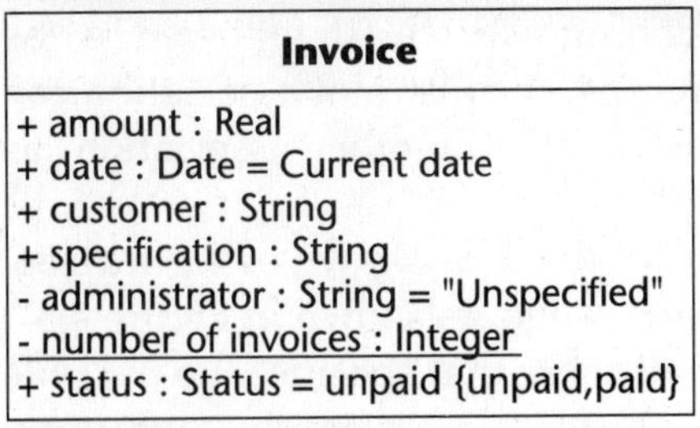

Invoice
+ amount : Real + date : Date = Current date + customer : String + specification : String - administrator : String = "Unspecified" - number of invoices : Integer + status : Status = unpaid {unpaid,paid}

Figure 4.56 Constraints on an attribute status.

Article
cost price sales price /profit

{profit = sales price - cost price}

Figure 4.57 A derived attribute profit, which is calculated from the cost and sales prices.

Operations also have constraints. An operation is specified with a signature (name, parameter-list, return-type) and can specify a precondition or postcondition.

- A *precondition* is one that must be true before the operation can execute. For example, it might be that a figure must be drawn before the resize operation can be called.
- A *postcondition* is one that must be true after the operation is executed. For example, a postcondition might state that after the draw operation is executed the figure must be updated (and that this doesn't happen later).

Some approaches to modeling stress preconditions and postconditions in the design so that the coding can contain the proper assertions to allow for testing and error handling in an efficient manner. Such design by contract can also improve the quality of the requirements and the finished product, provided the modeler captures the conditions in a manner that is easy to manage.

Any state change of the object may also be documented (for example, resize affects the object state). All of these specifications are done as constraints for an operation. The constraints are usually not shown directly in the class diagram, but rather are available from a tool (for example, clicking on an operation shows all constraints and their values).

Roles also can have constraints that restrict combinations of roles played by one object. For example, a person may normally not approve his own purchases.

When rules are expressed in constraints and expressions, they refer to model elements in a model. Along with UML, the OMG has defined an Object Constraint Language (OCL), useful for defining rules that apply to any level of model or type of diagram. Earlier versions of UML included the OCL as part of the specification. With the release of UML 2, OCL now has its own specification. UML does not require the use of OCL; a model can have constraints or expressions in any language. However, natural language is often ambiguous and if you need to produce a robust, platform-specific model that will work directly with code, it might be worth working with OCL. OCL is a pure specification language, so it has no programming syntax and cannot change anything in the model. OCL evolved from a business modeling language developed for IBM. For more details on OCL, see Chapter 8.

Interfaces and Ports

A package, component, or class that has an interface connected to it *implements* or *uses* the specified interface by supporting or relying on the behavior defined in the interface. Interfaces play an important role in well-structured systems by clearly showing the contracts between collaborating clusters of model elements. They represent an essential support for any component-based development, and in practical implementation interfaces provide a manageable way to maintain a system. The programming equivalents include OLE/COM, .NET, or Java interfaces, where a developer specifies an interface separately from any specific class and any number of classes (or packages or components) can choose to implement that interface. An interface cannot include real objects; rather, it contains only abstract operations. An interface, then, has a number of signatures that together specify a behavior that any element can support by implementing the interface. At runtime, other objects can then depend on the interface alone, without knowing anything more about the class; or they may depend on the entire class. A port is like an interface but also shows the provided and required features of the environment, or context.

A model can show an interface in two ways:

- It can be shown with notation where the interface looks like a ball (or a lollipop). If describing provided and required interfaces (see later in this section) , this can look like a ball and socket. You connect an interface to its model element via a solid line (it is an association that always has the multiplicity 1 to 1).

- A model can show an interface as a rectangle stereotyped as <<interface>> connected via a dependency relationship (a dashed line arrow). The dependent class may call the operations published in the interface, which are not directly shown in the diagram. To show the operations in an interface, the interface must be specified as a class with the stereotype <<interface>> using the ordinary class rectangle, (see Figure 4.58).

An interface can be specialized just like a class. The inheritance between interfaces is shown in a class diagram with the symbols used for classes. All interfaces have the stereotype <<interface>> but can also be represented as a ball, or lollipop as in Figure 4.59. Interfaces can use this ball-and-socket notation to show whether the interface is provided or required.

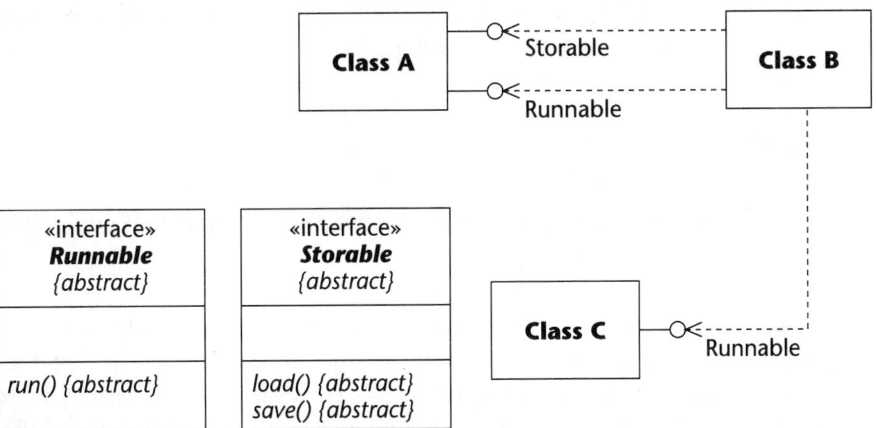

Figure 4.58 Class A implements the interfaces Runnable and Storable. Class C implements the interface Runnable. Class B uses the interface Runnable and Storable from A, and Runnable from C. The interfaces are specified as classes with the stereotype <<interface>> and contain the abstract operations that the implementing classes must implement.

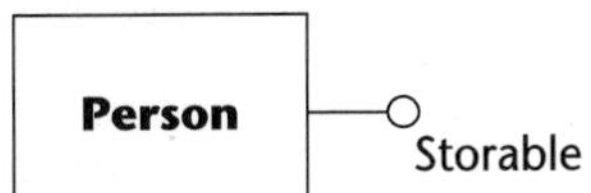

Figure 4.59 A class Person that implements an interface Storable.

For a required interface, this shows that a class depends on a specific interface to execute its responsibilities. This dependency uses notation showing the interface as a half-circle, or socket, rather than a circle. For a provided interface, this is still shown as the circle or lollipop. When one class requires an interface and the other provides the interface, those can be presented with combined ball-and-socket notation, as in Figure 4.60, indicating how directions are given to a spaceship in a videogame. Increasingly, ball-and-socket notation is recommended to visually indicate the relationship between the elements. Depending on the type modeling task, use the notation that best conveys the information to your audience. In the following example, a spaceship requires directions to determine where to turn. In this case, a steering wheel implements the interface to provide instructions to the ship. Another class could implement the direction interface, say a joystick, and the spaceship would still know which way to turn. A user can show the same information using the standard <<interface>> stereotyped class rectangle with a dependency relationship.

Java Implementation

The Java code for declaring both the Storable interface and the class that it implements, as shown in Figure 4.59, might be:

```
interface Storable
{
     public void Save();
     public void Load();
}

public class Person implements Storable
{

     public void Save()
     {
          // Implementation of Save operation for Person
     }
     public void Load()
     {
          // Implementation of Load operation for Person
     }
}
```

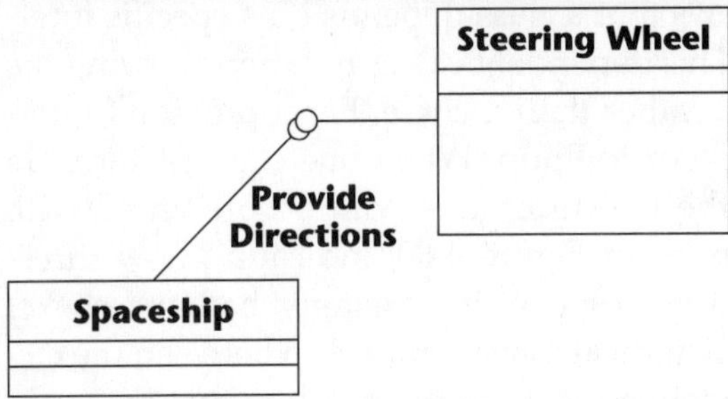

Figure 4.60 Example of ball-and-socket notation.

Ports

The interface supports plug-and-play components in software models, but it only goes so far since it says nothing about the environmental context. In addition to interfaces, UML provides a feature of a class, the port, to help model components by showing environmental requirements. This section reviews the basic features of a port as applied to a class.

CROSS-REFERENCE Ports are also found on other UML elements, not just classes. A port can model the relationship between the behavior of a classifier and its internal parts as part of a protocol state machine. This links a component to execution rules in the environment. For more on the protocol state machine, see Chapter 6.

The port allows the modeler to insulate the inner workings of a class from environmental variables. Such insulation keeps the developer focused on the responsibility of the class without concern for the deployment environment. So long as the deployment environment meets the port's specifications, the component will work.

To display a port on a class, draw a small square symbol on the edge of the class rectangle. The port name is placed next to the square with the multiplicity shown in brackets next to the name. To connect the port to the interfaces used and implemented by the class through the port, connect the box to the ball or socket interface icon with a line. When multiple interfaces connect to a port, write the name of each interface, separated by a comma, next to the ball or socket interface icon. A class can have more than one port. In addition, a port can connect to a state inside of the class rectangle. This shows a port with behavior dependent on the rules associated with the state of the class. The protocol state machine, as described in Chapter 6, uses this feature of ports.

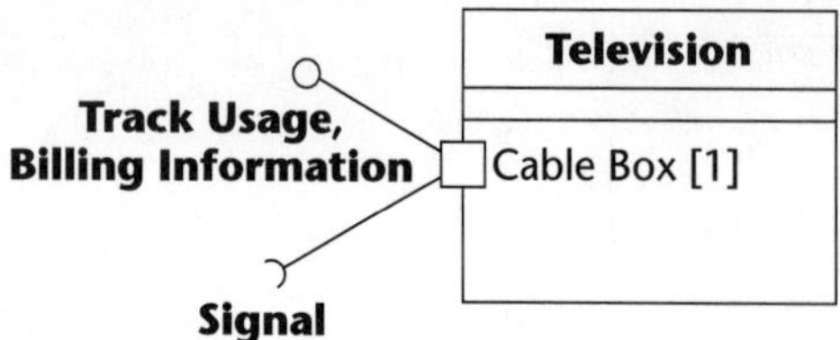

Figure 4.61 Example of port notation showing a cable box as a component with requirements in the external environment.

Figure 4.61 provides an example of a port. In the example, a television requires signal input from an external source, and a cable company wants to be able to track the usage of the television set. So, the cable box port provides this interface, while also implementing interfaces that allow the cable company to charge the user and track his or her television-watching history.

Packages

A *package* provides a grouping mechanism for organizing UML elements. In UML, a package is used to group elements and to provide a namespace for the grouped elements. All model elements that are owned or referenced by a package are called the *package contents*. As a grouping mechanism for model organization, the package does not have an instance. Thus, the packages often have a meaning during modeling that is not necessarily translated into the executable system. A package owns its model elements, and a model element cannot be owned by more than one package. If the package is removed from the model, then its owned elements are also removed. See Figures 4.62 through 4.66 for examples.

The package is shown as a large rectangle with a smaller rectangle (a tab) attached on the upper-left corner of the large rectangle (the common folder icon). If the contents (such as classes) of the package are not shown, then the name of the package is given inside the large rectangle; otherwise the name is given inside the small rectangle.

Owned and imported elements may each have a visibility that determines whether they are available outside the package. The visibility of a package element may be indicated by preceding the name of the element with a plus sign (+) for public, a minus sign (–) for private. The public contents of a package are always available through the use of qualified names.

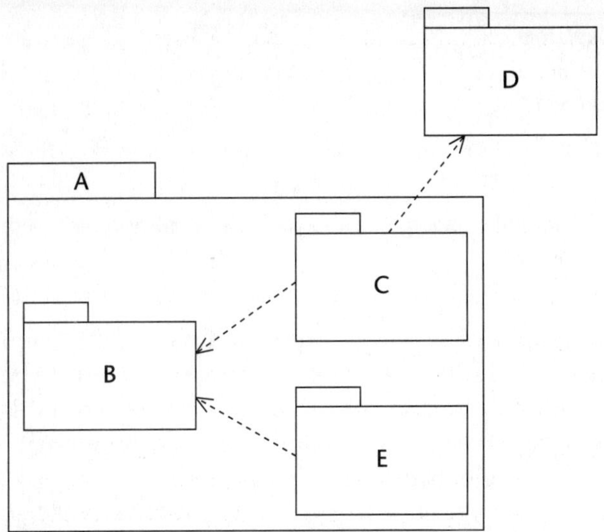

Figure 4.62 Package E is dependent on package B. Package C is dependent on packages B and D. Packages B, C, and E are inside package A.

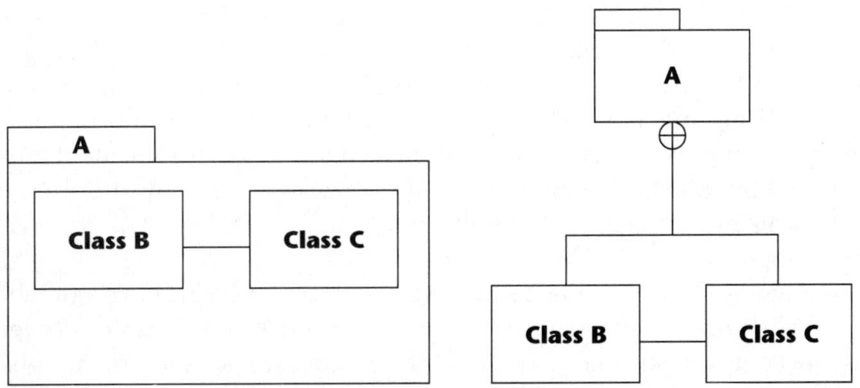

Figure 4.63 Two notations for indicating that package A contains classes B and C.

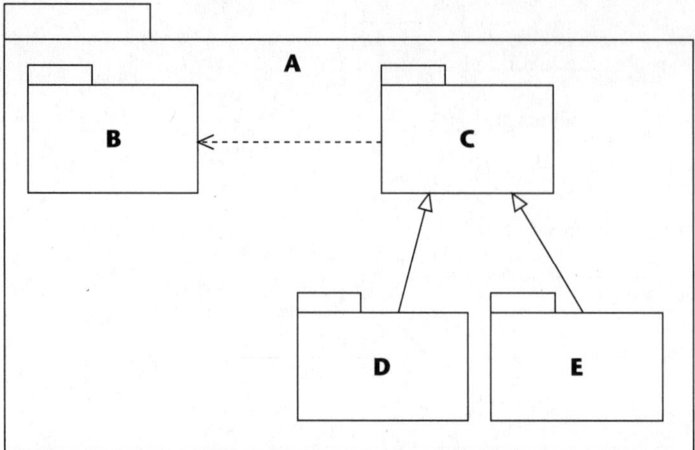

Figure 4.64 Packages D and E are specialized from the generalization package C. Packages B, C, D, and E are in package A. Package C depends on B (it typically has imported elements from it).

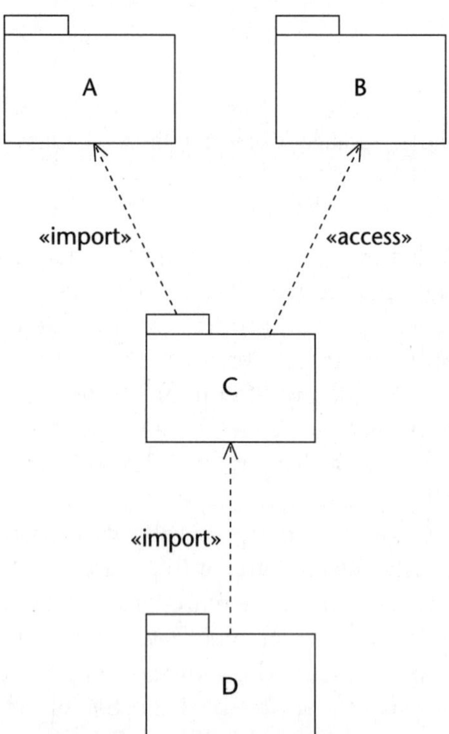

Figure 4.65 Elements defined in package A are imported publicly to package C. Elements in package B are imported privately to package C. Elements of packages A and C are imported into and are available to package D.

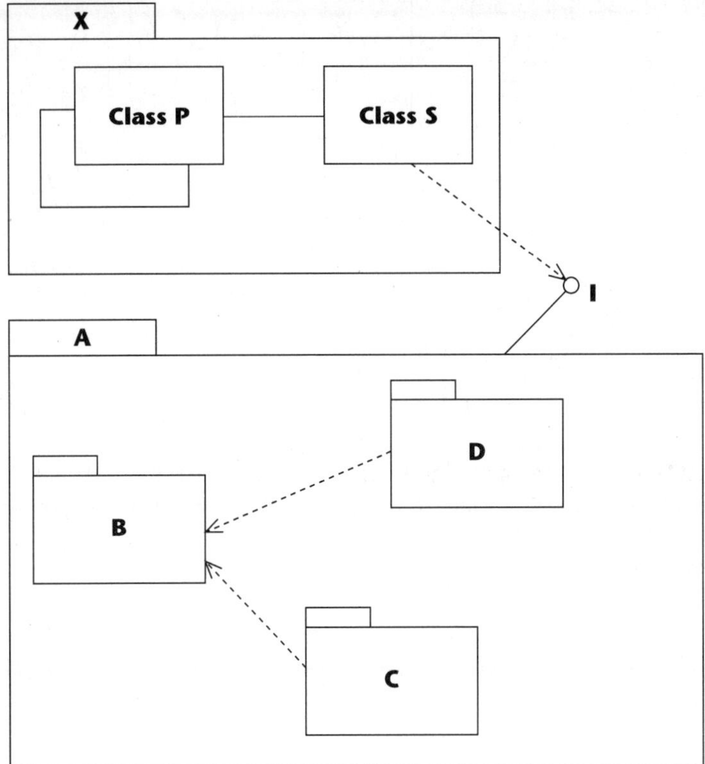

Figure 4.66 Package X contains classes P and S. Package A has an interface I. Class S inside package X is dependent on interface I in package A.

As is the case with most other model elements, you can have relationships between packages. The allowed relationships between packages are dependency, refinement, and generalization. Packages can import model elements from other packages. A package import (a dependency stereotyped as <<import>> for public import or <<access>> for private import) allows one package to import the members of another package, thereby making it possible to refer to elements of the imported package as if they were defined in the importing package (that is, without using qualified names).

A package merge (a dependency stereotyped as <<merge>>) allows the contents of the target package to be merged with the contents of the source package. It should be used when you intend to merge elements with the same name into a single element (see Figure 4.67). Merging two elements with the same name is a generalization from the source to the target. The source package also imports any elements that do not yet appear in the source package. See Figure 4.68 for the results of merging packages F, G and H from Figure 4.67.

The package has similarities to aggregation. If a package owns its contents, it is *composed aggregation;* and if it refers to its contents (that is, imports elements from other packages), it is *shared aggregation*.

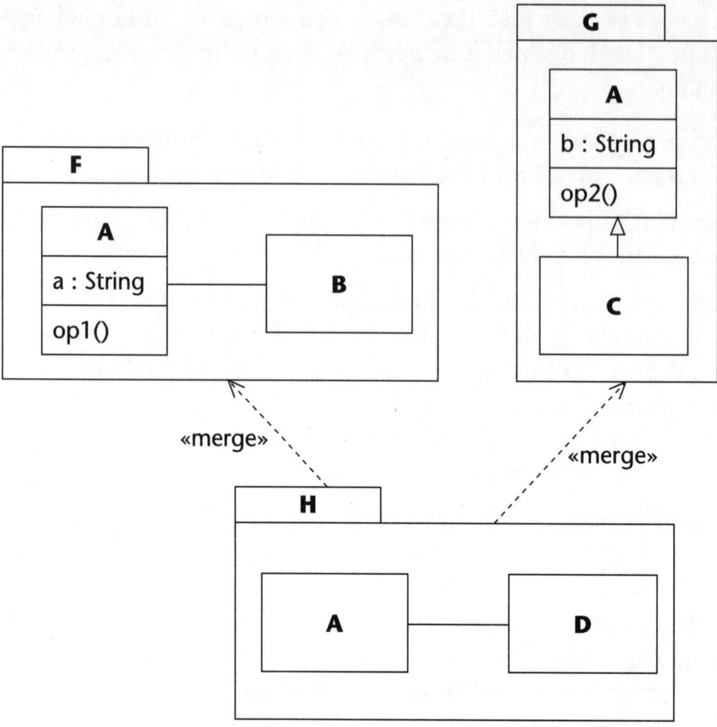

Figure 4.67 Source package H is merging all contents of target packages F and G.

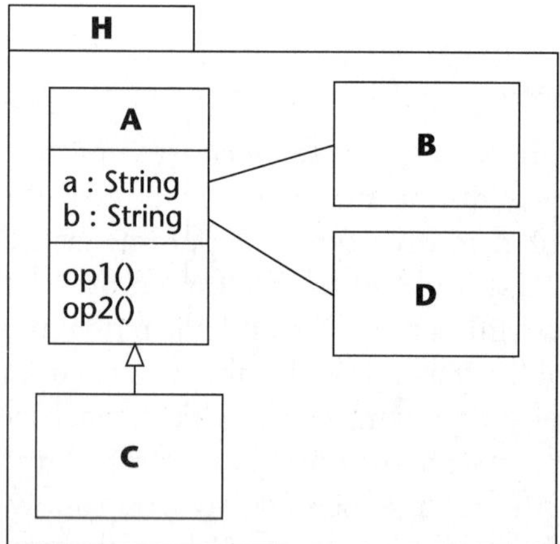

Figure 4.68 The transformed package H. Note that class A has merged classes F::A and G::A into H::A. Classes B and C are imported into package H.

A package may have visibility just like classes, showing how other packages can access its contents. UML defines four degrees of visibility: public, private, protected, and package.

- The default visibility for a package is public. Public visibility means that other elements can see and use the contents in the package.
- Private means that only the package that owns an element or a package that imports the model element can use it.
- If the visibility is protected, the package that owns or imports the model element can use it, and it is also possible for specialized packages to access the model elements inside the generalized packages. The difference between private and protected visibility for packages is the inheritance: Only packages with the protected visibility can use model elements from the generalization package.
- The last visibility is package. Package visibility is similar to private, but model elements that have a dependency to a package cannot use the elements inside that package if it has package visibility. Importing from a package is described as a dependency (with the stereotype <<import>> or <<use>>), which means that if a package has package visibility, no other package can import from that package.

A package may have an interface that publishes its behavior. The interface is shown with a small circle connected via a solid line to the packages. Typically one or more classes within the package then implement that interface.

Templates

In UML, a modeler can use a template to show a class or set of classes not fully specified. Parameters to the template provide the final specification of the class. These parameters can be classes or primitive types. A parameterized class can also be an array. The created classes of the template then are also arrays, providing a set of cars, a number of different colors, and so on depending on the parameters passed to the template. If a class is like the cookie cutter that produces specific types of objects, then a class template acts like a machine that makes cookie cutters according to the instructions (or parameter) sent to the machine. So, for example, a cookie cutter template could produce a snowman cookie cutter class when passed the proper parameter. The class produced by the template is called a *derivation*, or *derived class*. This derived class functions like any other class. In this case, the class produces the snowman cookie objects just as if it had been created without a template.

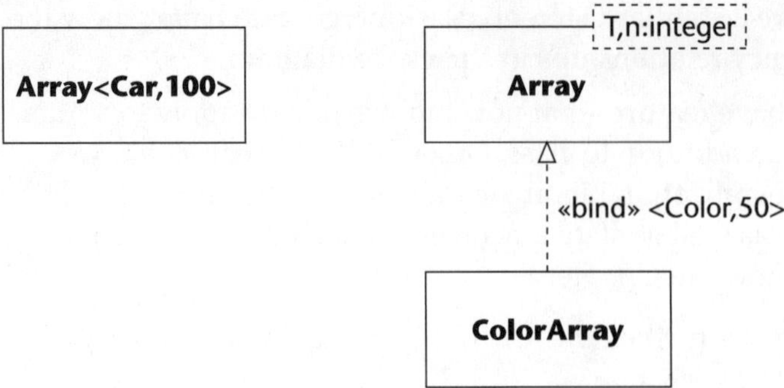

Figure 4.69 A parameterized class Array with the parameters T (a class) and n (an integer). Two instantiations are shown, one just by specifying the name of the template and the parameters within a class symbol, and the other by specifying a refinement relationship from the instantiated class to the template.

Figure 4.69 shows a template. UML displays a template with a small dashed rectangle containing the relevant parameter list placed on the upper-right corner of the class. This parameter list starts with the parameter-kind (a class if left blank), followed by the parameter name, followed by the type constraint on the parameter, optionally followed by a default value. A template parameter can include 1...* parameters in the list. A relationship between a derived class and the template is shown by a refinement relationship, using the stereotype <<bind>> followed by the actual parameters used in the class.

Relevant Changes in UML 2

Although the basic concept of class and association has not changed much from UML 1.*x*, a number of features make the description options more robust.

- The generalization set provides a tool for clarifying the different types of generalizations. A class can clearly have two or more types of generalization relationships to different sets of classes. The powertype allows for further definition of the generalization relationship. The generalization set replaces the "discriminator" attribute of a generalization from UML version 1.*x*.
- An interface can now use "ball-and-socket" notation to show a usage relationship between a class and an interface, in addition to the implementation relationship.
- The port provides a feature of a class to show environmental dependencies and links to internal behavior. The port can also be used with a protocol state machine to show the deployment rules for a component, based on the state of the application as well as the environment (see Chapter 6 for more on protocol state machines).

- Packages can take a standard stereotype <<merge>> to better show the type of dependency relationships in a package diagram.
- Many elements have features that now more explicitly apply to a number of classifiers in addition to class. Other UML elements can take advantage of generalization hierarchies and defined relationships. For example, signals as well as state machines can be redefined through inheritance, as shown in Chapter 6.

Many of these features further the UML 2 goal for enhanced support of components.

Summary

When you model, you portray the details of what you are analyzing. Thus, it is very important that the model capture the essence of the object of study. An object is something you can say things about and manipulate (in some way). An object exists in the real world (or more precisely, your understanding of the real world). An object can be a part of any system in the world—a machine, an organization, or a business. A class is a description of zero, one, or many objects with the same behavior. You use classes and objects to discuss systems.

UML provides the syntax and semantics to create a model. The modeling language, however, cannot tell you whether you have done a good job. You must strive to make all models easy to communicate, verify, validate, and maintain.

UML supports static, dynamic, and functional modeling. Static modeling is supported by class diagrams, which consist of classes and relationships between them. The relationships could be associations, generalizations, dependencies, or abstractions of some kind.

- An association is a connection between classes, which means that it is also a connection between the objects of those classes.
- A generalization is a relationship between a more general element and a more specific element. The more specific element can contain only additional information, while inheriting the elements from the parent class. An instance (an object is an instance of a class) of the more specific element might be used where an instance of the more general element is allowed.
- Dependency is a relationship between elements, one independent and one dependent. A change in the independent element affects the dependent element.
- An abstraction shows the relationship between two descriptions of the same thing, but at different levels. Abstractions such as realizations help maintain model consistency and clarity.

UML also allows the specification of constraints and rules to provide greater detail on how to implement a software system. Interfaces and ports are features that allow a modeler to focus on the specification of one class, leaving the implementation details of the environment and other interfaces to one side. So long as other software units abide by the specification, the relationships function without error. Package diagrams also help the analyst organize the model into coherent units. UML also includes features for modeling templates of classes.

CHAPTER

5

Dynamic Modeling

All systems have static structure and dynamic behavior; the UML provides diagrams to capture and describe both these aspects. Class diagrams are best used to document and express the static structure of a system—the classes, objects, and their relationships. State, activity, and interaction diagrams are best used to express the behavior of a system, to demonstrate how the objects interact dynamically during execution.

Class diagrams model intellectual and physical things and the relationships between those things. Describing the static structure of a system can reveal what the system contains and how those things are related, but it does not explain how these things cooperate to manage their tasks and provide the functionality of the system.

Objects within systems communicate with each other; they send messages to each other. For example, the customer object Joe sends a message Buy to the salesman object Bill to do something. A message is typically just an operation call that one object invokes on another object. How objects communicate and the effects of such communication are referred to as the *dynamics* of a system; that is, how the objects collaborate through communication and how the objects within the system change state during the system's lifetime. Communication among a set of objects to generate some function is called *interaction*.

The dynamic diagrams described in this chapter are:

- **State machines.** These describe which states an object can have during its life cycle, and the behavior in those states along with what events cause the state to change; for example, an invoice can be paid (state paid) or unpaid (state unpaid).
- **Activity diagrams.** These show communication in a system, but they focus on workflow. When objects are interacting with each other, the objects also perform work in terms of activities. These activities and their order are described in activity diagrams. Activity diagrams do not have to reference a specific object but can just reference a high-level flow.
- **Interaction diagrams.** These describe how objects communicate with each other. The sequence diagram shows how a sequence of messages is sent and received between a set of objects in order to perform some function. The interaction overview diagram shows interaction diagrams as part of a larger flow. The communication diagram focuses on the relationship between interacting objects.

Since the interaction and activity diagrams both show communication between objects, often you must make a choice as to which diagram to use when documenting a system. Your decision depends on which aspect is considered the most important, whether the set of actions occurring in a workflow is the focal point or whether the collaboration among the objects is the focal point.

In addition to the static structure and dynamic behavior, functional views can be used to describe systems. Functional views illustrate the functionality a system provides. Use cases are functional system descriptions; they describe how actors can use a system. As is discussed in an earlier chapter in the book, use cases are normally modeled at an early stage (for example, while gathering requirements) to describe and capture how an actor might use a system. Use-case models capture only how an actor might use a system, not how the system is built. Classes and actions implement use cases in the system. The actions are elaborated in interaction or activity diagrams; thus, a link exists between a functional view and a dynamic view of the system. The classes used in the implementation of the use cases are modeled and described in class diagrams and state machines (a state machine is attached to a class, subsystem, or system).

CROSS-REFERENCE **Use cases and their relationships to other diagrams are described in Chapter 3.**

State Machines

UML defines two kinds of state machines—behavioral state machines and protocol state machines. Behavioral state machines capture the life cycles of objects, subsystems, and systems. They tell the states an object can have and how events (received messages, time elapsed, errors, and conditions becoming true) affect those states over time. A behavioral state machine should be attached to all classes that have clearly identifiable states and complex behavior; the state machine specifies the behavior and how it differs depending on the current state. It also illustrates which events change the state of the objects of the class as well as any preconditions that must be in place to allow a transition. These state machines have also provided the foundation for "executable" UML, or xUML, when connected to an action language. See Chapter 9 for more on xUML. Protocol state machines are used to express the legal transitions that might occur in an abstract classifier such as an interface or a port. Several extensions were made to UML 1.*x* to support guidelines for working with components. Protocol state machines can provide clearer rules for component use.

CROSS-REFERENCE **The description and usage of protocol state machines, as well as concurrent state machine modeling, are found in Chapter 6.**

States and Transitions

All objects have a state; the state is a result of previous activities performed by the object and is typically determined by the values of its attributes and links to other objects. A class can have a specific attribute that specifies the state, or the state can be determined by the values of the "normal" attributes in the object. Examples of object states are:

- The invoice (object) is paid (state).
- The car (object) is standing still (state).
- The engine (object) is running (state).
- Jim (object) is playing the role of a salesman (state).
- Kate (object) is married (state).

An object transitions (changes) from one state to another state when something happens, which is called an event; for example, someone pays an invoice, starts driving the car, or gets married. The dynamic behavior has two dimensions: the interaction and the internal state changes. Interactions describe the object's external behavior and how it interacts with other objects (by sending messages or linking and unlinking with them). Internal state changes describe how objects are altering states—for example, the values of its internal attributes. State machine diagrams are used to show how objects react to events and how they change their internal state; for example, an invoice changes state from unpaid to paid when someone pays it. When an invoice is created, it enters the state of unpaid (see Figure 5.1).

State machine diagrams can have a starting point and several endpoints. A starting point (initial state) is shown as a solid filled circle, and an endpoint (final state) is shown as a circle surrounding a smaller solid circle (a bull's-eye). A state is shown as a rectangle with rounded corners. The name of the state is shown with text inside the rounded rectangle or as a name tab attached to the rounded rectangle, as shown in Figure 5.2.

Between the states are state transitions, shown as a line with an arrow from one state to another. The state transitions may be labeled with the event causing the state transition, as shown in Figure 5.3. When the event happens, the transition from one state to another is performed (it is sometimes said that the transition "fires" or that the transition "is triggered").

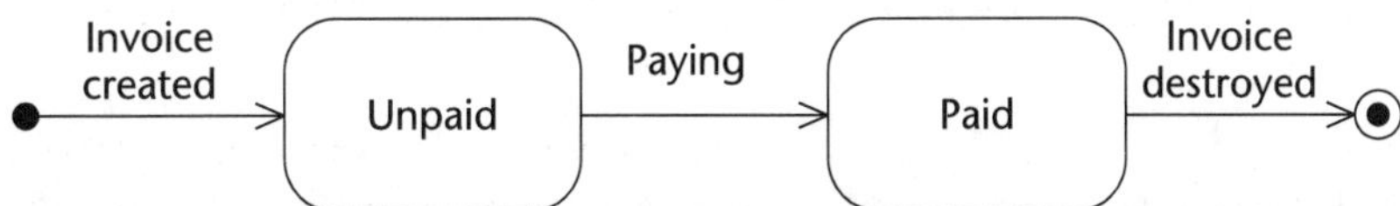

Figure 5.1 A state machine diagram for invoices. The solid filled circle indicates the starting point of invoices (object created). The circle surrounding the solid filled circle indicates the endpoint (object destroyed). The arrows between the states show state transitions and the events that cause them.

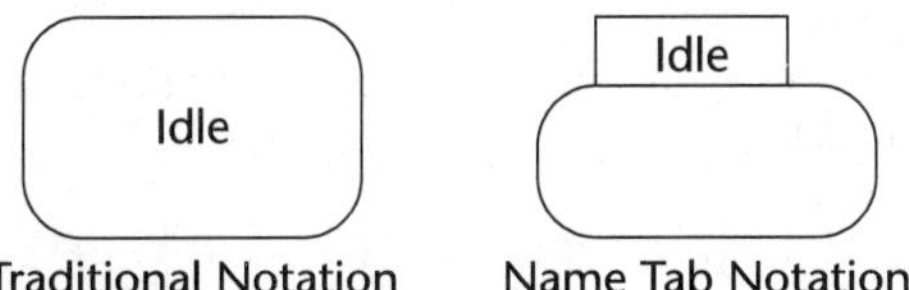

Figure 5.2 Alternate representations for a state named Idle.

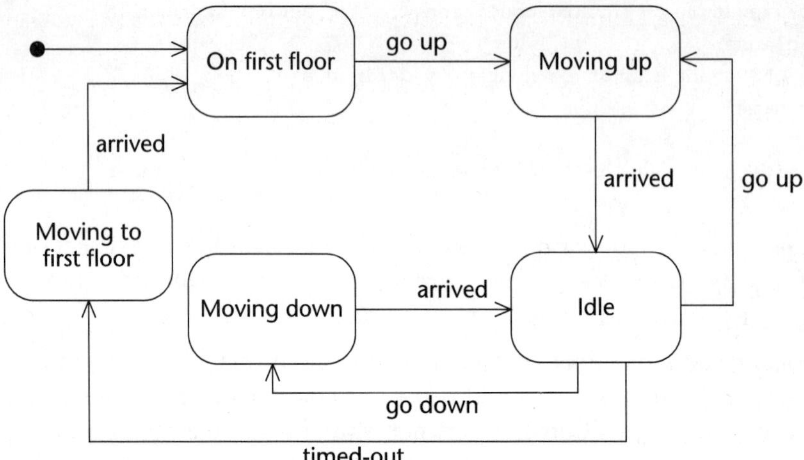

Figure 5.3 A state machine diagram for an elevator. The elevator starts at the first floor. It can be moving up or down. If the elevator is idle on one floor, a time-out event occurs after a period of time and moves the elevator back to the first floor. This state machine does not have an endpoint (final state).

A state may contain three kinds of compartments, as shown in Figure 5.4.

- The first compartment shows the name of the state, for example, idle, paid, and moving.
- The second compartment is the optional activity compartment, which lists behavior in response to events. You can define your own event, such as selecting a Help button, as well as the activity to respond to that event. Three standard events names are reserved in UML: *entry*, *exit*, and *do*.
  - The *entry* event can be used to specify actions on the entry of a state; for example, assigning an attribute or sending a message.
  - The *exit* event can be used to specify actions on exit from a state.
  - The *do* event can be used to specify an action performed while in the state; for example, sending a message, waiting, or calculating.

  These standard events cannot be used for other purposes. The formal syntax for the activity compartment is:

  ```
  event-name argument-list '/' action-expression
  ```
- The third compartment is the optional internal transition compartment. This compartment contains a list of internal transitions. A transition can be listed more than once if it has different guard conditions. The formal syntax for specifying a state transition is as follows:

```
event-signature '[' guard-condition ']' '/' action-expression '^'
send-clause
where the event-signature syntax is defined as:
event-name '(' parameter ',', ...')'
and the send-clause syntax is:
destination-expression '.'destination-event-name '(' argument ','
...')'
```

The destination-expression is an expression that evaluates an object or a set of objects. Examples of event-signatures, guard-conditions, action-expressions, and send-clauses are given next.

- Composite state machines have an additional optional decomposition compartment. This compartment is used to show the composition of the state. Since decomposition compartments might be too large graphically to display conveniently, they can be elided and represented as a graphical icon composed on two circles connected by a line (similar to a dumbbell in appearance).

The event-name can be any event, including the standard events, entry, exit, and do. The action-expression tells which action should be performed (for example, operation invocations, incrementing attribute values, and so on). It is also possible to specify arguments to the events (entry, exit, and do events do not have any arguments; see Figure 5.5).

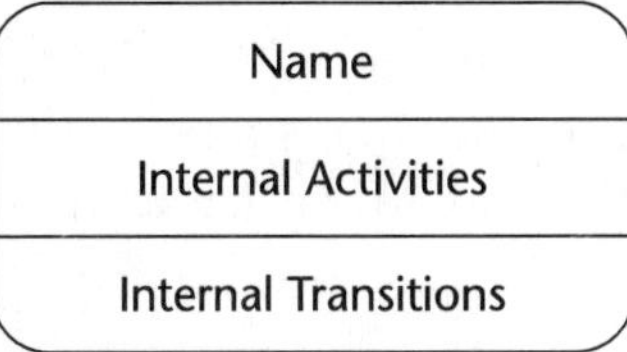

Figure 5.4 Name, state variable, and activity compartments. Note that the Name compartment cannot be used if the alternate name tab notation is used.

Login

entry/type 'login'
exit/login (username, password)
do/get username
do/get password
help/display help

Figure 5.5 A state called login, where a number of actions are performed on entry, on exit, and while in the state. The help/display help is a user-defined event and action within the action compartment.

A state transition normally has an event attached to it, but it is not necessary. If an event is attached to a state transition, the state transition is performed when the event occurs. A do-action within a state can be an ongoing process (for example, waiting, polling, operation control, and so on) performed while the object is in the given state. A do-action can be interrupted by outside events, meaning that an event on a state transition can interrupt an ongoing internal do-action.

If a state transition does not have an event specified, the attached state changes when the internal actions in the source state are executed (if there are any internal actions such as entry, exit, do, or user-defined actions). Thus, when all the actions in a state are performed, a transition without an event is automatically triggered (see Figure 5.6).

Event-Signature

Figure 5.7 shows an event-signature, which consists of an event-name and parameters, specifying the event that triggers a transition, along with additional data connected to the event. The parameters are a comma-separated list of parameters with the syntax:

```
Parameter-name ':' type-expression, Parameter-name ':' type-expression
...
```

The parameter-name is the name of the parameter and the type-expression is the type of the parameter, for example, integer, Boolean, and string. The type-expression may be suppressed, that is, not shown.

Examples of state transitions with event-signature are as follows:

```
draw (f : Figure, c : Color)
redraw ()
redraw
print (invoice)
```

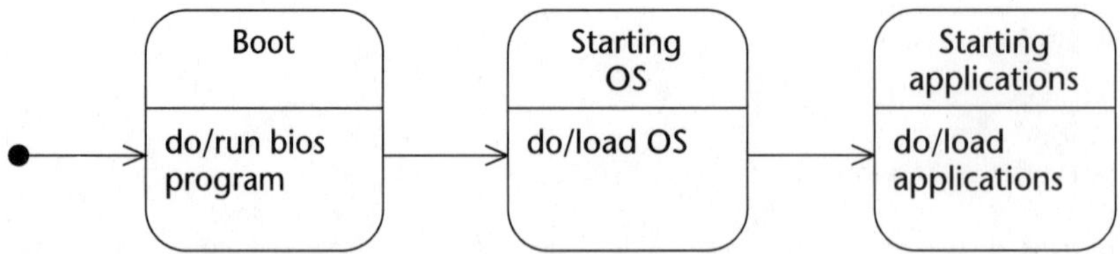

Figure 5.6 State transitions without explicit events. The transitions occur when the activities in each state have been performed.

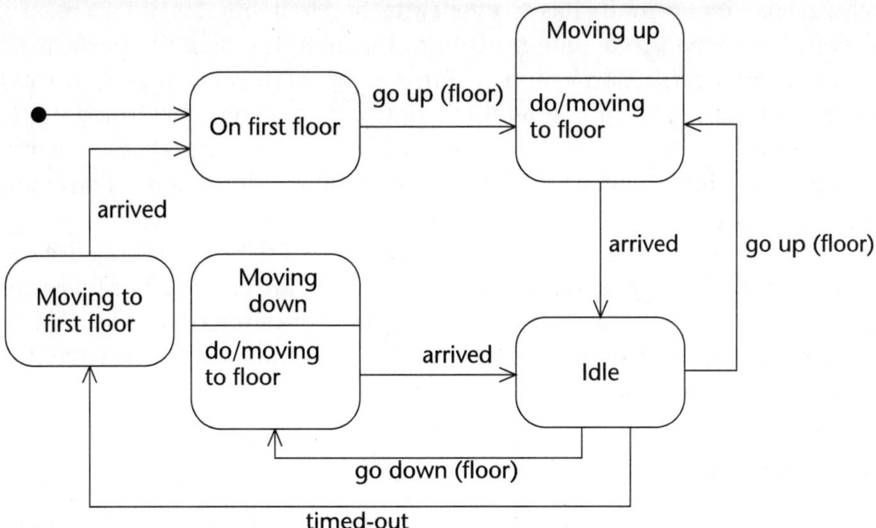

Figure 5.7 The event of the transitions between the On first floor and Moving up states has a parameter, floor (the type of the parameter is suppressed), as has the transition between Idle and Moving up and between Idle and Moving down.

Guard-Condition

Guard-condition is a Boolean expression placed on a state transition. If the guard-condition is combined with an event-signature, the event must occur, *and* the guard-condition must be true for the transition to fire. If only a guard-condition is attached to a state transition, the transition fires when the condition becomes true (see Figure 5.8). Examples of state transitions with a guard-condition are as follows:

```
[t = 15sec]
[number of invoices > n]
withdrawal (amount) [balance >= amount]
```

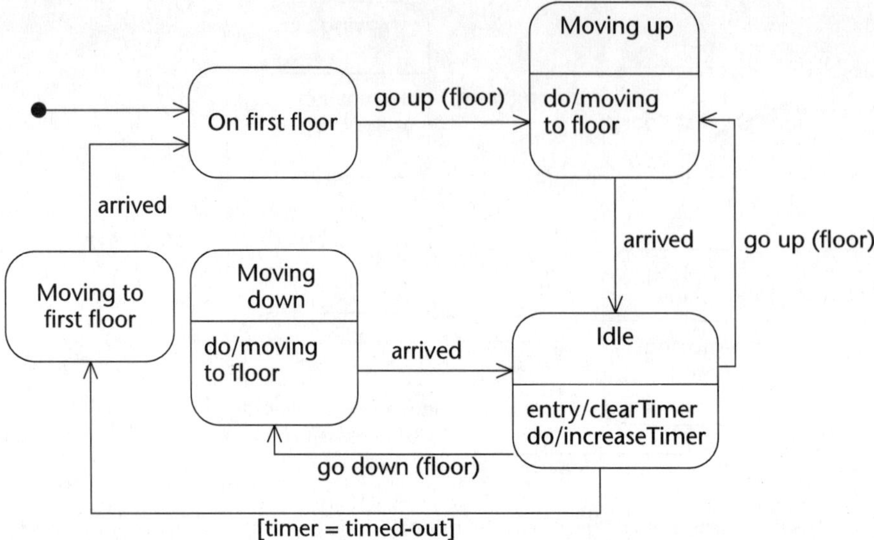

Figure 5.8 The Idle state assigns zero to the attribute timer; then it increases the timer continuously until the event go down or go up occurs or until the guard-condition timer = time-out becomes true.

Action-Expression

Action-expression is a procedural expression executed when the transition fires, as shown in Figure 5.9. It may be written in terms of operations and attributes within the owning object (the object that owns all of the states) or with parameters within the event-signature. It is possible to have more than one action-expression on a state transition, but they must be delimited with the backward slash (/) character. The action-expressions are executed one by one in the order specified (from left to right). Nested action-expressions and recursive action-expressions are not allowed. It is, however, possible to have a state-transition that contains only an action-expression. The action expression can rely on an action language that conforms to the UML action semantics. The action language has the precision needed to produce executable code in some circumstances. For more on using UML to produce executable code, see Chapter 9. Examples of state transitions with an action-expression are as follows (:= is used for assignment):

```
increase () / n := n + 1 / m := m + 1
add (n) / sum := sum + n
/flash
```

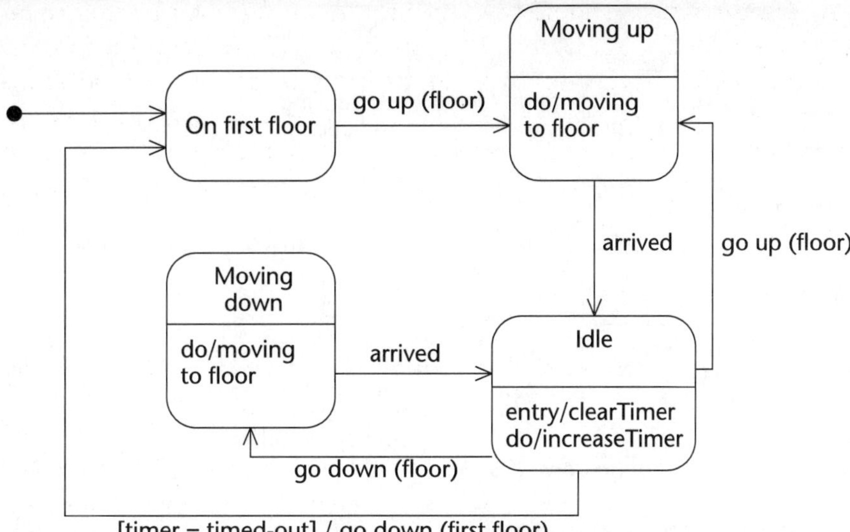

Figure 5.9 The state transition between the Idle and On first floor states has a guard-condition and an action-expression. When the timer attribute is equivalent to the time-out constant, the action *go down* (first floor) is performed; then the state is changed from Idle to On first floor.

Send-Clause

The send-clause is a special case of an action. It is an explicit syntax for sending a message during the transition between two states. The syntax consists of a destination-expression and an event-name. The destination-expression should be one that evaluates an object or a set of objects. The event-name is the name of an event meaningful to the destination object (or set of objects). The destination object can also be the object itself.

```
[timer = Time-out] / go down (first floor)
```

can be translated to a send-clause as:

```
[timer = Time-out] ^ self.go down (first floor)
```

Other examples on state transitions with a send-clause are:

```
out_of_paper()^indicator.light()
left_mouse_btn_down(location) / color:=pick_color(location) ^
pen.set(color)
```

State machine diagrams should be easy to communicate and understand (as all models should), but sometimes it is tricky to express complex internal dynamics (the object's internal states and all the state transitions) and at the same time create a model that is easy to communicate. In each situation, the modeler must decide whether to model all internal dynamics as they appear, in detail, or to simplify them to make it easier to understand the model (a simplification could be temporary).

Events

An event is something that happens and that may cause some action (see Figure 5.10). For example, when you press the Play button on your CD player, it starts playing (provided that the CD player is turned on, a CD is loaded, and the CD player is otherwise in order). The event is that you press the Play button, and the action is that it starts playing. When there are well-defined connections between events and actions, this is called *causality*. In software engineering, we normally model causal systems in which events and actions are connected to each other. It is not causal, for example, if you drive too fast on the highway and the police stop you, because the action of the police stopping you is not sure to happen; thus, no absolute connection exists between the event (driving too fast) and the action (the police stopping you).

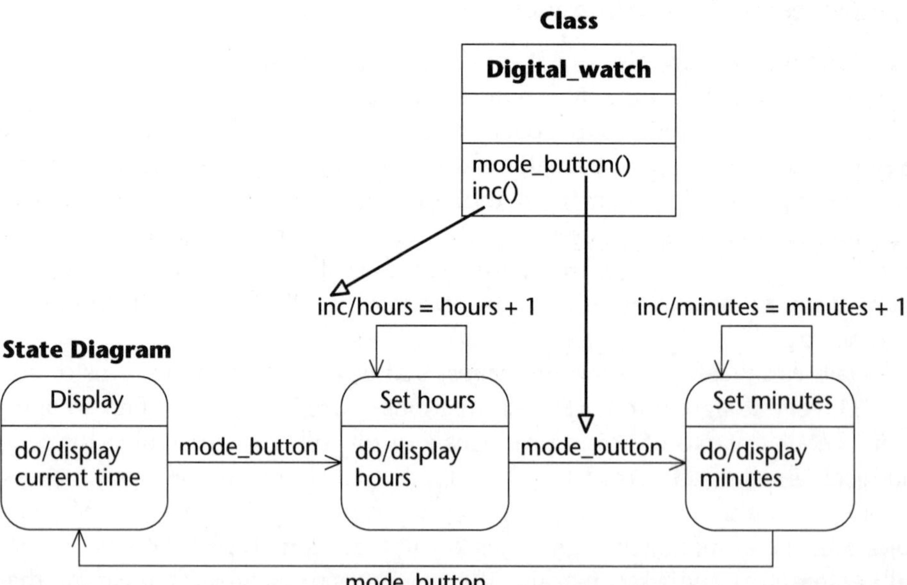

Figure 5.10 The Digital_watch class with its corresponding state machine diagram. The figure shows how events in the state machine are related to operations within the class. The watch has three states: its normal display state showing the time, and two states for setting the clock (hours and minutes, respectively).

The definition of an event can be found in the *Cambridge Dictionary of Philosophy* (Audi, 1995), by looking at the definition of entity (under metaphysics):

> *Every entity must be either an individual thing (e.g., Socrates and this book), or a property (e.g., Socrates' color and the shape of this book), or a relation (e.g., marriage and the distance between two cities), or an event (e.g., Socrates' death), or a state of affairs (e.g., Socrates' having died), or a set (e.g., the set of Greek philosophers).*

UML has four types of events, also referenced as triggers because the event triggers behavior that depends on how you build the system.

- **A condition becoming true.** This is shown as a guard-condition on a state transition.
- **Receipt of an explicit signal from another object.** The signal is itself an object. This is shown as an event-signature on state transitions. This type of event is called a message.
- **Receipt of a call on an operation by another object (or by the object itself).** This is shown as an event-signature on state transitions. This type of event is also called a message.
- **Passage of a designated period of time.** The time is normally calculated after another designated event (often the entry of the current state) or the passage of a given amount of time. This is shown as a time-expression on state transitions.

Note that errors are also events and can be useful to model. See Chapter 6 for more on error handling in dynamic models.

It is important to know some basic semantics about events. First, events are triggers that activate state transitions; these events are processed one at time. If an event potentially can activate more than one state transition, only one of the state transitions is triggered (which one is undefined). If an event occurs, and the state transition's guard-condition is false, the trigger does not fire (the event is not stored, triggering the transition when the guard-condition later becomes true).

A class can receive or send messages, that is, operation invocations or signals. The event-signature for state transitions is used for both. When an operation is called, it executes and produces a result. When a signal object is sent, the receiver catches the object and uses it. Signal classes are ordinary classes, but are used only for sending signals; they represent the unit sent between objects in the system. The signal classes may be stereotyped with the <<signal>> stereotype, which constrains the semantics of the objects, meaning that only they can be used as signals. It is possible to build signal hierarchies supporting polymorphism, so that if a state transition has an event-signature specifying a specific signal, all the subsignals are also receivable by the same specification (see Figure 5.11).

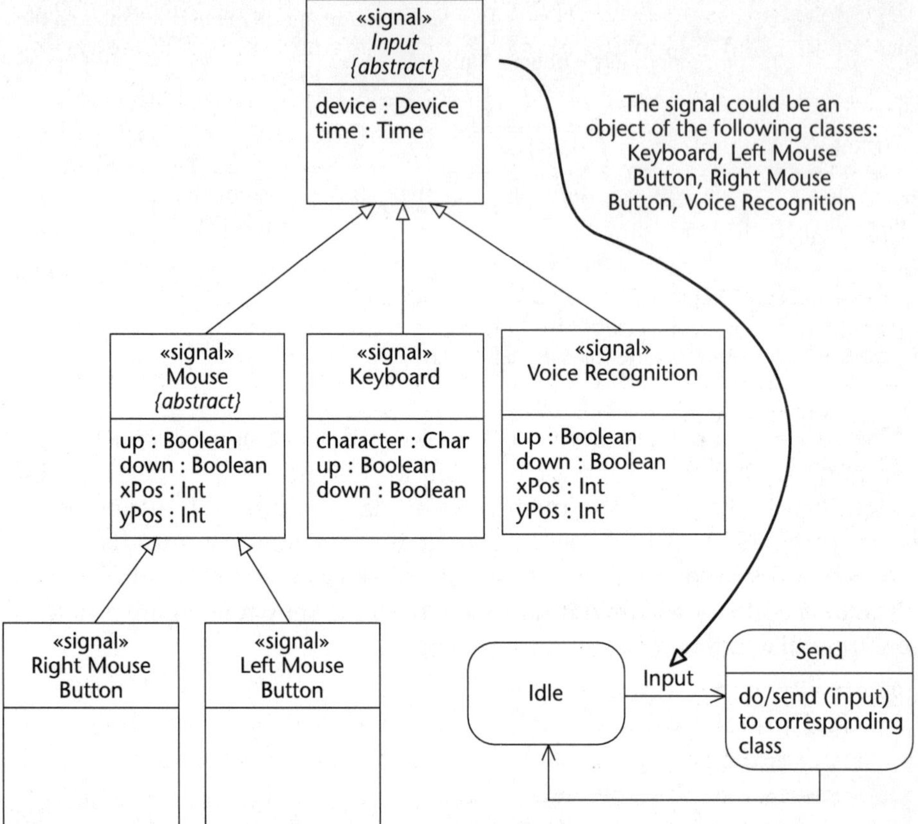

Figure 5.11 A signal class hierarchy with an abstract superclass. The state machine diagram on the right-hand side receives input signals (including subsignals to the Input class). Only concrete signals may be sent (because the abstract signal class does not have any instances).

Java Implementation

State machine diagrams are in some cases redundant information, depending on whether the operations within the classes have specified algorithms. In other words, a class behavior might be specified within operations as algorithms or explicitly by state machines (or both). When state machines are implemented in an object-oriented programming language, they are implemented either directly in the algorithms (with case statements and so on) or they are implemented with separate mechanisms, such as finite state machines or function tables. It is outside the scope of this book to describe this in detail; however, Figure 5.12 illustrates the principles for implementing a state machine directly in the operations of the class.

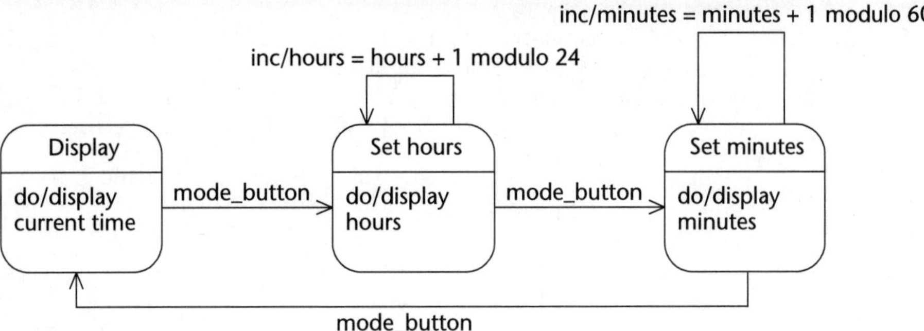

Figure 5.12 A state machine for a digital watch.

UML does not give any advice on how to implement signal events in a programming language. Nevertheless, implementing the signals is rather straightforward: They are implemented as classes with both attributes and common operations. The classes that are to receive the signals must have a corresponding operation that receives the signal object as an argument.

The Java code for a class with the state machine shown in Figure 5.12 looks something like the following:

```
public class State
{
     public final int Display = 1;
     public final int Set_hours = 2;
     public final int Set_minutes = 3;
     public int value;
}

public class Watch
{
private State state = new State();
private DigitalDisplay LCD = new DigitalDisplay();

public Watch ()
     {
              state.value = State.Display;
              LCD.display_time();
     }

public void mode_button ()
     {
               switch (state.value)
               {
               case State.Display :
                        LCD.display_time();
                        state.value = State.Set_hours;
                        break;
```

```
            case State.Set_Hours :
                   LCD.display_hours();
                   state.value = State.Set_minutes;
                   break;
            case State.Set_minutes):
                   LCD.display_time();
                   state.value = State.Display;
                   break;
      }
public void inc()
      {
            case (state.value)
            {
            case State.Display :
                   ;
                   break;
            case State.Set_hours:
                   LCD.inc_hours();
                   break;
            case State.Set_minutes:
                   LCD.inc_minutes();
                   Break;
      }
 }
```

Sending Messages Between State Machines

State machines can send messages to other state machines. This process is shown either by actions (that is, specifying the receiver in the send-clause) or with dashed arrows between the state machines. If dashed arrows are used, the state machines must be grouped inside their objects (the class rectangle symbol is then used). The rectangle symbol might also be used for modeling subsystems or systems (a sort of macro class). Two different techniques can be used to draw dashed arrows between state machines that represent messages:

- The first way is to draw the dashed arrow from a transition within the source object to the border of the target object (this is the alternative to the text syntax in the send-clause). Then, a transition is drawn within the target object, which corresponds to and catches the specified message.
- The second way is to draw a dashed line from the source object to the target object, indicating that the source object is sending the message some time during its execution. However, the target object must also have a corresponding transition signature to catch the message (see Figure 5.13).

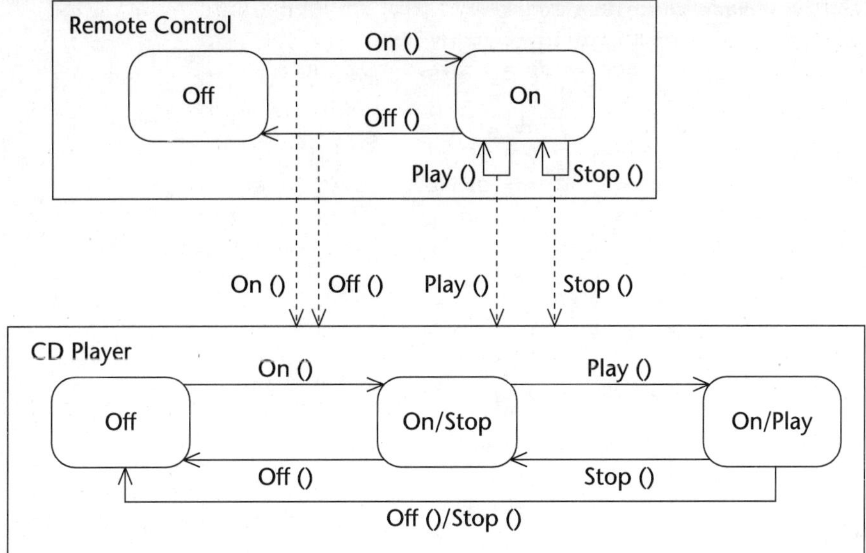

Figure 5.13 The remote control sends messages to the CD player.

Substates

A state may have nested substates, whereby internally the state has its own substates that can be shown in other state machines. UML 2 defines orthogonal (more clearly understood as "or-substates") and nonorthogonal ("and-substates") substate machines.

- An **or-substate** indicates that a state has substates, but only one at a time, as shown in Figure 5.14. For instance, a car may be in the running state, which has two different substates: forward and backward. These are or-substates because they cannot be true at the same time. The nested substates can be displayed in another state machine by expanding the running state in the initial state machine.

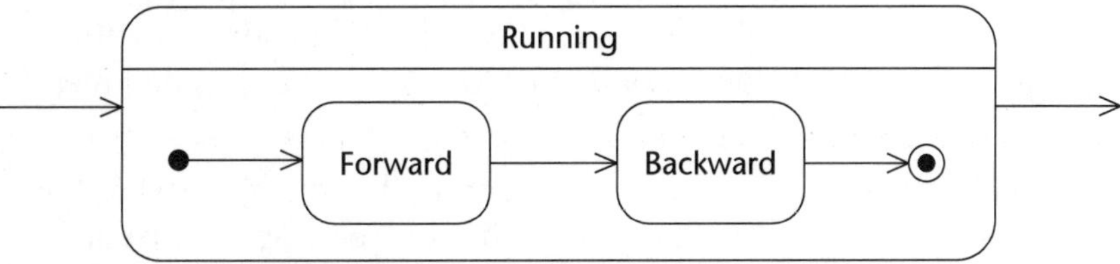

Figure 5.14 An or-substate.

- On the other hand, the running state can also have many concurrent substates (*and-substates*): forward and low speed, forward and high speed, backward and low speed, backward and high speed. When a state has and-substates, several of them can be true in parallel, indicating that a state can have substates that are both or-substates and and-substates, as shown in Figure 5.15. And-substates are also called concurrent substates and can be used when modeling the states of concurrent threads. This topic is discussed in more detail in Chapter 6.

Entry, Exit, and Terminate Indicators

The entry, exit, and terminate indicators are used to indicate points at which a corresponding transition enters a state machine.

- The *entry* point is used to describe actions that must occur on entry into the state machine. The entry point indicator is shown as a small circle on or optionally within the border of a state machine.
- The *exit* point is used to describe actions that must occur at the completion of a state machine. The exit point indicator is shown as a small circle with a cross on or optionally within the border of a state machine.
- The *terminate* point allows a transition out of the state machine and implies an immediate termination of the object whose behavior is represented by the state machine. The terminate indicator is shown as a cross within the border of a state machine.

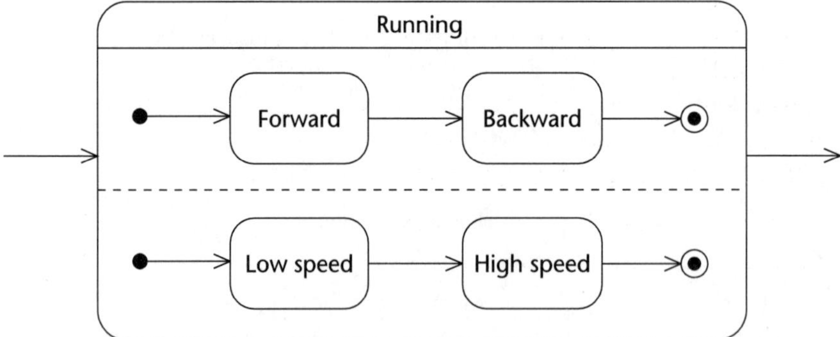

Figure 5.15 An and-substates (combined with or-substates).

History Indicator

A history indicator is used to memorize internal states; for example, it remembers a state so that it's possible to go back to that state at a later time, in case an activity has to be interrupted or reversed. A history indicator applies to a state region, in which it is placed. There are two types of history indicators, shallow history and deep history. If a transition to a history indicator fires, the object resumes the state it had last within that region.

- If the indicator is a shallow history indicator then the transition is to the most recent state of the immediately enclosing state machine. A shallow history indicator is shown as a circle with an H inside.
- The deep history transition is identical to the shallow history with the exception that the transition is applied recursively to all the enclosing state machines. A deep history indicator is shown as a circle with an H* inside. Both shallow and deep history might have several incoming transitions, but no outgoing transitions (see Figure 5.16).

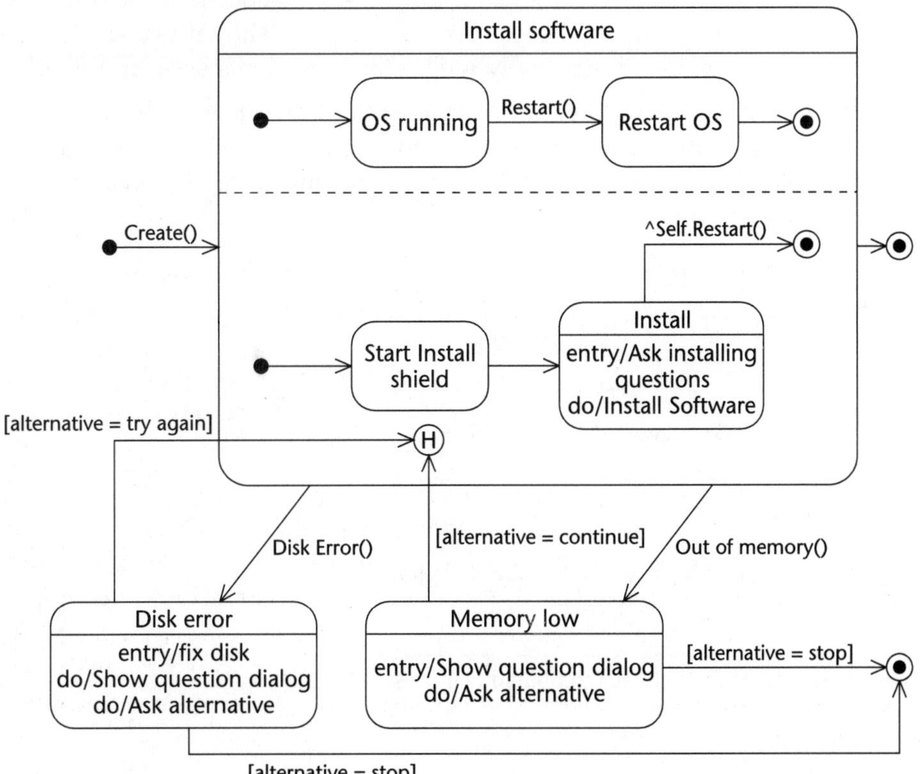

Figure 5.16 An install program. The shallow history indicator is used to handle errors such as "out of memory" and "disk error," when some specific error states handle these errors. After the error states have been performed, the shallow history indicator is used to go back to the state that applied before the error.

Activity Diagrams

Activity diagrams capture actions and their results. The activity diagram is similar to a state machine, but has a different purpose, which is to capture actions (work and activities that are to be performed modeled as executable activity nodes) and their results in terms of object-state changes. The actions in the activity diagram can transition to the next stage directly when the action has been completed (without requiring any events as in state machines). Another difference between activity diagrams and state machines is that the actions can be placed in *activity partitions.* An activity partition groups activities with respect to who is responsible for them or where they reside in an organization. An activity diagram is a way of describing system flow, with the possibility of expressing how actions are taken, what they do (change of object states), when they take place (action sequence), and where they take place (activity partitions).

Activity diagrams can be used for different purposes, including:

- To capture the work (actions) that will be performed when an operation is executing (the instance of the operation implementation).
- To capture the internal work in an object.
- To show how a set of related actions can be performed and how they affect objects around them.
- To show how an instance of a use case can be performed in terms of actions and object state changes.
- To show how a business works in terms of workers (actors), workflows, organization, and objects (physical and intellectual factors used in the business).

Actions and Edges

An action is performed to produce a result. The implementation of an operation may be described as a set of related actions, which is later translated to code lines. An activity diagram shows the actions and their relationships and can have a start and an endpoint. A start point is shown as a solid filled circle; the endpoint is shown as a circle surrounding a smaller solid circle (a bull's-eye). The actions (executable activity nodes) in an activity diagram are drawn as rectangles with rounded corners (the same notation used in state machines; see Figure 5.17).

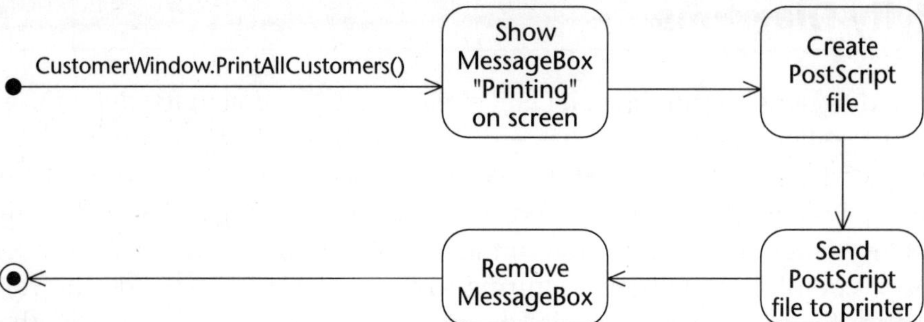

Figure 5.17 When someone calls the PrintAllCustomer operation (in the CustomerWindow class), the actions start. The first action is to show a message box on the screen, the second action is to create a PostScript file, the third action is to send the PostScript file to the printer, and the fourth action is to remove the message box from the screen. The transitions are automatic; they occur as soon as the action in the source state is performed.

Within the action, a text string is attached to specify the action or actions taken. The edges representing transitions between the actions have the same syntax as in state machines, except for events. Events are attached only to the transition from the start point to the first action. Activity edges are shown with an arrow, to which guard-conditions, a send-clause, and an action-expression can be attached. Often nothing is specified, indicating that the edge is triggered as soon as all the activities in the action have been performed (see Figure 5.18).

An edge can be protected by a guard-condition, which, as noted previously, must be true for it to trigger, using the same syntax as guard-conditions in state machines. Decisions are made using guard-conditions, for example, [yes] and [no]. A diamond-shaped symbol is used to show a decision node, and the decision condition is shown as an attached note stereotyped as <<decisionInput>>, as shown in Figure 5.19. The decision node can have one or more incoming edges and two or more outgoing edges labeled with guard-conditions. Normally, one of the outgoing edges is always true.

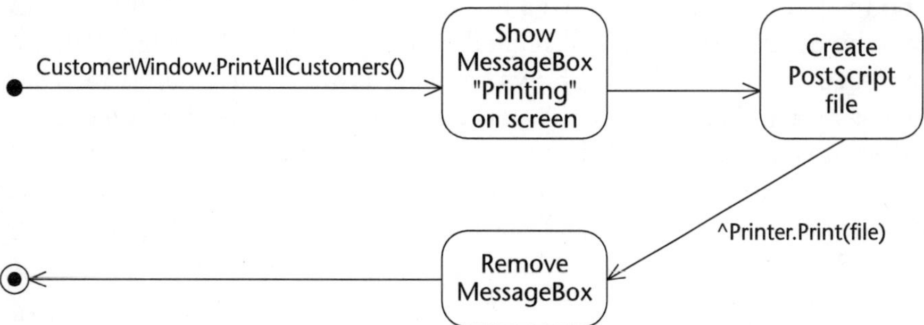

Figure 5.18 The activity edge between the second and the third actions has a send-clause that sends a Print(file) message to the Printer object.

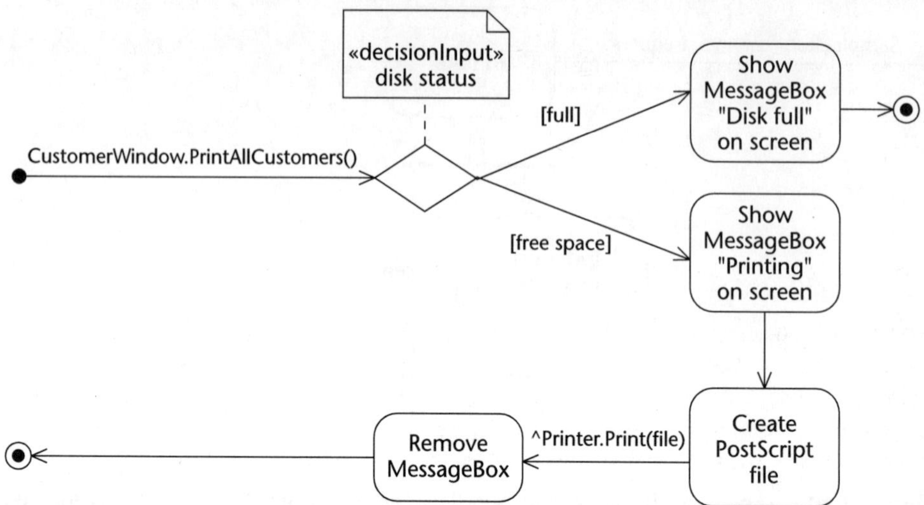

Figure 5.19 If the disk is full, MessageBox "Disk full" is shown. Otherwise, MessageBox "Printing" is shown.

An edge can be divided into two or more edges that result in parallel actions. The actions are executed concurrently, although they can also be executed one by one. The important thing is that all the parallel edges be performed before they unite (if they ever unite). A bold line is drawn to show that an edge is divided into several branches and shows the actual split into parallel actions. The bold line is also used to show the unification of the branches (see Figure 5.20). To model the end of one branch while still allowing other activities to continue, a special flow final state shown as a circled X can be used. For more on parallel, or concurrent, flow in an activity see Chapter 6.

Connectors can be used when the set of edges becomes too complicated to diagram. Connectors add no real semantic value; they just allow one to simplify a diagram. Each connector with an incoming edge must be paired with exactly one identically labeled connector with an outgoing edge. Figure 5.21 is semantically the same as Figure 5.19, but the connector was just used to allow the reorganization of the diagram visually, and the decision node was reworked to remove the need for the decisionInput note.

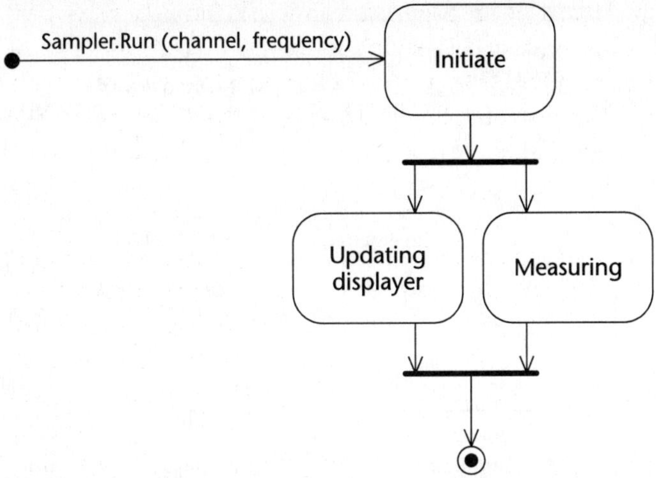

Figure 5.20 When the Run operation is called, the first action to take place is Initiate. Then, the actions Updating display and Measuring are performed simultaneously (concurrently or by alternating them).

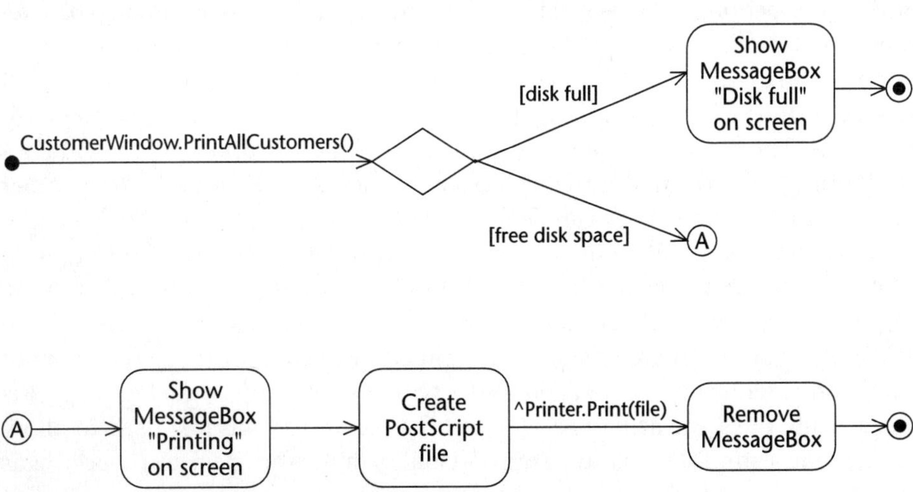

Figure 5.21 "Disk full" activity diagram reorganized with a connector.

Activity Partitions

As stated earlier in the chapter, activity partitions group actions, normally with respect to their responsibility. They are used for several different purposes; for example, to show explicitly where actions are performed (in which object), or to show in which part of an organization work (an action) is performed. A common usage of activity partitions is to show them as "swimlanes" drawn as vertical rectangles. The actions belonging to a swimlane are placed within its rectangle. The swimlane is given a name that is placed at the top of the rectangle (see Figure 5.22).

Activity partitions can be organized in other ways. When one is modeling business flows, it is common to use left-to-right lanes. Partitions might be further broken down into composite subpartitions. You can partition the activities in two dimensions, perhaps organizing one axis around who performs the activities and another around where they are performed. Because the visual modeling of activity partitions can get complicated, you can alternately denote the partition textually within the action in parentheses. The textual notation can be used in conjunction with the placement of actions in activity partitions to override the location of an action node appearing in a diagram. Figure 5.23 is semantically the same as 5.22.

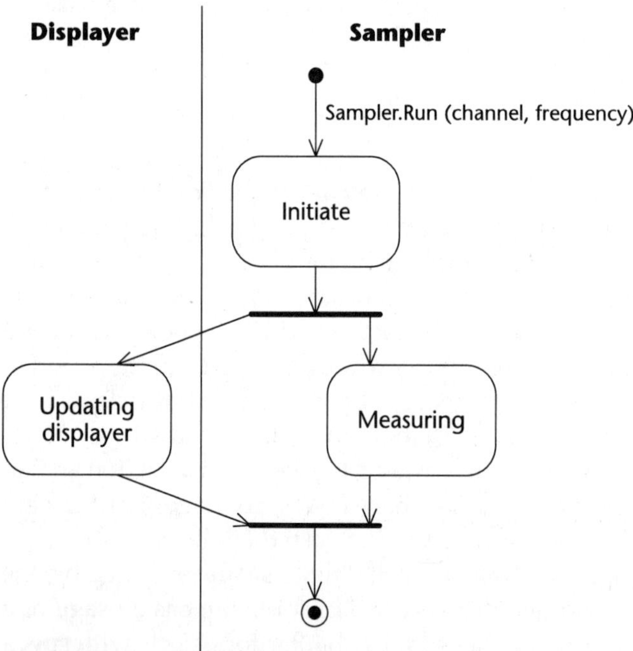

Figure 5.22 The Updating displayer action is performed within the Displayer. The Initiate and Measuring actions are performed within the Sampler.

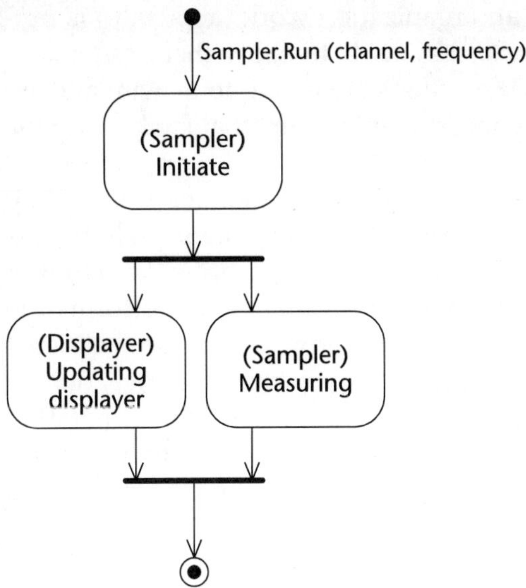

Figure 5.23 The Displayer/Sampler activity diagram with partitions specified textually.

Objects

Objects can be shown on activity diagrams. They are either input to or output from the actions, or they can simply show that an object is affected by a specific action. Objects are shown as object rectangles with the object and/or class name inside them. When an object is input to an action, it is shown with a flow line and arrow extending from the object to the action; when the object is output from an action, it's shown with the line and arrow extending from the action to the object. Optionally, the state of the object can be shown below the class name and inside the brackets, such as [planned], [bought], [filled], and so on.

In the underlying model of UML, the arrowed line between an action and an object is considered an object flow rather than an activity edge. But they are visually the same, and we do not distinguish between them here.

An object can be used represent a *datastore* that retains values created by one action to be consumed by another. See Figure 5.24 for some basic usage of a datastore object, and see Figure 5.26 later in the chapter for objects with specified states.

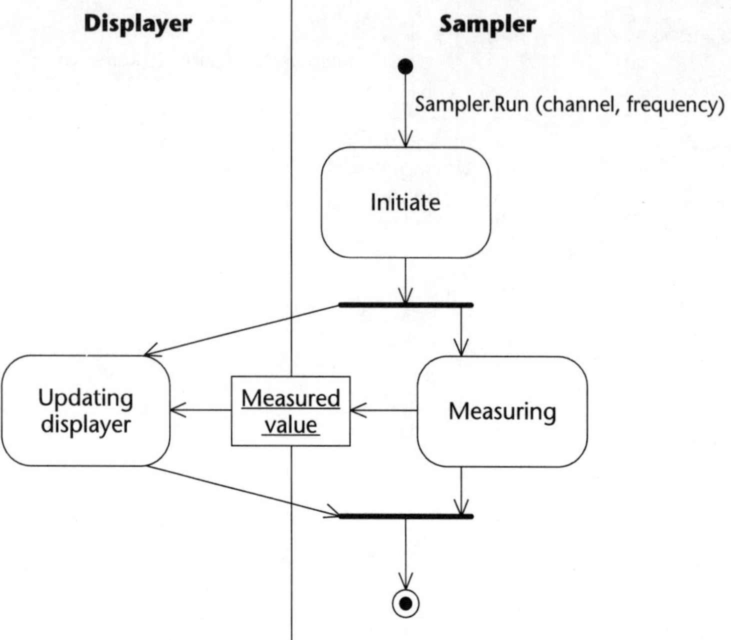

Figure 5.24 The Measuring action supplies the Updating displayer action with measured values (measured value is an object).

Signals

Signals can be sent or received in activity diagrams (signals were described earlier in this chapter). You use two symbols for signals, one for sending and one for receiving a signal. The send symbol corresponds to the send-clause attached to an edge. As with the send-clause, both the send and receipt symbols are attached to an edge; however, graphically, the edge is divided into two edges with a send or a receipt symbol in between.

The send and receipt symbols can be attached to the objects that are the receivers or the senders of the messages, which is done by drawing a dashed line with an arrow from the send or receipt symbol to the object. If it is a send symbol, the arrow points to the object; if it is a receipt symbol, the arrow points to the receipt symbol. Showing the objects is optional. The send symbol is a convex pentagon; the receipt symbol is a concave pentagon, as shown in Figure 5.25.

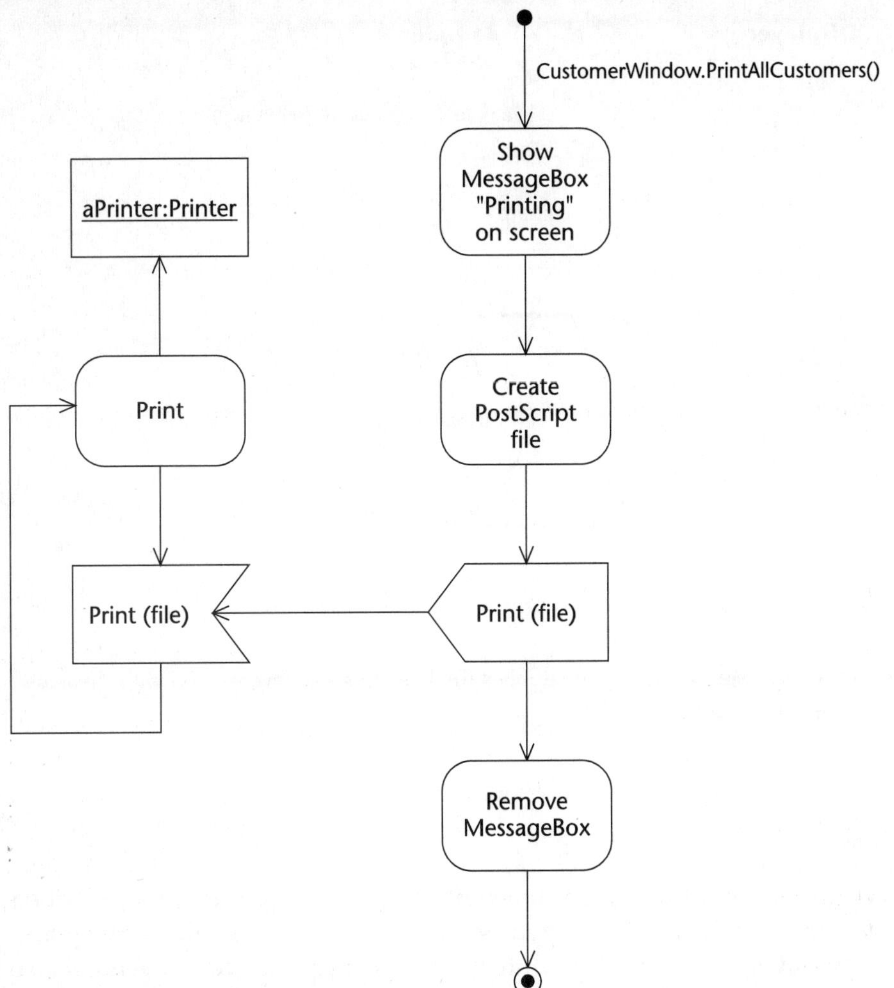

Figure 5.25 Between Create PostScript file and Remove MessageBox, a Print signal is sent. The signal contains a file that is received and printed in the Printer object.

Pins

Rather than just having an activity initiated when some preceding activity is completed, the semantics of initiating the activity can be formalized through the use of pins.

A *pin*, shown as a small rectangle attached to an activity, shows values an activity accepts (input pins) and values it produces (output pins). The input pins compose part of the prerequisites for an activity to execute. An activity cannot execute until it has tokens on each of its input pins.

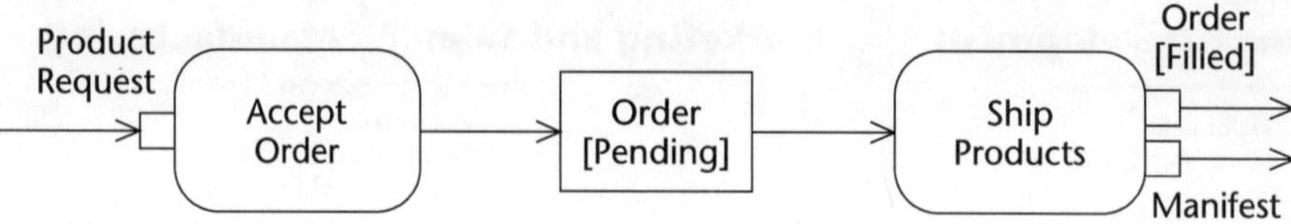

Figure 5.26 Pins.

When an output pin of one activity is then shown as an input pin to a subsequent activity, a standalone pin can be placed on the flow between the two activities. In this standalone pin form it is shown as we discussed earlier in the section on objects. Figure 5.26 shows an Accept Order action with an input pin, a standalone pin between the actions, and then two output pins from the Ship Products action.

Chapter 6 goes into more detail on pins, tokens, and other features that add fidelity to activity modeling.

Business Modeling with Activity Diagrams

According to Nilsson (1991), when one is modeling businesses, these important aspects should be studied and described in the models: resources, rules, goals, and actions (workflow). Two kinds of resources exist: physical and information. Workers (actors within the business) are examples of resources; they are physical objects. Other physical objects might be items that are produced, consumed, or handled. Information objects are often objects that are handled within an information system. Information objects carry information about the business. The business rules restrict the use of the resources, both physical items and information. For instance, one rule might be that a physical item must not be damaged during delivery. Another rule might be that some information is strategic and must be kept confidential. The use of these resources is the actual work, called the workflow.

The goals of the business motivate the workflow, where the resources are used in accordance with specified rules. In business modeling, it is often important to separate physical objects from information objects. Physical objects are those that exist in the real world (or our understanding of the world), for example, cars, customers, and contracts. Information objects carry information about the business, whether about work or physical things (objects). Thus, customer objects in an information system are not the actual customers; they contain information about the actual customers. Stereotypes can be used to separate physical objects from information objects within activity diagrams. For example, the stereotype <<Information>> might be used to indicate that an object is an information object; similarly, the stereotype <<Physical>> might be used to indicate that an object represents the actual physical object. When objects are handled, produced, or consumed, they are changing their states, which can be described in activity diagrams (see Figure 5.27).

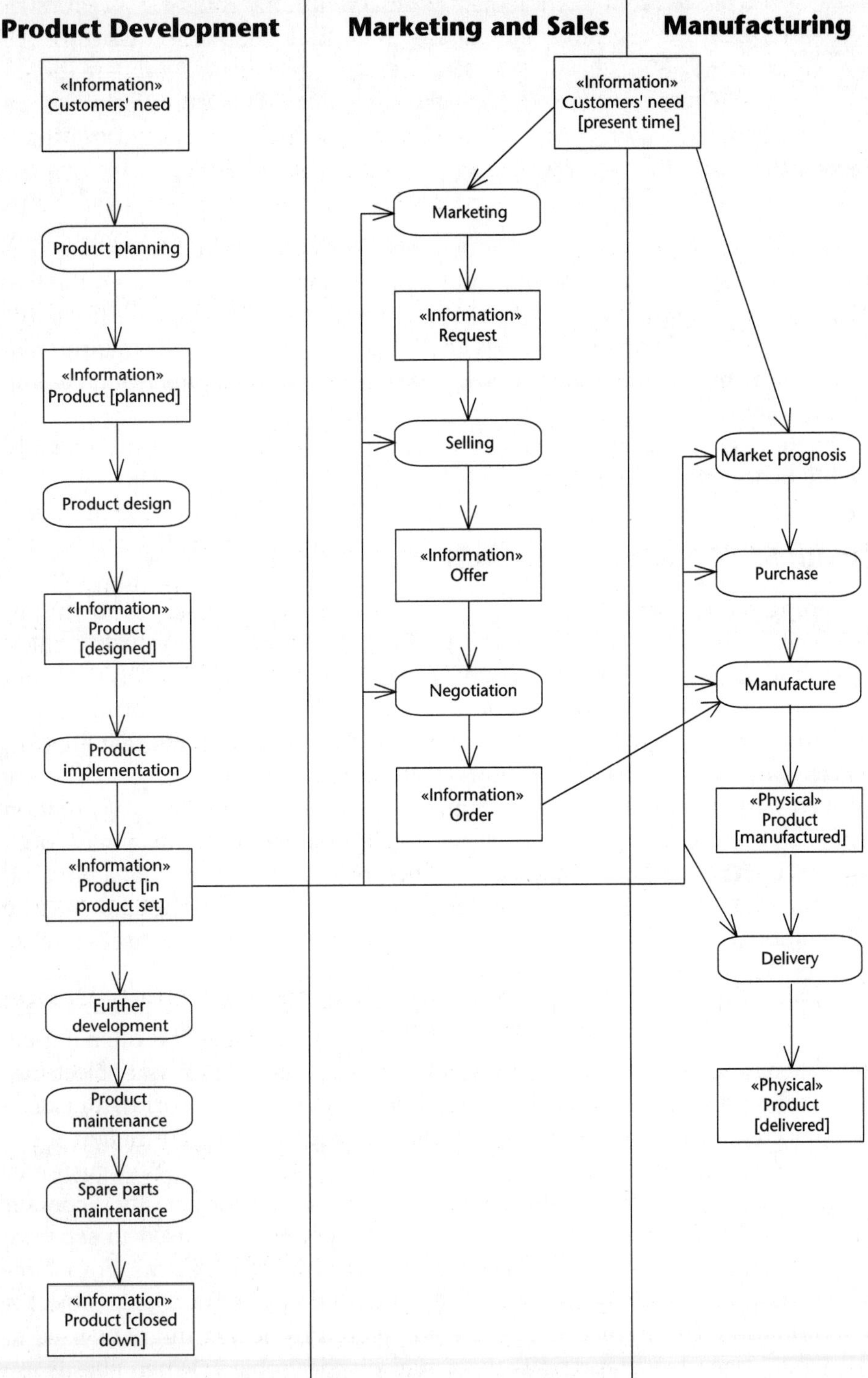

Figure 5.27 A business pattern for manufacturing described with an activity diagram.

The approach to modeling business with activity diagrams can be complemented by use cases or other techniques to capture the requirements of the system (the business system). Note that with this approach, objects are identified and classified into information or physical items. The identified information objects can become a proper foundation for analyzing and building a system to support the modeled business. Using activity diagrams has similarities to implementing workflow techniques such as IDEF0 (a standard visual process modeling language). Therefore, the actions might be described as in those techniques.

Actions can be described in many ways. One practical approach is to describe them with the following headings:

- **Definition.** A formal or informal description of the action.
- **Purpose.** A description of the purpose of the action.
- **Characteristic.** Typically repetitive or one-time shot.
- **Method of measurement.** When it is possible and desirable to measure the actions, the method of measurement should be described.
- **Actors/Roles.** Which actors and roles are required to perform the action.
- **Information technology.** What kind of information system support is required.
- **Rules, policies, and strategies.** Any documents, strategies, or policies that restrict the performance of the actions.

Interaction Diagrams

UML provides four types of interaction diagrams.

- The main diagram is the *sequence diagram*, which shows objects interacting along lifelines that represent general order.
- The *communication diagram* shows the messages passed between objects, focusing on the internal structure of the objects.
- The *interaction overview diagram* treats a sequence diagrams as the unit for a modified activity diagram that does not show any of the interaction details.
- The *timing diagram* shows interactions with a precise time axis.

The interaction diagram is displayed with the name of the diagram shown in a pentagram in the upper-left corner prefixed by *sd*. The use of *sd*, which can stand for sequence diagram, shows the prime place the sequence diagram has in the set of interaction diagrams.

For timing diagrams and advanced features of the other diagrams, see Chapter 6. This section covers basic features starting with the core interaction diagram, the sequence diagram.

Sequence Diagrams

Sequence diagrams illustrate how objects interact with each other. They focus on message sequences, that is, how messages are sent and received between a number of objects. Sequence diagrams have two axes: the vertical axis shows time and the horizontal axis shows a set of objects. A sequence diagram also reveals the interaction for a specific scenario—a specific interaction between the objects that happens at some point in time during the system's execution (for example, when a specific function is used).

A sequence diagram is enclosed by a rectangular frame with the name of the diagram shown in a pentagram in the upper-left corner prefixed by *sd*. On the horizontal axis are the objects involved in the sequence. Each is represented by an object rectangle with the object and/or class name underlined. The rectangle along with the vertical dashed line, called the object's lifeline, indicates the object's execution during the sequence (that is, messages sent or received and the activation of the object). Communication between the objects is represented as horizontal message lines between the objects' lifelines. To read the sequence diagram, start at the top of the diagram and read down to view the exchange of messages taking place as time passes.

Generic and Instance Form

Sequence diagrams can be used in two forms: the generic form and the instance form.

- The *instance form* describes a specific scenario in detail; it documents one possible interaction. The instance form does not have any conditions, branches, or loops; it shows the interaction for just the chosen scenario.
- The *generic form* describes all possible alternatives in a scenario; therefore branches, conditions, and loops may be included.

For example, the scenario "opening an account" in a sequence diagram using the generic form is described with all possible alternatives: where everything is successful, where the customer isn't allowed to open an account, where money is immediately deposited in the account, and so on. The same scenario documented with the instance form of a sequence diagram chooses one specific execution and sticks to that case; for example, one diagram might show the successful opening of an account. If all cases must be shown using instance form diagrams, a number of them have to be drawn.

A message is a communication between objects that conveys information with the expectation that action will be taken. The receipt of a message is normally considered an event. Messages can be signals, operation invocations, or something similar (for example, remote procedure calls [RPCs] in C++ or Remote Method Invocation [RMI] in Java). When a message is received, an activity starts in the receiving object; this is called *execution occurrence*. An execution occurrence shows the focus of control, which object(s) execute at some point in time. An activated object is either executing its own code or is waiting for the return of another object to which it has sent a message. The execution occurrence is optional on the diagram; when shown it is drawn as a thin rectangle on the object's lifeline. The lifeline represents the existence of an object at a particular time; it is drawn as an object icon with a dashed line extending down to the point at which the object stops existing (or to the bottom of the diagram if no destruction is shown). The messages are shown as arrows between the object lifelines. Each message can have a signature with a name and parameters, for example:

```
print (file : File)
```

The messages can also have sequence numbers, though they are not required because the sequence is given explicitly in the diagram. Reply messages (from synchronous messages such as operation invocations) are also shown as arrows (using a dashed-line arrow), but replies are rarely shown. Figure 5.28 shows an example with synchronous messages, each shown with a filled arrowhead.

A message can be sent from an object to itself, in which case, the message symbol is drawn from the object symbol to itself, as shown with the Printer invoking its own Initialize method in Figure 5.29.

Figure 5.29 shows the concepts used in a sequence diagram. This introduces the asynchronous message, shown as an open-headed arrow.

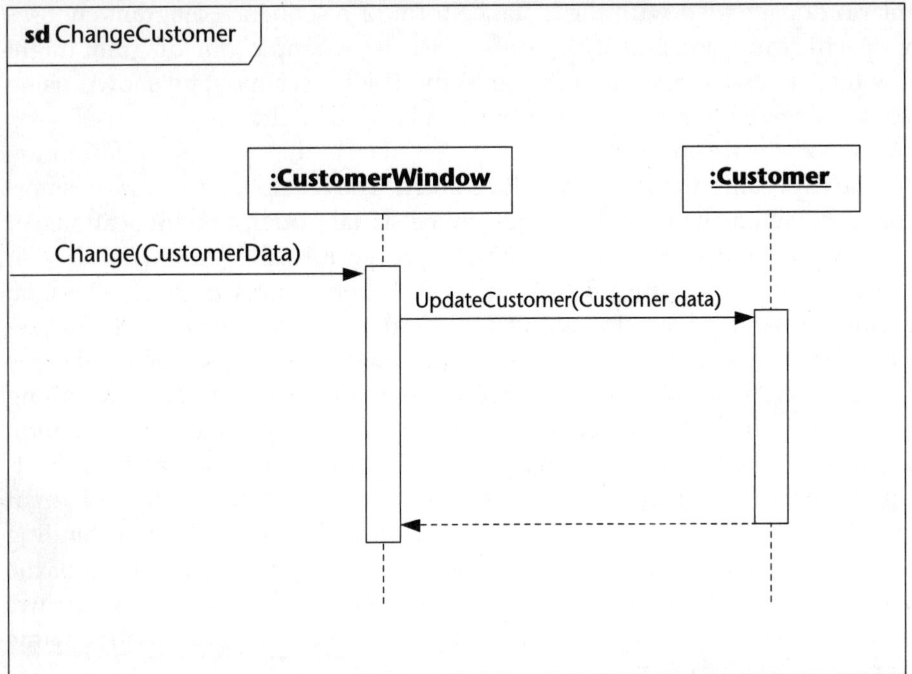

Figure 5.28 A sequence diagram with one scenario starting with the Change message. The reply from the UpdateCustomer message is shown.

Concurrent Objects

In some systems, objects run concurrently, each with its own thread of control. If the system uses concurrent objects, this is shown by activation, by asynchronous messages, and by active objects. This topic is discussed further in Chapter 6.

Combined Fragments

Sequence diagrams can be broken up into chunks called *fragments*. A combined fragment encapsulates portions of a sequence diagram. These fragments are surrounded by a frame like the one around the whole diagram; the specifier in the upper-left corner represents an operator that prescribes how the fragment is handled. Within the fragment are one or more operand regions tiled vertically and each separated by a horizontal dashed line.

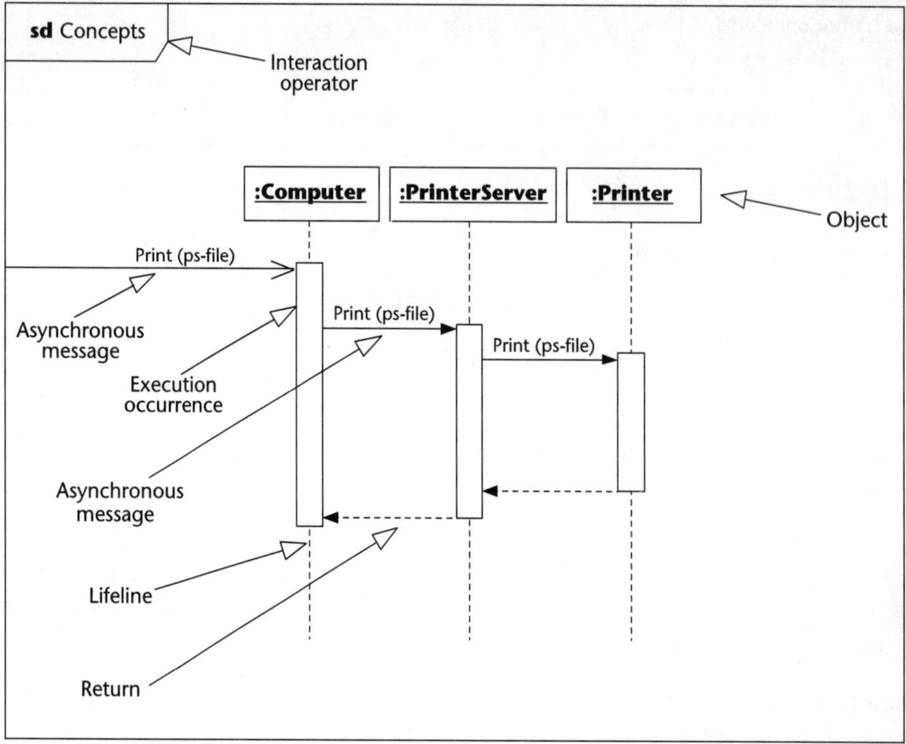

Figure 5.29 The concepts used in a sequence diagram.

When showing conditional behavior, the interaction operator keyword *alt* is put in the pentagram, the fragment is partitioned horizontally with a dashed-line separator, and constraints are shown in square brackets as has been described in previous sections. This fragment with multiple separate flows through it is called a *combined fragment*. At most one of the alternatives occurs; an else condition can be put on the final alternative to represent the negation of the disjunction of all other guards. Figure 5.30 shows a conditional fragment with two alternatives.

Loops are designated by placing the interaction operator keyword *loop* in the pentagram. Textual syntax of the loop operand is "loop ['(' <minint> [, <maxint>] ')']" or a Boolean expression can be placed in the conditional. When a loop operator is used, there is no need to separate the rest of the contents into separate operands; there is no horizontal dashed line. Figure 5.31 shows a simple example of two operations being repeated five times.

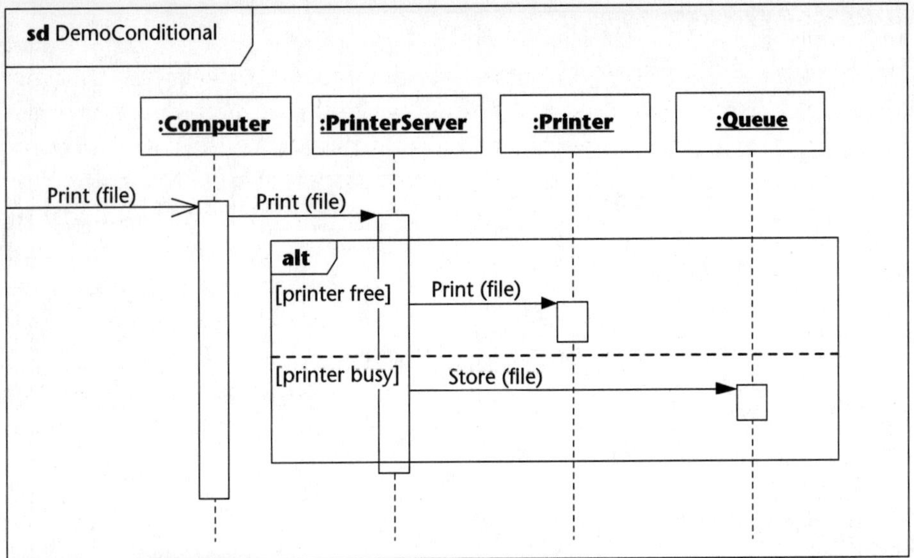

Figure 5.30 The messages from the PrinterServer to the Printer show how alternatives are described in a sequence diagram. Either the Print message to the Printer or the Store message to the Queue is sent.

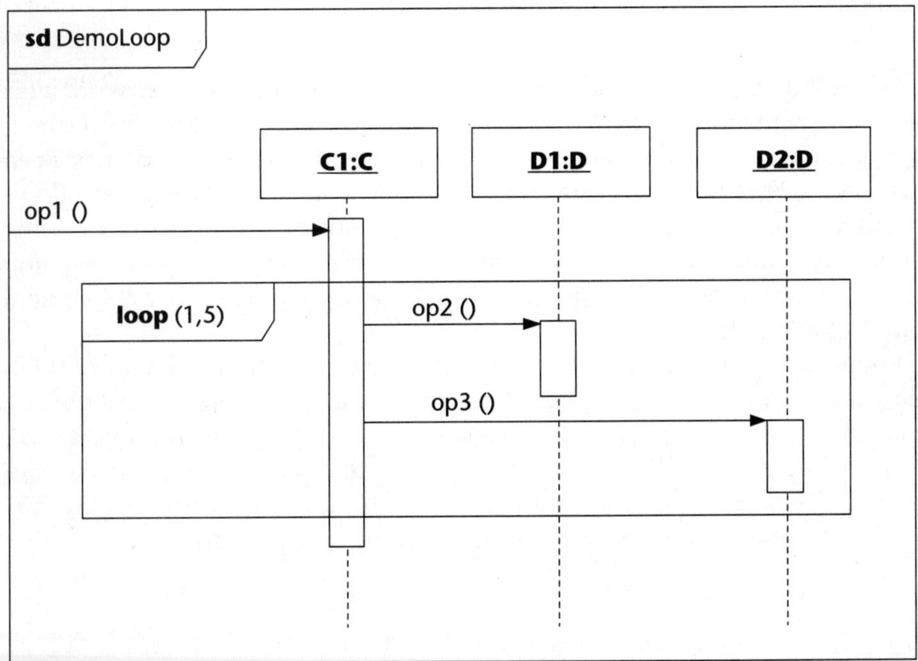

Figure 5.31 Iteration expressed with a loop operand.

Interaction Occurrences

It is common to want to share portions of an interaction between several other interactions. An interaction occurrence allows multiple interactions to reference an interaction that represents a common portion of their specification. When referencing a fragment as an interaction occurrence, the interaction identifier *ref* is placed before the name of the fragment. When one is modeling operations using sequence diagrams, the operation signature can be placed with the name in the pentagram. When one is showing such a sequence diagram as an interaction occurrence within other diagrams, the invocation of the operation with all the parameter values can be shown.

Figure 5.32 shows a simple sequence diagram for the findPrimaryKey operation on TitleMgr. The details of how TitleDAO builds the object is in a separate interaction referenced here.

Creating and Destroying Objects

Sequence diagrams can show how objects are created and destroyed as part of the scenario documented. An object can create another object via a message. The object created is drawn with its object symbol placed where it is created (on the vertical time axis). The message that creates the object is shown as a dashed-line, open-headed arrow. When an object is destroyed, it is marked with the stop symbol, a large X; the destruction is further indicated by drawing the lifeline of that object only to the point at which it was destroyed (see Figure 5.33).

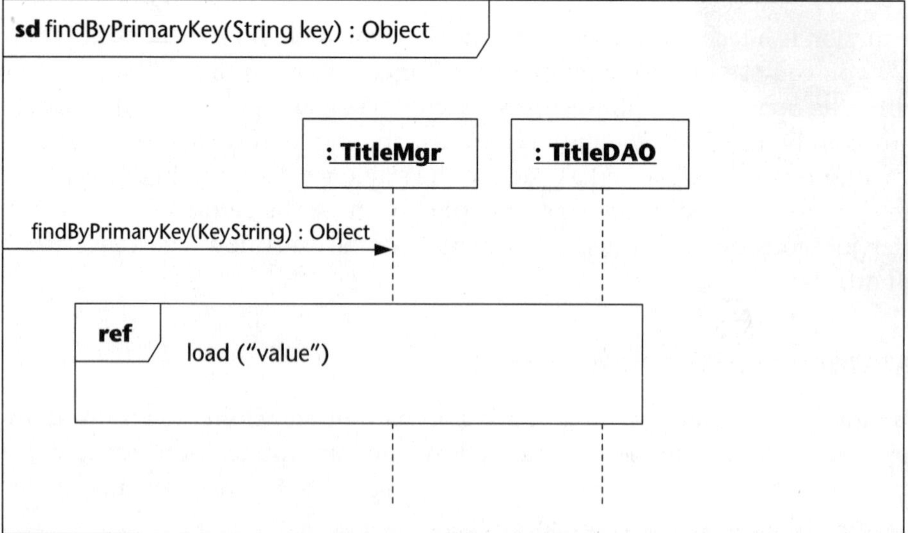

Figure 5.32 An operation that invokes another interaction.

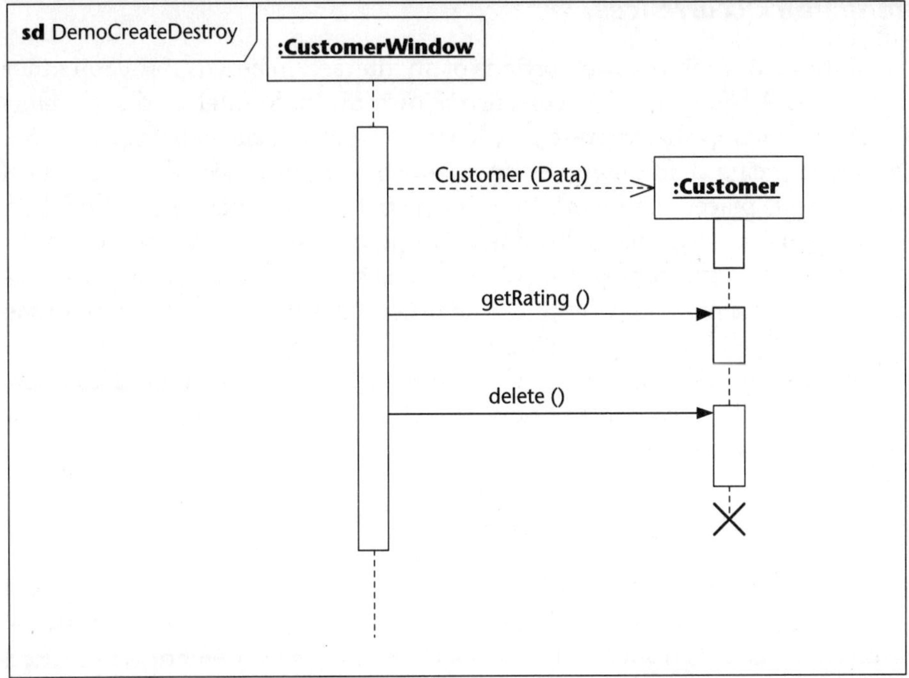

Figure 5.33 The Customer message creates a new object of the Customer class (this is typically handled by the constructor of the Customer class, which has the same name as the class). The delete operation destroys a customer object.

Recursion

Recursion is a technique used in many algorithms. If you look back at Figure 5.29 you can see an object invoke one of its own operations, Initialize, from within its operation Print. Recursion occurs when an operation calls itself, as shown in Figure 5.34. The message (when an operation calls itself) is always synchronous and is marked as such in the sequence diagram. In this case, we are showing the reply message to explicitly show the returns. This reply is often just considered implied by the bottom of the execution occurrence and is left off.

Interaction Overviews

The interaction overview diagram is a variant of an activity diagram that is appropriate to discuss here. Various flow of control nodes from activity diagrams can be combined with sequence fragments to create an interaction overview diagram.

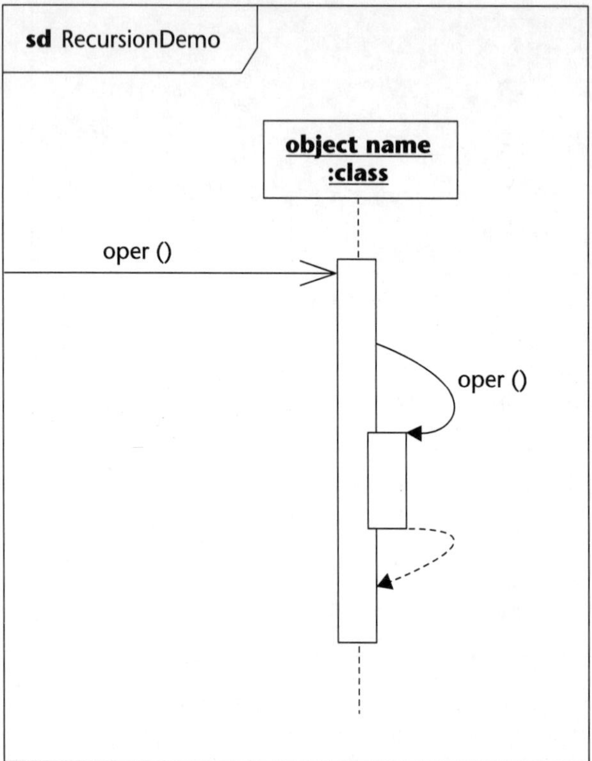

Figure 5.34 The oper () operation calls itself. There must be a condition in the operation that stops the recursion. The reply is explicitly shown.

These diagrams show how a set of fragments might be initiated in various scenarios. Interaction overview diagrams focus on the overview of the flow of control where the nodes are interactions (sd) or interaction occurrences (ref). The lifelines and the messages do not appear at this overview level. Interaction overview diagrams are framed by the same kind of frame that encloses other forms of interaction diagrams. The heading text might also include a list of the contained lifelines (which do not appear graphically). Figure 5.35 shows an interaction that just comprises references to two other interactions with some flow of control placed around them.

TIP **As a rule of thumb, the diagram is most understandable if you use just occurrences here, while keeping all actual sequence diagram modeling in detail outside of this diagram**

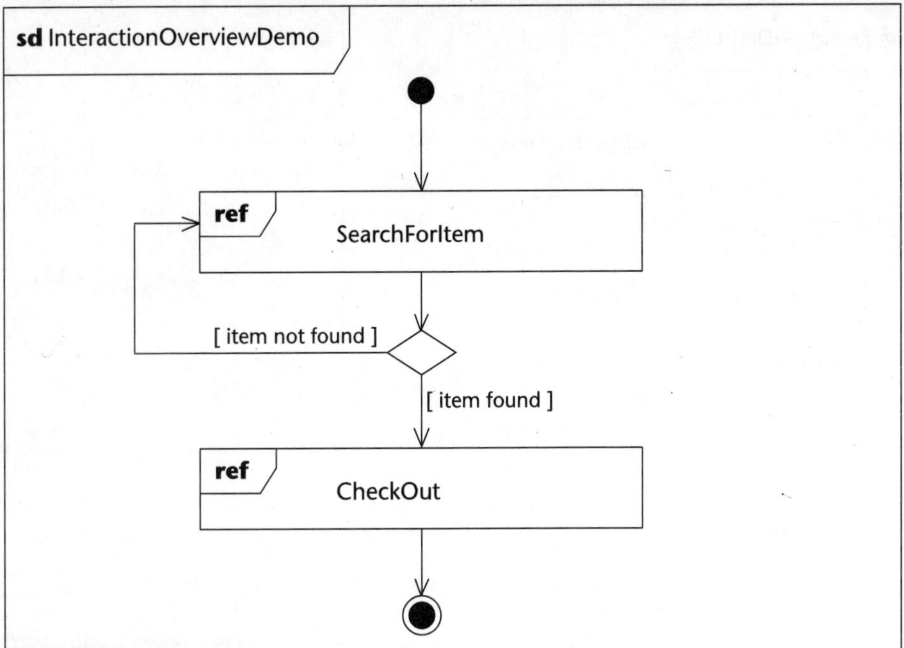

Figure 5.35 Interaction overview.

Communication Diagrams

Communication diagrams focus both on the interactions and the links among a set of collaborating objects. While the sequence diagram focuses roughly on time, the communication diagram variant focuses on space.

Communication diagrams show objects and how messages are sent between the linked objects and thereby imply their relations. The objects are rendered graphically as in sequence diagrams, but they are typically not placed across the top of the diagram. Objects are placed on the page in a way that best supports showing their relation to one another. Rather than being modeled as lines between two lifelines as in sequence diagrams, the messages are shown as lines between the actual objects. Therefore, the messages show how the objects are related to each other. The message line is not adorned with an arrowhead; instead, a small arrow is placed alongside the line for each actual message that is being modeled between the two objects. On the message arrow is a message label that defines, among other things, a sequence number for the message. The label requires a special syntax, given shortly in the section "Message Labels." Figure 5.36 shows a simple communication diagram with a set of messages initiated by any anonymous actor object.

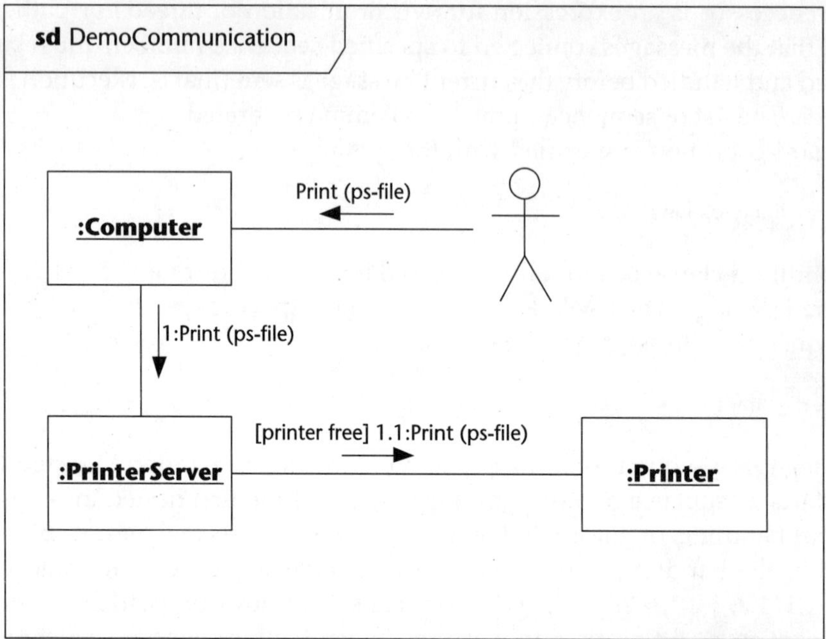

Figure 5.36 An actor sends a Print message to the Computer. The Computer sends a Print message to the PrinterServer. The PrinterServer sends a Print message to the Printer if the printer is free.

As with sequence diagrams, communication diagrams can be used to illustrate the execution of an operation, a use-case execution, or simply an interaction scenario in the system. But communication diagrams cannot show structuring mechanisms such as conditional or reference fragments.

Message Labels

A message label (the label placed on a message) in a communication diagram is specified with the syntax:

```
predecessor guard-condition sequence-expression return-value :=
signature
```

where the predecessor is specified with the syntax:

```
sequence-number ',' ... '/'
```

The predecessor is an expression for synchronization of threads or paths, meaning that the messages connected to specified sequence-numbers must be performed and handled before the current message is sent (that is, execution is continued). The list of sequence-numbers is comma separated.

The guard-condition is specified with the syntax:

```
'[' condition-clause ']'
```

The condition-clause is normally expressed in pseudocode or an actual programming language. The UML does not prescribe a specific syntax.

The sequence-expression has the syntax:

```
[integer | name][recurrence] ':'
```

The integer is a sequence-number specifying the message order. Message 1 always starts a sequence of messages; message 1.1 is the first nested message within the handling of message 1; message 1.2 is the second nested message within the handling of message 1. An example sequence is message 1, message 1.1, 1.2, 1.2.1, 1.2.2, 1.3, and so on. Thus, the numbering can delineate both the sequence and nesting of messages (when the messages are synchronous, nested operation invocations and their replies). The name represents a concurrent thread of control; this idea is discussed further in Chapter 6. For instance, 1.2a and 1.2b are concurrent messages sent in parallel. The sequence-expression should be terminated with a colon (:).

Recurrence represents a conditional or iterative execution. Two choices exist:

```
'*' '[' iteration-clause ']'
'[' condition-clause ']'
```

The iteration-clause is used to specify iteration (repeated execution), where the iteration-clause is a condition for the iteration, such as [i := 1...n]. For example, a message label containing an iteration can be shown as:

```
1.1 *[x = 1..10]: doSomething()
```

The condition-clause is normally used for specifying branches, not for guard-conditions. [x<0] and [x=>0] are two condition-clauses that can be used for branching, in which only one of the conditions is true; thus, only one of the branches is executed (sending the message connected to that branch). Both condition-clauses and iteration-clauses are meant to be expressed in pseudocode or in the syntax of an actual programming language.

The return value should be assigned to a message-signature. A signature is comprises a message-name and an argument list. The return value shows the value retrieved as the result of an operation call (a message). An example of this is the message label 1.4.5: x := calc (n) (see Figure 5.37). Examples of message labels are as follows:

```
1: display ()
[mode = display] 1.2.3.7: redraw()
2 * [n := 1..z]: prim := nextPrim (prim)
3.1 [x<0]: foo()
3.2 [x=>0]: bar()
1.1a,1.1b/1.2: continue()
```

Using Communication Diagrams

Communication diagrams can be used to show quite complex interactions between objects. However, learning the numbering scheme of messages can take some time, but once learned, it is rather easy to use. The main difference between communication diagrams and sequence diagrams is that communication diagrams show the actual objects and their relations (the "network of objects" that are communicating with their relations implied by the paths of communication), which in many situations can ease the understanding of the interaction. The time sequence is easier to see in the sequence diagram, where it can be read from top to bottom. When deciding which diagram to use to show an interaction, the general guideline is to choose a communication diagram when the objects and their links facilitate understanding the interaction and to choose a sequence diagram when only the sequence needs to be shown.

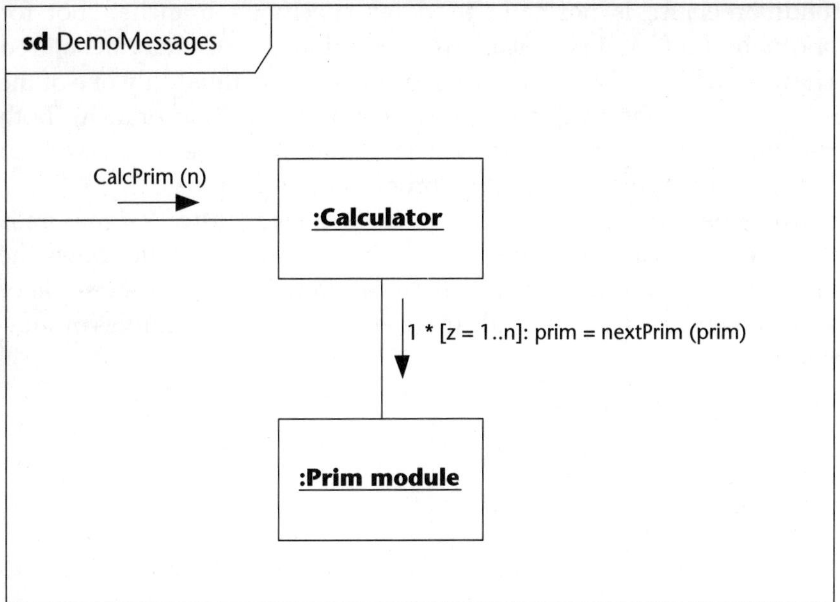

Figure 5.37 Iteration and return-value shown in a communication diagram.

Figure 5.38 shows a more complex communication diagram. A Sales Statistics window (message 1) creates a Statistics Summary object (1.1), which collects the statistics to display in the window. When the Statistics Summary object is created, it iterates all salespersons to get the total order sum (1.1.1) and the budget (1.1.2) for each salesperson. Each salesperson object gets its order sum by iterating all its orders, getting the amount for each (1.1.1.1), and adding them together, and gets its budget by getting the amount from a budget sales object (1.1.2.1). When the Statistics Summary object has iterated all salespersons, it has been created (the return of message 1.1). The Sales Statistics window then gets the result lines from the Statistics Summary object (the result line is a formatted string describing the result of one salesperson) and shows each line in its window. When all the result lines have been read, the show operation on the Sales Statistics window returns and the interaction is finished.

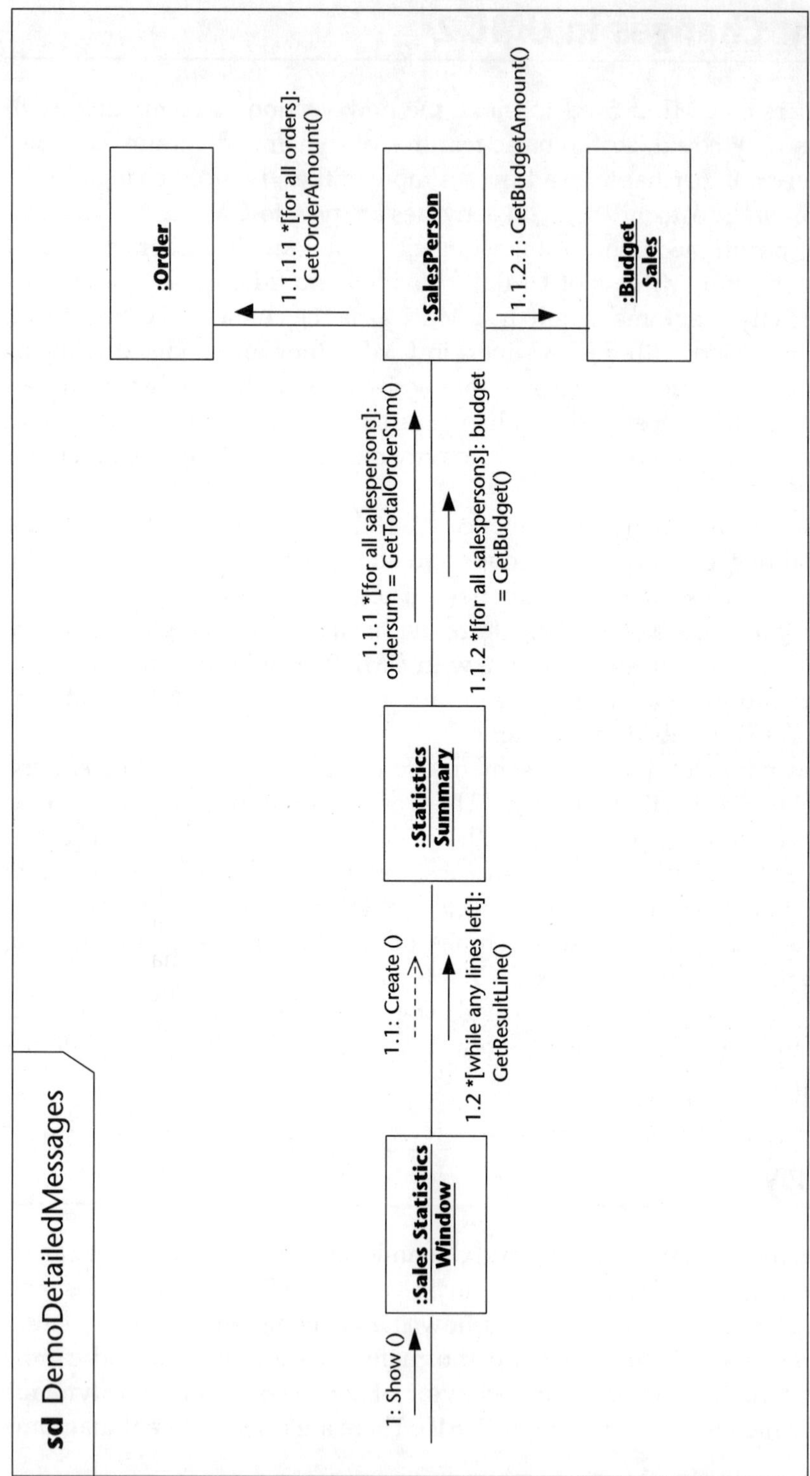

Figure 5.38 A communication diagram that summarizes sales results.

Relevant Changes in UML 2

The designers of UML 2 tried to make the new version as compatible with UML 1.*x* as they could, so the basic features of dynamic diagrams have not changed very much. Chapter 6 addresses more of the advanced changes.

Local pre- and postconditions on activities are new to UML 2. Activity diagrams were partitioned in one dimension with swimlanes in earlier versions of UML; the activity partitions of UML 2 provide extra fidelity. The Flow Final node on activity diagrams is new in UML 2 as is the connector. Object flows used to be modeled with dashed-lines; in UML 2 they are modeled with the same lines as other flows. The pins that assist in describing what makes an action start are new. Most of these changes are part of a significant increase in the depth of activity modeling. More activity modeling features are described in Chapter 6.

The notion of fragments in sequence diagrams is new in UML 2. All the related notations for representing loops and alternate sequences as well as the interaction overview diagram are new. These fragments provide clearer semantics for how the behavior transpires within a sequence diagram. And the use of interaction occurrences, also new in UML 2, enables decomposition of interactions into reusable chunks. Again, additional new features for modeling interactions are described in Chapter 6.

UML now has a defined action semantics that can be used for action expressions in a compliant action language. These action semantics were introduced with UML version 1.5 in March 2003, released during the final approval process of UML 2. These action expressions often go with transitions on state machines. State machines now have a clearer link to an action language with these defined semantics. State machines have additional features to make them more reusable, as is discussed Chapter 6.

Collaboration diagrams from earlier versions of UML have been renamed communication diagrams. They are now just considered a type of an interaction diagram.

Summary

All systems have a static structure and dynamic behavior. The structure can be described with static model elements such as classes, relationships, nodes, and components. The behavior describes how the elements within the structure interact over time. These interactions normally are deterministic and can be modeled. Modeling the dynamic behavior of the system is called dynamic modeling, which is supported by the UML. There are three different diagrams used for dynamic modeling, each with a different purpose: state machine, activity, and sequence.

- The state machine is used to describe the behavior of and the internal states within a class (it can also be used for subsystems and entire systems). It focuses on how objects over time change their states, depending on events that occur, the behavior and the actions performed in the states, and when transitions occur. An event can be a condition becoming true, the receipt of a signal or an operation call, or just passage of a designated period of time.
- The activity diagram is used to describe how things are done, the work that is performed. Activity diagrams can be used for operations, classes, or use cases, but they can also be used just to show workflow. Activity diagrams can be used to model businesses where work and workers, organizations, and objects are shown.
- The sequence diagram is used to describe how a set of objects interact with each other in a specific scenario. It focuses on message sequences, that is, how messages are sent and received between a set of objects. Sequence diagrams have two axes; the vertical axis shows time, and the horizontal axis shows the objects involved. The primary aspect of the sequence diagram is time.
  - The interaction overview is a variant of the activity diagram that uses control nodes from activity diagrams to show how sequence fragments can be put together.
  - The communication diagram is a variant of the sequence diagram that is used to describe how objects interact in space, meaning that besides the dynamic interaction, it also explicitly shows how the objects are linked to each other. No axis for time exists; instead, the messages are numbered for sequence.

CHAPTER

6

Advanced Dynamic Modeling Illustrated by Real-Time Systems

This chapter explores advanced mechanisms for showing dynamic behavior illustrated by real-time systems. We seek to provide you enough information to diagnose issues and to decide on the advanced "tool" from the UML toolkit you need. Even modelers who think they will never need real-time features will benefit from this chapter because all complex systems rely on the elements discussed in this review. UML has more advanced options than we can cover in this chapter, including dynamic modeling with components, working with Web services, and advanced development with the UML action semantics. Given the general nature of real-time issues, we concluded that this theme provides the best focus for advanced features in the complete UML diagram set.

This chapter investigates common issues in real-time systems and explores related concepts used in UML diagrams. The diagram section relies on practical examples, including an alarm system and an investment simulation game. Finally, the chapter considers advanced design and implementation issues, including suggestions on when to use the different UML diagrams.

What Is a Real-Time System?

No set definition of a real-time system exists. The term has come to stand for a system concerned with performance, scheduling, and timing. Even a simple

Internet application has real-time elements with performance over a distributed network. Any time a system must handle external events within constrained time limits, execution is concurrent, or the performance of the system needs to be "fast," you can benefit from real-time modeling features.

Attributes of a Real-Time System

A real-time system has the following attributes.

- **Timeliness is important.** The system performs its functions within specified time limits ("response time"). All specified time deadlines must be handled by the system.
- **It is reactive.** The system is continuously responding to events from the external environment that trigger the execution of the system.
- **It contains concurrently executing control processes, where different parts of the software run in parallel.** Concurrency enables an efficient utilization of the hardware and is used in creating good models of systems where external events occur in an unpredictable manner.
- **It has very high requirements in most of the non-function-related areas such as reliability, fault tolerance, and performance.** This makes almost all Internet applications in need of some form of real-time modeling.
- **It is not deterministic.** It is difficult to formally prove that the system will work in all situations under all conditions, due to the complexity of concurrency, the unpredictable events, and the hardware involved.

Types of Real-Time Systems

A real-time system is often highly integrated with its physical environment, receiving events and information through sensors and controlling devices through actuators. The system often works closely with specialized hardware and has to handle low-level interrupts and hardware interfaces, or ports. A system that involves tightly integrated specialized hardware and software is called an *embedded system*. Embedded systems can be found in cars, consumer electronics, manufacturing machines, and many other places. An embedded system often uses a small real-time operating system that uses limited memory. An embedded system must be fast enough to control its hardware and to handle all the events, even in a worst-case situation when everything happens at once.

Real-time systems are often divided into *hard* and *soft* categories. In a hard real-time system, a late (or incorrect) response is considered an unacceptable error that can result in loss of life. Examples of hard real-time systems are airplane control software, life surveillance systems, battlefield target control, and automatic train control systems. Soft real-time systems can accept a late response occasionally, for instance, in a digital telephone system: it may take a long time to connect a call, or the connection may fail; neither scenario is considered a serious or dangerous error, but they are situations the company wants to avoid. Real-time systems, then, require excellent design. How does UML address these demands?

Concepts in UML for Real-Time Systems

This section presents the basic concepts needed for modeling a real-time system in UML. Later in the chapter we show you how these are handled in UML diagrams. The mechanisms presented include the definition of active classes and objects (concurrency), communication between active objects, the synchronization of active objects, and fault tolerance.

Some real-time systems get very complex. The issues explained here are the more common. The Object Management Group (OMG) has a set of standard extensions for real-time systems called the profile for schedulability, performance, and time. This can help with advanced real-time modeling concepts, such as those involving complex latency and relative time. For more on profiles and how they extend UML, see Chapter 8. Here our focus relates to the basic issues in the core of UML that illustrate advanced dynamic modeling, not a review of advanced profiles.

CROSS-REFERENCE **For more advanced real-time features, review the profile for schedulability, performance, and time from the OMG.**

Active Classes and Active Objects

The key structure in a real-time system is the active class or object. An active class owns an execution thread so that all instances of that class, or the active objects, can initiate control activity. An active object can execute in parallel with other active objects and initiates actions by itself, in its own code or by sending messages. The active object executes its specified behavior until it is completed or terminated by an external force. The active object determines the reaction to external communication; the external object does not invoke the behavior or the active class. The active class represents the unit that executes concurrently. In contrast, a passive class has instances that can execute only when some other object performs some operation on it (sends a message to it).

Active Class Implementation

An active class usually is implemented as a process or a thread. A thread is a more "lightweight" unit of control. The important difference between process and thread is that a process normally encapsulates and protects all its internal structure by executing in its own memory space, while a thread executes in a memory space shared with other threads; this memory space can contain shared information (such as other objects). A thread may require less resources, but this means the shared resources must be managed.

Active classes are typically implemented through a class library with a superclass for the active class or an interface that an active class can implement. This superclass contains the mapping of process or thread operations such as start, stop, suspend, resume, priority handling, and so on to the corresponding operating system calls that implement these functions. See the Java implementation later in the chapter for an example.

Active Object Interactions

Once you have an object that can control a thread or process, it increases the options for interaction. With such options arise issues of communication between these active objects and the synchronization of resource usage. These concerns form the heart of real-time systems and dominate the rest of the chapter.

Active objects generally require more resources than passive objects because they own or reference a number of other objects. Sometimes a package or component is controlled through an active object that makes the package run concurrently with other packages. However, it is important to realize that even in a hard real-time system, there are a lot more passive objects than active objects. A cost is connected with creating a thread, and the system becomes overly complex and slow if too many active objects are defined.

An active class is shown in UML as a class rectangle drawn with an extra vertical line on the inside. If the name inside the rectangle contains a class name, the symbol represents an active class; if the name is underlined with a colon showing the class and the instance, the symbol represents an active object (see Figure 6.1). Without the underlining, the symbol represents an active part. When instantiated, a part functions in this context like any other active object (see Chapter 7 for composite structure diagrams and parts).

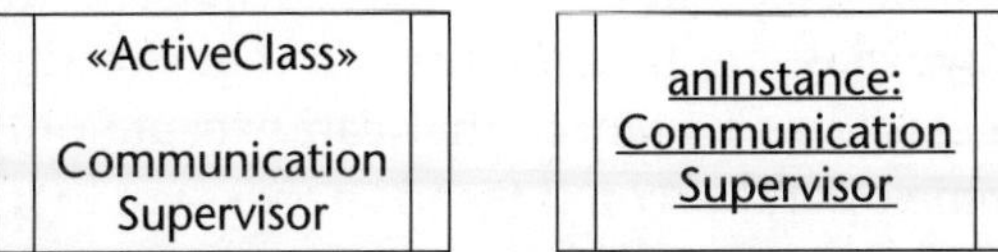

Figure 6.1 An active class and an object of that active class.

An active class, part, or object is often depicted with its internal structure embedded, as shown in Figure 6.2, and typically uses several other classes to define its internal structure. These internal classes can be both active and passive. Because active classes might manage a wide array of low-level behavior, they can have complex internal structure. Knowing the internal structure gets you to the first step in assessing a real-time system. Understanding how these active and passive objects communicate presents the next major hurdle.

Communication

Understanding the difference between asynchronous or synchronous communication is essential for real-time design.

- *Asynchronous communication* is unpredictable—that is, an event can occur at any time in the execution of the system, and it is not possible to know when a specific behavior will be triggered by an event.
- *Synchronous communication* is predictable in that it can occur only at specified times in the execution of the system (which can be identified by reading the control flow in the code).

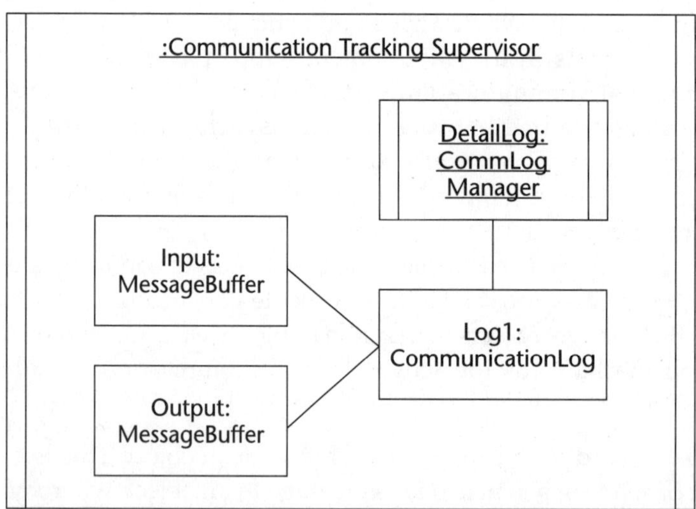

Figure 6.2 An active object with its internal structure in terms of other active or passive objects.

Passive objects normally use the synchronous approach to communicate with each other through operations (synchronous message sending). One object calls an operation (sends a message to) another object, and the calling object waits for the operation to execute (possibly along with a return value from the operation). As part of the operation call, data can pass between the objects. Such communication is not advanced. An object sends a message and waits for a return, like someone ordering a book from a mail-order company. Once a reader has ordered the book, the reader must wait for the book to arrive before he or she can start reading that book.

Of course, only a fool would stop reading entirely until the book arrived; people have libraries and other books they can read until they get the book they ordered. In contrast to the single option in synchronous communication, active classes and objects have far more communication options, so the modeling will show greater complexity. Messages will not necessarily occur in a particular order, and you need to model the system response to a message based on the current state. Depending on the priority for the book ordered from the mail-order company, when the book finally arrives, the reader either starts reading as soon as possible or puts it on the shelf for later. Of course, the decision gets more complicated if the reader gets three books on the same day. In a similar manner, systems using asynchronous communication must handle messages and triggers.

A real-time system uses both asynchronous and synchronous communication. Typically, external events in the environment happen asynchronously, while parts of the internal communication in the system are synchronous. When discussing message sending between objects, asynchronous and synchronous communications have also come to indicate whether the sending object waits for the message to be handled (synchronous message sending) or not (asynchronous message sending).

A number of strategies can be used to enable active objects to communicate with each other. Active objects must be able to execute concurrently and to send messages to other active objects without having to wait for a return value. Some common mechanisms for active object communication include the following.

- **Operation calls.** An ordinary call on an operation in an object. This is the equivalent of sending a synchronous message to an object, whereby the caller waits for the operation to finish and return.
- **Mailboxes/message queues.** A technique that defines mailboxes or message queues. A message is placed in the mailbox and at some point read and handled by the receiver. This technique allows for asynchronous messages; a sender can place a message in the mailbox and then continue to execute. This is often called the publish/subscribe model, whereby an object will send a message to a common destination and other objects will subscribe in order to get the message.

- **Shared memory.** A block of memory is reserved for communication, so that two or more active objects can write and read information. The block has to be guarded so that concurrently executing objects don't access the information at the same time.
- **Rendezvous.** A technique by which specific rendezvous points in the execution of two threads are defined. The first thread to reach the rendezvous point stops and waits for the other thread. When both threads are at the rendezvous point, they exchange information and then start to execute concurrently again.
- **Remote procedure calls (RPCs).** RPCs handle distribution of concurrent threads. The calling thread identifies an operation in an object and then furthers this request to the RPC library. The RPC finds the object in the network, packages the request, and sends the request over the network. On the receiving side, the request is translated to the format that the receiving object wants, and the call is made. When the call is finished, the result is returned in a similar manner.

To describe these strategies, modelers rely on showing communication with triggers, signals, and messages.

Events and Triggers

In UML, an event can provide a trigger to cause the execution of a behavior. An event is something that occurs in the system or in the environment. A well-designed system handles effectively the set of possible events. The behavior triggered by the event is often connected to the state of an object; the same event can cause different behaviors, depending on the state. An event can also trigger a transition from one state to another. As discussed in Chapter 5, UML defines four triggers related to four types of observable events.

- **Change trigger.** When a Boolean value expression is set to "true" because of some change, this represents a change that could trigger something for an object. So, for example, a guard condition that becomes true is considered a trigger that will have consequences. Once a change event prompts a change trigger, that change trigger remains active for the behavior until completion, even if the expression associated with the change event returns to false.
- **Signal trigger.** The receipt of an asynchronous signal can trigger behavior. Receiving a signal is called an AcceptEventAction, showing that the action will act on the event. See the section below for more detail on signals.
- **Call trigger.** One object calls an operation in another object or an object calls an operation of its own. This operation call, which is considered a

synchronous message, passes information through parameters and the return value. The call trigger represents the reception of a request to invoke an operation. The trigger indicates the behavior invoked in response to this call event, which can include state transitions or other behavior after the invocation of the called operation.

- **Time trigger.** A specified amount of time passing or reaching a specified deadline also represents an event. The time trigger can be relative to the execution of some system element. A time trigger can also respond to absolute time, such as a tax program requiring you to file by midnight on April 15.

Events can also be divided into logical and physical categories. A physical event is low level, at the hardware level, while a logical event is a higher-level representation of that occurrence. For example, the physical event "interrupt on port 4H" can be translated into the logical event "alarm from the infrared sensor device." Because logical events are at a higher level of abstraction, defining your model with logical events is preferable to defining it with low-level physical events. Physical events should be translated into logical events as close to their detection as possible. Properties such as a categorization of the event, priority, time-handling requirements, and administrative information can be defined for the classifiers that respond to the event.

Signals

Signals in UML specify the classifier passed between objects for communication. The signal can have attributes and operations to carry both information and behavior. Signals are passed between objects in the system asynchronously. On an interaction diagram, a message can represent a signal as well as an operation call. Signals can also be shown on transitions in state machines, and they can be shown on activity diagrams.

Because a signal is a classifier and a generalizable element, it uses class notation and inheritance (see Chapter 4 for an overview of generalization). These features make it possible to group a number of signals under a common superclass. A receiver of a signal can then specify that it accepts objects of a specified superclass or any of its specialized subclasses. A superclass in such a hierarchy can also contain general information about the signal.

A signal can be shown with special notation if desired. The receipt of a signal can be a rectangle with a notch in the side in the form of a triangle. The sending of a signal can be a rectangle that has a triangular point protruding from one side. A signal can also be shown as a classifier with the stereotype <<signal>>. Figure 6.3 shows a sample hierarchy of signal classes.

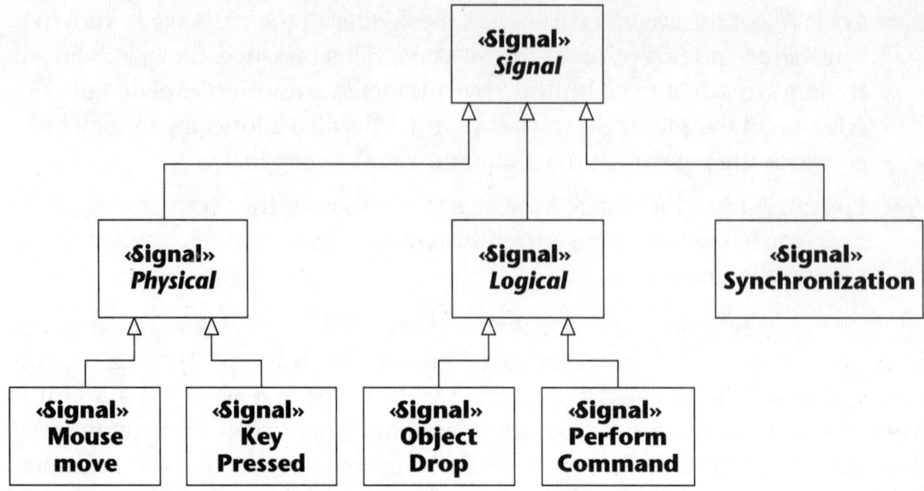

Figure 6.3 A hierarchy of signal classes.

Signals can be either logical or physical signals carrying low-level hardware information or a higher-level interpretation of what the event means in terms of the execution of the system.

Messages

Objects interact through messages. A message can be implemented by a simple operation call, or as a signal object that can be put in a mailbox or queue. A message can also be used to send a communication to create or to destroy an instance. The receipt of a message represents an event that can trigger a behavior. These messages used to communicate come in a few different types, as explained in the following:

- **Synchronous.** A synchronous message between active objects indicates wait semantics; the sender waits for the message to be handled before it continues to execute. This typically shows a method call.
- **Reply.** This shows the return message from another message.
- **Create.** This message results in the creation of a new object. The message could call a constructor for a class if you are working with Java, for example. The create message used in UML 2 has the same format as the old return message in UML 1.*x*, making this message not backward compatible with older sequence diagrams.
- **Asynchronous.** With an asynchronous flow of control, there is no explicit return to the caller. An asynchronous message between objects indicates no-wait semantics; the sender does not wait for the message before it continues. This allows objects to execute concurrently.

- **Lost.** A lost message occurs when the sender of the message is known but there is no reception of the message. This message allows advanced dynamic models to be built up by fragments without complete knowledge of all the messages in the system. This also allows the modeler to consider the possible impact of a message's being lost.
- **Found.** A found message indicates that although the receiver of the message is known in the current interaction fragment, the sender of the message is unknown.

Other message types are extensions to basic UML, such as a *balking* message (a message that is sent only if the receiver is ready to accept it) and a *time-out* message (which is canceled if it is not handled within a specified amount of time). These message types and other, similar variants can be stereotypes of messages found in a profile or implemented in some design tools as additional features. See Figure 6.4 to see how these messages are usually displayed.

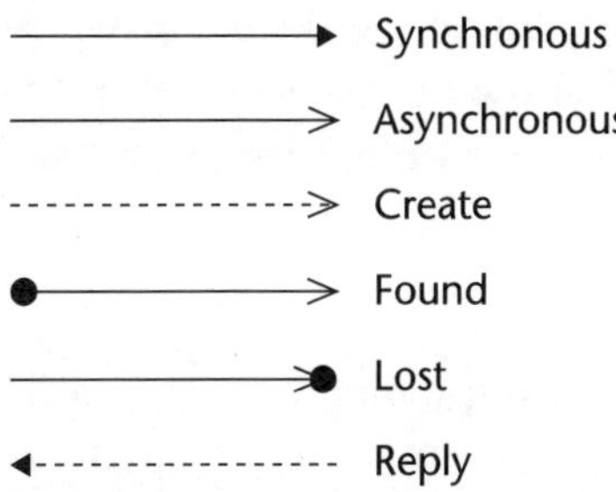

Figure 6.4 Common notation for messages.

Synchronization and Concurrency

Synchronization is the process of coordinating concurrently executing threads so that they interact effectively and efficiently. For example, threads should not try to access a shared resource at the same time.

WARNING Don't confuse synchronous communication and synchronization. Synchronization represents a coordinating activity for system resources, not messages between objects. Any system that has concurrent execution requires synchronization.

Synchronization Issues

Synchronization is not easy. A brief review of synchronization issues underscores the importance of good modeling in a real-time system.

- **Incorrect shared access.** Resources or passive objects shared between active objects can cause problems if accessed concurrently. If one thread calls an operation in a passive object, the operation could set attributes in the object, but not complete before another thread alters the same information. The attributes of the object have changed, and the final result of the operation is undetermined. What is needed is *mutual exclusion* so that only one thread at a time executes the operation and no other thread can access that operation until the first thread has finished.
- **Inefficient resource usage.** One thread might depend on another thread to make some preparation of the data it is using. The first thread might be continuously executing in a busy-wait loop, checking over and over again to determine whether the other thread is finished. This is a big waste of machine resources. A better solution is to have a synchronization mechanism to coordinate the thread with the preparing thread, to ensure that it is not scheduled to execute until it has been notified that the first thread has finished its work.
- **Deadlocks.** A deadlock occurs when a number of threads all are waiting for each other. As an example, a system could have two communication ports, A and B, guarded by some synchronization mechanism. Two threads at some point need both of these communication ports. One thread manages to reserve port A, and the other manages to reserve port B. The first thread now waits for port B to be released, and the second thread waits for port A, and meanwhile neither of them is releasing the port it has reserved. This is a deadlock, which totally stops the system.
- **Starvation.** A starvation problem occurs when one thread never gets to run. It occurs when the priorities of the threads are defined in such a way that it is impossible or very difficult for one thread to ever get control. Consequently, the task of the thread is never performed.
- **Priority inversion.** In a complex system with many objects that compete for resources locked for exclusive use, a priority inversion can occur. Objects have a priority that allows them to run, but a lower-priority object might already hold a portion of the resources needed, stalling the high-priority object. The higher-priority object still runs, but not according to the defined priority scheme.

A variety of design patterns expressed in UML address these typical issues. For a review of these design patterns, see *Real-Time Design Patterns: Robust Scalable Architecture for Real-Time Systems* (Douglass 2002). We discuss some of these in terms of managing synchronization.

Synchronization Mechanisms

The mechanisms used to synchronize threads guard a specific code block so that only one thread at a time gets access to it. The code block then contains the code to reserve or use a resource such as a device or a shared object. A mechanism could also have operations to wait for a resource to be released without continuous "busy waiting," which wastes processor resources. Typical guard mechanisms are such things as semaphores, monitors, and critical regions.

Resolving the synchronization problems described calls for the scheduling of threads, which is done through setting priorities. The simplest place to control the scheduling is in the code of the active objects, where they can voluntarily give up the control by calling functions such as sleep or by using a communication or synchronization mechanism such as a mailbox or semaphore. The programmer can control the scheduling in some operating systems, normally by setting priorities of the threads or by setting parameters of the scheduling algorithm. In a complex situation where detailed control of the scheduling is needed, a *supervisor thread* can be designed. The supervisor thread, given maximum priority, gives the control to the application threads according to the algorithm defined in the supervisor code.

In UML, the priority of an active object is most suitably noted as a tagged value of the active class. There is no predefined tagged value for such a value, but you can add it using the UML extension mechanisms. The value range depends on the implementation in the operating system.

A class or an operation can have its concurrency requirements defined with the possible values Sequential, Guarded, or Concurrent. If a property is set for a class, it affects all operations in the class; otherwise only the operation for which the property is set is affected. The meanings of the values are as follows.

- **Sequential.** The class/operation is intended only for use in a single thread of control (not concurrently by several threads).
- **Guarded.** The class/operation works in the presence of multiple threads of control, but it needs an active collaboration of the threads to achieve mutual exclusion. The threads normally have to lock the object or operation before using it, and unlock it afterward.
- **Concurrent.** The class/operation works in the presence of multiple invocations of a behavior to one instance, and these can occur simultaneously.

The built-in support for synchronization in UML can be extended using stereotypes or properties. For example, if synchronization must be indicated more explicitly, a semaphore class can be defined and instantiated to semaphores whenever the synchronization between active objects has to be shown. Another possibility is to define a stereotype <<semaphore>> that is used for all classes that should be guarded by a semaphore.

Fault Tolerance

Fault tolerance is the ability of a system to function in the presence of hardware and software failures. In many systems, a failure is simply not acceptable under any circumstances. If the software controls a missile-defense system, failure can mean the difference between life and death. The system must gracefully handle errors and be something that users can depend on. A number of techniques can help achieve this status:

- **Error and exception handling.** Certain aspects of fault tolerance can be handled through "normal" error and exception handling. Most programming languages support error handling in some form. In Java, for example, the programmer indicates what errors a certain block of code might throw, with instructions for how to handle the situation. Such exception handling can be modeled in activity diagrams, state machines, and sequence diagrams.
- **Multiple systems.** A technique involving multiple systems is used in applications, such as that implemented in the space shuttle, where both the hardware and software is doubled or even tripled. In multiple systems, malfunctioning hardware or software is directly replaced with its backup unit. On a smaller scale, a system can have a supervisor process that monitors the execution of the system; in case of a serious situation, the supervisor can take charge, causing an alarm or a possible restart of the system. Such a system can require complex state machine modeling to make sure that all states have been handled.
- **Formal proofs.** Mathematical methods used to analyze concurrent execution and message exchange can detect common problems such as deadlocks, starvation, concurrent use, and priority inversions. Such formal models can be used to detect possible error situations. As systems become more complex, such proofs become more important. As UML becomes more sophisticated, it will be easier to use your model as part of such testing.

Implementation in Java

The Java programming language has built-in support for threads and exception handling. The upcoming code shows an active class that inherits from a predefined Thread class (part of the Java API). As part of that inheritance, the abstract run operation must be implemented in the class to define the thread. An eternal loop is defined in the code, and inside the loop, some synchronous and asynchronous message sending is done. The loop sleeps for 10 milliseconds.

The thread objects are instantiated in the static main function. In this main function, two objects of the `DemoThread` class are created and started; they run in parallel execution, sharing the processor and being scheduled by the operating system. This execution takes place in a Java `try-catch` block, indicating that this will catch an `InterruptedException` to handle as an object called *e*. Using Java, the different real-time constructs are relatively easy to map to code.

```
class DemoThread extends Thread
{
    public void run()
      {
        try
    {
            // Do forever
            for (;;)
            {
                // Synchronous message to System.out object
                System.out.println("Hello");

                // Asynchronous message placed in Global_mailbox
                // Needs definition of Signal and Mailbox elsewhere
                Signal s = new Signal("Asynch Hello");
                Global_mailbox.Put(s);

                // Waits for 10 milliseconds
                sleep(10);
            }
        }
        catch (InterruptedException e)
        {
        }
    }
    public static void main(String[] arg)
    {
        // Create an instance of the active class (thread).
        DemoThread t1 = new DemoThread();
        // Start execution.
        t1.start();
```

```
            // Create another instance of the active class.
            DemoThread t2 = new DemoThread();
            // Start execution.
            t2.start();
        }
    }
```

Since Java does not support multiple inheritance, it also allows the definition of a class that implements the runnable interface. A class that implements runnable uses the interface to start the thread controlled by the active class.

UML Time Elements

UML 2 adds some simple definitions to provide common ways to handle time and durations. Any of the dynamic models can use these features. A modeler can note a single moment in time using a time observation. This assigns a time expression value to a write-once attribute, usually referenced as *t* and indicated with a line to the named element. The time expression can contain arithmetic operators. The example in Figure 6.5 shows part of a sequence diagram for the confirmation of a bid on an Internet auction system. The time `t = now` shows a time observation indicating the time of bid submission. In this case, the system does not accept a bid after the closing of the auction, which is defined as closingTime. The constraint here is on the message to submit the bid after the internal verification. A more complete sequence diagram would show the alternatives for a trace through the system that did not pass this constraint.

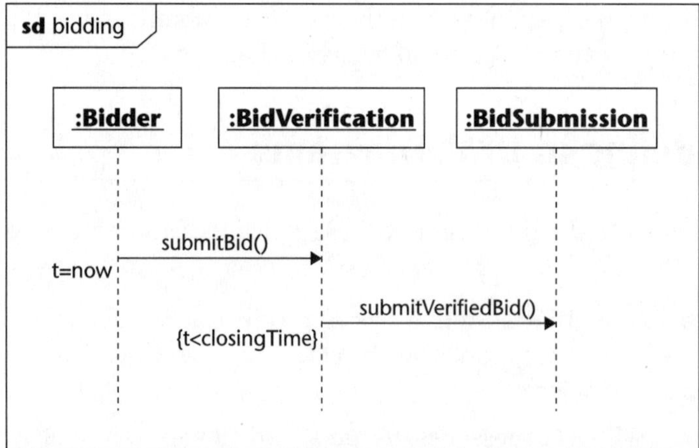

Figure 6.5 Sequence diagram with timing indicator and constraint.

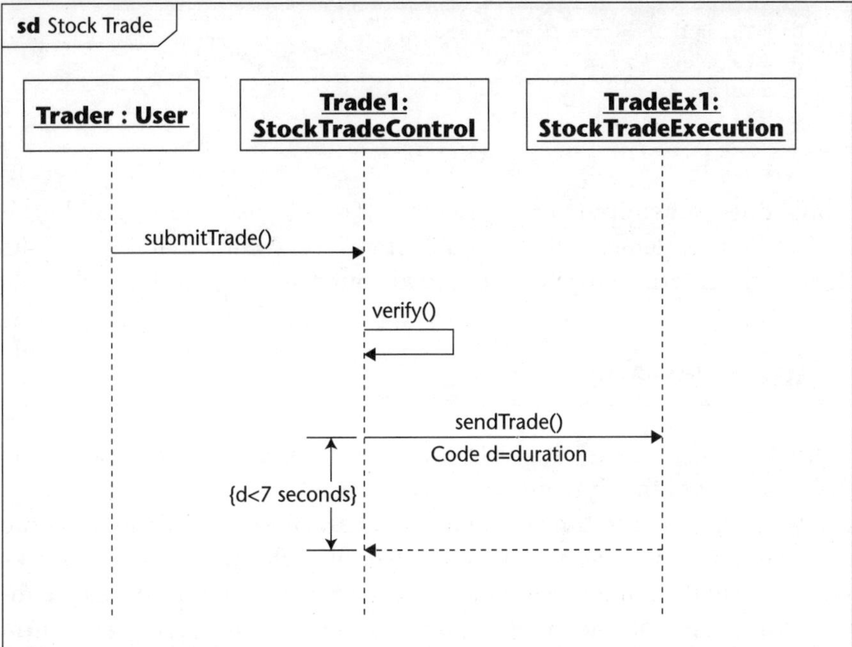

Figure 6.6 Sequence diagram with durations and timing constraints.

In addition to observing specific points in time, UML has actions defined for observing a duration. A duration constraint allows the modeler to show rules related to the duration. In the example in Figure 6.6 showing a portion of an Internet trading application, a user must have a confirmation for executing a stock trade in 7 seconds. Note that in this example the duration starts after the submitted trade has been validated, not when the user first submits it.

These basic time features can be used in all behavior diagrams.

Real-Time Modeling in UML Diagrams

This section shows how UML diagrams handle these concepts, as summarized in the following list.

- **Active class and active objects.** Active classes produce active objects, which have control over execution. The objects require more system resources than passive objects.
- **Communication.** UML uses messages, triggers, and signals to model synchronous and asynchronous communication. Advanced dynamic diagrams need to show the type of messages sent between threads or triggered from asynchronous events or signals in the environment.

- **Synchronization.** Synchronization coordinates executing threads. A system requiring synchronization raises a number of issues. Modelers have come up with mechanisms to address these, such as indicating priority with a tagged value or with guarding mechanisms, such as critical regions.
- **Fault tolerance.** The complex communication and synchronization strategies in real-time systems demand good exception handling. Systems should recover effectively from all potential error situations.

This section reviews how UML deals with these issues, focusing on some practical examples of activity diagrams, static structure diagrams, state machines, protocol state machines, and interaction diagrams.

Activity Diagrams

Activity diagrams focus on the dynamic flow of a system. While interaction diagrams focus on messages between instances and state machines show the life-cycle progress of a classifier, activity diagrams capture movement and process without having to reference a class or object. Activity diagrams provide an ideal mechanism for the review of comprehensive system requirements. In addition, activity diagrams can also convey precise technical information and link to specific classifiers, if desired. The activity diagram provides the best starting point for reviewing how UML deals with communication, fault tolerance, active elements, and synchronization. Activity diagrams did not always have such a position in the UML world.

The first edition of this book portrayed activity diagrams as the real-time weakling, stating that an activity diagram "is not as important as the other dynamic diagrams in terms of real-time specification." UML 2 changes that—activity diagrams now address complex flow. A complex flow occurs when each activity is influenced by events in the other activity, with multiple paths through the system. To take advantage of industry work on modeling concurrent systems, UML 2 imported many concepts used in Petri Nets. Developed by Carl Adam Petri in the 1960s as a way to model concurrent flow, Petri Nets model a process in terms of control tokens flowing through a system. In Chapter 5, we reviewed the basic activity diagram with pins, edges, and nodes. In this chapter, we consider what happens when many things go on at the same time and when you have to indicate how to deal with concurrent flows.

The Token Flow Model in Activity Diagrams

Activity diagrams portray multiple flows through the system with tokens. On an activity diagram that allows for multiple executions, imagine the edges, pins, and nodes of the activity diagram teeming with tokens, like amoeba in a pond or electrons moving across a wire to bring electricity to a light bulb. The elements of the activity diagrams provide rules for handling these tokens.

Although unseen on the diagram, the tokens provide the vehicle to move information and events through the system. The tokens are generic with no variation, although extensions to UML could make control tokens or tokens with their own rules. Tokens can carry objects or values. Because tokens are highly distributed, they are subject to timing and synchronization issues.

Activities have edges for carrying tokens. Activities consist of a number of actions resulting in a behavior. Ideally, you should use the same activity in many places in your model. An action inside an activity can start once the incoming control edges and input pins all have object tokens. If an action is missing one required token, then the other tokens accumulate until the system has the right combination of tokens to continue the flow. Once the action execution starts, this consumes the tokens, taking them out of circulation. On completion, the action offers tokens to the output pins and outgoing control edges. So, tokens reflect elements flowing through a system. Just because one token goes in does not mean only one comes out. The action produces as many tokens as needed to carry the elements produced as a consequence of the action's execution.

These unseen tokens provide the support structure that allows activities to communicate about complex concurrent flows. The next sections review examples to illustrate how activity diagrams model concurrency, exception handling, synchronization, and messages.

Chocolate Factory: Streaming Input and Output Example

Figure 6.7 shows the activity for boxing chocolate, which takes in individual chocolates and produces a wrapped box of high-quality chocolates. The flow begins with chocolate candy put into the system. The <<precondition>> at the top of the activity indicates that only fresh chocolate of high quality can make it into the system. An implementation that complied with this diagram would have to provide a mechanism to check chocolate quality before entry into the activity. The notation {stream} indicates that the parameter entering the activity is streaming, so we effectively have a conveyor belt delivering chocolate to the process. An activity with the stereotype <<singleExecution>> would allow only one path through the activity.

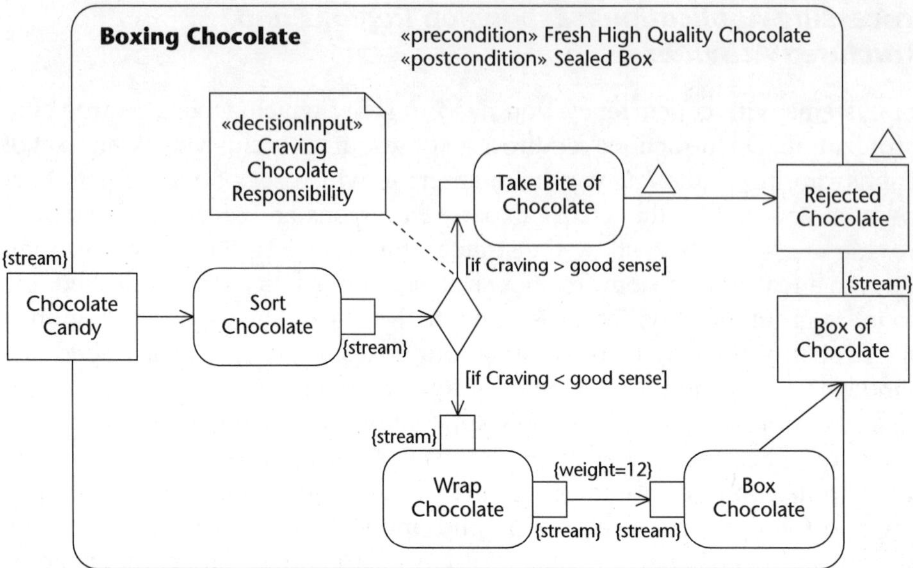

Figure 6.7 Managing the boxing of chocolate.

Some people first sort the chocolate. As the chocolate leaves this action, it is still streaming, so the output pin on the action shows {stream}. The pins all along the main flow are part of the stream, so they show {stream} as well. With no indicator, by default UML assumes pins are not a part of a stream, so you must provide the {stream} to show this type of ordering.

Depending on how much the people sorting crave the chocolates, they will take a few bites. These partially eaten chocolates show an exception in the process, indicated by a triangle along the edge that carries the exception and/or a triangle on the node for the exception. The half-eaten chocolates are moved outside the flow of high-quality chocolate to avoid boxing them with the high-quality chocolates.

The main flow sees the chocolates wrapped rather than eaten. After wrapping, those sorting then package the chocolate, with 12 chocolates in each box, as indicated on the diagram by {weight=12}. Weight indicates how many tokens are needed on the edge before the next action can execute. So, in this case, the flow does not move on until accumulating 12 tokens, with each token carrying one chocolate. The box chocolate action then executes and produces as an output, a box of chocolates. Even though 12 tokens come in, only one came out, but as a box of 12 chocolates.

Processing Applications: Expansion Regions and Structured Activities

For systems with concurrency, you need to show which actions require synchronization. Do the actions require a set of resources exclusively? Can a set of actions run in parallel? If you have an error, which set of actions gets shut down as you handle this error? Expansion regions and structured activities provide mechanisms to show the strategy for managing the synchronization issues in a real-time system. To show a structured activity, draw a dashed line around a group of activities, as is done in Figure 6.8. The expansion region, a type of structured activity, has a set of four boxes placed along the dotted line to indicate a collection used to enter or to exit the region.

The example of an organization's application-processing system illustrates a structured activity. In this example, the organization must accept an electronic application, review the eligibility of the application, store the application, and then confirm receipt of a valid application. The top section on the diagram shows an expansion region, a type of structured activity that handles the input and output of collections with multiple executions. In this case, you see the collection as two sets of four boxes on the top and one at the bottom showing the application, the personal information, and the verified applications. The italicized word in the upper-left corner shows that this expansion region allows multiple executions to the actions to occur in parallel, or concurrently. The action executions do not have to follow any ordering on the entering collections. You can also use *iterative* to show the region only allows one set of actions to execute at a time or *streaming* to show execution in the order of the collection.

The system also relies on information from a database about the person. When combined with the eligibility rules for the application, shown on the diagram as a <<decisionInput>>, the organization filters out ineligible applications and sends the application on for storage.

NOTE Take notice here that in this process it appears that ineligible or incomplete applications just go into the trash, because the diagram does not handle paths for these options. It's good practice to confirm that the client wants this model and not one that logs a rejection for an ineligible application and sends a notification. In many cases, clients want such a feature and appreciate the insight and the method that made you bring up the point. Raising such questions politely and clearly helps establish trust with the client that the modeling helps build a better system.

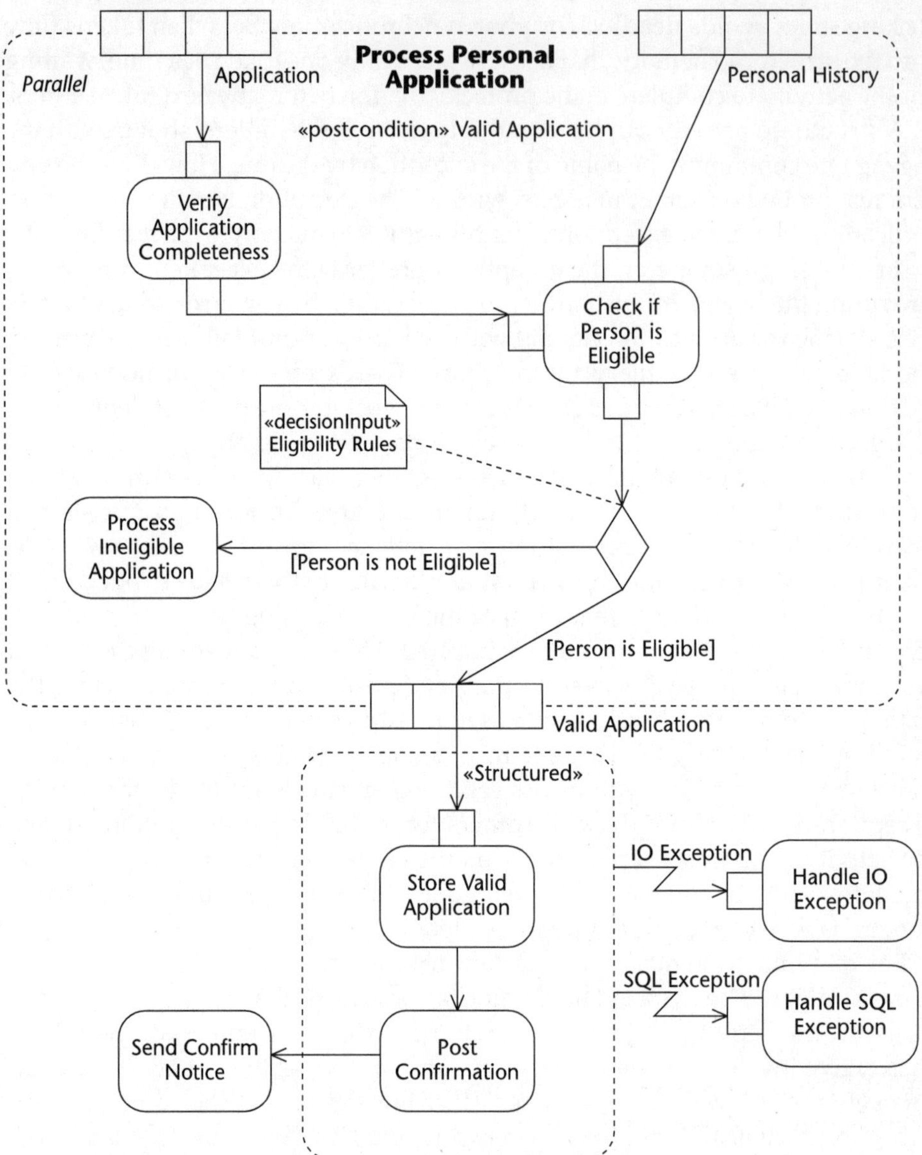

Figure 6.8 Managing applications for monetary grants.

Once it is deemed valid, the application then goes to the data warehouse for the organization. The activities for storing and posting the application take place inside a basic structured activity shown with the keyword <<structured>>. Inside this activity, the action locks any elements used during application storage and confirmation. Where users might compete for resources, locking them avoids deadlock or poor synchronization. So, when tokens flow into the structured activity, that activity takes only one token at a time, waiting for the activity to complete in the protected region before the next token enters.

A structured activity can have multiple exception handlers, shown with the zigzag line containing the name of the exception by the line. How does the system respond when something goes wrong? The exception handler shows this, indicating the type of exception it handles as it takes action to recover from the error. The small square on the exception handler is the exception input node, providing the object for the handler to work with when an error occurs. In this case storing the application can fail with an input/output failure or an error in the language used to query the database. The exception input node would include the offending language that did not work for purposes of debugging.

A modeler could display these exceptions more generally as "storage failure" to keep the model more abstract. Usually an activity diagram stays at a high level, showing the system designers the areas to focus on but staying away from explicit implementation instructions. However, as shown in the diagram, UML gives the activity diagram the ability to provide explicit detail if wanted. That said, note that most of the error handling needed for the system shown in the diagrams remains implied. Those implementing the system would need to enforce the preconditions and postconditions defined as well as manage access to the shared resources in the structured activity. Whether such details make the diagram harder to read and less valuable as a communication device depends on the type of project. Some clients want to see the explicit exception-handling design, while others leave that to implementation detail. On activity diagrams, keep the focus on the high-level flow and not the implementation details, unless you have a good reason to show that detail. Make sure to have exception handling in the detailed design.

For real-time systems, it is important to get a grasp on the exception-handling strategy. The system should not fail in a way that brings down other users. In the activity diagram, the exception firing terminates all the tokens then active inside the protected regions, shown here as the dotted line area. If this activity allowed multiple tokens flowing through at the same time, an exception such as that previously shown would shut down all other activities. General exception handling in the expansion region means a failure that stopped all processing of applications entering the system. Avoid such a situation if possible. Look to isolate or encapsulate known failure points. The handler should know how to notify the users of the problem, hopefully with information that makes it easy to recover from the problem. The handler can also go to a redundant system. In a large transaction system, such as an online bookstore or auction house, the handler can spark failover, which allows for recovery from an application server failure. In our example, for a more modest application without failover, the user receives a detailed error message telling him or her to contact the help desk or try again later.

Investment Simulation: Interruptible Regions and Storage

The third example in Figure 6.9 shows an activity diagram for an investment simulation game in which a group of players make complex investment decisions in a competitive environment. Each round produces scores that the players can review to decide if they need to change their decisions. The game manager signals the end of the round. If the game is over, the players can still review their final score. Since each action is influenced by the other actions in the system, an activity diagram is a good choice to show the flow through the system.

By default, multiple flows coming in or out of an activity show the *and* condition. In this case, the activity for managing investment decisions has two mutually exclusive entry paths. The activity diagram relies on parameter sets to show an *either/or* condition: the activity starts execution when the tokens have been collected on one parameter set or the other, but not both. The parameter set called economic information actually contains three pins, as shown on the diagram. To keep the diagram legible, the names of these three pins have not been shown, but in an automated tool you should be able to store that information even if you don't show it on the diagram. The input pins could reflect actual objects defined in the model. Clicking a pin could then provide the details of the attributes and operations of the objects entering the activity. In this case, clicking the pins shows an object for current players' scores, one for current economic indicators, and one for the set of players' decisions from the previous round. These objects ride on the tokens onto the node. The system tracks the round number to indicate if the information is current, enforcing the precondition of the activity. Once all three tokens arrive, the activity starts.

For the three pins of the top parameter set, activity execution starts by showing the current users' scores. In contrast, the parameter set final scores actually reflects two objects, one with final round scores and the other with the complete set of game decisions. Once the tokens arrive for this parameter set, the flow then goes to an activity final that shuts down the whole activity, destroying all tokens located anywhere else in the activity.

Be careful when using the activity final, because once any token reaches final, this shuts down the entire activity. However, there are times when you want to indicate the completion of one process that is a part of a number of simultaneously executing actions, such as checking out a library book, without shutting down the whole activity. When you need to show just one path through the activity, rather than the whole activity, use the flow final displayed as a circle with an X inside. Here, with final scores posted, we do want to end the entire activity.

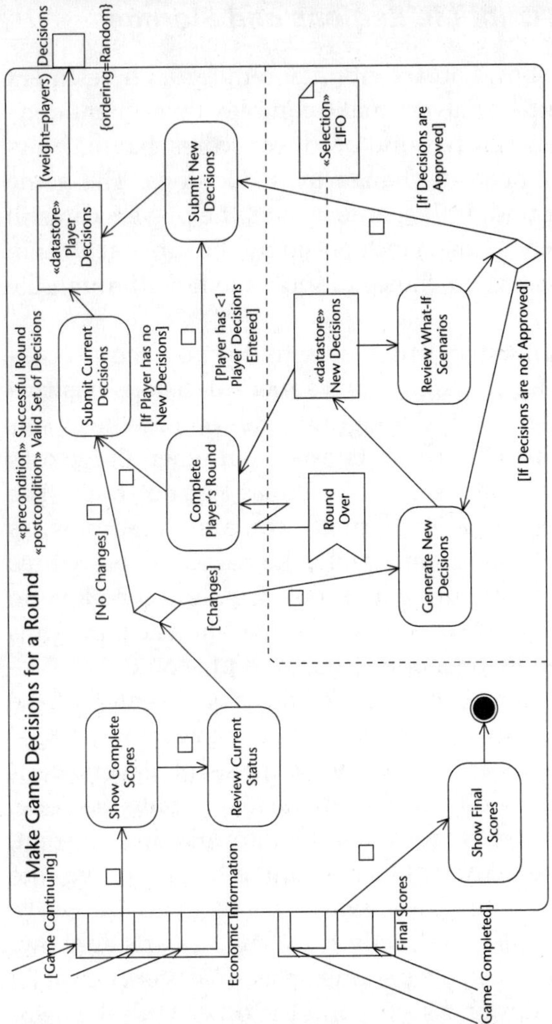

Figure 6.9 Activity diagrams for an investment game.

Back on the game path, once the system posts the current scores in an active game, players can review their status, their investment decisions, and economic indicators from the simulated economy. A number of players participate in the game, so review current status produces a number of output tokens. These tokens then move through the rest of the diagram like tiny bacteria on a laboratory slide. We could explicitly show the input and output pins, but that would clutter up the diagram. To show that the pins exist, but have been left off the diagram, show a small box on the flow, as is done in the example. A UML tool can manage the details of the objects flowing along these edges, and you can drill down to get this information as needed.

After reviewing the current score, a player decides whether or not to change his or her investment decisions. If the player decides not to change, the player submits those decisions to a datastore as the official decisions for the next round. The datastore, shown on the diagram as <<datastore>>, acts as a buffer to store objects. This keeps any decisions permanently even in the event of system failure or the end of the activity. In other words, once an object reaches a datastore, it has a more permanent home than riding on the back of a token. Even if the token disappears for some reason, the object, or more precisely the information the object contains, remains safe in storage.

Each entry into this database produces one output token to travel along the edge that leads to the output pin from the activity. This edge has a constraint that the weight, or the number of tokens, equal the number of players. The pin on the output node has ordering information indicating that a random order of players is sent on from this activity to the simulation engine. Because it is an advantage to have your decisions processed first by the dynamic simulation engine, the client does not want to set up a race to see who submits first. In the module, a player submitting first waits until all players complete their activities before moving randomly to the next activity. The player could end up waiting for a while, because players can engage in a number of activities to assess and then to create an alternate set of investment decisions.

A player can enter a new set of decisions. These decisions go into a datastore and provide a token to the activity to review the what-if scenarios. The scenarios estimate the performance of the new set of investment decisions, given user-entered economic assumptions and predicted behavior from other players. If the player does not like the new set of decisions, he or she can make another set. If the player likes what they see, he or she can submit the new decisions to the datastore, then wait along with the other players for everyone to finish. Note that if a player continually ran what-if scenarios in a loop, this would effectively halt the system. To handle this situation, the game needs a mechanism to get all the player tokens into the final datastore. The interruptible activity region provides the tool for this job by isolating activities that you need to stop.

To show an interruptible activity region, draw a dashed line setting off the activities you want to manage. This region allows for the halting of all activity when a token travels along the "interrupt edge" over the dotted line boundary and to an activity outside the interruptible region. Once that interrupt edge executes, the tokens inside the region are all destroyed. This leaves the persistent datastore, which represents a collection of stored objects, not tokens. The interruptible activity region can be used in any circumstance to isolate behavior in a real-time system. It can be an effective device for enforcing communication patterns, as in the rendezvous approach discussed previously.

In this example, the game manager presses a button to indicate that the round is over. This signal is received and handled as shown on the diagram. This signal can also be sparked by time, giving players 20 minutes to complete new decisions, for example. Having the signal controlled by a human being gives the system the flexibility to allow for different round lengths. The round over signal triggers an interrupt. When this happens, new decision building stops and the system uses the new decisions built during the round. The <<selection>> method of last in first out, abbreviated as LIFO in UML, indicates that the most recent set of decisions will be handled first. By default, the selection will be first in first out (FIFO), so if the diagram says nothing about ordering, assume FIFO.

The system, then, automatically completes the player's round for that person, using the most recent set of decisions stored for the what-if scenario or using the last round's decisions if a player did not build a new set of decisions. The conditions along the edge show these rules for how to handle each player's decisions from this activity. If a player already has decisions stored in the final datastore, then the output of complete player's round will not pass the condition to move to the submit new decisions activity. Once the number of decisions equals the number of players in the final datastore, the activity sends off the decisions for processing in a random order. Once processed by the simulation engine, the results are returned for a new round. This continues until the activity receives the tokens for the parameter set for the final decisions. The activity is then over.

Activity diagrams elegantly provide high-level information. You can use the diagram before mapping out the detailed class implementation. That said, the activity diagram can still handle technical detail. After we review static diagrams for a house alarm system, we will show an activity diagram for a detailed implementation.

House Alarm: Static Structure for Dynamic Messages

A house alarm illustrates many real-time features. The system cannot operate by synchronized function calls to objects. Instead, an alarm system requires a number of sensors with a central control that knows what to do when a sensor is triggered. In addition, the house alarm must handle failure, because it is likely that a burglar will try to thwart the system.

Static Diagrams

Figures 6.10 through 6.13 show the static diagrams associated with selected examples of a home alarm system. The system consists of a main unit with a number of sensors and alarms. The sensors detect movements in the guarded area, and the alarms generate sounds and/or lights to scare off an intruder. The total area that can be guarded is divided into cells, where a cell contains some sensors and some alarms that guard a specific area. When a cell is activated, the alarm functionality is on; when it is deactivated, it is not guarding the area.

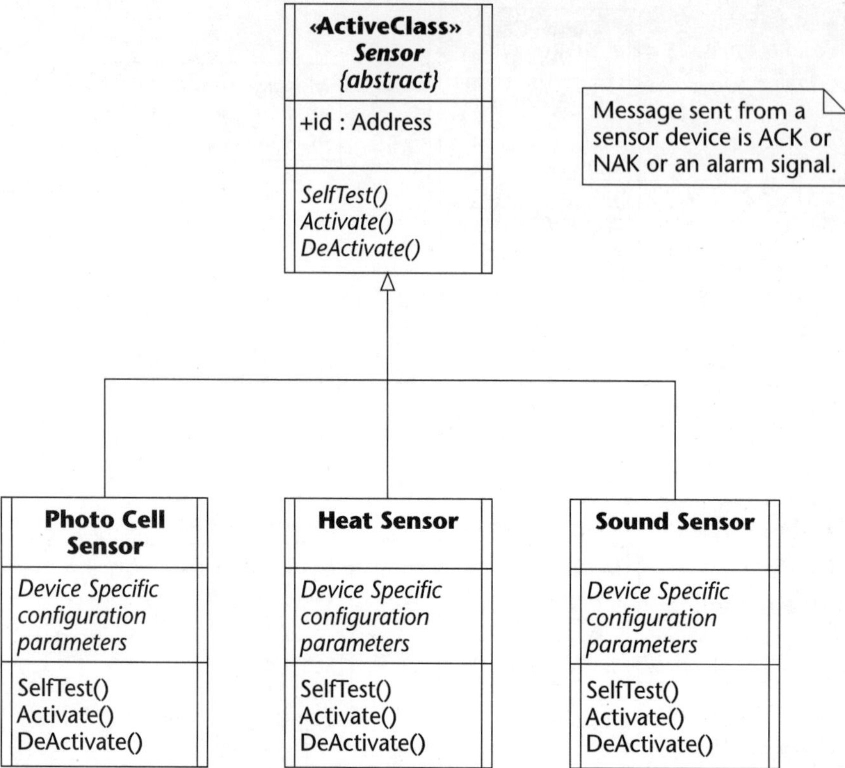

Figure 6.10 The alarm system has sensors.

The sensors detect activity in a specific area. In the model, they specialize an abstract Sensor class. The Sensor class is active; it has its own thread of control that handles the low-level interrupts from the actual device. A sensor can be activated or deactivated, it can be tested, and it can generate signals abbreviated as ACK, NAK as well as an alarm signal.

The alarms are devices to scare off an intruder by means of sound and light effects, or by calling and sending information to the police station via a phone number. An alarm can be triggered or turned off and it can be tested; the signals it can generate are either ACK or NAK. Like the sensors, the alarms are modeled as active classes that handle the low-level communication with the device. To show the full detail of that low-level communication, you can drill down into the internal structure of those active classes.

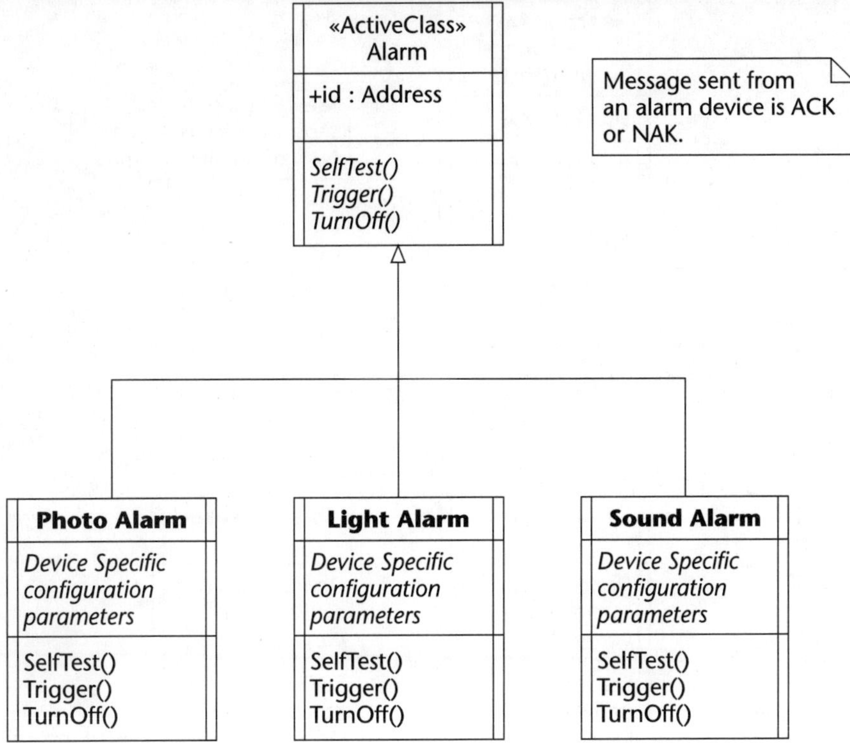

Figure 6.11 Alarms.

A class diagram of the system in Figure 6.12 illustrates how the sensors and alarms are integrated in the solution. Sensors and alarms are connected to a Cell Handler, an active class that handles a specific cell. A Cell Handler object reads its configuration from a persistent object holding the current configuration of the cell (the sensors and alarms it is connected to and other configuration parameters). The Cell Handler is connected to the System Handler, which is an active class that handles the user communication through a user panel that has a display and a small keyboard. Through this user interface, the system can be configured, activated, and deactivated. When you come home from work, you would use this to avoid having the police arrest you as a burglar, so long as you remember your password to shut the system off.

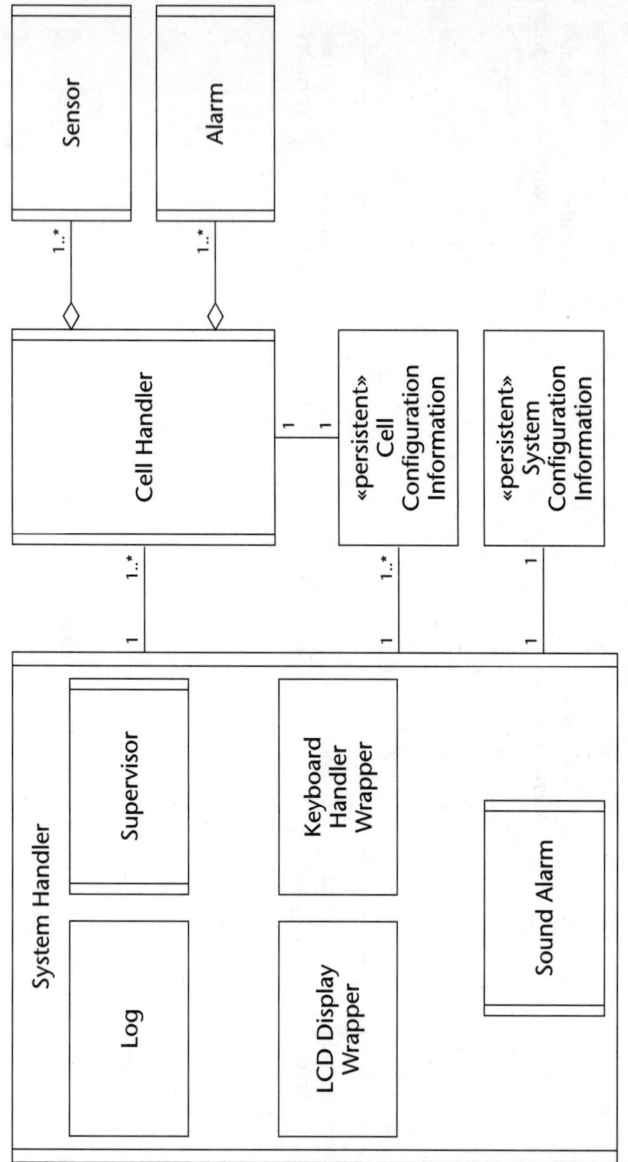

Figure 6.12 Active and passive objects in the home alarm system.

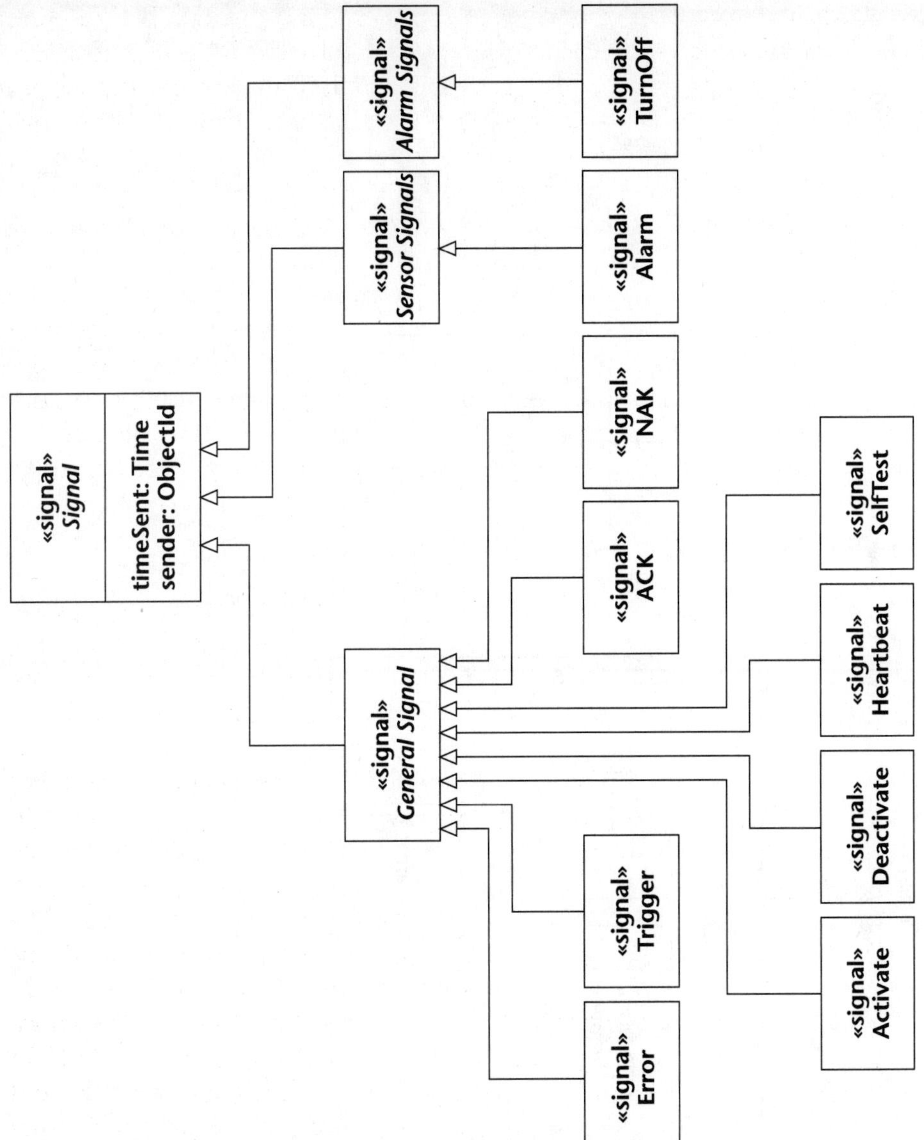

Figure 6.13 A signal hierarchy for the home alarm system.

Changes to the configuration are stored in cell and system configuration information classes. The System Handler also contains a supervisor thread, which continuously communicates with all the Cell Handlers. The supervisor performs self-tests on the devices and receives "heartbeat" signals from the

Cell Handler (signals sent from the Cell Handler to indicate that it is running correctly). It also receives an alarm signal from a cell, in which case it normally broadcasts a trigger signal to other cells, causing all alarms in the entire system to start. The System Handler has a log in which it stores all events; it also has an internal sound alarm that can be used under all circumstances, even if the connections to the other alarms have been cut (the main unit has a battery unit in case of power failure). This keeps a burglar from robbing you by first cutting the power.

The signals in the system compose part of the static structure of the home alarm system. They are collected into a hierarchy, whose organization is open to discussion. In the solution in the house alarm example, three types of signals exist: general, sensor, and alarm. The general signals can be used both between the System Handler and the Cell Handler, as well as with the devices. All asynchronous communication in the system is done using these signals.

Detailed Activity Diagram Showing Message Handling

The activity diagram can also demonstrate the sending and receiving of messages. The action state symbols can be complemented by symbols indicating that a signal is being sent or received. Dependency arrows can be drawn from these symbols to the objects that are the senders or receivers of the signals.

Although activity diagrams are usually meant for modeling higher-level concepts, they can apply to lower-level implementation details as well. For example, one possible use of the activity diagram in real-time systems is to specify the run operation of an active class, because this operation shows the concurrent behavior of the objects of that class. Figure 6.14 shows the run operation in the Cell Handler, in which the eternal thread loop can be seen. The operation waits for signals and, depending on the signal received, performs some activities to handle it. It then sends a heartbeat signal to the System Handler, requests a time-out signal from the operating system so that it is guaranteed to receive a signal in that time, and returns to waiting for a new signal. In Figure 6.14, the activities for handling the activate, deactivate, and time-out signals have been collapsed into superactivities to prevent the diagram from becoming too complex.

The activity diagram shows how these signals interact. For more detailed review of messages between instances, use the UML interaction diagrams.

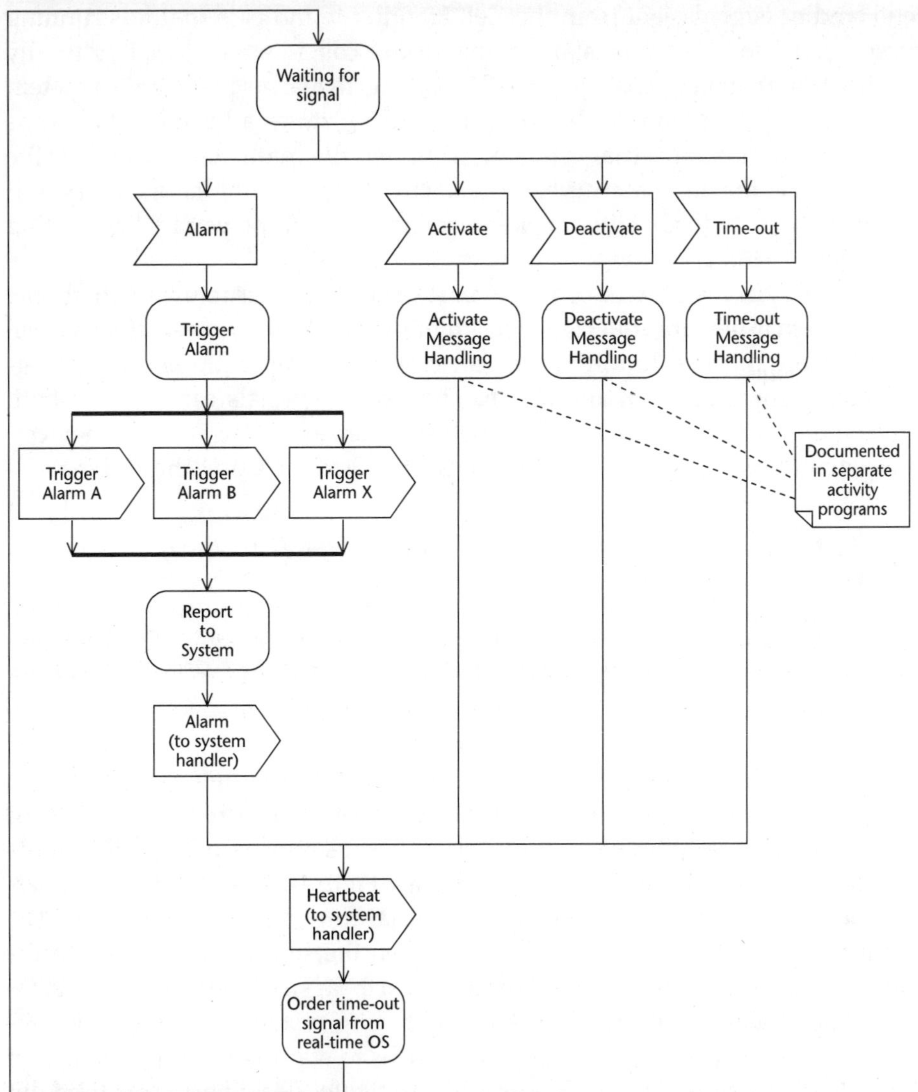

Figure 6.14 The run operation defined for the active Cell Handler class. Parallel activities can be shown in the activity diagram along with the synchronization of those activities (the triggering of alarms). The handling of the activate, deactivate, and time-out messages have been collapsed here, but they can be expanded into a separate activity diagram or an interaction diagram to show the details.

Interaction Diagrams

UML provides four types of interaction diagrams useful in advanced modeling.

- The *sequence diagram* shows objects interacting along lifelines, showing the general order of this interaction.
- The *timing diagram* shows interactions with a precise time axis.
- The *interaction overview diagram* allows a modeler to look at the interactions from a high level. These interactions are viewed on something like an activity diagram with many of the detailed elements not shown.
- The *communication diagram* shows the messages exchanged between objects, focusing on the internal structure of the objects.

The sections that follow discuss each of these diagrams in turn, starting with communication diagrams.

Communication Diagrams

A communication diagram shows both a context (a set of objects and their relationships) and an interaction (how the objects cooperate to perform a specific task). The diagram can show both active and passive objects. More than one thread of execution can be shown in the same diagram, as well as the parallel sending of messages. The message sequence is identified by numbering the messages with labels. Messages can also be nested by providing outline-style numbering and naming, so message 3.12 comes before message 3.2 or 4. Communication diagrams do not model complex systems when the reception order of messages is unknown at design time. Such systems require advanced sequence diagrams with combined fragments (discussed later in the chapter). A communication diagram is excellent for showing the interaction between a set of active objects, along with the internal structure of those active objects (often composed of passive objects).

The message types are the same as in the sequence diagram and have the same meanings and symbols. The label containing the message sequence replaces the vertical time sequence in the sequence diagram. Messages sent in parallel can be described using letters in the sequence number expression. For example, the sequence numbers 2.1a and 2.1b of two messages in the communication diagram indicate that those messages are sent in parallel. The message label can also implicitly contain synchronization information through the predecessor specification. A predecessor specifies other messages that must be performed before the message flow is enabled (that is, the message is sent). That means that the predecessor can be used to synchronize active objects so that the work is performed in the right order even if several active objects execute concurrently. A message label can also have a guard condition requiring that a resource be available before it is used.

Consider the house alarm system discussed earlier. The communication diagram for the alarm system provides a good example of how a system can mix synchronous and asynchronous messages. Figure 6.15 shows the interaction when a sensor detects something. The sensor then sends an asynchronous alarm signal to the Cell Handler. Such a signal must be asynchronous given the requirements of a sensor, which does not need to wait for a return signal and is used to alert the system to an external event. Next the Cell Handler sends in parallel trigger signals to all alarms (in this case, a phone and a sound alarm) and an asynchronous alarm signal to the System Handler. Inside the System Handler, the alarm signal is handled synchronously—the supervisor thread first calls the internal sound alarm and then writes the event to the log. A communication diagram provides a good picture of both the structure of the involved objects and their interaction.

Basic Sequence Diagram

A sequence diagram shows how objects interact in a specific situation. Sequence diagrams provide an approximation of time and the general sequence of these interactions by reading the diagram from top to bottom. The sequence diagram has no units associated with the amount of space used on the diagram from top to bottom, which is why the description of time is notional.

In the sequence diagram, communication between the objects can be shown with distinct message types. A synchronous message indicates wait semantics. An asynchronous message reveals that the sending object does not wait, but continues to execute immediately after having sent the message (any result is typically sent back as an asynchronous message as well). Transmission delays can be depicted by a slanted message arrow, indicating that the message is received at a later time than when it is sent (the maximum duration can be specified as a constraint, as in Figure 6.6 earlier in the chapter).

CROSS-REFERENCE **The branching, iteration, recursion, creation, and destruction of objects have the same notation as they do for systems that don't model concurrency, and are described in Chapter 5.**

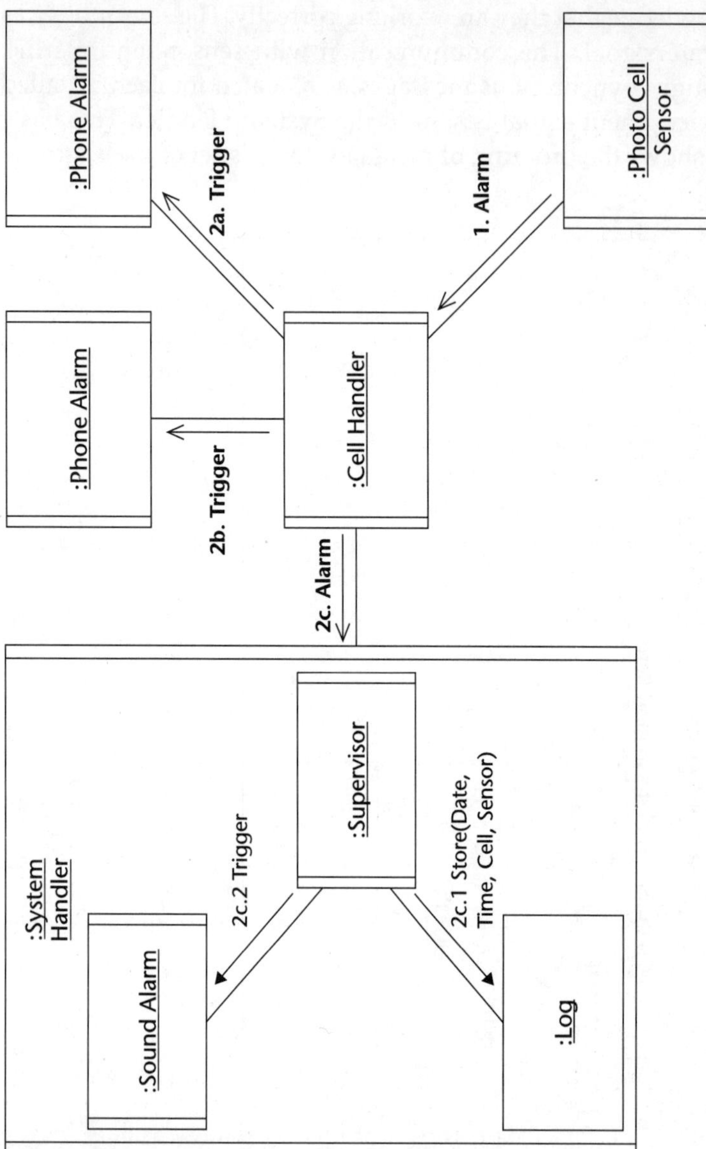

Figure 6.15 A sensor has detected a movement and initiates an alarm in the system that is documented in a communication diagram.

With the home alarm system, we can review the activation sequence. Figure 6.16 provides a sequence diagram showing one path, or trace, through the system, whereby the System Handler gives an order to the Cell Handler to activate itself. The Cell Handler then sends a synchronous message (makes an operation call) to the Cell Configuration object asking for information; it returns the configuration data. The Cell Handler then sends self-test signals to all devices to acknowledge that they are working correctly. The sensor devices also need an activate signal. The communication with sensors and alarms, which is done through asynchronous messages, is repeated for each installed device. An acknowledgment signal is sent to the System Handler. This basic sequence diagram shows the ordering of messages for this set of messages.

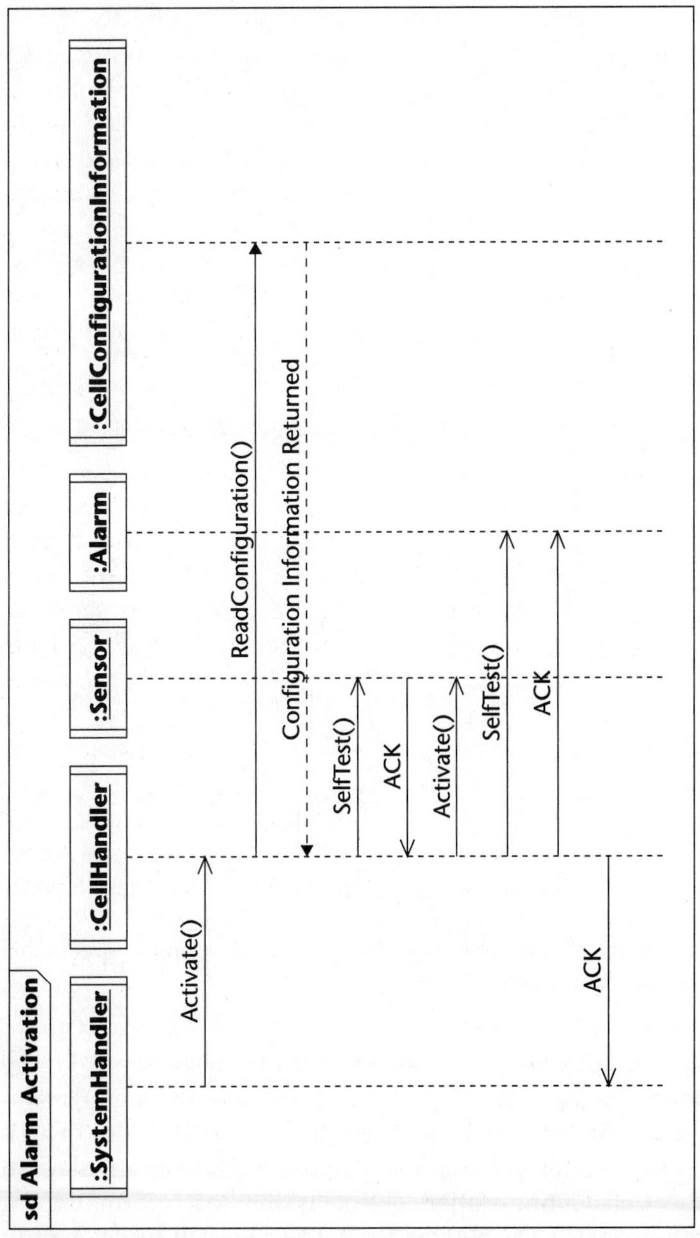

Figure 6.16 The alarm activation sequence documented in a basic sequence diagram.

Advanced Sequence Diagrams with Combined Fragments

Sequence diagrams can be broken into combined fragments of interactions. The ability to break these diagrams into separate fragments allows for substantial reuse of certain fragments and more concise models. In addition, combined fragments can take an interaction operator to indicate precise rules for each fragment. Most important for real-time systems, these rules can include sequencing guidelines and critical regions.

A modeler represents the time element on sequence diagrams by the order of the messages running down the pages. UML provides no clear definition of the units represented on a sequence diagram. On basic sequences, it is not possible to show the precise ordering of messages in the actual system, especially if response times and event triggers are unknown. Basic sequence diagrams also offer no mechanism to show when a sequence must follow an exact order. Combined fragments allow the modeler to issue instructions regarding these situations. In addition, the modeler can show an action execution on the sequence diagram, linking the specific sequence to an action on an activity diagram.

The interaction operator shown in the upper corner of the interaction (the "clipped pentagon" in the corner) provides an advanced feature to define how to read the message sequence on the diagram. The operator seq on a sequence fragment indicates weak sequencing between the messages. Under weak sequencing, the order of the messages must remain the same within each operand, while on different lifelines message sending and receiving can occur in any order. Strict sequencing is shown by the operator strict. Strict sequencing shows that the message sending and receiving indicated in the entire fragment must occur in the specified order. With strict sequencing, you are sending instructions about all the events in the diagram, not just about the single lifeline. The real power of strict sequencing lies in enforcing sequence rules across multiple elements, or multiple lifelines.

Some messages within fragments or specific actions can occur in any order. The interaction operator parallel merge applies to these circumstances. A parallel merge, shown by the interaction operand "par," indicates that the events of each participant in the interaction can have messages that can be interleaved in any fashion during run time and still maintain the order of the actions. In a sequence diagram, interleaving describes a situation in which messages can come in any order within a particular action or operand. Interleaving does not mean two events happen at the same time, but that the order at a low level will not disrupt the higher-level sequence of actions. Shuffling a deck of cards provides a good example of interleaving. Once shuffled, the order of the cards in the deck is changed, but it still has 52 cards, or messages, arranged in random order. These messages reference processes that can occur in parallel; the system does not care about the sequence of the behavior so long as the end result of the action remains the same. In this case, you will complete the action of shuffling with a deck of 52 cards. The parallel merge fragment indicates acceptable combinations of concurrent messages.

Figure 6.17 illustrates sequencing and concurrency with the same basic sequence from Figure 6.16. This time, there is more detail about message-ordering rules. The first three messages now belong to a strict sequence fragment. When the system handler looks to activate the system, the next message must be reading the configuration files. Those configuration files must also return before the cell configuration can send off any other message. The next message is part of a weak sequencing operand. The messages in this operand must follow the sequence, although the alarm and cell configuration do not have to follow this sequence if they are to get other messages in a variant of this sequence diagram.

The SelfTest message sent to the alarm causes the alarm to test and to validate results it has from the police station and the electrical battery. Because the alarm gets updates from the police station periodically, it might not have to send out a test; on the other hand, it might. So the order of the messages is unclear. Furthermore, this sequence diagram fragment does not know about the police station and electrical system, so the messages in this section are "lost" and "found." The par fragment, for parallel merge, shows that these messages can be interleaved. Whatever order the tests and validations occur in, the alarm can send off an acknowledgment to the cell manager after those processes have been completed. The parallel merge fragment also happens after the strict and weak sequenced fragments. The whole activation sequence should happen within 5 seconds, as shown by the duration constraint.

The critical region operator shows the times when there can be no parallel processing with other events or messages on the lifelines, even if they are within a parallel merge. To stay with the alarm system example, this could happen during the system's effort to get a heartbeat from all the sensors, as shown in Figure 6.18. The messages responding to the cell handler that indicate all is okay can stay within the parallel merge. However, if a message comes in showing an alarm situation, the system must immediately handle that message and take control over all needed resources. The critical fragment shows the critical region for the alarm system when checking the heartbeat of the system. If the alarm system is to fulfill its primary function, or use case, of alerting you, the police, and any intruder of a problem, then the design should account for critical regions where messages get high priority.

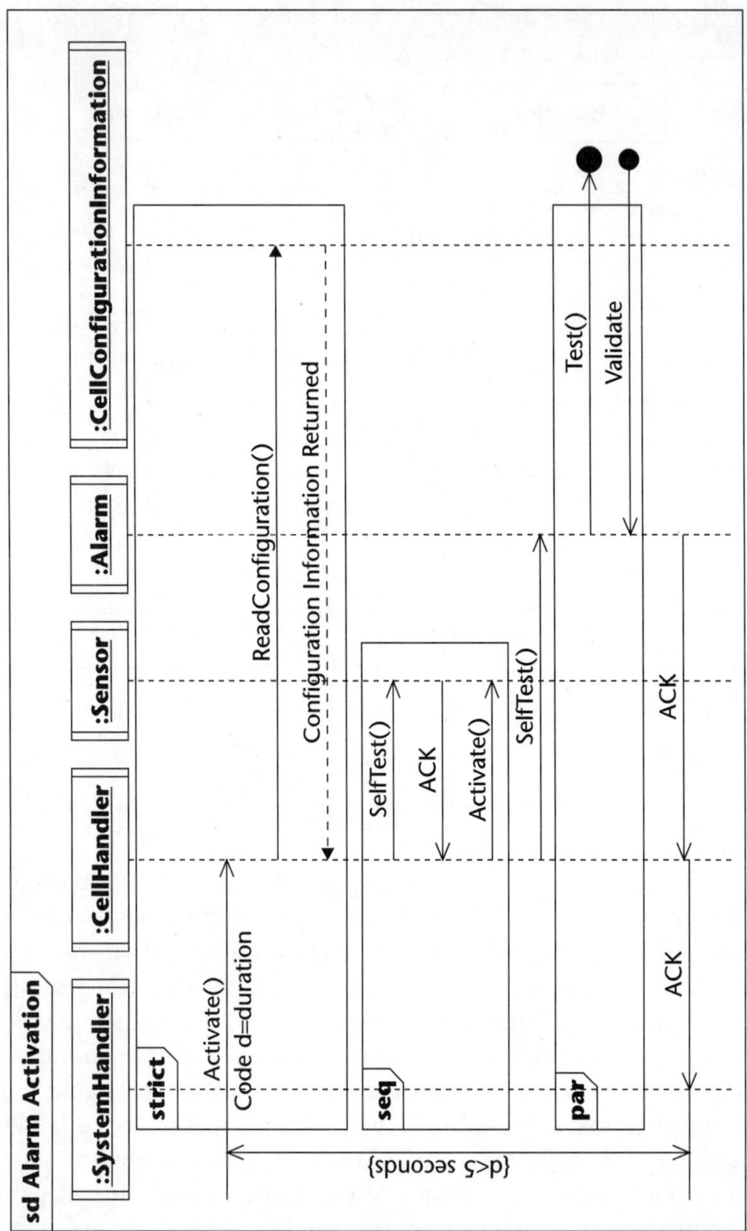

Figure 6.17 Example of strict sequencing and parallel merge in the alarm system.

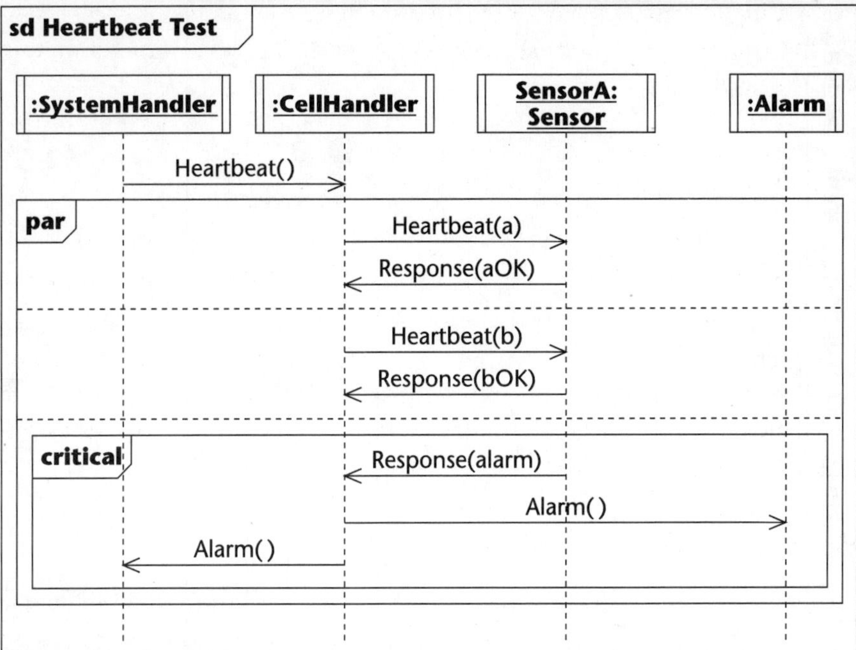

Figure 6.18 The critical region in the home alarm system.

Timing Diagrams

A timing diagram allows you to show the interaction of objects and changes in state for those objects along a time axis. A timing diagram provides a convenient way to show active objects and their state changes during their interactions with other active objects and system resources. The X-axis of the timing diagram has the time units, while the Y-axis shows the objects and their states.

Figure 6.19 shows a case where two active objects share a common resource. In this case, both objects show a trade that requires the execution engine for some time. One object is for a "platinum" user who is guaranteed a trade within 10 time units, and the other is a "gold" user who has no performance guarantee. The user objects have a waiting and executing state along with an idle state. The execution engine has a processing state that takes five time units for each trade and an executing state that takes two time units. In this case, the executing state is a strictly sequenced operation that could not be stopped, so a platinum priority user still has to wait at any point that the execution engine is in the executing state, even if a lower-priority object holds that engine. If the execution engine is only processing, the higher-priority object secures the resource, and the lower-priority object has to wait. Timing diagrams can also be expressed in a compact form where a value is written as text between two parallel lines. When the parallel lines cross, this indicates an event that changes that value.

Timing diagrams provide a helpful tool for sorting out race conditions, priority inversions, deadlocks, and other communication issues. When you are trying to sort out such complex executions, use a timing diagram.

Behavioral State Machines

A behavioral state machine identifies the range of states for a class. Unlike an activity, which can show a general process and workflow, a state machine must relate to a classifier. The other type of state machine, the protocol state machine, which focuses only on the rules for transitions linked to the environment of the classifier, is discussed later in this chapter.

Handling Active Classes and Objects

Chapter 5 reviewed the basic state machine, without reference to whether the classes and objects involved were active or passive. An active object often changes its behavior depending on some internal state (or in some cases, on the overall state of the system). The states of an active class and its behavior are modeled in a state machine. The state machine shows the possible states of the active class—which events are accepted in each state and the transition and actions performed when a specific event occurs (see Figure 6.20).

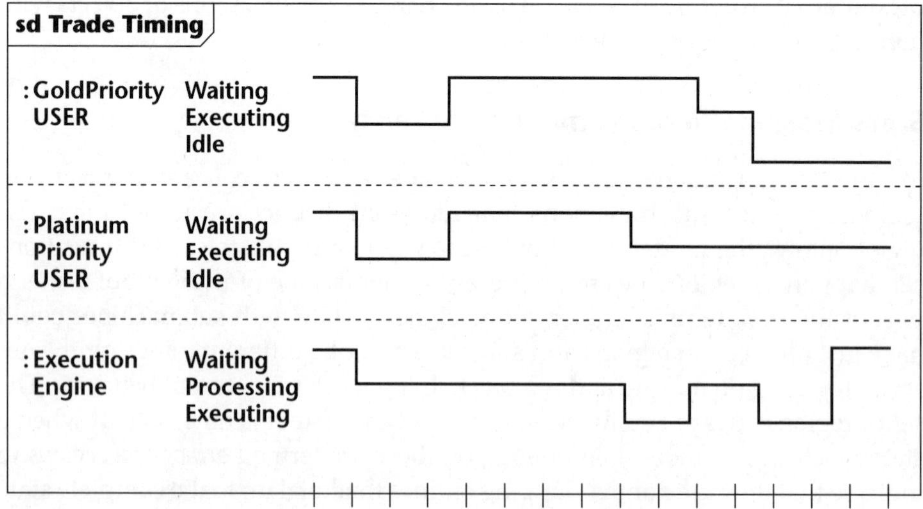

Figure 6.19 Different priority objects shown on a timing diagram.

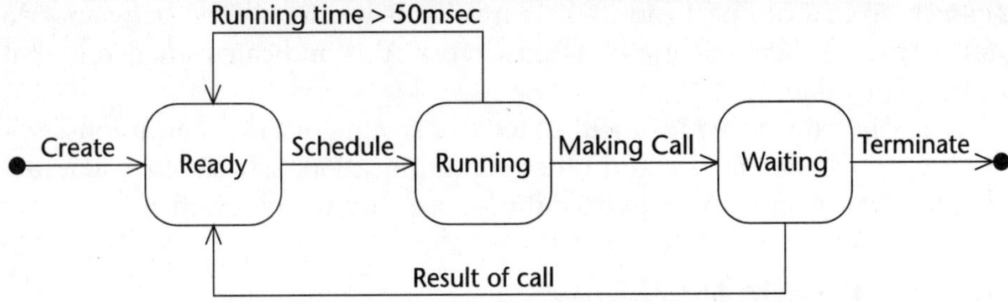

Figure 6.20 States of an active object with the triggers that cause transitions.

A state machine can also have a TimeTrigger relative to the entry of a state, showing how a state responds after a certain amount of time. For example, a TimeTrigger on a state for the final verification of an online transaction might be set to 5 minutes, so if the user does not verify the sale, a trigger fires, leading the user to a "timed out" state.

For complex systems, a state machine must consider active objects with an internal structure with both active and passive elements. To show such complexity, you can refine an active object's state into substates. UML provides the ability to model submachines and in this way indicate the rules for execution and event handling on each submachine. The sum total result of the nested submachines determines the overall state of the object. Each submachine is effectively a substate state machine with start and stop states, and each submachine can maintain a state for long periods of time (for example, for the total execution of the system). The submachines don't have to be executing in their own threads, though that is often the case. So, for active objects with complex internal structure, the state machine handles constellations of objects with defined transitions between states.

State Machine Regions and Concurrency

In order to show concurrency, state machines apply the concept of a *region* to define the states and transitions that represent distinct execution units. The region allows the modeler to show areas where a set of states and transitions can happen. A region does not represent a submachine of its own but rather a part of the existing machine or submachine. A state with submachines could have just one region: regions and substates describe different things, with substates focusing on nesting and regions helping model concurrent behavior. The set of regions always equals the sum total of the state machine, so that when a state machine has more than one region these are termed *orthogonal regions* to indicate that they are nonoverlapping entities that total up to the complete state machine. The state is then an orthogonal composite state, meaning that the state machine allows concurrent execution. To model orthogonal regions and composite states, simply use dashed lines to divide the state machines into regions. In UML 1.*x* this was a concurrent substate (see Figure 6.21).

UML allows a modeler to nest the various composite, orthogonal, and simple state machines into a complex hierarchical structure that will show how concurrent actions can happen. UML refers to such structures as state configurations. State configurations have rules for handling conflicts arising within the nested structure with concurrent behavior. Imagine a state machine diagram for a complex telephone exchange system with calls entering a variety of states, either active, waiting, busy, or delayed. When a call enters one of these states, that state is called the "active" state. Active in this context does not mean active as related to active objects and classes. Rather, in the context of state machines, a state is active when the state has been entered.

Showing which state can have activity is essential. For most simple systems with no concurrency this is not a problem: If a composite state that has just one region active, one and only one of its substates is active, so no concurrent behavior is possible. The introduction of concurrent states brings complexity, but the UML rules on this remain pretty straightforward. For an orthogonal composite state (one with concurrency), all of the regions are active if the composite state is active. Whether defined explicitly or not, each region of the composite state is entered when the state becomes active, and they are all exited before the composite state can terminate.

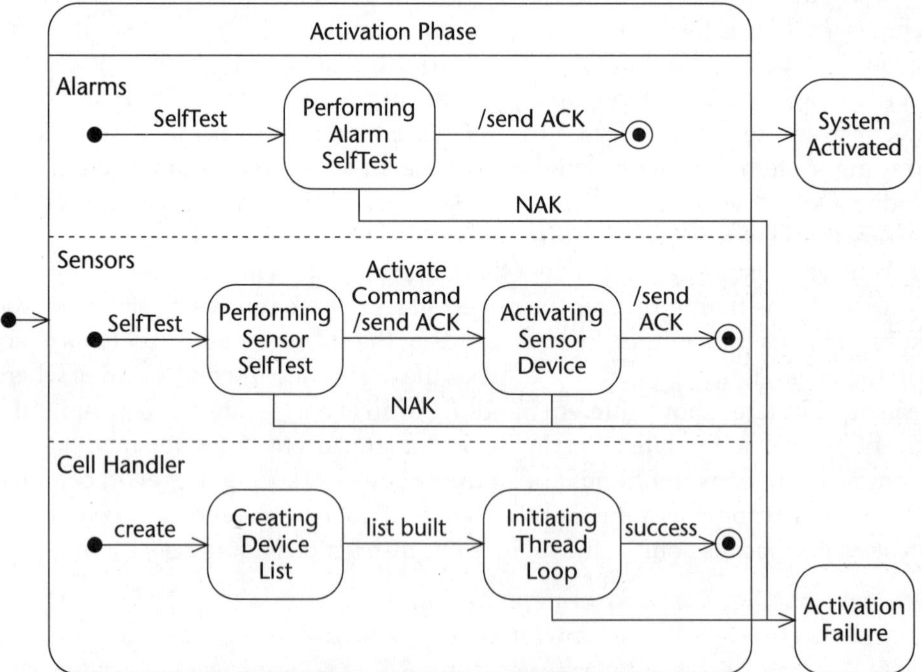

Figure 6.21 Orthogonal regions in a state machine showing an orthogonal composite state. The state machine describes the activation of the entire system.

The alarm system has concurrency, as shown in Figure 6.21. With orthogonal composite states, the submachines show the actions and states of interest for the alarms, the sensors, and the Cell Handler. Only if and when all these substates have reached their stop state has the overall state of the system been activated; otherwise, the system has been placed in an activation failure state. The substates are in this case also performed concurrently.

For concurrency, we can move from the home alarm system to another type of example. Musical notation includes a tremendous variety of timing signals designed to allow cooperation among different musicians. In many ways, the idea behind complex real-time modeling is not that different. Musical notation has conquered time synchronization for centuries, so there is hope UML can advance as well. Figure 6.22 shows a group playing in concert a song along with an automated backing track; they all want to move to the state of playing at the same time, preferably while the curtain is up, the power is on, and the lighting fits their requirements. Not only that, they hope to be playing the same tune. This state machine reflects the behavior of the classifier called "Concert."

Handling Triggers on Events in Composite States

The actions inside a state machine handle events according to a variety of factors. For a system with no concurrency and no submachines, the model for this is straightforward. However, in a system with concurrent states and submachines, handling these events can become complex. Some states might defer action on a trigger, while others seek to act on that trigger, or *consume* the event. UML terms this *consuming* the event because acting can remove the event from the list of deferred events in waiting. So, for example, in a stock-trading system, one action might consume an event from a time trigger that indicates trading in a particular market has stopped, while another action defers this event.

When a substate defers an event that the composite state consumes, UML follows a scheme that prioritizes the nested states over the enclosing states. So, the substate wins this conflict. In other words, if the substate has instructions to act on the event, it does, regardless of what the other state intends. In cases where concurrent states show different handling of an event, a state that consumes the event overrides the state deferring it. So, for concurrent states, the modeler can assume event consumption if one of the regions has such a trigger. In contrast, the modeler cannot assume that an event will not be consumed in a concurrent system just because one of the regions has instructions not to act.

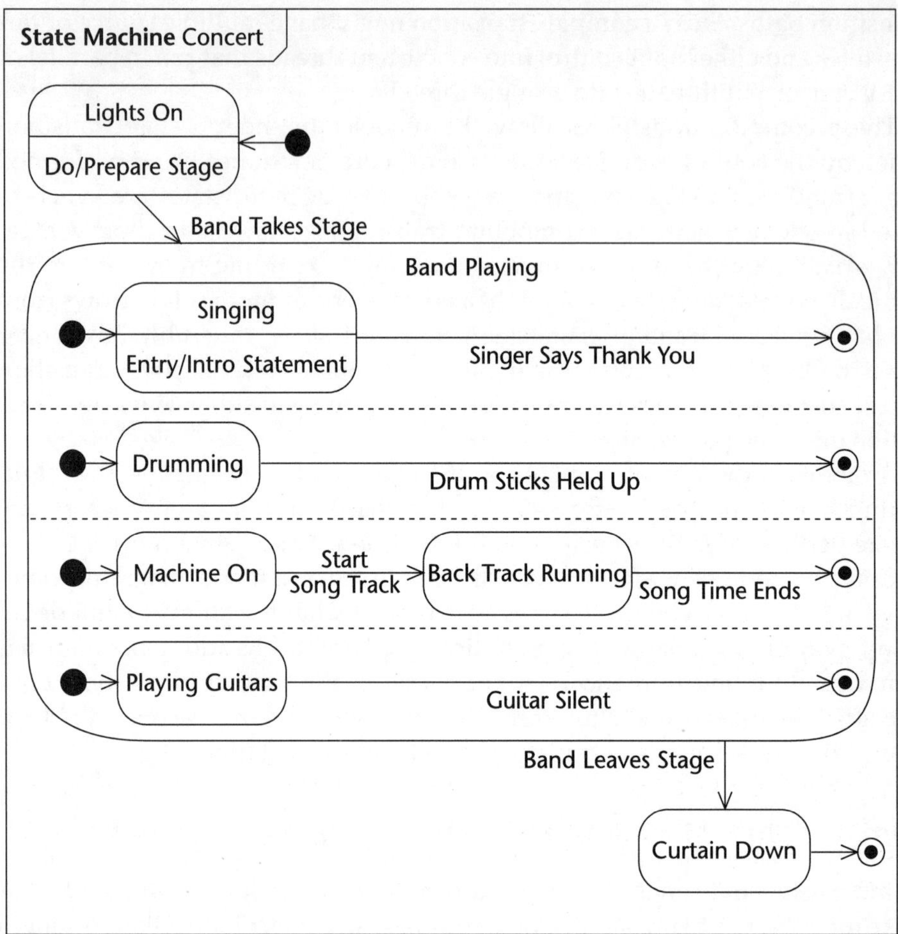

Figure 6.22 Concurrent or orthogonal composite states in a song played by a band during a concert.

Transitions and Synchronization

In composite states, transitions also require an extra layer of complexity. Any transition coming from a composite state is called a *high-level* or *group* transition. If a high-level transition has a target outside the composite state, this implies that the exit actions for that composite state execute with that transition. A high-level transition can also have a target inside the composite state that does not invoke the exit activities. UML also offers the notion of a compound transition, which will move a state machine between state configurations. A compound transition will employ joins and forks to show multiple transition paths. Such a complex transition might have multiple source or target states and either split control into concurrent threads that run in parallel or unify concurrent threads into a single thread.

These complex transitions allow the modeler to show a state transition whereby the control is divided into two or more new states being performed concurrently, or a state transition whereby two or more states are synchronized in one new state. The compound transition is shown as a short vertical bar, which might have one or more solid arrows extending from states to the bar (called the source states). It might also have one or more solid arrows from the bar to states (destination states). A transition string might be shown near the bar. Only when the object is in all of the source states and the transition guard string is true does the transition fire, which means that concurrent execution either begins or ends.

A model of the activation phase of the alarm system example shows compound transitions (see Figure 6.23). For the guard conditions, only when they all are performed is the transition to the system-activated state complete.

Complex composite states can be difficult to see on a model diagram. Sometimes it helps to model these states as composite, but not show the full detail on all models. UML has an icon to indicate that a state has additional information, usually found in the lower-right corner of the state. It looks something like a pair of glasses and should indicate two state rectangles connected by a line. Figure 6.24, shown later in the chapter, has this notation.

Complex State Machines and Run-to-Completion Semantics

Complex state machines also can require a lot of information for full and complete modeling. When you develop a complete state machine, it is important to realize whether the state has more information inside or is an atomic element. State machines have "run-to-completion" semantics. As a state consumes events, the state machine puts in motion the entire scripted behavior for that state. For example, in Figure 6.22 shown earlier in the chapter, once the "Band Playing" state has been entered, the musicians and automated soundtrack complete the song. Once triggered, a state goes until finished with its set of instructions. So, if a modeler forgets to indicate additional information, a reader can assume run-to-completion semantics. In the song example, if a modeler wants to provide the ability to stop a song, new states handling an "off" instruction or an exception event such as a cut in power to the amplifiers must be added. You could model this by showing special exit points, as is done on the submachine in Figure 6.24.

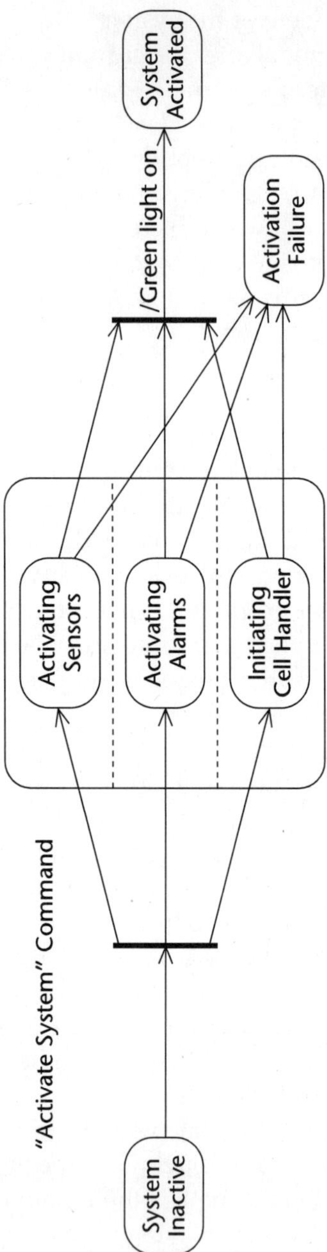

Figure 6.23 A complex transition where the control flows are divided into concurrent units that run in parallel and later become synchronized again.

To model the complete universe of options in a state machine, the modeler needs to add a number of elements and decide whether to actually show these on the diagram depending on the circumstances. Use the features that satisfy the goals of your project and provide a complete view of the system. A complete view helps those who need to maintain the model after the current project. Make sure to review the state machine in terms of run-to-completion semantics to see if the resulting behavior excludes options clearly needed, such as stopping a song or handling an application exception. The state machine might require more detailed decomposition. If you are going to use a state machine on a project, make it useful and know how complete it is. If you know you are not covering something, at least provide a stub or a note that provides this information. For the external reader, it is hard to know what is covered and what is not covered without such explanation.

State Machine Redefinition and Reuse

The object or class that owns the state machine might have parents or children in an inheritance hierarchy. When extending a state machine, the child has all the elements of the parent state machine and any additional elements desired. UML does not constrain you to the state configuration of the parent, so you can add regions and substates as needed. In cases of multiple inheritance, where a state machine inherits from more than one parent, the state machines come into the child state machine each as a region in an orthogonal composite state. In the language of states, such inheritance is also referred to as *redefinition,* where a state inheriting behavior has great flexibility redefining the parent state. For example, a modeler can redefine a state and add regions, creating a composite state or an orthogonal composite state.

To indicate an "inherited" state, draw that state with a dashed line. For an extended state machine, use the keyword {extended} on the state machine, and in a similar way to show an inherited transition, use {extended}. If you do not want to allow any future extension of a state element, use the keyword final on the state. So, for a state machine that extends a base machine, but should not itself be further extended, the keywords are extended and final. Figure 6.24 shows the concert class used previously in the chapter extended to handle a satellite feed and exception conditions while the band is playing.

Figure 6.24 includes a submachine for the band playing state with multiple entry and exit points. This submachine redefines the band playing composite state from Figure 6.22. On the state machine, a submachine has the notation stateName: submachineName. Here, In this case, the band playing state has a further-defined state machine called bandPlayingSM. That state machine provides the entry and exit point pseudostates corresponding to the entry and exit points on the submachine. In this example, the band can exit the playing state by stopping in the middle or by ending their set of songs after leaving the stage.

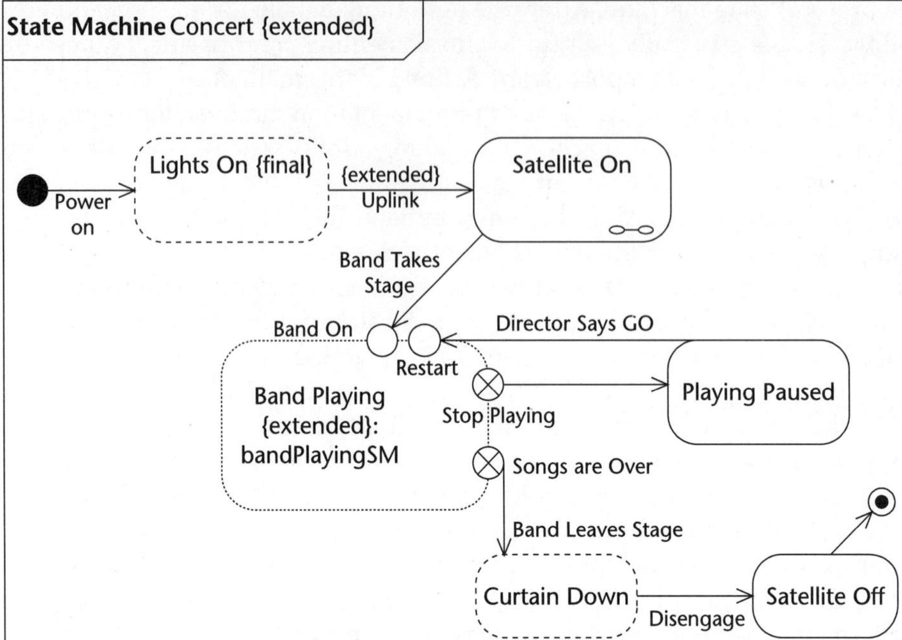

Figure 6.24 State machine with extended elements and a submachine.

The defined entry and exit points make it possible to reuse the submachine in many contexts and show alternate or exception paths. The defined entry and exit points provide convenient notation to place the submachine on other state machines. For real-time systems, this can be used to model common mechanisms or to show the ways the system handles an exception. Note that when extending a submachine, you can add entry and exit points, but you cannot take any away or rename them.

Protocol State Machines

A special type of state machine called the protocol state machine allows you to review the states of a classifier at a high level related to the environment. The protocol provides the rules for how the classifier can execute behavior. A protocol state machine can show the potential life cycle of an instance as it responds to external events. This life cycle emerges from the progression of conditions on a classifier's operations.

The protocol state machine does not define the detailed behavior elaborated inside a state; that is the function of the behavior state machine. A behavior state machine can conform to a protocol state machine, at which point the behavior state machine has valid transitions between all states that abide by the rules of the protocol. The protocol state machine usually relates to a specific interface or port, although any classifier can have a protocol state machine. Such a port, for example, has the execution ordering rules defined by the protocol state machine. After rule definition, detailed implementation can follow. This is especially helpful for implementing components, because the rules for working with a port can be defined in this manner.

Don't let the focus on the detailed implementation diminish the importance of a sound protocol state machine for making a solid system, especially where performance and time represent key features. The protocol state machine provides instructions regarding the environment, the sequencing, and the pre- and postconditions for the operations of a classifier. The transitions between states on the protocol state machine can also include guard conditions. When owned by an interface or a port, the protocol state machine indicates the rules that all implementations must enforce in order to use the feature. In the case of ports, two connected ports must have protocol state machines that conform to each other. With ports, a protocol state machine allows the enforcement of context-specific rules related to the physical environment of the deployment.

A protocol state machine should include all possible transitions for a classifier. Protocol state machines vary in the detail of the conformance rules provided. A declarative machine specifies the contract for the user of the classifier, while an executable protocol state machine includes the definitions of triggers for transitions and other details closer to the execution of code.

A protocol state machine looks much like a behavior state machine but has the keyword "protocol" placed in braces next to the state machine name. A well-formed machine includes all the legal transitions for each operation. Unexpected behavior and events can be handled in different ways, depending on the tool used; as far as UML is concerned, failure to handle all possible events indicates a poorly formed model.

A transition for a protocol state machine includes the syntax of a precondition in brackets, followed by an event with a slash and then a postcondition following the operation. The trigger for the event can be any trigger. The precondition functions as the guard condition for the operation.

The example in Figure 6.25 shows a model for a simple trading system that indicates the circumstances when a user can execute a trade. The classifier involved is the component that executes the trade. In the initial state after log in, the user can gather real-time information about stock prices. There is a guard condition, which means that the user must be a valid user of the system. They can also set up a trade and put in a bid to purchase the stock under certain constraints, namely they have to have enough money to execute the trade, shown as a guard condition on the transition to bidding. While in the bid state, the object can move to execute the trade only if the bid meets the guard conditions on the execute trade state. Trade execution relies on an active and valid connection to the trading engine. This connection can happen only under the circumstances and rules described in the protocol state machine. A component working with this system needs to know these rules, but no more detail than these rules.

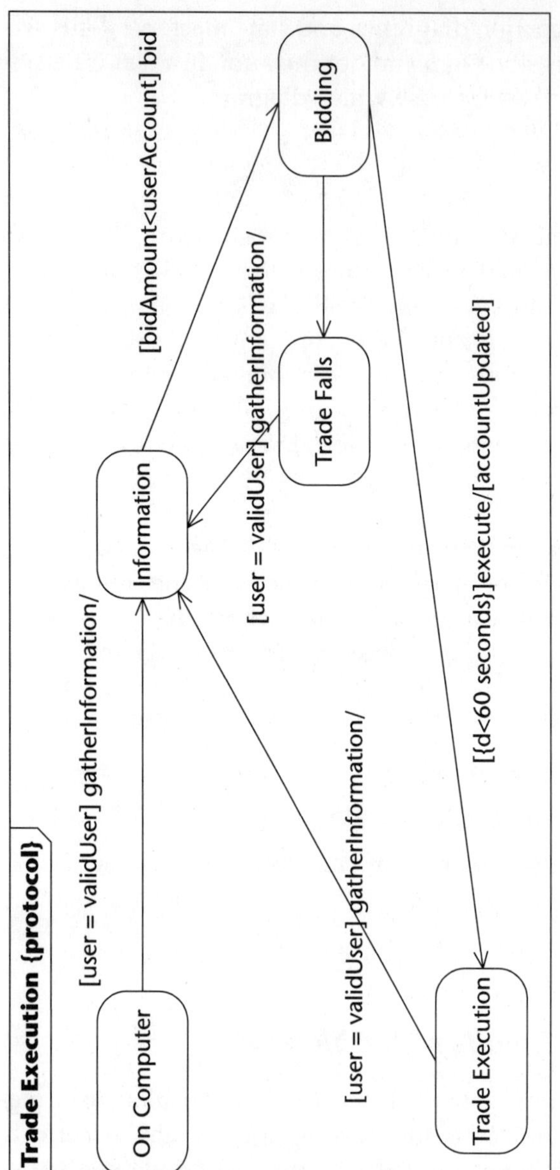

Figure 6.25 Protocol state machine for a simple trading system.

Advanced Modeling, Design, and Optimization

So far, we have reviewed how UML deals with active classes, communication, synchronization, and fault tolerance and seen how to handle these in activity diagrams, static diagrams, interaction diagrams, and state machines. This section focuses on the special issues of design and optimization in a real-time system, with general guidelines on when to use which diagram.

Design Overview

Like all other systems, real-time systems have a static structure in terms of classes and objects, which are related to each other using associations, generalizations, and dependencies. And a real-time system has a behavior that can be described using dynamic models, and a development and a deployment view that can be modeled in component and deployment diagrams. It is important to understand that even the most specialized real-time systems also have static structures and deployments, which can be modeled with UML. For deployment diagrams, see Chapter 7.

NOTE Real-time systems use more than just dynamic UML diagrams. Real-time systems require the designing of active classes and components, given the importance of optimizing system resources for performance and timely responses. This illustrates the relationship between the different diagrams.

The special design concerns for real-time systems are as follows:

- Determining the model for separating processes/threads and objects
- Identifying and defining active classes
- Mapping the real-time aspects to the implementation environment
- Using complex behavioral models to make rules about concurrency, parallel processing, and exception handling clearer

Modeling Processes and Threads with Objects

Since processes and threads are similar to objects (they encapsulate information and behavior, and communicate using messages), you can effectively model them. Concurrency in object-oriented systems can be viewed either through the explicit or the implicit concurrency model (Awad et al. 1996).

- The *explicit concurrency model* describes concurrency separately from the objects by defining processes at an early stage of analysis and then treating processes and objects as separate modeling entities. The system is decomposed into a number of processes, and each process is internally modeled as an object-oriented system to design the internal structure (naturally, classes can be reused in several processes). The process and object concepts are separated, and the system is divided so that each process is modeled internally as an object-oriented system of its own.

- The *implicit concurrency model* delays the design of concurrency. The system is modeled as objects, and in an early analysis, all objects are considered to have their own execution threads, that is, they are active objects. Gradually, through architecture and detailed design, the ideal analysis models are mapped onto an implementation with the support of services from the underlying operating system. In the end, only implement as active those objects that require such control.

Although UML can support both the implicit and explicit concurrency models, it has better support for the implicit concurrency model. Generally, for an object-oriented approach on a smaller system, follow the implicit concurrency model. The system is then totally described by active classes in object-oriented models. Active classes, asynchronous communication, and synchronization can be modeled in early phases and gradually translated into the services and capabilities of the implementation environment. For the explicit approach, this can work if you have a large system that needs a number of processes. In the explicit approach, every process is a system so process and object concepts are handled separately. In such a system, the processes are better viewed as components.

Designing Active Classes

The reasons for identifying a class as active typically are as follows:

- **Asynchronous events in the environment.** When the environment undertakes events asynchronously, and there are hard-time requirements for reacting to these events, active objects must be introduced to handle these events in the real world.
- **Periodic handling.** Work that must be performed periodically is normally modeled with active classes that sleep for a prescribed amount of time, wake up, perform their work, and then go back to sleep again.
- **Time-critical functions.** Functions dictated by time constraints can be modeled as an active class given higher priority than others.
- **Computational tasks in background.** Tasks can be considered background work, which can be performed in isolation and usually at lower priority. Such tasks include printing, collecting statistics, or doing other computational work that isn't time critical. This kind of work can be placed in an active object with lower priority, which executes only when there's time "left over" from the system's normal execution.

When the active classes have been identified, the issues of communication and synchronization immediately arise. Typically, the communication between active objects is asynchronous, while the internal communication in an active object is synchronous. Make sure that the model has protection against concurrent use for those passive objects that share two or more active objects.

Design and the Implementation Environment

An object-oriented real-time method must take into consideration the implementation environment. Sometimes, the performance requirements dictate the features to optimize in the implementation solution.

Hardware handling can be done through hardware wrapper classes, which are designed to present interfaces to the hardware and to model the capabilities and requirements of the hardware. The port (see Chapter 4) provides a modeling element to show the relationship between a classifier and the hardware environment. These hardware wrappers handle the communication protocol used with the device and the interrupts that the device can generate. Using such hardware classes enables the low-level protocol to be hidden and a low-level interrupt to be quickly translated into a higher-level event in the rest of the system.

A distribution mechanism includes packing and unpacking complex objects to and from streams of bytes (sometimes called *serializing*) that can be sent on a communication line. It also includes the task of instituting a global object identification system, so that objects can address each other without knowing exact locations. There must also be server processes or threads to enable the object to register and then resolve requests to that object into actual operations on the object.

In distributed systems today, many advanced application servers allow for "failover." When designing for such a system, you need to know which elements are serializable, where they can be moved between servers to maintain their state even with the collapse of the system.

Approaches to Showing Behavioral Diagrams

As we have seen so far, UML 2 includes support for a variety of dynamic behavior diagrams. How do you decide which to use? Few clients hire a modeler to see how well they use all the features of UML. Those who do hire based on such considerations probably won't be in business too long. A client quickly tires of model after model, illustrating the architect's arcane knowledge of UML elements if those models don't raise the system issues that need a solution for a successful project

NOTE Although many people expressed frustration that UML 1.*x* presented too many diagrams and was too complex, UML 2 did not improve this situation, but made it worse. As each diagram has improved in capability, we have seen more overlap and potential confusion among diagrams. The ability to translate these diagrams into a tabular form and exchange them using the standard format of XMI provides a long-term solution for this overlapping, though the translation is not yet fully realized in any UML tools. Common storage helps enforce the design principle of only entering information once. This approach is more efficient than duplicating information in models.

In terms of which diagrams to use, the bulleted list below provides suggestions. Whatever helps the project succeed you should pursue. Again, do not duplicate information unnecessarily. Look for the most elegant way to capture the system and communicate with the project's stakeholders.

- The *use-case diagram* references behavior through a set of activities. Use this diagram to make certain that the work remains in scope. The stickmen and circles provide a good scoping mechanism for the project, but do not have the ability to show detailed flow. Do not misuse this tool and try to turn it into a flow or business-analysis mechanism.
- The *activity diagram* provides a high-level overview of a system not tied to system classifiers. Use this diagram to show the flow of a system, even for things going on outside of the system you build. The diagram can provide a useful "you are here" map for everyone communicating about the project. In addition, the diagram can help in the definition of domain entities with the input and output pins that can link to real system elements.
- *Object diagrams* and *internal structure diagrams* can provide some important information about which classes have active behavior. These diagrams provide a required input for the interaction diagrams and state machines.
- The *interaction diagrams* can show the detailed messages that occur in a specific action or set of actions. Such detail gets very close to the code level and provides a good way to communicate about the interaction between objects. Use this diagram for review of issues closer to the implementation code. You can link the sequence to an action in your system, which lets you move easily from an activity diagram down to a sequence diagram.
- The *state machine* shows the complex life cycle of an object. Use this to review active objects or the internal dynamics of the more complicated objects in your system. Some use state machines as the core diagram for code generation.
- The *protocol state machine* shows how an entity relies not only on the environment but also on the current circumstances for execution. Use this machine to show how components work with ports in a distributed environment.

UML 2 introduced the notion of ports as well as protocol state machines, which modelers use to show how classes relate to their environment and to behavior. These new features support object-oriented methods specifically targeted at real-time systems not well supported in UML 1.*x*.

Much of the modeling with ports reflects approaches long pursued by other designers and only recently explicitly imported into the core of UML. In particular, the ROOM (Real-Time Object-Oriented Modeling) language is a mature modeling approach (Selic et al., 1994) complemented with heuristics and work organization guidelines for creating models of real-time systems. This approach provides the main influence on the ports and protocol state machines in UML 2. The language is based on an actor concept (not to be confused with actors in use cases) that is an active class. These actors, or active classes, are described as a state machine that can have nested substates. The active class is defined with interface components called ports. Each port defines a protocol: input and output messages and their legal ordering. An active class can have several ports and can thus reflect different roles of that class. Passive data objects can also be modeled, and the active classes can be placed in layers. If you review the protocol state machine, it is easy to see the influence of the ROOM method.

Other approaches that might be of interest to those who want to pursue the intellectual tradition of this topic include OCTOPUS (Awad et al., 1996), which is an adaptation of OMT (Rumbaugh et al., 1991) to real-time systems. A more recent approach to real-time development emphasizing UML in a more lightweight process is ROPES (Rapid Object-Oriented Process for Embedded Systems). Whatever approach and diagrams you decide to pull from the toolkit, they should further the goals of the project. For the discussion of the importance of process in software development, see Chapter 10.

Performance Optimization

The use of pure forms of abstraction can unfortunately lead to degradation of performance. When performance optimization is important, a conflict might arise between the "ideal" object-oriented model on one hand and performance on the other, so that the actual implementation has to be optimized. That includes taking shorter routes in the communication between objects (so that an object gains direct access to an object to which it normally does not have access) and merging classes to decrease the number of layers between different parts of the software. This strategy can improve the performance, though at the cost of decreasing the modularity of the software. The emphasis in UML on components helps to address these trade-offs; a well-designed system of components (including Web services) can provide optimal behavior.

Given the complexity of real-time systems, the need to design precise and descriptive models is more important than it is in normal systems. Good models, even if complex, allow a client to understand the trade-offs made during optimization. If the decision has an impact on the client's business, the modeler has the responsibility to communicate the options clearly. As usual, optimizing in one area requires a trade-off in another part of the system.

Design Optimization

As part of optimization, review the active objects. Preferably, review the design with an internal group to walk through the system before presenting to a client. Also, consider using one of a variety of automated tools to assess the performance of the existing program. If possible, active objects should be implemented as threads rather than as processes. Threads can execute together in the same memory space are definitely "cheaper" for the operating system in terms of performance. It is also necessary to check if active objects can be merged, thereby avoiding the sharing of passive objects, with all the synchronization handling this requires. Other guidelines for achieving higher performance include:

- Using synchronous communication (for example, operation calls) instead of asynchronous communication
- Reusing message objects or other frequently used objects instead of continuously recreating them
- Avoiding copying objects between different memory spaces

TIP **To guide you to the "right" places, consider a tool such as a profiler (a profiler shows where the processor spends its execution of a program, that is, which parts of the program are most often used). Make sure to review the new design and your assumptions with other software architects.**

Such detailed optimization work might be necessary when trying to achieve maximum performance. However, the first place to look for optimization possibilities is at the overall design level. Often an improved overall design can mean huge gains in performance, gains that are almost impossible to achieve by optimizing the lowest level. That said, if your design is deployed in an environment that does not effectively support your strategy for handling your active objects, performance still suffers.

Optimization and the Operating System

Complications arise when the underlying environment does not have adequate support for real-time constructs, such as processes or threads as well as communication and synchronization mechanisms. Real-time operating systems also require optimization and trade-offs. A tight system such as that used for embedded systems might perform very fast but might not extend to other environments so easily.

The operating system can be either a standard system that supports real-time constructs, such as Windows, Linux, or Unix, or a specialized operating system optimized for embedded systems. The operating system could also be a Java Virtual Machine running on one of these systems. The quality of the real-time services (performance, reliability, ease of programming) depends on the operating system used and is not a property of the object-oriented language or method. Object-oriented design models the system under construction and maps models onto the services provided by the operating system. With a platform-specific model, as used in Model Driven Architecture, or MDA (see Chapter 9), the model can fit very closely with the platform's method of handling these constructs, by employing the correct set of UML extensions.

Whatever system you use, focus on the performance elements most needed for achieving the system's goals. Modeling helps communicate issues and helps validate ways to solve problems. Review the use cases to make certain that the design is not missing something crucial that the users need from the system. Keep the client's goals in mind when deciding on how to optimize a system. Present the trade-offs and walk the client through the implications of the different strategies. If the client wants 99.99 percent availability, for example, walk them through the design implications of such performance and see if their system really needs such support.

Relevant Changes in UML 2

This chapter reflects more change from the first edition than any of the other chapters so far. UML 2 now handles a number of concepts related to complex design in dynamic systems. Relevant changes include the following:

- Activity diagrams have been rebuilt so they now provide powerful tools to model concurrent behavior. Based on Petri Nets, the new activity diagrams model dynamic flow relying on the notion of tokens. Activity diagrams can now easily show interruptible activities, multiple flows, exception handling, and protected regions.
- Active classes and objects are now represented with the addition of a thin vertical line in the class rectangle rather than as a thick line.
- Sequence diagrams now include defined combined fragments that show areas where message ordering is critical. Sequence diagrams can also show areas where parallel processing is possible.
- Concurrent execution in a state machine and parallel processing is now shown by orthogonal regions on a composite state. These orthogonal regions add up to the total state machine for a classifier.
- The protocol state machine includes firmer definitions of the rules for the ordering of operations for interfaces and ports. This feature helps when working with components.

- The new timing diagram provides a way to handle time along one axis of an interaction diagram. This diagram allows for mapping state and behavior to clear time units, which helps in the analysis of real-time design issues.
- A state machine has clearer extension rules so that portions of a state machine can be used in a number of places and can work with a classifier that is part of an inheritance hierarchy.
- A substate machine has clear rules for entry and exit points, making it easier to reuse the submachine in different diagrams.
- The new interaction overview diagram provides an advanced way to model all the issues for a given interaction. This diagram helps consolidate the many different strands and fragments of interactions the modeler needs to review for UML 2.
- Events are now called triggers to emphasize it is how the event is handled, not the event itself, that drives behavior.
- UML now includes standard features for observing and creating constraints based on the time and duration of behaviors.

Summary

To specify a model for a real-time system, you must consider time requirements, concurrency, asynchronous communication, and synchronization. A real-time system is often embedded, meaning that the software is tightly integrated with specialized hardware. UML has concepts to address these real-time issues.

Real time and object orientation are integrated through the definition of active classes and objects. An active class has its own thread of control and thus can initiate actions by itself. That is in contrast to "normal" passive objects, which execute only when some other object performs some operation on it and passes back the control when the operation returns. Active classes and objects are implemented through processes or threads supported by the operating system.

Active objects communicate either through ordinary operation calls (called synchronous messages in the object-oriented world) or through specialized mechanisms such as mailboxes or message queues in which messages can be delivered asynchronously. An asynchronous message means that the sender doesn't wait for the receiver to be ready to accept the message, nor does it automatically wait for any return result. The behavior of active objects is modeled using triggers that launch events.

Synchronization mechanisms are things such as semaphores or critical regions that protect a specific code area, which in turn protects some shared resource, such as a passive object or a device. Synchronization mechanisms are used to prevent problems such as conflicts in parallel usage of shared objects, deadlocks, or just inefficient resource usage of the processor caused by having threads executing in endless "busy wait" loops.

UML can let you work with basic real-time constructs in a variety of diagrams. Activity diagrams provide the high-level workflow with the ability to model concurrency. Static diagrams are needed to show the active and passive classes. The interaction diagrams provide detail on the messages between actual system objects. The state machine shows the transitions in the life cycle of a class or object. The protocol state machine shows the rules for shifting between states often used with ports to help show the environmental requirements.

In designing a real-time system, it is important to determine a basic model for separating processes/threads from objects. You need to identify and define active classes, and communication among and synchronization of the active classes. Be ready to recognize the trade-off between performance and design, discussing the options openly with the client.

This chapter has focused on the static and dynamic modeling required by real-time systems to illustrate advanced features. With the emergence of distributed enterprise computing and Web applications, deployment architecture has become critical to project success. The next chapter looks more closely at how you can use UML to model the logical and physical architecture of your system.

CHAPTER

7

Representing Architecture

A *system architecture* is a blueprint of the parts that together define the system: their structure, interfaces, and the mechanisms that they use to collaborate. By defining an appropriate architecture, you make it easier to navigate the system, to find the location of a specific function or concept, or to identify a location to which to add a new function or concept so that it fits into the overall architecture. The architecture must be detailed enough so that it can be mapped to the actual code. An architecture that is both easy to navigate and sufficiently detailed must also be scalable, meaning that it can be viewed on different levels. The architecture, for example, should provide a top-level view that includes only a few parts. From there, the developer should be able to select one part and examine its internal architecture, which consists of more parts. Using a tool, it should be possible to "zoom into" different parts of the system to study them in greater detail.

A well-defined architecture allows the insertion of new functions and concepts without imposing problems on the rest of the system. This is unlike an old monolithic system where one small change in one part of the system could cause something seemingly unrelated to stop working because of complex relationships across the system.

The architecture serves as a map for the developers, revealing how the system is constructed and where specific functions or concepts are located. Over time, this map may have to be changed because of important discoveries and experiences along the way. The architecture must "live" with the system as the system is being developed and constantly reflect the system's construction in all phases and generations. Naturally, the base architecture is defined in the first version of the system, and the quality of this initial architecture is vital for enabling developers to change, extend, and update the functionality of the system. In private communication, Grady Booch, one of the leaders of the definition of the UML, has said, "It is possible for an inexperienced team to succeed within a well-structured architecture, while an expert team will be hard pressed to succeed without such a roadmap."

The UML definition of architecture is as follows (as taken from the UML 1.4 specification):

> *Architecture is the organizational structure and associated behavior of a system. An architecture can be recursively decomposed into parts that interact through interfaces, relationships that connect parts, and constraints for assembling parts.*

Frank Buschmann and his coauthors in the text *Pattern-Oriented Software Architecture, Volume 1: A System of Patterns* (Buschmann et al., 1996) offer another definition of software architecture:

> *A software architecture is a description of the subsystems and components of a software system and the relationships between them. Subsystems and components are typically specified in different views to show the relevant functional and nonfunctional properties of a software system. The software architecture of a system is an artifact. It is the result of the software design activity.*

Although the architecture must have sufficient detail, it must also serve as an abstraction of the detailed design. Len Bass and his coauthors in their text *Software Architecture in Practice* (Bass et al., 1997) remark as follows:

> *Software architecture must abstract away some information from the system (otherwise there is no point looking at the architecture, we are simply viewing the entire system) and yet provide enough information to be a basis for analysis, decision making, and hence risk reduction.*

While one must be able to demonstrate that the architecture can support the functional requirements of the system, other systemic concerns *drive* architectural decisions. A particular architectural element or architectural pattern might have been selected to best support the basic precepts of quality engineering such as loose coupling, understandability, and minimal redundancy. Other architectural decisions can be traced to specific nonfunctional requirements such as performance, scalability, or security.

The architecture is described in a number of views, and each view concentrates on a specific aspect of the system. The complete picture of the system can be made only by defining all views. In UML, these views are usually defined as follows:

- Use-case view
- Logical view
- Concurrency view
- Component view
- Deployment view

A broader separation usually divides the architecture into the following:

- Logical architecture
- Physical architecture

These architectures are described further in this chapter.

So, with all these definitions in mind, what constitutes a good architecture? Here are some guidelines for answering that question:

- A correct description of the parts that define the system, both in terms of the logical architecture and the physical architecture.
- A map of the system within which a developer can easily locate where a specific functionality or concept is implemented. The functionality or concept may be either application oriented (a model of something in the application domain) or design oriented (some technical implementation solution). This also implies that requirements of the system should be traceable to the code that handles it.
- Changes and extensions should be easy to make in a specific location, without the rest of the system being negatively affected.
- Simple, well-defined interfaces and clear dependencies between different parts are provided so that an engineer can develop a specific part without having a complete understanding of all the details in the overall system.
- Reuse is supported by both incorporating reusable parts into the design and allowing the design of generic parts that can be used in other systems.

An architecture that comprises all these qualities is not easy to design, and sometimes compromises have to be made. But defining a good base architecture is one of the most important steps in the development of a successful system. If it is not done conscientiously, the architecture comes to be defined from the bottom up by the code, resulting in a system that is difficult to change, extend, maintain, and understand.

Logical Architecture

The *logical architecture* contains the application logic, but not the physical distribution of that logic into different environments across different computers. The logical architecture gives a clear understanding of the construction of the system to make it easier to administrate and coordinate the work (to use the human developer resources as efficiently as possible). Not all parts of the logical architecture have to be developed within the project; class libraries, binary components, and patterns can often be bought.

The logical architecture answers questions such as:

- What is the overall structure of the system?
- What functionality does the system deliver?
- What are the key classes, and how are those classes related to one other?
- How do these classes and their objects collaborate to deliver the functionality?
- How are common mechanisms applied consistently across the design?
- What would be a suitable plan for a number of developers to follow to develop this system?

Remember that the logical architecture is not the complete logical design; the architecture as described in these diagrams provides focus on the answers to the questions posed in the preceding bulleted list. The architecture introduces organization, constraints, and a set of common tools to the design. While a complete design might be described as an "as-is" model describing a system, the architecture always has a "to-be" tone. The architecture doesn't so much say, "Here it is," as it says, "This is how you do it."

In UML, the diagrams used to describe the logical architecture are class, state, activity, and sequence. These diagrams have all been described in previous chapters.

Logical Architecture Structure

Class diagrams describing architecture can focus on the structure of the overall system by showing packages, components, and their dependencies and interfaces.

A common architecture is the three-layered structure where the system is divided into a presentation layer, an application layer, and a domain layer. A diagram showing such a logical architecture is shown in Figure 7.1. From the packages, other diagramsthat describe the classes in each package and their internal collaboration can be reached.

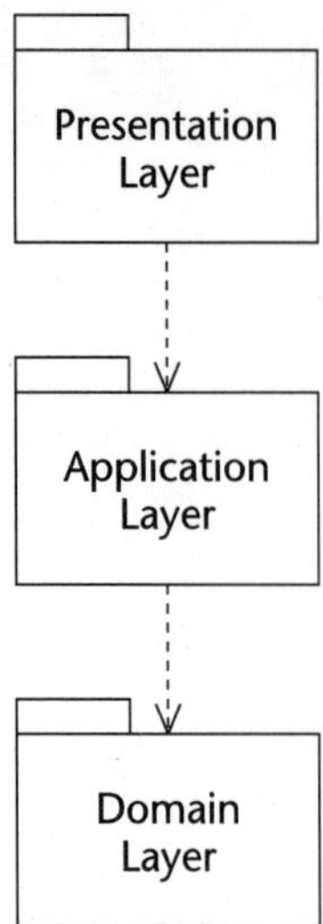

Figure 7.1 A simple three-layered architecture shown as UML packages with dependencies.

Components

As we discuss in Chapter 4, UML provides packages as a grouping mechanism that provides controlled visibility. When taking an architectural view of system decomposition, you can use the component as a more semantically rich grouping mechanism. A *component* is a self-contained unit that encapsulates the state and behavior of a set of classifiers. Contrary to how packages contain modeling elements, all the contents of the components are private—hidden inside. Also unlike a package, a component realizes and requires interfaces. This full encapsulation and separation of interface from implementation enables a component to be a substitutable unit that can be replaced at design time or run time by another component that offers equivalent functionality.

An important aspect of component-based development is the ability to reuse preexisting components. A component is encapsulated and its dependencies are designed so that it can be treated as independently as possible. As a result, components can be reused flexibly and replaced by connecting ("wiring") them together via their provided and required interfaces. This concept extends to run time and is revisited when we discuss physical architecture later in this chapter.

The external (or black box) view shows the interfaces that a component provides and requires. The component is shown as a classifier rectangle with the keyword <<component>>. Optionally, in the upper-right corner a component icon can be displayed, a classifier rectangle with two smaller rectangles protruding from its left side. Figure 7.2 shows a simple component providing one interface and requiring another.

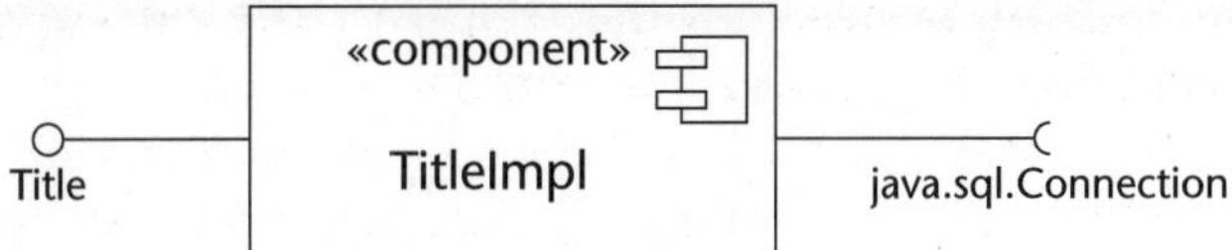

Figure 7.2 External view of a component.

The internal (or white box) view shows the internal classifiers, how they are connected, and how they collaborate to realize the interfaces. A component can use ports to formalize its interaction points. The internal elements (for example, classes or subcomponents) have the semantics of the ports delegated to them. Figure 7.3 shows the internal view of a component where the interfaces have been formalized as ports and delegated to internal classifiers. Among the components, some have been shown with the textual stereotype, some with the embedded icon, and some with both; these are all valid forms.

The particular example shown in Figure 7.3 is a twist on what was actually implemented in the case study. This component-centric design of the Title provides a well-encapsulated chunk of design that contains a number of classes. When we were designing the case study, it was determined that the more significant design issue was the separation of the business logic from the data access objects that would be implemented in support of various specific databases. So an architectural decision was made to stress the separation of technical concerns across layers rather than to stress the separation of business concerns across components. Architecture design is full of such trade-offs.

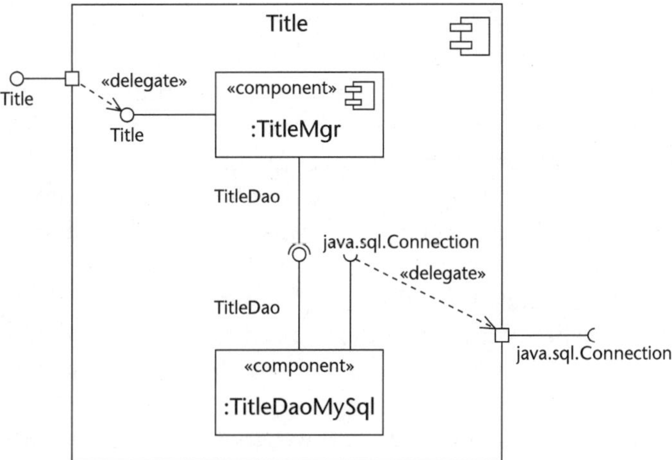

Figure 7.3 Internal view of a component.

Components promote a plug-and-play design within which a component can be replaced by a different component that matches the external view with no ripple effect. To support this design, a component comprising only an external view can be created. Such a component will be stereotyped as <<specification>>.

Collaborations

Logical architecture is structured by more than just these static elements. A dynamic *collaboration* is a key part of an architecture that communicates how a system should be designed within it. A collaboration is not instantiable. Collaborations enable you to describe only the relevant aspects of the cooperation of a set of instances by identifying the specific roles that the instances play.

A collaboration is shown as a dashed-line use case. Its contents can optionally be shown in a second compartment under the name. Figure 7.4 shows a collaboration that contains two roles. Other behavior specifiers, such as interaction diagrams, can be attached to the collaboration to show clearly how the roles deal with one another in various scenarios.

While the collaboration itself is not instantiable, a collaboration icon can show the use of a collaboration together with the actual classifiers that occur in that particular application of the collaboration. Figure 7.5 shows the collaboration with classes attached that play the particular roles. In this example, the second compartment of the collaboration has been excluded.

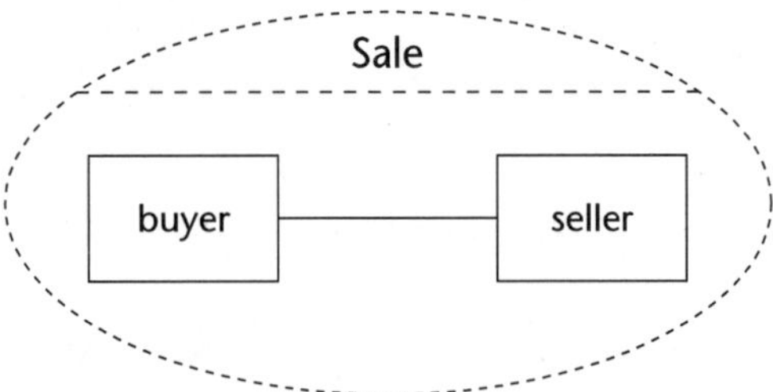

Figure 7.4 Collaboration.

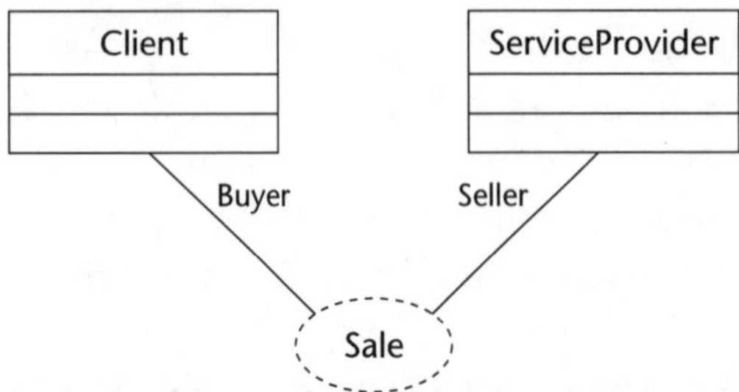

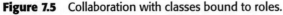

Figure 7.5 Collaboration with classes bound to roles.

Composite Structure Diagrams

The composite structure diagram provides the modeler with a mechanism to describe the connections between the elements that work together within a classifier. For example, the elements might work together on the tasks of a collaboration or in support of the needs of a class.

Though similar to a class diagram, a composite structure diagram shows parts and connectors. The parts are not necessarily classifiers in the model, and they do not represent particular instances; they are roles that classifiers will play. Parts are shown in a similar manner to objects, but the name is not underlined. The diagram specifies the structural features that will be required to support the enclosing classifier.

Figure 7.6 shows how the tires work together supporting a car. In an overall class model the tire class might support numerous configurations, but this is how the tires will be put together when they are used as parts of a car. On its own, the tire has no concern for enforcing this particular structure; it is within the context of a car that this structure is enforced.

This diagram can be used in diverse ways to show the runtime architecture of any kind of classifier.

Patterns in Architecture

Design patterns have received a lot of attention in the object-oriented community, because they represent a breakthrough in the development of software. Design patterns are smart, generic, well-proven, simple, reusable design solutions for object-oriented systems. The following list examines these characteristics individually:

- **Smart.** Design patterns are elegant solutions that a novice would not think of immediately.
- **Generic.** Design patterns are not normally dependent on a specific system type, programming language, or application domain. They are generic for a specific problem.
- **Well-proven.** Design patterns have been identified from real, object-oriented systems. They are not just the result of academic thinking, but have been successfully tested in several systems.
- **Simple.** Design patterns are usually quite small, involving only a handful of classes. To build more complex solutions, different design patterns are combined and intermixed with application code.
- **Reusable.** Design patterns are documented in such a manner that they are easy to reuse. As mentioned, they are generic; therefore, they can be used in all kinds of systems. Note that the reuse is on the design level, not on the code level. Design patterns are not in class libraries; they are for the system architects.

- **Object-oriented.** Design patterns are built with the basic object-oriented mechanisms, such as classes, objects, generalization, and polymorphism.

The core of a design pattern is a problem description and a solution. The *problem description* states when the pattern is used and which problem it tries to solve. The *solution* is described as a number of classes and objects, their structure, and dynamic collaboration. All patterns have names.

The documentation of a design pattern varies in different books and papers; sometimes it is only given in text, sometimes it is a combination of text and models in a modeling language. Patterns provide object-oriented software developers with:

- **Reusable solutions to common problems.** These solutions are based on experiences from the development of real systems.
- **Names of abstractions above the class and object level.** With design patterns, developers are able to discuss solutions at a higher level, for example: "I suggested that we use a Bridge or possibly an Adapter to solve that" (Bridge and Adapter are the names of two design patterns).
- **Handling of both functional and nonfunctional aspects of development.** Many patterns specifically address some of the areas that object-oriented programs are good at: separating interfaces and implementation, loose dependencies between parts, isolation between hardware and software platforms, and the potential for reuse of design and code.
- **A base for developing frameworks and toolkits.** Design patterns are the basic constructs used in designing reusable frameworks.
- **Education and training support for those who are learning object-oriented programming and design.** By studying design patterns, you can gain an understanding of the basic properties of good design, which you can then emulate in your own designs.

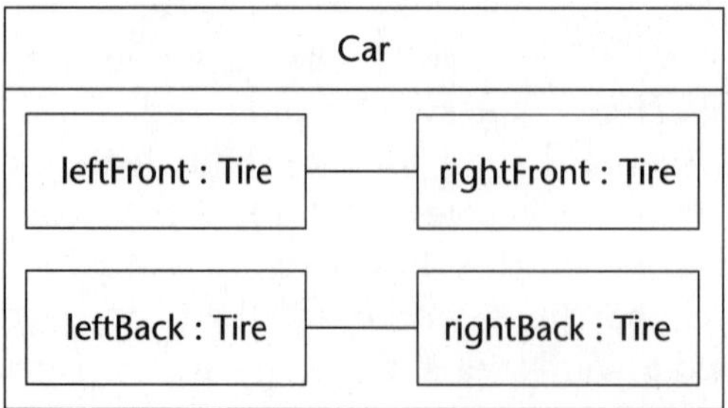

Figure 7.6 Parts and connectors inside a car.

Design patterns in the software community were inspired by the work of the architect Christopher Alexander. Alexander has defined a "pattern language" to describe successful architecture in buildings and cities. His language describes how "good" buildings are constructed (a "good" building is one in which the visitor or inhabitant feels alive and whole), and although the patterns can appear in many variations, they are always present in successful architectures. Alexander's work has had a significant impact not only within his own discipline, but also on other disciplines where pattern languages have been identified to describe general and good designs.

Many people in the software industry found Alexander's work very appealing, and that appeal led to discussions about applying patterns in software in the early 1990s. In August 1994, the first Pattern Languages of Programs (PLoP) conference was held. It prompted a lot of work on producing patterns for software. Though the idea of using patterns for software is not necessarily related to object orientation, it became clear that the modeling capability of objects enabled object-orientation to capture design abstractions; hence, most design patterns are related to object-oriented development. In the beginning of 1995, a group referred to as the "Gang of Four" (Erich Gamma, Richard Helm, Ralph Johnson, and John Vlissides) released the book *Design Patterns: Elements of Reusable Object-Oriented Software* (Gamma et al., 1995), which contained a basic catalog of design patterns and established patterns as a new research area for the software discipline. The pattern movement in the software industry is, however, still in its early stages, and not nearly as complete, mature, and consistent as Alexander's work in architecture.

The interest in patterns has since resulted in a number of other books applying patterns to a number of different areas, such as CORBA (Common Object Request Broker Architecture) and project management. Some of the more interesting work is concerned with the move to pattern systems that attempt to identify patterns at different levels, where together they form a complete system of patterns. Of particular interest is the research into high-level patterns, such as the architectural patterns described by Frank Buschmann in *Pattern-Oriented Software Architecture* (Buschmann et al., 1996). The architectural patterns describe fundamental schemas for organizing a system: subsystems, allocation of responsibility and rules, and guidelines for how subsystems communicate and cooperate. These top-level patterns are a very important step toward achieving higher-quality architecture of the systems produced.

Experienced developers sometimes seem to have a "magic" ability to define good architectures. This skill comes from having designed a lot of systems, experience that gives them knowledge for which solutions work and which don't. They typically reuse solutions that have worked well in the past. Recently a lot of work has been directed toward trying to identify architectural patterns or frameworks ("solutions") that are repeatedly used by experienced developers when designing software architectures. Buschmann and his coauthors in the text mentioned in the previous paragraph have defined the following architectural patterns:

- **Layers pattern.** A system decomposed into groups of subtasks in which each group of subtasks is at a particular level of abstraction.
- **Pipes and filters pattern.** A system that processes a stream of data, where a number of processing steps are encapsulated in filter components. Data is passed through pipes between adjacent filters, and the filters can be recombined to build related systems or system behavior.
- **Blackboard pattern.** A system where several specialized subsystems assemble their knowledge to build a partial or approximate solution to a problem for which no deterministic solution strategy is known.
- **Broker pattern.** A system where decoupled components interact through remote service invocations. A broker component is responsible for coordinating communication and for transmitting results and exceptions.
- **Model-view-controller pattern.** A system that divides an interactive system into three components: a model containing the core functionality and data, one or more views displaying information to the user, and one or more controllers that handle user input. A change-propagation mechanism ensures consistency between user interface and model.
- **Microkernel pattern.** A system that separates a minimal functional core from extended functionality and customer-specific parts. The microkernel also serves as a socket for plugging in these extensions and coordinating their collaboration.

Further descriptions of these patterns and frameworks can be found in the Buschmann text. Naturally, no system uses just one of these frameworks or patterns. Various patterns are used in different parts of the system and at different scales. A layers pattern can be used to define the architecture of a specific subsystem, while in one of the layers in the subsystem another pattern can be used to organize it internally. To become a good software architect, you must know the design of the architectural patterns, when they should be used, and how to combine them.

The Proxy Pattern

The Proxy pattern is one of those given in the Gang of Four's *Design Patterns* book. Proxy is a structural pattern that separates an interface from an implementation into different classes. The idea of the pattern is that a proxy object works as a surrogate object for another real object; the proxy controls access to this "real" object. Thus, it solves the problem when an object (the real object) cannot always be instantiated directly due to performance, location, or access restrictions. It is a rather simple pattern, but it suits the purposes of describing and demonstrating patterns in UML. Figure 7.7 shows a class diagram for the Proxy pattern in UML.

The representation of this pattern has been modified slightly from that which was presented in the *Design Patterns* text so as to best fit how it would be represented in the Java language. There are two classes and one interface involved in the Proxy pattern: Proxy, RealSubject, and Subject. The Client class in the diagram shows the use of the pattern; in this case, the Client class always operates on the interface Subject. The operation declared in the Subject class is implemented in both the RealSubject class and in the Proxy class. The RealSubject class implements the operations in the interface, while the Proxy class only delegates any calls it receives to the RealSubject class. Through the interface, the Client class will always work against a Proxy object, and thus the Proxy object controls the access to the RealSubject object. This pattern is used in several ways, depending on the problem that needs to be solved:

- **Higher performance and efficiency.** A system can instantiate a cheap Proxy until the real object is needed. When an operation is called in the Proxy, it checks whether the RealSubject object is instantiated. If not, it instantiates it and then delegates the request to it. If it is instantiated, it immediately furthers the request. This pattern is useful if the RealSubject object is "expensive" to create, that is, has to be read from a database, requires complex initialization, or has to be fetched from another system. By using Proxies for all such objects, the system instantiates only the objects necessary for a specific execution of the system. Many systems with lengthy start-up times can gain significant boosts in performance in terms of start-up time by using the Proxy pattern.
- **Authorization.** If it is necessary to check that the caller is authorized to call the RealSubject object, that check can be made by the Proxy. In that case, the caller has to identify itself, and the Proxy has to communicate with some kind of authorization object to decide whether access is allowed.
- **Localization.** The RealSubject object is located on another system, and a local Proxy only "plays its role" in the system, and all requests are actually furthered to the other system. The local client is unaware of this and sees only the Proxy.

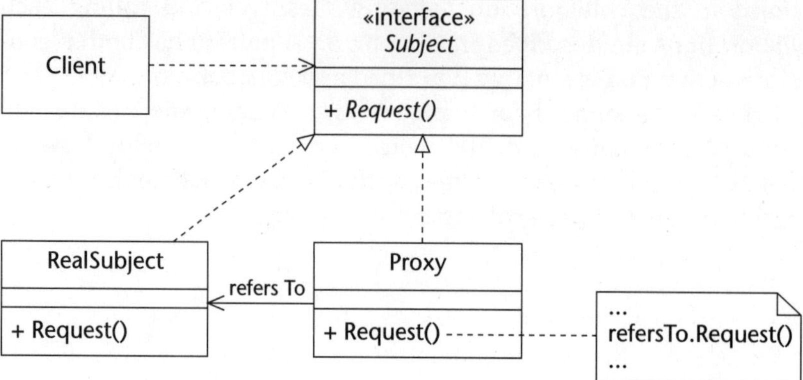

Figure 7.7 The Proxy design pattern described as a UML class diagram.

The Proxy pattern is varied in even more ways: It can contain additional functionality that it performs without delegating it to the RealSubject; it can change the types of parameters or the operation name (in which case, it becomes a lot like another pattern, an Adapter); or it can perform some preparation work to reduce the workload of RealSubject. All these variations demonstrate the idea behind patterns: the pattern offers the core of a solution that can then be varied, adapted, or extended in a multitude of ways without removing the basic solution construction.

The code for the pattern is often very simple. The Java code for a Proxy class that instantiates the RealSubject on demand simply looks like this:

```
public class Proxy implements Subject
{
    RealSubject refersTo;
    public void Request()
    {
        if (refersTo == null)
            refersTo = new RealSubject();
        refersTo.Request ();
    }
}
```

Modeling Patterns in UML

A pattern is documented as a collaboration in UML. A collaboration describes both a context and an interaction. The context is a description of the objects involved in the collaboration, how they are related to each other, and of which classes they are instances. The interaction shows the communication that the objects perform in the collaboration (sending messages and calling each other). (Collaborations are described in Chapter 5.) A pattern has both a context and an interaction and is suitably described as a collaboration.

Figure 7.8 shows the symbol for a pattern in a collaboration (a dashed ellipse) with the pattern name inside it. When you are using a tool for drawing the diagrams, the symbol can usually be expanded, in which case the context and the interaction of the pattern collaboration are shown.

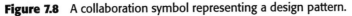

Figure 7.8 A collaboration symbol representing a design pattern.

An object diagram for the Proxy pattern is shown in Figure 7.9. To understand the object diagram fully, a reference to the class diagram describing the classes of the objects must also be available. The object diagram for the Proxy pattern shows how the Client object has a link to the Proxy object, which in turn has a link to the RealSubject object.

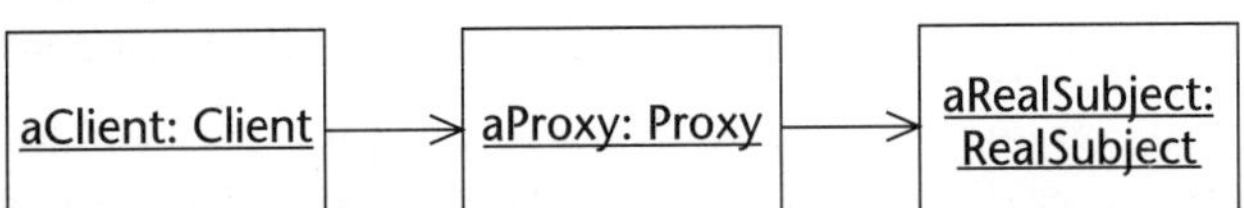

Figure 7.9 The context of the Proxy pattern described as an object diagram.

When you are describing the Proxy pattern, the interaction shows how the objects interact when the client makes a request. The sequence diagram in Figure 7.10 shows how the request is delegated to the RealSubject object and how the result is returned to the client.

A communication diagram can show both the context and the interaction in one diagram. The context from the object diagram in Figure 7.9 and the interaction shown in Figure 7.10 are condensed into one communication diagram in Figure 7.11. The decision to use a communication diagram or to divide it into an object diagram and a sequence diagram depends on the situation. (A discussion about the differences between these diagrams is found in Chapter 5.) A more complex pattern may need to describe several interactions to show different behaviors of the pattern.

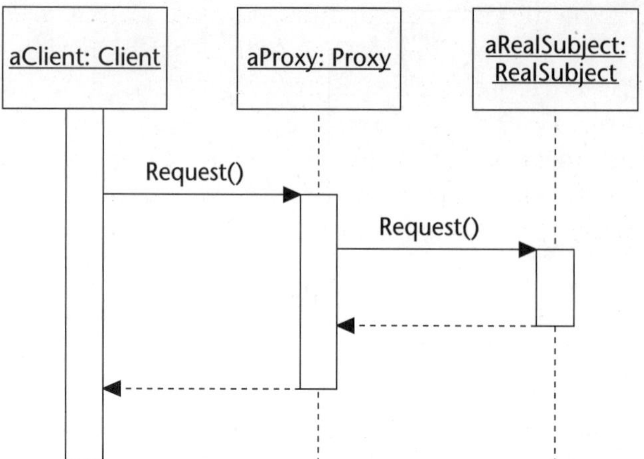

Figure 7.10 The interaction in the Proxy pattern described as a sequence diagram.

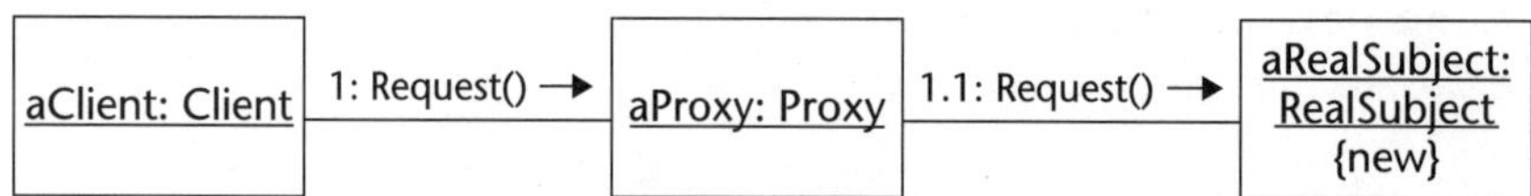

Figure 7.11 The interaction in the Proxy pattern described as a communication diagram.

One can show how a pattern is applied among actual participants within a design. The participants in a design pattern are the application elements that play the roles defined in the pattern; for example, in the Proxy pattern, the classes that act as the Subject, Proxy, or RealSubject class. The participants are illustrated by drawing lines from the pattern symbol to the elements that play the different roles in the patterns. The line is annotated with the participating role name, which describes which role the class "plays" in terms of the design pattern.

If the collaboration is expanded in a tool, both the context and the interaction of the pattern are shown in terms of the participating classes. In Figure 7.12, the names of the classes that are participants are deliberately different from the roles they play to illustrate that the role name of the dependency defines what its task is in the pattern. In practice, the classes are often named to suit the pattern; for example, the Sales class is called SalesProxy, the SaleStatistics class is called SalesStatisticsSubject, and so on. However, that is not possible if the classes are already defined or if they participate in several patterns. If the collaboration is expanded, the participants are shown "playing" their roles in the pattern, as shown in Figure 7.13.

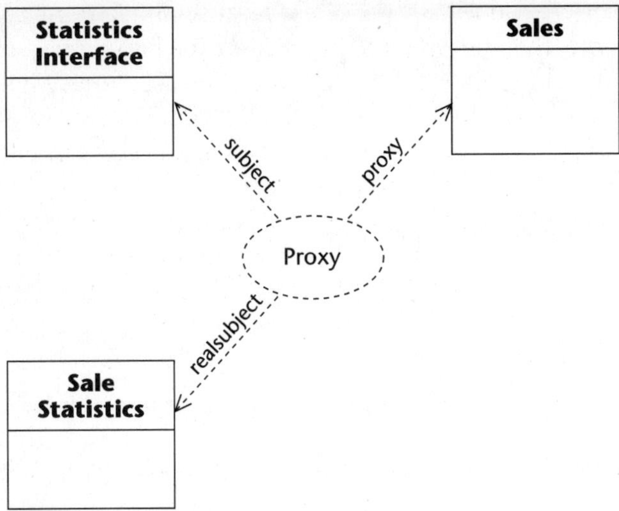

Figure 7.12 The Proxy pattern used in a class diagram, where the Statistics Interface class has the participating role of subject, the Sales class has the participating role of proxy, and the Sale Statistics class has the role of realsubject.

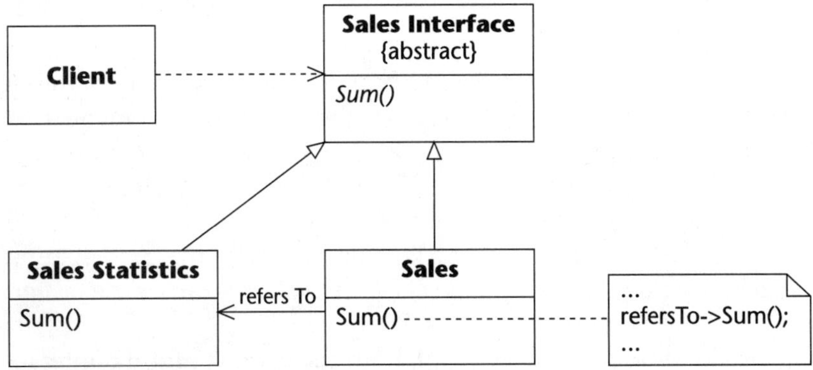

Figure 7.13 The Proxy pattern expanded with participants from Figure 7.12.

Showing Patterns in Diagrams

By defining patterns as collaborations, you can use them as full-fledged design constructs where they represent a design construct at a higher abstraction level than the basic elements. They can be used repeatedly in designs and, as long as they are well established, they can simplify the models because not all parts of the design have to be shown. The context and interaction in the pattern is implicit; therefore, patterns can be seen as generators of design solutions. Figure 7.14 shows a number of classes in which parts of their context and collaboration are described by using patterns. In a tool it's possible to access details about the patterns by expanding the collaborations.

When a pattern is used in a tool, a developer sees the pattern in a diagram that he or she can expand to reveal the context and interaction that the pattern represents. The pattern is viewed in terms of the participating classes that play roles in the pattern. A tool can also be used to capture and document patterns in a repository, where new patterns are described, stored, and made available to other projects. The patterns are naturally described as collaborations in UML.

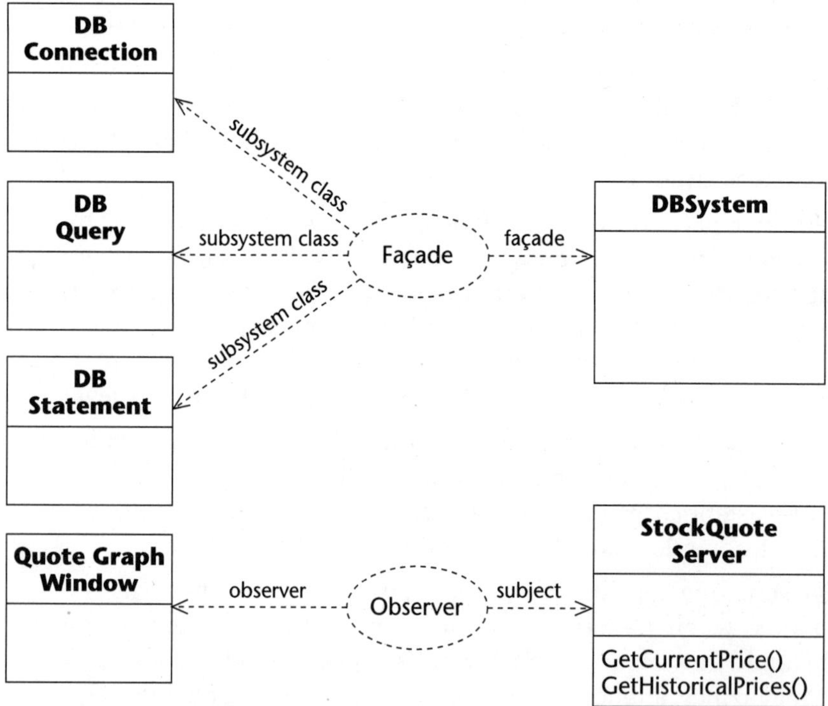

Figure 7.14 Patterns as generators.

Here are some suggestions for using design patterns:

- **The name of the pattern is important.** The name represents abstraction at a higher level than the design elements in the pattern, and the ability to communicate and discuss abstractions at a higher level is a very important property of design patterns.
- **Make sure that everyone understands the patterns used in a project.** Some patterns are treacherously simple, and a developer may think he or she understands all the implications of using such a pattern, even when that is not the case. Good documentation and training are important activities when using patterns.
- **Adapt or modify patterns, but don't change their basic properties.** A pattern can be adapted or varied in a number of ways, but the fundamental core of the pattern should never be altered. The core is often the primary reason to use that specific pattern, and therefore, it shouldn't be removed or changed.
- **Don't overuse patterns.** Patterns can be used in any system development effort, but they should never be regarded as a "silver bullet." Eager developers sometimes overuse patterns, so that everything is designed as patterns.
- **Emphasize patterns as reuse of design.** Many organizations try to transform patterns into reusable code (classes, libraries, and programs). That often means that a pattern has one specific implementation, and that none of its variations can be used. It also means that the documentation of the pattern is transformed into detailed code documentation. A pattern should be reused at the design level, not at the code level.
- **Describe patterns as part of your architecture.** The logical architecture of the system includes the patterns that will be applied to the design. The consistent usage of these patterns is part of what will make an architecture understandable, maintainable, and consistent.
- **Have someone monitor the pattern community.** New patterns and new areas where patterns are applied are constantly appearing. Someone should be assigned to track what's happening by reading books and magazines, attending conferences, and searching the Internet.

Patterns and Use Cases

When examining patterns more closely, it's possible to see a resemblance between patterns and the realization of use cases. They have these characteristics in common:

- **Context.** Both are described as a network of objects related in some kind of structure.
- **Interaction.** Both have one primary interaction as to how the objects collaborate (their behavior in the pattern or the use case).
- **Participants.** Both are "instantiated" with a number of application classes that play a specific role in the pattern or use case.

Furthermore, use cases are realized and patterns are documented in the same way in UML. A collaboration can be either the documentation of a pattern or the description of how a use case is realized. The name of the collaboration is the name of the pattern or the use case and the collaboration has dependencies to the participating classes. A pattern can be viewed as a generic collaboration that can be used in a number of systems, while a use case is an application-specific collaboration typically used in only one system (see Figure 7.15).

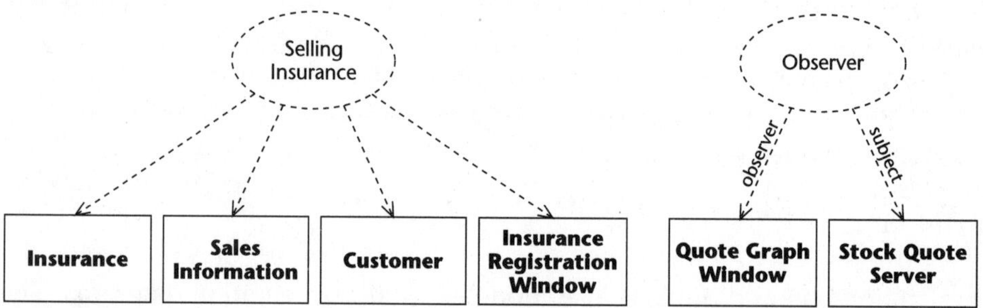

Figure 7.15 A use-case collaboration and a pattern collaboration with relation to classes that are participants.

Physical Architecture

The *physical architecture* deals with a detailed description of the system in terms of how the software artifacts are assigned to the physical nodes. It reveals the structure of the hardware, including different nodes and how these nodes are connected to one another. It also illustrates the physical structure and dependencies of the software artifacts that manifest the concepts defined in the logical architecture and the distribution of the runtime software in terms of deployed artifacts. The physical architecture attempts to achieve an efficient resource usage of the hardware and the software.

The physical architecture answers questions such as:

- Which computers and other hardware devices are in the system, and how are they connected to each other?
- What are the executable environments within which various parts of the system run?
- On which computers are the various executable artifacts deployed?
- What are the dependencies between different code files? If a specific file is changed, which other files have to be recompiled?

The physical architecture describes the decomposition of the software and hardware. A mapping is drawn from the logical architecture to the physical architecture, whereby the classes, components, and mechanisms in the logical architecture are mapped onto artifacts, processes, and computers in the physical architecture. This mapping allows the developer to "follow" a class in the logical architecture to its physical implementation, or vice versa, to trace the description of a program or a component back to its design in the logical architecture.

As previously described, the physical architecture is concerned with the implementation and, thus, is also modeled in implementation diagrams. The implementation diagrams in UML are the component and the deployment diagrams. The component diagram shows how the physical artifacts implement the components. The deployment diagram shows the runtime architecture of the system, covering both the physical devices and the software allocated to them.

Hardware

The hardware concepts in the physical architecture can be divided into the following:

- **Devices.** The physical computational resource with processing capability upon which artifacts can be deployed for execution. These are the computers that execute the programs in the system.

- **Communication paths.** Processors have connections to other processors. They also have connections to devices. The connections are represented as a communication mechanism between two nodes and can be described as both the physical medium (for example, optical cable) and the software protocol (for example, TCP/IP).
- **Execution environments.** Typically modeled as subnodes within devices, these provide an execution environment for specific types of components that are deployed within the environments in the form of executable artifacts. Though not physically a hardware device, an execution environment details how the hardware is configured to host the software elements.

Software

Traditionally, the software in a system architecture was rather loosely defined as consisting of "parts." A common name for the modular unit handled in the architecture is *subsystem*, a miniature system within a larger system. It has an interface and is internally decomposed either into more detailed subsystems or into classes and objects. Subsystems can be allocated to executable environments within which they execute (and the executable environments are allocated to devices on which they execute).

In UML, a subsystem is modeled as a component stereotyped as <<subsystem>>. A subsystem is different from a package, which organizes a number of classes into a logical group but defines no semantics for the group. In the design, it is often cleaner to define one or more interfaces as the facade to a subsystem. By using a facade, the subsystem becomes a very modular unit in which the internal design is hidden and only the facade interface has dependencies from other elements in the system. When viewing the subsystem, it is the facade that is interesting for those who want to use the services of the component, and typically only the facade needs to be shown in diagrams. Subsystems are used both in the logical design, where a number of classes can be grouped into a unit, and in the physical architecture, where a subsystem is directly manifested by an artifact that is deployed on a device.

The main concepts used in describing the software in the physical architecture are the following.

- **Components.** A component in UML is defined as "a reusable part that provides the physical packaging of a collection of model element instances." This definition means that a component is a physical implementation (for example, a source code file) that implements logical model elements as defined in class diagrams or interaction diagrams. A component can be viewed at different stages of the development, such as at compile time, link time, and run time. In a project, the definition of a component is often mapped to the implementation environment (that is, the programming language and tools used).

- **Artifacts.** An artifact represents a physical piece of information that is used or produced by a software development process and that can be deployed to nodes. Examples of artifacts include model files, source files, scripts, and binary executable files.
- **Deployment specifiers.** A deployment specification specifies a set of properties that determine the execution parameters of a component artifact that is deployed on a node. A deployment specification can be aimed at a specific type of container.

Component Diagram

The component diagram shows the organizations and dependencies among components and artifacts. The components represent cleanly grouped and encapsulated elements from the logical architecture. The components are typically implemented as files in the development environment; these are modeled as artifacts.

An artifact can be:

- **A Source artifact.** A source artifact is meaningful at compile time. It is commonly a source code file implementing one or more classes.
- **An Executable artifact.** An executable artifact is an executable program file that is the result of linking all binary components (either static at link time or dynamic at run time). An executable component represents the executable unit that is run by a processor (computer).

Specific profiles are expected to extend the breakdown of artifacts in ways more relevant to their corresponding technology. For example, an EJB profile might define <<EJB>> as a subtype of <<executable>>.

As stated earlier in the chapter, a component is shown in UML as a rectangle with the stereotype <<component>> and/or a special component icon in the square (this is the symbol that was used in earlier versions of UML for components). An artifact is shown as a rectangle with the stereotype <<artifact>> and/or a "file icon" in the corner. If one is applying subtyping among artifacts, the appropriate stereotype (for example, <<executable>>) can be used.

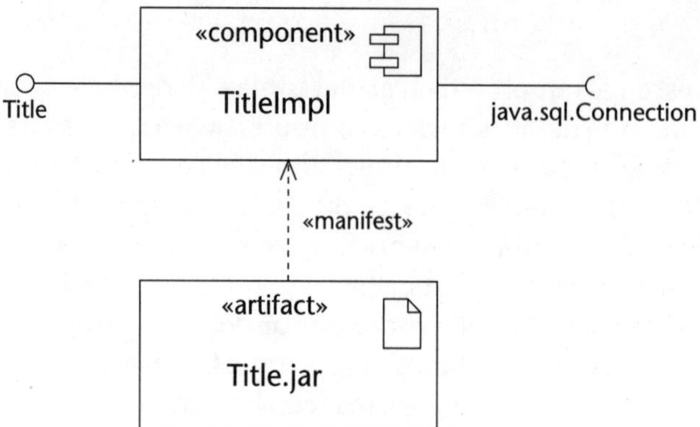

Figure 7.16 Components and artifacts.

An artifact represents the physical manifestation of a component (or any packageable element, such as a simple class). This manifestation is shown as a dashed line with an open arrow stereotyped as <<manifest>>. A dependency connection can also be shown between artifacts. Shown as a dashed line with an open arrow, this dependency means that one artifact needs another to be able to have a complete definition. A dependency from one source code artifact A to another artifact B means that there is a language-specific dependency from A to B. In a compiled language, it could mean that a change in B will require a recompilation of A because definitions from component B are used when compiling A. If the artifacts are executable, dependency connections can be used to identify which dynamic libraries an executable program needs to be able to run. Figure 7.16 shows a component and the artifact that manifests it at execution time.

Deployment Diagram

The deployment diagram depicts the runtime architecture of devices, execution environments, and artifacts that reside in this architecture. It is the ultimate physical description of the system topology, describing the structure of the hardware units and the software that executes on each unit. In such an architecture, it should be possible to look at a specific node in the topology, see which components are executing in that node and which logical elements (classes, objects, collaborations, and so on) are implemented in the component, and finally trace those elements to the initial requirement analysis of the system (which could have been done through use-case analysis).

Nodes

Nodes are computational resources upon which artifacts may be deployed for execution. These resources include devices such as computers with processors, as well as card readers, mobile devices, communication devices, and so on. They also include subnodes within those devices that reflect disparate executable environments such as J2EE container, workflow engine, or database.

A node can be shown both as a type and an instance (a node is a classifier), where a type describes the characteristics of a processor or device type and an instance represents actual occurrences (machines) of that type (see Figure 7.17). The detailed definition of the capability of the system can be defined either as attributes or as properties defined for nodes. A node is drawn as a three-dimensional cube with the name inside it, and just as for the notation of classes and objects, if the symbol represents an instance, the name is underlined.

When nodes are used to represent physical computational resources, they are shown with the <<device>> stereotype. Distinct execution environments within these nodes are shown with the <<execution environment>> stereotype (see Figure 7.18).

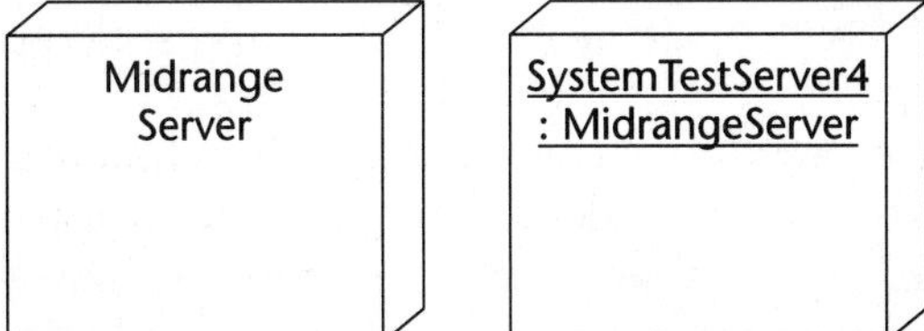

Figure 7.17 The MidrangeServer is a node type, and SystemTestServer4 is an instance of that type.

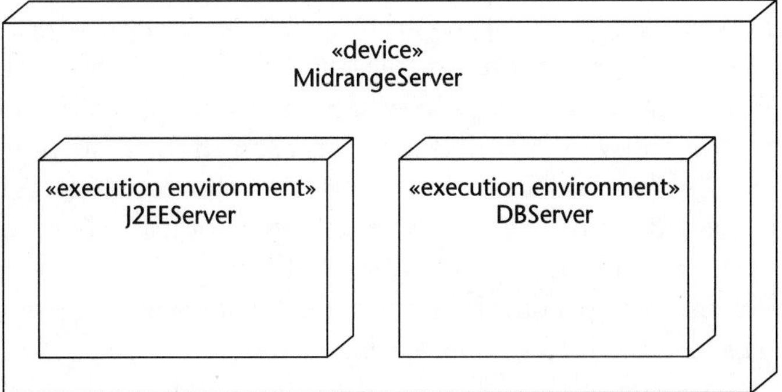

Figure 7.18 Device nodes with embedded execution environments.

Communication Paths

Nodes are connected to each other by communication paths, as shown in Figure 7.19. They are drawn as normal associations with a straight line, indicating that there is some sort of communication between them and that the nodes exchange objects or send messages through that path. The communication type can be represented by a stereotype that identifies the communication protocol or the network used.

Deployed Artifacts

Artifacts can be deployed onto nodes. Using the classifier/instance idiom, these artifacts are shown with their name underlined.

An artifact deployed onto a node might be presented with a set of properties describing execution parameters for that artifact on that particular node. This set of properties can be modeled either directly within the deployed artifact as properties or separately as a deployment specification. When a deployment specification is shown, it is modeled as a simple classifier rectangle with the stereotype <<deployment spec>>.

Dependency relationships can be modeled between deployed artifacts. A deployment specification is related to a deployed artifact with a unidirectional association. A deployment specification might also exist within an artifact, as might other artifacts; in this case, the icons for the contained modeling elements are shown within the icon representing the enclosing deployed artifact.

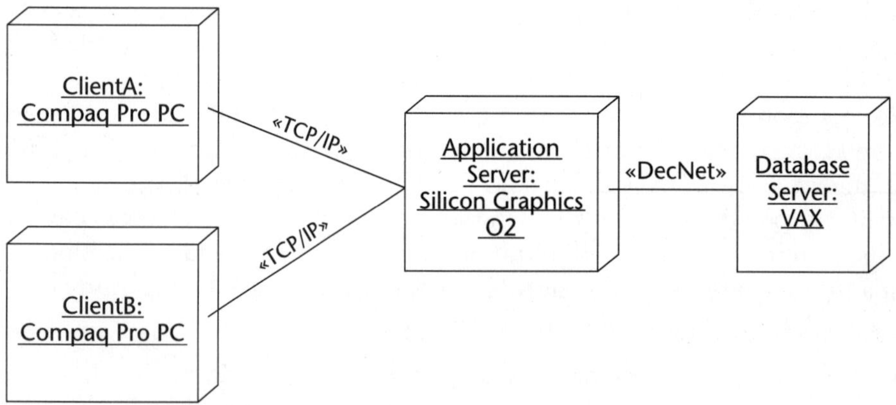

Figure 7.19 Communication associations between nodes.

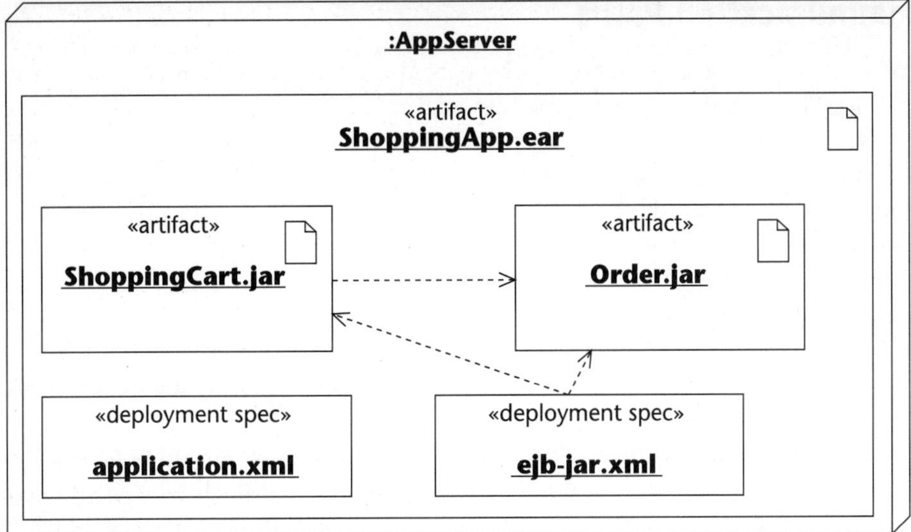

Figure 7.20 Artifacts deployed within nodes.

Allocating Artifacts to Nodes

Classes and collaborations, as defined in the logical design, are allocated to components within which they reside. The allocation is driven by the programming language used. For example, Java implements a class in a source artifact code file (.java). Then, a group of classes, within a package or a component, has their source files compiled and put into a jar executable artifact file (.jar).

So, components that reside within the executable architecture are implemented by artifacts, and artifacts are deployed on nodes. A deployed artifact executes on at least one node instance, and possibly on several. The allocation of artifacts to nodes can also affect the actual topology, so that changes have to be made to the proposed configuration in terms of nodes and connections to best suit the runtime communication among artifacts. Consider a number of aspects when allocating components to nodes:

- **Resource usage.** One of the main goals when determining the physical architecture and the allocation of components is the resource usage of the hardware. Hardware should, of course, be utilized in an efficient manner, to the full capacity of each node (without overusing, which results in poor performance).

- **Geographical location.** Decisions have to be made regarding where specific functionality is required (on which nodes), and what functionality must be available locally (because of performance, or if it must be available even if other nodes are not operating).
- **Access to devices.** What are the needs for a specific device on a node? Can the printer be connected to the server, or does every client need a local printer?
- **Security.** Which architecture handles access rights and protection of information in an optimized and efficient way? Access control may concern both geographical location (having the server in a secure place) and the communication solutions (using secure hardware and software to communicate).
- **Performance.** The need for high performance sometimes affects the location of a component. It is possible to improve performance by creating proxies on a local node, substituting them for the real component available on another node.
- **Extensibility and portability.** When different nodes have different operating systems or machine architecture, you must consider which components can be dependent on a specific operating system and which must be portable to a number of operating systems. This affects the location of those components and perhaps the programming language for implementation as well.

Iterative design is required to produce the deployment diagram. Various solutions have to be tested, first by discussion during the modeling phase and later by implementing prototypes. Ideally, the system will be flexible so that a specific component can be moved between different nodes. A distributed object system such as J2EE or .NET enables the creation of such systems.

Relevant Changes in UML 2

Earlier versions of UML called out a special modeling element called a subsystem that was both a classifier and a package. Furthermore, these earlier versions used components only to structure the model in the physical architecture. UML 2 consistently uses components across all parts of the model and so there is no need for a special subsystem modeling element.

In UML 2, a component is notated by a classifier symbol that no longer has two protruding rectangles. Instead, a <<component>> keyword notation is used. Optionally, a component icon that is similar to the UML 1.4 icon can still be used in the upper-right corner of the component symbol.

Earlier versions of UML had a special icon for parameterized collaborations; that icon was used when patterns were expressed. UML 2 uses the standard collaboration icon for these modeling elements.

The composite structure diagram is a new addition in UML 2 and is used to show the runtime architecture for a particular classifier. The nodes on this diagram, parts, are also new.

UML 2 adds fidelity to how deployment issues are described with the addition of the deployment specification. Execution environments are also new in UML 2.

Finally, the UML 2 concepts of profiles and model-driven architecture can produce significantly more robust designs than are covered in this chapter. Consider the level of architectural modeling described here as just a starting point.

Summary

The system architecture can be divided into logical and physical categories. The logical architecture shows the key classes and objects, along with their relationships, that together support the functional and technical aspects of the system. It shows the high-level structure of the system via packages and components. The logical architecture is documented in class, state machine, sequence, and activity diagrams.

The logical architecture is also represented by collaborations showing how the system supports various mechanisms and patterns. These collaborations represent more abstract designs, typically showing how classifiers playing particular roles relate to one another statically and dynamically in support of some architectural need. In a system design, collaboration occurrences show which actual classes or components play which roles to carry out the work of the collaboration. The classifiers playing parts within a collaboration can be rendered in a composite structure diagram.

The physical architecture deals with the structure of the code components and of the hardware that constitutes the system. It details the physical implementation of the concepts defined in the logical architecture. Classes and components are allocated to the artifacts that implement them. Artifacts and components and their relationships are shown in a component diagram in UML.

A deployment diagram depicts the nodes and their connections to each other. A node can be either a physical object such as a computer or a partition within that physical object. Nodes can be described both as types and as instances. Connections between nodes are represented by associations, indicating that the nodes can communicate with each other. A stereotype on the association can identify the protocol or physical medium used, such as <<TCP/IP>>. Executable artifacts can be allocated to the nodes within which they execute. A deployment diagram can map all the way from the physical appearance of the system, via the artifacts that execute within executable environments on the computers, to the logical design of the system, as shown in use-case, class, and interaction diagrams.

CHAPTER

8

Extending UML

To avoid making UML overly complex, the designers left out details available in more targeted modeling notations. However, they made UML extendable so that modelers can adapt the language to fit a specific method, organization, or user. Through the extension mechanisms provided in UML, a user can define and use new elements appropriate to the problem at hand. This chapter reviews these mechanisms, providing a number of examples of standard extensions packaged with UML. The chapter ends with a high-level overview of the UML language architecture. We suggest that those who plan to create a number of their own extensions learn the language structure in more detail.

UML explicitly supports these extension mechanisms, so a proper way to add new semantics or content to the modeling language exists. New semantics can take the form of a redefinition, an addition, or some kind of constraint on an element's usage. In other words, users can create a stereotype of an existing element, add tagged values to an element, or put constraints on an element. If done properly, tools will also support these extensions. Architects can bundle these extensions into profiles, creating new "dialects" of UML tailored to a specific environment.

For advanced modeling that requires abstractions not easily covered by the extension mechanisms, the UML 2 architecture now resides in a wider modeling universe that provides almost unlimited options. Modelers can define language variants, or "cousins," making UML potentially a "family of languages." So, unlike version 1.*x*, UML is no longer defined in terms of UML but rather in terms of a more abstract modeling language, the Meta-Object Facility (MOF). This feature provides the opportunity to create related, interoperable "languages" with common tool support, since they all relate back to a common set of modeling constructs. UML will benefit from being under a broad umbrella of languages, allowing for common ways of communicating models. Because this book focuses on UML, we don't explain the details of how to use MOF, but rather focus on how this relates to UML. In a later section, this chapter reviews the Object Constraint Language (OCL) as an example of a modeling language important to users of UML now moving toward definition in terms of MOF.

To summarize, UML provides two ways to extend the language:

- First, modelers can add stereotypes, tagged values, and constraints to model elements to extend the power of UML. Users will find sets of these extensions bundled together as profiles as well as a few of these used by the UML designers as standard extensions. The first part of this chapter reviews these mechanisms, using the standard extensions as examples.
- Second, modelers can use a variant of UML that is a new instance of MOF. Individual users are unlikely to create a UML variant but rely on one managed by the OMG, such as OCL. User should be aware of the options available with a modeling notation that is MOF-compliant.

Standard Extensions Overview

UML relies on its own extension mechanisms to define additional features. When the designers use the extension mechanisms, these are called standard extensions or standard stereotypes. The evolution of UML has seen the rapid expansion of the standard extensions. We refer to the extensions by one modeler as *user-defined extensions*. This chapter looks at a few of the standard extensions along with some instructions on how to implement your own user-defined features. The three main extension elements for practical use are tagged values (properties), constraints, and stereotypes:

- *Tagged values* are properties attached to UML elements. An author tag with a value of the class author is an example of a tagged value.
- *Constraints* are rules that restrict the semantics of one or more elements in UML. Constraints can be attached to classes or objects and are often attached to relationships, where they constrain the classes or objects that can participate in a relationship.

- A *stereotype* represents the main extension mechanism. It provides a method to extend a metaclass, creating a new metamodel element. Stereotypes can add new or extra semantics to any UML element (see the "Language Architecture and Kernel Overview" section in this chapter for more details). For example, in a Web application you can define a new type of class, such as <<JSP>>. Then, you can show a JSP class by applying the <<JSP>> stereotype, applying any linked rules you might have for this type of class you have defined.

There are a number of reasons to extend UML. For example, the method being used might have some special concepts not directly supported in UML. The application domain or the organization might have some common concepts that are important enough to be defined in the modeling language. Alternately, you might want to create more precise and clear models, possibly to make the model generate better code.

You can bundle sets of these extensions into profiles to handle specific environments. For example, users modeling for a .NET system could then use the .NET profile that would provide modeling elements suited to that environment. A section later in this chapter will review profiles. But first, the next three sections review the main user customization features of UML, starting with tagged values.

Tagged Values and Properties

A *property* represents a value connected to an element. Properties add information to model elements, and with tagged values, the information can be used both by human beings and machines. Human beings can use them to add administrative information about the models, such as author of a model, the time it was last modified, and so on. Machines can use them to process the models in a certain way; for example, code generation might be parameterized by properties in the model to indicate what kind of code to generate. Note that properties are normally not present in the finished system. They contain information about the models and the elements *in the models*, not information that should be handled by the final system.

A *tagged value* explicitly defines a property as a name-value pair. In a tagged value, the name is referred to as the tag. Each tag represents a particular kind of property applicable to one or more kinds of elements. Both the tag and the value are encoded as strings. The notation for a property is `{ tag = value}` or `{ tag1 = value1, tag2 = value2...}` or `{ tag}`.

The property or properties are displayed inside braces, with a tag and a value. If the tag is a Boolean flag, then the default value is true if the value is omitted. Tags of types other than Boolean require explicit values. A value can be defined as uninterpreted (typically a string), which means that there is no formal definition of the syntax for the value. Such values are typically meant to be read by a human being, who then interprets the value as a free text string and, where the tag name defines a context, gives a meaning to the tagged value. For example:

```
{ status = "under construction", system analyst = "Bob Smith"}
```

Properties (including tagged values) can be shown in the diagrams or be separately documented. When shown, properties are enclosed within braces inside or close to the element for which they are defined. Most UML tools have a property window that can be revealed by executing a command on an element. This window lists all the properties of the element with their values. A method or tool using UML can add more tagged values to adapt UML to the method or the deployment platform.

Standard Tag Value Examples

The set of tag values available on all attributes of classes as well as associations provides a good example of how to use the tag value extension. These tag values all have the type Boolean, so to show them, simply include the item as {*tagged value*} next to the attribute or on the association end. The range of tagged values includes the following:

- The *union* tag indicates a derived value from a union of subsets. The *subsets <property-name>* tag shows the opposite, that the attribute or association represents a subset of the named property. These tag values allow the modeler to clearly define the specific elements in a composition relationship.
- Modelers can show whether they have redefined an attribute or an association end with the tag *redefines <property-name>*. This allows a modeler to indicate which elements have a name change. In the example in Figure 8.1, the parent class Car has an aveSpeed attribute that the Racer child class redefines to lapSpeed. The redefines tag tells the viewer that in the model those attributes can be handled in the same fashion. In contrast, the driver attribute in the child class does not inherit from the parent class. However, the Taxi child class does have a driver attribute that redefines owner from the parent class. This indicates that the race car driver is not a type of owner, unlike the taxi driver. The example shows the power of the redefinition tag for clarifying the meaning of attributes. A redefinition of a property can also include

new defaults. If the attribute retains the same default, then you don't need the redefinition tag, as shown with the maxSpeed default value in Car and Racer. If desired, the modeler can also redefine attributes in the subclass to make these attributes derived values.

NOTE **A Boolean tagged value when "true" can function as a constraint on the element, showing that all values must correspond to the property.**

Tag Value from a Profile

Although you can add a tag value to a specific class, you can also make a name/property pair that is defined generally from a profile. For example, a simple Enterprise JavaBean (EJB) profile shown in Figure 8.2 creates a tagged value for StateKind as part of a stereotype. The state kind is an enumeration that shows the possible values for the StateKind tagged value. In this case, an EJB session bean can be either stateless or stateful, depending on the tagged value. So, if you are using a profile, look for these tagged value options when you apply the stereotype.

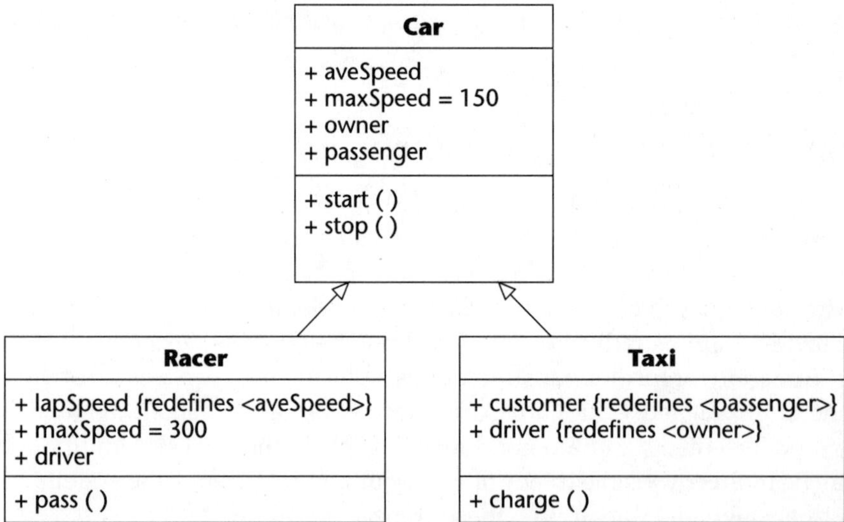

Figure 8.1 Example of redefining properties in an inheritance relationship, in this case an attribute. Note that the child class automatically inherits everything from the parent class not explicitly entered.

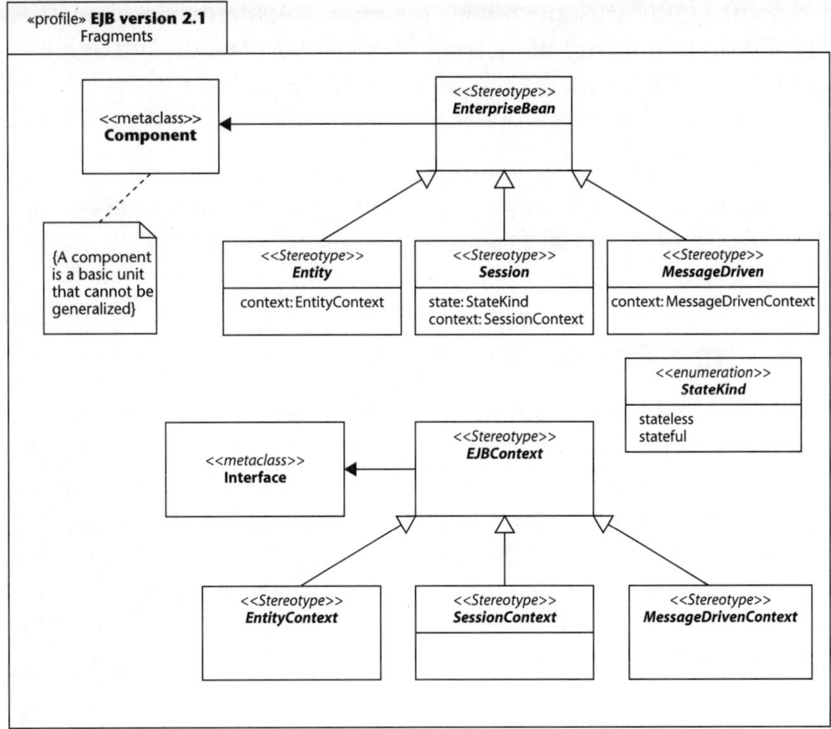

Figure 8.2 EJB simple profile showing a definition of StateKind tagged value. A full EJB profile will be larger.

Defining Your Own Tagged Values

Tagged values become a useful method to mark up a model to provide additional information. As has been discussed, a tagged value has a name (the tag) and a value (of a type) and can be connected to all kinds of elements. A tagged value adds extra semantics to an attached element. User-defined tagged values could be used to add administrative information about the progress or status of a project, or information for further transformations of the models such as code or database generation. Tagged values are extra information needed about the models and the model elements and are not directly visible in the final system (though they may be indirectly visible if they affect the implementation of the system).

To define a tagged value, follow these steps:

1. Investigate the purpose of the tagged value.
2. Define the elements it may be attached to.
3. Name the tagged value appropriately.
4. Define the type of the value.
5. Know who or what will interpret it, a machine or a human being. If it is a machine, the value must be specified in a more formal syntax (for

example, in a formal language such as C++, algebraically, using predicate logic, and so on). If it is a human being, the value can be more loosely specified (for example, an uninterpreted string).

6. Document one or more examples showing how to use the tagged value.

Two examples of possible user-defined tagged values are standard algorithm and author. The standard algorithm should be attached to an operation within a class. The name of the tag is standard algorithm and the value is a string. The value is the name of the standard algorithm. This tagged value can be used in software development tools to generate code or as an instruction to a human being. Examples of standard algorithms are quick sort and FFT. For example:

```
{ Standard algorithm = "Quick sort"}
```

The author tagged value can be attached to any element. It tells the name of the author (the person who modeled an element, such as a class diagram, an operation, and so on). The value is a string. This tagged value can be used together with a configuration-management tool to track those who work on the element. For example:

```
{ Author = "Peter Smith"}
```

Stereotypes

All languages have their restrictions and limits, especially when it comes to the things you can express with the language. When the semantics of a language are too general, they undermine the possibility of making distinct and sharp statements about systems. Conversely, if the semantics are too specialized, they limit the possible statements. Specialized languages also tend to be too large and complex. C++ can be seen as a modeling language, but it is specialized for programming and is not that powerful for business modeling. With stereotypes, a modeler can specialize UML. The stereotype represents the core mechanism for extending UML and is defined in its own package of the central language architecture, called the profile package. You will want to organize complex sets of stereotypes in profiles or rely on a library of profiles. This section focuses on the basic stereotypes. Profiles are covered in a later section.

Creating a Stereotype

Stereotypes provide the main vehicle for customization in UML. A stereotype extends a metaclass, or another stereotype, resulting in a new metaclass, allowing an acceptable way to extend the UML metamodel. UML has no limit on the number of times a metaclass can be extended by a stereotype, nor do the rules limit the number of classes that can apply a stereotype. If a class represents some form of template or cookie cutter, the metaclass provides a way of defining the type of cookie cutters or templates you produce at a high level. For some factory methods, you will probably want to use the less drastic notion of a class template, saving the stereotype for a real extension to the core concepts in the modeling domain. Once again, UML provides a number of ways of communicating similar information. Look for the best way to communicate your core concepts; don't apply a stereotype just because you can; rather, apply the stereotype when your model needs a new concept for communication with machines or human beings.

UML 1.4 had a substantial number of predefined standard stereotypes, and as is the case with tagged values and constraints, it is also possible to have user-defined stereotypes. The designers have retired some of these features in UML 2 and allowed others to move to core model elements. For example, the notion of a powertype has moved from a stereotype to a defined feature in UML 2. The new UML architecture seeks to stem the geometric expansion of standard stereotypes as features of the core specification, instead putting them into managed profiles. Stereotypes have notation, which is the text string <<name of the stereotype>> (the characters used before and after the string are guillemets, << >>). The notation (the stereotype string <<name>>) is generally placed above or in front of the name of the element on which it is based. An element can have more than one stereotype. Since stereotypes can extend the UML metamodel, a modeler should be able to have a stereotyped version of every aspect of UML.

You can associate a graphical icon with a stereotype, but this is optional. The graphical icon can include color. In UML tools, you find different ways of using icons together with stereotypes. One way is to display the icon inside the stereotyped element. If a class is stereotyped, an icon can be attached to the name compartment in the class rectangle symbol (the view element). If the icon is displayed directly in an element, you can display either both the icon and the stereotype name or just the icon. The second way of displaying icons is to collapse the stereotyped element into the icon itself, with the name of the element above or below the icon (see Figure 8.3).

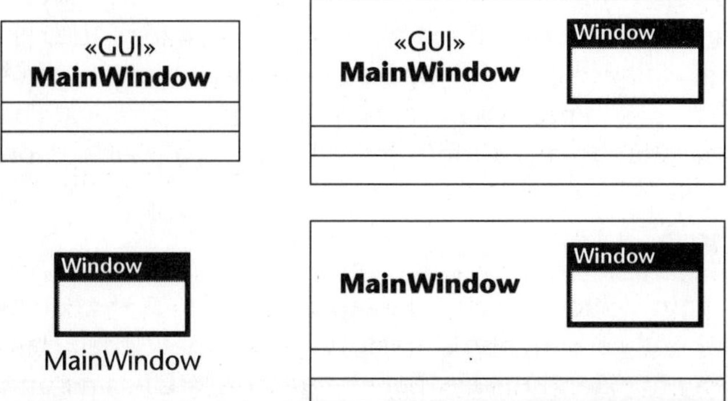

Figure 8.3 Varieties of stereotype notation for the stereotyped MainWindow class. The class is of the stereotype <<GUI>>that has a graphical window icon as its visual representation. In many UML tools, architects can often choose their own notation for a stereotype.

Examples of UML Stereotypes

The following section reviews some of the more common UML stereotypes. Some of these are referred to as standard stereotypes.

Metainformation

This chapter has already employed the metaclass concept. A *metaclass* is a class whose instances are classes. Thus, a metaclass creates instances that are not objects but rather classes. A metaclass is the core model element that a stereotype extends. A metaclass may be applied to all kinds of UML elements. The metaclass does not have a standard icon; it is just marked with the string <<metaclass>>. Metaclasses can also be implemented in programming languages such as Smalltalk. At a package level, metaclasses reside in a <<metamodel>>, another standard stereotype. A metamodel defines a set of metaclasses for use by a modeler. All modeling languages require a metamodel to provide the rules for how the modeling language behaves.

Discussion of UML extensions includes the notion of the meta-metamodel, which is a set of models defining how to define a metamodel. Because all models require a model to define their structure, the modeling discipline does discuss the structure of these meta-metamodels. Information technology and software development have had great success handling higher levels of abstraction, leading many to focus on manipulating knowledge at this super-abstract level. However, at this level of abstraction, you quickly get into something of a "chicken and the egg" brain teaser, because you always need something to give birth to the current model. As a practical matter, the easiest thing is to accept the current metamodel universe and leave it to the high priests of the Object Management Group (OMG) to battle over the definitions of the meta-metamodel. Ultimately, it is the power any model gives you to achieve something that dictates success, not the structure of language formalisms.

Dependency Stereotypes

A modeler can stereotype a dependency in a number of ways.

- A *call* is a usage dependency connecting operations. If a class A has a call dependency to a class B, operations in class A might call any of the operations in class B within scope.
- *Refine* is a type of dependency that shows a model element that further elaborates another element. Refinement and its usage are described in more detail in Chapter 4 in the discussion of abstractions. Refinement is a good example of how UML is bootstrapped from a small kernel of model elements.

- *Send* is a stereotyped dependency where the source is an operation and the target is a signal. The operation sends the signal.
- A *trace* is a stereotyped dependency from one model element to another model element. The elements traced to each other can be in the same diagram or in different diagrams. The trace indicates that the source traces conceptually back to the target. The trace stereotype can be used to show that one diagram is a more detailed description of another diagram or that a design diagram can be traced back to an analysis diagram of the same thing. This stereotype rarely results in code and typically is used informally.
- With a *derive*, UML can show a dependency that indicates you can compute the element from some other element or that the client can be computed from the supplier. The formula showing this derivation can be included as an expression on the model element. For example, an attribute can be derived from other attributes, as shown in Figure 8.4. The derivation is a stereotyped dependency.
- An *instantiate* is a subclass of a usage dependency, showing that an operation on the client creates one or more instances of the supplier.

Customization with Components

A component allows for a "plug-and-play" environment where clear rules for communication and deployment make it easy for different teams to develop compatible software. A component provides an excellent example of a standard iconic notation that you will typically use as part of your diagram. You will usually indicate a component with the keyword <<component>>, while showing the component icon in the classifier rectangle (see Figure 8.5). Because a component has so many associated elements it must handle, you can show a number of these in the class rectangle for clarity, applying the proper stereotype to the property.

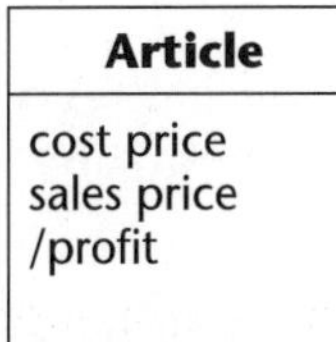

{profit = sales price - cost price}

Figure 8.4 The profit is a derived attribute. The formula (rule) for the derivation can be shown within braces. Derivation is indicated by the / in front of the operation.

Components have two very important stereotyped properties.

- The <<*required interface*>> tells you what the component needs to work.
- The <<*provided interface*>> indicates what the component gives to a system.

The component rectangle, as shown in Figure 8.5, can also show the realizations for the component, the interfaces (or also ports) needed, as well as the artifacts required for the physical manifestation of the component. In this case, the component for statistical analysis requires a portfolio interface, while providing an interface for data entry and analysis. It will be deployed in the jar file stats.jar. This same information can also appear with different notation in an internal structure diagram for a component that more clearly shows the connection between required and provided interfaces. Such a diagram uses the assembly connector notation designed to show the "wiring" of the component.

Stereotypes Applied to Deployment Artifacts

Several stereotypes can be applied to the deployment and execution environment. They help clarify the picture of a deployment by showing what each artifact represents in the real world. An *artifact* represents something that exists that can be used to implement a component. In a deployment, an artifact is generally a manifestation of some other model element. Artifact rests at the top of a large generalization hierarchy, as outlined in the following in these elements that inherit from artifact.

- The stereotype <<executable>> represents an executable program.
- The stereotype <<file>> represents any system file and has many subclasses.
- The stereotype <<library>> is a subclass of <<file>> that represents a static or dynamic library.
- The stereotype <<document>> is a subclass of <<file>> that shows that the file contains documentation for use by human beings rather than any information for the machine to interpret.
- In contrast, the stereotype <<source>> shows a type of file that can be compiled into an executable, at least once you have fixed all the compile errors in the code.
- The stereotype <<script>> also indicates a file for machine interpretation, but the system can interpret the information without need of a compiler.

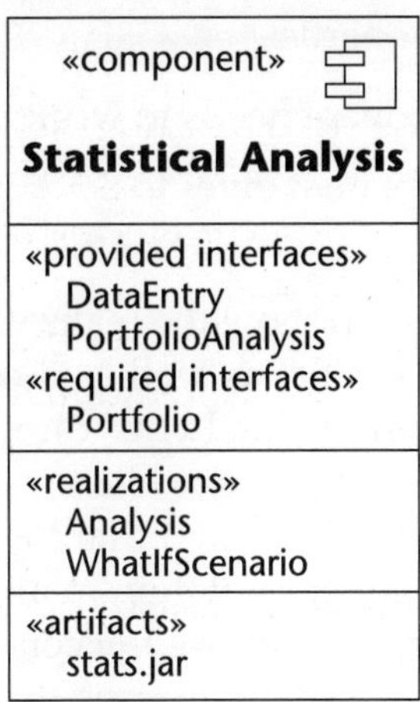

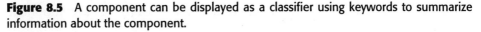

Figure 8.5 A component can be displayed as a classifier using keywords to summarize information about the component.

The deployment of artifacts represents an area well suited for further extensions to fit the deployment environment. For a Java Web application, for example, one might see jar files, deployment descriptors, Web-inf files, or anything else needed to clarify the physical deployment of the application. Obviously, such a proliferation of stereotypes helps the management of middleware, but it requires excellent model management. Sets of managed stereotypes, or profiles, guided by the Model Driven Architecture initiative (see Chapter 9) help manage these assets.

Utility

A *utility* is a stereotyped type that contains only class-scope operations and attributes. The utility doesn't have any instances; it's only a set of class-scope operations and attributes accessed through the type, not through any instance. A class-scope operation is called by specifying only the class name and the operation name, such as in MathPack::sin(3.14). The utility is normally applied to classes, as shown in Figure 8.6.

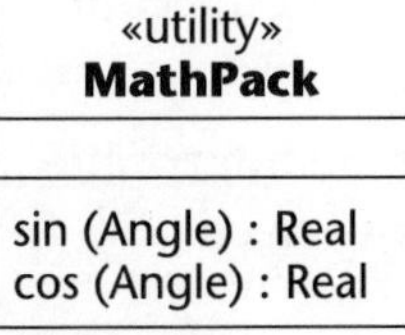

Figure 8.6 A utility class for mathematical functions that are grouped together in a class and made available as class-scope operations.

Use Case Stereotypes

Extend is a stereotyped relationship between use cases implemented to specify that one use case might incorporate the flow of another use case, diverging at an extension point to model a specific flow. The main use case incorporates the supplementary use case, depending on the condition found at the extension point. In contrast, the *include* stereotyped relationship indicates that one use case incorporates the supplementary use case entirely. Include helps support reuse in a use case model, while extend allows the modeler to easily show variants based on different conditions.

CROSS-REFERENCE **Use cases with the extend and include relationships are described in Chapter 3.**

Signal

Signal is a stereotyped classifier that constrains the semantics of the instances so that they can be sent only as signals, as shown in Figure 8.7. Signals are used in systems where asynchronous messages are sent between different active objects, so in a distributed environment they have become quite common. It's possible to build hierarchies of signals supporting polymorphism so that if a state transition has an event-signature specifying a signal class, all the subclasses of that signal class are also receivable and accepted. A signal represents a separate object from the entities sending and receiving it.

In UML, the *receptions* owned by a classifier indicate the signals that the classifier can handle. So, an object sends a signal, and the receiving object responds to the signal according to the receptions defined for the receiving entity. In other words, you can detail the signals that a classifier can receive by showing the receptions on the classifier. As shown in Figure 8.8, show the receptions on a classifier in the operations compartment of the classifier using the stereotype <<signal>>. Such notation means the classifier has a method to handle the signal. Combined with hierarchies of signal classes, you can show of the many ways to handle messages in a distributed system.

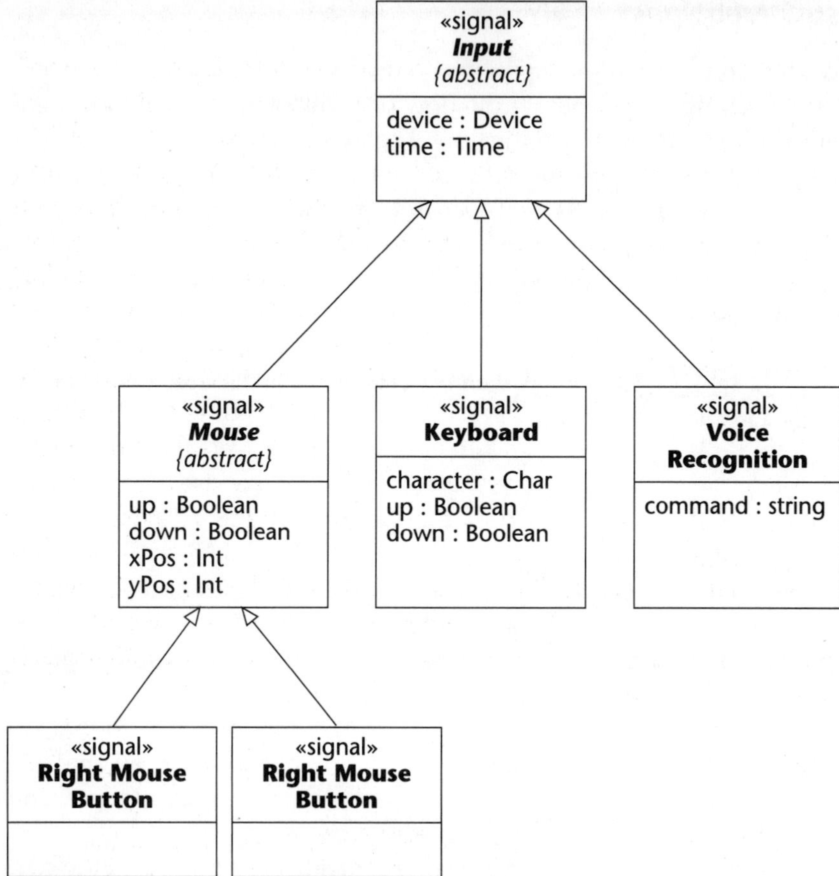

Figure 8.7 A hierarchy with signal stereotyped classes.

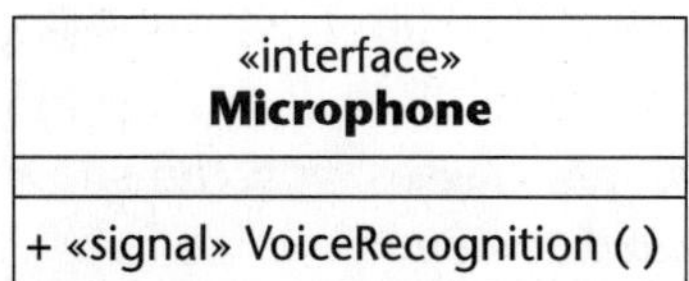

Figure 8.8 A classifier showing an available reception expressed with the stereotype <<signal>>. This shows that the microphone interface can interpret voice signals. This would indicate that this interface is not able to interpret keyboard or mouse signals.

Control, Boundary, and Entity

Classes can be stereotyped as control, boundary, and entity. These stereotypes are used to increase the semantic meaning of the classes and their usage in modeling situations. These stereotypes are not found in the core of the UML specification. Rather, they are common stereotypes implemented in many UML tools and used during the design and analysis phase. They are based on the model-view-controller concept, where the entity is the model, the control is the controller, and the boundary is the view. The model-view-controller (MVC) concept, shown in Figure 8.9, is a well-used solution (pattern) for building systems with an entity model, which is presented and manipulated via a graphical user interface (GUI). Because these stereotypes are based on the MVC concept, they are very useful when dealing with GUI-based systems and also Web application frameworks, such as Struts, that implement the MVC pattern. These stereotypes are used to analyze and to realize use cases in more detail. The analysis classes are an entity class (something to be stored in the system and implemented in many use cases), a boundary class (used to communicate with the external actors), or a control class (used to handle a specific use case or scenario, typically specialized to only one or a few use cases). For an example of implementing these stereotypes on a real software deliverable, see the case study in Chapter 11.

- The *boundary* stereotype specializes in using the class for presentation and manipulation. Boundary classes present and communicate the information in a system to another system, such as a human or a machine (that is, actors). The boundary classes can also enable the manipulation of the information (through well-defined rules in the entity objects). Boundary classes are typically windows, dialog boxes, or communication classes, such as TCP/IP.
- The *entity* stereotype is used to model business objects (the core concepts) such as debt, invoice, insurance contract, and so on. They are typically persistent so that they can be stored in the system.
- The *control* stereotype is used to connect boundary objects with their entity objects and to handle a sequence of operations inside the system. The entity objects carry the information that is presented and manipulated through boundary objects. Control objects typically handle the processing of the information in the entity objects, along with the functionality sequences that involve a number of entity objects.

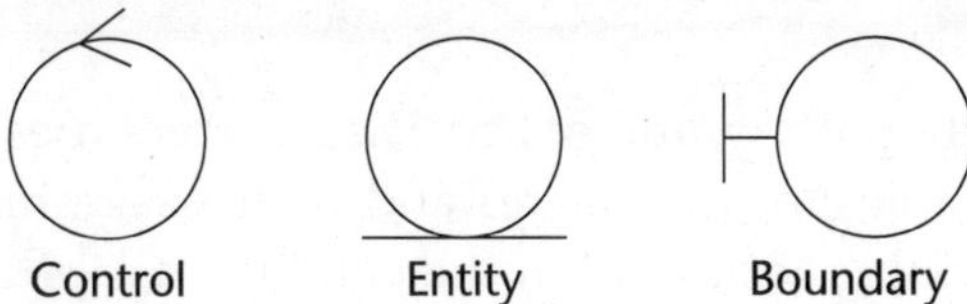

Figure 8.9 The typical icons for the control, entity, and boundary stereotypes.

By including these three simple stereotypes, a class diagram can be made more precise and easier to understand for the reader. The purpose and responsibility of a class is indicated by its stereotype and is immediately visible in the diagram. A more detailed description of the class can be accessed through the documentation and responsibility properties of the class. Furthermore, the relationships between classes are easily understood; for example, if a boundary class has an association to an entity class, it's usually the information in the entity class that is shown or manipulated through that boundary class.

UML includes a standard stereotype <<entity>> that indicates a component that provides persistent information related to a business. In other words, the class <<entity>> from the analysis level quickly translates into the component entity and then from there into some persistent entity, taking advantage of the platform used to deploy the application. So, for a project using Enterprise JavaBeans, for example, these will become some form of bean.

Users can define new stereotypes for classes, defining common roles used in a specific application domain where classes of a special type have their own icons and semantic meaning. For example, in the financial domain, possible stereotypes are <<Asset>>, for describing classes that represent an item that has a price, and the stereotyped dependency <<Affects>>, for showing that the price calculation of a instance of one class is affected by the price of an instance of another class. For example, the price of a stock option is affected by the price of the underlying stock. The organization that uses the stereotype decides how formal and extensive the semantics of a stereotype are. However, the meaning of the stereotype needs to be well known by everyone reading the models in which the stereotype is used (see Figure 8.10).

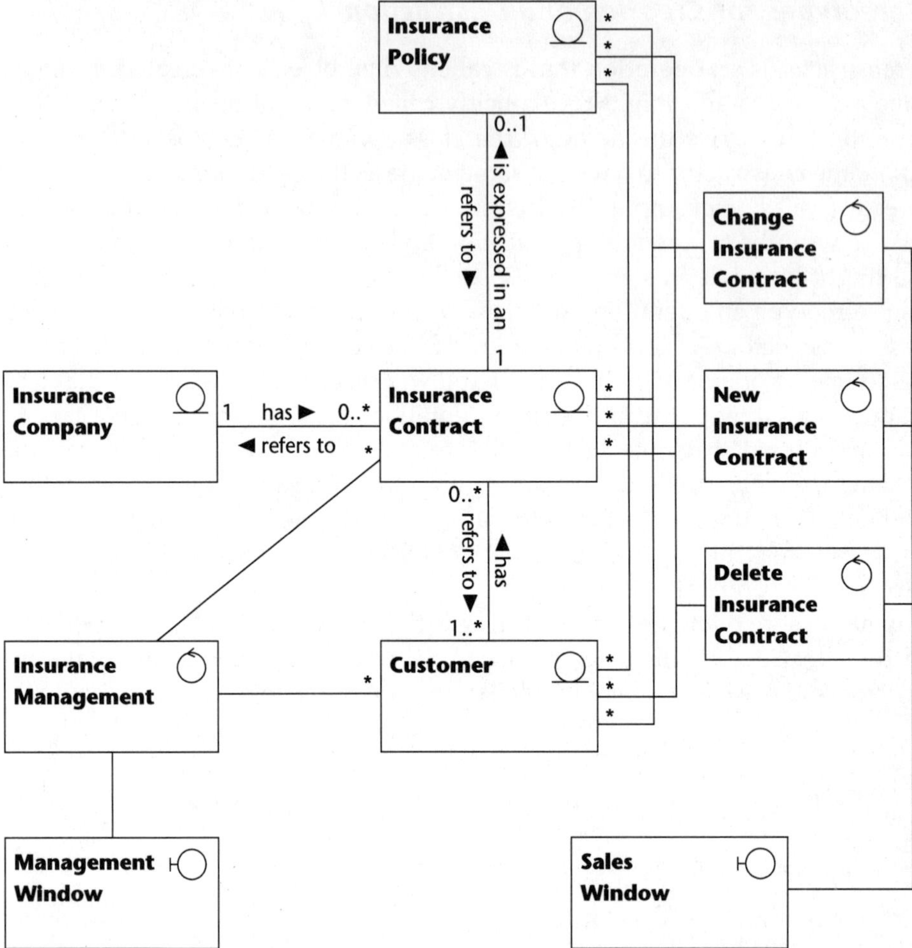

Figure 8.10 The entity classes capture the core business, in this case, the insurance business. The entity classes are Insurance Policy, Insurance Contract, Customer, and Insurance Company. The control classes Change Insurance Contract, New Insurance Contract, and Delete Insurance Contract serve the boundary class Sales Window. The control class Insurance Management serves the Management Window with Customers and Insurance Contracts.

Stereotypes for Creation and Destruction

A *constructor* is an operation that is called when objects are created. It might have arguments and might be explicitly called. It might have any name, but commonly it carries the name of the class (languages such as C++ or Java *require* the constructor to have the same name as the class) or simply the name "create (...)." For example, the Invoice class may have a constructor called invoice with the arguments specification and amount. An explicit constructor call might look like this: invoice ("A dell computer", 2000 $). A modeler can also stereotype an operation on a class with <<create>> to indicate that it is a class constructor. At the opposite end from construction, the modeler can stereotype an operation to indicate that it will destroy the instance of the class that it relates to with the <<destroy>> notation.

In an internal structure diagram, the modeler can show the constructor for an instance with a dependency arrow with the <<create>> notation pointing to the specific operation that acted as the constructor for the instance. The arrow can cross the rectangle boundary of the class and point to the exact operation. See Figure 8.11 for an example of this notation. In some cases, a class may have more than one constructor, resulting in a different object, depending on the constructor called. So, for example, you could have a different constructor in those cases where the dollar amount of the invoice is not shown.

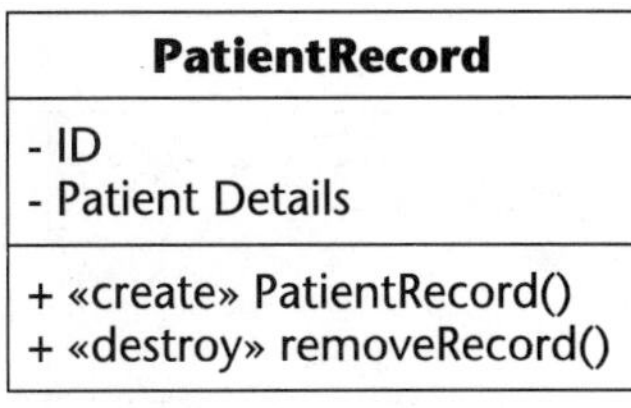

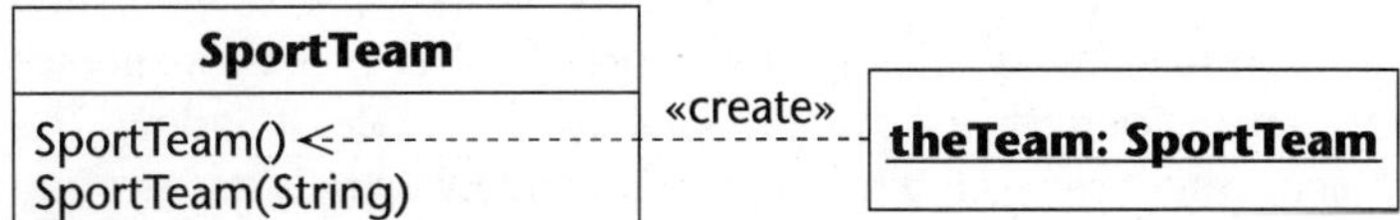

Figure 8.11 Operations that can create and destroy instances of the owning class. The first figure shows a patient record. Note that now in most modeling tools you do not need to show the get and set methods for a private property because most tools will generate that automatically. Also, the other figure is an instance showing a <<create>> dependency on a class operation, in this case a sports team created in a fantasy sports league tracking program.

Retired Standard Stereotypes

The architectural redesign of UML for version 2 promoted some of the more commonly used stereotypes from version 1.*x* into full-blown UML elements, while leaving other stereotypes relatively unchanged and still others irrelevant. For example, powertype now is included in UML with the notion of a generalization set. Stereotyped constraints should be replaced by OCL. Table 8.1 shows the retired stereotypes organized by the base element type.

Defining Your Own Stereotypes

In user-defined tagged values or constraints, value and semantics are added onto an element; a new type of element is defined, although it is always based on an existing element. A stereotype also has its own notation, and it can have an icon that represents the stereotype element in diagrams. The definition of stereotypes is typically supported by a development support tool that allows this capability, along with an icon used for display.

Table 8.1 Stereotypes No Longer Official UML Standards

BASE ELEMENT	STEREOTYPE RETIRED OR PROMOTED
Package	<<appliedProfile>>, <<facade>>, <<profile>>, <<stub>>, <<topLevel>>
Permission	<<access>>, <<friend>>
AssociationEnd	<<association>>, <<local>>, <<parameter>>, <<self>>
Flow	<<copy>>
CallEvent	<<create>>, <<destroy>>
Constraint	<<invariant>>, <<postcondition>>, <<precondition>>, <<stateInvariant>>
Class	<<powertype>>
Abstraction	<<realize>>
Comment	<<requirement>>
ObjectFlowState	<<signalflow>>
Artifact	<<table>>
Classifier	<<thread>>

User-defined stereotypes are often implemented when adapting UML to a specific method or to the application domain that an organization uses. Concepts used in the method, or common elements or relationships used in the application domain that are not supported in the standard UML, are usually defined as stereotypes. As noted earlier, stereotypes have been added to the UML to make it easier for the UML designers to answer the question: "Why isn't the concept X or Y defined in UML?" They can always say: "Define a stereotype for it, and it's there!"

When defining stereotypes, you need to describe:

- On which element the user-defined stereotype is based
- The new semantics the stereotype adds or refines
- One or more examples of how to implement the user-defined stereotype

Figure 8.12 shows some examples of the user-defined stereotypes <<time>>, <<semaphore>>, and <<GUI>>. (Note that although UML has other ways to show time, this system required a special stereotype and that these are *not* standard stereotypes but customizations for this specific model presented in a realistic example.)

- The *time stereotype* applies to associations, specifying that there is a time dependency. A time-stereotyped association must have the multiplicity one-to-many, where the many side is many over time. For example, a shelf might be placed in many bookcases, but only one at a time.
- The *semaphore stereotype* applies to classes. A semaphore class is one whose object guards a resource and allows access to only one or a specified number of users of that resource at a time. A printer should be used only by one thread in the system at a time and, thus, can be guarded by a Printer Queue class with the stereotype <<semaphore>>. The semaphore semantics indicate that only one thread at a time gains access to the printer queue and, consequently, prevents several threads from concurrently trying to write information to the printer.
- The *GUI stereotype* is a specialization of the boundary stereotype. It has the same functionality and purpose as a boundary class, but concerns only graphical user interfaces (a boundary class also involves any other means of communication with users or other systems). Consequently, a GUI class must be part of a graphical user interface, for example, a window or a message box. The GUI stereotype in Figure 8.12 is an example of a stereotype defined as a specialization of another stereotype (since stereotypes can inherit from each other).

For more detail on how to specify a stereotype as a profile element, see the section on profiles later in this chapter.

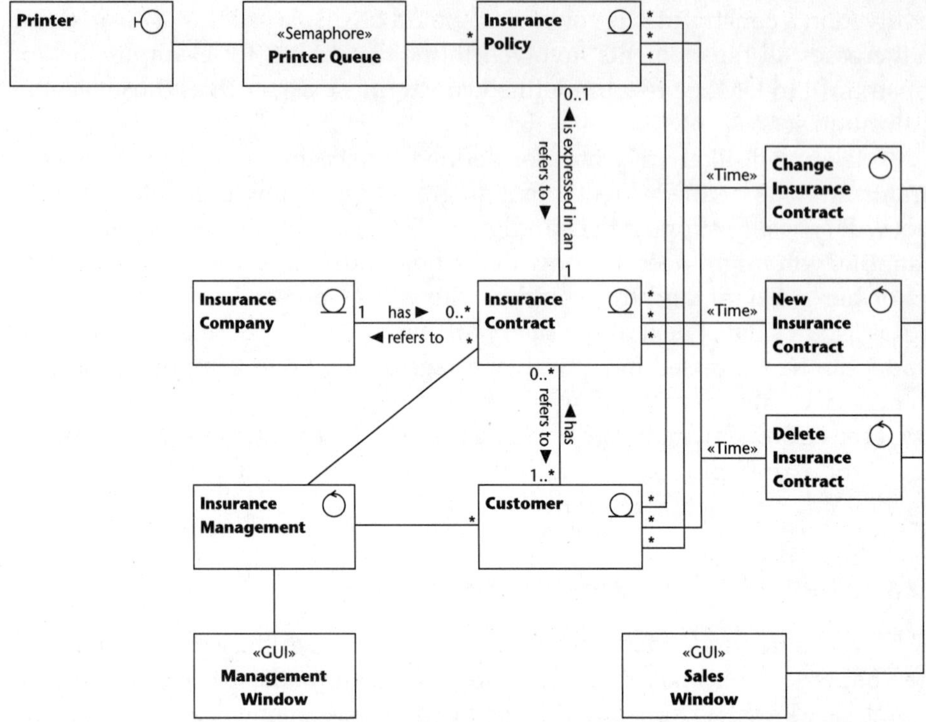

Figure 8.12 An example of implementing user-defined stereotypes. The Printer Queue class is a semaphore; it connects the Insurance Policy class with the Printer by controlling the access via the Printer Queue. The associations between the controller classes and the Insurance Contracts are stereotyped with time. The Management Window and Sales Window classes are GUI stereotypes.

Constraints

A *constraint* is a semantic condition or restriction on elements. Constraints are applied to elements using an expression; one constraint applies to one kind of element. Thus, while a constraint can involve many elements, they must be of the same kind (for example, associations, as in the xor constraint). The constraints are displayed in braces ({ constraint}), either directly in the diagrams or separately (typically available through a constraint window in a development support tool). A constraint can be displayed directly in the diagram next to the view element it constrains. If many elements of the same kind are involved in a constraint, the constraint should be displayed near a dashed line that crosses all the elements involved in the constraint (for example, the xor constraint). In UML, a few predefined constraints exist, such as those on generalization sets.

Modelers will likely rely on user-defined constraints quite often. The constraints may be defined directly in a diagram near a view element. The UML tool will typically support the handling of the rule with the related entity. For example, you might need to show that a boss must have a higher salary than his or her assistant, and this could be shown as { person.boss.salary >= person.assistant.salary} next to the salary attribute. The rule defined between the braces can be expressed in natural language or any other computer language identified by the modeler. For constraints within UML that execute in the model environment, many recommend the use of the OCL as a specialized language for expressing constraints. The UML specification uses OCL to express constraints on modeling elements.

Examples of UML Constraints

UML has some predefined constraints, as were shown throughout the previous chapters of this book. This section reviews some of these to show how constraints work when applied to different UML model elements.

CROSS-REFERENCE For additional standard constraints not shown here, see the time constraints in Chapter 6 and the constraints on generalization covered in Chapter 4.

Recognize that for constraints, the power of the construct usually rests in the ability of the modeler to apply his or her own rules wherever needed. Therefore, modelers tend to develop their own constraints. While the UML specification includes hundreds of constraints, almost all are user defined for the specific entity. In contrast, UML uses stereotypes in a more standard manner as a managed resource; the modeler does not make up so many new stereotypes. Consequently, the number of standard constraints is smaller than the number of standard stereotypes. However, constraints represent a more commonly used feature to customize the model to fit the circumstances.

Constraints for Associations

The *xor constraint* specifies that a set of associations has constraints on their links. The xor constraint is applied where an association connects a single class to a set of other classes. The xor constraint specifies that an object of the single class is connected (linked) to only one of the associated class objects (on the opposite side of the association). For instance, a person can have many (zero or more) insurance contracts, and a company can have many insurance contracts, as shown in Figure 8.13. The model doesn't indicate whether an insurance contract can be owned by both a person and a company at the same time. To specify that an insurance contract can be owned only by either one person or one company, the xor constraint is used to restrict the associations between Insurance Contract and Person and between Insurance Contract and Company.

Constraints for Association Roles and Properties

The *ordered constraint* is a standard constraint for association roles. An ordered association specifies that there is an implicit order between the links within the association. Windows are ordered on a screen, for example; one window is on top, one window is at the bottom, and so on. Therefore, the association between the screen and the windows is ordered. The default value for an association is unordered, meaning that the links can be in any order. In addition, ordered indicates that the set has only one instance of each value. In contrast, *bag* used as a constraint indicates that the collection can repeat a value, with *seq* or *sequence* indicating a specific order to the bag. The constraint is displayed in braces near the association, as shown in Figure 8.14. Both ordered and unordered constraints can be shown explicitly, though unordered is the default constraint for all associations, and doesn't have to be specified. The constraint can also apply to all properties, so you can use ordered or sequence to define the nature of an attribute on a class as well.

Another constraint typically used on a property and used as a standard in UML is *readOnly*, which indicates that the element cannot be overwritten. Note that in such cases a Boolean tagged value indicating a true property functions just like a constraint in terms of the model, showing that all instances of the elements with the constraint must have those tag values.

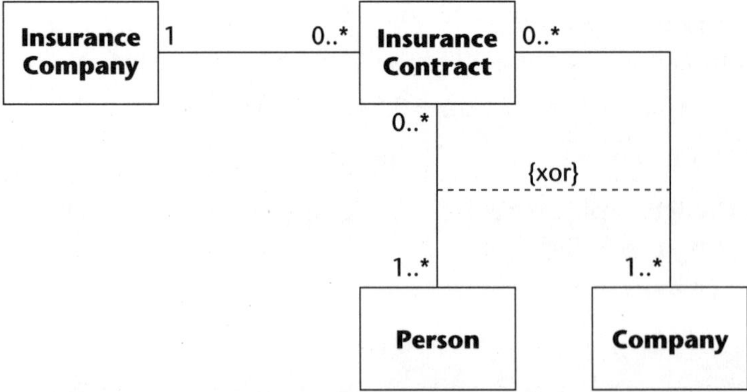

Figure 8.13 A Person/Company can have zero or more Insurance Contracts. A contract can be owned by one or many Persons or by one or many Companies. Without the xor constraint one or many Persons *and* one or many Companies can own the Insurance Contract. If multiplicity were changed at the Person or Company side (to say zero or more), this change would affect the semantics, allowing an Insurance Contract to be owned by no one.

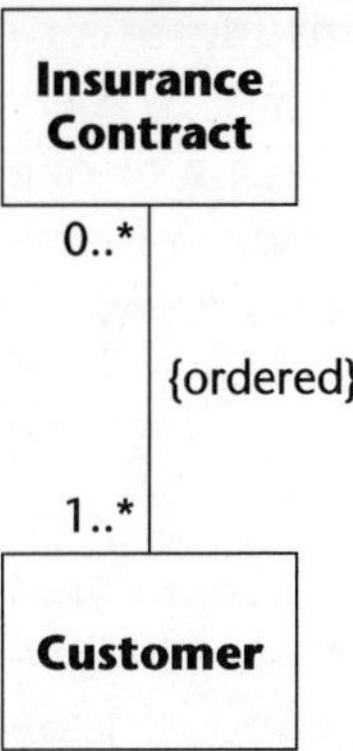

Figure 8.14 The constraint { ordered } specifies that there is an explicit order between the links. The exact order can be shown inside the braces as a user-defined constraint, for example, { ordered by increasing time }.

Defining Your Own Constraints

As noted, user-defined constraints are common. A user-defined constraint is specified for the element to which it applies. The semantic impact—what it means to apply the constraint to an element—is also specified. Constraints are used to limit element semantics in terms of conditions or restrictions of the semantics, and in some cases can represent an advanced feature of your model. Consequently, when you need one of the more advanced constraints (more than just a simple rule), it's important to evaluate all the effects it might have. As with all types of specifications, it's useful to give examples of how the constraint can be used. Thus, to specify an advanced constraint, it's necessary to describe the following:

- To which element the user-defined constraint applies
- The semantic impact on the element of the user-defined constraint
- One or more examples of how to apply the user-defined constraint
- How the user-defined constraint can be implemented

An example of a more complex user-defined constraint, Singleton, that can be applied to classes is shown in Figure 8.15 and described in the following paragraphs.

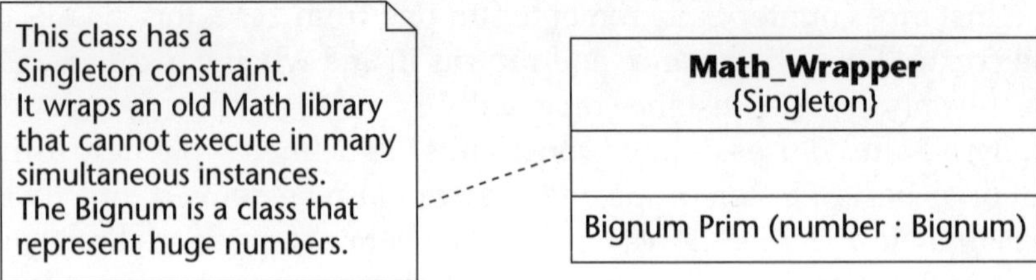

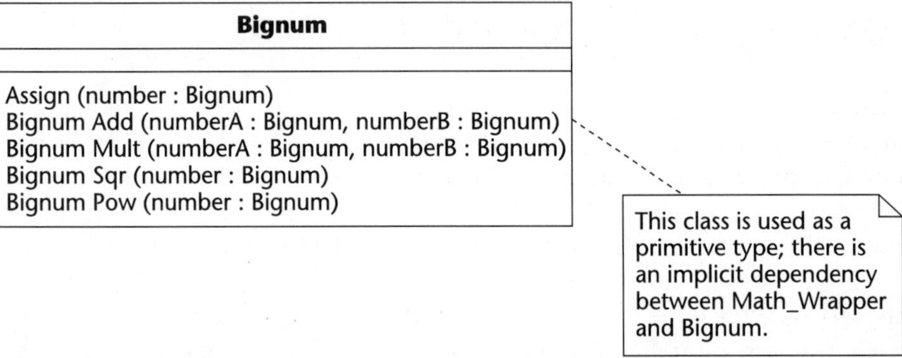

Figure 8.15 An example with a Singleton class. The Math_Wrapper wraps an old Math library that cannot execute in many simultaneous instances. The Math_Wrapper class has a Singleton constraint.

A class with the Singleton constraint has a restriction on the number of objects it may have at the same time. The Singleton class can have only one object at a time. Singleton classes can be used for wrappers where many coexisting objects can be problematic. For example, if you wrap legacy C code, the code might cause problems when executed in many simultaneous instances. Singleton classes are also used frequently in Web applications to define one object that handles communication with other systems, such as a database connection pool. Singleton classes, typically available throughout the system, can also be used for global configuration objects that should exist only in one instance.

A Singleton class can be implemented with a class-scope attribute, which is used as an instance counter. The class constructor increments the class-scope attributes value every time it is called, that is, every time someone creates an object of the class. The destructor, which is in the class, decrements the class-scope attributes value every time it is called—every time someone destroys an object of the class. The default value of the class-scope attribute's value must be zero because no objects exist before the class; when the class-scope attribute's value is other than zero or one, an exception is thrown. A variant of this is to provide a class-scope operation to access the Singleton instance.

When the instance counter is incremented to one from zero, this class-scope operation creates the only instance and returns it; and when it is called again, it returns the only existing instance repeatedly.

Generally, advanced user-defined constraints are defined separately using a UML tool or as part of a stereotype, but they can also be defined directly in a diagram near a view element. An example of constraints specified directly in a diagram are rules that constrain attributes or links.

A Language for Expressing Constraints

UML used to include the Object Constraint Language (OCL), a standard way to express constraints with UML that tools could also interpret. Modelers had the option of expressing constraints as strings using natural language or using OCL. Now, OCL receives a first-class definition because it has its own metamodel. Still, users of UML do not have to use OCL. However, for those who use MDA or seek to have their models execute in any way, OCL provides the standard and sanctioned method for articulating constraints on UML models.

OCL is no longer defined as part of the basic UML language but rather represents an extension of MOF, providing a real example of extension through the creation of another member of the UML family of languages. Understanding how OCL relates to UML illustrates the first class extensions, while also showing the core elements of this constraint language, which is becoming a common way to express rules in a system.

OCL Metamodel

When the OCL definition was a part of the UML specification, it guaranteed a certain amount of interoperability at a cost of making OCL a less sophisticated construct. Now, OCL attains interoperability through a mapping to the same abstract modeling language, MOF. What is it about OCL that makes it need its own metamodel?

OCL provides a good candidate for a full-blown extension. Given that UML is set up to use OCL for machine-readable information, the two languages must operate in a synchronized manner. However, UML does not have as a core a focus on the definition of a constraint language; attaching such features to the UML core would distract from the purpose of the language. The constraint language has distinct enough requirements that it makes more sense to define it outside UML. Theoretically, one can define the constraint language within UML, but that does not allow for reuse and ties the definition to a lot of elements not central to the expression of constraints.

Now, with OCL as a separate construct, language architects have been able to more clearly focus on improving language features such as the handling of collection types. OCL now handles fully nested types, where before OCL flattened out all types. Certainly, such improvements could have been made within the UML specification; however, these improvements would start to make UML more complex with a difficult combination of tools to wield. Better to have a clear construct for handling constraints outside UML than a set of packages in UML for constraints not as clearly and efficiently designed.

A constraint language exists as a pure specification language defined outside UML for use within UML. OCL only exchanges information about associated elements. These expressions are guaranteed to have no side effects; the constraint language does not change model elements. OCL is used to make expressions that can return a value with a type and has mechanisms to handle such things as pre- and postconditions for an operation.

The OCL metamodel has two main packages, a types package that shows the main collections and primitive types available, and an expressions package. The OCL metamodel extends classifier to define the OclMessageType and the OclModelElementType to provide distinct core language types along with the data type elements brought in from the MOF. The expressions package extends Model Element from the infrastructure library of MOF to define the abstract base class for expressions, like OclExpression. As shown in Figure 8.16, the expressions package includes a number of features. This is not the place to go in detail through these elements in the OCL metamodel. The diagram, however, illustrates an instance of the language architecture of UML where OCL expressions and types, rather than relating to UML definitions, relate to their own metamodel with interoperability aided by MOF.

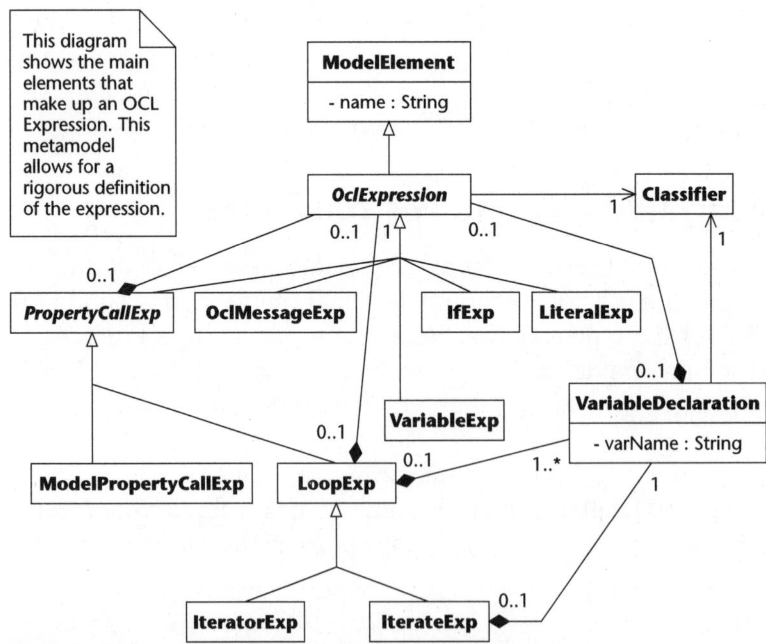

Figure 8.16 Detail of the OCL expression package.

Basic Structure of OCL Expressions

Any UML element that can use an expression can use an OCL expression. OCL expressions relate to a specific place in the UML model, such as a precondition related to a class. OCL can be quickly grasped but has features that take extensive training to master. This section shows OCL at a high level.

An OCL expression has a context, which is a classifier name as well as the keyword "self," which is the instance of the classifier. An OCL expression relates to a package, so it can have a namespace. In the example that follows this paragraph, the initial value, shown by init:, for a player in this economic simulation game, equals the total value of the bank times the stake in the bank that the player has at the start of the simulation.

```
Package simulation::banking::person

context Player:: value: Integer
init: Bank.toalValue * self.bankStake

End Package
```

OCL provides syntax to allow a modeler to specify invariants, preconditions, postconditions, guards, targets for messages, definitions, derivation rules, initial values, and general constraints using this basic approach with, on the whole, intuitive notation. For a full review of OCL, see the most recent version of the specification on the OMG Web site (www.omg.org). OCL support for invariants, preconditions, and postconditions replaces the stereotypes for these elements in earlier versions of UML. These constraints, taken together, help support a "design by contract" approach to software development; they are important constraints for UML. UML users are encouraged to use the OCL syntax for expressing these constraints, as shown in the next section.

Invariants, Preconditions, and Postconditions

Invariant applies to a type. It specifies a property that is preserved over the lifetime of an instance of the type. The property is usually some kind of condition that must be valid for the type instance. Some languages, such as Eiffel, have built-in support for invariants, and they can be directly implemented in the final code. The syntax of the value is uninterpreted and usually is not shown in the diagram.

For example, a value for an invariant constraint to a color attribute in a class named Car is, in natural language, that the value of the attribute color cannot change during the lifetime of the object or the speed of the car can never be negative. In OCL, the car speed is expressed as follows, using inv: to show an invariant. The package notation is optional and not shown in this example.

```
Context car inv:
CarSpeed >= 0
```

Precondition applies to an operation. It is a condition that must be true before the operation is invoked. The value is uninterpreted and typically not shown in the diagram. For example, a value for a precondition attached to the operation calculateFinalScore() that takes a person *only if* that person has completed the game and provides their final score as an integer might be as follows.

```
Context Player::calculateFinalScore():: Integer
Pre: self.isComplete = true
```

Postcondition also applies to an operation. It is a condition that must be true after the completion of an operation. The value is uninterpreted and usually not shown in the diagram. For example, a value for a postcondition tag attached to an operation that processes game events for a player and returns the value of the number of choices that should be remaining for the player might be as follows. (Note that the *result* key word is designed to reference the result of the expression.)

```
Context GameEvent::processPlayerChoices():: Integer
Post: result = 0.
```

CROSS-REFERENCE **These simple examples show the possible features that OCL can include. For more on OCL, see the specification on the OMG Web site (www.omg.org).**

Invariants, preconditions, and postconditions are often used together to implement the technique known as *programming by contract* and, by extension, design by contract. An invariant is a condition that the *class implementor* guarantees to be true throughout the execution of the system. A precondition is one that the *caller* of an operation guarantees to be true before the operation is called, and the postcondition is one that the *operation implementor* guarantees to be true after the operation has been executed. Should anyone break any of these "contracts," the system might throw an exception (typically indicating an internal programming error in the system). Making certain that the invariants, preconditions, and postconditions have been defined in the model almost always improves the software development effort dramatically. Whether these constraints should be expressed in OCL or in another language depends on the needs of the project.

Language Architecture and Kernel Overview

To implement user-defined extensions, it is important to familiarize yourself with the UML's semantics or at least the core semantics. Although most of this book focuses on the UML superstructure, this section focuses on the UML infrastructure and the language kernel. This structure carefully defines extension mechanisms, making UML a modeling language that essentially can extend itself. Both syntax—which indicates the form for stating information—and semantics—which indicate the content of a statement—are formally defined.

As an aid, this section provides a simplified description of the main UML elements. Again, we recommend that you have a basic knowledge of the core semantics before you create your own stereotypes or profiles. This section also helps you to understand the underlying model of the UML and what it means for the modeler.

High-Level Language Constructs

As shown in Figure 8.17, the language architecture starts from the infrastructure library package, which contains two packages; a core, which has the main language elements, and profiles, which define the ways to extend language elements, making it easier for tools to support these features. From such a small seed, a number of language constructs grow with automated support. The MOF uses the infrastructure library as a metamodel, or a model used to define other models. The MOF represents a special type of metamodel used to define other metamodels, what you could theoretically term a meta-metamodel. The UML metamodel then relies on MOF.

What does MOF supply UML? MOF provides the rules for the reflective interfaces in a reflection package, as well as rules for the exchange of XML definitions of a model using XML Metadata Interchange (XMI). Thus, MOF makes it easier to share models between different development support tools as it defines the rules for automated querying of model elements and the exchange of information. This architecture also defines different compliance points, so tool vendors can easily identify the features they support. A "basic" package sets out a minimum expected level of compliance for tool vendors. The emphasis on having compliance checked by XMI means that UML can be defined automatically without references to the visual information. For mapping to the visual information, UML has a diagram interchange specification.

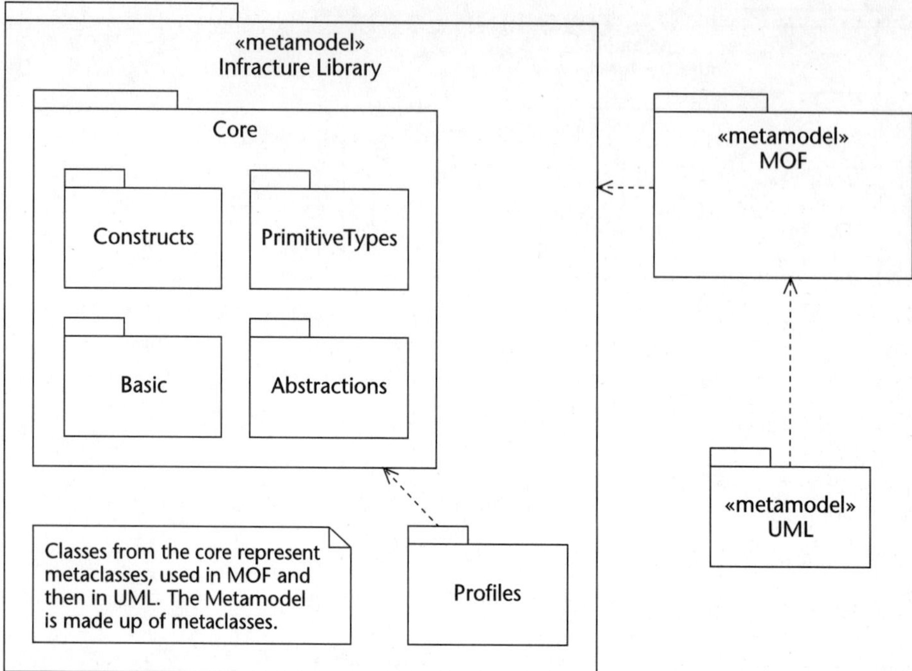

Figure 8.17 High-level UML architecture.

The core UML elements from the infrastructure library provide the foundation for the UML superstructure. Because MOF maps precisely to the infrastructure library, UML also maps to MOF. As Figure 8.18 shows, the UML superstructure uses the class package as a set of metaclasses to map to the core concepts of the metamodel. The other top-level packages use the class package to provide the language definition. Within the class package, the kernel package represents the core elements of UML. The kernel combines the many separate packages found in the infrastructure library, designed atomically to allow for reuse and flexibility, into a coherent modeling language designed to model software. This complex exercise in object-oriented modeling has evolved to provide more abstract modeling mechanisms, while at the same time providing a clearer definition of the core of UML itself. Finally, at that point, we arrive at constructs recognizably UML.

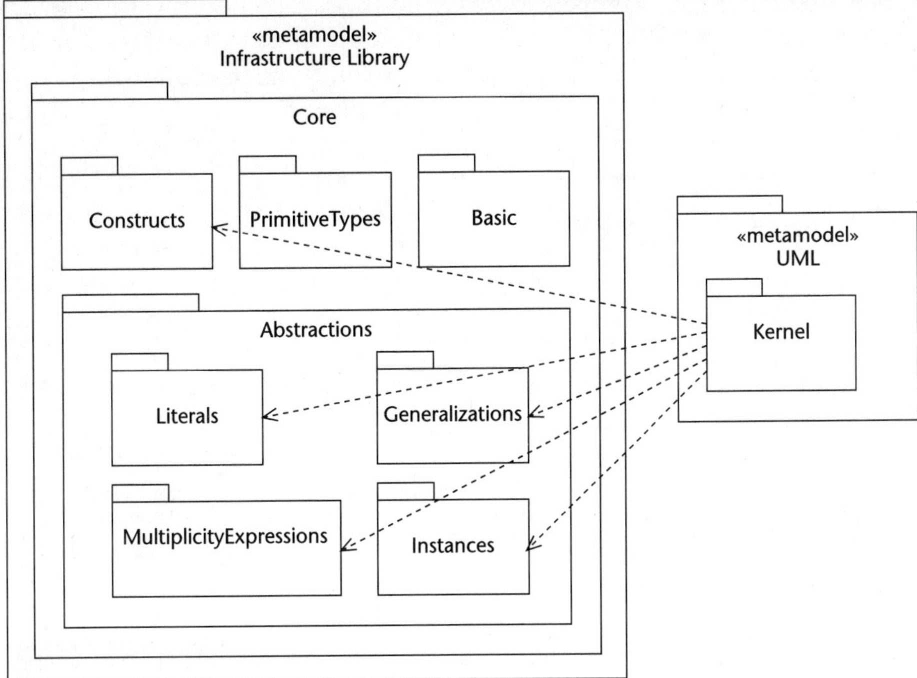

Figure 8.18 Use of the infrastructure library.

Reviewing the UML Kernel

To extend UML constructs, it is worth looking more closely at the kernel package and how UML specifies model elements. As mentioned, the kernel includes the core of UML so it represents a large selection of classes in one package. To organize these classes, the specification breaks their relationships down into a number of class diagrams, rather than packages. At the very root of the kernel is a class called element, which is used in most of these diagrams.

An *element* is the abstract base class for UML. It acts as an anchor to which you can attach a number of mechanisms. The kernel extends the base class element in a number of different ways. For example, Figure 8.19 shows the main features from the kernel in a class diagram for the familiar construct of classifier and how it extends from element. As is shown, a classifier is a packageable element as well as a redefined element and a namespace. The definition of a class thus extends classifier to include the additional features that make up a UML class. The kernel provides a rich array of model element subclasses. If an architectural group wants to define a cousin to UML, they derive their own model elements, extending the MOF and infrastructure library where needed. However, if they only require a variant of a construct already defined in UML, they can use a profile to extend a metaclass from the metamodel.

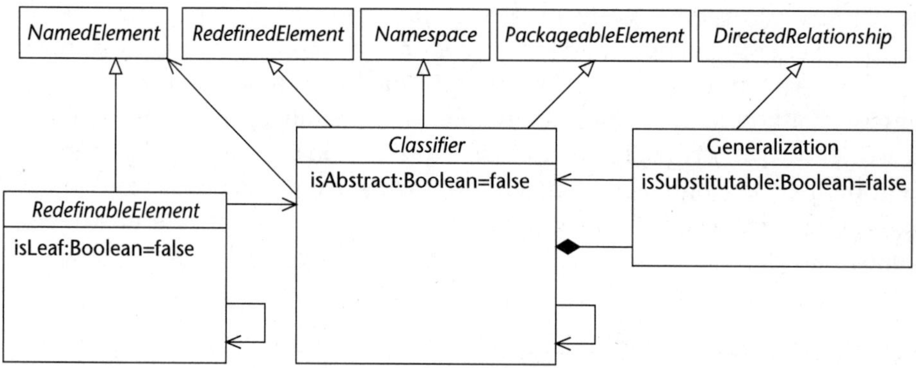

Figure 8.19 Basic kernel diagram for a classifier.

Model elements are specialized to artifacts that are useful when modeling systems. Most model elements correspond to some diagram that represents them. However, certain model elements exist without defined notation, and with UML 2, models include additional syntax for clarity that may or may not be displayed on a tool, depending on the vendor. With UML 2, though, the modeler will always have access to this information using XML.

The following high-level overview of model elements shows the type of semantic constructs found in UML. Note that this list moves, generally, from abstract to concrete and so should be read in order, not as some type of glossary. (See Appendix B for a glossary of important terms.) How UML arrives at the specific model constructs already described in this book should become increasingly clear as you proceed, just as your vision becomes clearer as an optometrist starts applying corrective lenses during an eye examination. Given the complex relationship between abstract UML elements, the order of the list at times reflects convenience, so the reader may experience a sense familiar to those who have had vision-correcting eye examinations: the inability to discern any difference after the introduction of a new lens or filter. We suggest that you read through the whole list, remembering that the goal is to understand UML's core abstractions as a foundation for developing strategies for applying the language to new environments. Do not get caught up in asking "Is it clearer now?" after each entry. If you have an appetite for digging deeper into these abstractions, consult the UML specifications on the OMG Web site (www.omg.org).

- **Element.** As indicated, element is the common superclass for the UML kernel. An element has no notation defined. Subclasses of element define notation. The immediate subclasses of element have clearly descriptive names, such as PackageableElement or GeneralizableElement representing, respectively, an element you can package and one you can generalize.
- **Relationship.** The next most important abstract class after element, a relationship is an element that provides the common superclass for indicating a connection between model elements. A number of items in the core extend relationship, such as dependency and generalization.
- **Multiplicity Element.** This abstraction allows an element to have information specifying the number of allowed elements when instantiated.
- **Namespace.** An abstract metaclass that allows for a named model element to own a set of named modeled elements. This abstraction allows for hierarchical organization of model elements.
- **Expression.** A string that evaluates to some value in a given context. Expression has an attribute to indicate the language used by the string.

From these high-level abstractions, we move to look at how UML handles more information attached to these model elements.

- **Package.** A concrete implementation of namespace that provides a container for those elements that can be packaged.
- **Value specification.** This abstraction starts the definition of values. Classes defining object instances and data values use this abstract metaclass.
- **Literal specification.** Abstract specialization of value specification to identify the values modeled. The UML kernel further specializes this to include specifications for Boolean, integer, string, unlimited naturals, and null.
- **Instance specification.** A single member or individual entity of a model element described by the model. For example, an instance of a class is an object. A *slot* on an instance specification indicates if an instance specification has values for a structural feature of the model element.

Now, the list turns to classifiers and features as UML starts to come into focus.

- **Classifier.** An abstraction that classifies instances, including the information needed to define the classification. A classifier can contain a generalization relationship, making it possible for a class, for example, to implement a generalization hierarchy, as discussed in Chapter 4.
- **Association.** A relationship between two classifiers that has a property on both ends of the relationship to show how the classifiers participate in the relationship.
- **Link.** An instance of an association.
- **Dependency.** A relationship where a model element requires other model elements to function. As shown in Chapter 4, UML includes a number of different types of dependency relationships, such as usage, realization, and substitution.
- **Feature.** An abstract class used to characterize a classifier. A behavioral feature describes dynamic elements, while a structural feature provides the abstraction needed for showing the descriptive elements of a classifier.
- **Property.** A structural feature of a classifier. For example, when owned by a class, it is an attribute. When owned by an association, it is an association end.
- **Parameter.** The specification of a variable or argument used as input or output with a behavioral feature. Parameters can reference an operation and indicate a direction.

Finally, we turn to the more recognizable model elements.

- **Class.** A classifier that has attributes and operations as its features.
- **Operations.** Owned by a class, this defines a service provided and can include preconditions and postconditions as UML-defined constraints.
- **Attribute.** Owned by a class, this defines the structural features of the class. Use data type to show the type of values available for the structural feature.
- **Data type.** An abstract classifier that includes properties and operations to show the nature of the value specification with no specific identities. So, an operation for a data type might add two integers and return an integer, but it does not indicate the specific values returned. Profiles for specific languages typically extend data type to fit the platform.
- **Enumeration type.** Extension of data type that allows for user-defined sets of values or model elements.
- **Primitive type.** Base class to allow for definition of primitive types such as Boolean, integer, or string.
- **Interface.** A classifier that declares a set of public features and obligations. An interface must be reached by an instance of a classifier.
- **Implementation.** A specialized realization relationship between a classifier and an interface.
- **Association class.** A model element that is both a class and an association. In other words, it has the features of both class and association.
- **Powertype.** A classifier that has a group of generalizations in a generalization set.

This completes the overview of the core elements of UML. The additional model elements in UML, such as those used in sequence diagrams and state machines, rely on constructs from the core. These other model elements are part of the UML specification, but they are not part of the UML kernel, or metamodel. This fact does not make them any less a part of UML; it just means they are not covered in a section on core elements. Figure 8.20 shows how UML extends the metaclass "classifier" into many of the elements found in UML.

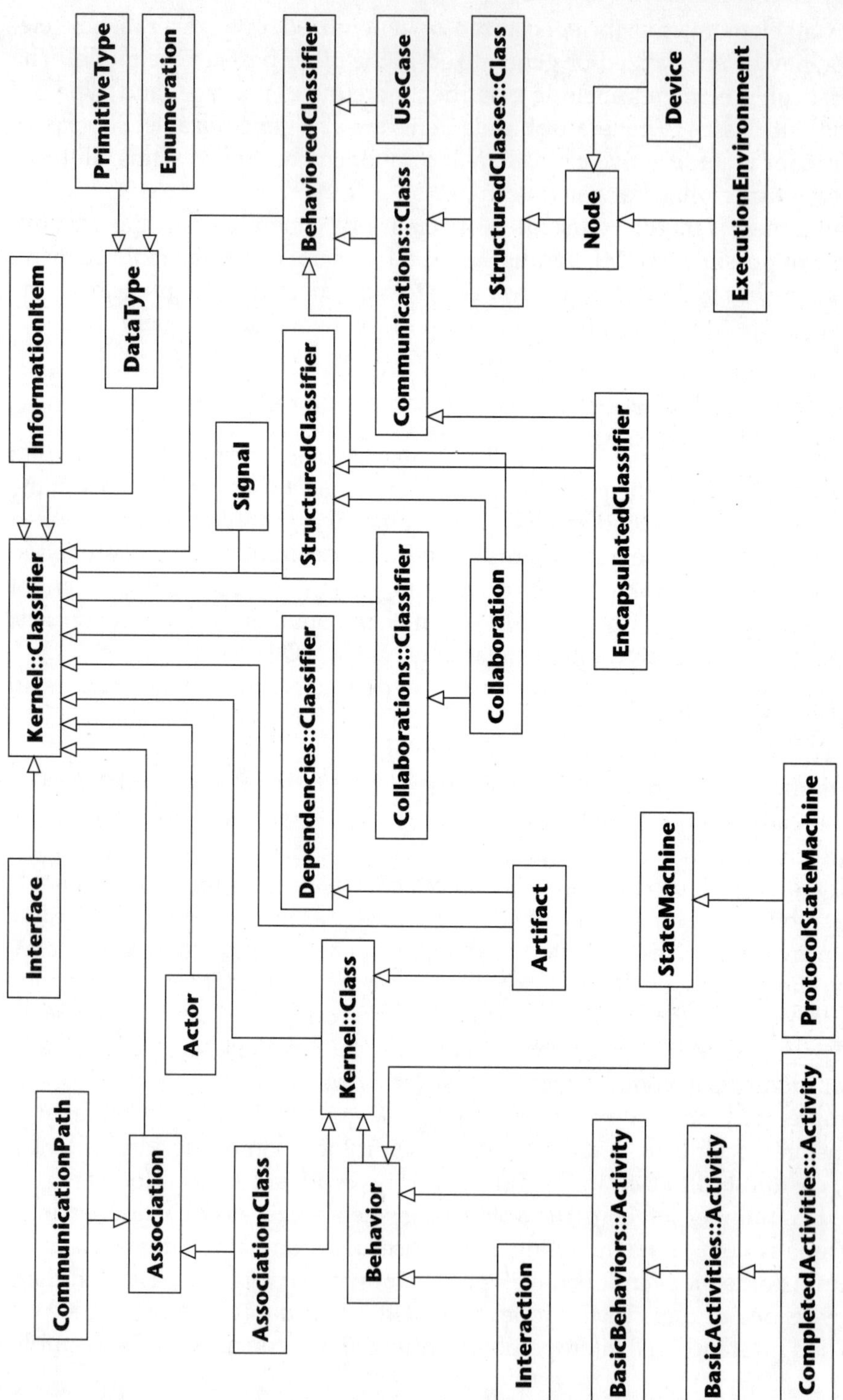

Figure 8.20 Use of Classifier as a Superclass for UML Elements.

Not all elements may be specialized or generalized; only generalizable elements may be specialized or generalized in the other parts of the model. The generalizable elements include classifier, stereotype, package, and type. Of course, subclasses to generalizable elements are also generalizable. Subclasses of classifier include active class, signal, component, and node. Thus, all these classes are specialized or generalized.

Sometimes, it might be useful to specialize or generalize associations, but this is not possible in UML because association is not a generalizable element. If someone has to do this, he or she needs to construct a new language from the infrastructure library that has association as a generalizable element.

The Profile Package

The infrastructure library and MOF have their own extension mechanism that UML inherits, called the profile package. An architect uses the elements in the profile package to extend models. Put another way, profile structures, when used by a modeler, contain variants of the UML metamodel elements tuned to a specific need. A profile relates directly to a reference metamodel; it cannot create new constructs not defined in a single metamodel. For new constructs, an architect has to create a new metamodel using MOF. The definition of OCL reviewed earlier represents the approach of defining entirely new concepts. In terms of UML, however, the profile mechanism supports most of the extension needs of UML users.

In addition, users of UML might not need to define their own profiles. Others have already spent a lot of time and effort testing the profiles so that they work effectively, and tool vendors package the more common of these with their UML tools. UML profiles represent an effective way to manage the inevitable adaptations users must make to adapt the UML metamodel, while at the same time providing consistent automated support. Given the proliferation of platforms and the pace of technological change, no modeling language can provide the semantic detail to apply across platforms. Profiles as a fully defined high-level package much improve the extension mechanisms in UML, making it easier for modelers to communicate with synchronized models.

Profiles have become more prominent, in part due to the popularity of extension mechanisms and UML. With the proliferation of user-defined variants, custom-built UML in 1.*x* did not always work smoothly. Modelers produced a number of constructs covering such areas as Web applications, real-time systems, data modeling, Enterprise JavaBeans, and framework architectures. Some tool vendors developed their own variants and packaged them into versions of their UML model tools. Understandably, because these profiles had no standards, interoperability emerged as a concern. So, for example, one user might have a particular definition of an <<EJB>> stereotype, while another modeler might use the same stereotype tag defined in a slightly different manner, perhaps for a different version of Enterprise JavaBeans. UML 1.*x* profiles had particular problems as platform-specific information changed as language versions altered the meaning of the platform-specific concepts over time.

Currently, OMG seeks to manage approved profiles to help improve interoperability. Already, OMG has an approved profile for Common Object Request Broker Architecture (CORBA), and their Web site has draft specifications for such things as Enterprise Application Integration (EAI), as well as schedulability, performance, and time specification. A profile for Enterprise JavaBeans, the wider Java language, and .NET are in the works.

The requirements for UML 2 made it clear that the new version needed to support a general mechanism to allow users to adapt the language, while allowing them to manage conflicting extensions. The profile mechanism coupled with the requirement to express models using XML realizes this requirement for casual UML users.

It is possible to extend any element in the UML metamodel with a profile. To model such an extension, use features from the profiles package. In creating a stereotype, a user can also define a set of properties or constraints on that element. The example shows a definition of a stereotype and then an application of that stereotype. Figure 8.21 shows a stereotype extending a metaclass. In this case, the model defines a stereotype "primate." This stereotype takes one property, chromosomes, with a type of integer, which shows how many chromosomes the primate has. Figure 8.22 shows the stereotype in action, with the Ape and Human classes both with the primate stereotype. A fully compliant UML tool knows to look for the defined property of chromosome. In a profile, an extension has special notation, shown as an arrow with a solid black triangle on the end pointing toward the metaclass that the stereotype extends. A tagged value is a user-defined property of a stereotype, applied to the model element when the base metaclass is extended.

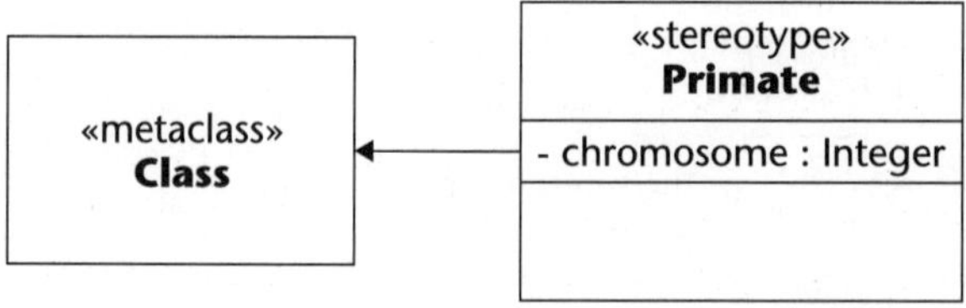

Figure 8.21 Sample stereotype extension.

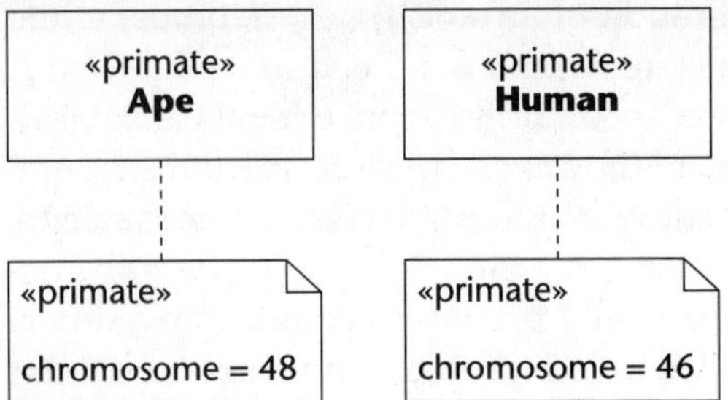

Figure 8.22 Classes built from a defined stereotype.

In UML, a modeler applies a profile to his or her model using a dependency relationship with a stereotype of <<apply>>. Figure 8.23 shows an example of how to apply a profile, showing the reference metamodel and the profile. The relationship between the profile and the reference metamodel can be modeled with more specific information. Such a relationship defined at a high level will help the UML tool manage which profile you are using on a specific model, avoiding the problem of conflicting names. However, do not attempt to redefine the name of the existing standard stereotypes in UML, because all these stereotypes are applied automatically.

CROSS-REFERENCE For an updated list of available profiles, visit the OMG Web site (www.omg.org).

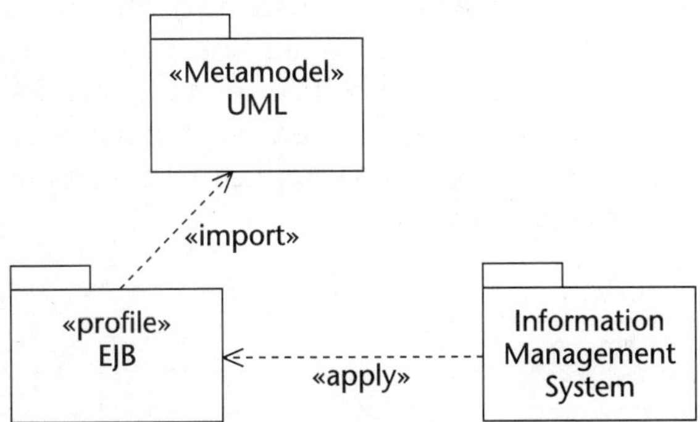

Figure 8.23 Applying a profile that uses UML as the reference metamodel.

Architecture Overview Summary and Observations

The element is the abstract base class for most constituents of the UML; it provides an anchor to which a number of mechanisms may be attached. The metamodel specializes element into model elements, relationships, namespaces, value specifications, classifiers, classes, and so on, with the UML specification producing a large number of subclasses that define the constructs explained in the book as part of the UML toolkit, such as use cases, components, classes, state machines, activity diagrams, sequence diagrams, and deployments. The breakdown in this section illustrates the many different levels on which to approach UML. Those using a modeling tool for a basic class diagram need not know how UML was built, just that it allows the display of a class rectangle that also links to the code for that class in an implementation language.

This definition of UML in terms of general modeling concepts makes it more likely that vendors will enable model sharing and support user-defined adaptations of UML. So, for most users of UML, this means it will be easier to share models with others and have the tools understand what they mean. Of course, if the modeler can't communicate using these tools, then this is an opportunity wasted. The goal for these extensions is to enable communication and targeted customization, not abstraction for its own sake.

This discussion of the metamodel shows how the designers of UML allowed for user input. If a tagged value, stereotype, or constraint is attached to a model element, a specialization to that model element has the same tagged value, stereotype, or constraint. For most purposes, modelers should use these features to improve their models. However, avoid using these features to clutter a model with excessive detail that is not needed. These extensions have practical purposes, and modelers should always look for the reasons for applying an extension or profile before they take the trouble of integrating the new material into their model. As with everything in UML, just because the language offers you a feature does not mean that using that feature will bring project success. For more on model quality, see Chapter 10.

Relevant Changes in UML 2

UML 2 presents the modeler with a rather different extension architecture designed to provide more options, smoother tool support, and clearer definitions for machines. No longer does UML use UML to define its own model. The core UML metamodel now reflects another set of modeling concepts in the MOF, giving the modeling community the ability to supplement UML by creating a cousin of UML. This new ability to create another member of the UML family of languages has resulted in the separate specification of a constraint language with OCL, no longer defined in the UML specification. The profiles mechanism, a less drastic way of extending UML, also has a clearer definition, showing the way a stereotype maps to an element in the metamodel.

With the requirement to express these extensions using XMI, UML now has a standard that makes it easier for tool vendors to support common extensions. Under UML 1.*x*, tool vendors added in their own special extensions to UML, but a modeler using a different tool would not be able to understand those elements. With UML 2, a modeler can explicitly indicate which profile his or her model applies, so any other user can get the same profile for the system to work. This language architecture is designed to support a proliferation of model extensions as architects seek to extend UML concepts to new domains. This flexibility has helped UML expand; now, the extensions can be more clearly managed.

A number of standard elements from version 1.*x* have been retired or promoted. The long-range vision for these extensions involves coherent and controlled packaging of extensions into profiles. UML still uses its own stereotypes and profiles and will continue to do so, but these should support UML's core aim as a language to model systems that use information technology. Constructs, such as constraints or data-modeling tools, will, in the future, reside not in UML but in cousins that also use MOF as the defining modeling language.

Why does UML 2 need such extension features? Why did the designers of UML 2 put so much effort into redefining the language architecture to allow such extensions? The next chapter on MDA helps to explain the larger knowledge management goals of the UML community and how the new internal architecture supports these ambitions.

Summary

All model languages have restrictions and limits. When a language is too general, it undermines the possibility of making distinct and sharp statements; when it is too specialized, it limits the possible statements. C++ can be seen as a modeling language specialized for programming but not that powerful for business modeling. Therefore, UML is defined with a limited number of general elements and armed with extension mechanisms.

UML uses profiles as an internal way to organize the three main extension mechanisms: tagged values, constraints, and stereotypes. These mechanisms are used to define a set of standard extensions included in UML, to which new extensions may be added (user-defined extensions). Extensions are typically added to adapt UML to a method, an organization, or a specific application domain.

Profiles extend the UML metamodel as their starting point. UML also offers a more elaborate extension mechanism to specify a completely new modeling language, separate from UML but related by a common parent. For both of these extension strategies to work, the modeler needs to have a firm grasp of the details in the UML high-level model.

Tagged values are a mechanism for adding extra information to the models and their elements. The information may be intended both for human beings and for machines (such as code generators or UML tools).

Constraints are used to restrict the semantics of the elements within the UML. A constraint might not add extra meaning, only limit the existing semantics of the elements. OCL provides the supported way to express constraints so that tools can interpret these rules.

Stereotypes are used for specializing semantics of the UML metamodel. They enable you to define and model with higher precision. Bundled into profiles, stereotypes are the core extension mechanism within UML. Modelers should use these extension mechanisms to improve model quality and avoid the temptation to model to a degree of precision not needed for project success.

The changes in the language architecture for UML 2 do have a practical purpose. UML 2 requires such support for extensions in response to the problem of the proliferation of middleware platforms. Modelers can use these features as they try to extend UML to help it address complex information management systems, deployed systems that need to change platforms, and dispersed systems such as Web applications. The MDA initiative provides the guiding architectural statement that organizes these features into a coherent approach to software development. The next chapter provides an overview of MDA.

CHAPTER

9

Model Driven Architecture

The Model Driven Architecture (MDA) initiative seeks to make UML models more useful for the distributed and integrated software systems so prevalent today. MDA places the model at the center of information management, applying UML models to manage complex systems. Such a prominent effort from the keepers of UML raises some questions for users of UML tools, like the following.

- What does MDA have to do with UML?
- What drives the MDA initiative?
- What role does UML play in the structure of MDA?
- How does MDA influence the revisions to UML?
- Looking to the future, what type of evolution might you anticipate from UML/MDA?

These questions define this chapter. For a more complete review of MDA and the latest case studies, see the OMG Web site. Here, the focus is on MDA as an architectural strategy that has influenced and continues to influence UML. After a review of MDA goals and definitions, the chapter looks at the varying types of modeling activities that MDA emphasizes at different levels of abstraction. MDA will likely require modelers to change their emphasis, so this chapter summarizes some of the modeling demands of the MDA environment. The chapter concludes with a brief assessment of the relationship between MDA and UML and the opportunities for the future.

MDA Evolution and Goals

What is MDA? MDA is an architectural statement by the OMG that provides guiding principles to coordinate a variety of activities under the umbrella of making modeling artifacts capable of doing more work to solve integration problems. Although MDA is recent, the general trends it represents are not.

Background and General Goals

With a white paper in November 2000, the OMG first proposed MDA as a way to use advanced modeling technology to address the confusion caused by the proliferation of middleware platforms. In February 2001, the OMG formally put their efforts behind the initiative and began work on elaborating the vision from this initial white paper. Unlike UML, which produced specification documents numbered in the hundreds of pages, MDA uses short documents that focus on important themes. MDA themes have appeared in a number of books and articles to promote this approach to using models. OMG committees have worked on short "technical perspective" documents as well as some general framework models to provide greater definition. In May 2003 the OMG published version 1.0 of the MDA Guide to reflect these efforts. Large companies, already in pursuit of MDA goals, have joined in the effort through the OMG and have helped shape UML to support MDA.

MDA resembles a previous initiative. In 1990, the OMG had an Object Management Architecture (OMA) as an architectural statement to provide guidance on how to address integration issues. This related to the work defining the Common Object Request Broker Architecture (CORBA) that helped solve a number of integration issues. MDA provides a similar architectural statement but one that addresses integration issues on the complex enterprise systems now deployed. With the expansion of UML specifications and the growing number of profiles, the relationship between the different groups of OMG standards becomes complex. For example, how does the latest profile on enterprise application integration relate to OMG's goals? How will the modeling community assess these efforts? How does the Meta-Object Facility (MOF), the language used to define UML, help those producing software? MDA provides a common background and vision that explains the purpose of these varied initiatives.

Works on MDA portray the initiative as the next step in the evolution of software development. Software, the argument goes, has successfully moved to higher levels of abstraction, building on the work of others to create software that can do more things. From initial computers that required detailed programming of quite specific machine instructions, software languages have provided easier ways to access the power of computers. As software becomes more abstract, those developing instructions for the computer can start to ignore the specific code at the more detailed level; this code has been around long enough with predictable behavior that a developer can access it using a shorthand notation provided by a language. By storing well-defined snippets of code that deliver functionality in a specific environment, it is possible to set up commonly used libraries. As these become difficult to manage, many people start using object-oriented languages that import and extend a variety of core classes, which enables developers to create their own classes to execute a set of instructions written in a human language such as English, not in terms of specific machine instructions. MDA comes as the next level of abstraction, as developers will over time replace today's source code with automated compilers that generate the predictable elements in the code. The model layer will provide human beings with the ability to manage and to monitor higher level concepts without getting bogged down in implementation detail.

Although software has succeeded in building on layers of abstraction, this point can take the industry only so far. As members of practical software delivery teams, we emphasize the evolutionary power of managed "cut and paste" as a core driver of increased efficiency in delivering software projects. Once someone finds a particularly good approach to solving a problem, such as session management on a Web application, others cut and paste this solution, using effective tools such as UML to communicate. To the extent that the higher levels of abstraction manage this evolution effectively, they help deliver better software. Abstraction for the sake of abstraction, with no practical application, does not help deliver better software.

Although MDA reflects trends long apparent in software development, it provides a new package for these ideas. The OMG's MDA logo, complete with trademark, summarizes the initiative and gives it a public emphasis like that of UML (see Figure 9.1). Taken as a whole, the logo appears vaguely like the steering wheel on a ship's helm, or maybe a bull's eye or round brain-teasing puzzle. As you read from the outside in you move through layers. At the outermost layer you find business sectors or verticals, indicating MDA's goal of applying to many industries. The "more" indicates that this list is not exclusive in any way: MDA applies many places. The next circle in shows the set of pervasive services relied on by these industries. In turn, the next circle in shows the platforms needed for these services, such as Java or .NET. Most industries rely on a mixture of these platforms. The next layer is not a band but a central sphere, perhaps a core brain that can manage all these different elements. On the central sphere, you find the architectural languages specified by the OMG, brought together under the guiding intelligence of MDA. Not shown are the many software development tools essential to MDAs' playing such a central role, but it might be helpful to view those tools as the glue that holds the whole thing together.

On a more technical level, MDA seeks to address the problem of integration and interoperability by making UML models and modeling artifacts more executable. As David Frankel, a leading technical expert observed, "MDA is about using modeling languages as programming languages rather than merely as design languages." (Frankel 2003). This effort has been a part of UML since the start. Tools such as Rational Rose used UML as a basis for automatic code generation, adding features to work with Java and C++. The ability of models to reach their potential with code-generation tools ran into limits given the complexity of different platforms and the lack of precision in earlier versions of UML.

To give UML more precision, a number of companies created variants of "executable UML" (xUML) that rely on state machines and an executable action language to generate full systems. Some companies, such as Kennedy Carter (www.kc.com), have demonstrated success with xUML on large defense projects. In March 2003, the release of UML 1.5 introduced a definition of UML action semantics providing a general statement of how these action languages should work, but without definition of a specific language. The main action languages used to define the action semantics include Action Specification Language (ASL) in the public domain, BridgePoint Action Language (AL), and Kabira Action Semantics (Kabira AS). (For more on xUML, see *Executable UML: A Foundation for Model-Driven Architecture* by Stephen Mellor and Marc Balcer (Mellor and Balcer, 2002)). Although executable UML has worked on some projects, it has not found wide commercial application, especially outside of the defense industry. MDA is not simply xUML with new clothing but a broad enough initiative to include both xUML and the folks trying to manage complex distributed systems important to a business. The conceptual approach to solving business problems adds a distinct layer to the initiative. MDA instructs a modeler to break up a system model into a set of models with clearer responsibilities and deployment strategies. This breakup results in model layers, with some layers focused on the semantic precision needed for code generation in some form and other layers focused on the needs of the business without reference to the delivery mechanism. The approach means to provide clear instructions on how to approach modeling to improve communication about business needs, while also enabling better management of coding best practices (or better cut and paste).

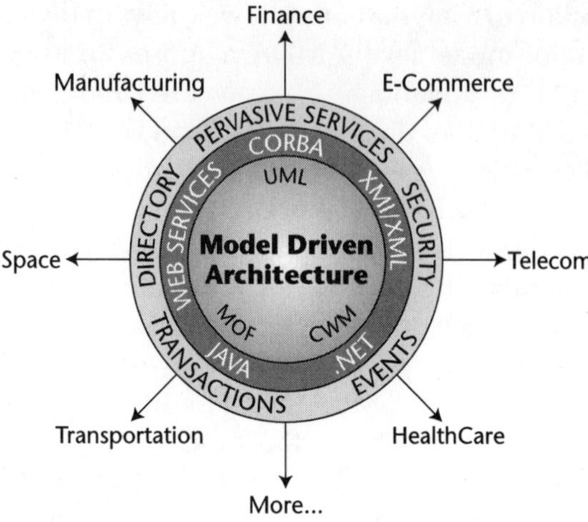

Figure 9.1 MDA logo.

Model Levels

MDA starts with a fundamental distinction between two different types of models:

- First, the *Platform Independent Model*, or *PIM*, aims to capture implementation-independent information about the system and business process modeled.
- Second, the *Platform Specific Model*, or *PSM*, aims to provide the implementation detail tuned to a specific deployment environment.

In this context, a platform represents the engineering details that do not matter to the actual functionality of the system: A clock can deliver time from a variety of platforms. By encouraging such a fundamental break between the PIM and PSM, MDA continues the traditional object-oriented emphasis on proper definition before launching into code. This core distinction between the PIM and PSM helps organize MDA, but it is not the only distinction between model types.

MDA asserts a fractal approach to modeling, moving away from one supermodel representing the system to a number of supporting models. MDA looks for varying models applied at different levels of abstraction related to each other through clearly defined relationships. Just as modelers can break down a system by defining certain core classes and relating them within a model, MDA breaks down a larger system into component models that retain a link. These separate models are more than just separate views of the same system;

each model also has its own collection of views and might well rely on different UML profiles. With the variety of model levels, MDA proposes an information-management system that takes advantage of automated modeling tools to achieve interoperability; MDA applies object-oriented standards but at a higher level, tuned for large and complex systems. To model a simple system to manage, say, your recipes, you are unlikely to need MDA.

Given the focus on relationships among a number of models, MDA requires rigor in the definition of mapping rules. If MDA is not to become bogged down in a confused proliferation of models, the architect needs to map not only between the different model levels in a system but also between the different views in the model itself. MDA relies on UML support for mapping different types of abstraction to automate and to manage this process.

MDA envisions multiple model levels. However, beyond the PIM and PSM, what other levels of abstraction will emerge in a typical industry? Figure 9.2 shows the basic layers of MDA. Complex systems have models at higher levels of abstraction and at greater detail than the PIM and PSM. MDA literature stresses that the PIM should include computational detail. The PIM does not, then, represent the highest level of abstraction. Above the PIM one can find a computation-independent business model or a domain model setting out the major elements of a system.

Unfortunately, MDA cannot resist another three-letter acronym, and many refer to the Computation Independent Model as the CIM (pronounced SIM). In conversation, those working in MDA pronounce the many acronyms for model levels as complete words, resulting in sentences that sounds like this: "After we defined the 'simm' our 'pimm' did not map well to our 'pissimm' because we did not have a 'moth' (pronunciation of MOF) compliant' metamodel." (Fortunately, folks still pronounce UML by speaking out the letters, not as "ummmmal.") MDA has far more going for it than the production of new code words; try to get past the explosion of acronyms and the often-silly buzz words to look at how the effort to handle these different model layers influences how you can work with a firm to manage information and software.

MDA enables exciting work on executable models targeted at the business level, to provide an accurate picture of crucial concepts. Architects can use UML tools to generate a cost-aware model at a higher level that can help the assessment of system cost in the weighing of different options. UML can be used at these different layers of modeling to deliver better information-management systems. Both the PIM and the CIM model processes without reference to platform.

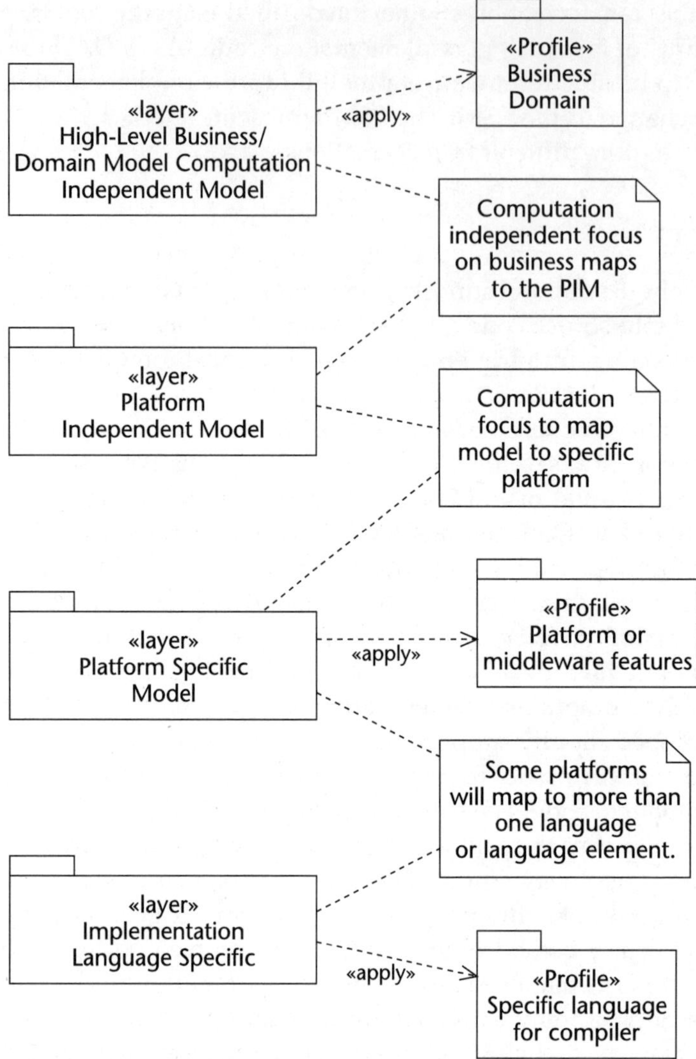

Figure 9.2 Layers in a typical MDA project.

On the more detailed side, the PSM does not necessarily provide all the detail needed to allow the model to execute. For technical implementation detail, a platform remains independent of software languages. Some platforms, then, require drilling farther down into different types of implementation. MDA refers to this next level as the "implementation language environment." PSMs can be implementation-language-environment-specific or -independent. The main cog in the modeling structure is found with the model compiler, or the transformation engine, the detailed mapping tool that does the heavy lifting of producing implementation code. As MDA tools improve, the goal is to be able to move from the PIM to the implementation code without much change to the PSM. The PSM represents another view of the code that will not require difficult transformations.

Model Compilers

UML has always sought to support round-trip engineering, where an architect can translate a model into source code and back again. A variety of software-support tools support such round-trip engineering. The model compiler is the tool that allows for this translation. The model compiler takes the defined model and generates source code, at least in skeleton form.

Since the introduction of UML, development support tools have rapidly added features to enhance the model compilers available for standard languages such as Java or C++. On the more detailed side, integrated development environments support model elements on their end to make coding more efficient. For example, Rational's main modeling tool, Rational Rose, evolved into an integrated development environment, called Rational XDE. Eclipse, a basic standard Java development environment, includes plug-ins that support basic UML diagrams. Model compilers, then, are not new to MDA and have developed rapidly supported by UML.

Under MDA, however, the model compiler becomes critically important as the tool to map the model to code. The software architect working in the MDA environment needs to develop the skill to assess the type of profile needed to best support efficient code generation. The model compiler increasingly resembles an automated set of coding standards. The compiler generates the main elements of the source code, leaving particularly complex portions for human coding or high-performance tuning of the model compiler.

In information technology, any activity that becomes repetitive and predictable immediately emerges as a candidate for automation. As patterns and frameworks seek to make certain common features repetitive, an architect can look for ways to automate the implementation of this standard pattern. UML tool vendors will continue to produce easy implementations for common patterns, such as an online shopping cart. The model compiler contains this logic tuned to a specific platform.

An architect has standard profiles to select from, but the architect still needs to have a tool ready to modify elements of the profile to fit the specific environment. UML now has a number of features designed to help architects work with a model compiler, including enhanced support for collaborations, better template mechanisms, and stereotypes to help indicate which classes require hand-coding and which fit the predictable elements of the pattern to allow automatic code generation.

When viewed from this perspective, the focus of UML on unambiguous definitions with a rigorous XML Metadata Interchange (XMI) specification appears quite helpful. The model compiler, by definition, requires some sort of software tool for implementation. An architect can work on extending a model and defining new elements and can still easily communicate information about this model using the common rules for interchange.

Building a model compiler represents substantial work. Most executable UML model compilers work from the structural class diagrams and associated state machines, which, when supported by a detailed action language, provide the type of detail needed for such engineering. However, it will take some time for model compilers to use fully the behavior-modeling features now in UML for code generation.

As a matter of practical application, the model compiler brings with it a trade-off with coding activities. To the extent that the model contains the exact same semantic meaning as the code, the code can be written either in a modeling tool or directly, depending on circumstances. You could say that in MDA terms developers represent, essentially, walking model compilers who find it easier to sketch out ideas in code rather than in an abstract model. The risk in all model- driven projects is that the model gets out of step with the code. The advantage of more automated links between code and model is that this gap between model and code will slowly narrow and take less time to manage.

Tools that allow for increased use of UML diagrams in the development environment provide a variant of the model compiler, furthering the MDA aim of making the model more executable but falling short of the dream of 100 percent code generation from UML. Making coding environments that support UML diagrams encourages greater use of modeling. When developers can work more quickly because of UML, it is likely these MDA features will expand rapidly.

Model translation, either in a model compiler or in a development environment, provides a core feature of MDA. It provides the automation that theoretically reduces production costs and makes software more manageable.

Mapping the Many Elements of MDA

If MDA is to work, the mapping between the PIM and PSM, as well as the other model elements, needs to work very smoothly. Figure 9.3 shows mappings required by MDA. The MDA world refers to the process for mapping a PIM to a PSM as marking, where the modeler marks the PIM to indicate the mapping rules used. As shown in this figure, MDA requires effective management of multiple metamodels. Here, the focus on the Meta-Object Facility (MOF), as described in Chapter 8, helps to manage these relationships. With all metamodels referencing MOF, the modeler soon has standards for querying and validating models. Each type of metamodel used should be MOF-compliant, as shown in the diagram. With such standards, tools are able to gather tremendous amounts of information about the system from these models.

MDA seeks to improve software development by providing a way to organize the abstract information about the business domain, functional needs, and implementation language in a manageable fashion. By making UML more of a programming language that can implement standard features in a variety of languages, MDA provides a set of goals that keeps the OMG and software architects busy for years to come. Signs that MDA is on the road to achieving success will be an increasing library of varying types of profiles and model compilers that architects use to make their own projects efficient. A sign of MDA failure will be a number of projects failing to deliver any working software, while delivering an excellent specification showing what they were supposed to deliver. The next section provides a practical example to illustrate how to move between separate layers in a large organization.

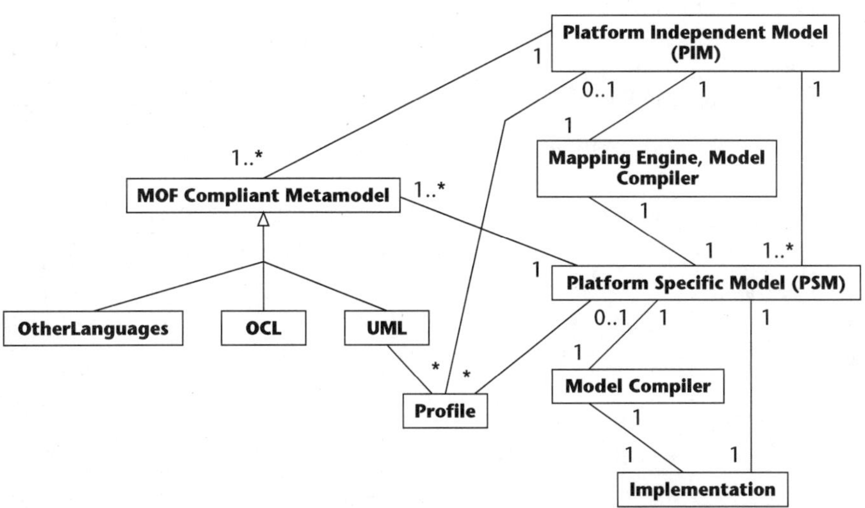

Figure 9.3 PIM and PSM mappings for an MDA project. The PIM will rely on one or more MOF-Compliant Metamodels for expression. Typically this will include both UML and OCL. The may also rely on a profile for domain information. The mapping engine or model compiler provides the rules to transform the PIM into a PSM. The PSM has the same relationship to metamodels as the PIM, relying on the model compiler to produce the implementation. Note that as the PSM relationship to implementation becomes more predictable, the main transformation will be from PIM to PSM, with projects effectively going directly from PIM to implementation code.

From the Business Model to PIM and PSM

Imagine that you have been hired to review the information technology and management needs of a small college. The college has a variety of information technology needs and wants to know the best areas to focus their budget. The first step is to review the major inputs and outputs of all the different users to see what information they use. At this level you build a CIM that reviews the enterprise and the main domain objects. Later, you will drill down into the areas most in need of new technology.

This example is not meant as a full case study and does not include nearly enough diagrams to portray the system with the full power of the language. Rather, the emphasis here is on explaining one example of how to use an architecture driven by sets of models to help an organization use technology effectively. The example reflects actual work done with clients.

The High-Level Review

After you conduct a number of interviews, a picture of the college business emerges. Figure 9.4 shows a high-level diagram representing the main elements of the college with the user-defined package stereotype of <<College Unit>>. The dependency arrows at the package level indicates a relationship from one of the diagrams in the package to one of the diagrams in the other package. Each of these packages holds diagrams to show use cases, domain entities, activities, and some notes that provide more detail on the main responsibilities of each unit. For the business, as shown by the high-level diagram, many programs and workflows rely on the registration and student records section. At this level, the modeling acts as a diagnostic tool; it does not contain the information needed to build a system nor does it have the computational detail needed to apply the model to a platform.

The analysis also includes a high-level review of domain entities in a class diagram. Additional work on the domain model would further clarify the main entities in the system. The client did not want to work on a general domain model for the higher education industry. Such a general model would have been helpful, but requires cooperation out of the scope of most projects. To provide such general domain models, the OMG has task forces for key industries, such as health care. This layer represents the outer ring of the MDA logo. Absent such a general domain model, you can still provide the client with a quick but complete review of the entire system with a package diagram. MDA encourages such a global view.

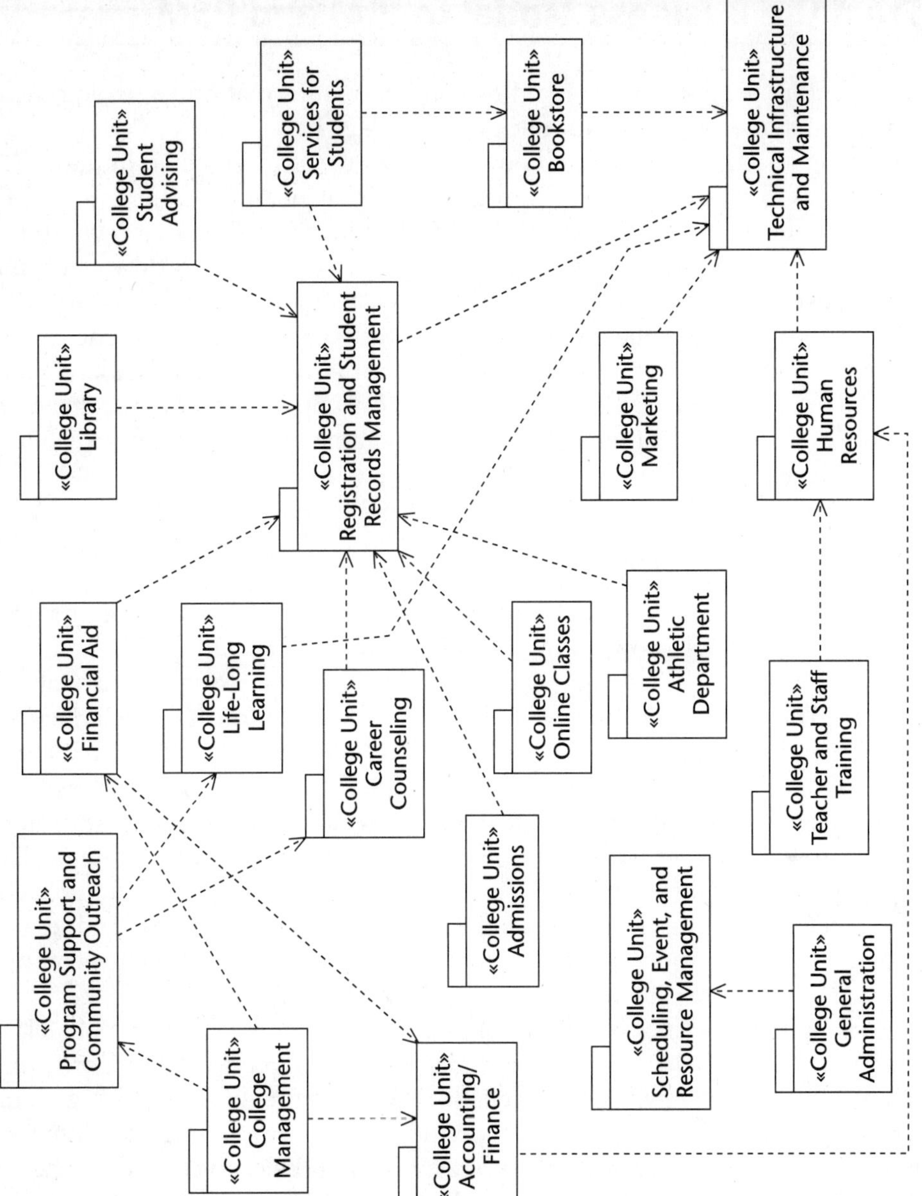

Figure 9.4 High-level model showing business units of a small college, stereotyped as <<College Unit>>. The model also shows some dependency relationships at a high level. This information could also be expressed as a domain model, but this version communicates the information in the best manner for this client.

If you look into the packages and review the detail, it becomes clear that not only do a number of software efforts rely on the student records unit but also the notes show that these software efforts use a variety of different middleware platforms and architectures. Not surprisingly, many started from disparate department initiatives fulfilling a variety of goals. The notes from the interviews indicate an excessive focus on platforms, which the consultant will need to correct in the next stage. The high level overview of the firm reveals the following.

- Student Services wants registration information for their campus portal based on a WebSphere platform.
- The Career Counseling service needs access for their Web-based system based on Cold Fusion that interfaces with community businesses.
- The online classes package uses a .NET package.
- The Athletic Department wants to know about student eligibility.
- The government wants information about scholarships and the status of foreign students.
- The bookstore wants to be able to order books based on a student's class.
- The library wants to move from their client-server package to an Internet platform and wants to know which platform to use to best work with student information.
- The registration and student records reside in an Oracle database, but it is not managed effectively and few can use the information.
- Accounting manages payment and does not have a good way to provide updated information about student status to the records section.
- The stressed technical team speaks of a nightmare of confused applications, poor security, and a lack of interoperability. They are also concerned about a lawsuit from a disgruntled student whose personal contact information appeared without permission on the campus portal.
- The university wants a Web application that allows all these different systems to access and update student records, with full security.

Figure 9.5 shows the use cases involved in the Registration and Student Records Management unit. These remain at a high level, but show the amount of interaction between these units. Also, a number of the other units, as shown by the earlier Figure 9.4, rely on this key unit. The use cases are supported by activity diagrams showing the workflow as well as a few more detailed requirements. For more on use cases, see Chapter 3.

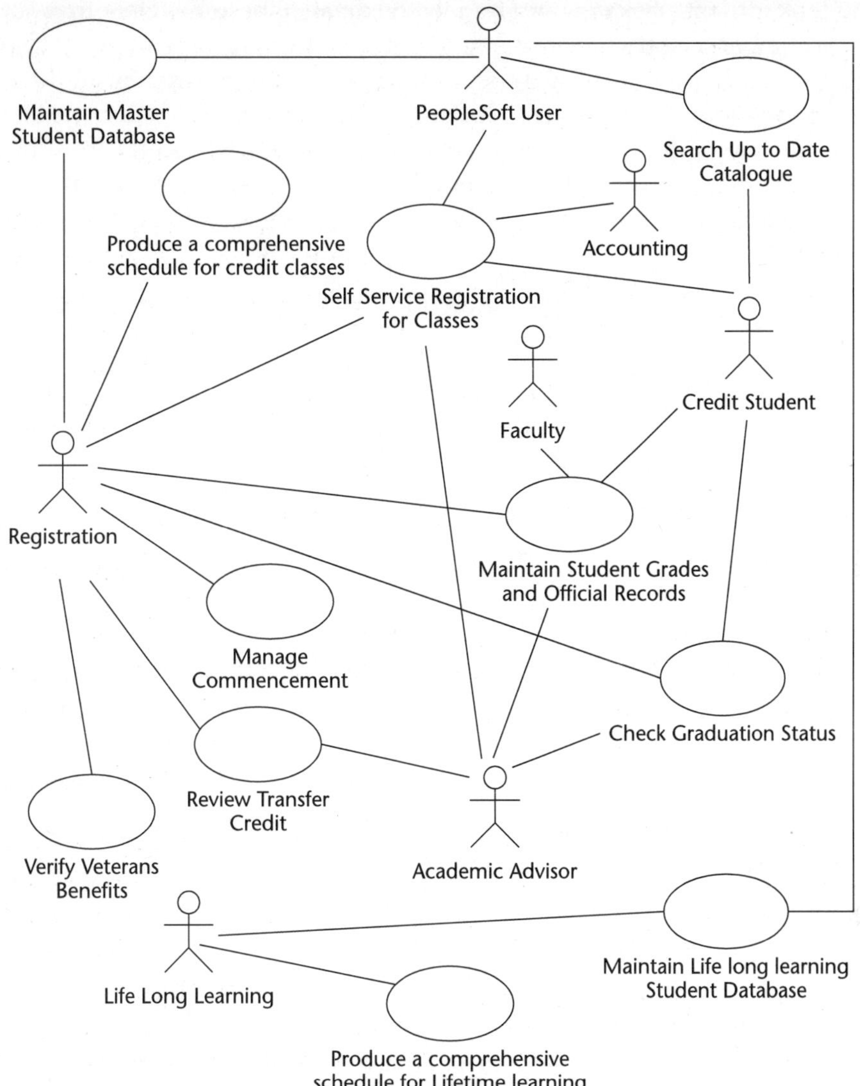

Figure 9.5 Basic use cases for student records.

Among those working in this environment, the technology discussion focused on the best middleware platform to use as a portal as a point of integration. In some cases, the problems of interoperability were real. In other cases, the technical discussion prompted a discussion of workflow issues, requiring a new business process that could achieve the client's goals. Once the business process works properly, then technicians can look for the way to automate the system. Automating a system that does not work merely replicates the workflow problems. Either way, the organization benefited from a review of the business issues to manage access to student records. This initial high-level modeling effort served the purpose of identifying a good candidate for process improvement and information technology. Making this assessment can involve injecting into the high-level model some cost assumptions and equations to indicate the best general area in which to move forward. In addition, technical improvement can make possible new business arrangements not considered before, such as managing information over the Internet. So, it is not always possible to separate out entirely the business model from the implementation details. As a practical matter, however, the point is to avoid excessive discussion of technical details, while focusing on the business process that needs fixing. At this point, in MDA terms, we have a CIM. After review of the CIM and the main notes from the clients, work began on the PIM for the student records section, with detailed review of the functions needed.

Defining Functionality with No Platform

The consulting architect manages to steer the discussion away from which platform to use and toward the question of what functionality is needed. More detailed activity diagrams help to show the boundaries and bridges between the different systems and encourage the new focus for the users. The discussion soon moves to the management of a variety of student record classes. Each of these student record classes extends a base student record class that defines some general features of these records, such as permission rules and attributes. State machines introduce difficult questions, because school officials have a variety of interpretations on the rules for state changes. Tremendous effort goes into clarifying the preconditions and postconditions of each state as well as any invariants. The organization soon recognizes that a good portion of their problem reflects contradictory or vague rules about how to manage student records. These rules must be defined independent of any platform the client might use.

With these rules coming into focus, it becomes easier to isolate the areas where information technology can most improve the process. With this PIM, you can recommend against fighting to get a single integration platform throughout the school. In this case, the timing of registration and the notification of class changes represent areas where the University needs to reduce cycle time. The reduced cycle time in informing system clients of student status will ease the impact of a number of "limbo" states found throughout the system when no response or an outdated response comes from the student system. Although the client expressed initial reluctance to allow online registration due to security concerns, it becomes apparent that the direct updating of the student record database is essential for the rest of the university. Activity diagrams and package diagrams showing dependencies helped to make this point clear to the user community.

The PIM has further defined a number of areas, each of which can take a separate PSM. For this system, the platform for the online learning module does not have to be the same as that for student record management. Rather, the software designed to link that module to the student records information must work properly according to the rules defined in the PIM, regardless of the platform. By focusing on functionality, the needs of the enterprise as a whole come into focus. This moved the discussion away from technology platforms toward needs.

Platform-Specific Models

Suspend your critical thought for a moment and imagine now that one can choose between a variety of robust UML profiles that provide the implementation detail for all platforms considered. Not only that, but each of these platforms has a model compiler that produces pretty good code. After a little work marking, the model compiler has what it needs to lay out sets of student record classes complete with a security model and timing rules keyed to specific messages.

Unfortunately, most of the elements in the above paragraph do not yet really exist. However, this result is the goal of the MDA initiative. With improvements in platforms, such as with Java application servers, such mapping gets better with each passing month. As the way to address the needs of the industry become standard, increasingly automated solutions will become common. MDA encourages this process.

Once at the level of the PSM, architects still have a variety of modeling tasks to perform even after the profile and model compiler have been chosen. They have to review and define the classes for the system in a way that makes sense for the mapping to the PIM as well as the model compiler. No matter how good the profiles and model compilers get or how great the PSM is, you always encounter some conflicts when trying to map the PIM and PSM.

As a practical matter, MDA implementation will often be incremental, focusing first on the repeatable areas of the code that have been used many times before. Larger projects will have the economies of scale needed for this much effort. To finish up our example, the PSM for the student record system might have ended up using a J2EE platform that applied a factory method pattern to produce the different student classes needed in this system as Enterprise JavaBeans (EJBs). The system extends a central controller to manage the state changes, data conflict issues, and security for the student beans. The specific type of J2EE platform employed is WebSphere, but can easily be any other platform. Data access is managed through a series of Data Access Objects (DAO) that primarily go to an Oracle database but also rely on a Lightweight Directory Access Protocol (LDAP) directory accessed through Java Naming and Directory Interface (JNDI) for information about system users and the levels of their permissions. Figure 9.6 shows the various model levels and how they rely on profiles in order to implement a system more efficiently. In this case, the system uses different profiles for the implementation of connections to data sources in the LDAP as well as Oracle. The profile mechanism allows a model to apply a profile, but the model does not lose coherence if the modelers remove the profile. In the case of the lower-level implementation layers, the profiles provide the semantic detail to allow the model compilers to work more smoothly in producing code.

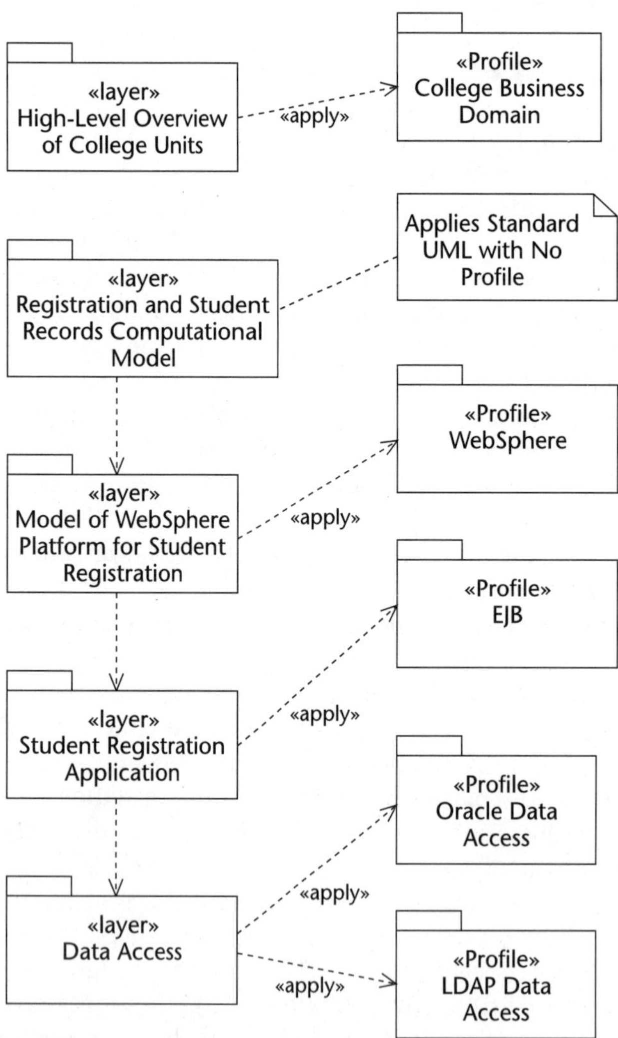

Figure 9.6 Overview of model levels for a college.

The use of standard patterns for creation of value objects to hold data (factory method) and for defining application control (the model-view-controller (MVC) pattern) and for data access (the DAO pattern) has a practical importance in the platform model. Such common patterns are more likely to generate useful code from the compiler because they reflect the collected wisdom of many software development efforts. As in most cases, the patterns take the system only so far. In recognition of this fact, the architect tags those classes in the platform model that appear to need custom coding due to special features. In this case, the hand-off of the student bean to the Career Center requires some special permissions and handling because of its use of the .NET platform and its participation with a wide network of community-based business users.

Information Management Solution

In the example we have been discussing involving the university, MDA clarifies the nature of the information-management issues, opening solutions not initially considered by the client. More than likely, and certainly in our experience, such an information-system review can become a debating society regarding the adoption of a common platform throughout the organization. Some tool vendors support such a view of information management. Although the modeler stresses interoperability and interfaces, the organization tends to look for a common structure. MDA can provide this common structure without demanding the unrealistic imposition of a common platform. By focusing on interoperability to achieve the organization's functional objectives laid out in a PIM, MDA provides for an organization's information-management strategy.

So long as the system delivers the functionality wanted by the organization in a cost-effective manner, the organization can function fine without a common platform. That said, many scenarios require a common platform as the best solution. To assess the different technical solutions effectively and see if the delivery cost associated with a PSM is worthwhile in terms of savings in the business model, MDA models at a high-level need to include information about cost. Such a cost-aware MDA points to areas that provide the most bang for the buck. In this case, the timely management of student information had an impact on many of the organization's systems. This fact emerged clearly even without detailed workflow analysis.

What other solutions might such a client receive? If the client talks primarily to vendors of specific platforms, they get sales pitches on those platforms and the interoperability solution specific to the platform. They might also receive a mismatched collection of different software packages with nobody focusing on interoperability. Some consultants might be so tied into a specific platform that their approach becomes "show me your problem, and I will tell you why our implementation of platform X solves your problem." This approach is often less effective than the vendor-neutral solution usually offered by MDA. That said, as MDA progresses, vendors will likely find it in their interests to support the common interoperability guidelines, or at least claim to. By being vendor neutral, MDA does not mean to be vendor hostile. A vendor delivers a platform, but MDA allows for multiple vendors to work with each other in one system. Ultimately, the competitive market helps determine what types of approaches work. If MDA can better deliver solutions, organizations will increasingly use it.

Finally, the MDA solution focused on interoperability rather than a common platform provides the organization with a clear and coordinated evolutionary path. Today's best platform or portal technology likely will not remain at the leading edge for long. In a creative organization with a lot of different independent actors, such as the university in the example, the best system provides a framework to harness this creativity in a common direction. MDA and UML put the focus on the type of activities that make this pushing in a common direction more likely to occur. With a focus on functional delivery and semantically rich models delivering solutions more efficiently, or at least more measurably, MDA offers an effective architectural approach for enterprise solutions as opposed to that offered by a consultant pushing a particular platform.

Tips for Modeling in the MDA World

This section reviews the practical impact that MDA is likely to have on those who work at different levels of modeling using UML. Each of these users, the business analyst, software architect, and developer, are modelers in this context. They all produce models meant to help deliver successful software.

Modeling for Business and Functional Analysis

Business-analysis modeling has to become more rigorous and dependable in the collection of information. MDA relies on useful information in the CIM and PIM, structured in such a way that it can be executable down the line. Those doing business and functional analysis probably need to have programming skills or at least the aptitude for programming. To work well with automated tools, the MDA modeler probably uses the OCL, loosely under the UML umbrella, as the way to express constraints.

The business analyst, as a practical matter, also understands at a high level the structure of the model of the platform. By understanding the way the PSM is organized, the business analyst can have visibility into the entire system. In addition, he or she can ask for attributes and stereotypes that help him or her to assess the amount of effort needed to implement a PSM. MDA stresses the separation of concerns between the PIM and PSM, so the business analyst should understand the PSM well enough to keep platform information from polluting the PIM.

The business analyst needs to have an interest in technology, and it will be increasingly difficult for the business analyst to function as a salesperson for a particular vendor platform. Most IT managers have honed their ability to detect those not interested in making a better system; IT managers can tell the difference between someone pushing a platform agenda and someone really interested in making a better system built for long-term health. Too many managers have been burned adopting a proprietary solution. The emphasis on interoperability in MDA means that business analysts need to show more flexibility in working with different technologies.

Modeling for the Software Architect

Architects need to learn more about metamodeling strategies. They need to decide when they need a new profile versus just using UML as it is and extending a few classes. They need to know enough about the UML metamodel to know the options for making their own profiles (see Chapter 8). Architects might even need to assess whether to rely on one of the cousins of UML, another modeling language that maps to MOF, such as the Object Constraint Language.

As the architect takes on a more prominent role in a project's success, they increasingly play roles coordinating a number of different components. They need to be able to assess the weak points of available model compilers and intelligently assign for human coding those sections that require such coding.

Depending on the skill set of the business analyst, an MDA approach might require the architect to more carefully review the PIM in terms of the clarity of the expressed constraints. The architect is the pivotal person, the driver, the only one who really is able to understand the translation of the notional business models into hard code.

UML and MOF used to have certain features that were not well aligned, such as association classes, while other UML elements lacked the semantic clarity for model compilers, such as aggregation and navigable associations. Architects working with model compilers built before UML 2 need to avoid using association classes and to try to employ MOF constructs, such as a reference or an isUnique property, rather than aggregation.

Architects then need to understand some specific features of the wider modeling universe. To continue the example of aggregation, modelers need to be careful how they define shared aggregation and composite aggregation; MOF does not have a precise definition for shared aggregation, so it is treated like any other association with no aggregation semantics. With UML 2, architects should understand when they should rely on new ways to indicate composition in the composite structure diagram (see Chapter 7), rather than on the UML 1.*x* composition relationships. Because those composite structure diagrams map more cleanly to MOF, the architect should use them for any complex structure, particularly if they need to express a structure that exists when the system is running. For domain modeling, the traditional aggregation relationship more elegantly communicates the concept. This provides one example of the many trade-offs architects can make between semantic precision and the ability to communicate the purpose of their model to their client. UML 2 has precise alignment with MOF that fixes many of these specific "features" found in UML 1.*x* structures. However, the MDA initiative, if it is growing and thriving in new environments, will uncover more such issues. Architects need to know the anomalies of the profiles, patterns, and metalanguages used as they affect the generation of code. This is but one detailed example of the features bound to exist in the effort to coordinate so many different model types automatically.

Modeling for the Developer

For developers, an MDA world means that they need to learn UML. Unlike some initial UML models, there should now never be a gulf between the UML model in an automated support tool and the development environment. The model in UML becomes a development artifact. Developers, then, actually need to use UML rather than leaving it as the special language of the architect.

For those who enjoy coding, the best introduction to UML is through plug-ins or extensions to standard integrated development environments. With UML providing clearer specifications for tool vendors, you can anticipate the increased use of UML as a different take on the source code.

MDA does not make developers obsolete. Hopefully, it makes their tasks less boring. Repetitive and predictable implementations of patterns can be done with the common code generators, leaving developers to focus on special cases. However, developers have to pay more attention to UML if they want involvement in the interesting decisions about a system. UML provides the mechanisms to capture key system decisions and implement these when possible using automated support tools.

Many developers have had disdain for the procedures of high-level modeling, seeing the effort as a waste of time, producing artifacts that don't help make software. As Leon Starr put it in his excellent *Executable UML: How to Build Class Models,* the elaboration of use-case scenarios is "stupid" (Starr 2002). Although we do not agree with this sentiment and find the issues uncovered during use-case analysis essential to project success, Starr's larger point has merit. Architects need to find better ways to maintain this information efficiently and not create throw-away models. The ability of UML 2 to link use cases to other model elements makes these artifacts more useful. In other words, integrating the essential modeling decisions down to the code level makes the system more efficient. The gap between design and implementation should narrow with MDA.

NOTE To reinforce the point that development is not a separate activity from modeling in UML, MDA defines a model as any formal specification of a system, textual or graphical. Under this definition, source code is just another type of model, a model that provides instructions to the computer translated by the development language into a form so that the machine can deliver value from the instructions. UML, under this definition, becomes another, more powerful, language.

While most software methodologies stress planning, modeling, and design, a large number of developers still love to code and naturally gravitate toward this activity. If forced to produce a model, many first produce the code and then reverse engineer a model. Often, this method even produces a better system than if you have forced someone who thinks in code to think in terms of a model. Such an approach is not ideal, but a reverse-engineered model used to analyze a legacy system is better than no model at all. It still recognizes the practical utility of having a UML representation of a system. The model starts to reflect the source code and can be used to explain the system to others, with some modifications by the architect.

On the other hand, the general preference of developers not to code in terms of the model reflects a practical weakness in using earlier versions of automatic code generators. As a practical matter, the evolution from thinking in terms of source code to thinking in terms of a model takes time, but will not take forever. Information technology automates repetitive processes, so developers can expect this to happen to their own tasks as well as the tasks automated in the software systems they build. Those embarking on a software-engineering career can expect the demand for implementation language skills to fluctuate dramatically, while the ability to use effectively the set of tools found in UML retains importance. As models become more executable with MDA, software developers can come to appreciate the time saved with automation and increasingly used models. Just as modern software development projects no longer need bit-shifting skills, it is likely that the next generation of software development engineers will require a new set of skills.

MDA calls for a number of platform and language experts who are able to move between the architect level and the source code, opening up a lot of work for developers. Tasks for people with these skill sets include working on model compilers and coding standards to optimize code generators. Some software development processes encourage the promotion and publication of official coding standard documents. MDA allows for the opportunity to integrate these standards directly by using elements at the model level to enforce certain rules on the code. Again, as with so many things in MDA, this characteristic is not something new that comes only with MDA. The software industry is already moving in this direction. For example, most development environments now support the automatic generation of getters and setters for beans. In addition, frameworks, such as Struts, enforce syntax rules on bean access during compile time for a JavaServer Page (JSP). Such constraints make software more reliable.

High-Level Assessment of MDA Opportunities

MDA offers a substantial number of opportunities. This section outlines a few notions about what makes MDA compelling as a future direction for software development, but focuses at a higher level than the previous section, discussing it as an intellectual construct and not as a practical initiative that will change the lives of analysts, architects, and developers. This discussion is tempered by some warnings about areas where MDA may not be a full success. You are no doubt able to add to both the opportunities and warnings in this section from your own thoughts and experiences without much effort.

Opportunities

Given the reliance of all organizations on information-management structures, MDA has an excellent opportunity to succeed. If MDA in practice can effectively address the issues associated with interoperability, many people will find the investment in MDA worth the effort. In addition, MDA with the enhanced power of UML 2 offers a platform that allows thought to flourish in ways not initially anticipated. For example, the semantic richness of UML and the automated capacity of PSMs make it possible to assess more accurately the business impact of changes to information-management systems.

A Necessary Evolutionary Step for Increased Coordination

The MDA is designed specifically to address the difficulty of operating in environments with a proliferation of middleware. With even simple systems relying on a number of different distributed servers, the industry needs some standards to address the problem. MDA has strengths as a candidate for this standard because it promotes a vendor-neutral approach with enough extension mechanisms to allow adaptation. With adoption by a number of prominent vendors, such as IBM, MDA can be the mechanism of choice for resolving interoperability problems in complex systems.

That MDA represents the OMG's response to the compelling problem of interoperability in software development indicates that UML and MDA remain vibrant and alive. The history of software development contains a number of bleached bones on the side of the road—interesting for those with the taste of a collector, but irrelevant for those who want to produce software more efficiently. Although it might be interesting to learn about old operating systems such as CP/M or old ground-breaking languages like LISP, these are dead in terms of addressing current problems. MDA remains vibrant and alive, and it is injecting the energy into UML to keep it vibrant and alive.

As an intellectual construct, MDA has the value of flexibility. MDA does not assert a dogmatic control designed to limit options. Rather, MDA offers a strong framework to enable software engineers to share information. This information sharing in a visible manner provides a critical opportunity. With models easier to exchange and share and with the feedback loop that forces a model to improve to succeed, modelers can deploy the tested intellectual artifacts of a huge number of brilliant analysts. With MDA, the notion of the super IT man is put to rest. People provide coordinating functions, acting as judges and assessors. The architect on a successful project is not able to act as God. With the complicated systems today, no person can sit down and code all the instructions. MDA and UML provide the common guidelines to allow for clear communication using automated tools.

Cost-Aware MDA

MDA requires cost justification for skeptical managers who have been burned adopting the latest technical flavor of the year. That MDA is designed to specifically address this problem in a vendor-neutral manner might not be convincing by itself, given that the marketing of every major platform and tool makes similar claims. So why does MDA make a difference? Why is it worth the investment?

Although one might think a way to address this question is to run an MDA project and compare it to the cost of another, similar control project, such a strategy actually will not help. An accurate estimation/cost model has eluded the software industry for years, making such efforts prone to exaggeration and to manipulation. No real control project exists in software development. Success relies on so many discrete factors with technological inputs changing so rapidly that to make any assessment of a "control" project resting outside time is impossible.

The ability of information technology to rapidly alter the very nature of production functions does more than make a control study unconvincing. Information technology leaves traditional methods of microeconomic analysis behind. This problem was a theoretical one recognized by one of the founders of mathematics-based microeconomics from the nineteenth century, Alfred Marshall from Cambridge. Marshall saw that economic growth stemmed from the ability to lower production costs. The calculus used in microeconomics required a fairly static production function. In situations of technological change, Marshall recognized that different analytical tools were needed to assess investment strategies. This recognition has remained among many growth economists and economic historians, while many mainstream economists and econometricians have persisted in the use of old microeconomic assumptions based on differential calculus to assess investment in information technology. The inability to accurately model economic investment strategies helps to explain the wildly divergent assessments of value found in the so-called new economy of the late 1990s. Lately, consultants and advanced economic modelers have been addressing these issues with quite complex models recognizing the dynamic nature of modern technologies. These models need the type of data accuracy and ability to model different scenarios that MDA can provide.

UML and MDA provide modeling mechanisms that can start to address these issues with a cost-aware MDA. Cost-aware MDA requires enhancements to all MDA model types. At a high level, you can see UML models built to allow for the collection of economic information and the modeling of different assumptions about external activities, using an industry-specific profile where needed (the outer ring of the MDA logo discussed earlier in the chapter). At the more specific level of the PSM, this modeling offers the opportunity to collect a number of clean, natural data points about software implementation as input to assessing cost. This data can be collected automatically at little additional cost and is not prone to human manipulation, so it is likely to be more accurate than other software productivity models. Also, depending on the nature of the enterprise, this information can be collected in close to realtime, allowing for decisions based on real information.

MDA provides the tools to allow an organization to assess the return on investment and assets not only in terms of the software effort but also in terms of the impact of that software on a business process by linking to the PIM and the higher-level domain model. In other words, MDA can help a business answer the key question of any technological change: Does this approach lower production costs? Rather than focusing on individual projects with faulty cost assumptions to promote MDA, it is worth proposing MDA as a method for assessing business assets as circumstances change. With MDA you can collect accurate information about the technological landscape of the firm.

A successful MDA effort, then, is one that provides complete transparency to the development process and the ability to summarize this information in a form useful for executive decision makers. With that information, a decision maker can actually determine what form of MDA and information technology benefits their business.

Warnings

MDA supported by UML, while a very promising initiative, also has some pitfalls. Do not assume that the widespread adoption of UML and the trend toward MDA-type approaches to software development makes MDA and UML automatically successful. Indeed, in some ways MDA has influenced UML 2 so much in the redefinition of the language architecture and enhancements to business modeling that if MDA falls apart, UML will also suffer. If one looks at the adoption of UML as it currently stands, many opportunities for improvement exist. Will UML with MDA address these problems or make them worse?

NOTE These warnings also bring their own opportunities, but we list them here as warnings because they represent some of the barriers UML faces in trying to achieve its goals.

Too Much Modeling Overhead and Complexity

A PIM that requires definition in a constraint language of sufficient rigor to allow automatic execution of code represents a substantial amount of abstract programming. On the one hand, such work might tax the skills of some business modelers who may not have skills related to programmatic execution. On the other hand, it might take developers away from implementing source code.

Another form of modeling overhead involves the additional metamodeling activities needed to derive and review profiles. Although eventually MDA will be able to provide successful profiles, early adopters of MDA have to shoulder the cost for this early profile generation. In addition, and as is clear from a quick review of this book (which reviews only the main features of the language), UML requires experience and training to implement effectively.

Some complain that the complexity of earlier versions of UML resulted in a variety of model types and views that cannot be effectively used in most circumstances. Some organizations relied primarily on a small portion of UML, such as class diagrams or deployment diagrams, and never fully integrated UML into the development process. UML with MDA increases the pressure to more fully integrate UML into software development, but for some, such integration might be too complex and not cost-effective.

Lack of Universality in Tool Implementation

If the OMG cannot effectively manage profiles to attain useful standards, the modeling community might face a resurgence of the method wars that UML solved. Even if OMG defines a standard, it does not mean that all vendors and clients will adopt the standard. The focus on exploding the number of modeling options and tailoring them to specific environments encourages models with implementation detail, but not necessarily model quality. Many implementing MDA will not find it worthwhile to use a standard for the sake of using a standard if it comes at the cost of modifying a profile or an extension used in their business. The best response to this danger is in the common XMI definition to allow for communication between tools. With UML tools supporting any user-defined profile, the lack of universality can at least be managed by providing a common platform to allow communication about these models.

Untested Behavioral Modeling

MDA implementations so far have worked mostly from structural diagrams. UML 2 offers a number of enhancements for those modeling behavior. MDA has a clear need for better modeling of behavior and workflow. However, how these elements translate via a model compiler into code is less clear. UML's behavioral modeling features are relatively untried for code generation when compared with class models. This observation reveals an opportunity as much as a danger because there is a lot of work to do to make behavioral modeling executable. The outstanding question remains whether it is worth the cost to develop.

Misuse of MDA

The OMG draft overview of MDA observed that they had the technology to implement MDA. For them, the main barrier for MDA was that a gap existed "in knowledge of how to use the technology" as well as a lack of "universal" tools supporting the technology (OMG MDA 2001). We would add that if MDA is not part of a process that supports teamwork toward clear goals, it will be hard to achieve the track record necessary to attract folks to MDA. If key industry players decide not to go with MDA and UML or implement them poorly, they will soon become hollowed-out intellectual constructs built to accommodate the improving modeling ideas of hundreds of intelligent people, with no content. Future versions will stagnate and an ambitious effort to communicate about information management will become yet another bleached bone by the side of the road. What can stop this from happening is the effective use of UML and MDA to solve real problems. If modeling does not address real problems, it is no more than an intellectual curiosity. This makes managing models with a process that keeps everyone focused on the most important issues key for using UML and MDA successfully. The next chapter focuses on these process issues.

Summary

After this brief overview of the issue of MDA and UML answers to the questions posed at the beginning of the chapter emerge. The OMG drives the MDA initiative to address the problems posed by the proliferation of middleware and the pace of technological change. With a flexible, but semantically rich modeling structure guiding a series of models addressed to different goals, MDA can help organizations manage complex structures.

UML plays a central role in MDA. The modeling language encourages the abstraction of different processes as well as the arrangement of different views of the same system. MDA has adopted this approach and even implemented it on a larger scale, stressing a number of different models in addition to the number of different views that make up a single UML model. MDA very much relies on the use of UML and the support given the language by automated development support tools. This support provides a foundation for MDA that makes it possible to envision such an approach to software development.

The sentiments driving MDA have found expression in a number of the requirements for UML. MDA requires a flexible modeling language that can adapt to different levels of analysis while maintaining a logical connection between elements. The language also requires a clear extension mechanism that can be supported by automated tools. In general, MDA requires greater rigor and less ambiguity from the modeling language to have enough constructs to be able to produce software code.

This chapter ended with some speculation about how UML and MDA might develop and the opportunities and pitfalls associated with the initiative. What is less speculative, however, is that UML and MDA continue to help many produce software. The most likely scenario for the future involves an incremental adoption of MDA, with large projects looming as the candidates likely to find the best trade-off between model overhead and improved implementation quality. On the more detailed side, development environments can increasingly use UML for reverse engineering and generating code. With UML, the OMG provides substantial support for MDA as a future evolutionary path for large-scale software development.

The emphasis on any notation or approach to modeling will fail without a method that encourages quality and supports successful teamwork. The next chapter focuses on these issues of process and quality.

CHAPTER

10

A Process for Using UML

The UML comprises notations and rules that make it possible to express object-oriented models. It does not, however, prescribe how the work should be done, that is, the process or method for working with the language. Instead, it was designed for use with many processes, different in both scope and purpose. Nevertheless, to use the UML successfully, some sort of process is necessary, especially when designing large models that require a team effort. Everyone's work must be coordinated, and everyone must be aiming in the same direction. Using a process also makes it more efficient to measure progress and to control and improve the work. In addition, a process, particularly in the field of software engineering, more fully enables reuse, in terms of both the process itself and its parts (models, components, conclusions, and so on).

Simply, a process describes what to do, how to do it, when to do it, and why it should be done. It describes a number of activities that should be done in a certain order. As a result of the process, documentation (models and other descriptions) about the system being built is produced, and a product that solves the initial problems is introduced and delivered. Just as a modeling language needs tool support, a process needs tools to support its inherent activities. Unfortunately, such tools are not as widely available as tools for modeling.

When the named activities of a process are complete, an explicit goal is achieved. A process should result in value for its customer (user). To that end, the process consumes resources in terms of human beings, computers, tools, information, and so on. There are rules for this resource utilization, and an important part of describing a process is to define these rules. A process is normally divided into nested subprocesses. At the bottom level, a process is atomic, meaning that it cannot be divided and broken down any further.

In contrast, a method is normally also considered a set of related activities, but without explicit goals, resources, and rules. In software engineering, both methods and processes need a well-defined modeling language to express and communicate their results. A number of sources attempt to define the meaning of "process" and "method," including the differences between the terms. However, for the most part, no significant differentiation is made between the terms in this chapter; process will be used primarily. Some processes are of general interest, such as management processes, quality processes, manufacturing processes, and development processes. In this chapter, software development processes are discussed, in particular, the development of software systems using the UML.

Defining and Understanding Software-Engineering Processes

Defining a process for software engineering is not easy. It requires understanding the mechanisms behind the work of software development and knowledge of how the work *should* be done. At this juncture, we must introduce some general aspects of processes for software engineering. The ideas in this section have been derived from N. Jayaratna (Jayaratna, 1994) and his work on the Normative Information Model-based Systems Analysis and Design (NIMSAD) framework for defining and comparing processes. The terminology used here is also from NIMSAD.

Certain object-oriented methods on the market today, such as The Unified Process, might be considered processes. However, other lightweight methods, such as Extreme Programming (XP), are not robust enough to be considered processes in the way we use the term here. Although they provide a valuable set of interrelated techniques, they are often referred to as "small m methodologies" rather than as software-engineering processes.

Our intention in this section is to open up the discussion of software engineering and process/method support. There is always need for structured ways of working and thinking, either explicitly as guided by a process or implicitly as guided by thought. With that in mind, a process can be viewed from the following aspects:

- **Process context.** Describes the problem domains in which the process can be used
- **Process user.** Gives guidelines for how the process should be adopted and used
- **Process steps.** Describes the steps (activities) to be taken during the process
- **Process evaluation.** Describes how to evaluate the results (documents, products, experience, and so on)

The next sections of the chapter delve into each of these aspects.

Process Context

A process must describe its context, the problem domains in which it is applicable. Note that it might not be desirable (or even possible) to develop or choose a generic process that handles all potential problems. It is important only that the problems in a specific problem domain be properly handled by the process. However, this creates a dilemma—often the problem domain is not completely known until *after* the process has been completed.

The problem domain, also called the process context, is part of an organizational or business context composed of people, power, politics, cultures, and more. The business has goals, and the information systems that are developed should support these goals. At least four reasons to regard a problem domain (related to an information system) as part of an organization or a business exist:

- Efficiency in an information system can be measured only by the contribution it makes to the business.
- To be able to develop information systems, the developers must interact with the people within the business.
- To solve a problem, the problem solver (the process user) must be introduced to the business and understand how it works.
- When a problem solver is introduced to a business, interpersonal relationships are formed between the people in the business and the problem solvers.

The term *business* should be considered in a general sense because there is no model or process that can capture all aspects of a business. This limitation must be documented within a process for software engineering. A well-known technique for describing a business is to describe it with metaphors, such as machines, organisms, a rational control structure, social culture, political systems, psychic prisons, flux and transformations, instruments of domination, and others (Morgan, 1986).

Process User

A process for software engineering must include guidelines for its use. These guidelines refer not only to the process itself, but also to the person or people using the process, the intended problem solver(s). We humans have mental constructs that affect how we think, including how we think about using tools such as a process. These mental constructs can be divided as follows:

- Perceptual process (how one picks up information)
- Values and ethics
- Motives and prejudices
- Reasoning ability
- Experiences
- Skills and knowledge sets
- Structuring ability
- Roles (played in our society and business)
- Patterns, models, and frameworks that are "in one's head"

So, all these constructs affect your interpretation of process descriptions. For instance, your experience of a process might affect the way you structure things even if the process gives you a different direction. Your values and ethics might restrict you from taking certain process steps, such as reorganizing or negotiating (especially in regard to processes for developing and improving businesses). A well-defined process, then, must guide its users to avoid misuse caused by mental constructs.

Process Steps

Most processes for software development consist of at least three basic phases (some processes might have more). They are *problem formulation, solution design*, and *implementation design*.

- The problem-formulation phase helps you to discover and formulate the problems.
- In the solution-design phase, you formulate solution to the problems.
- The implementation phase introduces and implements the solution, thereby (ideally) eliminating the problems.

In a software-engineering process for object-oriented systems, the steps could easily translate into *analysis, design*, and *implementation*.

Problem Formulation

Problem formulation consists of five general steps, which are all well-defined processes or methods for system engineering:

1. Understanding the domain of concern
2. Completing the diagnosis
3. Defining the prognosis outline
4. Defining the problems
5. Deriving notional systems

The first step is to understand the problem domain; otherwise, it is difficult to describe the problems therein. It is important to investigate the nature of the problems to avoid a problem formulation that does not include the most important problems, which can happen if the problems are described just as they appear. Note that problems are related to each other, and consequently, it is not always easy to capture the underlying issues that may be at the root of the obvious ones. Problems may be described within problem hierarchies. For example, a problem may be that the logistics in a company do not work. But the *underlying* problem might be that the actors that handle the logistics do not have sufficient knowledge, in which case, no information system will help solve the problem unless the actors are trained. The training can be done by means of information systems, but that software cannot be built until the real problem is discovered and described.

The second step is to complete a diagnosis, meaning that the present domain should be described in terms of what was discovered in the first step. Again, the previous step is to know and understand the domain of concern; the purpose of this step is to summarize and document it. The documentation is called a diagnosis. A diagnosis might be that your systems are in some aspects not efficient compared to those of your competitors.

The third step is to formulate a prognosis outline, in which the desired future domain is described. This description should list where you want to be, why you want to be there, and when you want to be there. The prognosis outline might be that you need more efficient systems (in the aspects diagnosed in Step 2) than your competitors, because you believe that such efficiency is a competitive strength. A prognosis should list which aspects in your systems should be improved, what advantages this improvement brings you, and when you want this achieved.

The fourth step is to describe how to go from the present domain to the desired future domain. This step normally requires itemizing steps and subgoals necessary to reach the final goal, the desired future domain. These steps and subgoals can, for instance, express functions to add or to improve in the system and how to implement those functions as quickly as possible.

The final step is deriving the notional systems. A notional system is one that is formulated from your mental constructs, which, if designed and implemented, you believe would eliminate the identified problems within the problem domain.

Solution Design

The solution design normally consists of two main steps:

- Completing a conceptual/logical design
- Drawing a physical design

The conceptual and logical design models (expresses) the notional system using a modeling language. The physical design is constructed of the nonfunctional aspects, such as performance, capability, and so on. The purpose of a conceptual and logical design is to create a model that is easy to implement, for example, with an object-oriented programming language. The purpose of the physical design is to create a model that captures nonfunctional aspects and leads to efficient use of your resources, for example, computers, printers, networks, and so on. The UML works perfectly for both these steps; the implementation is then straightforward.

Implementation Design

The last step is to implement the models produced in the solution design phase; in software-engineering terms, they are programmed. Implementation also means that the system is introduced to the customer, so this step also covers documentation, online help, manuals, user training, converting parts of old systems and data, and more.

Process Evaluation

It is important to evaluate everything that is done and everything that might affect your work. Only by evaluation can you learn from your work and continue to improve. Thus, the process user, the process itself, and the process results are continuously evaluated, because you never know whether the real problems have been captured (it is easier to capture the symptoms than the cause). Furthermore, new problems might reveal themselves during the work. Often, after the customers or users describe the problem domain, an experienced developer investigates whether their description really captures all of the problems (the customers' needs).

Both during and after projects, evaluate results. Results may be seen as the products delivered by the project (models, software components, and so on). The products are specified and developed to eliminate problems detected within the problem domain, so they must be evaluated in terms of how well they solve problems. In short, if the problem domain isn't carefully evaluated, the products cannot be evaluated; and if the products cannot be evaluated, then the customer/user might not be satisfied with the final system.

To improve your work, the process and the process user also need to be evaluated, particularly under the current circumstances. Evaluating the results (the products) along with the reactions and experiences of the process users (the developers) can help you assess the process and its users. It is important to evaluate how the user actually uses the process. Ask questions such as these:

- Did the user follow all the process's steps?
- Did the user comply with the process's intention?
- Were the results as expected?
- What problems did the user experience when implementing the process?

Unfortunately, evaluating the process user is not done on a regular basis in many of today's software-engineering processes. Only through evaluation can the process be tuned and improved. No process is perfect, and even if one were, it wouldn't be perfect forever.

The Basis for a UML Process

Although UML is considered generic for object-oriented modeling, its designers had to have some kind of process in mind when they designed it. The acceptance of UML as a standard was followed quickly by The Unified Software Development Process text, written by the same key visionaries. This text described The Unified Process and benefited from years of process-related work by such methodologists as Philippe Krutchen and Walker Royce, as well as the three key visionaries of UML. The Unified Process uses UML as its modeling language. However, any object-oriented method or process can use UML. The basic characteristics that the designers had in mind for a process using UML are that it should be use-case-driven, architecture-centric, and iterative and incremental. These characteristics will now be studied in more detail one by one.

Use-Case-Driven Systems

In UML, use cases capture the functional requirements of the system; they "drive" the development of all subsequent work products, or *artifacts*. Thus, use cases are implemented to ensure that all functionality is realized in the system, and to verify and test the system. Because the use cases compose the functional requirements of the system, they affect all disciplines and all views, as shown in Figure 10.1. During the capturing of requirements, they are used to represent the required functionality and to validate the functional requirements with the stakeholders. During analysis and design, the use cases are realized in UML models that demonstrate that the requirements can be met and can be reasonably implemented. During implementation, the use cases must be realized in the code. And, finally, during testing, the use cases verify the system; they become the bases for the test cases.

Processes in which use cases are the dominant concept, such as the Unified Process, also prescribe that the work be organized around use cases. While fitting it into an overall architecture that might be driven by nonfunctional requirements of the system, designers design the system use case by use case. And then implementers build the system in a similar vein. Incremental builds of the system are defined and verified by the use cases supported. In the project-management discipline, which plans, monitors, and transcends the modeling-centric activities described within this text, use cases become the lynch pin by which all activities are defined and then are linked together.

Architecture-Centric Approach

A process that uses UML is architecture-centric. This characteristic means that you consider a well-defined, basic system architecture important and that you strive to establish such an architecture early in the process. A system architecture is reflected by the different views of the modeling language, and it is usually developed through several iterations. It is important to define the basic architecture early in the project, then to prototype and evaluate it, and, finally, to refine it during the course of the project (see Figure 10.2).

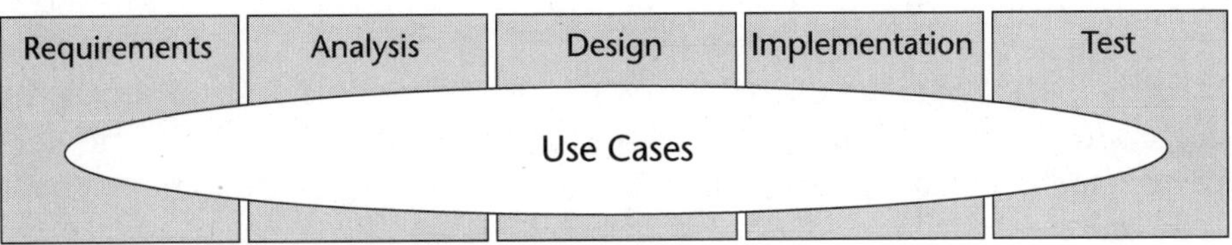

Figure 10.1 Use cases bind the process.

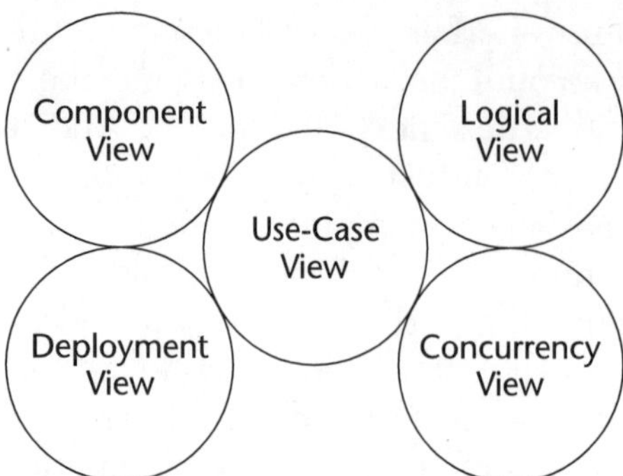

Figure 10.2 The UML views reflect the system architecture.

The architecture works as a map of the system that defines the different parts of the system, their relationships and interactions, their communication mechanisms, and the overall rules for how parts may be added or changed. A good architecture must demonstrate that it can support the functional aspects of the system, but it is driven more by nonfunctional issues. It is especially important to define a system that can be modified, that can be understood intuitively, and that enables reuse (either into or out of the system).

The most important aspect of creating a good architecture is to divide the system logically into subsystems, in which the dependencies between different subsystems are simple and sensible. Dependencies should usually be of the client/server type, where one package knows about the other, but not vice versa (if they both depend on each other, they are very hard to maintain or separate). Packages are also often organized in layers, where different layers handle the same thing but in various degrees of abstraction (a layer of business objects can be placed on top of a persistence handler layer, which in turn is placed on top of an SQL-generation layer, and so on).

Iterative Approach

Building models with UML is best done in a number of iterations. Instead of trying to define all the details of a model or diagram at once, the development is a sequence of steps, whereby each iteration adds some new information or detail. Then, each iteration is evaluated, either on paper or in a working prototype, and used to produce input for the next iteration. Thus, a process that uses iterations provides continuous feedback that improves the process itself, as well as the final product.

An iteration exercises the appropriate amount of each discipline of system development: requirements, analysis, design, implementation, and test. At first glance, you might consider a process that has the team gathering some requirements, then doing some analysis, then doing some design, and then implementing and testing. This sort of mini-waterfall idea is shown in Figure 10.3. But this approach does not take into account the fact that team members might be specialized (requirements analysts, designers, and so on). And it does not properly take into account the fact that early iterations focus more on requirements activities, while later iterations focus on implementation.

Although it is true that requirements must feed analysis, analysis feeds design, and so on down the line, it is not true that each iteration goes in lock-step through the activities associated with each of those disciplines in a "stop this, then start that" mode. Figure 10.4 shows a set of notional iterations over time and how the team might exercise the disciplines. In each iteration after the first one, a backlog of input lets the activities associated with any particular discipline start right away. For example, in iteration two, analysis starts immediately on some requirements that were gathered late in iteration one; requirements gathering also continues on from the start of iteration two, but some of those requirements might not be analyzed until iteration three. The mini-waterfall idea holds true in the dependencies among the disciplines; it just does not hold true in how the tasks are carried out across a project.

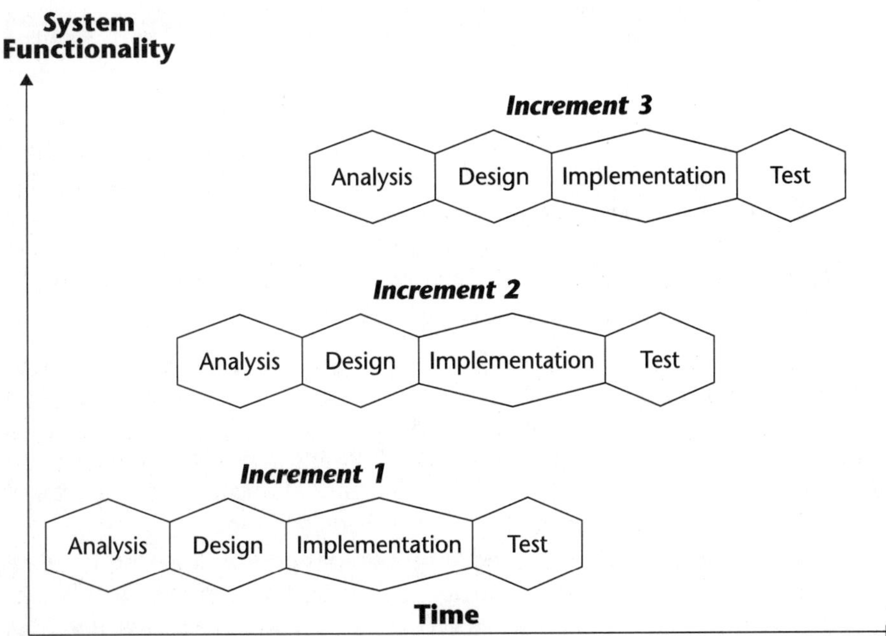

Figure 10.3 Iterations seen as mini-waterfalls.

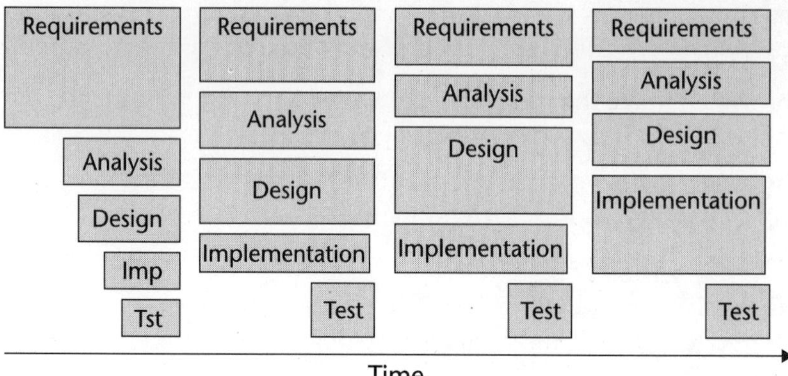

Figure 10.4 A more realistic view of iterations.

Incremental Approach

Each iteration should produce an executable result that can be tested to verify forward progress. An increment is a step in the evolution of the system, sometimes called a version of the system. When developing iteratively and incrementally, the development is based on the definition of a number of steps. A step is "delivered" and evaluated according to its technical, economical, and process merits. When the system is delivered, it doesn't necessarily mean that the software is sent to a customer; in many cases, it is an internal release to the software department. When they deliver it, the development team should, however, hand over the system in its current state to someone who validates the progress made. Therefore, it is imperative that each iteration have appropriate testing activities at the end (see Figures 10.3 and 10.4).

Early iterations should be organized around producing increments supporting architecture and attacking risk. When you are deciding what to include in an early iteration, focus on the activities that will have the greatest impact on the architecture or mitigate the highest level of risk. Although the architecture must be verified based on its ability to support the functional requirements, the earliest increments don't necessarily provide significant end-user functionality. Early iterations should tackle the big problems, not postpone them. Some deliverables from early iterations might also be considered prototypes to be thrown away if they do not produce the desired results.

Later increments build on the architectural baseline, adding end-user functionality. Although the early increments are demonstrated via the implementation of threads through use cases, in these later increments, the key unit of delivery is a system *fully* supporting a selected set of use cases.

The delivered increment is always tested and evaluated, typically with the software team involved in the evaluation process. These questions are posed:

- Does the system have the functions that were supposed to be included in this step, and do they work as expected?
- Does the system satisfy nonfunctional attributes such as adequate performance, reliability, and user-friendliness?
- What risks were mitigated, and what new risks have been unearthed?
- Was this step developed within the time estimated, and was the resource budget adhered to—was the step developed within the economic constraints?
- Were there problems in the process/method during this step? Does the process/method have to be clarified, or do actions have to be taken, say, to substitute or add new resources?

Other questions can be added. It is important that the steps be used to evaluate the entire development process—the functional and nonfunctional aspects of the product, as well as the process and the work of the software team. After each step, you can take actions to correct any problems, and the experiences from each step can be input into the next step. Once a problem is identified, it doesn't necessarily lead to dramatic actions. It may simply indicate that overly optimistic and incorrect estimates were made and that they are the reasons for the failure of the increment. During the course of the project, the steps are meant to tune the product and the process so that the result is successful.

Every step should add new functionality or attributes to the product. Their contents must be planned; they shouldn't just be what the developers felt like including. As previously discussed, functions that have the greatest impact on the end user or pose the greatest risk should be put in first. An increment can also be delivered to the actual end users. The advantage of this action is that user opinions of the product and the interface are received early enough to be taken into account.

Opponents of iterative and incremental development often claim that this method makes it more difficult to plan and precludes long-term planning. But iterative and incremental development is more economical and predictive than the waterfall model, and when implemented correctly, creates a self-improving process of the overall software development.

The opposite of incremental development is the aforementioned waterfall model, in which each phase is performed only once, and the system is released in what is called a "big bang." The entire system generation is analyzed in an analysis phase, designed in a single design phase, and implemented and tested in a construction phase. The risks posed by this model are apparent:

- Feedback and experiences during the development process can't be taken into account (at least not in an organized manner). Such experiences may concern both the product and the way it is being produced (the development process).
- A test to determine whether the analysis and design assumptions are correct is not done until very late in the project, when it might be too late to correct problems.
- Maintaining the schedule might be very difficult because, during the construction phase, someone might realize that the plans are too optimistic, by which time it's too late to revamp them.
- The risks of the project are not pushed to the front, and thus they might reveal themselves late in the project as unpleasant surprises.

WARNING **Some practical observations: Even though most proponents of object-oriented methods talk about and advocate incremental and iterative development, in practice, many use the waterfall method. Just because the system is being programmed in a number of releases (for example, alpha, beta, pilot, and so on), doesn't mean that the development is incremental. Remember, each increment must add some new functional or nonfunctional aspects to the system, and not be just a set of bug fixes. Each step must be evaluated properly and used as input to the next step.**

A Traditional Object-Oriented Method

This section looks at the different activities typically performed when using an object-oriented method, as shown in Figure 10.5. This is not an attempt to create a new method, nor to capture one specific method in detail. It's a generic description of the activities usually performed in a method. The models in object-oriented methods are organized around requirements, analysis, design, implementation, and deployment. These have been traditionally called phases; we refer to them as disciplines here to remove the issue of where they fit into an end-to-end schedule. These disciplines are supported by less model-centric disciplines such as test and project management. The next section introduces a macroprocess that contains phases within which these disciplines are exercised.

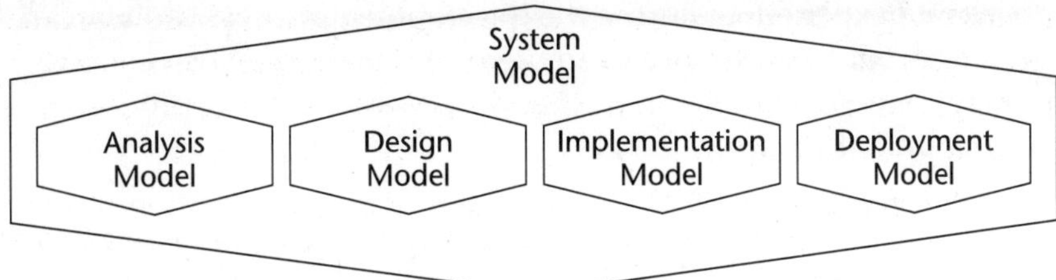

Figure 10.5 The disciplines and models in a traditional method/process.

Each of the disciplines produces its own model, which consists of some diagrams. It's possible to introduce new functions by adding them to the requirements model and then to each of the other models in turn. In addition to the contents of these disciplines, other activities are present throughout the project, including walkthroughs and reviews, project planning, quality measurement, and so on. A process can also contain descriptions of how these vertical procedures are performed.

Requirements

The requirements discipline generates an agreement between the stakeholders and the supplier of the system. Stakeholders can include the actual customer that is paying for the system, future users of the system, or others with authority over requirements, such as members of a systems security team within the organization. The customer may be a user within the same organization as the supplier or separate companies where detailed business contracts are written based on the requirements documents. The requirements should be as detailed as possible, although it's usually impossible to define everything in such a document. When it's not possible to go into detail in the requirements artifact, the document should express an intention or an idea to be invoked when a conflict between the customer and supplier arises. The requirements discipline is often integrated with business modeling, where business resources, rules, goals, and actions are modeled. (Business modeling is discussed in Chapter 5.)

The requirements activities utilize use cases, business processes, or plaintext to describe the functions required of the system. The system is viewed from the outside; requirements do not delve into how things are done technically. The practical work consists of discussions and negotiations between the stakeholders and the supplier.

Along with the functional aspects, it is important you remember the nonfunctional requirements as well. Issues such as performance and reliability should be discussed, even though it is difficult at this early stage to write business contracts based on numbers here. Other constraints of the system should be made: size, technical environment, necessary integration with legacy systems, products and languages to use, and others.

The requirements discipline results in a specification upon which the stakeholders and supplier agree. To that end, a simple glossary and/or conceptual model of the basic entities used in the system is helpful. Naturally, if use cases have been used to capture the functional requirements, they are the focal point of all this documentation.

The UML diagrams created in requirements activities include use-case diagrams, some simple class diagrams, and possibly some state machine or activity diagrams. The activity diagrams might be used to specify the internals of a particular use case or to show how the use cases relate to one another in a business flow.

Analysis

Analysis generates models of the problem domain: classes, objects, and interactions that model the "real-world" entities. An analysis should be free from any technical or implementation details and should constitute an ideal model because it is the representation of the problem to be solved. This model deals with acquiring the necessary knowledge about the domain.

Some typical activities in an analysis are as follows:

- Domain knowledge is acquired from requirements specifications, use cases, models of the business processes, a glossary, descriptions of existing systems, and interviews with users and any other interested parties of the system. This is a research activity.
- Candidates for suitable classes are found, often in a brainstorming session, during which possible classes are listed. When the session ends, a critical review of all candidates is given and certain classes are removed from the list for a number of reasons (for example, they are functions, they are duplicate classes with different names, they don't have the characteristics of a class, they're not within the domain, they can't be defined in a concrete manner, and so on). The list of classes in the system typically changes throughout the development, as new experiences lead to the insertion or deletion of classes.
- Use-case analysis uses a set of heuristics to distribute the responsibilities of the realization of a use case among classes stereotyped as <<entity>>, <<boundary>>, and <<control>>.
- The static relationships between classes are modeled in terms of associations, aggregations, generalizations, and dependencies. Class diagrams are used to document the classes, their specifications, and their relationships.
- The behavior and collaboration between objects of the classes are described using state machine, sequence, communication, and activity

diagrams. As part of use-case analysis, scenarios of the use cases are modeled in sequence and/or communication diagrams. Note that no technical solutions are modeled, that is, technical logic or factors such as database access are not described.

- When enough diagrams have been developed (usually very iterative work where things constantly change), the overall model is verified by running the system "on paper." The entire model is presented to domain experts and discussed. The scenarios are "played," and the experts are asked whether this is a natural model for solving the problem.
- The basic user interface can be prototyped, though not necessarily in detail (for example, finished window layouts). The overall structure—the navigation between windows, metaphors used, and the basic contents of the main windows—is prototyped, tested, and discussed with representatives of the users.

The analysis documentation consists of a model that describes the problem domain to be handled in the system, along with the necessary behavior of the analysis classes to provide the required functionality. Again, the documentation should describe an "ideal" system, without taking the technical environment and its details into consideration.

The UML diagrams created in an analysis are class, sequence, communication, state machine, and activity diagrams, and their focus is on the problem domain, not on a specific technical solution.

Design

The design is a technical expansion and adaptation of the analysis result. The classes, relationships, and collaborations from the analysis are complemented with new elements, now focusing on how to implement the system in a computer. All the details of how things should work technically and the constraints of the implementation environment are taken into consideration. The results of the analysis are carried over to the design and maintained in the center of the system. To maintain their basic properties and behavior, the analysis classes (also known as business objects) should not be tampered with unless absolutely necessary. Instead, the analysis classes should be embedded in a technical infrastructure, where technical classes help them to become persistent, to communicate, to present themselves in the user interface, and so on. By separating the analysis classes from the technical infrastructure, it is much easier to change or update either of them. In the design, the same diagram types are used as in the analysis, although new diagrams have to be created and modeled to show the technical solution.

Typical activities in a design are as follows:

- Architectural design introduces design elements to support technical issues. Design elements supporting technical issues and nonfunctional requirements, such as security, communication, and database persistence, are called architectural mechanisms. They might be manifested in the design as a set of helper classes; they might be a set of interfaces and other framework elements to which the other classes must conform. The architectural mechanisms typically require both static class diagrams and dynamic object diagrams to be fully described in the design.

- Model partitioning divides the analysis classes into functional packages (if this has not already been done in the analysis). New packages for technical areas such as the user interface, database handling, and communication are added. The analysis package might use technical services from these packages, but otherwise should remain as unaffected as possible. The communication mechanisms between different packages are established (striving for client/server relationships in which the functional analysis packages are servers).
- The concurrency needs are identified and modeled through active classes, asynchronous messages, and synchronization techniques for handling shared resources (as described in more detail in Chapter 6).
- The detailed format of the output from the system is specified: user interface, reports, and transactions sent to other systems. The user-interface design may be viewed as a separate design activity, considering its importance.
- Necessary class libraries and components that enhance the architecture and minimize implementation work are acquired. Their designs are introduced into the model and related elements are fit into these design constraints.
- If you are using a relational database, the classes in the system are mapped to tables in a traditional relational model. The mechanism for reading from the database is also established in the architectural design.
- Special consideration is taken to handle exceptions and faults in the system. This consideration normally includes both "normal" error handling (errors that can be anticipated in the course of performing the system's functions) and abnormal errors (those that can't be anticipated and must be handled by some generic exception mechanism).
- The classes are allocated to source code components, and executable components are allocated to nodes, using component diagrams and deployment diagrams.

A detailed design activity includes specification of all classes, including the necessary implementation attributes, their detailed interfaces, and descriptions of the operations (in pseudocode or plaintext). The specifications should be detailed enough so that, together with the diagrams in the model, they provide all the necessary information for coding.

When performing design, remember:

- **Traceability.** Document all decisions so it's apparent on what basis they were made and from where the original requirement was generated. Separate analysis, design, and implementation models from each other.
- **Interfaces.** Create simple, complete, and consistent interfaces so that all component services can be easily understood and used.
- **Performance.** Do not overemphasize performance at an early stage (it's easier to increase performance in a working system than to improve a fast but nonworking system).
- **Simplicity.** Strive to create simple implementations that are sure to be understood and used by all developers, rather than creating "ingenious" solutions that only a few can understand.
- **Documentation.** Keep notes about everything that happens in the development process so that all events are documented and all problems can be traced.

The UML diagrams created in while designing are class, sequence, communication, state machine, activity, component, and deployment diagrams. Their focus is a detailed technical solution to provide the basis for the implementation discipline.

Implementation

Implementation is the actual writing of the code. If the design has been done correctly and with sufficient detail, the coding should be a simple task. This step involves making the final design decisions and translating the design diagrams and specifications into the syntax of the chosen programming language (which hopefully is an object-oriented language). It also involves the practical development process to iteratively compile, link, and debug components.

NOTE While the Model Driven Architecture approach provides means to transform aspects of a properly structured design all the way forward into a platform-specific implementation, we assumed here that a need exists for some amount of manual programming.

The work is supported by programming rules that attempt to standardize code developed by different programmers, and to prevent dangerous or unsuitable implementations in the language. Code inspections or reviews, formal or informal, facilitate standards being followed and improve the overall quality of the code.

The implementation activities are usually very popular among programmers and managers. The programmers feel that this is the area with which they are familiar (making models is often regarded as abstract and unnecessary), and the managers feel that until the coding has started no real work has been done. When object-oriented analysis and design is introduced, it is not uncommon for managers to walk around demanding, "Why haven't you started coding yet?"

In most cases, the rush to start coding the system is a mistake. Obviously, the analysis-and-design decisions have to be made at some point; the choice is to make them using a well-composed team in a structured modeling process or to have them made implicitly by disparate programmers during the coding. Wiser decisions usually are made in a structured manner. That said, remember to conduct the overall development process in an iterative manner. Having performed some analysis and design, verify the decisions via targeted implementation and test activities. Furthermore, certain key architectural features of the system should be analyzed, designed, and implemented early in the life cycle, while other functional areas are still having their requirements specified. No one discipline should be performed for long in absence of the others. If any one of the activities takes too long (for example, analyzing use cases for months), it could lead to too much administration and documentation, resulting in a decrease in the efficiency of the process.

Very few new diagrams are created as part of implementation; rather, the diagrams created in the design are detailed or corrected when necessary.

Test

The aim of testing is to identify errors in the code. Finding an error is thus considered a success, not a failure. A test consists of a number of test cases, where different aspects of the part under test are checked. Each test case tells what to do, what data to use, and what result to expect. When conducting the test, the result—including any deviations from the planned test case—are noted in a test protocol. Normally, a deviation indicates an error in the system (although sometimes the test case could be wrong and the system right). An error is noted and described in a test report, after which a responsible programmer is assigned to correct the bug for the next version of the system. Errors can be functional (for example, a function is missing or incorrect), nonfunctional (for example, performance is too slow), or logical (for example, a user-interface detail is not considered logical).

Significant automated support exists for the test process; this support includes both tool support for specifying and running the tests, and administrative support for the overall test process. In an iterative process, automated regression testing is key.

A number of different types of tests exist.

- A *unit test* is one of a component or a set of components, often done by the developer of the components.
- An *integration test* is one of packages that are put together, where the interfaces of the packages and their collaboration are validated. A special integration test team, whose members have good knowledge of the architecture of the system, typically does the integration test.
- A *system test* is a functional test of the entire system as viewed by end users and is typically done with the requirements specification (with use cases) as the basis. The system test verifies that the system delivers the specified functionality to the end user.
- A variation of the system test is the *acceptance test*, which is done by the receiver of a system in order to determine whether to accept the delivered version.
- A *regression test* is a technique to handle changes in systems. A regression test is run after changes have been made to the system; it is actually a series of tests run on the entire system to determine whether any other functionality has been incorrectly affected by the changes. It is very common that a change in one part of the system has unexpected effects on some other part (though the risk diminishes with object-oriented technology). Continuous regression tests unveil such problems. Regression tests are often automated. They are run by a tool, and the tool signals any differences in relation to the expected result.

The use-case diagrams created while gathering requirements are used in the test discipline to verify the system's proper functioning. The deployment, sequence, and communication diagrams created during analysis and design are typically used as the basis for integration tests. Testers can use UML to represent facets of their test model in the form of state machines, activity diagrams, and use-case diagrams.

NOTE Because testing can require significant code, and even whole test frameworks, test code can warrant its own complete UML design.

The Unified Process

In tandem with their initial textbooks on the UML, the three most recognized UML leaders, Grady Booch, Ivar Jacobson, and James Rumbaugh, introduced The Unified Software Development Process (Booch, Rumbaugh, and Jacobson, 1999) based on work done within a process group at Rational Software Corporation. More commonly called The Unified Process, it is becoming recognized as a premiere process for developing complex systems when using UML. Each of these three methodologists already had his own processes; this process pulls together the best features from each and adds more industry-recognized best practices.

NOTE Although this process is often used when developing object-oriented systems modeled with UML, we must stress that the process does not come from the OMG, nor is it the only process available for UML modelers.

Rational Software Corporation has created a branded version of this process that is called the Rational Unified Process. It is sold as a product with artifact templates and a huge volume of information detailing the process from many perspectives. This text describes the process as it was described by Jacobson, Booch, and Rumbaugh in their book. A number of minor differences are apparent, but the concepts and issues are the same.

The Unified Process is really a macroprocess for development, aimed at both managers and technicians. Microprocess activities organized around requirements, analysis, design, implementation, and testing are still present, but are placed in a larger framework for producing commercial software.

Here are the basic ideas behind the Unified Process:

- **Based on models of systems to be built.** The models reveal different views of the system, each detailing a specific aspect of the system. The views create a balance when defining the system to prevent the developer from overemphasizing any one part of the system. Naturally, UML is the language used. The views and their purposes in UML are described in Chapter 2.
- **Process oriented.** The work is done according to a well-defined set of activities that are repeatable by different teams in different projects. The work is not done individually, to preclude each project or participant from doing things in conflict.
- **Iterative and incremental.** The work is done as a number of iterations; the final product is developed incrementally.

- **Risk driven.** The process focuses on minimizing risk by promoting regular risk analysis and by pushing high-risk activities to early iterations.
- **Tailorable.** The process is a process framework that should be applied as appropriate, based on such issues as business context, organizational factors and attitudes, and size and degree of novelty of the system being built.

The Life Cycle

The life cycle of the Unified Process governs the product life from conception to development completion. The life cycle consists of a number of cycles, each of which produces a generation, a release or version of the product. Every cycle consists of phases, and each phase consists of a number of iterations. Figure 10.6 shows how the disciplines of the Unified Process are exercised across one release cycle.

The phases performed in every generation cycle are seen from a macroperspective—management. The work disciplines include the same activities found in object-oriented software development—requirements, analysis, design, implementation, and testing—although they are performed in an iterative manner within the macroprocess.

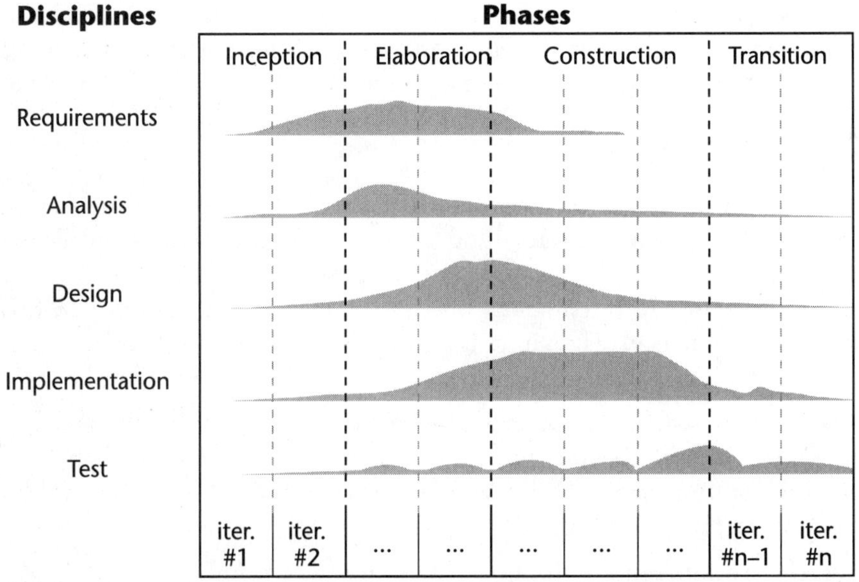

Figure 10.6 Phases, iterations, and disciplines of the Unified Process.

The phases are as follows:

- **Inception.** Makes a business case and defines the scope and goals of the project.
- **Elaboration.** Establishes a sound architectural foundation and captures detailed requirements. Planning for the overall project is done, amplified by the definition of the functionality and architecture.
- **Construction.** Develops the product in detail through a series of iterations. This involves more analysis and design, as well as actual programming.
- **Transition.** Delivers the system to end users (including activities such as marketing, packaging, support, documentation, and training).

Each phase in the cycle is performed as a series of iterations. The amount of time spent in each phase depends on the project (is it a contract job for subcontract, is it being done internally, and so on), the size of the project, how much new technology is used, and the general experience within the application domain. It also depends on which generation of the system is developed; the first generation typically needs more time in the inception and elaboration phases.

A number of milestones are defined at the end of a phase or an iteration, and these milestones are used to track the progress of the project.

Inception

The inception phase is when a vision of a product is created. If it is the first cycle, the inception phase contains the establishment of all the basic ideas about the product: its functionality and capability, its performance and other nonfunctional properties, and the technology to be used. In the second cycle and beyond, the inception phase is when the ideas to improve and enhance the product are formulated.

The inception phase is intended to result in a plan of what to build in this cycle, followed by a study determining whether it can be built and how it should be built (the feasibility of the project). The inception should also contain a basic domain analysis and architectural ideas. Typically, the most primary functions and actors are described in use cases. The plan must also include business arguments for the product, in terms of estimated development costs, market potential, risk analysis, and competitive products.

When the plan has been made, it is presented to the decision makers who, based on the product, the technical analysis, and the business arguments, make a decision whether or not to go ahead with the project.

The inception phase can be rather lengthy for the first cycle of a new product, but it is often not as extensive when new generations are produced.

Elaboration

The elaboration phase consists of a more detailed analysis of the system/generation to be built, along with a plan detailing the work to be done. Both the functionality and the problem domain are analyzed in more detail (using use cases, class diagrams, and dynamic diagrams), and a system architecture is baselined. The architecture is not just modeled; an executable architecture that can be verified against a number of architecturally significant use cases is built.

A project plan is drawn up to include an overall estimate of resources and a schedule. A preliminary draft, itemizing how the work should be divided into iterations, is also written, in which the impact on the system and risk are the dominant factors for the assessment of the early iterations.

Following this phase, a more detailed plan of the system/generation to be built is available, and a decision is made whether or not to further pursue this cycle.

Construction

The construction phase is carried out as a series of iterations. The inception and elaboration phase only define a basic system architecture that is refined and detailed incrementally during the construction, which means that altering the architecture and ideas from earlier phases is allowed.

In this phase, the main activity is normally programming, but test specification and actual test work are also large parts of the construction phase. It is expected that additional specifics of requirements not detailed in the earlier phases will be recorded and that the analysis and design models will continue to be refined. Another important construction activity is writing the documentation of the system, including both the development and use of the system.

The construction phase delivers a constructed system (in the current generation) in its final iteration, along with development and user documentation of the system.

Transition

The transition phase delivers the product to the end users; it takes the system from the development team and puts it into real use. The transition phase involves everything around that process, including:

- **Marketing.** Identifying the potential users and selling the product to them
- **Packaging.** Giving the product an attractive package
- **Installation.** Defining the correct installation procedures for all environments

- **Configuration.** Defining all the possible configurations of the system
- **Training.** Writing course materials and planning the training of end users
- **Support.** Organizing support around the product so that users can get their questions answered and their problems handled
- **Maintenance.** Organizing the handling of problem reports, which will often be turned into error reports that must lead to bug-fix updates of the system (meaning that development resources must still be available in this phase)

The user manuals written in the construction phase are often expanded or complemented by materials from the marketing, installation, configuration, and support activities. These phases are also performed in iterations, where the marketing and support materials are continuously improved and bug-fix updates are released.

Comparing the Unified Process to a Traditional Process

Even though the Unified Process has different phases in its generation cycle, the activities normally done in traditional development are also present. They are, however, done in iterations that are part of the phases of the process. A mapping of the traditional activities places them primarily in the following phases:

- **Inception.** Consists of project planning, analysis, and architectural design on a very high level, where the focus is on creating a vision of a product rather than on specifying any details.
- **Elaboration.** Consists of project planning, analysis, architectural design, and design work, where the vision is elaborated and the foundation for an actual implementation of the system is created.
- **Construction.** Consists of architectural design, design, implementation, integration, and testing. This is the actual construction work, when the final details are worked out and the system is programmed and integrated into a current generation and finally tested.
- **Transition.** Consists of implementation, integration, and testing in a delivered format, including the maintenance of reported bug fixes and release of maintenance versions of the system. This phase also accounts for activities not normally described in object-oriented software engineering methods, such as packaging, marketing, and training.

One very positive aspect of the Unified Process is that the iterative nature of the development process is clearly visible. Another advantage is that the cycles present one view for the managers (the inception, elaboration, construction, and transition phases) while another view, consistent with the first, is presented to the technicians in terms of a series of iterations containing requirements, analysis, design, implementation, and testing.

Process Tools

Ideally, tools used in the development process should support the modeling language and the programming language, as well as the process. Today, most tools are based heavily on supporting a programming language, though new tools are being constructed to support visual modeling languages such as UML. In fact certain modeling/implementation tools blur the line between building models and authoring code. Still, the support for the process is lacking in most tools (which can be explained by the fact that it is more difficult to define generic processes that can be used by everyone than it is to define generic programming and modeling languages).

The following features are envisaged for support for a process in a tool:

- **Knowledge of the process phases.** The tool should know the phases of the process, and if the tool is used in more than one phase, it should adapt its behavior and provide support for the phase in which it is currently being used.
- **Online help and guidelines support.** The tool should be able to provide online support, citing a list of the activities to perform in the current phase, along with guidelines for how to do them.
- **Support for iterative development.** The tool should be able to iterate the work, supporting a series of iterations. In a modeling tool, this could mean support for code generation and reverse engineering of modified code.
- **Team support.** The tool should support teamwork, enabling each team member to work on his or her part without disturbing the others.
- **A common system repository.** The tool should be able to share a common repository with other tools, so that all the tools have a shared global image of the system.
- **Integration with other tools.** It should be possible to integrate the tool easily with other tools. This integration can require coverage across disciplines; for example, a design tool might need to have links back to requirements and forward to testing.

Naturally, some tools have a very specialized task and are involved in only one phase or in one activity. In that case, the tool doesn't need all the capabilities just described, but it should support how that one phase or activity is normally performed, for example, iteratively, with input from the previous phase, checking consistency, and so on. Figure 10.7 shows the tools that are usually involved in the development process. They are:

- **Requirements-management tools:** Support tools for capturing and describing the requirements of a system and relating them to each other and other artifacts.
- **Visual-modeling tools.** Tools to create UML diagrams supporting requirements, analysis, design, and implementation models.
- **GUI builders.** Tools to build and prototype user interfaces and to deploy them in the system.
- **Language environment.** Editor, compiler, and debugger for the chosen programming language.
- **Test tools.** Support for different tests and for administration of the test process.
- **Configuration and change management.** Tools for handling different configurations and versions of the product, including support for handling concurrent development by several developers.
- **Documentation tools.** Support for automatic or easy production of development or user manuals. With strong requirements, analysis, and design models, various documents can be generated as a report from the model rather than handwritten.
- **Profiling and metrics tools.** Produce a quantifiable view of the application to support quality and provide insight into performance.
- **Project-management tools.** Help the project manager to plan and track the development process.

One can see that the tools naturally align themselves along the disciplines being described in this chapter. These disciplines are a key way to organize both activities and artifacts within any development process.

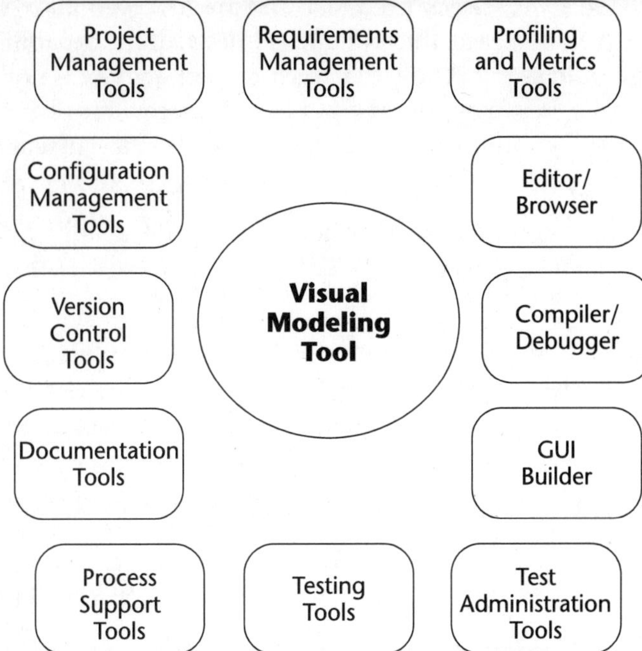

Figure 10.7 Tools used in the development process.

Model Quality

Within the process of using UML, we should discuss the issue of examining the quality of UML models. How do you know if a model is good or not? A modeling language can give you syntax and semantics to work with, but it cannot tell you whether a good model has been produced. This reality opens the very important subject of model quality. What is important when you design models is what you are saying about reality. Models give expression to whatever it is you are studying (reality, a vision, and so on).

In a model, it is very important to capture the essence of the problem domain. For example, in financial systems, invoices are often modeled, but the debt is not. However, in most businesses, the invoices as such are of no real importance, but the debts are. An invoice is just a representation of a debt, so it should be modeled to reflect that. Another example is bank accounts. During the 1970s and 1980s, many banks modeled bank accounts. The customers (bank account owners) were just a part of the bank accounts (a bank account was modeled as a class or an entity and the customer as an attribute). The first problem with this model was that the banks could not handle a bank account with many owners. The second problem was that the banks could not conduct marketing work involving customers without a bank account because they did not have the addresses. Neither of the sample models discussed truly captured the essence of the problem domain.

Thus, one dimension of model quality must be the relevance of the model. A relevant model captures the important aspect of whatever is being studied. Other dimensions of model quality are that the model be easy to communicate, have an explicit goal, be easy to maintain, be consistent, and have integrity. Different models of the same thing but with different purposes (or perspectives) should be support being integrated (model integration).

No matter which method and modeling language you have used, other modeling problems exist that you must address. When you make the models, you become a part of the business, which means that you must consider the effects of your intervention on the business. It is very important to handle all aspects of your intervention such as politics, culture, social structure, and power. If you fail to do this, you might not be able to discover and capture all the real needs of the customer (note, the stated requirements are not always the same as the customers' needs). In particular, you must take into consideration problems with internal politics, social patterns, informal structure, and power surrounding the customers.

What Is a Good Model?

A model is good when it is possible to communicate it, when it fits its purpose, and when it has captured the essentials. A good model takes time to create; it is normally done by a team, one composed to fit a certain purpose. One purpose might be to mobilize the forces to discover the needs of an organization. Other purposes might be to model a requirement specification, perform an analysis, or draw a technical design for an information system. When people are allocated to teams, it must be done with the team purpose in mind. Teams for modeling a business or an information system might be composed of customers, modeling experts, and problem domain experts.

Can You Communicate the Model?

Why must models be easy to communicate? All projects, large and small, are about communication. People are talking to each other. They are reading each other's documents and discussing their contents. Thus, the primary idea behind models is to be able to communicate them. If you are creating models that no one reads or understands, then it doesn't make sense to do them at all. Models are not done because a method or a project leader stipulates it. Models are done to communicate with and unite your forces to achieve the highest productivity, efficiency, and quality as possible.

When you are modeling with UML, many diagrams make up the model. One diagram might examine a part of the system from one aspect; another diagram might focus on another. Make sure each diagram communicates a digestible amount of information.

The model structure can make the design clear or muddy. Make sure key design decisions are easy to find. In larger models, consistency can play a significant role in producing a model that communicates well. Design standards that cover, among other things, how the model is laid out can provide consistency and higher quality models.

Does the Model Fit Its Purpose?

A model should have an explicit purpose that everybody using it recognizes. All models have a purpose, but often that purpose is implicit and that makes it harder to use and understand them. Analysis and design models might be models of the same systems, but they are still different models and focus on different topics (or details). It is also necessary to have an explicit purpose for the model in order to verify and validate it. Without an explicit purpose, you might, for example, verify an analysis model as if it were a design model.

This concept can be taken one level down in abstraction with respect to areas of the model. One set of diagrams might be intended to show how the domain classes fit into the security framework, while another set might show how those same classes support persistence. These separate areas might each be complete from their particular aspect, but they will not cover other issues outside of their area of concern.

Does the Model Capture the Essentials?

Many models just involve documents in the business—for example, invoices, receipts, and insurance policies. If the models just involve documents, what happens when the business changes? In practice, this change is a huge problem. It is necessary to capture the essence of the business (the core) and model around those core concepts to be able to handle changes properly. Model the core business and then model the representation of that core business. If the core (for example, debt) is modeled, small changes in the business can be handled by alterations in the classes that represent the core classes (for example, an invoice as a representation of debt).

Naming Conventions

The names of the model elements should be derived from the problem domain; they should not have a prefix or suffix. It is important that elements be assigned relevant names, especially classes, associations, roles, attributes, and operations. When elements are named from the domain, it is easier to communicate the model.

Model Coordination

Different models of the same thing must be able to integrate and relate to each other. One aspect of model coordination is integration. Integration means that if a number of models have the same purpose (although they may have different perspectives, for example, dynamic, functional, static) and represent the same thing, it should be possible to put them together without introducing inconsistencies.

The relationships between the models on different levels of abstraction are another important aspect. It is one of the keys to succeeding with traceability in software engineering. Relationships between different levels of abstraction can be visualized with the refinement relationship in UML. This refinement relationship means that models are coordinated at each level of abstraction and between the different levels of abstractions.

Model Complexity

Even if the models you design can be communicated, have an explicit purpose, capture the essentials in the business, and are coordinated, you can still run into problems if the models are too complex. Extremely complex models can be difficult to survey, verify, validate, and maintain. Often it is a good idea to start with a simplification, and then go into greater detail, using model coordination. When the problem domain is very complex, divide the models into more models (using submodels—for example, packages) and through that process control the situation.

Summary

A process is a group of activities that, if done correctly, achieves an explicit goal. There are many types of processes: management processes, manufacturing processes, sales processes, and so on. A process for developing software should be described along with the process context (when the process can be used), the process user (providing guidelines for how the user should use it), and the steps to take within the process. The basic steps in all processes are problem formulation (understanding and formulating the problem), solution design (creating a solution to the problem, both conceptually and physically), and implementation design (actual implementation of the solution).

The UML is designed for a process that is use-case-driven, architecture-centric, iterative, and incremental.

- A use-case-driven process means that use cases, describing the overall functionality, are used throughout the process as input to the work and to verify the models.
- Architecture-centric means that there is an emphasis on the definition of a well-defined architecture that is easy to modify, extend, and understand.
- An iterative and incremental process is one in which the product is developed in a series of iterations, and each iteration adds some incremental value to the product. Each increment is evaluated in terms of technology, economy, and process, and the result is used as feedback for the next step.

A traditional object-oriented method (process) is divided into requirements analysis, analysis, design, implementation, and testing.

- The requirements analysis captures the functional and nonfunctional requirements of the system to be produced.
- The analysis models the problem domain and creates an "ideal" model of the system without taking the technical environment into consideration.
- The design activity expands and adapts the analysis model into a technical environment, where the technical solutions are worked out in detail.
- The implementation consists of writing the actual programs.
- The test activity tests the system on different levels (unit, integration, and system) to validate and verify the system that has been produced.

The Unified Process consists of both a manager view and a technical view of the development. The technical view uses the traditional analysis, design, and implementation activities, while the manager view uses the following main phases in the development of each generation of a system:

- **Inception.** Makes a business case and defines the scope and goals of the project.
- **Elaboration.** Establishes a sound architectural foundation and captures detailed requirements. Planning for the overall project is done, amplified by the definition of the functionality and architecture.

- **Construction.** Develops the product in detail through a series of iterations. This involves more analysis and design, as well as actual programming.
- **Transition.** Delivers the system to end users (including activities such as marketing, packaging, support, documentation, and training).

Each phase in the cycle is performed as a series of iterations. Each iteration typically consists of traditional activities such as analysis and design, but in different proportions, depending on the phase and which generation of the system is under development.

Modern tools should support not only the modeling or programming language used, but also the process used to develop a system. That support includes knowledge of the phases in the process, online help, guidelines for the activities in each phase, support for iterative development, team support, and easy integration with other tools.

UML models should be examined to make sure they are high quality. They can be examined from a number of angles, all relating to correctness and understandability.

CHAPTER

11

Case Study

This chapter presents a case study to demonstrate how UML is used in an application. As discussed throughout this book, the requirements for an application are described with use cases and possibly domain analysis. These are analyzed, producing an object-oriented analysis model. It is then expanded into a design model that describes a technical solution. Finally, it is programmed—in Java within this case study—to create an application that is ready to run. Most case studies discuss an application and include a few examples but don't include additional models and diagrams. On the CD-ROM accompanying this book, additional elements of the requirements, analysis, and design models are supplied, along with all the code for the application.

This case study is a Web application that automates something with which everyone is familiar: a library. As you might imagine, it provides capabilities to search, reserve, and borrow items, as well as supporting capabilities to manage inventory and the users of the library. It is a relatively simple application, and at the end of this chapter, a number of exercises are provided to enable you to extend the system in more advanced directions. In this chapter, we are walking a fine line of good design versus a more minimalist approach, but we did want to address the areas of opportunity you have to enhance the design based on common practices in the industry, such as the use of certain design patterns. The purpose of the case study is twofold:

- To show the usage of UML in a complete application, tracing the models from requirements to analysis to design to the actual code and then into a running application.
- To give you an opportunity to invoke UML in an existing model by going through the exercises at the end of this chapter. The exercises provide opportunities to extend and improve the application. You can choose to do the exercises only in analysis and/or design, or if you know how to program in Java, you can evolve the actual code to incorporate the changes.

The initial diagrams are available on the CD-ROM that accompanies this book. At the time of this writing, there are no widely used modeling tools that support the UML 2 specification, so a modeling tool is not provided with this book. (However, we have included a set of links to vendor sites on the CD for this book. With the speed of development of these tools, we are confident that the reader will find demonstration versions that support UML 2 at practical levels.) This chapter discusses only certain diagrams from the case study, but additional diagrams are on the CD-ROM and can be studied and printed. You are encouraged to examine and experiment with the diagrams.

Before getting started, we need to discuss some terms related to Web development with Java that might not be familiar to you:

- **JavaServer Pages (JSP).** The JSP specification provided by Sun Microsystems provides the presentation mechanism that allows you to combine HTML and Java code to present information to the user dynamically.
- **Servlets.** Information appearing on java.sun.com states that "Servlets provide a component-based, platform-independent method for building Web-based applications, without the performance limitations of CGI programs."
- **Taglibs.** Sun Microsystems indicates on java.sun.com that JSP tag libraries define reusable functionality. Per Sun, "Tag libraries reduce the necessity to embed large amounts of Java code in JSP pages by moving the functionality provided by the tags into tag implementation classes."

Just as in a real-world solution, we utilize a number of tools commonly used in developing Java Web applications today, such as the following:

- **Eclipse.** This is the integrated development environment (IDE) used for editing Java code and managing all of the development of the application.
- **MySQL.** An open-source relational database management system.

- **J2SE.** As Sun Microsystems indicates on java.sun.com, the Java 2 Standard Edition (J2SE) provides a "solution for rapidly developing and deploying mission-critical, enterprise applications, . . . compiler, tools, runtimes, and APIs for writing, deploying, and running applets and applications in the Java programming language."
- **Log4j.** Part of the Apache Jakarta project. It is used to log information for development and runtime environments
- **Ant.** Part of the Apache project. It is a build tool, similar to `make`, for the purpose of building and deploying code in a platform-independent manner.
- **J2EE.** The Java 2 Enterprise Edition. Provides enterprise services such as Servlets, JSP, and Java Database Connectivity (JDBC).
- **Tomcat.** Part of the Apache Jakarta project. It is an open-source Web container that supports the Servlet and JSP specifications provided by Sun Microsystems.
- **Struts Framework**. Part of the Apache Jakarta project. It is used to build J2EE Web applications by providing the presentation and control mechanisms to handle common patterns in Web development.

The primary focus of this case study is to demonstrate the use of UML, so we do not favor one implementation over others. We chose not to use Enterprise JavaBeans (EJB) in the example so as not to get hung up in too many implementation details. In practice, we could create a better, more elegant J2EE solution for the Web; however, for this case study it was more important that we focus on demonstrating how to use the UML diagrams to implement a J2EE Web solution.

NOTE Throughout this chapter and on the CD-ROM, remember that what's shown is only *one* possible solution. There is no right solution for all circumstances. If you want to make some changes to the initial models, feel free to do so. The goal is to produce a system that satisfies the requirements and that works well, not to produce diagrams that are perfect in all their details.

Requirements

Various means to elicit, capture, and communicate the requirements of the system exist. Among the more prominent means are the system vision (communicated in a document) and the system's use cases (communicated in UML as a use-case model, and in a series of use-case specifications, that detail the core functionality of the system in a language and manner that emphasizes user-to-system interaction). Other common requirements artifacts include things like a glossary of terms and supplementary specifications (where we put requirements that transcends use cases) but, for this case study, we limited the robustness of the requirements artifacts.

In a real project, it is essential to engage the system's stakeholders to support the production, approval, and inevitable evolution of the requirements.

In addition to the vision and use cases we also demonstrate a simple domain model, often used to define the key domain classes and their relationships. The domain model, like the requirements artifacts, should limit itself to terms that are understood by users of the system and others who understand the system's domain, but who are not necessarily programming experts.

Developing a Vision

Before delving into detailed requirements that prescribe what the system shall do, it is a good idea to gather a set of higher-level requirements that assist in scoping the effort. These high-level requirements constitute the vision of the system to be developed and assist in achieving agreement on what will be developed.

A lightweight set of features for the first version of the library application might look like this:

- It is a support system for a library.
- The library lends books and magazines to borrowers, who are registered in the system, as are the books and magazines.
- The library handles the purchase of new titles for the library. Popular titles are bought in multiple copies. Old books and magazines are removed when they are out of date or in poor condition.
- The librarian is an employee of the library who interacts with the customers (borrowers) and whose work is supported by the system.
- A borrower can reserve a book or magazine that is not currently available in the library, so that when it's returned or purchased by the library, that borrower is notified. The reservation is canceled when the borrower checks out the book or magazine or through an explicit canceling procedure.
- The librarian can easily create, update, and delete information about the titles, borrowers, loans, and reservations in the system.
- The system can run on all popular Web browser platforms (Internet Explorer 5.1+, Netscape 4.0+, and so on).
- The system is easy to extend with new functionality.

To give some business context, we explain portions of the library inside and outside the application. In the first version, the borrower is able to access the application from any of the PCs within the library. In later versions, enhancements are made to the business processes and the application so that borrowers can access the application from anywhere they have access to a supported Web browser. The borrowers are able to check out items and pick them up at a later time.

The first version of the system doesn't have to handle the message that is sent to the borrower when a reserved title becomes available, nor does it have to check that a title has become overdue. Additional requirements for future versions are available in the exercises at the end of this chapter.

Modeling Use Cases

The first step in use-case modeling is to define the actors that represent those who interact with the system and the use cases that describe what the library system provides in terms of functionality to those actors—the functional requirements of the system. While identifying the use cases, you must read and analyze all specifications, as well as discuss the system with potential users of the system and all stakeholders.

The actors in the library are identified as the librarians and the borrowers, because both are users of the system. The librarians have management capability to add borrowers, titles, and items. The borrowers are people who check out and reserve books and magazines. Occasionally a librarian or another library can be a borrower. Finally, we have a Master Librarian actor—this role is capable of managing the librarians as well. It is possible to add a title to the system before the library has a copy (an item), to enable borrowers to make reservations.

The use cases in the library system are as follows:

- Login
- Search
- Browse
- Make Reservation
- Remove Reservation
- Checkout Item
- Return Item
- Manage Titles
- Manage Items
- Manage Borrowers

- Manage Librarians
- Assume Identity of Borrower

Note the difference in concepts between "title" and "item." Because a library often has several copies of a popular title, the system must separate the concept of the title—the name of a book and the book's author—and a separate physical copy of the same title, which is an item.

To pragmatically limit the complexity of this case study, we do not perform an implementation for some of the "Manage" use cases such as Manage Librarians and Manage Borrowers. As in a real-world effort, the scope of what can reasonably be built using available resources must be weighed against what is needed to have the software succeed. For example, rather than implement Manage Librarians, we expect those designated as Master Librarians to be able to manage librarians by editing the database directly. As potentially dangerous as that is, it is a risk worth taking until a foolproof implementation can be provided.

The library functional requirements are documented in a UML use-case diagram as shown in Figure 11.1. Each of the use cases is documented with text, describing the use case and its interaction with the actor in more detail.

The outline of the basic flow for the use case Checkout Item (which means that a Borrower can check out an Item) is described as follows:

1. The borrower chooses to perform a "Search" for desired titles.
2. The system prompts the borrower to enter Search criteria.
3. The borrower specifies the search criteria and submits the search.
4. The system locates matching titles and displays them to the borrower.
5. The borrower selects a title to check out.
6. The system displays the details of the title, as well as whether or not there is an available item to be checked out.
7. The borrower confirms that he or she wishes to checkout the item.
8. The system checks out the item.
9. Steps 1 to 8 can be repeated as often as desired by the borrower.
10. The borrower completes checkout
11. The system notifies a librarian that the borrower has concluded the checkout item session and displays instructions for the borrower to collect the contents.

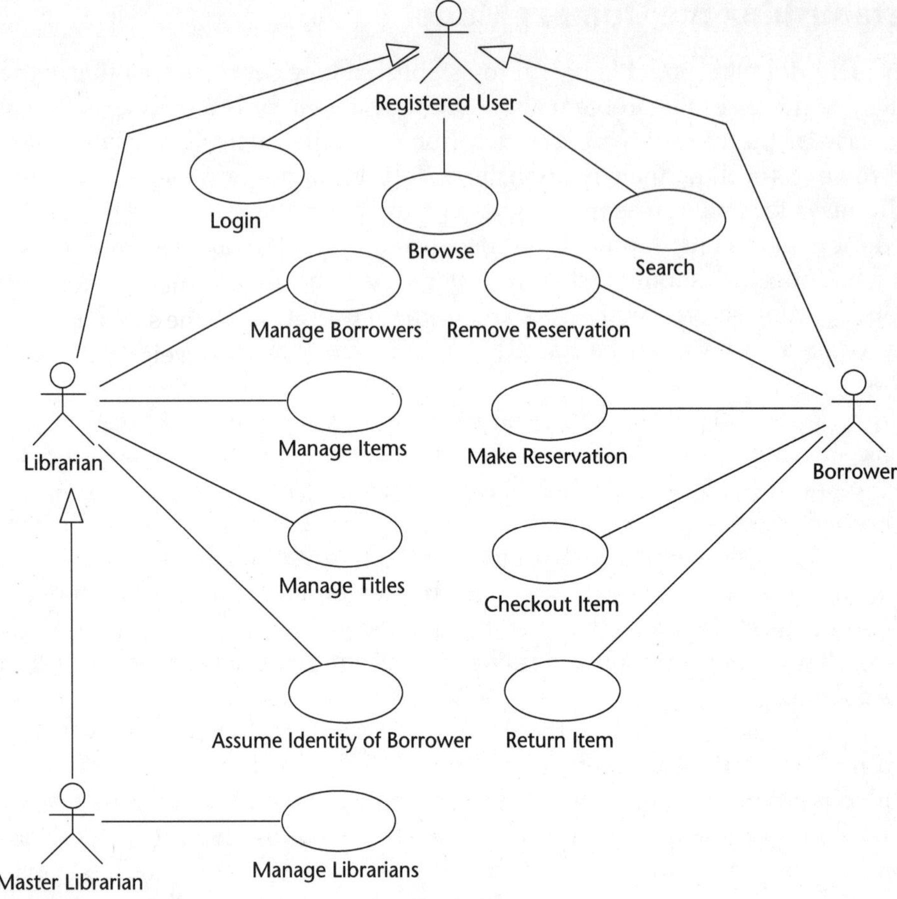

Figure 11.1 A use-case diagram for the library system.

NOTE **Several alternative and exception flows for this use case exist.**

The description of this use case and others are included in more formal detail in the use-case model on the CD-ROM. A team implements use cases throughout the development of the system to provide descriptions of the functional requirements of the system. They are used in the analysis to check whether the appropriate analysis classes (discussed later in the chapter) have been defined, and they are used during the design process to confirm that the technical solution is sufficient to handle the required functionality. The use cases can be visualized in sequence diagrams, which detail their realization.

Establishing the Domain Model

An early domain model is useful to establish a core set of classes that represents the things in the problem space of the system to be built. For example, in the case of the library, you see such things as Title, Item, Reservation, and Borrower as well as their relationships. To build a domain model, you typically need to have a reasonable grasp of the business domain of the system under development. You read the specifications and the use cases and look at which "concepts" should be handled by the system. You might also organize a brainstorming session with users and domain experts to try to identify all the key concepts that must be handled, along with their relationships to each other.

The domain classes in the library system are as follows: Borrower, Title, Book Title, Magazine Title, Item, Reservation, and Loan. They are documented in a class diagram along with their relationships, as shown in Figure 11.2. Everyone's practices vary slightly, but you can formally model a business model or simply perform some domain analysis with the intent of identifying entities of the system. We chose to use the stereotype "entity" for each of our domain classes. Typically, you use the stereotype "entity" to illustrate that a class is likely in the domain and is likely persistent (that is, instances are stored in a database).

It is important to note that the detail of classes modeled evolves over time. You might be pleased to see good names, with clear definitions, and only a hint of relationships, operations, and attributes during the early stages of a project. But, as you conclude other supporting steps, or even complete iterations of development, you see the classes evolve, become refined, even explode into numerous classes or disappear as you move further into understanding of both the problem and solution space.

You build UML state machine diagrams for those classes with interesting states. The diagrams show the different states that objects of those classes can have, along with the events that make them change their state. The state machine diagram for the Title class is shown in Figure 11.3.

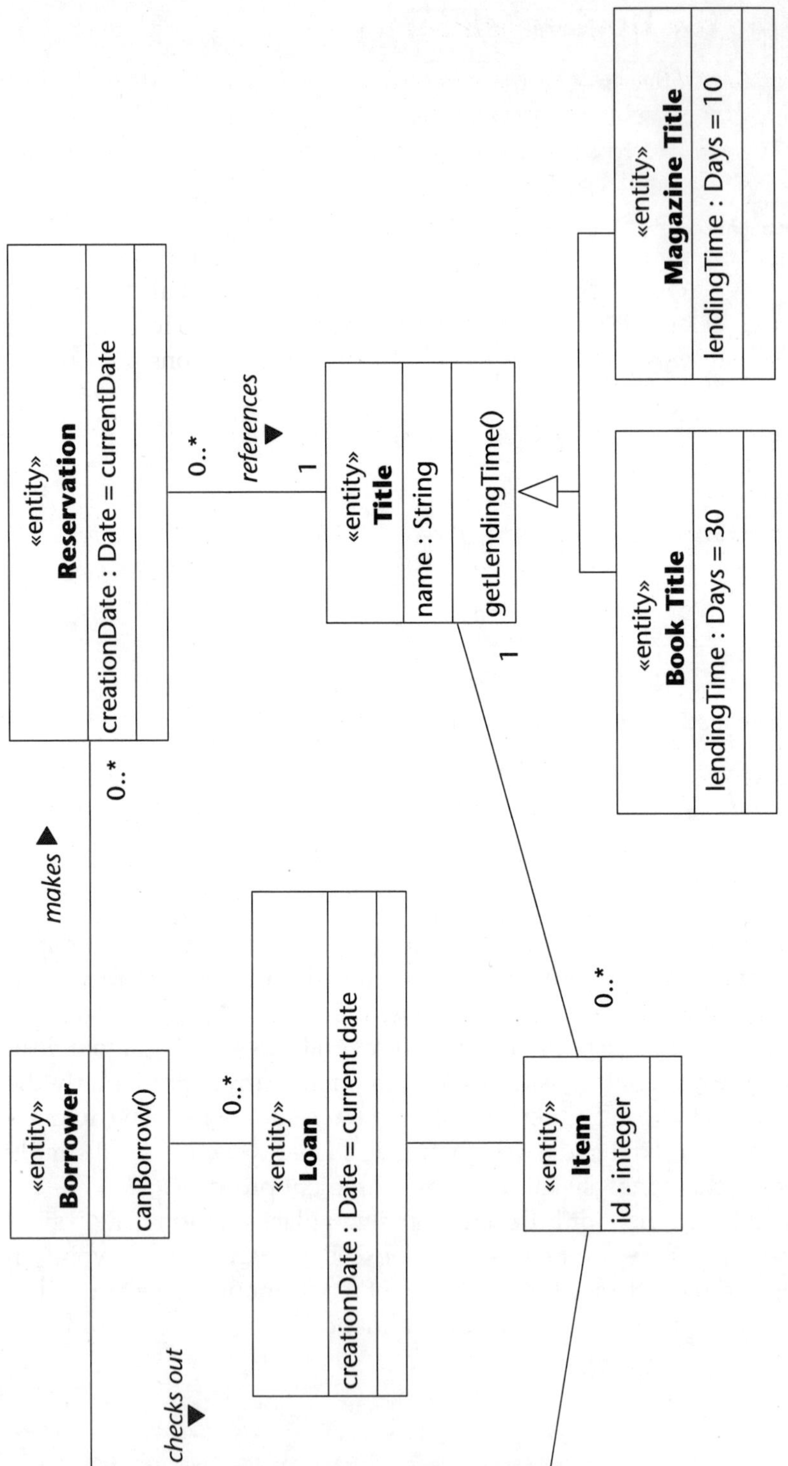

Figure 11.2 Key domain classes for the library system.

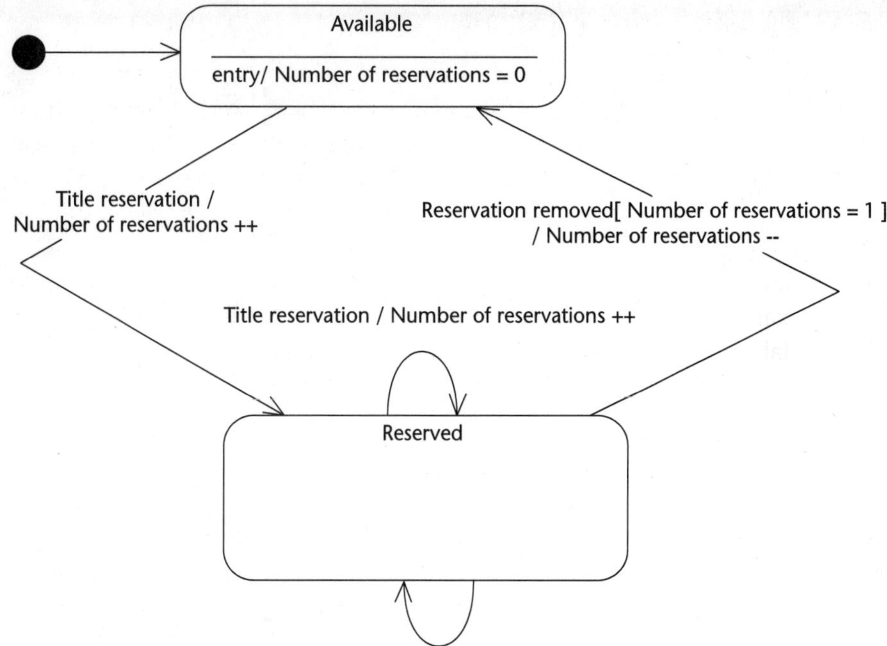

Figure 11.3 State machine diagram for the Title class.

Analysis

As you move closer to developing a solution to your problem, you begin to exploit more of UML to represent unambiguously and consistently your understanding of the problem space in ways that easily translate into proposed solutions. You can perform analysis in several ways, and as a matter of fact, the lines between analysis and design are often blurred, particularly the further into a project you get. Often, it is simply too resource-intensive to manage both an analysis model and a design model, so many teams would simply stop maintaining their analysis model as development proceeds.

Regardless of how much (or little) emphasis you place on formal analysis, a technique known as use-case analysis is an excellent way to get beyond an empty canvas and begin to see the formation of a rich enough object model so that design can proceed with a degree of confidence.

Performing Use-Case Analysis

Assuming that you have done some domain analysis, you have a simple set of classes that begin to demonstrate the analysis classes involved in your system. That is a good start, but to really enrich your model you perform use-case analysis to refine the classes, add additional classes, and add operations and attributes to these classes, so that each helps to represent what goes on during the execution of the various paths through your use cases.

You use static diagrams (for example, class diagrams) and dynamic diagrams (for example, sequence diagrams) to illustrate how classes and their instances collaborate to perform the actions required by the use cases. Analysis classes are typically organized as one of the following:

- **<<entity>>.** As you have already seen, entity classes represent those classes that have meaning in the domain and are likely have long lifetimes in your system. The reality of *long lifetime* is that they require some form of persistence so that they can exist beyond the execution of a single use case or session with a user. In the majority of applications today, you can infer that some form of database is used to support the persistence of entities.
- **<<boundary>>.** Boundary classes are used to represent those things that are necessary to provide a means for actors to communicate with the system. In the case of an interactive user, boundary classes represent their user interface mechanisms (for example, a form or page). In the case of noninteractive users, like an external system or device, you can typically expect some protocol-based interface to shuttle communication between the system and the nonhuman actor. During use-case analysis, you generally create a single boundary class for every actor-system relationship found in the use-case model.
- **<<control>>.** Control classes are used as the placeholder of the coarse-grained logic of a use case. You usually start out by creating a single control class for each use case you are analyzing.

To describe the dynamic behavior of the analysis classes, a variety of the dynamic UML diagrams can be used: sequence, communication, or activity. The basis for the sequence diagrams are the use cases, where each use case has been described with its impact on the analysis classes, to illustrate how the analysis classes collaborate to perform the use case inside the system. When modeling these sequence diagrams, you discover new operations and add them to the classes. Though there are now more precise operations, some even with hints of arguments, you are far from a fully defined set of classes. You complete things like operation signatures, and review classes for completeness, sufficiency, and primitiveness during individual class design.

A sequence diagram for the basic flow of the use case Checkout Item is shown in Figure 11.4.

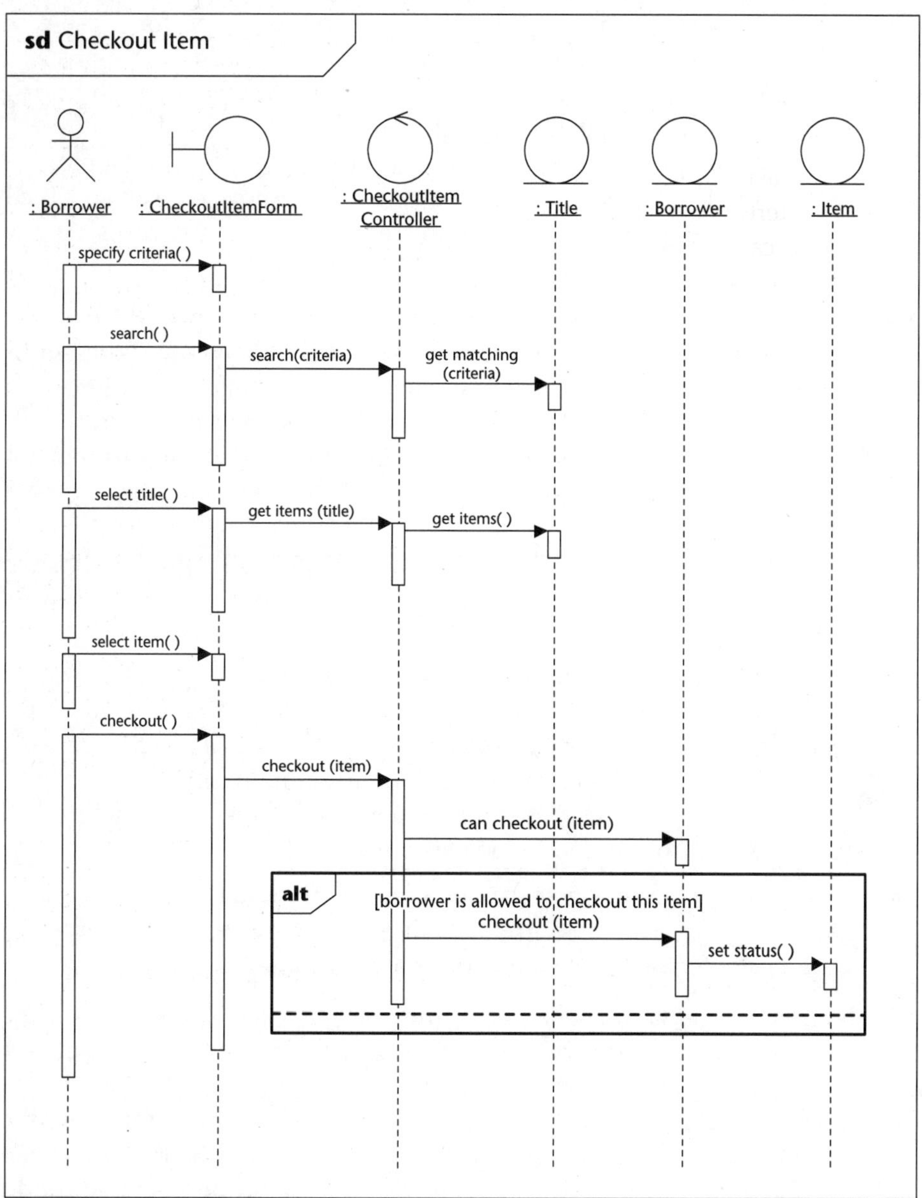

Figure 11.4 A sequence diagram for the use case Checkout Item (the borrower does not have a reservation for the title).

How much is enough? When performing use-case analysis, typically look for a class diagram representing the View of Participating Classes (VOPC) for each use case modeled. Each VOPC depicts the classes, relationships, operations, and attributes necessary to support its associated use case. If you can derive that class diagram without once modeling a sequence or communication diagram, then good for you. However, most of you will like to do a few interaction diagrams just to ensure you can trace through the various flows of a use case. As such, we recommend developing a sequence diagram for each primary (or basic) flow of a use case and supporting those with occasional diagrams for interesting or potentially ill-understood alternative or exceptional flows. These can be supplemented by communication diagrams that better demonstrate the links required between the objects to support the use case. Ultimately, these diagrams might be treated as mere scaffolding, but it is certainly a reasonable check during the early stages of development. You should be able to see clearly that the VOPC diagram is robust enough to support all the other dynamic diagrams.

Figure 11.5 shows a communication diagram that is semantically equivalent to the sequence diagram shown in Figure 11.4.

Figure 11.6 shows a View of Participating Classes diagram that shows which classes participate in the Checkout Item use case and which relations and operations are exercised. We have dropped off the actor because that relationship is not part of the final technical design, but otherwise one can clearly see that this diagram parallels Figure 11.5. In addition to the classes and operations obvious from the communication diagram, we have added some fidelity to the associations modeled. Multiplicity has been specified on the associations. Based on the directions of the messages in the communication diagram, the associations are predominantly unidirectional. We have left the association between Title and Item—already in our model from the domain modeling effort—as bidirectional; we are confident we will need to traverse in each direction as we model the rest of the system. On the other hand, to minimize dependencies, we have changed the association between Borrower and item to be unidirectional. This is a natural way a model is refined over time.

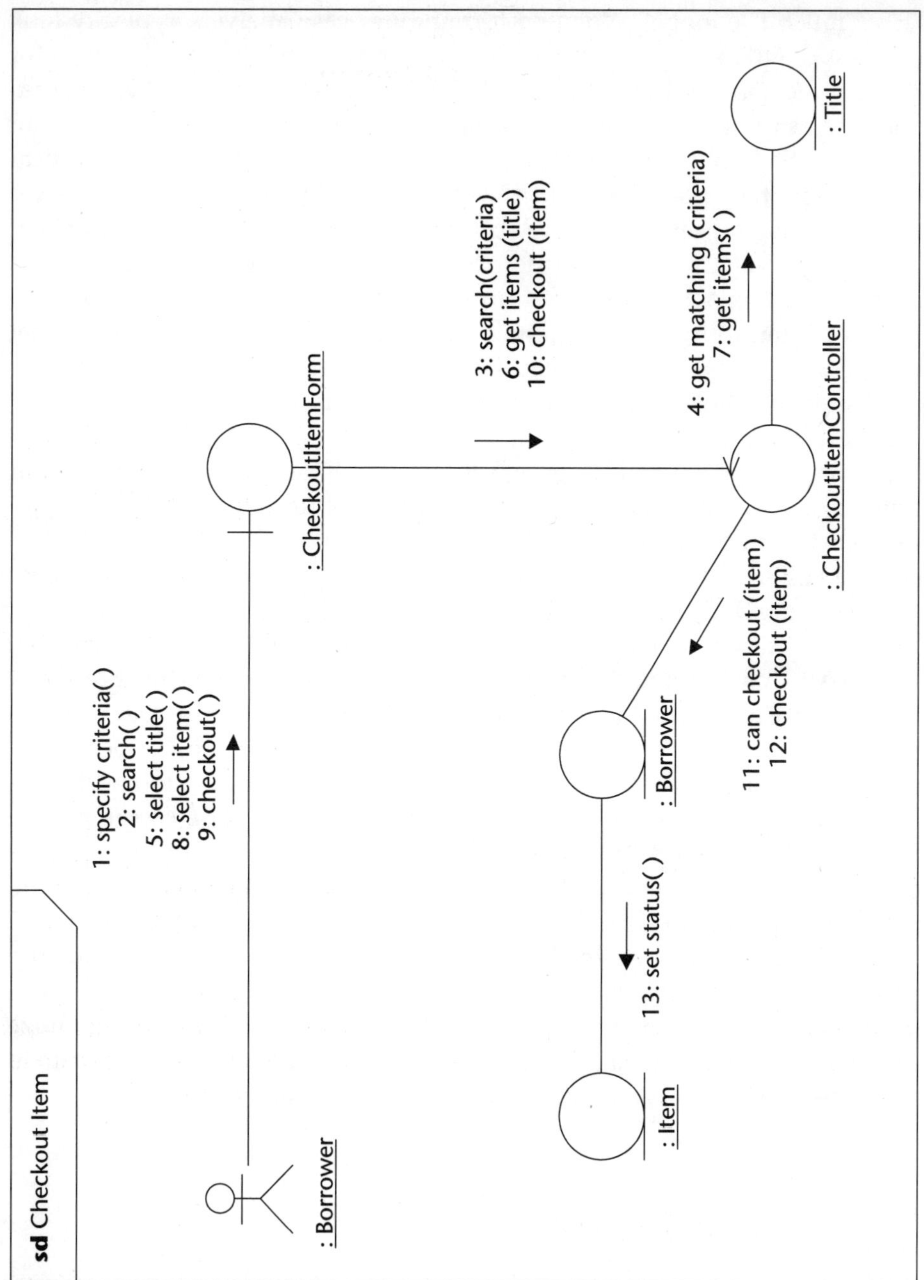

Figure 11.5 A communication diagram for the use case Checkout Item (the borrower does not have a reservation for the title).

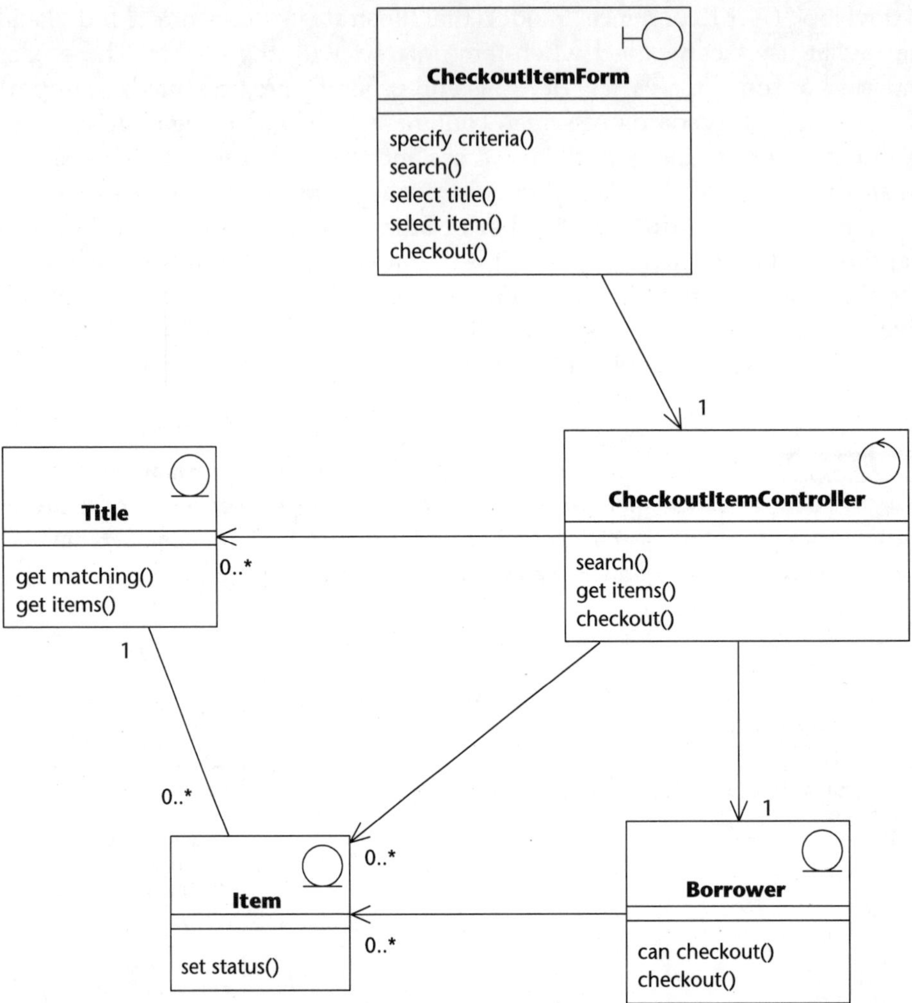

Figure 11.6 Shows the VOPC for the use case Checkout Item. Note that it covers the needs of these sequence diagrams, plus some others—not shown here—that are associated with this use case.

Not UML? How Can That Be?

We all love UML and want to think it is all you ever need to model a software system properly. However, the cold hard reality (apologies to all zealots out there) is that there are other tools you can use that are extremely helpful as well. Somewhere between analysis and design, for example, you usually want to develop "User Experience" models that illustrate in a very direct and visual way what users can expect when they interact with the system. These user experiences come in a variety of forms and generally are presented in support of use cases. Storyboards of screen content, action, and navigation are very useful in ensuring that both the use cases and the subsequent use-case analysis are grounded in tangible reality. Additionally, simply having an occasional, tangible screen shot, double-edged sword that it is, serves to move the understanding and agreement process. (It is a double-edged sword because on the one side it gives something the users can easily grasp, but on the other it can give a false sense of progress to an unmanaged client.) Figures 11.7 and 11.8 show examples of a storyboard and comp (cool user interface lingo short for "composition"), respectively.

WARNING **The use of such client-friendly diagrams must be tempered with a good deal of management of customer expectations. In other words, once the clients see nifty stuff, they'll want more, and it is up to the development team to keep the focus on productive and semantically valuable stuff.**

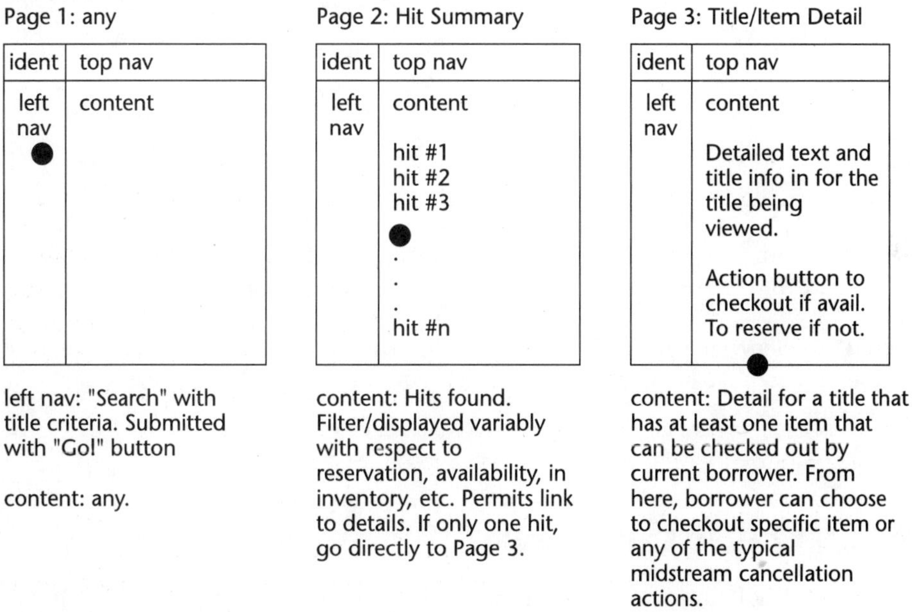

Page 1: any

ident | top nav
left nav | content

left nav: "Search" with title criteria. Submitted with "Go!" button

content: any.

Page 2: Hit Summary

ident | top nav
left nav | content
hit #1
hit #2
hit #3
.
.
.
hit #n

content: Hits found. Filter/displayed variably with respect to reservation, availability, in inventory, etc. Permits link to details. If only one hit, go directly to Page 3.

Page 3: Title/Item Detail

ident | top nav
left nav | content
Detailed text and title info in for the title being viewed.
Action button to checkout if avail. To reserve if not.

content: Detail for a title that has at least one item that can be checked out by current borrower. From here, borrower can choose to checkout specific item or any of the typical midstream cancellation actions.

Figure 11.7 A sample storyboard to help flesh out the user experience.

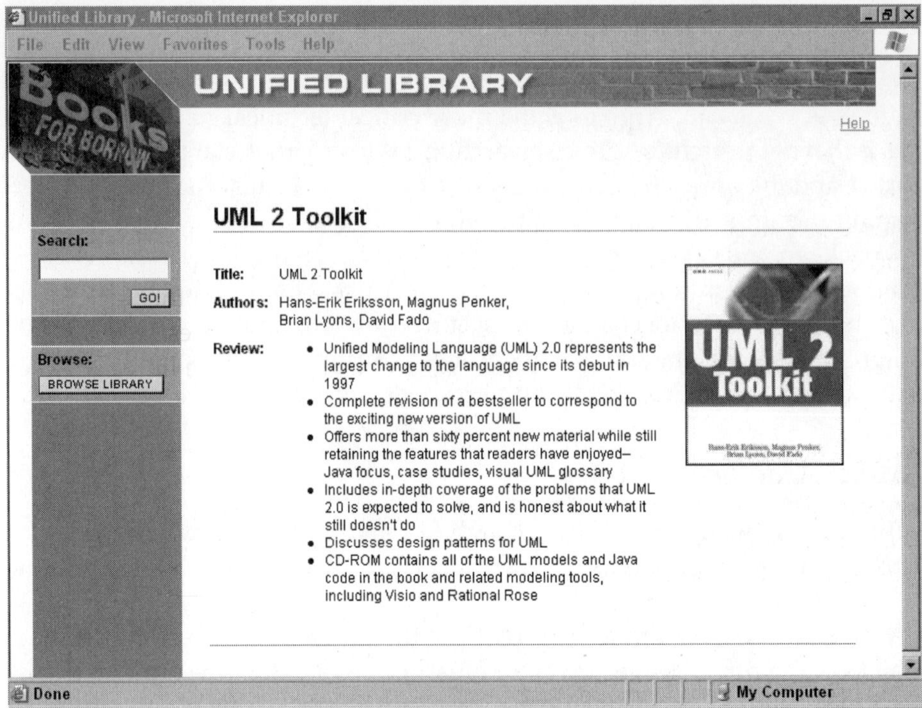

Figure 11.8 A comp that tangibly sets context for users.

Design

The application of the design discipline and the resulting UML model expands and details the analysis model by taking into account all technical implications and restrictions. The purpose of the design is to specify a working solution that can be easily translated into programming code. The classes defined in the analysis are detailed, and new classes are added to handle technical areas such as database, user interface, communication, devices, and more.

The design can be divided into two segments:

- **Architectural design.** This is the high-level design where you define the packages (subsystems), including the dependencies and primary communication mechanisms between the packages. Naturally, a clear and simple architecture is the goal, where the dependencies are few and bi-directional dependencies are avoided if at all possible.
- **Detailed design:** This part details the contents in the packages, so that all classes are described in enough detail to give clear specifications to the programmer who codes the class. Use dynamic models from the UML to demonstrate how objects of the classes behave in specific situations.

Designing the Architecture

A well-designed architecture is the foundation for an extensible and easily maintainable system. Arguably, the most critical technical role on most projects is that of the architect. To be an architect is to be a rock star (in the software world), and the time when architects earn their pay most is when they are performing design activities of architectural breadth and depth. Such things as key package and layer structure, selecting or designing large-scale reusable components, committing to key patterns for critical and repeated functionality (like the persistence mechanism or security model), and simply driving the design and coding standards to be upheld during the life of the project are each examples of critical architectural responsibilities.

System Structure

In this section, we put on the hat of architect and try to separate the system at hand into large chunks (packages) that serve to both layer and partition the system under development.

A simple class diagram representing the essence of these packages is depicted in Figure 11.9. Figure 11.10 illustrates to another level of detail how those packages expand both internally and through relationships with implementation mechanisms (in this case, several preexisting standard Java and J2EE packages). Notice that the static architecture has no bidirectional dependencies between packages (avoiding packages' becoming forever coupled) and an implied build dependency exists between the packages. This example is a simple case of the sort of implicit rule by which architects abide.

The packages that provide layering for the library system are as follows:

- **presentation.** This contains classes for the entire user interface, to enable the user to view data from the system and to enter new data. The standard for presenting this information to the user in a Java Web application is to use JSP. This package cooperates with the business objects (via the Value Objects) and the controller packages. The user interface package uses the Value Objects and posts data so that it can be sent to the Controller package.
- **controller.** The classes in this package are responsible for most of the application control and also provide "traffic cop" mechanisms to help delegate dependencies to and separate them between the presentation and domain packages.

- **business.** This includes the domain classes from the analysis model such as Borrower, Title, Item, Loan, and so on. These classes are detailed in the design so that their operations are completely defined. The business object package cooperates with the database package via an associative relationship.
- **dao.** Named *dao* because it contains a Data Access Object (DAO) that represents a commonly used design pattern that encapsulates all data-related activity into discrete classes. This is the means to firewall or limit the knowledge of how things are persisted.
- **vo.** The *vo* package is so named as it contains simple Value Objects, which are lightweight representations of domain-related things. The Value Object (VO) is yet another common pattern used to limit the passing of heavyweight objects and traffic across enterprise systems.

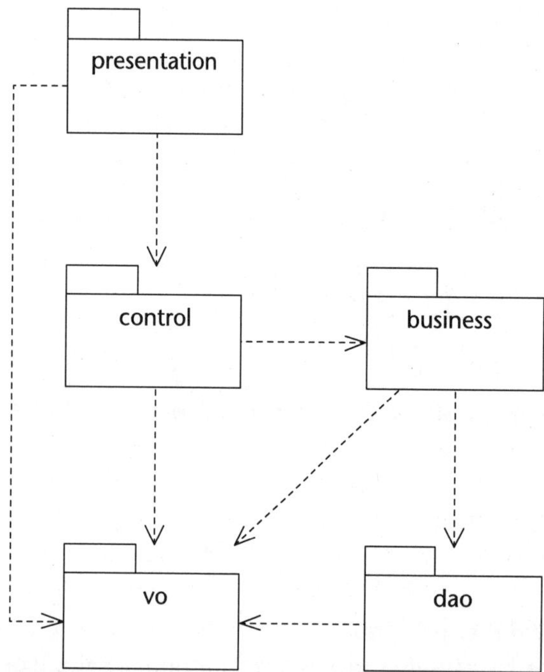

Figure 11.9 An easy-to-grasp class diagram showing an architectural overview with the library system packages and their dependencies.

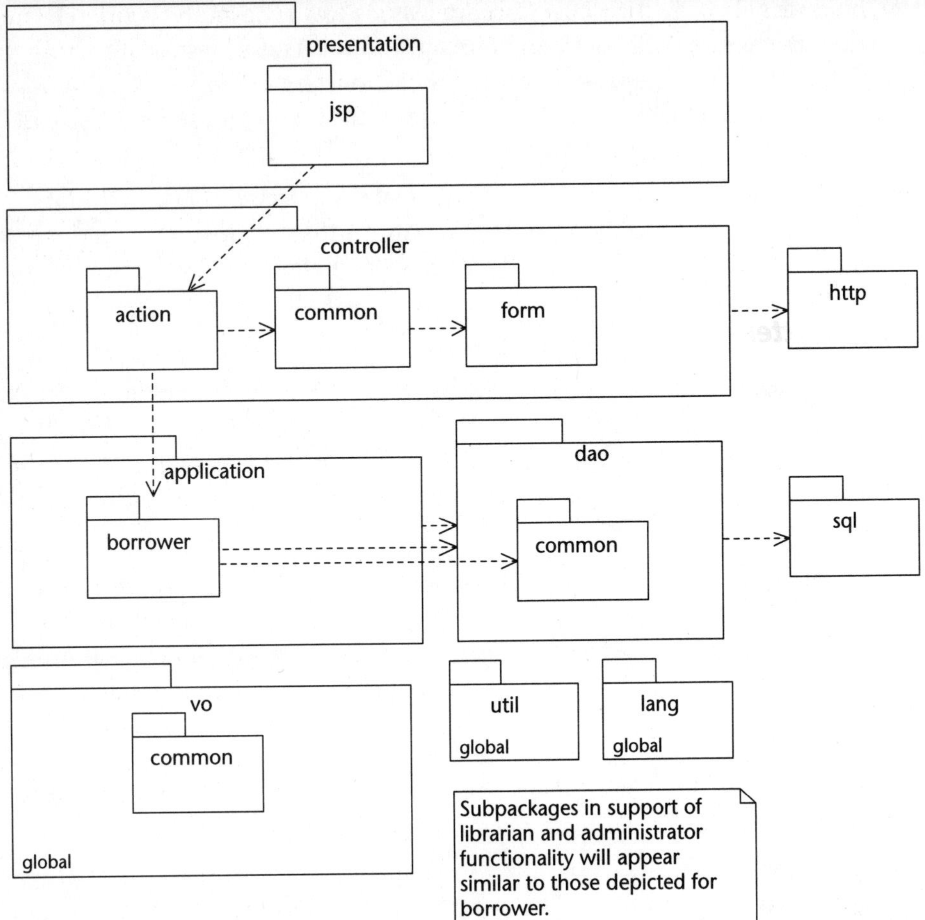

Figure 11.10 A more detailed class diagram showing an architectural overview with the library system packages and their dependencies.

Architectural Mechanisms

Architectural mechanisms describe the techniques to deal with, among other things, persistence, security, error handling, and system interfaces. Architectural mechanisms must be modeled to give the architect(s) and developers a view on common mechanisms that transcend any one-use case.

The application must have objects stored persistently; therefore, a database layer, called the dao package, must be added to provide this service. The solution for a complex application is to use a commercial database; typically this database is a relational database management system (RDBMS) such as Oracle or SQL Server. However, because this case study application is intended to be portable, we chose to use an open-source database tool you may be familiar with called MySQL. The data is manipulated using DAOs, implementing a common interface to call common operations such as `create()`, `store()`, `remove()`, and `load()` on the objects. Figure 11.11 illustrates a pattern specified by the architect to be used for data storage and retrieval. The diagram reflects both how DAO and VO patterns are blended to work together. Figure 11.12 is a variant on the 11.11 sequence diagram, using a class diagram instead.

Design Patterns

As we discussed in Chapter 7, design patterns are, among other things, well-proven, reusable solutions used to solve a particular problem. In designing the case study, we made a decision to use many of the patterns applied to the design good Web applications. Among other patterns, we are using these patterns in the design of this application:

- **Model-view-controller (MVC).** The MVC pattern is more of an architectural pattern that uses design patterns to enforce its high-level pattern. Nicholas Kassem and the Enterprise Team at Sun Microsystems state in *Designing Enterprise Applications with the Java 2 Platform, Enterprise Edition*, "The MVC architecture allows for a clean separation of business logic, data, and presentation logic." The model contains the business data, the view (that is, JSP) renders content of the model, and the controller defines the application behavior (Kassem, 2000).
- **Front controller.** This design pattern is provided by the Struts framework that supports the MVC pattern. As Alur and his coauthors describe in *Core J2EE Patterns: Best Practices and Design Strategies*, the front controller provides the first point of contact for handling incoming requests to the application (Alur et al., 2001).
- **Data Access Object (DAO).** Alur and his coauthors also state that a DAO is used to "abstract and encapsulate all access to a data source." (Alur et al., 2001). This allows you to go to one place to make data changes and does not have an impact on the business or presentation layers. You use a DAO Factory so that you can conditionally access data from multiple datasources, such as a Properties file or the MySQL database, thus promoting the tenets of polymorphism.
- **Value Object (VO).** According to Alur and his coauthors, a VO is "used to encapsulate business data" (Alur et al., 2001). In the Unified Library application, VOs are used by the business objects, DAOs, and the JSP.

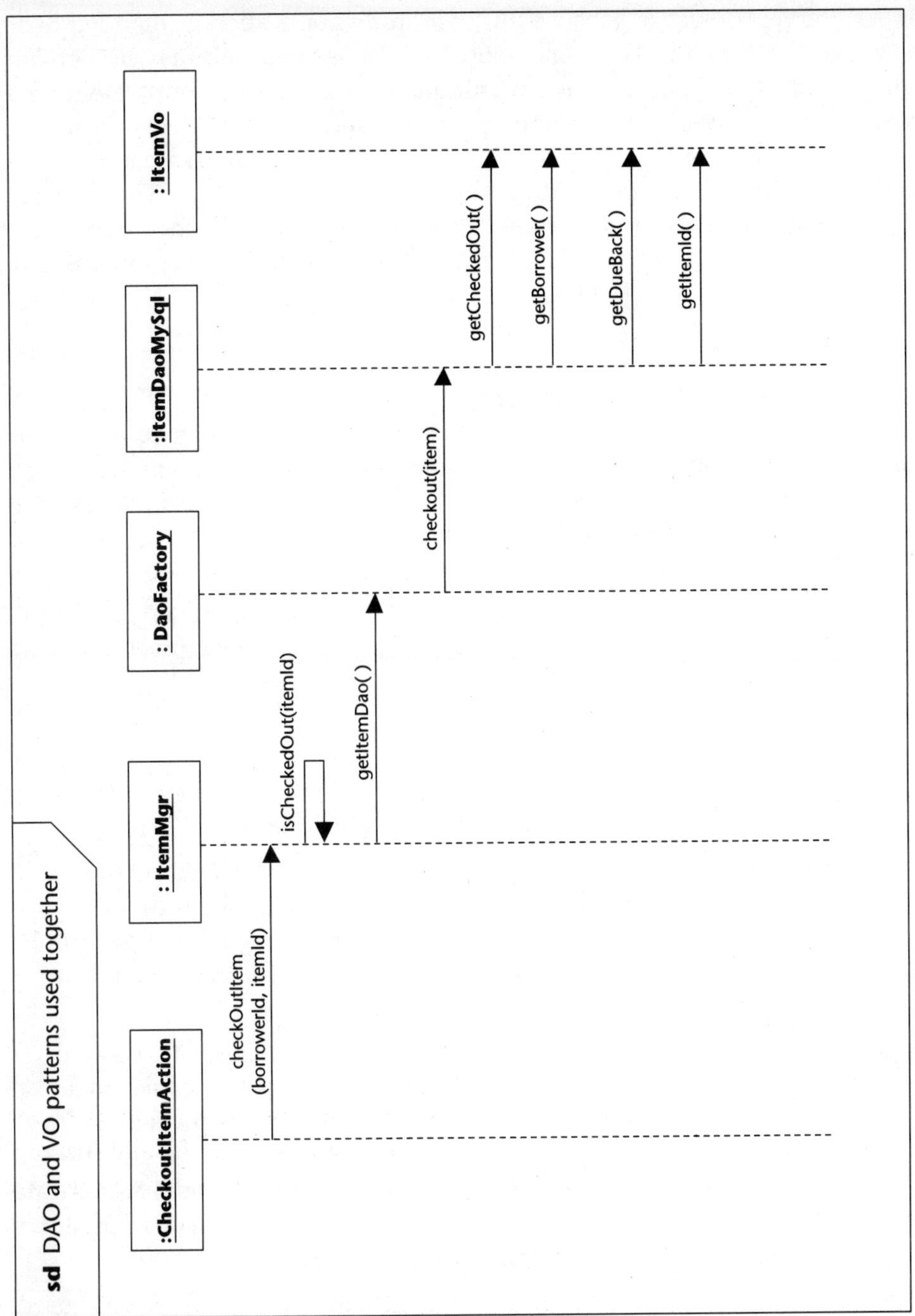

Figure 11.11 A sequence diagram that highlights both VO and DAO use on the library system.

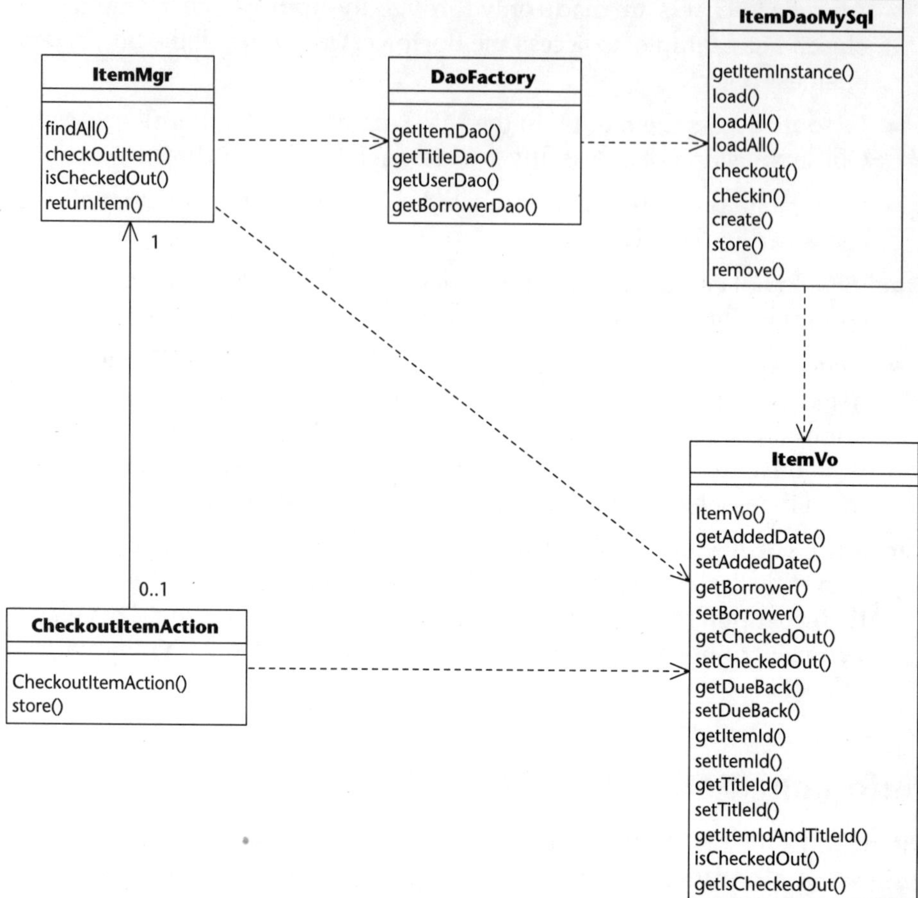

Figure 11.12 A class diagram depicting a VOPC for the key VO and DAO pattern usage.

Design Policies

We establish certain policies on the project to enforce the principles of the architectural design. You can see many of these identified in the architectural detail diagram in Figure 11.10. Here, you identify that the following rules are established:

- Loose coupling between the architectural layers:
  - A change to one layer does not necessitate a change elsewhere in the application.
  - Separation of concerns. This allows developers and designers to focus on what they know best.

- All calls to DAOs are made only through the appropriate business object. For example, to access the BorrowerDao, you call the Borrower business object.
- JSP only access the model (in the MVC architectural pattern) via a Value Object. JSPs do not access any business-related objects directly.
- JSP contain only presentation-related code. No business functionality is contained in the JSP.
- JSPs do not contain any Java scriptlet code. Instead, they use taglibs to conditionally show or hide certain presentation-related data.
- Action classes supported by Struts framework contain only code related to extracting the data from the request objects, passing data to the appropriate business object, and returning to the appropriate JSP. There is no business code in these action classes. This enables you to support more than one type of client (other than a Web browser).
- Since FormBeans are an implementation mechanism of the Struts framework, we chose to link the FormBeans to the Value Object and then act upon the Value Object elsewhere in the application. This way if you need to use a different framework, you can do so with minimal impact.

Performing Detailed Design

The purpose of the detailed design is to employ the strategic architectural design and all of its associated implicit guidance (like key patterns for frequently performed or critical functionality) and adhere to it while evolving the results of analysis, or even earlier iterations, into a precise and semantically rich representation of what you want to build in code. This gets pretty detailed, including such things as refining individual class specs to ensure that they are complete, meeting the policies of the project for exception propagation, reporting, general handling, and so on.

After a few iterations, the design model should be detailed enough so that you can hand the model to a tool, and an appropriate compliable specification so that its classes can be generated with a click of a button.

Clearly, the visual parts of UML are insufficient to depict all that is needed; however, the combination of graphical elements and nongraphical UML elements are sufficient to achieve the goal.

The following sections describe the nature of detailed design considerations and activities on a key package-by-package basis. As a part of this discussion, we focus on the business and presentation packages described in some of the detailed design decisions based on original analysis.

business Package

The business package is primarily composed of control-type classes that represent the coarse-grained logic within the application. All business object classes interact with DAOs from the database package and implement the necessary read and write operations.

The operations from the analysis have been detailed, which means that some of them have been translated into several operations in the design model and some have changed names. Additionally, as a part of the detailed design, all operations in the design model must have well-defined signatures and return values.

NOTE **Not even UML 2 diagrams provide a consistent or elegant visual means to depict all the detail you might capture in the detailed design of a single class operation, and you invariably need to specify details of the operation's signature in its nonvisual specification.**

Note these changes between the design and the analysis:

- The current version of the system does not have to handle checks on whether an item is returned in time, nor does the system have to handle the ordering of reservations. Therefore, the date attribute in the Loan and Reservation classes has not been implemented.
- The handling of magazine and book titles is identical (it would be different if a lending period were in our requirements, but it isn't), so separating the subclasses for Magazine and Book Title is deemed as unnecessary during the analysis. Only a type attribute in the Title class specifies whether the title refers to a book or magazine. There's nothing in object-oriented design that says the design can't simplify the analysis!

Both of these simplifications can be removed easily if deemed unnecessary in future versions of the application.

presentation Package

The presentation package is "on top" of the other packages. It presents the services and information in the system to a user. As noted, this package contains JSP. It is a good idea to limit the amount of Java code contained within your JSP. Also, since you plan to support multiple Web browser platforms, you perform the validation code on the server, thus reducing the amount of client-side code (that is, JavaScript).

Use-Case Design

Having analyzed the use case, and then made various architectural decisions, we need to delve into more detail by further elaborating on the use case using dynamic diagrams.

The sequence diagram created during use-case analysis was of a reasonable size, but as more detail is added in design, it becomes unwieldy. Furthermore, as we have created other analysis-level sequence diagrams, we have found significant overlap in behavior. For example, both the Checkout Item use case and the Manage Items use case have requirements regarding searching for a title. Based on these issues, we created an Interaction Overview diagram to partition the diagram into manageable, reusable chunks. Figure 11.13 shows the Interaction Overview diagram for Checkout Item; although it is very simple with no particularly interesting control flow, it greatly improves the understandability of the model as we delve into more detail.

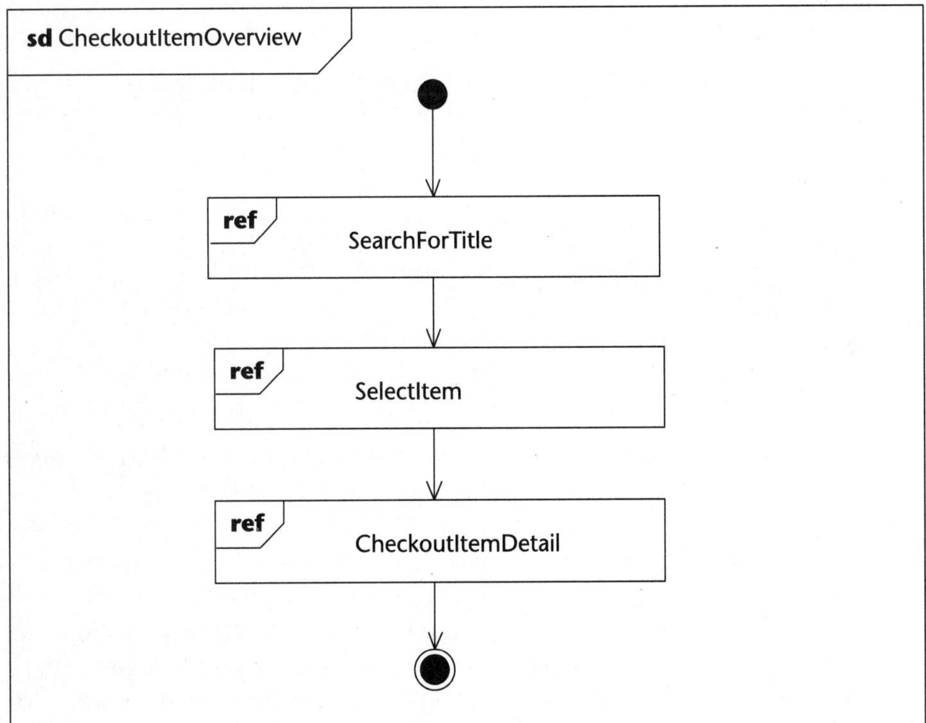

Figure 11.13 Interaction overview diagram for Checkout Item.

Each of the interaction occurrences in the interaction overview will be designed in its own sequence diagram. It is important to remember that these are not disparate visual diagrams; as we work on each of the detailed sequence diagrams, we are updating the overall model. As new operations are identified while building these dynamic diagrams, they are added to static diagrams and the underlying model. As we walk through these detailed scenarios, we make numerous design decisions, break apart and combine classes, identify relations, and so on. Keeping the model in synch across all the diagrams becomes challenging, but tool support helps.

Figure 11.14 shows the detailed sequence diagram for the `CheckoutItemDetail` fragment. The figure is worthy of significant explanation both in the area of UML usage and in the actual design being rendered.

This interaction starts with the Borrower actor sending a checkout message to a `CheckoutJSP` object. While messages typically represent an operation or signal, we have chosen to start this interaction with a checkout message that is not attached with an actual operation. Although in a strict technological sense it would be most accurate to show the actor submitting an HTTP POST, that would not best communicate what is happening. So the interaction is shown as being initiated via a "checkout" message. Since this is not associated with an actual operation within the design, the parentheses have been excluded from this message signature.

We added a note to remark on the store operation initiated on the `CheckoutItemAction` object. In our use of the Struts framework there is a lot that goes on in constructing the object and getting the method invoked. But we are not authoring that design here, we are just working within it. Rather than show all those details, we are just showing the message as going straight from `CheckoutJSP` to `CheckoutItemAction` with the explanation that there are details not shown here.

It would rarely be appropriate to create a sequence diagram that shows every small step involved in a complicated interaction. The designer must decide what to include and what to exclude from a diagram. Here, we are excluding the steps involved in getting the borrower identifier and the item identifier from the request object in the `CheckoutItemAction` class. (Any coder familiar with the `HttpServletRequest` object will be familiar with how to do this, and it is not worth the space it would take up on this diagram.)

We didn't worry about when objects are created during use-case analysis. In any design, and especially in a Web-based design, you need to make sure that you know when each object is created and who creates it. Here, you can see the `ItemMgr` created by the initiation of a static `getInstance` method on the class. The constructors of the other objects are also shown with the exception of `DaoFactory`. The `getItemDao` operation is also a static method.

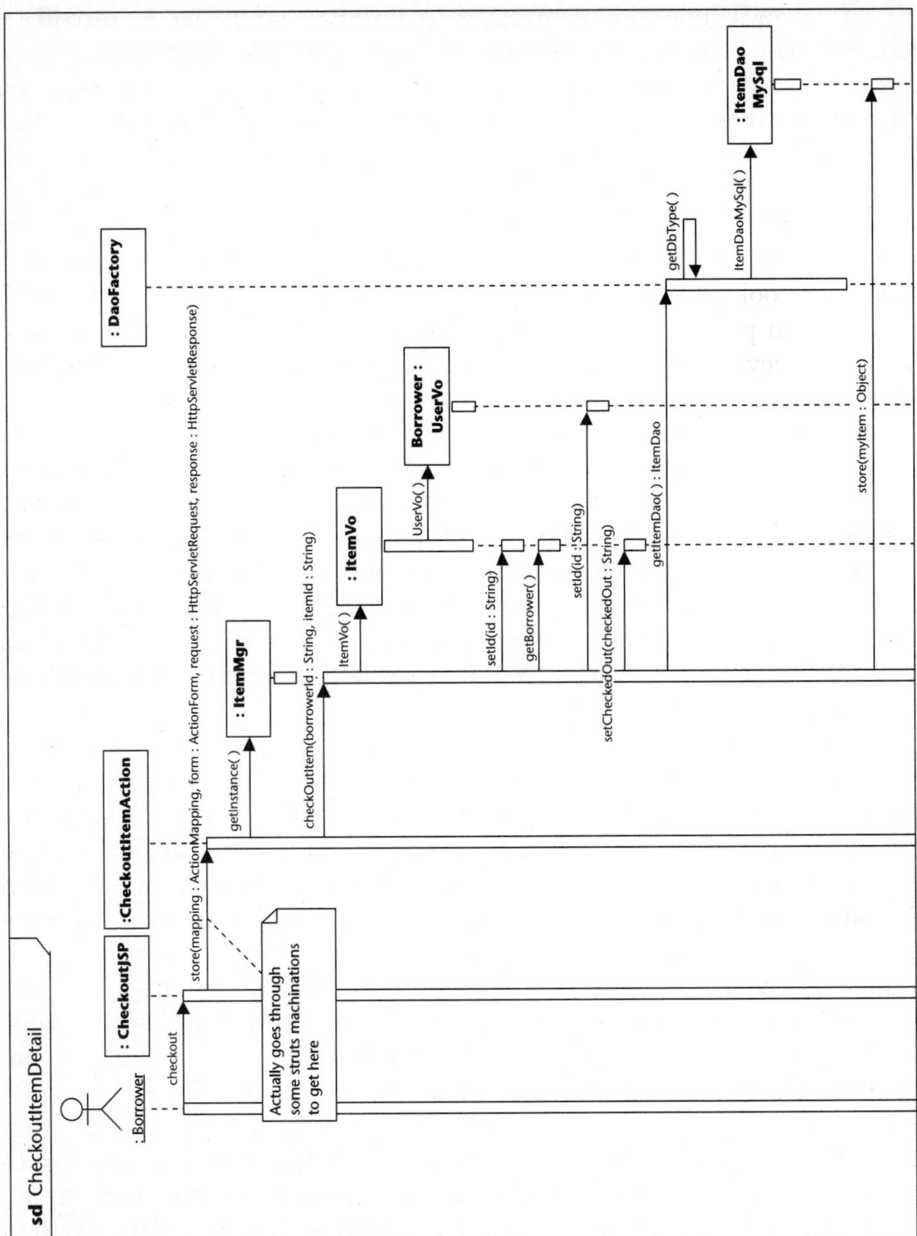

Figure 11.14 CheckoutitemDetail sequence diagram.

The `DaoFactory` is a notable part of this design. As described earlier when discussing the architectural design, we have an `ItemDao` interface and different classes implementing it for each database we use. Here we are showing that the `ItemMgr` asks the factory for an `ItemDao`, the factory figures out what kind of database we are using, and the `ItemDaoMySql` is created and returned. The `ItemMgr` is sending a message directly to the `ItemDaoMySql` object, but actually has no idea what concrete object is implementing the `ItemDao` interface.

Designing the User Interface

A special activity carried out while designing is the creation of the user interface—the "look and feel." Initiated during analysis, you perform this separately but in parallel to the other design work. (Creating a successful user interface is beyond the scope of this book; consult other sources devoted to this topic for more information.)

JSPs are used to display the information and capture the data entered by the user; in short, they act as an interface to the user. Because of the support for multiple Web browser platforms, we made a design decision to put as little Java code as possible within the JSP. Regardless, the decision should always ensure that the requirements for the application are met. In this case, we chose to use the taglibs provided by Struts so that the Java code is not included directly in the JSP. Ultimately, this choice allows for a more readable JSP for purposes of this case study, because certain implementation details are not performed in the JSP.

The resulting Unified Library application user interface is composed of a main page (`Main.jsp`), featuring a menu and an appropriate graphic, from which all other pages in the application can be reached. The other pages typically present a service of the application and are mapped to a particular use case. In some cases, a single user interface, or page, might map to multiple use cases. You might recall from Chapter 3 how the actors interact with use cases, just as in analysis the borrower interacts with a boundary class in the sequence diagram. In design, the borrower boundary class from analysis becomes a JSP.

Implementation

The implementation activities constitute the actual programming of the classes. One of the reasons to use Java to implement a system is because it works with multiple processors and operating systems. When you use Java, you find a natural progression from the logical classes that were created in the design to the code components during implementation because there is a one-to-one mapping of a class to a Java code file (and a one-to-one mapping to a Java executable .class file). Java also specifies that the name of the file be the same as that of the class it contains.

A component diagram helps in visualizing the physical representation as mapped from the design model. The design was set up to manage the dependencies on particular database products. For each entity there is a manager class that depends on a specific DAO interface. Then, the interface is realized by separate classes supporting each of the databases, but the manager does not really depend upon those classes. Instead, they all depend upon the interface. Figure 11.15 shows a class diagram and the corresponding component diagram, which shows the artifacts that manifest those classes. Although the dependencies of the physical code files can be surmised by an educated viewer of the class diagram, the component diagram shows them explicitly.

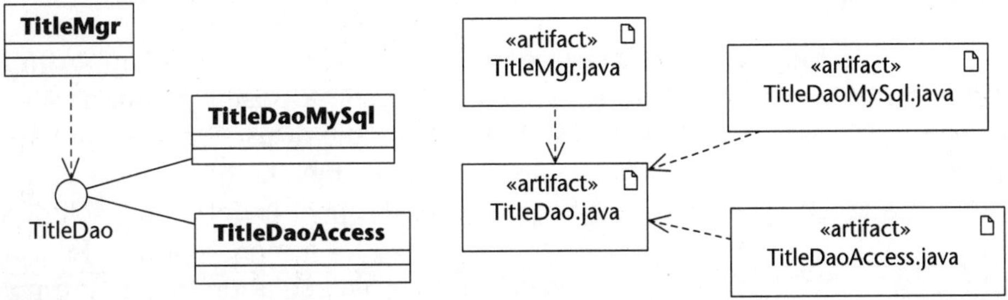

Figure 11.15 A class diagram and corresponding component diagram showing the dependencies among a number of title classes.

For coding, the specifications are collected from the following diagrams in the design model:

- **Class diagrams.** The class diagrams in which the class is present, showing its static structure and relationship to other classes.
- **State machine diagram.** A state machine diagram for the class, showing the possible states and the transitions that need to be handled (along with the operations that trigger the transitions).
- **Dynamic diagrams (sequence, communication, and activity) in which objects of the class are involved.** Diagrams showing the implementation of a specific method in the class or how other objects are using objects of the class.
- **Use-case diagrams and specifications.** Diagrams that show the result of the system give the developer more information on how the system is to be used when he or she might be getting lost in details—losing sight of the overall context.

During implementation, deficiencies in the design model surface. You might identify a need for new or modified operations, meaning that the developer has to change the design model. This happens in all projects. What's important is to synchronize the design model and the code so that the model can be used as final documentation of the system.

The Java code examples that follow demonstrate traversing the path from the presentation layer to the controller to the business to the data and back through the layers back to the presentation layer. This is a good example because other implemented use cases employ a pattern similar to this example. The Java code for the entire application is available on the accompanying CD-ROM. When studying the code, read it with the UML models in mind and try to see how the UML constructs have been realized in the code. Consider these points:

- The Java package specification is the code equivalent for specifying to which package in the component or logical view the class belongs.
- The private fields in Java correspond to the attributes specified in the model, and the Java methods correspond to the operations in the model.

This example demonstrates the checkout of an item from the View Items page (`ViewItems.jsp`). The first code snippet contains the HTML and the Struts taglibs used for the `ViewItems.jsp`. This JSP enables a user to enter and submit the data. The JSP sends the request data to the server.

```
// ViewItems.jsp
...
<logic:equal name="item" property="isCheckedOut" value="false">
<td><html:link page="/Checkout.do?subAction=store" name="item"
property="itemIdAndTitleId">Checkout</html:link></td>
</logic:equal>
...
```

Once the request is sent to the server, the `CheckoutItemAction` object processes the request by executing the appropriate business method, providing the necessary data. `CheckoutItemAction` uses the Struts framework, which employs the front controller design pattern in conjunction with a Struts ActionForm to retrieve data from the request and to send processing on to the next page as necessary.

```
// CheckoutItemAction.java
...
ItemMgr.getInstance().checkOutItem(user.getId(),request.getParameter(Con
stants.ITEM_ID));
...
```

ItemMgr is called by CheckoutItemAction and performs the business-related functionality for items. ItemMgr abstracts out any of the HTTP- or Struts-related processing that takes place in CheckoutItemAction. ItemMgr calls on the DAO Factory to get the DAO interface. The Factory is responsible for determining which implementation to use. In this case, it chooses between a MySQL or an Access DAO.

```
// ItemMgr.java
...
if(this.isCheckedOut(itemId)){
  DaoFactory.getItemDao().checkout(item);
}
...
```

The ItemDao[Impl] DAO abstracts and encapsulates the data access code, given a populated Value Object, and sends control back to the business object that called it. In this application, the ItemDao[Impl] is either the ItemDaoMySql or the ItemDaoAccess implementation.

```
// ItemDao[Impl].java
...
PreparedStatement pStmt = conn.prepareStatement(CHECKOUT_STMT);
pStmt.setString(1, item.getCheckedOut());
pStmt.setString(2, item.getBorrower().getId());
pStmt.setString(3, item.getDueBack());
pStmt.setString(4, item.getItemId());
pStmt.executeUpdate();
conn.commit();
closeDbConnection(pStmt,conn);
...
```

As discussed earlier, the example code snippets displayed in this section are similar to how the other use cases are coded. The separation of layers helps promote encapsulation so that you can make a change to one of the layers without affecting the others. The use of the DAO Factory with a single interface promotes polymorphism so that the clients of the Factory do not need to know the underlined implementation. By using the Struts taglibs, we reduced the need to write Java code within the JSP, which makes the maintenance of the code easier to manage.

Test and Deployment

While testing requires significant attention and rigor, we are not going to describe any of the testing efforts in UML here. For this example, we used the original use cases to test the finished application to determine whether the use cases were supported by the application and can be performed as defined in the use-case descriptions. The application was also tested in a more informal way by putting it into the hands of a user.

NOTE A larger-scale application requires more formal specifications against which the software is tested and a defect tracking system.

The deployment of the system is the actual delivery, including the documentation. In a real-life project, user manuals and marketing descriptions are typically part of the documentation work. A deployment diagram should also be drawn of the physical architecture, as shown in Figure 11.16. This application can be used on any computer with the supported Web browser platforms. This diagram shows our simple deployment structure for this case study. The war file simply needs to be put in a J2EE application server on a machine to which clients can connect.

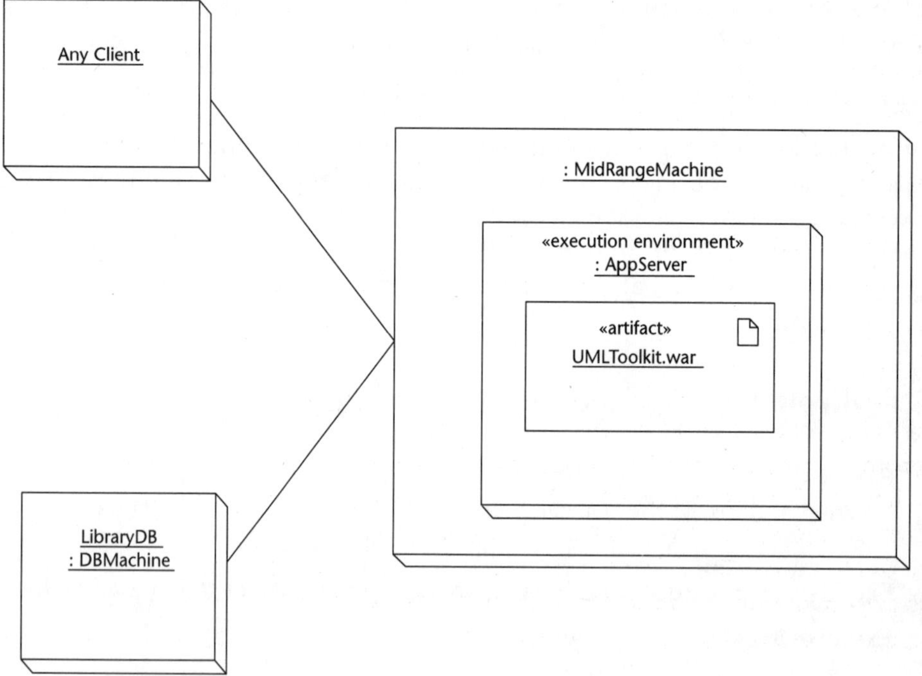

Figure 11.16 A deployment diagram for the library system.

Summary

This case study demonstrated how stakeholder requests of a system can be modeled with use cases, refined into an analysis model, expanded and detailed into a design model, and finally implemented and programmed in Java. The various parts of this case study were designed by a group who made every effort to work in the same manner they would have worked on an actual project. And though the different activities might seem separate and to have been conducted in a strict sequence, the work is more iterative in practice. The lessons and conclusions resulting from the design were fed back into the analysis model, and discoveries made in the implementation were updated and changed in the design model. This is the normal way to build object-oriented systems.

Exercises

The exercises presented here enable you to immediately begin to apply UML. They are divided into analysis and design/construction categories. The first category lists new requirements on the system that have to be analyzed, designed, and implemented in the system. The second category contains technical changes and improvements that primarily affect design and implementation. You can decide to what extent to implement the solutions to the exercises, but note that some can only be made in the analysis and design models. If you are proficient in Java, you can code and test the solutions in the final application. Look at the different views, the different diagrams, and the specifications.

Requirements and Analysis Exercises

Exercise 1: Introduce functionality to inform a borrower with a reservation when an item of the reserved title is returned to the library. The customer with the oldest reservation should be informed first.

Exercise 2: Introduce functionality to inform a borrower that a loan is due.

Exercise 3: Extend the system so that reservations are removed after a specified amount of time.

Exercise 4: Extend the handling of titles so that they can be placed in different categories and so that user-defined information can be added to each title (for example, a review of a book).

Exercise 5: Extend the system to administrate the purchases of new items.

Exercise 6: Introduce rules in the library model to constrain the loans. For example, restrict borrowers to no more than five reservations at the same time, or to no more than 10 loans at the same time. Make it easy to define such new rules.

Exercise 7: Enable a borrower to search for titles and items over the Internet.

Exercise 8: Rebuild the library model to support integration of other libraries using the same system. This means that one library should be able to search for a title or an item in another library. A library should be able to lend an item in another library by sending a message to that specific library, which then performs the loan procedure and sends the item by mail to the lending library. Show a deployment diagram for this new system.

Design and Construction Exercises

Exercise 9: Add the Book Title and Magazine Title classes to the design and add some new appropriate attributes to each of these classes. Make the existing Title class abstract and make sure the new classes can be stored persistently.

Exercise 10: Change the design of the search facility of objects, so that "wildcard" characters can be used when searching for titles, authors, or borrowers (for example, "UML*" returns all titles starting with "UML").

Exercise 11: Change the design of the search facility of objects, so that multiple search results are handled (currently only the first match is returned). The number of "hits" should be reported, and the user should be able to choose from among the result records.

Exercise 12: Add a new utility class for creating a log that can be used by all parts of the application to log either debug or trace messages. The type of information actually saved in the log should be configurable from the user interface.

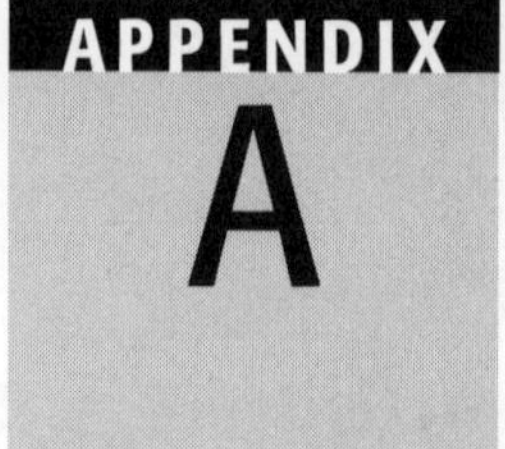

Visual Glossary

Activity Diagram

Action:

Action Name

Initial Node:

●

Activity Final:

◉

Flow Final:

Activity Edge, Control Flow or Object Flow:

Decision or Merge Node:

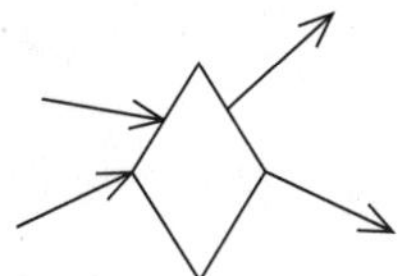

Decision Input

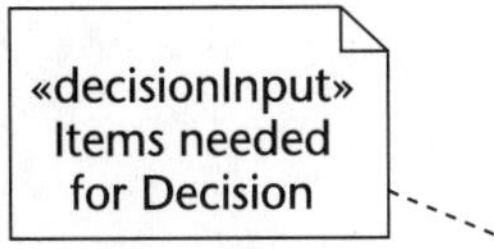

Input Pin

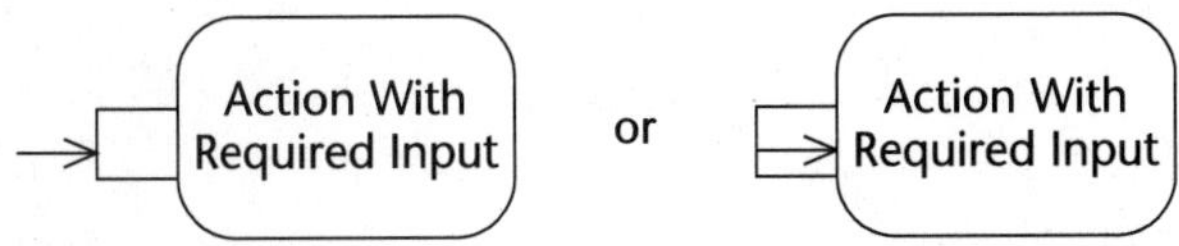

Output Pin

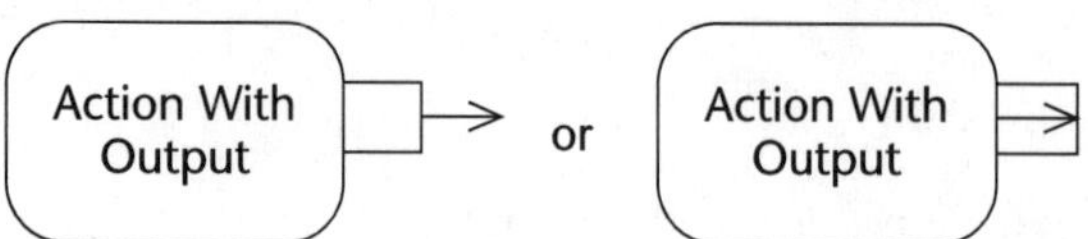

Streaming Pins

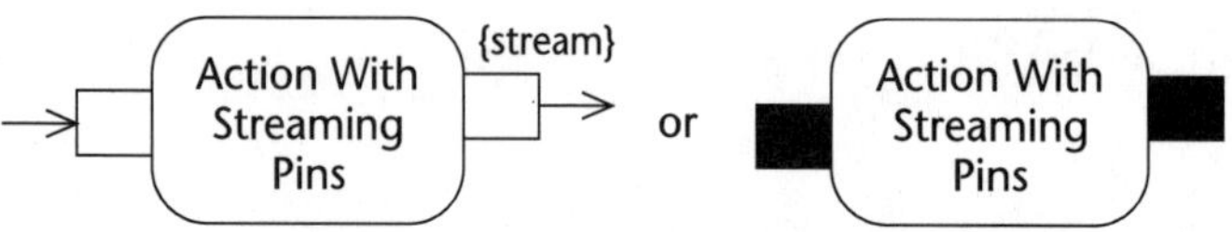

Activity Edge Connector

DataStore

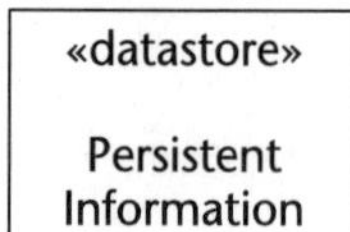

Conditions on Action

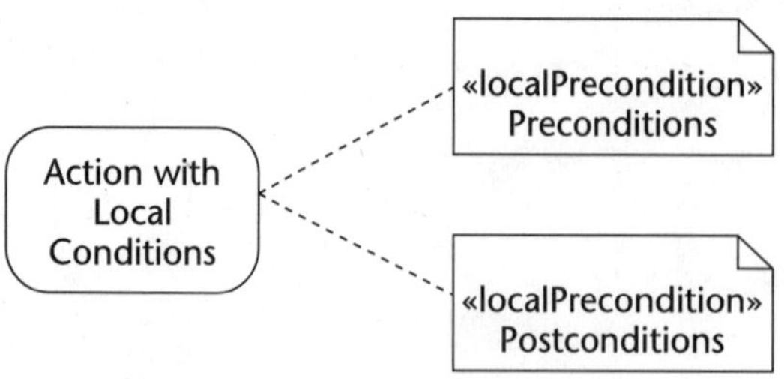

Structured Activity

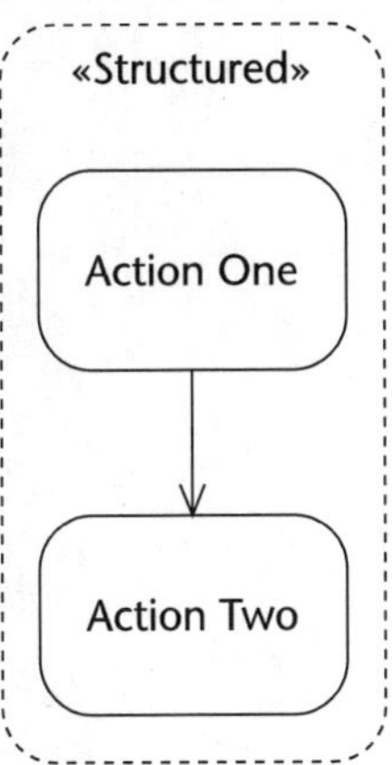

Expansion Region

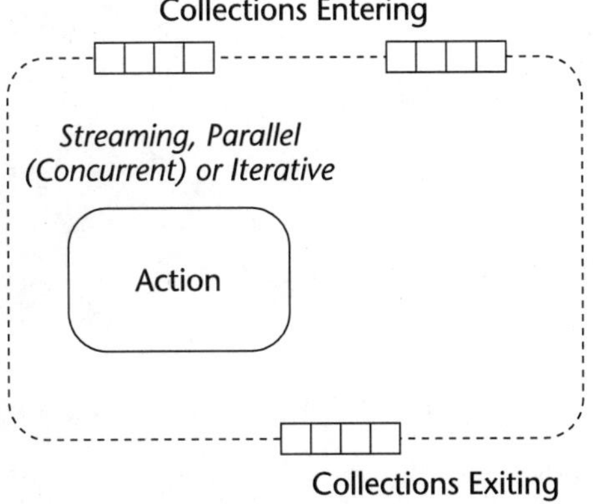

Edge Weight on Activity Edge

{weight = Number of Tokens Needed}

Exception Handler

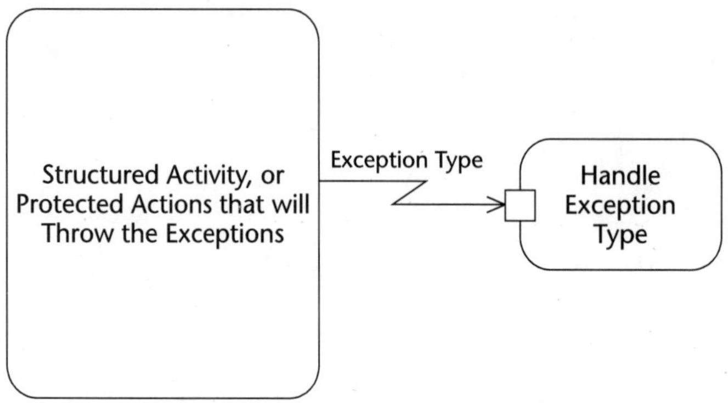

Interruptible Activity Region

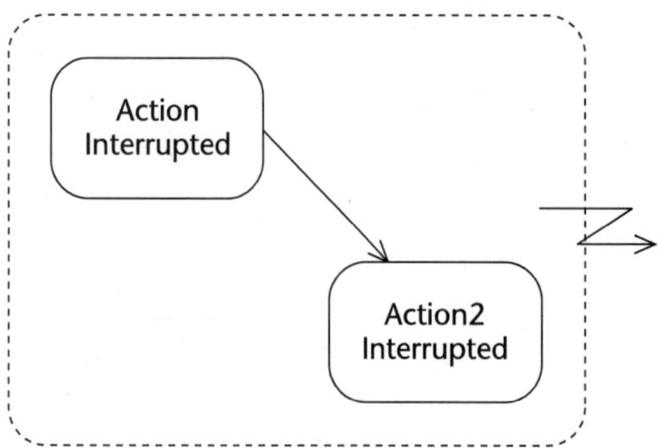

Time Trigger

Parameter Set

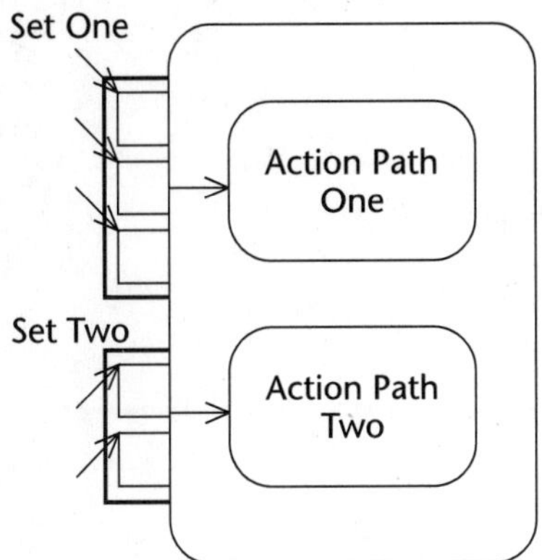

Exception on an Edge

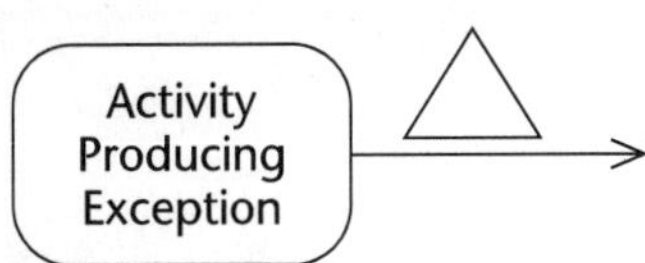

Activity Partitions:

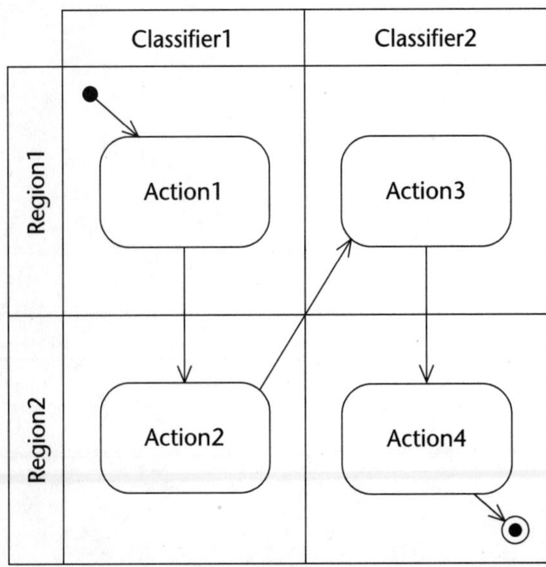

Object Node:

Object Name

Object Node with Signal as Type

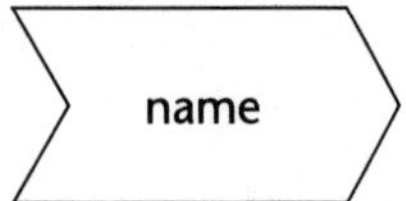

Send Signal Action:

Send Signal

Accept Signal Action:

Accept Signal

Fork Node:

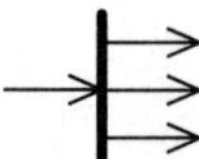

Join Node

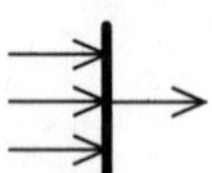

Class Diagram

Class:

ClassName

attribute1: type [multiplicity] = default
/derivedAttribute: type [multiplicity]
attribute2: type = default {property string}
classScopedStaticAttribute: type = default

operation1(param1, param2)
operation2(param1): {property-string}
operation3(param3: type = default)

Association:

Association Name →

Multiplicity:

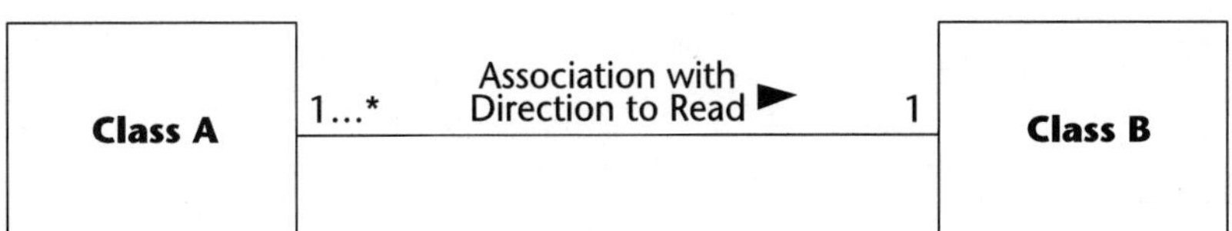

Named Association Ends:

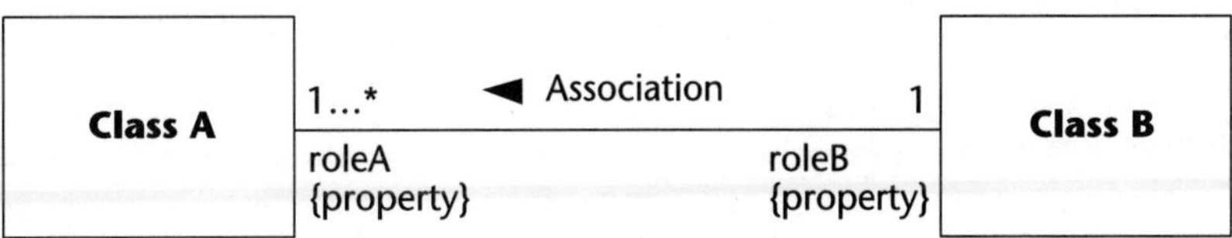

Association Class:

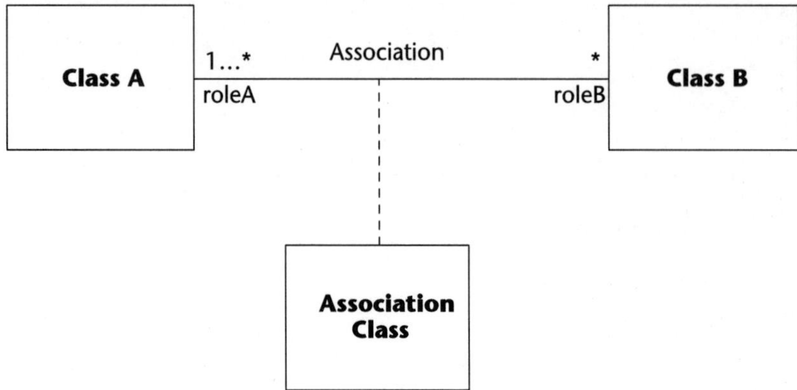

Qualified Association:

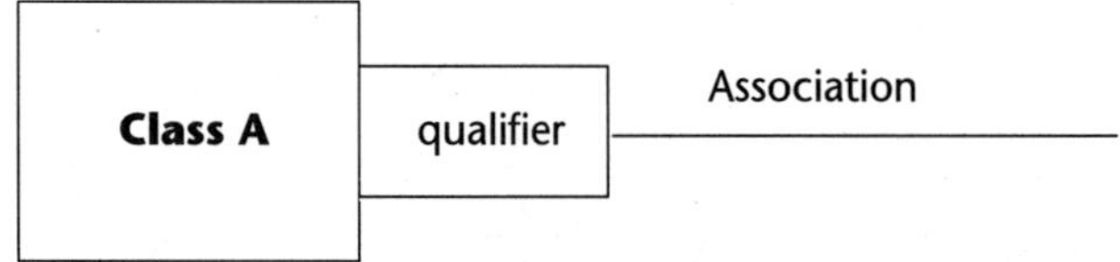

Xor-constraint (Between Associations):

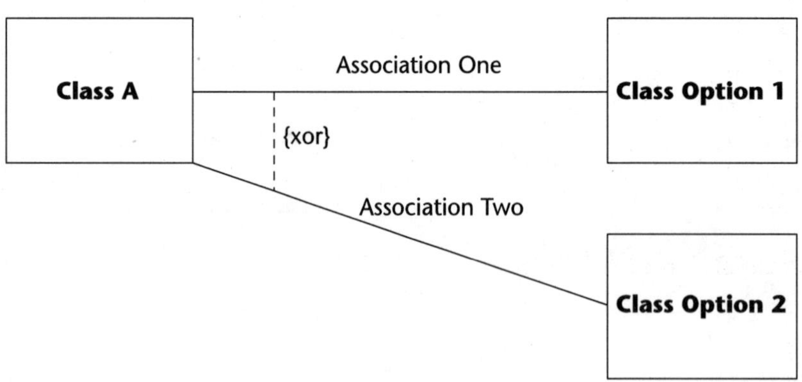

Ternary Association:

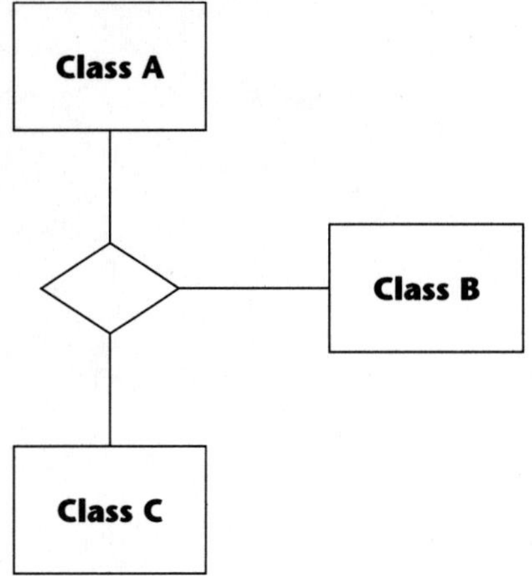

Aggregation:

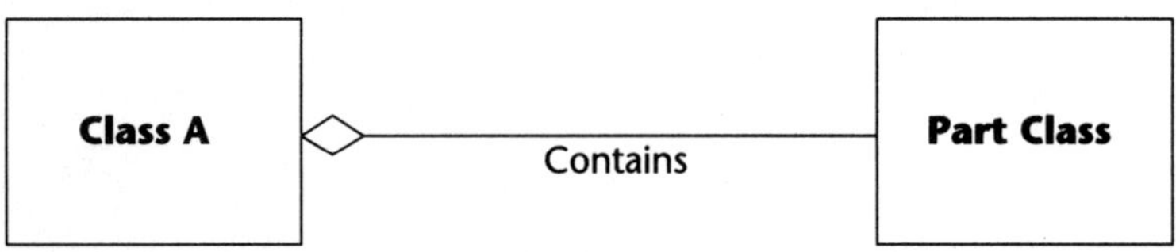

Composition:

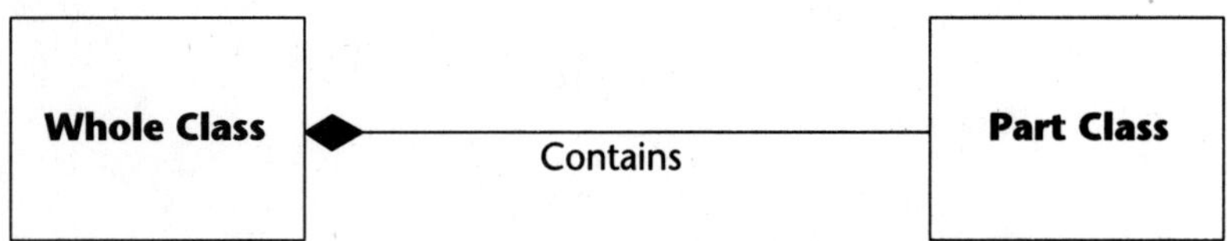

Generalization:

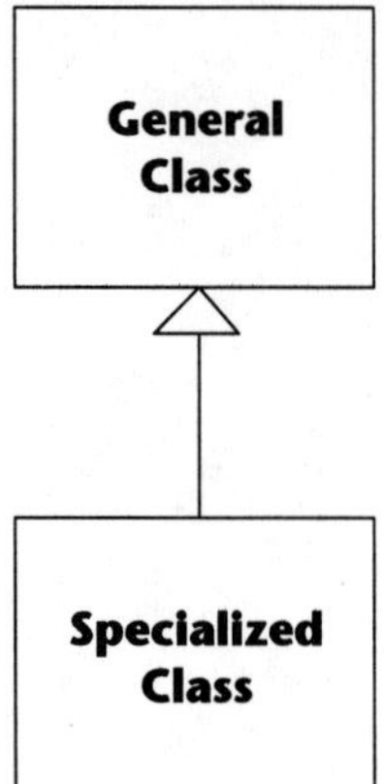

Abstract Class:

Class
{abstract}

Dependency:

Interface:

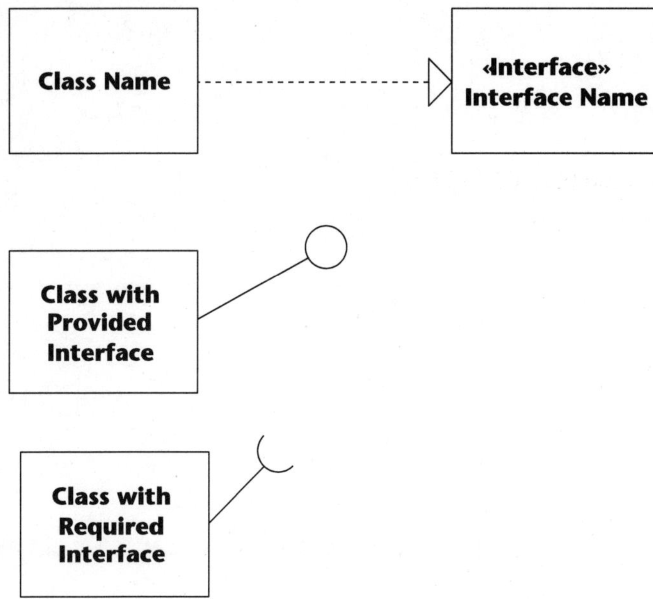

Interface, Provided and Required Notation:

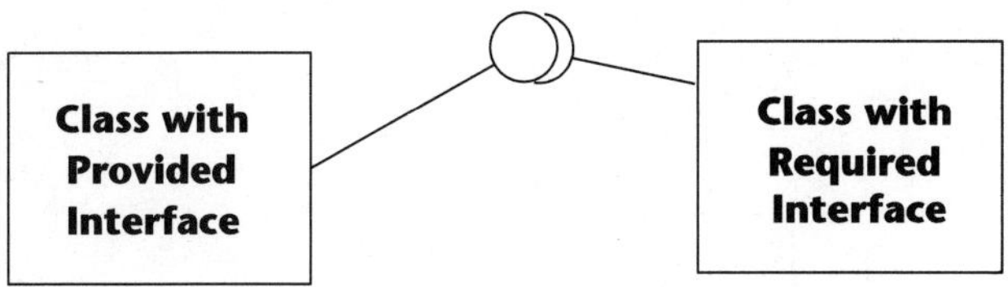

Parameterized Class (Template):

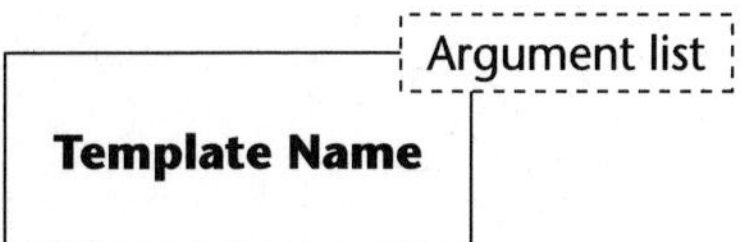

Instantiated Parameterized Class:

Template Name
<parameters>

Object or Instance Specification:

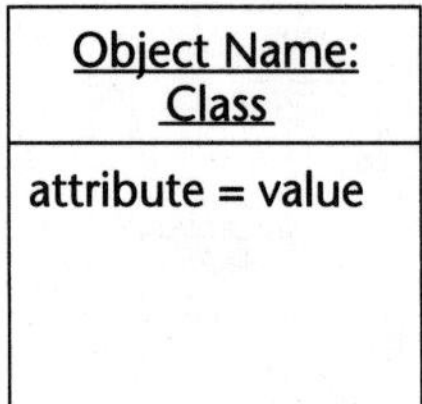

Realization

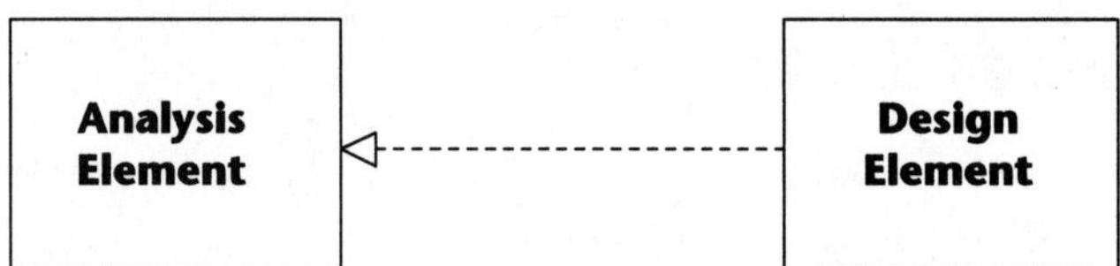

Active Class

Active Class

Powertype

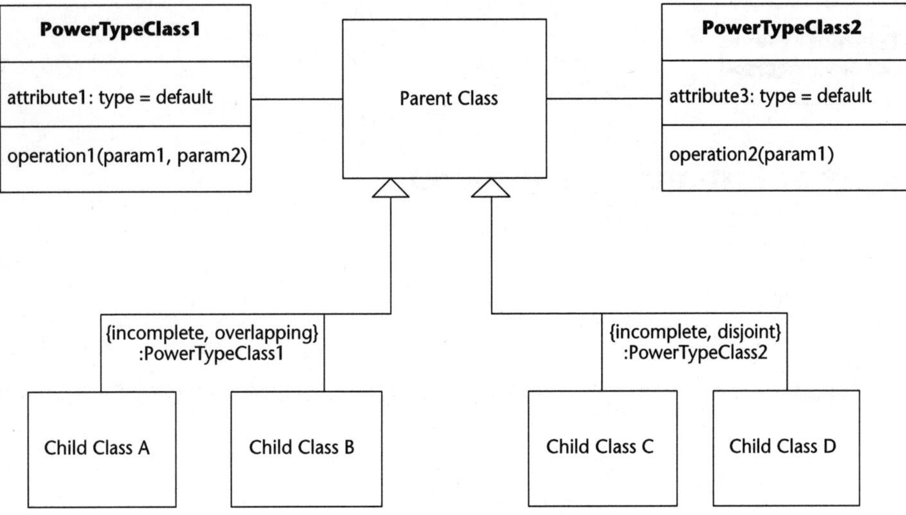

Port

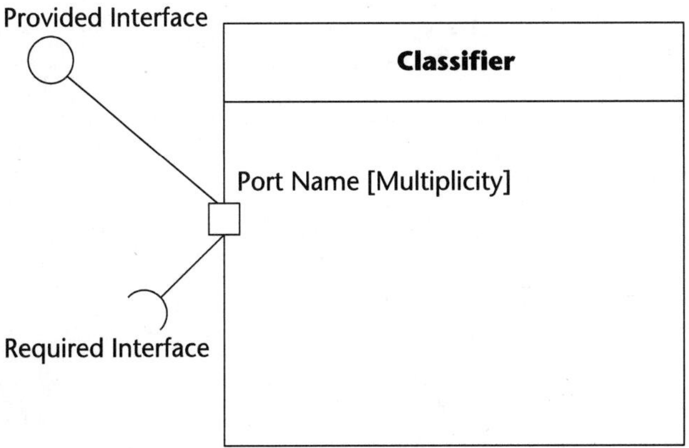

Component Diagram

Component:

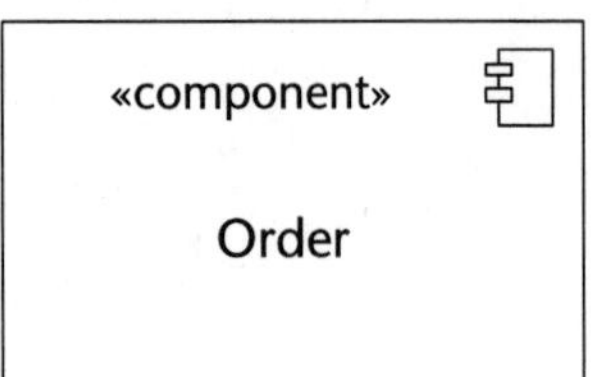

Component (with Provided and Required Interfaces):

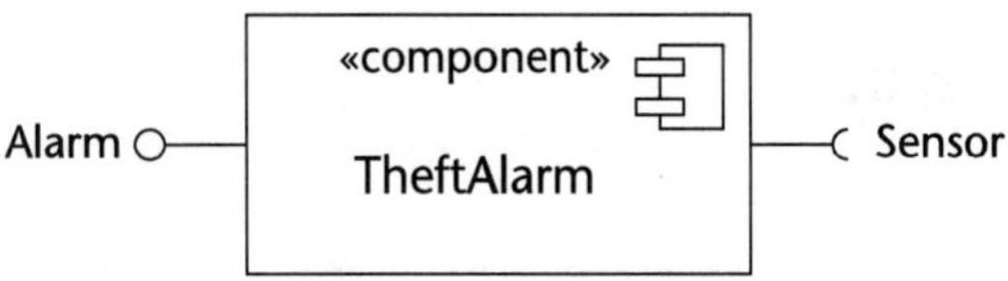

Artifact:

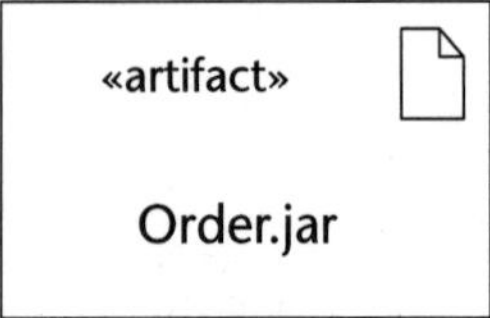

Manifestation:

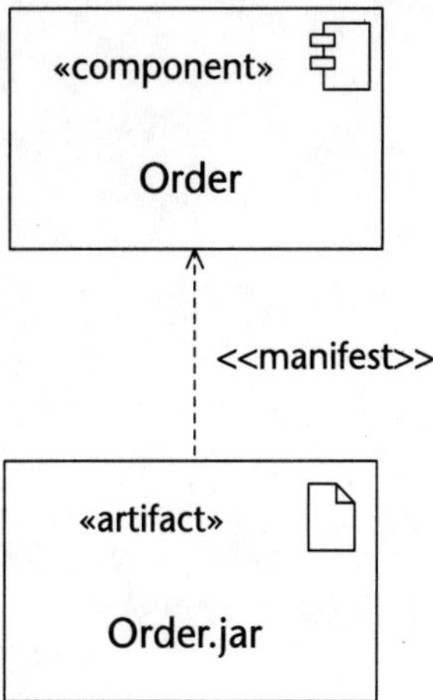

Composite Structure Diagram:

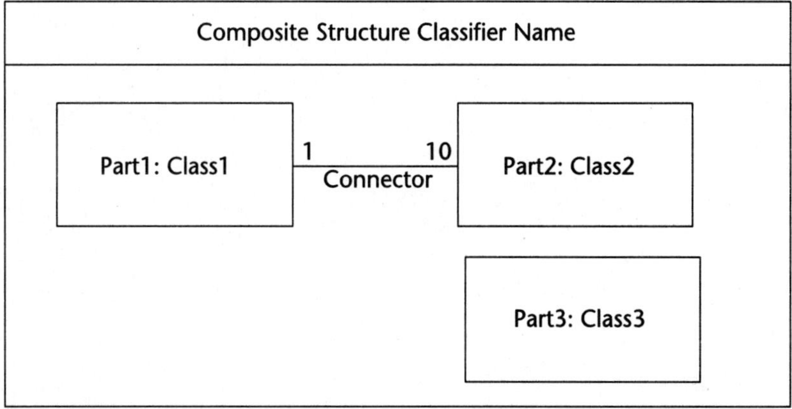

Deployment Diagram

Node:

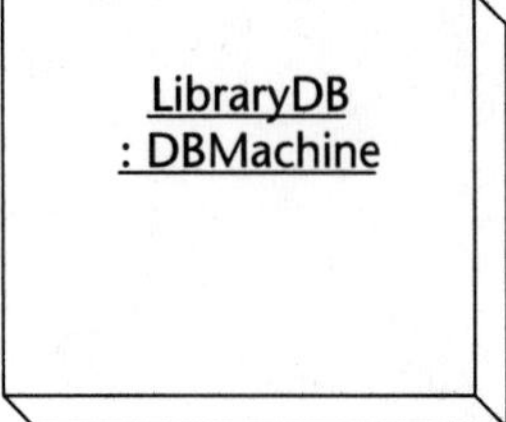

Communication Path:

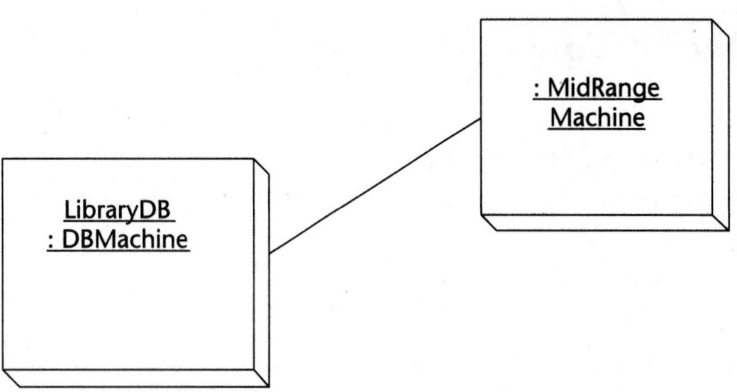

Execution Environment:

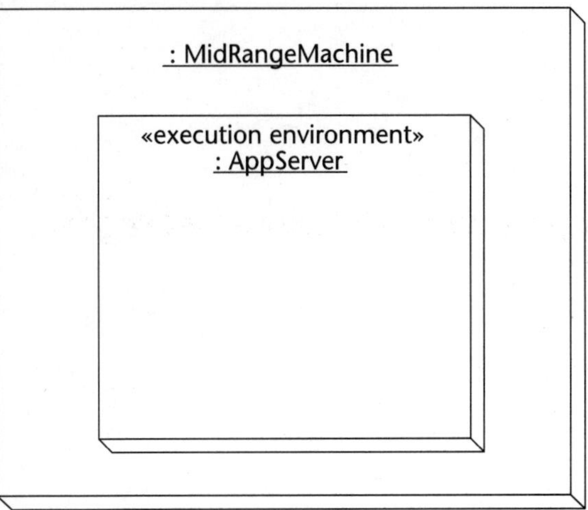

Deployment Specification:

«deployment spec»

application.xml

General Mechanisms

Comment or Note:

Package:

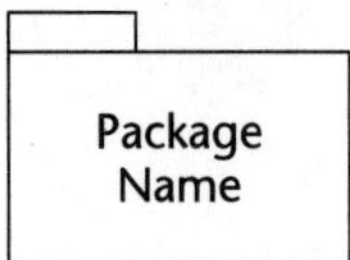

Nested Packages and Dependency Between Packages:

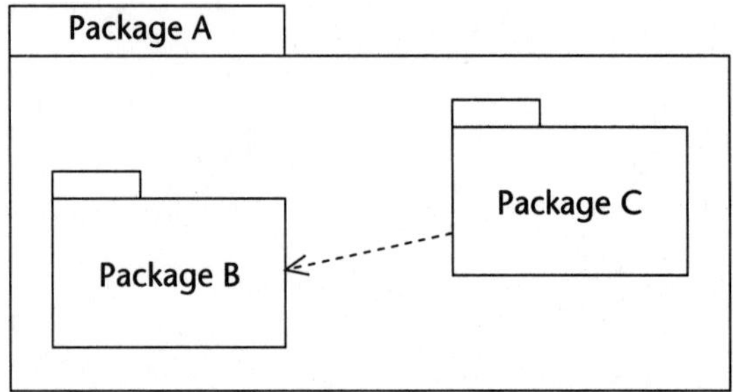

Alternative Package Content Display

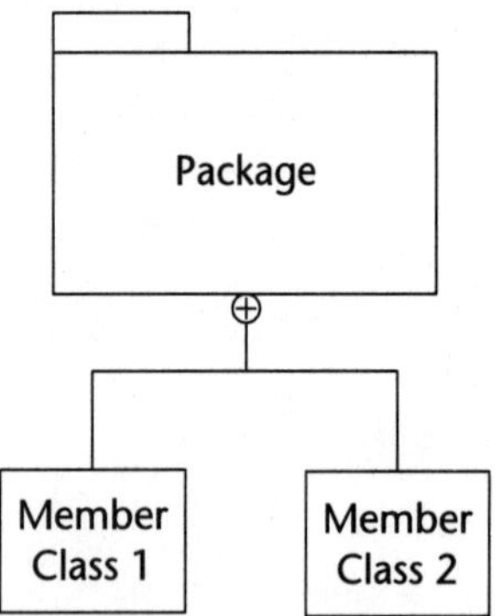

Diagram Frame:

Diagram Type Name of Specific Diagram

Frames can include the following diagram types:

Activity
Class
Component
Interaction (abbreviated as SD)
Package
State Machine (abbreviated as SM)
Use Case

Package Merge:

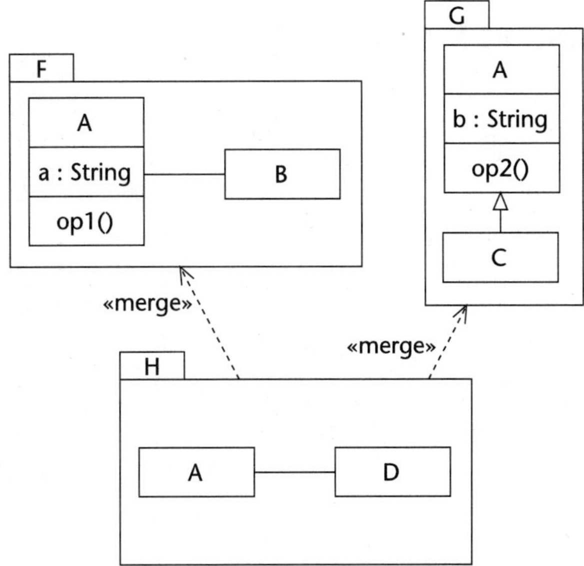

Package Import:

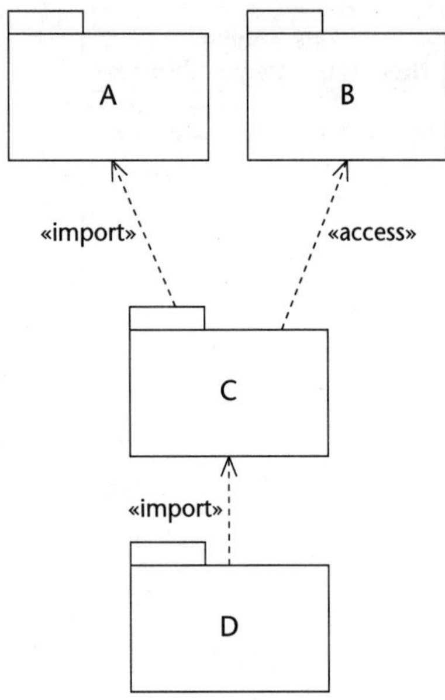

Stereotypes, Constraints, and Properties:

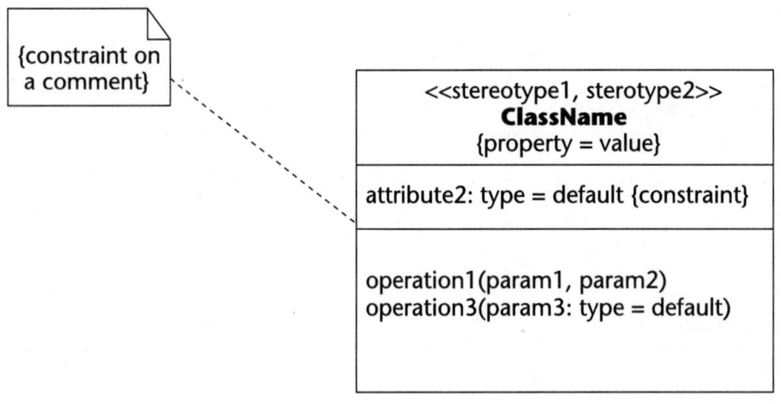

Extension of a Metaclass

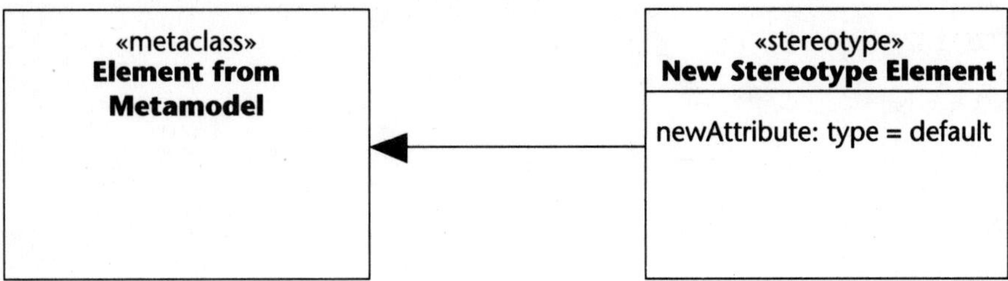

Application of a Profile

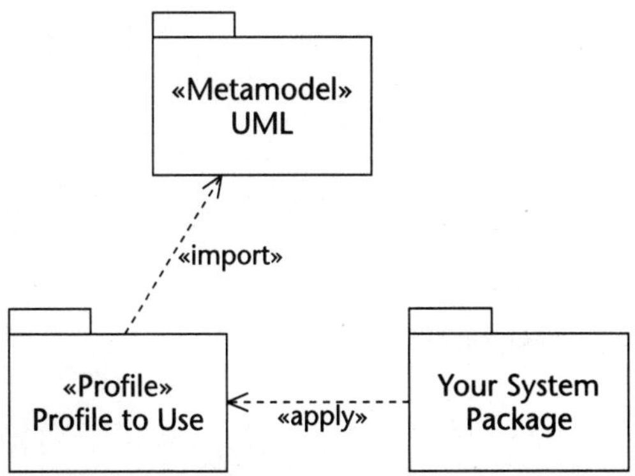

Interaction Diagram

Frame:

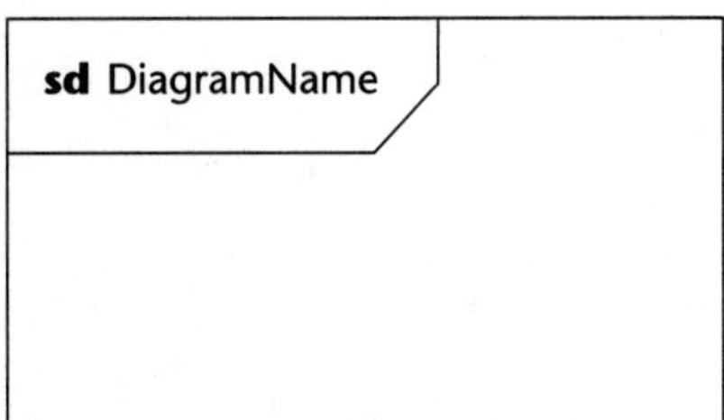

Object instance (with Lifeline):

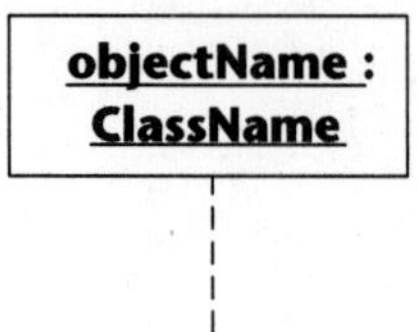

Message:

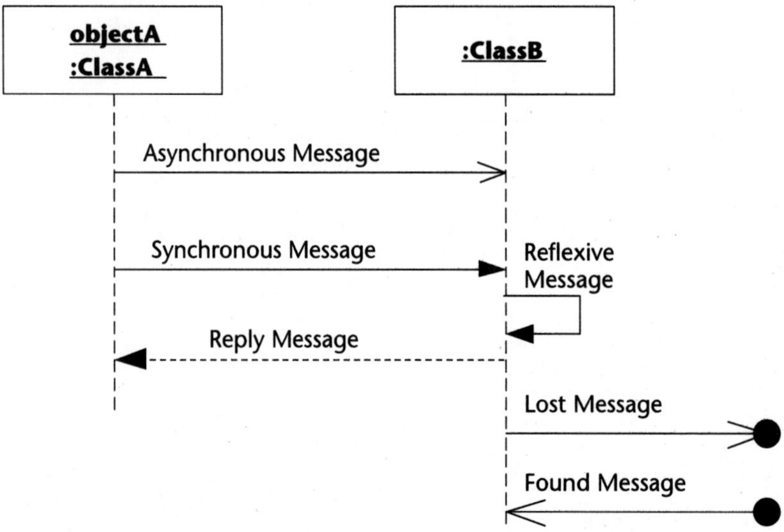

Message (on Communication Diagram):

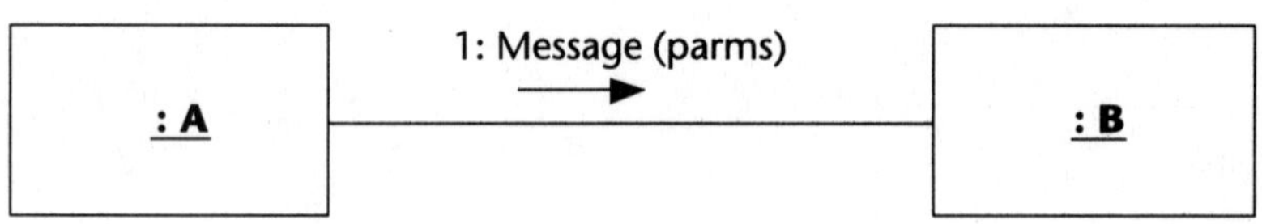

Execution Occurrence:

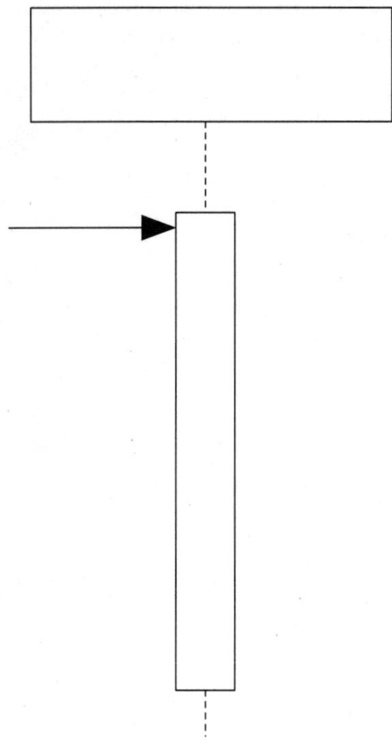

Creation and Destruction of Object:

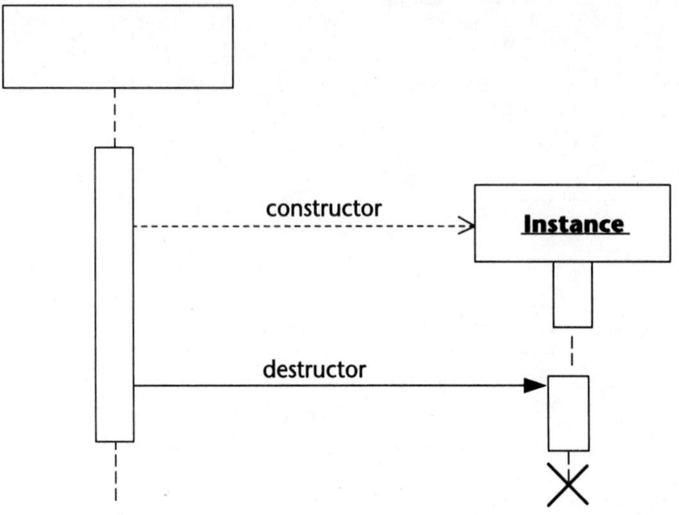

Interaction Occurrence:

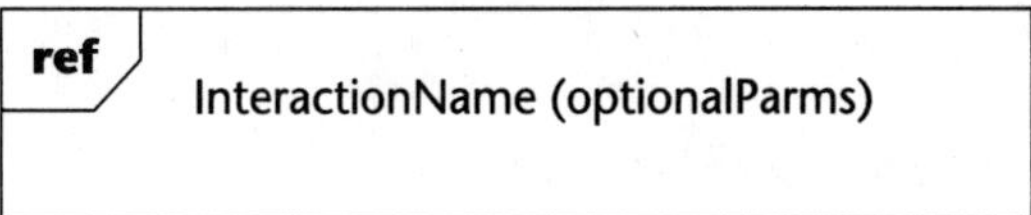

Combined Fragment (Alternative):

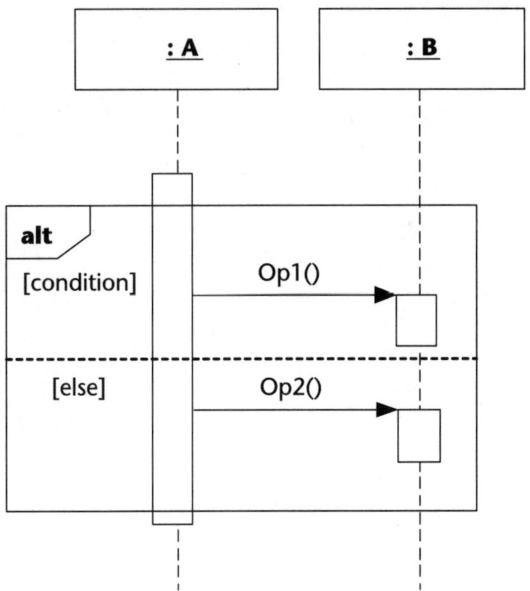

Combined Fragment (Loop):

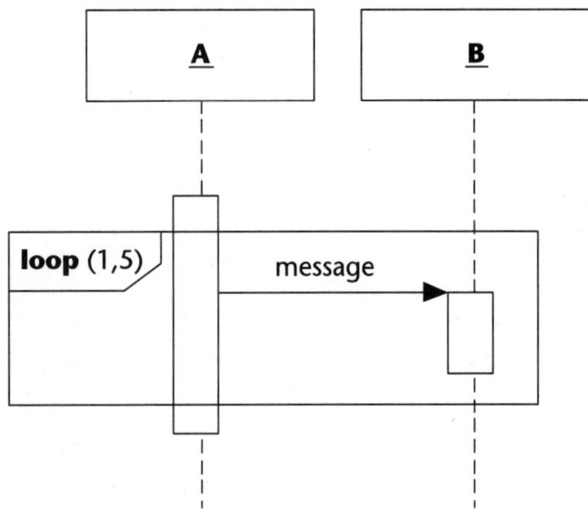

Duration Constraint:

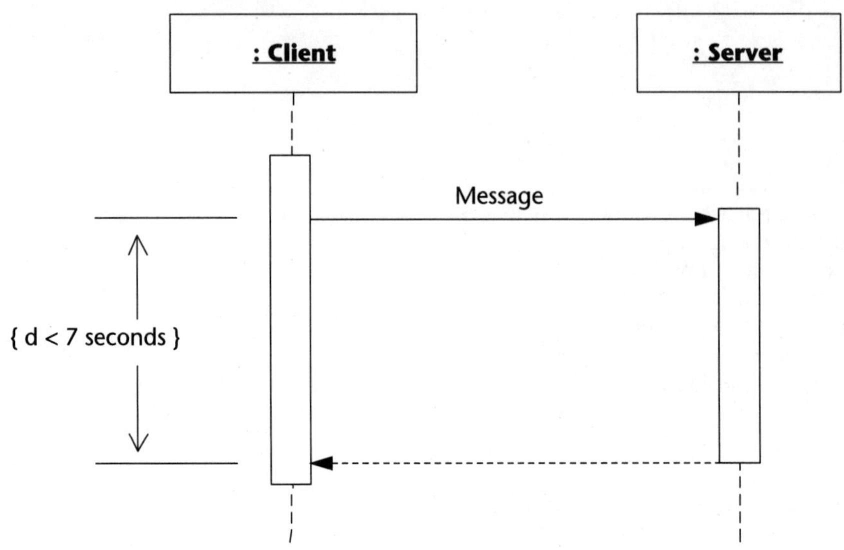

State or Condition Timeline:

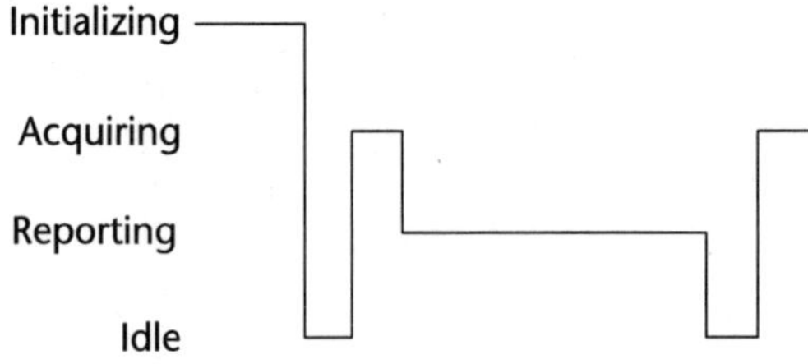

State Diagram

State:

Name

event1/internal activity name
event2/internal activity name
exit/exit activity name
enter/enter activity name
do/ongoing activity name

Internal Transitions

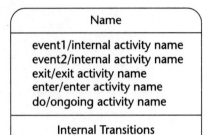

State with Name Tab Notation

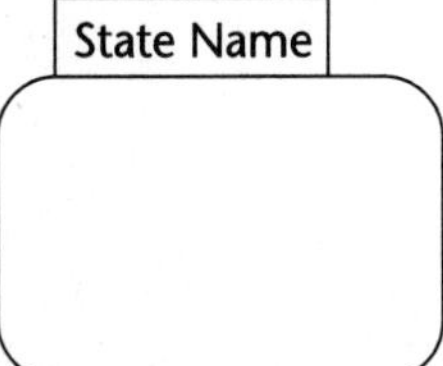

State Transition:

Trigger[guard]/Activity Expression

Entry Point:

Entry Point Name

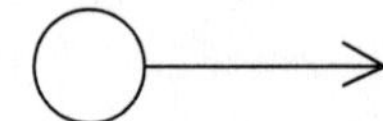

Exit Point:

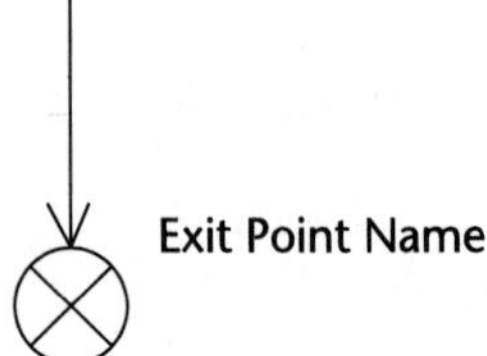

Initial Pseudo State:

Final State:

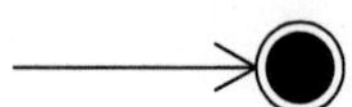

State Machine

[Guard Condition on Transition]

Substate Machine on State Machine

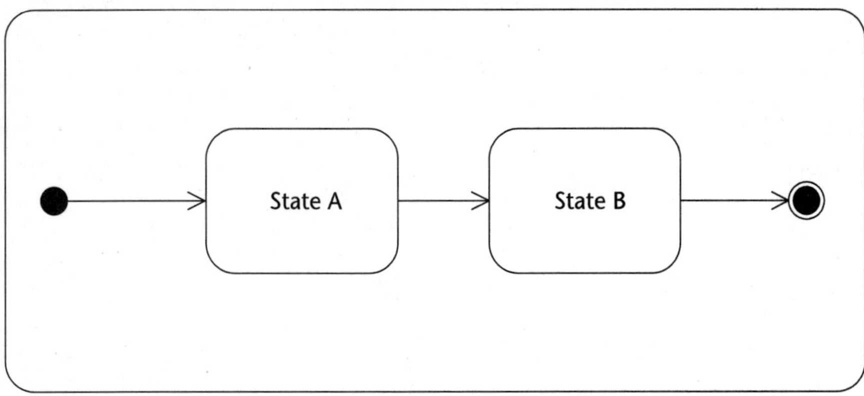

Shallow History Indicator:

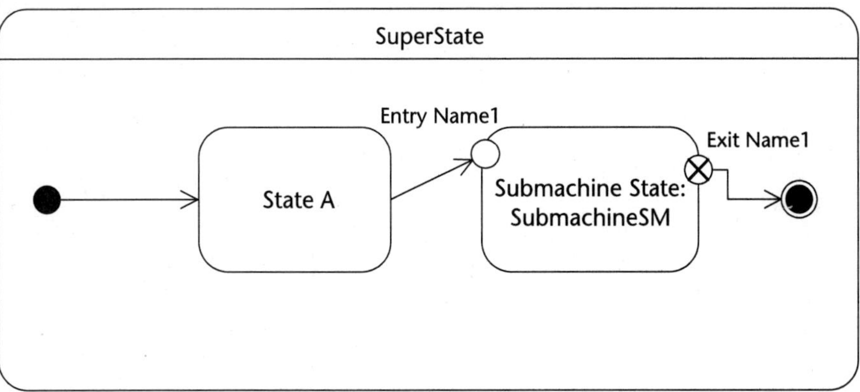

Deep History Indicator:

H

Composite State

H*

Composite State with Regions, or Orthogonal Composite State

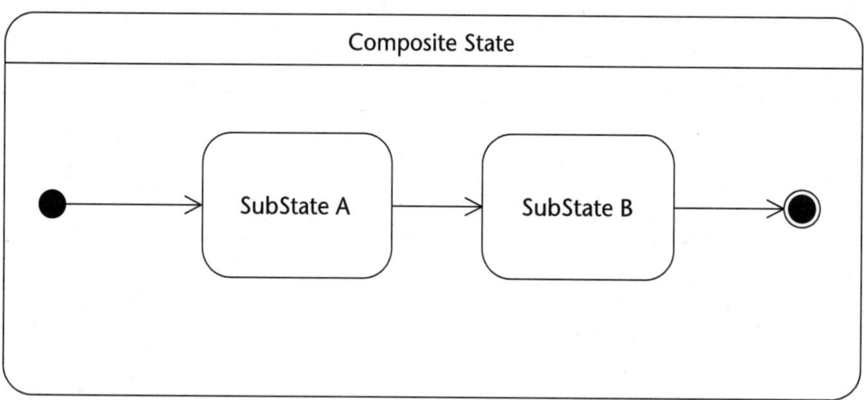

Protocol State Machine

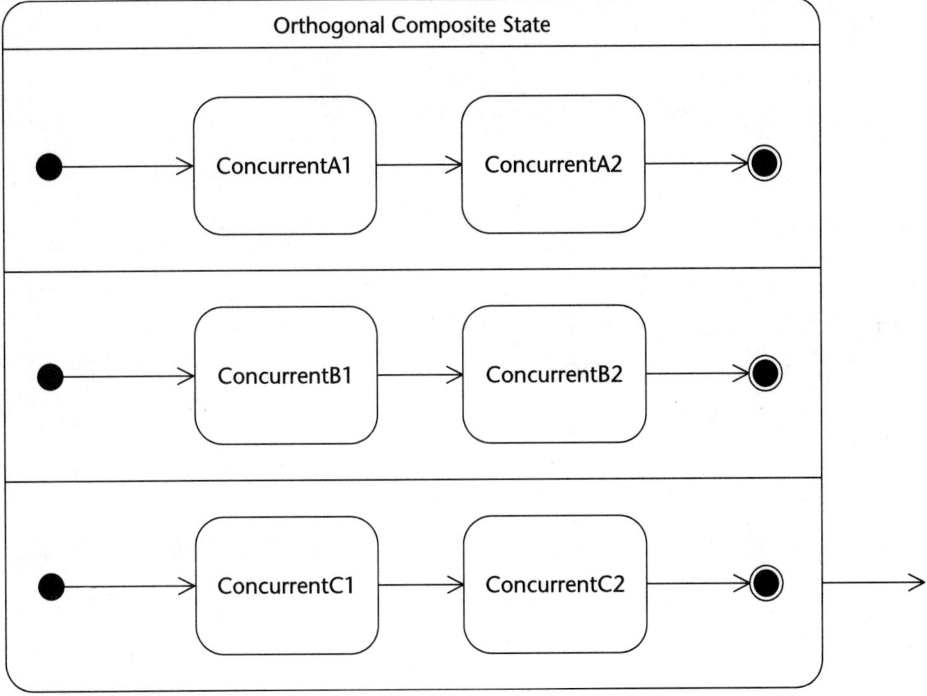

Port Connected to Behavior

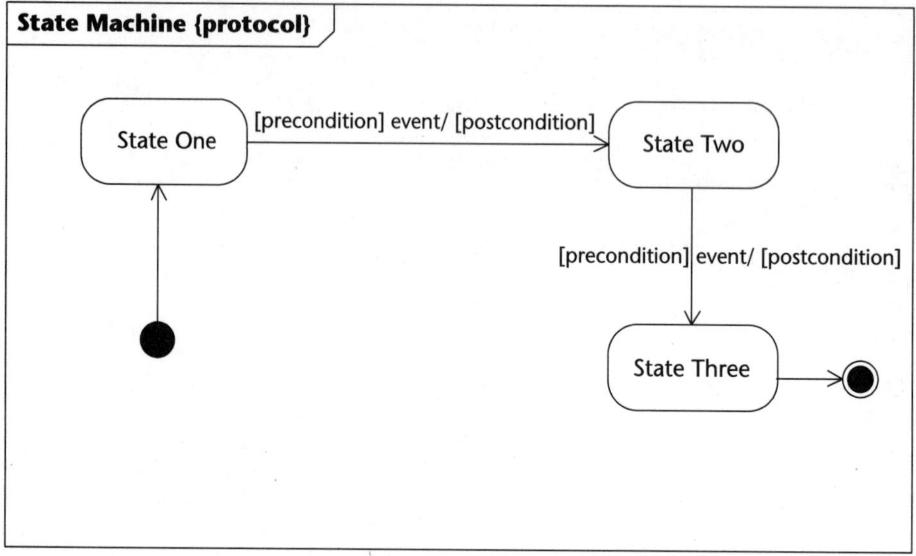

Generalization or Redefinition of State Machine

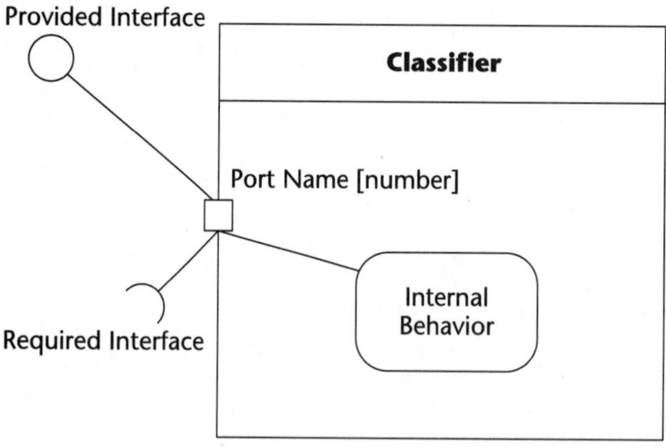

Use-Case Diagram

System or Subject:

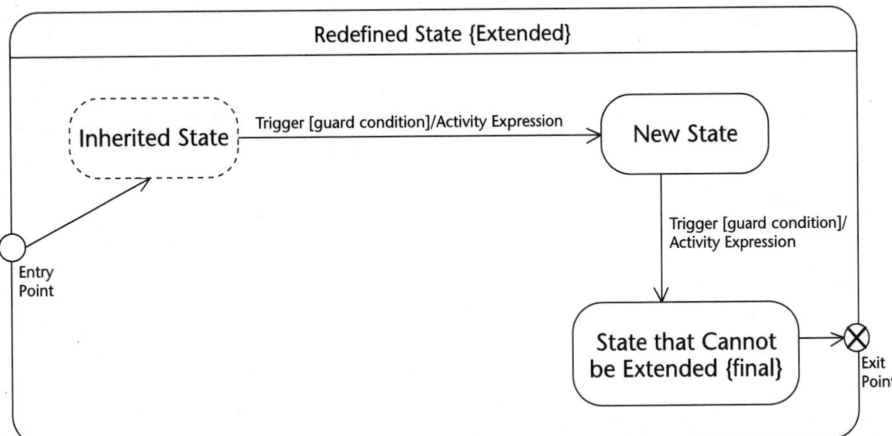

Actor:

System or Subject Name

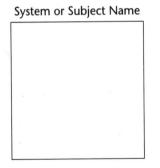

Use Case:

Use-Case Alternative Notation (with Extension Points)

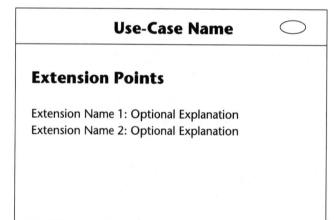

Association:

Use-Case Name 

Extension Points

Extension Name 1: Optional Explanation
Extension Name 2: Optional Explanation

Generalization:

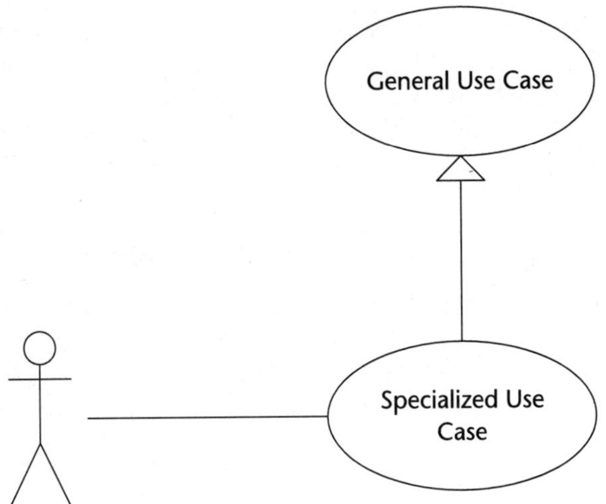

Include:

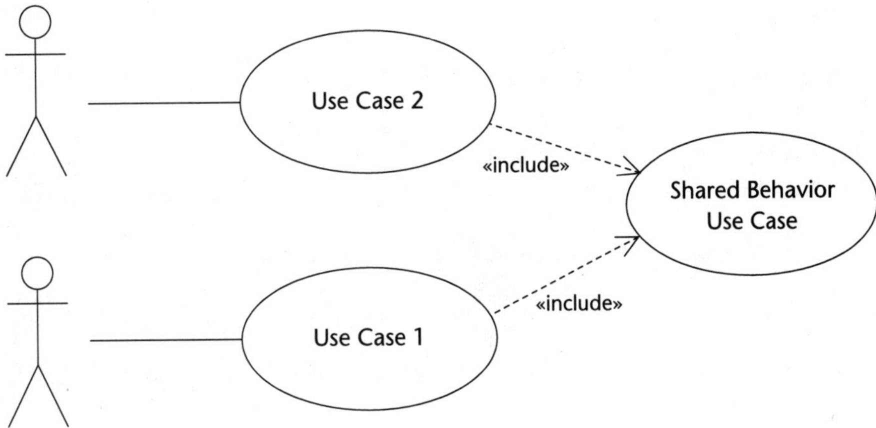

Extend (with Condition)

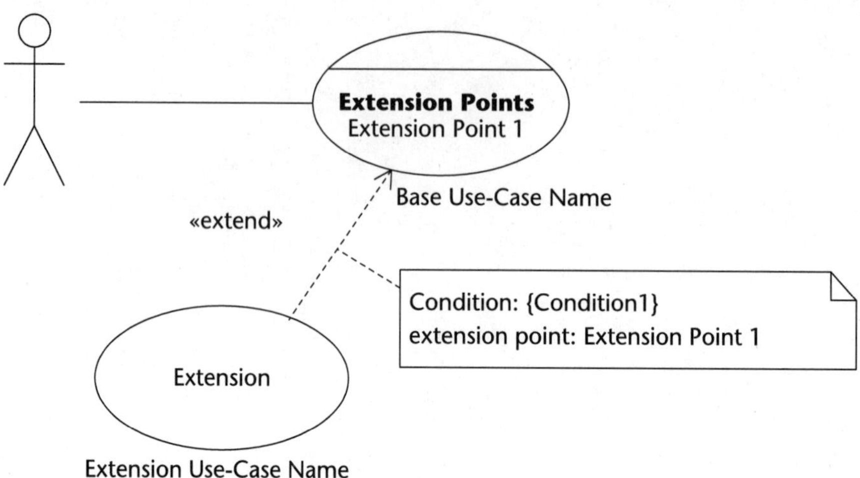

APPENDIX

B

Glossary

Abstract class A class that can have no instances. An abstract class is used only to inherit from.

Action A procedure of executable statements representing the atomic unit of behavior specification. Actions are the building blocks of activities and can be used on state machine transitions.

Action semantics The general model in UML for how an action language should work. This does not define a specific action language but provides guidelines for the existing action languages.

Activation The execution of an action. An object is said to be activated while it is executing.

Active class A class whose objects have their own thread of control.

Active object An object that has its own thread of control.

Activity Behavior specified by a workflow made up of actions, objects, and edges between actions.

Activity diagram A diagram that shows behavior, focusing on the work performed. The activity diagram displays a sequence of actions including alternative execution and objects involved in performing the work.

Activity partition A defined area in an activity diagram within which activities and actions reside. This can be associated with an actor or with a class or can be more loosely specified as in when partitions are used to specify an area within an organization or a physical location where something occurs.

Actor Something external that interacts with the system or subject. An actor can be a role played by a human being or another system.

Aggregation A relationship in which one class consists of another class. The relationship indicates a whole-part connection. Aggregation is a special case of association.

Analysis A discipline that examines a problem and produces a hypothesis or diagnosis of a solution. In object-oriented analysis, a model is created of all the real-world entities, including their relationships and collaborations independent of a technical solution.

Architecture The organizational structure of a system. This covers both the obvious aspect of structure manifested by cohesive chunks of the design with their interfaces and other design decisions with sweeping impact, such as the application of patterns.

Argument A value that is parsed to a parameter within an operation's signature.

Artifact A tangible entity used by a development process. In modeling this is often the physical manifestation of a design component that is deployed into an execution environment (for example, in Java a jar file).

Association A relationship that describes a set of links between classes (their objects). Used to describe that objects of the involved classes have some sort of connection to each other.

Association class A class attached to an association to provide extra information about the connection. The association class is just like a normal class; it can have attributes, operations, and other associations.

Association end name An association can have ends connected to each classifier involved in the association. The end indicates the role played by the class (and its objects) in terms of the association. The role names are part of the association, not of the classes.

Asynchronous message Asynchronous flow-of-control occurs when there is no explicit return to the caller and the sender continues to execute after sending the message without waiting for it to be handled.

Attribute A member within a class to store data. The attribute has a name and a type and may have a default value.

Behavior An observable effect, including its results.

Binary association An association relationship between two classes.

Bind A stereotyped dependency. The dependency connects types or collaborations and has arguments to match properties of the source to the target. A bind dependency specifies that the source is a binding of the target, where parameters are used to make the source definition complete. Typically used to show the instantiation of a parameterized class (template).

Boundary class A stereotyped class whose objects are used to communicate with actors.

Call A stereotyped dependency connecting operations in classes. If class A has a call dependency to class B, operations in class A can call any of the operations in class B.

Class A model element used to model things, both intellectual and physical. A class is a type (*see* Type) and can be instantiated to objects that are individual entities (objects) of the same class. A class is described with members that are attributes, operations, and relationships to other classes. The members are reflected in objects of the class. A class can be generalized and specialized; extension mechanisms can be attached to the class.

Class diagram A diagram that shows a static structure with classes and their definitions and relationships.

Classifier A general model element to indicate an entity that has instances with common features. Class, interface, signal, and node are all examples of classifiers.

Collaboration Describes how a set of objects interact to perform some specific function. A collaboration describes both a context and an interaction. The context shows the set of objects involved in the collaboration along with their links to each other. The interaction shows the communication that the objects perform in the collaboration.

Combined fragment A diagram that shows a distinct portion of an interaction on a sequence diagram that takes an operator to describe the nature of the interaction.

Comment A note attached to an element or a collection of elements. A note has no semantics.

Communication diagram A diagram that describes how objects interact, and focuses on the collaboration in space, which means that the relationships (links) between the objects are explicitly shown.

Communication path An association between two nodes through which they are able to communicate.

Complete inheritance The complete generalization constraint says that all subclasses in an inheritance relationship have been specified. No additional subclasses can be added.

Component A discrete module in a system with defined provided and required interfaces. Designed for "plug and play" use in many systems.

Component diagram A diagram that describes the organization and dependencies amongst software components and their relationships to artifacts.

Composite state A state that consists of substates (concurrent substates or sequential substates).

Composite structure diagram A representation that shows the run-time relationships, or connections, between a set of instances owned by a classifier.

Composition A composition aggregation is an aggregation where the whole owns its parts (strong ownership). The parts live inside the whole and are destroyed together with the whole.

Computation Independent Model (CIM) A model showing the basic domain concepts in a system or industry. Should be used across several specific projects. Similar to a business object model.

Concrete class A class that can have instances (objects). The opposite of an abstract class.

Concurrency When two or more activities execute simultaneously (in parallel).

Concurrent substate A substate that is part of an orthogonal composite state.

Connector An instance of an association in a composite structure. A link to allow communication.

Constraint A semantic condition on an element. Certain constraints are predefined in the UML; others may be user-defined. For example, a constraint can restrict which objects can be part of a specific association.

Context A description of a set of objects involved in collaboration, including their links to each other.

Control class A stereotyped class whose objects typically handle the processing and operational sequence of entity objects. A control object often controls the realization of a use case.

Creation message A message that results in the creation of an object.

Deadlock Occurs when a number of threads are all waiting for each other.

Dependency A relationship between two elements, in which a change to the independent model element affects the dependent model element.

Deployment diagram Shows the run-time architecture of nodes, execution environments, and the software components that execute in the architecture. It is the ultimate physical description of the system topology, including the structure of the hardware units and the software that executes on each unit.

Deployment specification A modeling element representing a set of properties that determine execution parameters of an artifact that is deployed on a node.

Design A discipline that describes how an analysis model can be implemented within a technical environment. A design model should provide enough detail so that the system can be implemented in a programming language.

Destroyed A constraint that affects the life cycle of objects. The constrained object is destroyed during the execution of an interaction.

Diagram A view element that shows (projects) a set of model elements.

Discipline A collection of activities relating to an area of concern such as the requirements of a software system.

Discriminator *See* Powertype.

Disjoint inheritance Subclasses inheriting from a common superclass cannot be specialized to one common subclass (using multiple inheritance). Disjoint inheritance is the default and is the opposite of overlapping inheritance.

Document The stereotyped artifact <<document>> is a general electronic file containing information rather than source code or an executable that could be compiled.

Edge A directed connection between two activity nodes used to mode control flow and object flow in activity diagrams.

Element The abstract base class for UML. The element class provides an anchor upon which a number of mechanisms can be attached. A model element is an abstraction drawn from the system being modeled (for example, a class, message, nodes, event, and so on). A view element is a projection (textual or graphical) of a single model element or a collection of model elements (when the view element is a diagram).

Entity object The entity stereotype is used to model objects that hold information, typically business objects such as debt, invoice, insurance contract, and so on. Usually, they are persistently stored in the system.

Enumeration A stereotyped primitive type, specifying a set of values (a domain) that are the allowed values for the enumerated primitive type.

Event A significant occurrence in time or space. In behavior diagrams, an event is related to behavior by triggers.

Event-Signature Consists of an event-name and parameters.

Exception A signal showing a fault or special circumstance to handle.

Executable A file that can run on a computer system. Indicated by the stereotyped artifact <<executable>>.

Executable UML (xUML) A variant of UML that relies on an action language usually connected to state machines to create code from the UML model.

Execution occurrence A unit of behavior within a lifeline represented on an interaction diagram.

Export A package can export its contents (the elements) so that the contents may be referred to and used in other packages.

Extend A relationship between use cases where one use case extends another by adding actions to a general use case. The extending use case can include behavior from the use case being extended (depending on conditions in the extension). This is indicated by the stereotype <<extend>>.

Extension point An aggregation that shows a stereotype extends the properties of a metaclass. Used only when creating a stereotype or building a profile.

Façade A stereotyped package that refers only to elements from other packages (imports, via friend dependency, and so on). The façade does not own any elements, but typically presents a view of the services provided by a package.

Feature A property of a classifier.

File The stereotyped artifact <<file>> represents any physical file in a system.

Fire The execution of a state transition.

Generalizable element A model element that can participate in an inheritance hierarchy.

Generalization A relationship between a general element and a more specific element. The more specific element is consistent with the more general element and contains additional information or behavior. An instance of the more specific element can be used wherever the more general element can be used.

Guard condition A Boolean expression of a state transition. If the guard condition is combined with an event-signature, the event must occur and the guard condition must be true for the state to change. However, only a guard condition can be attached to a state transition, meaning that the state changes when the condition becomes true.

History indicator Used to memorize internal states.

Implementation A discipline that comprises building the system based on the design model.

Import The stereotyped import dependency between packages means that a package imports and can access elements within another package that has public visibility.

Include A stereotyped relationship between use cases where one use case contains the behavior of another use case. This allows for reusing common behavior in a use case model.

Incomplete inheritance An incomplete generalization indicates that new subclasses may be added in the future. Incomplete generalization is the opposite of complete generalization and is the default.

Inheritance *See* Generalization.

Instance An individual member described by a type. An instance of a class is an object.

Interaction Shows how the classes/objects communicate to perform a specific functionality.

Interaction diagram A generic term for sequence, communication, timing, and interaction overview diagrams.

Interaction occurrence A shorthand for copying the contents of a referred interaction into another interaction being modeled.

Interaction overview diagram Provides an overview of cooperating interactions in a flow much like an activity diagram.

Interface This describes the externally visible and accessible behavior of a classifier.

Interface inheritance Generalization and specialization among interfaces (since interfaces don't have implementation, only the interface is inherited).

Invariant Applies to a type and specifies a property (that is, condition) that must be preserved over the lifetime of an instance of the type.

Iterative A software development process model in which a set of activities are performed again and again converging toward some goal.

Layer In the idiom of a layered architecture, the organization of classifiers or packages at the same level of abstraction representing a horizontal slice through the architecture.

Library The stereotyped artifact <<library>> shows that a component is a static or dynamic library. This is a subclass of file.

Lifeline A modeling element showing an individual participant in an interaction.

Link A semantic connection between instances; an instantiation of an association, or the actual connection between two (or more) objects.

Manifest A relation showing that a model element is embodied by a particular physical artifact.

Member A part of a type or a class denoting either an attribute or an operation.

Message A communication between objects that conveys information with the expectation that activity will ensue. The receipt of a message is normally considered an event.

Metaclass A class that can be instantiated to other classes (a class for classes). Shown in diagrams with the stereotype <<metaclass>>.

Metamodel A model that describes other models, expressed in a metalanguage. Metamodels are used to describe UML. When working with profiles or new UML variants, a metamodel is shown as <<metamodel>>.

Meta-Object Facility (MOF) The high-level language used to define other modeling languages. UML 2 is defined in terms of MOF.

Metatype A type whose instances are types.

Method The implementation of an operation.

Model An abstract description of a system, expressed with diagrams.

Model coordination Different models of the same thing must be able to be integrated and related to each other. Models should be coordinated on each level of abstraction (for example, structure and behavior) and between the different levels of abstraction (for example, system versus subsystem and analysis versus design).

Model Driven Architecture (MDA) An OMG initiative to allow the effective modeling of distributed systems. Also seeks to make UML more effective as a platform for producing executable artifacts.

Model element The concepts within the UML, for example, class, object, node, and state. Most model elements have a corresponding view element that shows their graphical appearance; they may, therefore, be projected within diagrams.

Model integration If a set of models have the same purpose and represent the same thing, it should be possible to put them together without inconsistencies.

Model quality (High) model quality means that all models must have an explicit and clear purpose and that they capture the essence of what is being studied and modeled. All models should be easy to communicate, verify, validate, and maintain.

Modeling language A language used to express models, defined with syntax and semantics. Some modeling languages also have pragmatic rules.

Multiple inheritance When a type is specialized from more than one supertype.

Multiplicity The range of allowed links and how they combine the objects at each end of the link. There is a range of nonnegative integers on each end in an association or aggregation, specifying the number of objects allowed in each role.

Name Text to identify a model element.

Node Physical objects (devices) that have some kind of computational resource. Includes computers with processors, but also devices such as printers, card readers, communication devices, and so on.

Object An instance of a class.

Object Constraint Language (OCL) A language built from the same metalanguage as UML, used for defining the conditions of execution for a model.

Object diagram A snapshot of a system execution, showing objects and their links.

Object lifeline A dashed line in a sequence diagram that represents the existence of an object.

Operation A feature of a classifier that performs actions. An operation is usually defined as a function with a signature and an implementation.

Orthogonal composite state Substates that are concurrent and add up to form one region. A non–orthogonal composite state is the opposite.

Overlapping inheritance Subclasses inheriting from a common superclass can be specialized to one common subclass using multiple inheritance. The opposite of disjoint inheritance.

Package A grouping mechanism to link elements, for example, to create groups of diagrams, classes, nodes, and so on.

Parameter The specification of a variable that can be changed, passed, or returned. A parameter can include a name, type, and direction. Parameters are used for operations, messages, and events.

Parameterized class An incomplete class that needs to be bound with a parameter (typically a type) to become complete. It is used to express generic classes that are filled with types (such as classes and primitive types) to instantiate other, more specialized classes. Parameterized classes are often an alternative to using inheritance. In C++, a parameterized class is called a template.

Part An element representing an instance playing a role within the context of a containing classifier. Parts can be joined connectors.

Pattern Smart, generic, well-proven, simple, and reusable solutions used to design object-oriented systems.

Persistence Applies to a type. Defining a class as persistent means that objects of the class can be stored in a database or a file and that the object can retain its value (state) between different executions of the program.

Petri Nets An approach to showing concurrent flow through a system started in the 1960s. UML 2 activity diagrams rely on many concepts from this approach.

Phase A major component in the schedule of a development effort that represents the time between two project milestones during which various disciplines are exercised to meet a set of objectives.

Pin A model element that represents either the data values passed into an action upon its invocation (Input Pin) or the data values returned from an action upon its completion (Output Pin). In the case of an Input Pin, it also contributes to the precondition of the behavior occurring.

Platform Independent Model (PIM) A model that defines an application independent of a specific platform. The PIM is applied to a more detailed model using a transformation mechanism.

Platform Specific Model (PSM) The model that includes elements from the implementation platform, often made more precise through the use of relevant stereotypes.

Port Shows the interaction between a classifier and the physical environment. Ports help in modeling plug and play component systems.

Postcondition A condition that must be true after the completion of some behavior.

Powertype When a generalization is specialized, a discriminator can be used to specify on what basis the inheritance is made. The discriminator is used to separate instances. The discriminator type is called a powertype. A powertype works at the type level, while the discriminator works at the instance level.

Precondition A condition that must be true before the behavior is initiated.

Primitive type A datatype without features of a class, such as an integer or an enumeration.

Profile A stereotyped package to manage sets of extensions for a specific domain or purpose. A profile includes stereotypes, constraints, and tagged values.

Property A general description for built-in characteristics, such as names on elements. A property may also be predefined and user-defined tagged values attached to model elements. Property lists specify the value domain for attributes.

Protocol state machine Shows the valid transitions allowed for an object. Focuses on the rules, or protocol, for the object changing state.

Pseudo-state A vertex that can act like a state in a state machine, but is not really a state of the classifier, such as an initial pseudo-state.

Qualifier The qualifier distinguishes among the set of objects at the many end of an association (for example, works as a key in navigation among the objects in the association).

Realization An abstraction relationship where one element implements, or realizes, the specification of another element.

Reception Indicates that the element can react to a signal.

Recursion When an operation calls itself (until a condition becomes true).

Refinement A relationship between two descriptions of the same thing, but at different levels of abstraction. One description provides more detail. The refinement is a stereotyped dependency relationship that can be used to connect an analysis description with the design description of the same thing.

Relationship A semantic connection among model elements. A relationship is specialized to such elements as generalization, dependency, association, transition, and link.

Reply Message A message that explicitly shows the return of control when an execution occurrence has completed.

Requirements A discipline that elicits needs from the stakeholders and formulates a set of technical requirements to which the system must conform. When modeling in UML, requirements will commonly take the form of use cases supplemented with more traditional textual specifications.

Role An association can have roles connected to each class involved, indicating the role played by the class in terms of the association. Roles are a useful technique to specify the context for a class and its objects. A role is equivalent to the association end.

Scenario An instance of a use case showing one sequence of actions to produce a result.

Scheduling A part of the synchronization between active objects is handled through the scheduling of active objects. Scheduling determines which thread should run next where a number of threads are conceivable.

Semantics Used to describe the meaning of something. Semantics may be seen as the link between a concept and the symbol for that concept.

Sequence diagram A diagram that describes how objects interact with each other. Sequence diagrams focus on message order, meaning they display when messages are sent and received.

Signal A stereotyped class whose objects are sent as messages.

Signature The name of an operation, along with a list of parameters and a return-type that make it unique within its context.

Starvation When one thread (active object) is never able to run. The problem occurs when the priorities of the threads are defined in such a way that it is impossible or very difficult for one thread to gain control.

State An object state is determined by its attribute values and links to other objects. A state is a result of previous activities in the object.

State diagram Captures object life cycles (also the life cycles of subsystems and systems). State diagrams illustrate how events (messages, time, errors, and state changes) affect object states over time.

Stereotype A type of modeling element that extends the semantics of the UML. Stereotypes must be based on elements that already are defined in the UML. Certain stereotypes are predefined in UML; others can be user-defined.

Subclass A class that is a specialization of another class.

Submachine state A state in a state machine that is described by another state machine.

Substate A state within another state. A set of substates is a composite state.

Subtype A type that is a specialization of another type.

Superclass A class that is a generalization of another class.

Supertype A type that is a generalization of another type.

Synchronization Synchronization mechanisms are objects used to control the execution of concurrent threads, so that there is no conflicting usage of shared resources or overall ineffective resource usage.

Synchronous message A nested flow of control, typically implemented as an operation call. The operation that handles the message is completed (including any further nested messages being sent as part of the handling) before the caller resumes execution.

Syntax The rules that restrict how concepts (elements) may be combined with each other.

System A set of items organized in some way, for example, information system, business system, or embedded system.

Tagged value The explicit definition of a property as a name-value pair. In a tagged value, the name is referred to as the tag. Certain tags are predefined in the UML. In UML, property is used in a general sense for any value connected to an element, including attributes in classes, associations, and tagged values.

Template *See* Parameterized class.

Test A discipline that devises a set of test cases based on requirements and executes the tests on a system to verify that the requirements have been met. When developing using UML, the tests are typically organized around the use cases.

Thread A process is a "heavyweight" thread of control, while a thread is a "lightweight" thread of control. The important difference between process and thread is that a process normally encapsulates all its internal structure and executes in its own memory space, while a thread executes in a memory space shared with other threads. Also, a stereotype for the implementation of an active object.

Time event Passage of a designated period of time after a designated event (often the entry of a state) occurs.

Time expression An expression for a time event.

Timing diagram Shows the change in state along a lifeline in terms of a defined time unit.

Token A mechanism on an activity diagram that carries objects, values, or a null value for consumption by actions.

Trace A stereotyped dependency from one model element to another model element. The elements traced to each other might be in the same diagram or in different diagrams. The trace indicates that the source can be traced conceptually back to the target, with no precise rules for this trace.

Transient A constraint that affects the life cycle of objects. Transient objects are created and destroyed in the same execution of a collaboration, so they do not continue after the collaboration occurrence.

Transition A relationship between two states where an element enters the second state when a specified event occurs, the state performs specified actions, and/or specified conditions are satisfied.

Type A description of a set of instances that share the same operations, attributes, relationships, and semantics. Primitive type, class, and use case are all types.

Uninterpreted Placeholders for types that do not have a specified implementation in UML. Often used for expressions or constraints giving the modeler flexibility to use a number of different languages where an uninterpreted string is specified.

Use case A description of how a system can be used (from an actor's point of view). Use cases show the functionality of a system and are described in terms of actors, use cases, and the system being modeled. A use case should yield an observable result of value to a particular actor.

Use-case diagram A use-case model is described as a use-case diagram, which contains elements for the system, the actors, and the use cases, and displays the different relationships between these elements.

Use-case model Describes a system's functional requirements in terms of use cases.

Utility A stereotyped type that contains only class-scope operations and attributes. A utility is never instantiated.

Value An element of a type domain. The type domain specified for a certain type; for example, the number 42 is in the type domain for integer.

Vertex A source or target of a state transition. A basic unit on a state machine.

Visibility An enumeration where the set of allowed values are public, protected, private, and implementation. The visibility specifies the allowed access to elements within types and packages.

Waterfall A software development process model in which the life cycle is broken up into phases that include distinct activities that are performed to completion and not expected to be performed again once the phase is over. A traditional waterfall process might be broken up into the phases Requirements, Analysis, Design, Code, Integration, and Test.

Xor constraint Applied to a set of associations that have constraints on their links. The xor constraint can be applied where an association connects a single class with a set of other classes. The xor constraint specifies that an object of the single class can be connected to only one of the associated classes objects (on the opposite side of the association).

APPENDIX

C

References

Standards and Specifications

OMG. *Common Warehouse Metamodel (CWM) Specification, Version 1.0.* OMG Document, October 2001.

OMG. *Final Report of the UML 1.4.1 RTF OMG UML 1.4.1 Revision Task Force.* ad/02-06-18 June 18, 2002.

OMG. *Model Driven Architecture (MDA).* OMG Document number omg/2003-05-01 Version 1.0, May 1, 2003.

OMG. *Model Driven Architecture (MDA).* OMG Document number ormsc/2001-06-01 Architecture Board ORMSC1 Draft 00.10, June 26, 2001.

OMG. *Response to the UML 2.0 OCL RfP (ad/2000-09-03) Revised Submission, Version 1.6.* OMG Document ad/2003-01-07, January 6, 2003.

OMG. *UML Profile for Schedulability, Performance, and Time Specification.* OMG Adopted Specification ptc/02-03-02, March 2002.

OMG. *Unified Modeling Language Specification, Version 1.4,* OMG Document formal/01-09-67.

OMG. *Unified Modeling Language: Infrastructure, Version 2.0.* OMG Document ad/2003-03-01 March 3, 2003 (submission).

OMG. *Unified Modeling Language: Superstructure, Version 2.0.* OMG Document ad/2003-04-01 April 10, 2003 (submission).

Books and Articles

Albin, S. T. *The Art of Software Architecture.* John Wiley & Sons, Inc., 2003.

Alur, D., J. Crupi, and D. Malks. *Core J2EE Patterns: Best Practices and Design Strategies.* Prentice Hall PTR, 2001.

Astrakan 97. *The Astrakan Method.* Sweden, Astrakan Strategic Development, 1997.

Audi, R., ed. *The Cambridge Dictionary of Philosophy.* Cambridge: Press Syndicate of the University of Cambridge, 1995.

Awad, M., J. Kuusela, and J. Ziegler. *Object-Oriented Technology for Real-Time Systems.* Upper Saddle River, NJ: Prentice Hall, 1996.

Bass, L., P. Clements, and R. Kazman. *Software Architecture in Practice.* Addison-Wesley, 1997

Booch, G. *Object-Oriented Analysis and Design with Applications.* Redwood City, CA: Benjamin Cummings, 1994.

Booch, G., J. Rumbaugh, and I. Jacobson. *The Unified Modeling Language User's Guide.* Addison-Wesley, 1999.

Buschmann, F., R. Meunier, H. Rohnert, P. Sommerlad, and M. Stal. *Pattern-Oriented Software Architecture, Volume 1: A System of Patterns.* New York: John Wiley & Sons, Inc., 1996.

Catalysis v0.8 97. Desmond Francis D'Souza and Alan Cameron Wills, USA, 1997, in press. *Component-Based Development Using Catalysis version Draft 0.8.* 1997.

Coleman, D., P. Arnold, S. Bodoff, C. Dollin, H. Gilchrist, F. Hayes, and P. Jeremes. *Object-Oriented Development: The Fusion Method.* Upper Saddle River, NJ: Prentice-Hall, 1994.

COMMA 96. COTAR. *Technical Report.* Sydney, Australia: Center for Object Technology Application and Research, School of Computing Sciences, 1996.

Douglass, B. *Real-Time Design Patterns: Robust Scalable Architecture for Real-Time Systems.* Boston: Addison-Wesley, 2002.

Eriksson, H-E., and M. Penker. *Objektorientering—Handbok och lexikon.* Lund, Sweden: Studentlitteratur, 1996.

Falkenberg, D., W. Hesse, P. Lindgreen, B. Nilsson, J. L. Han Oei, C. Rolland, R. Stamper, F. Van Assche, A. Verrijn-Stuart, and K. Voss. A Framework of Information System Concepts. *The FRISCO Report,* 1996.

Fontura, M., W. Pree, and B. Rumpe. *The UML Profile for Framework Architectures.* Boston: Addison-Wesley, 2002.

Frankel, D. *Model Driven Architecture: Applying MDA to Enterprise Computing*. John Wiley & Sons, Inc., 2003.

Gamma, E., R. Helm, R. Johnson, and J. Vlissides. *Design Patterns: Elements of Reusable Object-Oriented Software*. Reading, MA: Addison-Wesley, 1994.

Hubert, R. *Convergent Architecture: Building Model Driven J2EE Systems with UML*. John Wiley & Sons, Inc., 2002.

Hutt, A. *Object-Oriented Analysis and Design: Comparison of Methods*. New York: John Wiley & Sons, Inc., 1994.

Hutt, A. *Object-Oriented Analysis and Design: Description of Methods*. New York: John Wiley & Sons, Inc., 1994.

Jacobson, I., M. Christerson, P. Jonsson, and G. Övergaard. *Object-Oriented Software Engineering*. Reading, NY: Addison-Wesley, 1992.

Jayaratna, N. *Understanding and Evaluating Methodologies—NIMSAD, a Systematic Framework.* (New York: McGraw-Hill), 1994.

Kassem, N. and Enterprise Team. *Designing Enterprise Applications with the Java 2 Platform, Enterprise Edition.* Addison-Wesley, 2000.

Kruchten, P. A Rational Development Process. White paper from Rational Software Corp. Santa Clara, CA 1996.

Kruchten, P. The 4+1 View Model of Architecture. *IEEE Software*, IEEE, November 1995.

Leavitt, H. The Volatile Organization: Everything Triggers Everything Else. *Managerial Psychology*, 1972.

Malmberg, B. *Readings in Modern Linguistics*. Stockholmn, Sweden: Läromedelsförlagen, 1972.

Mellor, S., and M. Balcer. *Executable UML: A Foundation for Model Driven Architecture*. Addison-Wesley Professional, 2002.

Morgan, G. *Images of Organization*. Thousand Oaks, CA: Sage Publications, Inc., 1986.

Nilsson, B. On Models and Mappings in a Data Base Environment—A Holistic Approach to Data Modeling. Unpublished Dissertation, 1979.

Nilsson, B. Perspective on Modeling the Business and its IT Support. Presentation, Conference ER94, 1994.

Nilsson, B. Towards a Framework of Information Systems Concepts. Keynote presentation. Conference ISCO3, 1995.

Nilsson, B. Vision 95. CaiSE91 Conference on Advanced Information Systems Engineering, 1991.

OMG. *OA&D RFP Response*. IBM Corporation and ObjectTime Limited USA, 1997.

OPEN Modeling Language Reference Manual 1.0. Open Consortium (Contact: David Firesmith, Knowledge Systems Corporation, Cary, NC), 1996.

Penker, M. Report on NIMSAD. The Department of Computer Sciences, KTH—Royal Institute of Technology, Stockholm, Sweden, 1996.

Rumbaugh, J., G. Booch, and I. Jacobson, *The Unified Modeling Language Reference Manual.* Addison-Wesley, 1999.

Rumbaugh, J., M. Blaha, W. Premerlani, F. Eddy, and F. Lorenson. *Object-Oriented Modeling and Design.* Englewood Cliffs, NJ: Prentice-Hall, 1991.

Selic, B., G. Gullekson, and P. T. Ward. *Real-Time Object-Oriented Modeling.* New York: John Wiley & Sons, Inc., 1994.

Starr, L. *Executable UML: How to Build Class Models.* Prentice Hall PTR, 2002.

Steneskog, G. *Process Management.* Stockholm, Sweden: Liber, 1991.

Taylor, D. *Object-Oriented Technology: A Manager's Guide.* Reading, MA: Addison-Wesley, 1991.

Wilars, H. Amplification of Business Cognition through Modeling Techniques. IEA Congress, 1991.

APPENDIX

D

What's on the CD-ROM?

This appendix provides you with information on the contents of the CD that accompanies this book. For the latest and greatest information, please refer to the index.html file located at the root of the CD. Here is what you will find in this appendix:

- System requirements
- Using the CD with the Windows platform
- What's on the CD
- Troubleshooting

System Requirements

Make sure that your computer meets the minimum system requirements listed in this section. If your computer doesn't match up to most of these requirements, you may have a problem using the contents of the CD.

For Windows platforms:

- PC with a Pentium processor running at 500 MHz or faster
- At least 128MB of total RAM installed on your computer; for best performance, we recommend at least 256MB
- Ethernet network interface card (NIC) or modem with a speed of at least 28,800 bps
- A CD-ROM drive

NOTE The CD should work on all Windows platforms, but has been tested only on Windows 2000 and Windows XP.

Using the CD with Windows

To view the items on the CD to your hard drive, follow these steps:

1. Insert the CD into your computer's CD-ROM drive.
2. A browser window appears with the main page, index.html.
3. The page displays a list of key features on the companion CD:
   - Case study
   - How to get updates

If you do not have autorun enabled or if the autorun browser window does not appear, follow the steps below to access the CD:

1. Double-click on My Computer.
2. Double-click on your CD-ROM drive to view the contents of the CD.
3. Double-click on the index.html to open the companion CD main page.

What's on the CD

The following sections provide a summary of the software and other materials you'll find on the CD.

Case Study

The case study is located on the CD at *X*:\UML2Toolkit\chapter11\CaseStudy (where *X* is your CD-ROM drive letter). Additional diagrams that apply to the case study but aren't a part of the actual case study chapter can be found at *X*:\UML2Toolkit\chapter11\figures\additional_diagrams on the CD.

The case study—Unified Library application—is a fully implemented Java Web application that uses the UML 2 with fully documented source code. It utilizes many technologies such as J2EE (Servlets, JSP, and JDBC); Open Source (Tomcat, Struts, Ant, Log4j, MySQL, and Commons); XHTML; and Microsoft Access. In addition, the case study has implemented many design approaches and patterns such as Front Controller (using Struts), Data Access Object, Abstract DAO Factory, Value Object/Transfer Object, Form Bean to Value Object/Transfer Object, model-view-controller (Model 2), and dynamic sub action calls to concrete methods. The case study includes the following:

- Case study setup and instructions
- Use-case specifications (requirements)
- UML 2 figures from the case study chapter
- Additional UML 2 diagrams not included in case study chapter that further elaborate on the case study
- JavaDoc specifications
- Complete source code
- Instructions on how to modify source code and build the application

CROSS-REFERENCE **For more information about the Case Study, see Chapter 11.**

UML 2 Specifications

The CD also includes the current set of UML 2 specifications at time of publication from the Object Management Group (OMG). For latest version, visit OMG's Web site, `http://www.omg.org/`.

Included Software

Additionally, the following applications are on the CD:

- Adobe Acrobat Reader
- WinRAR
- Eclipse, version 2.1—Eclipse is an integrated development environment (IDE) for using in editing the Java source code in the case study
- MySQL version 4.0.1—Open source database
- Java(tm) 2 Platform, Standard Edition, version 1.4.1 for Windows
- Tomcat—JavaServer Pages—Implementation server and Java Servlet
- Apache Ant, version 1.5—Java-based build tool
- Jakarta Log4j, version 1.2.7—Java-based logging utility
- Jakarta Struts, version 1.1—release candidate 1—Open source framework for building Web applications

Shareware programs are fully functional, trial versions of copyrighted programs. If you like particular programs, register with their authors for a nominal fee and receive licenses, enhanced versions, and technical support. *Freeware programs* are copyrighted games, applications, and utilities that are free for personal use. Unlike shareware, these programs do not require a fee or provide technical support. *GNU software* is governed by its own license, which is included inside the folder of the GNU product. See the GNU license for more details.

Trial, demo, or evaluation versions are usually limited either by time or functionality (such as being unable to save projects). Some trial versions are very sensitive to system date changes. If you alter your computer's date, the programs will "time out" and will no longer be functional.

Note on UML 2 Tools

The authoring of this book coincides with the final review of the UML 2 proposal, so we did not have the benefit of UML 2 compliant tools. While we looked at a few early versions of tools, we did not find the support for features we are accustomed to in the current UML support tools. However, we have included a set of links to vendor sites on the CD. With the speed of development of these tools, we are confident that the reader will find demonstration versions that support UML 2 at practical levels.

Troubleshooting

If you have difficulty installing or using any of the materials on the companion CD, try the following solutions:

General Solutions

- **Turn off any anti-virus software that you may have running.** Installers sometimes mimic virus activity and can make your computer incorrectly believe that it is being infected by a virus. (Be sure to turn the anti-virus software back on later.)
- **Close all running programs.** The more programs you're running, the less memory is available to other programs. Installers also typically update files and programs; if you keep other programs running, installation may not work properly.

Frequently Asked Questions

- **Q:** What if the login page never displays?

  A: Another application may be using the port that Tomcat is attempting to use, by default, port 8080. See `http://jakarta.apache.org/tomcat` for more information on changing the port for your Tomcat server instance.

  A: It could also mean that you did not run the go.bat file located at C:\CaseStudy (assuming it was copied to the C: drive)

  A: It could also mean that all of the files from the CaseStudy folder on the CD were not copied over to your hard drive. Verify that all of the files have been copied over.
- **Q:** What if I can't get past the login screen?

  A: If you are using MS Access as the database, then you probably don't have the database ODBC System DSN configured correctly. It is possible that the auto-installation of the System DSN did not work correctly. Please confirm the location of the System DSN by going to the ODBC Administrator in Windows.

- **Q:** Why can't I check out an item, return item, reserve item, unreserve item?

  A: It is possible that the C:\CaseStudy\implementation\database\library.mdb file has a read-only attribute set on the file. You'll need to remove the read-only attribute and then you will be able to perform the aforementioned features.

- **Q:** Why can't I build the application?

  A: It is possible that the CaseStudy folder is located on your PC with an absolute path that contains white spaces. Make sure that you copy the CaseStudy folder to a path that doesn't contain white spaces.

  For example, a *bad* absolute path would be C:/Documents and Settings/administrator/desktop/CaseStudy.

  Whereas, a *good* absolute path would be C:/temp/CaseStudy.

If you still have trouble with the CD, please call the Customer Care phone number: (800) 762-2974. Outside the United States, call 1 (317) 572-3994. You can also contact Customer Service by e-mail at `techsupdum@wiley.com`. Wiley Publishing, Inc. will provide technical support only for installation and other general quality control items; for technical support on the applications themselves, consult the program's vendor or author.

Index

A

Wiley Publishing, Inc.
End-User License Agreement

READ THIS. You should carefully read these terms and conditions before opening the software packet(s) included with this book "Book". This is a license agreement "Agreement" between you and Wiley Publishing, Inc. "WPI". By opening the accompanying software packet(s), you acknowledge that you have read and accept the following terms and conditions. If you do not agree and do not want to be bound by such terms and conditions, promptly return the Book and the unopened software packet(s) to the place you obtained them for a full refund.

1. **License Grant.** WPI grants to you (either an individual or entity) a nonexclusive license to use one copy of the enclosed software program(s) (collectively, the "Software," solely for your own personal or business purposes on a single computer (whether a standard computer or a workstation component of a multi-user network). The Software is in use on a computer when it is loaded into temporary memory (RAM) or installed into permanent memory (hard disk, CD-ROM, or other storage device). WPI reserves all rights not expressly granted herein.

2. **Ownership.** WPI is the owner of all right, title, and interest, including copyright, in and to the compilation of the Software recorded on the disk(s) or CD-ROM "Software Media". Copyright to the individual programs recorded on the Software Media is owned by the author or other authorized copyright owner of each program. Ownership of the Software and all proprietary rights relating thereto remain with WPI and its licensers.

3. **Restrictions On Use and Transfer.**

   (a) You may only (i) make one copy of the Software for backup or archival purposes, or (ii) transfer the Software to a single hard disk, provided that you keep the original for backup or archival purposes. You may not (i) rent or lease the Software, (ii) copy or reproduce the Software through a LAN or other network system or through any computer subscriber system or bulletin-board system, or (iii) modify, adapt, or create derivative works based on the Software.

   (b) You may not reverse engineer, decompile, or disassemble the Software. You may transfer the Software and user documentation on a permanent basis, provided that the transferee agrees to accept the terms and conditions of this Agreement and you retain no copies. If the Software is an update or has been updated, any transfer must include the most recent update and all prior versions.

4. **Restrictions on Use of Individual Programs.** You must follow the individual requirements and restrictions detailed for each individual program in the About the CD-ROM appendix of this Book. These limitations are also contained in the individual license agreements recorded on the Software Media. These limitations may include a requirement that after using the program for a specified period of time, the user must pay a registration fee or discontinue use. By opening the Software packet(s), you will be agreeing to abide by the licenses and restrictions for these individual programs that are detailed in the About the CD-ROM appendix and on the Software Media. None of the material on this Software Media or listed in this Book may ever be redistributed, in original or modified form, for commercial purposes.

5. **Limited Warranty.**

   (a) WPI warrants that the Software and Software Media are free from defects in materials and workmanship under normal use for a period of sixty (60) days from the date of purchase of this Book. If WPI receives notification within the warranty period of defects in materials or workmanship, WPI will replace the defective Software Media.

(b) WPI AND THE AUTHOR(S) OF THE BOOK DISCLAIM ALL OTHER WARRANTIES, EXPRESS OR IMPLIED, INCLUDING WITHOUT LIMITATION IMPLIED WARRANTIES OF MERCHANTABILITY AND FITNESS FOR A PARTICULAR PURPOSE, WITH RESPECT TO THE SOFTWARE, THE PROGRAMS, THE SOURCE CODE CONTAINED THEREIN, AND/OR THE TECHNIQUES DESCRIBED IN THIS BOOK. WPI DOES NOT WARRANT THAT THE FUNCTIONS CONTAINED IN THE SOFTWARE WILL MEET YOUR REQUIREMENTS OR THAT THE OPERATION OF THE SOFTWARE WILL BE ERROR FREE.

(c) This limited warranty gives you specific legal rights, and you may have other rights that vary from jurisdiction to jurisdiction.

6. **Remedies.**

   (a) WPI's entire liability and your exclusive remedy for defects in materials and workmanship shall be limited to replacement of the Software Media, which may be returned to WPI with a copy of your receipt at the following address: Software Media Fulfillment Department, Attn.: UML 2 Toolkit, Wiley Publishing, Inc., 10475 Crosspoint Blvd., Indianapolis, IN 46256, or call 1-800-762-2974. Please allow four to six weeks for delivery. This Limited Warranty is void if failure of the Software Media has resulted from accident, abuse, or misapplication. Any replacement Software Media will be warranted for the remainder of the original warranty period or thirty (30) days, whichever is longer.

   (b) In no event shall WPI or the author be liable for any damages whatsoever (including without limitation damages for loss of business profits, business interruption, loss of business information, or any other pecuniary loss) arising from the use of or inability to use the Book or the Software, even if WPI has been advised of the possibility of such damages.

   (c) Because some jurisdictions do not allow the exclusion or limitation of liability for consequential or incidental damages, the above limitation or exclusion may not apply to you.

7. **U.S. Government Restricted Rights.** Use, duplication, or disclosure of the Software for or on behalf of the United States of America, its agencies and/or instrumentalities "U.S. Government" is subject to restrictions as stated in paragraph (c)(1)(ii) of the Rights in Technical Data and Computer Software clause of DFARS 252.227-7013, or subparagraphs (c) (1) and (2) of the Commercial Computer Software - Restricted Rights clause at FAR 52.227-19, and in similar clauses in the NASA FAR supplement, as applicable.

8. **General.** This Agreement constitutes the entire understanding of the parties and revokes and supersedes all prior agreements, oral or written, between them and may not be modified or amended except in a writing signed by both parties hereto that specifically refers to this Agreement. This Agreement shall take precedence over any other documents that may be in conflict herewith. If any one or more provisions contained in this Agreement are held by any court or tribunal to be invalid, illegal, or otherwise unenforceable, each and every other provision shall remain in full force and effect.

GNU General Public License

Version 2, June 1991
Copyright © 1989, 1991 Free Software Foundation, Inc.
59 Temple Place - Suite 330, Boston, MA 02111-1307, USA

Everyone is permitted to copy and distribute verbatim copies of this license document, but changing it is not allowed.

Preamble

The licenses for most software are designed to take away your freedom to share and change it. By contrast, the GNU General Public License is intended to guarantee your freedom to share and change free software—to make sure the software is free for all its users. This General Public License applies to most of the Free Software Foundation's software and to any other program whose authors commit to using it. (Some other Free Software Foundation software is covered by the GNU Library General Public License instead.) You can apply it to your programs, too.

When we speak of free software, we are referring to freedom, not price. Our General Public Licenses are designed to make sure that you have the freedom to distribute copies of free software (and charge for this service if you wish), that you receive source code or can get it if you want it, that you can change the software or use pieces of it in new free programs; and that you know you can do these things.

To protect your rights, we need to make restrictions that forbid anyone to deny you these rights or to ask you to surrender the rights. These restrictions translate to certain responsibilities for you if you distribute copies of the software, or if you modify it.

For example, if you distribute copies of such a program, whether gratis or for a fee, you must give the recipients all the rights that you have. You must make sure that they, too, receive or can get the source code. And you must show them these terms so they know their rights.

We protect your rights with two steps: (1) copyright the software, and (2) offer you this license which gives you legal permission to copy, distribute and/or modify the software.

Also, for each author's protection and ours, we want to make certain that everyone understands that there is no warranty for this free software. If the software is modified by someone else and passed on, we want its recipients to know that what they have is not the original, so that any problems introduced by others will not reflect on the original authors' reputations.

Finally, any free program is threatened constantly by software patents. We wish to avoid the danger that redistributors of a free program will individually obtain patent licenses, in effect making the program proprietary. To prevent this, we have made it clear that any patent must be licensed for everyone's free use or not licensed at all.

The precise terms and conditions for copying, distribution and modification follow.

Terms and Conditions for Copying, Distribution and Modification

0. This License applies to any program or other work which contains a notice placed by the copyright holder saying it may be distributed under the terms of this General Public License. The "Program", below, refers to any such program or work, and a "work based on the Program" means either the Program or any derivative work under copyright law: that is to say, a work containing the Program or a portion of it, either verbatim or with modifications and/or translated into another language. (Hereinafter, translation is included without limitation in the term "modification".) Each licensee is addressed as "you".

Activities other than copying, distribution and modification are not covered by this License; they are outside its scope. The act of running the Program is not restricted, and the output from the Program is covered only if its contents constitute a work based on the Program (independent of having been made by running the Program). Whether that is true depends on what the Program does.

1. You may copy and distribute verbatim copies of the Program's source code as you receive it, in any medium, provided that you conspicuously and appropriately publish on each copy an appropriate copyright notice and disclaimer of warranty; keep intact all the notices that refer to this License and to the absence of any warranty; and give any other recipients of the Program a copy of this License along with the Program.

   You may charge a fee for the physical act of transferring a copy, and you may at your option offer warranty protection in exchange for a fee.

2. You may modify your copy or copies of the Program or any portion of it, thus forming a work based on the Program, and copy and distribute such modifications or work under the terms of Section 1 above, provided that you also meet all of these conditions:

   a) You must cause the modified files to carry prominent notices stating that you changed the files and the date of any change.

   b) You must cause any work that you distribute or publish, that in whole or in part contains or is derived from the Program or any part thereof, to be licensed as a whole at no charge to all third parties under the terms of this License.

   c) If the modified program normally reads commands interactively when run, you must cause it, when started running for such interactive use in the most ordinary way, to print or display an announcement including an appropriate copyright notice and a notice that there is no warranty (or else, saying that you provide a warranty) and that users may redistribute the program under these conditions, and telling the user how to view a copy of this License. (Exception: if the Program itself is interactive but does not normally print such an announcement, your work based on the Program is not required to print an announcement.)

   These requirements apply to the modified work as a whole. If identifiable sections of that work are not derived from the Program, and can be reasonably considered independent and separate works in themselves, then this License, and its terms, do not apply to those sections when you distribute them as separate works. But when you distribute the same sections as part of a whole which is a work based on the Program, the distribution of the whole must be on the terms of this License, whose permissions for other licensees extend to the entire whole, and thus to each and every part regardless of who wrote it.

   Thus, it is not the intent of this section to claim rights or contest your rights to work written entirely by you; rather, the intent is to exercise the right to control the distribution of derivative or collective works based on the Program.

   In addition, mere aggregation of another work not based on the Program with the Program (or with a work based on the Program) on a volume of a storage or distribution medium does not bring the other work under the scope of this License.

3. You may copy and distribute the Program (or a work based on it, under Section 2) in object code or executable form under the terms of Sections 1 and 2 above provided that you also do one of the following:

   a) Accompany it with the complete corresponding machine-readable source code, which must be distributed under the terms of Sections 1 and 2 above on a medium customarily used for software interchange; or,

   b) Accompany it with a written offer, valid for at least three years, to give any third party, for a charge no more than your cost of physically performing source distribution, a complete machine-readable copy of the corresponding source code, to be distributed under the terms of Sections 1 and 2 above on a medium customarily used for software interchange; or,

c) Accompany it with the information you received as to the offer to distribute corresponding source code. (This alternative is allowed only for noncommercial distribution and only if you received the program in object code or executable form with such an offer, in accord with Subsection b above.)

The source code for a work means the preferred form of the work for making modifications to it. For an executable work, complete source code means all the source code for all modules it contains, plus any associated interface definition files, plus the scripts used to control compilation and installation of the executable. However, as a special exception, the source code distributed need not include anything that is normally distributed (in either source or binary form) with the major components (compiler, kernel, and so on) of the operating system on which the executable runs, unless that component itself accompanies the executable.

If distribution of executable or object code is made by offering access to copy from a designated place, then offering equivalent access to copy the source code from the same place counts as distribution of the source code, even though third parties are not compelled to copy the source along with the object code.

4. You may not copy, modify, sublicense, or distribute the Program except as expressly provided under this License. Any attempt otherwise to copy, modify, sublicense or distribute the Program is void, and will automatically terminate your rights under this License. However, parties who have received copies, or rights, from you under this License will not have their licenses terminated so long as such parties remain in full compliance.

5. You are not required to accept this License, since you have not signed it. However, nothing else grants you permission to modify or distribute the Program or its derivative works. These actions are prohibited by law if you do not accept this License. Therefore, by modifying or distributing the Program (or any work based on the Program), you indicate your acceptance of this License to do so, and all its terms and conditions for copying, distributing or modifying the Program or works based on it.

6. Each time you redistribute the Program (or any work based on the Program), the recipient automatically receives a license from the original licensor to copy, distribute or modify the Program subject to these terms and conditions. You may not impose any further restrictions on the recipients' exercise of the rights granted herein. You are not responsible for enforcing compliance by third parties to this License.

7. If, as a consequence of a court judgment or allegation of patent infringement or for any other reason (not limited to patent issues), conditions are imposed on you (whether by court order, agreement or otherwise) that contradict the conditions of this License, they do not excuse you from the conditions of this License. If you cannot distribute so as to satisfy simultaneously your obligations under this License and any other pertinent obligations, then as a consequence you may not distribute the Program at all. For example, if a patent license would not permit royalty-free redistribution of the Program by all those who receive copies directly or indirectly through you, then the only way you could satisfy both it and this License would be to refrain entirely from distribution of the Program.

If any portion of this section is held invalid or unenforceable under any particular circumstance, the balance of the section is intended to apply and the section as a whole is intended to apply in other circumstances.

It is not the purpose of this section to induce you to infringe any patents or other property right claims or to contest validity of any such claims; this section has the sole purpose of protecting the integrity of the free software distribution system, which is implemented by public license practices. Many people have made generous contributions to the wide range of software distributed through that system in reliance on consistent application of that system; it is up to the author/donor to decide if he or she is willing to distribute software through any other system and a licensee cannot impose that choice.

This section is intended to make thoroughly clear what is believed to be a consequence of the rest of this License.

8. If the distribution and/or use of the Program is restricted in certain countries either by patents or by copyrighted interfaces, the original copyright holder who places the Program under this License may add an explicit geographical distribution limitation excluding those countries, so that distribution is permitted only in or among countries not thus excluded. In such case, this License incorporates the limitation as if written in the body of this License.

9. The Free Software Foundation may publish revised and/or new versions of the General Public License from time to time. Such new versions will be similar in spirit to the present version, but may differ in detail to address new problems or concerns.

   Each version is given a distinguishing version number. If the Program specifies a version number of this License which applies to it and "any later version", you have the option of following the terms and conditions either of that version or of any later version published by the Free Software Foundation. If the Program does not specify a version number of this License, you may choose any version ever published by the Free Software Foundation.

10. If you wish to incorporate parts of the Program into other free programs whose distribution conditions are different, write to the author to ask for permission. For software which is copyrighted by the Free Software Foundation, write to the Free Software Foundation; we sometimes make exceptions for this. Our decision will be guided by the two goals of preserving the free status of all derivatives of our free software and of promoting the sharing and reuse of software generally.

No Warranty

11. BECAUSE THE PROGRAM IS LICENSED FREE OF CHARGE, THERE IS NO WARRANTY FOR THE PROGRAM, TO THE EXTENT PERMITTED BY APPLICABLE LAW. EXCEPT WHEN OTHERWISE STATED IN WRITING THE COPYRIGHT HOLDERS AND/OR OTHER PARTIES PROVIDE THE PROGRAM "AS IS" WITHOUT WARRANTY OF ANY KIND, EITHER EXPRESSED OR IMPLIED, INCLUDING, BUT NOT LIMITED TO, THE IMPLIED WARRANTIES OF MERCHANTABILITY AND FITNESS FOR A PARTICULAR PURPOSE. THE ENTIRE RISK AS TO THE QUALITY AND PERFORMANCE OF THE PROGRAM IS WITH YOU. SHOULD THE PROGRAM PROVE DEFECTIVE, YOU ASSUME THE COST OF ALL NECESSARY SERVICING, REPAIR OR CORRECTION.

12. IN NO EVENT UNLESS REQUIRED BY APPLICABLE LAW OR AGREED TO IN WRITING WILL ANY COPYRIGHT HOLDER, OR ANY OTHER PARTY WHO MAY MODIFY AND/OR REDISTRIBUTE THE PROGRAM AS PERMITTED ABOVE, BE LIABLE TO YOU FOR DAMAGES, INCLUDING ANY GENERAL, SPECIAL, INCIDENTAL OR CONSEQUENTIAL DAMAGES ARISING OUT OF THE USE OR INABILITY TO USE THE PROGRAM (INCLUDING BUT NOT LIMITED TO LOSS OF DATA OR DATA BEING RENDERED INACCURATE OR LOSSES SUSTAINED BY YOU OR THIRD PARTIES OR A FAILURE OF THE PROGRAM TO OPERATE WITH ANY OTHER PROGRAMS), EVEN IF SUCH HOLDER OR OTHER PARTY HAS BEEN ADVISED OF THE POSSIBILITY OF SUCH DAMAGES.

End of Terms and Conditions

D0521329